Peters

This book offers the most comprehensive characterization assembled to date of the historical, institutional, and economic forces affecting electricity regulation. Eminent economists organized by the University of California Energy Institute survey the United States, the United Kingdom, Scandinavia, Latin America, France, Germany, Japan, Canada, New Zealand, and Yugoslavia. Recent experiments with privatization, competition, and restructuring in electricity are contrasted with instances where government ownership and traditional vertical integration still dominate.

The introductory essay by Richard J. Gilbert, Edward P. Kahn, and David Newbery synthesizes individual country studies. In any regulatory system, the government must bargain with investors and consumers to satisfy conflicting interests. The opacity of information about cost constrains this process. Governments also impose multiple political and economic objectives on the electricity industry, which further obscures cost conditions. Privatization and deregulation tend to reverse these effects. Few countries, however, have managed to sustain private ownership in the long run.

International Comparisons of
Electricity Regulation

International Comparisons of Electricity Regulation

EDITED BY

RICHARD J. GILBERT
University of California, Berkeley

EDWARD P. KAHN
University of California, Berkeley

CAMBRIDGE
UNIVERSITY PRESS

Published by the Press Syndicate of the University of Cambridge
The Pitt Building, Trumpington Street, Cambridge CB2 1RP
40 West 20th Street, New York, NY 10011-4211, USA
10 Stamford Road, Oakleigh, Melbourne 3166, Australia

First Published 1996

Printed in the United States of America

Library of Congress Cataloging-in-Publication Data
International comparisons of electricity regulation / edited by
    Richard J. Gilbert and Edward P. Kahn.

      p. cm.
     ISBN 0-521-49590-3 (hc)
     1. Electric utilities—Government policy—Case studies.
    2. Electric utilities—Deregulation—Case studies.   3. Electric
utilities—Government ownership—Case studies.   4. Privatization—
Case studies.   I. Gilbert, Richard J., 1945-   . II. Kahn, Edward
(Edward Paul), 1944-   .
HD9685.A2I567   1996
333.79′32—dc20

                                          95-47279
                                               CIP

A catalog record for this book is available from the British Library

ISBN   0-521-49590-3   Hardback

Jacket photos: Artist's rendering of photographs produced from USAF DMSP
(Defense Meteorological Satellite Program) film transparencies archived at the
University of Colorado, CIRES/National Snow and Ice Data Center, Campus Box
449, Boulder, CO U.S.A. 80309.

Contents

Preface

When we began the research that has led to this book, we did not realize that reform of the electricity industry would become a worldwide phenomenon. The experiments in the U.K. were in their early stages, and the restructuring activities in Chile and New Zealand, to the extent they were known at all, were thought to be isolated, rather than seminal activities. Although intended as a largely academic inquiry into the nature and performance of alternative regulatory institutions, our efforts acquired a measure of direct relevance with the recent international movement to privatize, deregulate, and re-regulate electric power and other infrastructure industries.

The team of investigators assembled in this project was drawn largely from the economics profession, reflecting our particular interests in the economic determinants and outcomes of regulation. The country studies reflect the growing recognition that competition is feasible in significant segments of the industry. Yet the authors also appreciate that the electric power industry is beset with the traditional monopoly regulation problems of increasing returns and information asymmetries, which make it difficult to achieve the benefits of competition. These chapters also illustrate how variations in national experience, endowments, traditions, and political constraints have shaped existing institutions and how they are likely to affect the prospects for regulatory reforms.

Our efforts started in 1990 with the task of assembling an international team to investigate electricity regulation. Without the commitment of our co-authors over the years that this project has taken, we would never have finished this book. We are grateful for their insights, patience, and good will.

In May 1993 we met at the Institut d'Economie Industrielle at the University of Toulouse to exchange intermediate results. Jean-Jacques Laffont organized this meeting and made it a considerable success. Participation by many individuals in those discussions substantially improved the subsequent efforts. In addition to the contributors to this book, we would like to thank Sebastian Bernstein, Joel Dirlam, Tony Frayne, Alex Henney, Einar Hope, Tracy Lewis, Eileen Marshall, Stephen Peck, Bernard Tenenbaum, Jean Tirole, Rolf Weideswang, Roger Witcomb, and George Yarrow. We are particularly indebted to David Newbery, who helped to keep this project and the conference on track with his energy and enthusiasm.

We have also benefited from comments received in connection with presentations at the American Economic Association, the Econometric Society, the Department of Applied Economics at the University of Cambridge, the World Bank, the International Association of Energy Economists, the Canadian Bureau of Competition Policy, the Universidad Carlos III de Madrid, and the University of New South Wales.

We are grateful for financial support from the Electric Power Research Institute, Electricité de France, Hydro Quebec, Pacific Gas and Electric Company, the Public Utility Research Center of the University of Florida, and Gothenburg University. The authors of individual chapters were also supported by various institutions, which are acknowledged in their chapters. The continuing support of the University of California Energy Institute was fundamental to the successful completion of this project. We acknowledge the logistical support of Mike Lederer, Carol Kozlowski, and Linda Dayce, and the valuable research support provided by Steve Stoft and Haru Conolly.

Richard J. Gilbert
Edward P. Kahn

**International Comparisons of
Electricity Regulation**

CHAPTER 1

Introduction: International comparisons of electricity regulation

Richard J. Gilbert and Edward P. Kahn
University of California Energy Institute

David M. Newbery
Department of Applied Economics, Cambridge, United Kingdom

What is so special about electricity?

As the sun goes down in the evening sky, cities around the world are illuminated in electric light. Photos from satellites orbiting the earth show clearly the outlines of modern society etched against the darkness. We show these pictures on the cover of this book to underline the special role played by electricity in the contemporary world.

Yet, although electricity is a universal feature of modern society, should we expect the firms that produce this universal commodity to be organized along broadly similar lines internationally? There are prima facie arguments on both sides. On the one hand, common factors of production and technological history suggest broad institutional similarities. On the other hand, the influence of particular national traditions, political culture, and experience argue for differences. There is no definitive answer to this question, but it is becoming more and more interesting for those who follow institutional developments in the industry and those who seek to improve economic efficiency in the electricity sector.

The electricity industry in many countries is experiencing a wave of structural change. Much of this we document here. It is not immediately clear, however, why reorganization of this industry is occurring now, what is the driving force, and whether there will be an international convergence in its structure. Our inquiry will help to address these large and somewhat mysterious questions.

The research represented by this volume is a collaborative effort of academic investigators from around the world. Each chapter describes the electricity industry and its regulation in one country (or several geographically proximate countries). By its very nature electrification draws in government involvement. Public land must be used for establishing distribution networks. National resources, river basins, and subsurface minerals are frequently exploited as inputs to electric power production. There are natural monopoly features to the elec-

1

tricity industry in every country. Moreover, government is involved at every point in the determination of the framework in which these resources and opportunities will be employed. The interactions between government and the electricity industry vary widely from country to country. We will refer to these relations broadly as the regulatory structure of a particular country.

The regulation problem[1]

Natural monopoly and competitive elements

When a single firm can provide a range of specific goods or services at lower total cost than a set of firms can, we say that a natural monopoly condition exists. This cost condition is not itself sufficient to justify a monopoly structure. The cost advantage would need to be sufficient to offset the additional costs of regulating the resulting monopoly. More competitive structures may raise production costs but reduce regulatory costs or allocative inefficiencies sufficiently to provide the service at lower total social cost. Several countries are actively encouraging duplication of telephone lines to customers in the hope that the resulting competition will reduce the overall costs of service. There are even cases where this occurs in electricity.

Berg and Tschirhart (1988) cite Farrer's (1902) catalogue of typical characteristics of natural monopolies:

1. Capital-intensity and minimum economic scale.
2. Nonstorability with fluctuating demand.
3. Locational specificity generating location rents.
4. Necessities, or essential for the community.
5. Involving direct connections to customers.

Some of these attributes contribute directly to the likelihood that a single firm will have lower supply costs within a well-defined area. If the output can be stored or readily shipped to dispersed customers, then the size of the market in which firms may compete increases, and the larger market may be able to sustain more than one firm at minimum economic scale. The combination of necessity (i.e., low demand elasticity) and direct connection (i.e., specific investment) implies large potential exploitative power by the producer, ensuring that regulation or public ownership will be politically inevitable.

It is clear that electricity fulfills these conditions closely. Because electricity cannot be readily stored, supply must be continuously adjusted to varying demand. At one extreme, each customer could have a generator, but the spare capacity required to meet peak demands would be excessively costly, as would having inefficiently small plant. As a result, numerous consumers are supplied

---

[1] This discussion follows Newbery (1994).

by each utility through a distribution system. Up to some limit, the larger the number of consumers served, the lower the average operating and capital costs, for smaller proportionate reserve margins are required, whereas larger generating stations with lower running costs can be built and the benefits of scheduling stations of differing variable costs in a merit order can be realized. These scheduling advantages require central dispatch, and the full advantages of an integrated network system require coordination between investment in generation and transmission. The cost economies typically offset the cost of the network infrastructure. These facts were generally recognized at the level of municipal distribution by the last decade of the nineteenth century. By the second decade of the twentieth century, they were also apparent with respect to high-voltage transmission.

The demand for regulation

Network natural monopoly industries like electricity must inevitably be subject to social control. Scale economies and specific assets (those with high costs for consumers to switch suppliers), particularly in distribution, provide the network owner with considerable market power. The political and social demand for control of this market power arises from (1) the nonstorability of supply, (2) the dependence of the consumer upon the supplier, and (3) the essential nature of the service. Local or central governments have therefore always stood ready to require suppliers to guarantee access on fair terms. Because suppliers need rights of way, governments have the leverage to impose an obligation on supply.

There is a counterpart to this demand for regulation, for the electricity industry is capital-intensive, and its assets are durable, long-lived, and immovable. The political demands for access and "fair" or nonexploitative prices mean that investors must expect that after they have sunk their capital they will be limited in the prices they can charge, and subject to possibly onerous obligations to supply, to guarantee security, stability, and safety. Therefore the incentive to invest depends critically on expectations of the future pricing policy. Will it be set at a sufficiently remunerative level to justify the investment? There are reasons for doubt. Once the capital has been sunk, the bargaining advantage shifts toward those arguing for lower and possibly unremunerative prices. This is not baseless fear. There are numerous examples of countries failing to adequately index the prices of public utilities in periods of inflation (see the discussion in the section titled "Measures of performance").

In its extreme form, one might ask why should anyone sink money into an asset that cannot be moved and that would not pay for itself for many years? A confident investor would have to believe that the asset would not be expropriated, either explicitly, or implicitly through a stream of returns that would not be sufficiently remunerative. Durable investments thus require the rule of law, and specifically the law of property, which is a public good provided by the state. If the state exists primarily to enforce the rights of property owners, then there is no problem since the state just protects owners. But by the time electricity became important, the state also represented workers, voters, and consumers. The resulting conflicts of interest weakened property rights as the coercive power of the state could be used not only to enforce laws, but also to regulate economic activity, impose taxes, and even to expropriate property.

If the industry is to be successfully privately financed, then regulation must credibly satisfy the demands of both consumers and investors. Some countries, notably Germany, Japan, and the United States, have managed more or less to solve this problem by using different strategies (see the section titled "The organization of this book"), but many have failed. If it is not possible to create an efficient and credible system of regulation, then public ownership will be the only alternative. Indeed, the simplest explanation for Short's (1984) observation that throughout the world most network utilities exhibiting natural monopoly with significant specific assets are in the public sector is that it was not possible in the private sector to devise a satisfactory and credible system of regulation that would both attract finance and deliver the service at lower cost.

Each jurisdiction must therefore find a solution to the basic problems of reassuring consumers and investors (who may be the taxpayers), though not all solutions will be equally satisfactory. A good system of regulation will command the support of consumers, will provide sufficiently remunerative prices to enable investment to be financed, and will do so at low cost, which in turn means that investors have confidence that their investment will be able to cover its financial costs. In turn, investors will coordinate investment in transmission and generation to secure the least-cost expansion of the system consistent with adequate security against system failures, fuel shortages, and price shocks. Because electricity is vital to production, governments must also be convinced that its supply will be under adequate domestic control in times of international tension or conflict.

How can the regulatory system be designed to reassure private investors? The experiences documented in these chapters illustrate various solutions. One approach is to provide constitutional guarantees to a fair rate of return, as in the United States, upheld by an independent legal system that protects property rights, or by creating sufficiently independent regulatory agencies supported by appeal procedures to guard against expropriatory behavior. Another solution is a regulatory compact in which the costs to the government of intervening to impose tighter regulation outweigh the benefits in terms of lower prices and short-run voter support. Many countries in continental Europe have evolved systems of essentially self-regulation in which prices are kept remunerative but not exploitive and supply and quality are satisfactory, so that the government has little obvious reason to intervene. The self-regulation system is feasible under public ownership or under a system of mixed public and private ownership. What is critical is that there be some protection against political intervention. In the public ownership case particularly, such protection may be facilitated by the division of responsibility between the various tiers of government (central and local, or state and federal). The other principal protective mechanism under government ownership is the reliance upon political consensus (as in a coalition). The political equilibrium would be disturbed by intervention, or because the consequences of intervention would be self-evidently damaging.

Different regulatory solutions

The history of the electricity industry in various countries illustrates the variety of solutions that have been found to the problem of balancing the interests of consumers and governments while still enabling efficient investment. The solutions available to any jurisdiction are constrained by politics, history, endowments, technology, and the state of the economy. The solutions, formulated in terms of ownership structures, fall into three main types. The electricity industry may be entirely publicly owned and hence directly subject to political control and access to funds, or it may be entirely private but regulated either explicitly or implicitly, or it may be a mixed system in which the private sector is implicitly controlled by the potential of the remaining publicly owned system to take over its function. In addition, the type of regulatory system may be local, regional, or national.

Local (or municipal) regulation could function in principle so long as generating stations were small compared to local demand, but it became clear very early that there were substantial economies in building larger units and serving larger market areas by using higher-tension transmission systems. The main problem to solve was how to transfer responsibility for electricity supply from the local level to an authority covering a sufficiently large number of consumers. This transfer of authority was necessary to reap economies of scale while preserving satisfactory representation of local interests, without encouraging free-riding or appropriation of investment by other interests. Achieving scale economies requires solving the problem of coordinating investment in generation and transmission to secure least-cost delivery of electricity. The key to this was the creation of an integrated transmission system within some area, which in turn had responsibility for dispatching power stations in merit order, thus securing the least-cost generation of electricity.

The details of regulatory structure in various countries often stem from the different solutions found to the problem of breaking out of the constraints of the local municipal-based undertakings. The chapters themselves describe the historical and institutional factors that have influenced the present regulatory structure of each country. The British story, told in Chapter 2, is perhaps the most dramatic in the variety of structural reforms that have characterized its evolution. Other countries have typically adopted a more evolutionary approach to regulation, though several have found nationalization necessary to achieve the required structure to support subsequent coordination in investment and operation.

The monopoly regulation literature

Monopoly regulation has attracted the close attention of economists for decades, and there is an extensive theoretical and empirical literature that predates the more recent framework of economics of regulation. The chapter authors have written their contributions in the light of these precursors, which are briefly surveyed here.

Theory

The longest line of economic theory on regulation has emphasized normative aspects of natural monopoly pricing. In the 1970s a large amount of research was devoted to refining precise definitions of the natural monopoly concept (Baumol, Panzar, and Willig, 1982). The optimal pricing literature for natural monopolies emphasizes the efficiency benefits of pricing at marginal costs. This general notion was adapted to regulated industries characterized by the common capacity problem (i.e., where fixed facilities produce the same physical good at different times of the day or seasons of the year). Numerous authors developed the implications of this technological situation under the general framework of "peak-load pricing" (Boiteux, 1960). Where firms use marginal-cost pricing without government support for fixed-cost recovery, various nonlinear tariff schemes have been discussed to cover the potential revenue deficits (Brown and Sibley, 1986). Laffont discusses the application of these ideas to tariff design at Electricité de France in Chapter 10.

The older normative pricing literature presumes an exogenous cost function with managers and employees minimizing costs given the level of output. The first questions about managerial incentives were raised in the context of input choices by Averch and Johnson (1962). In their model, the regulator enforces a constraint on the rate of return the utility is allowed to earn. This constraint is set at a level above the cost of capital and creates an incentive for the firm to accumulate an excessive amount of capital relative to the cost-minimizing level. The Averch–Johnson paper stimulated a large literature drawing out the implications of the model for firm behavior and eliciting numerous efforts to provide empirical verification (for example, Courville, 1974).

One of the most prominent themes of the more recent literature on regulation is the application of the principal–agent framework to the relationship between the regulatory authorities and the utility (Laffont and Tirole, 1993). The basic insight on which this research program is built is the profound gap between the firm's knowledge of its costs and capabilities and the information available to the regulator. The regulatory problem is then defined as a trade-off between rent extraction and incentives. Regulators give the firms incentives to fulfill the social objective, and the price of this compliance is a rent allocated to the firm. We will find many aspects of these ideas reflected in the country studies.

Empirical studies

A substantial empirical literature comparing the performance of investor-owned electric utilities (i.e., privately owned) with publicly owned utilities (state or municipally owned) was surveyed in Vickers and Yarrow (1988, pp. 40–3). They conclude that there is little to choose between public and private ownership in terms of technical or cost efficiency, and caution against supposing that public ownership leads to greater allocative efficiency, which they argue is more dependent on the form of regulation. The majority of the studies focus on the United States, and any expected consensus about the superior performance of privately owned firms fails to materialize. Many of the early studies, such as Peltzman (1971), focus on prices as the main data from which efficiency is estimated. With increasingly sophisticated statistical techniques available, later authors began to examine reported costs. Representative studies include Pescatrice and Trapani (1980), who find greater cost-efficiency in the publicly owned sector of the U.S. electricity industry than in the privately owned sector. The opposite conclusion is found by Hollas and Stansell (1988), but their result is only short-run in nature – that is, they treat capital as a fixed input. This assumption ignores the whole set of issues raised by the Averch–Johnson paper.

These results are questioned by the findings of Atkinson and Halvorsen (1986), perhaps the most careful of the recent studies on U.S. data. The Atkinson and Halvorsen study eliminates biases in the specification of the cost model. Their result is that no efficiency difference can be detected between the privately owned and the publicly owned firms. The same conclusion is found by Hjalmarsson and Viederpass (1992) for their more limited study of electricity distribution in Sweden.

The most recent and thorough empirical investigation of electric utilities is provided by Pollitt (1993, 1994). He subjects two recent datasets to exhaustive comparisons of efficiency. Following Farrell (1957), technical efficiency is measured as the extent to which the utility reaches the technical production frontier, variously estimated, whereas cost efficiency is the extent to which the utility minimizes cost at prevailing input prices. A utility can be technically efficient but not minimize its costs. The first dataset is an international sample of 95 utilities operating in nine countries in 1986, and thus it is considerably more recent and comprehensive than the earlier studies, largely done on 1970s data and in the United States. Depending on the approach used, Pollitt finds evidence for no significant difference in technical efficiency between the two ownership types but some evidence for the superior cost-efficiency of private utilities. The second dataset is an international sample of 768 power plants in 14 countries in 1989, which together produced about 40% of world thermal electricity. This plant-level analysis, using four different methodologies for measuring technical efficiency, finds that private firms are statistically significantly more technically efficient than are public firms, once the efficiency scores are pooled (Pollitt, 1994). The failure to find significant differences in technical efficiency in the first (and other, earlier) studies reflects the inadequacy of their sample size for detecting rather small differences in measured technical efficiency, reducing cost by between 1 and 3%.

To measure cost efficiency, Pollitt then takes the 164 of the 213 base-load plants in the dataset for which input price data could be found. He rejects the hypothesis that public utilities are as efficient as private, finding private utilities to be more efficient both in minimizing costs and overall, though the difference is quantitatively small – perhaps 5% higher efficiency (the difference varies with the methodology employed). Well-run public utilities can certainly equal the performance of average private utilities.

The evidence from Britain is that privatizing the generators and forcing them to compete in the bulk electricity market resulted in dramatic improvements in labor productivity by halving the workforce within three years, and in much closer control over investment costs. It is noteworthy that the publicly owned company Nuclear Electric also improved its productivity quite dramatically, as did the publicly owned British Coal, both forced to sell into markets facing competition from private firms or imports. In Argentina, generation availability dramatically improved within a short period after the reforms, with Central Costanera improving availability from 20 to 50% with a doubling of output (Perez-Arriaga, 1994). Norway introduced competition into the bulk electricity market and created Statnett Marked (as a subsidiary of the state-owned owner of the transmission system Statnett) to operate the power pool in 1993 without altering the ownership structure of the industry. The effect has been to induce substantial trade across former franchise boundaries with a decrease in the dispersion of prices (Moen, 1994). In a hydro system like that in Norway, changes in patterns of supply will have negligible effects on short-run costs, and it is too soon to tell whether creating an integrated and competitive market will eliminate inefficient local investment in generation and induce moves toward more efficient-sized distribution companies, which was a large part of the goal of the reforms. In time, the Norwegian example should provide an important test of the relative importance of creating contestable power markets by restructuring the industry, compared to privatization. Note, however, that the Norwegian system allows private generation to compete with state- and municipally owned systems.

The English regional electricity companies (RECs, or distribution companies) remain natural monopolies, and their performance does not appear to have changed markedly since privatization, though neither has it deteriorated. The same seems to be true in Argentina and Chile judging from the case study of Enersis reported by Galal (1994). Because they do not have large investment requirements in Britain, their considerable ability to earn profits in a protected market has not been required to finance investment (as it has been for the privatized water companies with their large backlog of replacement and upgrading investment). The evidence from elsewhere is that the main requirement of the ownership structure of distribution companies is that they should be large enough to reap economies of scale, and they should ideally be subject to an element of benchmark regulation. Their role and ownership may also be influenced by the way in which transmission is organized and the form of the obligation to supply, which, in a de-integrated system, will need to be devolved to the distribution companies.

The Pollitt study, along with the preceding anecdotal evidence, is consistent with the view that the more important determinant of efficiency is the degree of competitive pressure put on the utility, which in turn depends on the extent to which a utility has to compete for its market, and on the quality of regulation, though private ownership appears to provide some additional improvement. Private owners typically perform better in competitive markets, particularly where innovation is important or least-cost solutions require careful and informed choices, and where costs need to be closely monitored. Generation is therefore a natural choice for private ownership, particularly if it is associated with open access to transmission. This combination would allow private enterprises that self-generate to sell surplus power and improve the competitiveness of the bulk electricity market.

A whole range of other empirical studies has been surveyed by Joskow and Rose (1989) in the context of regulated industries as a whole. Topics important in the case of electricity include the effect of regulation on input choices (i.e., biases regarding choice of capital, fuel, and labor) and the distributional impacts of regulation.

Comparative institutional approach

This book belongs to a genre that is intermediate between the standard theoretical and empirical approaches. We emphasize comparative institutional performance, giving due consideration to historical and political conditions.

There are costs and benefits to this approach. The authors make use of the insights provided by theory, but they frequently find that the stylized textbook models omit important features of reality. Similarly, although the empirical studies are also useful, most do not cover a range of different regulatory regimes, or transitions between different regimes, and frequently fail to find important effects. The advantage of the comparative approach adopted here is that the reader should be able to gain a sense of perspective of the major determinants of industry performance, and both the potential for and constraints on regulatory reform. Such reforms are increasing, and although the present form of some regulatory systems described here may well have changed by the time this book reaches the reader, the lessons from experience should endure.

The comparisons across countries suggest that economic institutions have an inertia and robustness that survive the inevitable twists and turns of debate on public policy. There is a danger in focusing on the immediate policy issues that the larger and longer-acting forces shaping the industry will be overlooked. It is our hope that this study of the institutional structure of the electricity industry will reveal something of these forces and thereby inform future theoretical enquiries into regulation and the more immediate policy debate.

Measures of performance: Excess capacity, relative prices, and long-term productivity

There is no consistent international database that would allow sophisticated statistical comparison of economic performance in electricity. As a substitute, however, we collected a small amount of data for the countries studied here to develop at least a simple picture of common trends and variations. Tables 1-1, 1-2, and 1-3 summarize our results for three performance measures: reserve margins, relative prices within a country, and long-term productivity. Each table tells a reasonably coherent story. Together they provide a global view of the investment process in electricity in the past three decades and some insight into its financing.

Reserve margins

Reserve margins in electric generating capacity are necessary to maintain reliability of service in face of the random breakdown of operating equipment. The high costs of storage make redundant capacity the only practical method for achieving reliability. The economic problem is to optimize reserves at a reasonable level. This optimization must account for both the electricity supply system characteristics and the cost of outages to consumers. Engineering

Table 1-1. *Reserve margins*

Country	Reserve Margin (Capacity) (Capacity − Peak) / Peak		
	1970	1980	1990
Chile	139.4%	90.4%	94.1%
Uruguay	25.9%	27.7%	67.6%
Canada	19.0%	28.0%	20.0%
France	Not Avail.	24.3%	27.1%
Germany	20.4%	39.2%	42.8%
Japan	3.4%	24.9%	4.0%
New Zealand	33.6%	52.3%	37.9%
Sweden	43.0%	58.0%	45.0%
United Kingdom	27.6%	33.1%	20.2%
United States	19.3%	30.4%	22.7%
Yugoslavia	41.0%	53.0%	80.0%

methods to characterize the probability of outages as a function of supply system parameters have been developed over decades (Billinton and Allen, 1984). The valuation of electricity outages, on the other hand, has been undertaken only more recently and requires expensive surveys and sophisticated analytical technique (see, for example, Woo and Train, 1988). Studies of the trade-off between outage costs and reserve capacity tend to result in optimal reserve margins in the 15 to 20% range for predominantly thermal power systems (Southern Company Services, 1991). For hydroelectric systems, these measures are less meaningful, since rainfall variation, not equipment breakdown, is the primary reliability problem.

Table 1-1 shows the data on aggregate reserve margins (i.e., capacity minus peak demand divided by peak demand) for each country where data were available for 1970, 1980, and 1990. These data show an underlying tendency toward apparent excess capacity (i.e., reserves above the 15 to 20% level). In some countries this tendency is minimal; in others it is more extreme. Of the industrialized countries, only Japan exhibits anything resembling potential shortages, presumably because of very rapid economic growth. The long lead time on power plant construction, particularly compared to turns in the cycle of economic activity, can result in mismatches between capacity additions and demand. The tendency toward excess capacity appears to result from an asymmetry between the social penalties of a shortfall (very severe) and those from excess capacity (only moderate). It is not an accident that firms would choose to err on the side of excess capacity.

Table 1-2. *Relative prices*

Country	Industry/Residential			Commercial/Residential		
	1970	1980	1990	1970	1980	1990
Argentina	0.54	0.45	0.93	1.29	1.18	1.93
Brazil	0.38	0.44	0.65	1.00	0.80	1.35
Chile	0.37	0.57	0.59	1.29	1.44	0.93
Uruguay	0.75	0.71	0.80	1.90	1.43	1.11
Canada	0.44	0.61	0.69	0.78	0.90	0.99
France	0.42	0.62	0.35	0.42	0.66	0.58
Germany	0.56	0.63	0.63	Not Available		
Japan	0.41	0.71	0.68	Not Available		
New Zealand	1.38	1.36	1.17	1.92	1.70	1.44
Sweden	0.48	0.45	0.43	0.70	0.75	0.63
United Kingdom	0.76	0.70	0.59	1.13	0.92	0.83
United States	0.79	0.88	0.86	0.96	1.02	0.93
Yugoslavia	0.35	0.74	0.70	Not Available		

The economic optimization framework from which one would derive an estimate of efficient reserve levels still has many conceptual problems. The surveys used to estimate outage costs may be unreliable, in particular because they fail to deal with adjustments consumers might make in anticipation of outages. Indeed, many very sensitive consumers already make such adjustments. Another conceptual problem is the valuation of social costs from widespread interruptions in electricity service. The disruption due to riots and looting during power outages is a real factor motivating government attitudes toward reliability, but this is never an explicit factor in the cost-benefit analysis of reserve margins. The aversion of governments to power outages is an intuitively meaningful factor in the behavior of firms; making it a coherent part of the assessment of excess capacity has not yet been done.

In Chapter 2, Newbery and Green offer an interesting account of the motivation for excess capacity in the United Kingdom. They attribute part of the responsibility for excess capacity to marginal-cost pricing. By pricing low in the face of excess capacity, the demand for electricity is stimulated, thereby justifying future capacity additions. This mechanism is really produced by a configuration in which managers want to oversee a large construction program of new capacity and in which no single regulatory authority is paying sufficient attention to prevent mispricing and excess investment. Waverman and Yatchew in Chapter 8 make similar observations about Canada. This measure of investment performance confirms the ability of all the regulatory systems

Table 1-3. *Historical trend in real prices*

| Country | Historical Trend in Real Prices Continuous Growth Rate | |
	1950–74	1974–90
Canada	−0.74%	2.09%
France	3.23%	−0.04%
Germany	−2.06%	0.27%
Japan	−1.75%	0.16%
New Zealand	−1.95%	1.11%
Sweden	−2.60%	−1.50%
United Kingdom	−2.99%	0.64%
United States	−2.55%	1.68%
Yugoslavia	Not Available	3.40%

examined to facilitate investment. How it is financed and whether it is efficient remain to be seen.

These data suggest no clear conclusion about such propositions as the claim that rate-of-return regulation, for example, induces excess capacity, which in some cases may appear to be higher reserve margins. Moreover, the various technology mixes across countries make even this observation imprecise.

Relative prices

A direct comparison of electricity prices in different countries would be a desirable way to compare performance, but there are conceptual and empirical problems associated with such exercises. Henney (1992), for example, compares prices for various kinds of electricity consumers in Western Europe using European Currency Units (ECUs) but removing the effect of taxes. Using currency exchange rates for broad international comparisons across widely differing economies is generally inferior to purchasing power parity (PPP) when nontradable goods are involved (Kravis, Heston, and Summers, 1978). Although PPP is an improvement over exchange rates, it is not a universal key to all interesting questions involving international comparisons (Sen, 1979). At the heart of PPP methods lie a number of index number issues that are difficult to resolve (Kravis, 1984). Rather than immerse ourselves in these, we adopt a simpler and somewhat less ambitious approach.

We address price performance in two different ways. First we look at potential cross-subsidization by examining relative prices. For each country we develop a measure of the average price paid by industrial, commercial, and residential customers. Table 1-2 displays these data expressed as ratios for the years 1970, 1980, and 1990. We examine long-term trends in average price in Table 1-3.

On the basis of first principles, we would expect industrial prices to be lower than commercial prices, and commercial prices to be lower than residential. There are two primary cost factors determining these relations. First, the ranking of industrial, commercial, and residential loads reflects a typical order of declining load factor. Load factor is the ratio of average to peak demand. All else equal, high load-factor loads have a lower cost of service than low load-factor loads because the facilities dedicated to their use are used more frequently off peak. Second, the cost of distribution facilities to serve industrial loads is low compared to that for other customers because they typically take service at higher voltages, so losses are less and step-down transformers and low-voltage lines are not required. The economics of distribution costs also favor commercial loads over residential loads for much the same reasons. On the demand side, Ramsey pricing principles and typical estimates of demand elasticity are also consistent with the same ordering of relative prices. The Ramsey price is a markup above marginal cost that is inversely proportional to the price elasticity and is the efficient method of meeting a breakeven constraint on revenue (Baumol and Bradford, 1970).

Table 1-2 shows a broadly consistent picture in which industrial consumers of electricity pay substantially less than residential consumers do. The only prominent exception is New Zealand, but as the discussion in Chapter 5 indicates, there are substantially lower prices for a small number of energy-intensive manufacturing firms. On the commercial side, the picture is more mixed. In some countries the prices paid by commercial customers are lower than those paid by residential customers; in other countries they are higher. Marginal-cost principles seem to be applied most systematically in France and Sweden. If we were to treat the pricing in France and Sweden as the closest to marginal cost, this would suggest that most other countries are cross-subsidizing residential consumers from the commercial customers. Further evidence for this conclusion comes from looking at the time trend in Chile and the United Kingdom. In both cases, the deregulation during the 1980s is consistent with lessening the burden on commercial customers.

The data in Table 1-2 must be treated with caution, because there is no consistent international classification of customers into tariff categories. Thus, some residential customers in large apartment buildings or some small manufacturing establishments may be billed under commercial tariffs.

Nonetheless, it appears from these data that the financial burden of investment is typically carried by smaller customers. In particular, the commercial class appears to bear a disproportionate burden in most countries. Most countries recognize an economic need to keep industrial rates relatively close to marginal costs. Politically, it is useful to provide some subsidies to residential customers. This leaves the financial burden with the commercials.

Historical trend in real prices

Table 1-3 shows the major adjustment problems faced by the electricity industry from the inflation and fuel price disruptions of the 1970s. For most countries, the period up to 1974 reflected a continuation of the long historical trend of declining real costs for electricity. Following 1974, however, most countries experienced some increase in real cost. Joskow (1987) made a careful study of this pattern for the United States.

The data in Table 1-3 reflect prices rather than costs. We assume, at least for the industrialized countries for which we have data, that the relation between price and cost is reasonably stable over this period. In most of the chapters, however, there are indications that governments suppressed electricity prices for some period following the OPEC oil price increases of 1973–4. This was a transient episode for most of the industrialized countries. For the developing countries, price suppression has been a much longer-term and more serious phenomenon. In these countries, rates of return have been falling steadily due to declining real electricity tariffs (Schram, 1993). Because of poor maintenance and operating procedures, costs in these countries have probably been going up at the same time that prices have been declining.

The data in Table 1-3 show emerging productivity problems in the electricity industry. These problems are a large part of the motivation for the radical structural reform that is documented in Chapters 2 (the United Kingdom) and 3 (Latin America). In both cases, however, the problems have a longer history than the disruptions associated with fuel price shocks of the 1970s.

Major themes

Certain commonalities emerge from examining the institutional experience in all the countries studied. These are not strictly consequences of the general regulatory problem as formulated in the section titled "The regulation problem" but seem to be peculiar to, or at least characteristic of, the electricity industry.

Information asymmetry

All the country studies in this volume illustrate one way or another the information problems inherent in electricity regulation. There are interesting variations in each context. These variations reinforce the notion that regulation is fundamentally constrained by the opacity of detailed information about cost.

This basic and ubiquitous insight, however, does not imply that the entire research program based on the Principal–Agent framework is a good description of the regulatory problem as it appears in practice. In some settings, it may be reasonable to assume that the principal has a single well-defined objective and substantial flexibility to design instruments that can achieve it. In most cases, however, this is a stylization at best. We document the range of government policy objectives imposed on the electricity industry in the next section. The first implication of this long litany of obligations is the fundamental importance of a multiplicity of objectives facing the regulated firm. Less concretely, but no less basic, are the implicit constraints on regulatory policy created by the political economy in particular countries. These arguments suggest that something like the voting and interest group models surveyed by Noll (1989) may be a better description of regulation in electricity.

The information asymmetry theme might have somewhat weaker implications for regulatory policy than those articulated by the formal Principal–Agent theory. In particular, the prospect for yardstick regulation on an informal international basis is one challenge that emerges from our study. Clearly, the ability to compare performance measures today in a systematic manner is quite limited. Our data collection exercise discussed under "Measures of performance" illustrates the problem. On the other hand, the movement toward privatization and competition has generated an increasing amount of information in those countries where it has taken hold. A new regulatory agenda for electricity, based on the general principle of yardstick comparisons (e.g., Schleifer, 1985), may well be possible if the trend toward privatization internationally produces as much information as the process in the United Kingdom seems to have done.

Relations between government and industry

The multiplicity of objectives that governments have imposed upon the electricity industry is impressive in its scope but somewhat depressing in its tenacity. We discuss these, emphasizing the common tendencies that emerge from the individual studies.

Fuel choice constraints imposed by government policy have influenced the electricity industry in most of the countries we have studied. The preference for indigenous or secure fuel supplies has been a strong feature of government pressure in France, Japan, Canada, and the United Kingdom, and a significant factor in Scandinavia and the United States. In many cases, this interest was translated into support for a nuclear energy program based on indigenous technology. International standardization of nuclear power design has been significantly missing. Instead, each country has pursued an independent path. The dynamic scale economies associated with nuclear technology make it strongly susceptible to "technological lock-in" (Cowan, 1990). Therefore, countries that start along separate paths find it difficult to adjust and learn from the experience of others. Interestingly enough, two of the countries with the most successful nuclear programs, France and Japan, both licensed imported technology and then ultimately adapted it to local engineering expertise (see Chapter 6, and David and Rothwell, 1993).

The fuel security issue is not limited to nuclear power. In several countries (e.g., Germany, the United Kingdom, and Yugoslavia), preference for local coal resources has been mandated, typically at prices above world market levels. In Japan, a remarkable dependence on imported liquefied natural gas (LNG) has developed. This fuel has not been popular in other developed countries because of perceived safety risks. In Japan, however, its low environmental emissions have given it a 20% share of the fuel mix, predominantly in the major polluted urban areas.

Electric utilities have also been encouraged to subsidize rural economic development. In some cases the mechanism has been the construction of hydroelectric facilities in remote locations (Canada and New Zealand). In the United States this function has been supplied directly by the national government, acting in regions largely neglected by private utilities and where federal authority over water rights is operative. Much more commonly, tariff policies have been used to subsidize rural electricity prices.

Several chapters in this volume indicate that environmental concerns are becoming a new source of social demand on the performance of the electricity industry.

Government intervention contributes to the opacity of information because it becomes increasingly difficult for anyone, either inside or outside the firm, to tell which costs are really attributable to which objectives. Conversely, privatization and increased competition make it difficult to sustain multiple objectives and require that governments either forgo them or pursue them with direct, and therefore more easily monitored, subsidies (e.g., the U.K. nuclear levy).

History, technology, and the prospects for institutional reform

The long shadow of nuclear power is seen prominently in these chapters. At once a central object of government policy, this Faustian technology bundles great opportunities with equally great challenges. International experience has been quite mixed. Operational results vary considerably. France, Canada, and Japan all seem to have gotten high levels of output from these assets. The utilization record in the United Kingdom has been disappointing. In all countries, costs have increased far beyond original expectations.

Among the more interesting lessons of the privatization experience in the United Kingdom was the impossibility of making nuclear power a commercial venture. A large part of the problem appears to have been the difficulty of getting realistic estimates of the liabilities associated with plant decommissioning costs and fuel reprocessing. Nuclear technology exhibits the combination of inherent technological uncertainty with the bureaucratic incentives to control information access by regulatory authorities. In many cases, it is almost as if the government has ended up colluding with the utilities to maintain ignorance about cost conditions. When serious discussions about privatization begin, however, such collusion is no longer sustainable. Along with Waverman and Yatchew in their discussion of Ontario Hydro in Chapter 9, we conjecture that dependence on nuclear power will seriously constrain, if not prevent, privatization.

On the other side of the technology equation, Newbery and Green suggest that the availability of new, efficient combined-cycle natural gas generation may facilitate privatization. The U.S. experience, as discussed in Chapter 5, is certainly consistent with this view. Wright, Culy, and Read also speculate that privatization in New Zealand will be accompanied by use of this technology.

The organization of this book

We present our studies along the ownership axis, starting from the major new experiments with private ownership, moving next to the systems of mixed government and private ownership, and ending with the countries where government ownership is complete.

The big experiments

We begin with Newbery and Green on the United Kingdom in Chapter 2. Although the broad outlines of the British experience are relatively well known, this chapter provides a wealth of historical detail that illustrates the institutional constraints on regulatory policy. The authors also articulate the trade-offs between public and private ownership in a way that provides perspective on the subsequent chapters. Newbery and Green are fundamentally historicist in perspective. Their view is consistent with the "path dependence" approach to the evolution of institutions associated with David (1992) and others. Among the many interesting conjectures that they draw from the U.K. experience is their notion of the "option value" of public ownership. The idea here is that public ownership makes far-reaching reforms generally easier than if private interests must be restructured.

Spiller and Viana present the public-private contrast for Latin America in Chapter 3. They emphasize the strength of property rights in the political economy of a nation as a principal determinant of the potential for successful private sector activity. By contrast with Newbery and Green, Spiller and Viana take a structuralist approach: The nature of institutions in one economic sector depends on the large space of political culture. The privatization and competitive structure of the electricity industry in Chile was the first major reorganization in the world. Its success has been one of the primary motivations for experimentation in other countries.

Mixed systems

The cross-sectional view of competition is also provided by Hjalmarsson's study of Scandinavia in Chapter 4. The unique feature of the electricity system in these countries has been the relative success of voluntary cooperative mechanisms, what Hjalmarsson calls "club regulation." This system has maintained coordinated dispatch among electricity producers of mixed ownership and widely differing scale. This has required solving a number of problems that are frequently managed by central control, such as optimizing the operation of large hydroelectric reservoirs and transmission capacity planning. Nonetheless, the system has resulted in excessive capacity expansion. This appears to have been the primary motive for introducing competition (though no accompanying movement toward substantial further privatization). The process is most advanced in Norway. Sweden and Finland have moved much more slowly along these lines.

In Chapter 5, Gilbert and Kahn present the United States, a mixed system of public ownership and heavily regulated private ownership. The pressure for more competition is quite substantial in the United States, and it raises questions about the viability of the current institutional structure. Restructuring arrangements for electricity transmission are the central focus of the discussion. Although similar issues have arisen in the United Kingdom, Chile, and New Zealand, the greater complexity of the network in the United States, very substantial private ownership, and the greater institutional fragmentation make these issues very difficult.

The Japanese electricity system, discussed by Navarro in Chapter 6, took its modern form after World War II. Although designed to resemble the U.S. system of regulated investor ownership, the Japanese government has ownership participation in several major wholesale power companies and strongly influences policies adopted by the large investor-owned firms regarding choices of fuel and pollution control technology. Nonetheless, the utilities have considerable de facto flexibility within explicit regulatory constraint.

In Chapter 7, Muller and Stahl discuss the electricity system in West Germany. The regulatory structure appears comprehensive, but in reality is quite lax. Federal institutions are unable to even enforce common accounting standards by which they might compare costs. Government influence, however, is quite pervasive, including substantial public control over the voting of shares and publicly mandated coal purchases from internationally noncompetitive sources. None of this, however, prevents substantial tariff preference for industrial customers.

Government ownership

Culy, Read, and Wright in Chapter 8 give a detailed look at the process of moving from state to private ownership in the case of New Zealand. The common story of substantial government intervention in the electricity industry is followed by steps toward privatization after a major change in political direction that occurred nationally in response to economic stagnation. Considerable efficiency improvements occurred in the "corporatization" period, when the electricity industry was removed from ministerial control and given commercial objectives. As of 1993, however, further progress toward complete transfer of the industry to private control was stalled by political factors.

The Canadian electricity system is studied by Waverman and Yatchew in Chapter 9. They find many of the classic problems of government ownership. Most of their analysis focuses on Ontario Hydro. They link the dependence of the utility on nuclear power to a substantial increase in the information asymmetry between the firm and the public authorities. This appears in the areas of both construction and operating costs. Because there is no single long-term regulatory agency in charge of monitoring Ontario Hydro, persistent high levels of staffing and compensation as well as unrealistic financial forecasting have gone on for long periods without effective constraint.

In Chapter 10, Laffont describes the French electricity industry. His discussion of the "contract plans" between the government and Electricité de France illustrates many of the difficulties created by multiplicity of objectives. He concludes that writing "contracts" between government and public industry is substantially easier when no major investment programs are required. This chapter also gives a very complete discussion of tariff design using marginal-cost principles, an activity in which France has taken a leading role.

Finally, in Chapter 11 Antic takes up the tragic case of Yugoslavia. The story involves most of the difficulties common to state-run economies. It also includes a record of substantial engineering accomplishment. This is all the more remarkable in the face of a bewildering array of institutional forces, both governmental and regional, pulling the industry in many different directions at once. Given the centrifugal pressures pushing toward parochial and even inconsistent goals, the industry was able to achieve significant interregional cooperation and integration. Unfortunately, these achievements have ultimately been undone by the destabilizing forces that have since eliminated Yugoslavia as a functioning national entity.

Conclusions

Our comparative study reveals few sweeping conclusions, but nonetheless does allow for some generalizations. Some of these are rather simple, some raise methodological questions, some point to unresolved issues.

At the most mundane level, we find that the electricity industry in almost all countries responds to the elastic demands of industrial customers by pricing their service below rates charged to others. There are differences in degree but not in kind. These price concessions are related to demand elasticity, but the overall pricing policy does not reflect Ramsey principles, because commercial customers appear to cross-subsidize others. The result is that the burden of capital recovery for the industry's fixed costs is largely borne by small customers, particularly commercial firms. Residential customers typically benefit to some degree from their political influence in the aggregate.

Another interesting universal appears to be similarity of the systems in response to exogenous shocks. In all the developed countries, the oil price disruptions of the 1970s caused a period of price suppression. This was a transient phenomenon, however, in all the countries that we have examined.

The role of government control is quite variable. It is difficult to find a common denominator in the government-owned systems, except perhaps a greater multiplicity of objectives than in those systems subject to more private sector forces. Otherwise, it is difficult to detect major differences in performance that result from ownership type. The results on power plant efficiency illustrate this point.

More fundamentally, we find that endowments matter. The traditional dichotomy between theoretical and empirical study of regulation suppresses the role of history in shaping the institutions and policies that characterize particular regulatory regimes. Thus, the fuel security concerns that we observe in many countries are tied both to natural resource endowments and to the political heritage of war. With the easing of international tensions, these objectives may diminish, facilitating a more commercial orientation for the electricity industry. The political systems of each country, however, are also an endowment of a sort, and these can either foster or impede competition in electricity.

The ubiquitous problem of information opacity is reduced by privatization and the regulatory concerns that accompany it. The regulators keep requiring that the managers of these systems respond to a continual pattern of questions about the cost basis of particular prices or services. Conversely, in public systems no one can really be sure what costs are incurred and for what purposes. This phenomenon seems linked to our next observation.

We find that privatization in electricity is accompanied by structural change. As opposed to the experience of privatization in many other industries, there seems to be more behind the process than the simple desire of governments to raise revenues by the sale of state-owned assets. It is not clear why this is the case. Perhaps governments recognize that productivity gains will come from competition, and this requires structural change. Perhaps investors see competition as more secure than a regulatory structure for a privatized monopoly. Since the only component of the electricity industry for which competition is feasible is the generation segment, the introduction of market forces requires some reorganization.

Finally, privatization and structural change are the most exciting developments in the electricity industry. It is uncertain whether they will become dominant trends or be confined to certain countries only. This uncertainty of outcome is linked with our incomplete understanding of exactly why they have emerged now. Although many plausible reasons can be offered in individual cases, these developments have had only partial and limited success to date.

REFERENCES

Averch, H., and L. Johnson. "The Behavior of the Firm Under Regulatory Constraint." *American Economic Review* 52 (1962): 1053–69.

Atkinson, S., and R. Halvorsen. "The Relative Efficiency of Public and Private Firms in a Regulated Environment: The Case of U.S. Electric Utilities." *Journal of Public Economics* 29 (1986): 281–94.

Baumol, W., and D. Bradford. "Optimal Departures from Marginal Cost Pricing." *American Economic Review* 60 (1970): 265–83.

Baumol, W., J. Panzar, and R. Willig. *Contestable Markets and the Theory of Industry Structure.* New York: Harcourt Brace Javanovich, 1982.

Berg, S, and J. Tschirhart. *Natural Monopoly Regulation.* New York: Cambridge University Press, 1988.

Billinton, R., and R. Allen. *Reliability Evaluation of Power Systems.* New York: Plenum Press, 1984.

Boiteux, M. "Peak Load Pricing." *Journal of Business* 33 (1960): 157–79.

Brown, S., and D. Sibley. *The Theory of Public Utility Pricing.* New York: Cambridge University Press, 1986.

Courville, L. "Regulation and Efficiency in the Electric Utility Industry." *Bell Journal of Economics and Management Science* 5 (1974): 53–74.

Cowan, R. "Nuclear Power Reactors: A Study in Technological Lock-In." *Journal of Economic History* 50 (1990): 541–67.

David, P. "Path Dependence and Predictability in Dynamic Systems with Local Network Externalities: A Paradigm for Historical Economics." *Technology and the Wealth of Nations,* edited by C. Freeman and D. Foray. London: Francis Painter, 1992.

David, P., and G. Rothwell. "Measuring Standardization: An Application to the American and French Nuclear Power Industries." Stanford University Economics Department Working Paper, 1993.

Farrell, M. J. "The Measurement of Productive Efficiency." *Journal of the Royal Statistical Society* A 120 (1957): 253–81.

Farrer, T. *The State in Its Relation to Trade.* London: Macmillan, 1902.

Galal, A. "CHILGENER," Ch. 9, and "ENERSIS," Ch. 10. In *The Welfare Consequences of Selling Public Enterprises,* edited by Galal, A., L. Jones, P. Tandon, and I. Vogelsang. New York: Oxford University Press, 1994.

Galal, A., L. Jones, P. Tandon, and I. Vogelsang. *The Welfare Consequences of Selling Public Enterprises.* New York: Oxford University Press, 1994.

Henney, A. *The Electricity Supply Industries of Eleven West European Countries.* London: Energy Economic Engineering Ltd., 1992.

Hjalmarsson, L., and A. Veiderpass, "Productivity in Swedish Electricity Retail Distribution." *Scandanavian Journal of Economics* 94 Supplement (1992): 193–205.

Hollas, D., and S. Stansell. "An Examination of the Effect of Ownership Form on Price Efficiency: Proprietary, Cooperative and Municipal Electric Utilities." *Southern Economic Journal* 55 (1988): 336–50.

Joskow, P. "Productivity Growth and Technical Change in the Generation of Electricity." *The Energy Journal* 8 (1987): 17–38.

Joskow, P., and N. Rose. "The Effects of Economic Regulation." *Handbook of Industrial Organization* II, edited by R. Schmalensee and R. Willig. Amsterdam: North-Holland, 1989.

Kravis, I. "Comparative Studies of National Incomes and Prices." *Journal of Economic Literature* 22 (1984): 1–39.

Kravis, I., A. Heston, and R. Summers. *International Comparisons of Real Product and Purchasing Power.* Baltimore: Johns Hopkins University Press, 1978.

Laffont, J., and J. Tirole. *A Theory of Incentives in Procurement and Regulation.* Cambridge, Mass.: MIT Press, 1993.

Moen, J. "Electricity Utility Regulation, Structure and Competition. Experiences from the Norwegian Electric Supply Industry." Oslo: Norwegian Water Resources and Energy Administration, NVE, 1994.

Newbery, D. "Regulatory Policies and Reform in the Electricity Supply Industry." *Regulatory Policies and Reform in Industrializing Countries.* New York: Oxford University Press, 1994.

Noll, R. "Economic Perspectives on the Politics of Regulation." *Handbook of Industrial Organization* II, edited by R. Schmalensee and R. Willig. Amsterdam: North-Holland, 1989.

Peltzman, S. "Pricing in Public and Private Enterprises: Electric Utilities in the United States." *Journal of Law and Economics* 4 (1971): 109–47.

Perez-Arriaga, Ignacio. "The Organisation and Operation of the Electricity Supply Industry in Argentina." London: Energy Economic Engineering Ltd., 1994.

Pescatrice, D., and J. Trapani. "The Performance and Objectives of Public and Private Utilities Operating in the United States." *Journal of Public Economics* 13 (1980): 259–76.

Pollitt, M. G. "The Relative Performance of Publicly Owned and Privately Owned Electric Utilities: International Evidence," PhD thesis. Oxford: Oxford University Press, 1993.

"Technical Efficiency in Electric Power Plants." Mimeo, Faculty of Economics. Cambridge, U.K.: Cambridge University, 1994.

Schleifer, A. "A Theory of Yardstick Competition." *Rand Journal of Economics* 16 (1985): 319–27.

Schram, G. "Issues and Problems in the Power Sector of Developing Countries." *Energy Policy* 21 (1993): 735–47.

Sen, A. "The Welfare Basis of Real Income Comparisons: A Survey." *Journal of Economic Literature* 17 (1979): 1–45.

Short, R. "The Role of Public Enterprises: An International Statistical Comparison." In R. Floyd, C. Gary, and R. Short (eds.), *Public Enterprises in Mixed Economies: Some Macroeconomic Aspects.* Washington, D.C., International Money Fund (IMF), 1984.

Southern Company Services. "An Economic Study of the Optimum Reserve Margin and Associated Reliability Indices for the Southern Electric System." Birmingham, Alabama, 1991.

Vickers, J. S., and G. K. Yarrow. *Privatization: An Economic Analysis.* Cambridge, Mass.: MIT Press, 1988.

Woo, C., and K. Train. "The Cost of Electric Power Outages to Commercial Firms." *The Energy Journal,* Special Electricity Reliability Issue, 9 (1988): 161–72.

World Bank. "The World Bank's Role in the Electric Power Sector." Washington, D.C., 1993.

CHAPTER 2

Regulation, public ownership and privatisation of the English electricity industry

David M. Newbery and Richard Green
Department of Applied Economics
Cambridge, United Kingdom

Introduction

The privatisation of the Electricity Supply Industry (ESI) of England and Wales not only transferred ownership from the public to the private sector but must rank as one of the most ambitious attempts anywhere to introduce competition into a normally vertically integrated natural monopoly. The high-tension transmission grid and the low-tension distribution system are classic examples of natural monopolies in which the costs of duplication make competition between alternative systems uneconomic. Between the date of nationalisation in 1948 and privatisation in 1990, the industry consisted of two vertically integrated, state-owned segments: generation and high-tension transmission were under the control of the Central Electricity Generating Board (CEGB) and its precursors, whereas distribution and supply were under the control of twelve Area Boards (ABs), which received electricity from the CEGB under the Bulk Supply Tariff. Both the CEGB and the Area Boards were represented on the coordinating body of the Electricity Council.

Recent theoretical discussions of regulation and privatisation typically work within a Principal–Agent framework and assume the existence of a single principal (normally taken as the state or party in power), with a coherent and well-defined objective and substantial powers to design systems of monitoring and incentives to best achieve that objective, constrained by the opacity and asymmetry of information about the regulated enterprise and the conflicting objectives of the owner, the manager, or both. A more realistic assessment would be that at each moment natural monopolies are constrained by a historically given politicoeconomic balance of interests that circumscribe the actions available to the principal and severely limit the possible changes in the system of regulation and the design of incentives.

The modern approach to the design of regulatory systems often overlooks the historical constraints placed on the options available for reform and implicitly assumes that the state of the industry is one of neutral equilibrium, in which any displacement will not set in train a sequence of subsequent changes that have long-term implications for the structure and performance of the industry. Privatisation in England was the most important such event but not the only one. It had the great advantage that the debate over restructuring was conducted in public and that within a very short time it precipitated consequential changes elsewhere in the industry and in the coal and gas industries that demonstrated how much the balance of interests had changed. It therefore provides a central object lesson in the potential for reforming the electricity supply industry.

The other main lesson from history and international comparisons is that the relative performance of the industry under public and private ownership does not involve a simple unchanging comparison of the two alternatives, but depends on the state of development of the industry, which owes much to history, technology, and the balance of political and economic forces shaping its development. Rather than asking which form of ownership is best, it is more interesting to identify circumstances under which public ownership appears to have a comparative advantage and circumstances under which private ownership is preferable. To simplify drastically, public ownership has a comparative advantage where coordination and restructuring are required, at least in the kind of economy exemplified by Britain. Private ownership on the other hand, especially when combined with competition, may be able to avoid some of the inefficiencies inherent in the lack of clear objectives that frequently go with the balancing of diverse interest groups under state ownership.

The history of the electricity industry in Britain can be divided into four phases. The early period until 1926 was decentralised, uncoordinated, with generation under both private and municipal ownership subject to loose regulation laid down by statute. There were examples of notable private sector success, but overall the industry fell behind best practice abroad and seemed locked in an unsatisfactory equilibrium. The creation of the Central Electricity Board as a public corporation in 1926, set up to build the high-tension grid, marked the start of the second phase, which reaped some of the benefits of coordination by public ownership of part of the natural monopoly element, with mixed ownership in generation and distribution.

The failure in this period lay in extending the benefits of coordination to distribution, when it became increasingly evident that voluntary negotiation would continue to be blocked by vested interests. Nationalisation in 1948 was the only way to resolve this deadlock, for central public ownership seemed to be the only way of coordinating the fragmented and largely municipally owned local distribution undertakings. Much of the political commitment to public ownership of the incoming postwar Labour Government derived from the unsatisfactory attempts to reform the industry by voluntary negotiation in the 1930s, whereas much of the opposition from the Conservative Party derived from the image of electricity and steel as central features of the Soviet planned economy. Although this period had its technical successes, the regulatory system reflected an inefficient equilibrium that only privatisation appeared capable of upsetting. The present phase of private ownership has set in train substantial changes in the structure and operation of the industry, and it raises the critical question whether the benefits of increased competition offset the difficulties of achieving the benefits of coordination.

Regulatory issues in electricity

The electricity transmission and distribution system is a natural monopoly, and in Britain one-half of the electricity is sold to small consumers who are poorly placed to choose between alternative suppliers. There are sound economic arguments for regulating natural monopolies such as the durable network utilities, and the main question is whether this regulation requires public ownership or whether the public interest can be adequately represented by a regulator who imposes conditions upon the activities of privately owned operators of the network.

Short (1984) provides a detailed study of the sectoral allocation of public enterprises and finds considerable similarities across both developed and developing countries in the pattern of public ownership. In particular, public ownership is common among the durable network industries and for other natural monopolies such as ports and airports. Given the alternative of regulating private enterprises, it is worth first asking why public ownership has been the preferred solution in so many cases. Consider what is necessary for private utilities to be willing to invest in the more capital-intensive industries (telecommunications, rail, water, electricity). It is unlikely under most systems of government that private operators would be free to charge monopoly prices, either because in a democratic form of government consumers would resist through the political process or in other forms of government the state would be reluctant to allow large rents to be generated beyond its control. There are some exceptions to this claim, but they are notably few. If, therefore, the utility owners rationally expect that their prices will be regulated in the future, they need the reassurance that the prices could be set at a sufficiently remunerative level to justify the investment. Once the capital has been sunk, the risk is that the balance of advantage would shift toward those arguing for lower and possibly unremunerative prices, and there are numerous examples of developing countries failing to adequately index the prices of public utilities in periods of inflation.

The problem can be posed more sharply. Why should anyone sink their money into an asset that cannot be moved and that would not pay for itself for many years? Investors would have to be confident that they had secure title to these returns and that the returns would be sufficiently attractive. Durable investments thus require the rule of law, and specifically the law of property, which is a public good provided by the state. If the state exists primarily to enforce the rights of property owners, then there is no problem, but by the time electricity became important, the state represented a wider range of interests and needed to balance the claims of property against those of workers, voters, and consumers. The resulting tensions weakened property rights because the coercive power of the state could be used not only to enforce laws but also to collect taxes, affect the purchasing power of the currency by issuing fiat money, and even, in extreme cases, to expropriate property.

One of the clearest examples of the effect of this shift in political power occurred in the British coal industry in the interwar period. At that time, the industry was privately owned and employed more than a million workers. The currency appreciation caused by the return to the gold standard in 1926 put huge pressure on export-oriented industries like coal. Wages were cut, and the General Strike was a direct result of the resistance by mineworkers. The class conflict between workers on the one hand and capitalist mineowners on the other hand was reminiscent of the recent Russian Revolution and was widely perceived as a serious threat to the political stability of the country. Nationalisation of the mines was called for and must have seemed attractive as an alternative to bloody revolution. Once the question of state intervention to regulate the struggle between miners and owners was posed so sharply, the genie was out of the bottle. The mineowners feared that an incoming Labour Government would nationalise the mines and that any investment would therefore be lost. Not surprisingly, they cut back investment and attempted to lower costs by reducing wages. British mining rapidly fell behind best practice elsewhere, and the less satisfactory was the performance of the privately owned coal-mining industry, the greater was the argument for nationalisation. The expectations of both sides were self-reinforcing, and in due course the mines were nationalised under the postwar Labour Government.

It might seem that all that is required to reassure private investors is sufficiently strong and legally enforceable guarantees that they are assured of a fair rate of return on their investment. The problem with this solution is the standard problem of rate-of-return regulation: If investors cannot lose, then they have little incentive to invest prudently and a temptation to overinvest or gold-plate the investment. The regulatory problem is therefore to devise a system that credibly rewards prudent investment while penalising inefficiency. One of the key tests of the efficiency of any regulatory regime is the extent to which it succeeds in resolving this dilemma.

The seriousness of the problem of regulatory commitment will depend on several factors. If the regulator represents the interests of capital or the industry owners and is secure against labour unrest or regime change, then the problem is slight, though the danger here is that the monopoly will overcharge and have little incentive for efficiency. There is a greater problem if regulation reflects wider interests, particularly when these are politicised and exercised through changing governments with short time horizons. The problem is reduced if it is self-evident that high rates of investment are required or if the investors alone have access to appropriate technology. The costs of underinvestment then would be too great relative to the short-term gains of lowering prices and transferring rents. Similarly, when the industry has the capacity to inflict large and rapid damage on the economy, it is more likely to be allowed to enjoy a reasonable return on its investment. This is most evident in telecommunications, where the software to manage the system can be erased overnight and the consequent collapse of communications within the country would be too awful to contemplate. Electricity has similar features in that power cuts are politically costly, though this countervailing threat is clearly not sufficient in many countries.

Finally, the more capital-intensive and durable the investment, the greater is the need for regulatory commitment. Until the recent introduction of combined-cycle gas turbine (CCGT) sets, generation was capital-intensive, with capital costs between 40% (fossil fuel) and 65% (nuclear) of total costs for base-load plant. The transmission and distribution systems are even more capital-intensive and account for nearly one-third of total delivered electricity costs. It is hardly surprising that electricity generation and transmission are frequently under public ownership in countries where the private sector lacks confidence in the regulatory system.

The advantages of coordination

Because electricity cannot be readily stored, supply must be continuously adjusted to varying demand. Efficiency requires centralized dispatch of generator units and coordination between investment in generation and transmission. The areas within which there is central dispatch can be small and numerous, perhaps with some power exchange between systems, in which case some of the network benefits will be forgone, or they may be extensive, possibly countrywide, as under the CEGB. It may be institutionally difficult to achieve these wide-area benefits through amalgamation or agreement, and a second test of the regulatory system is the extent to which it facilitates efficient wide-area coordination of grid expansion and use. The optimal degree of coordination or the optimal size of area over which central dispatch is exercised will depend on the benefits of central dispatch compared to the costs of the required restructuring.

The three factors influencing the cost savings of central dispatch are the degree of variation in short-run avoidable operating costs, the reserve margin required to reduce risks of shortages, and the degree of variation in demand over time and space. The steeper the short run marginal cost (SRMC) schedule and the greater the demand variability, the greater will be the price variability and the greater the prospects for beneficial trade between adjacent regions. If the shape of the SRMC schedules and the temporal pattern of demand were identical in each region, there would be no gains from trade, but this is unlikely. In Britain, most coal-fired plants are located near the coal-mining areas of the Midlands and Northeast. Oil-fired plants are located at refineries near oil terminals, and nuclear plants are normally located in areas of low population on the coast (for cooling water) close to demand centres. Different sizes and ages of plant have different short-run variable costs, and the merit order ranks stations in increasing order of SRMC: nuclear on base-load, followed by gas CCGT, coal, then oil, and finally gasoil (in open-cycle gas turbines).[1]

Greater diversity of fuels, plant sizes and ages, and demand variability argue for larger areas for central dispatch, as do plant-level economies of scale. Beyond some point these scale advantages become less important and may not justify the additional cost of expanding the grid (or reaching agreement over sharing access and centralising dispatch). The question is how the choice of regulation and the institutional environment affects the extent to which these scale and network economies are realised (or overinvested in).

One hypothesis to be tested against the evidence is that dispersed ownership of utilities that are vertically integrated into local transmission systems, whether municipal or private, will find it hard to realise network economies as they will find it hard to amalgamate or delegate central dispatch. Nationalisation may then be the simplest and possibly the only feasible method of achieving the required structural change. In a competitive market, takeovers and mergers can realise economies of scale, but regulation often discourages such market-based solutions. To the extent that corporatist states encourage self-regulation by cartels this problem may be avoided, and there are examples both in Britain and Germany suggesting that concentrated private ownership of natural monopolies may achieve some and perhaps most of the benefits of coordination, though there are equally counterexamples from Britain, both in electricity and also in railways.

The next two sections review the history up to the moment of privatisation, to examine the nature and efficiency of the regulatory equilibrium, and the ex-

---

[1] When it was abolished in 1990, the CEGB owned 34 coal, 6 oil, 5 dual-fired, 9 open-cycle gas turbine, 6 hydro, 1 wind, 2 pumped storage, 7 (nuclear) magnox, and 5 (nuclear) advanced gas-cooled reactor (AGR) stations (all located in England and Wales). The stations varied not only in fuel but also in size, age, and efficiency. The consequence was that variable costs varied widely from plant to plant so the network benefits were potentially large for Britain.

tent to which it encouraged efficient investment and achieved the potential network economies from coordination.

Fragmentation and disputation:
The first phase of development

The first small generators followed soon after the announced discovery of electromagnetic induction by Michael Faraday in 1831.[2] By 1857 generators were used to produce light in lighthouses, and by 1879 football matches were being staged under arc lights. The first central power station was water-powered, built by the German company Siemens, at Godalming in 1881. The first steam-powered generator was at Holborn Viaduct in 1882, financed by Edison. The 1882 Electric Lighting Act enabled companies to supply mains electricity but provided for maximum price regulation and the purchase by the local authority of companies established under the Act at written-down value after 21 years. In 1888 Parliament extended the purchase clause to 42 years, a clause that was to return to haunt the industry in the late 1930s. In 1889 Bradford became the first municipal electrical enterprise.

Initial progress in Britain was slow, for two interrelated reasons. Low demand at the initially high price meant small generating sets that failed to reap economies of scale. Small generating sets meant high costs, which restricted demand. The special problem faced in Britain was the competitive advantage that gas held over electricity in domestic lighting. Gas was relatively more expensive in the United States, enabling Edison to sell electric lighting at the "gas price" competitively and to break out of this constraint on market size. In the last decade of the nineteenth century all electricity was used for lighting, which led to very low load factors. Not until 1906 was the demand for power and traction equal to that of lighting, and with a more balanced load during the day, load factors dramatically improved. Combined with rapid growth in demand, the advantage of scale over transmission losses dictated larger generating stations.

One of the more successful examples of private supply extending over a significant area and reaping increasing economies of scale was that of the Newcastle-upon-Tyne Electric Supply Company (NESCo). In 1900 its distribution covered 16 square miles, but by 1914 it covered 1,400 square miles, mostly operating on three-phase 40 hertz AC at 20,000 volts. In 1903 NESCo started work on the largest power station in Europe, and it rapidly became the biggest integrated power system in Europe. It owed much of its success to the entrepreneurial talents of its chief engineer, Charles Merz, and in the decade to 1913 increased sales 32-fold, compared with only a fourfold increase in the rest of Britain.

---

[2] This section draws heavily on Hannah (1979).

NESCo was atypical. Elsewhere the country confronted a fundamental conflict. Cheap electricity, at a price low enough to make its use for power and traction (especially in trams and railways) economically attractive, required integrated distribution and large generating stations. These would logically be under single ownership – in short, as natural monopolies. Existing municipal undertakings could not expand into neighbouring jurisdictions. Relations between the public and private sector were perhaps more strained than in other countries, and the debate over public ownership more vigorous. Municipal undertakings appeared to maximise sales, charged lower prices, and had built up a better load factor and higher load than had private undertakings. Britain entered World War I with the conflicts between the small municipalities and the potentially larger (but on average smaller) private generators unresolved and with the resulting fragmented and inefficient supply and distribution system. This unsatisfactory equilibrium exemplified the characteristic malaise of British society, described as a "series of closed groups, ... stratified and cellular" (Williams, 1908, cited by Foster, 1993, p. 63).

The national grid and the Central Electricity Board

The 1914–18 war had demonstrated the relative backwardness of Britain in electricity supply and had created the need for rationalising supply from existing stations by some interconnection that allowed the higher load factors to be met from the more efficient stations. Reconstruction Committees were set up, with coal chaired by Haldane, who delegated work on electricity supply to Merz of NESCo. They reported in 1917 with a blueprint for the future of the industry – replacing the 600 undertakings with large power plants in 16 districts, modelled on NESCo. It was estimated that this would halve the cost of power. Although there were claims that the capital requirements of the new large stations and grid would require public ownership, opposition to government encroachment on the private sector was strong. Rationalisation, to be effective given the history of failure to cooperate, would require powers of compulsory purchase, and on this the government choked.

The 1919 Electricity (Supply) Act did empower electricity commissioners to refuse permission for uneconomic generating plant extensions and to require frequency change and interconnection for bulk supply where economical, but they had to be content with voluntary agreements between undertakings, not executive power. They sanctioned 11 new stations of 30 MW, authorised 30 expansions of the same size between 1919 and 1926, and closed down 101 small stations, though the lack of a grid meant many new small stations were still built. After seven years only 10% of electricity was sold under bulk supply agreements, and the net flow from the company to the municipal sector was only 2%, rather than the estimated economically justified transfer of 16%.

Faced with such slow progress, the Weir Committee was set up in 1925 and promptly produced a damning indictment of the power of local interests to block technical improvements. The committee argued for a national grid and suggested an ingenious compromise to the conflict between public and private interests. The Central Electricity Board (CEB) should build and operate the grid, while existing companies would build and operate stations and locally distribute power. New investment would be coordinated by the CEB, as would dispatch. Such a proposal was presented to Parliament in 1926 and bitterly opposed, although no private assets were to be transferred to public ownership. It finally passed in December with Labour support, with an additional clause (Section 13) limiting the bulk supply tariff to no more than the companies would have paid under independent operation had the Act not been passed – a subsequent lawyers' paradise.

The CEB was a statutory corporation modelled on the BBC, acting more like a commercial enterprise than a "nationalised industry." It had considerable autonomy, paid high salaries, and was financed by fixed-interest loans that were not guaranteed by the government as a policy decision to retain independence from the Treasury. It rapidly decided to standardize on 132 KV and 50 Hz for transmission, and financed the conversion from other frequencies out of levies that never exceeded 1% of total revenues. The grid was completed on 5 September 1933, and full grid trading over the whole country followed almost immediately. This meant that the CEB operated a "merit order" and directed the operation of all major power stations (which continued to be owned and operated by the undertakings). The grid was not initially intended to transmit power over long distances and can best be described as an interconnected set of local interconnection schemes.[3] Indeed, initially the seven grid regions were run as local systems, though in 1936 the complete grid was run experimentally for the first time as a whole – apparently the largest number of generators to run in parallel up to that date. By 1937 the North and South were regularly run as two main systems, and, faced with large power deficits in the South in 1938, the whole grid was again run as a single synchronised system, this time for lengthy periods.

Consequences of the CEB

The CEB paid all costs, capital and operating, and took responsibility for security of supply. The merit order concentrated generation on the most efficient plants, with 15 out of the 148 under CEB control accounting for half

---

[3] The transmission voltage of 132 KV was rather low for long-distance transmission, and proposals to move to 275 KV were delayed by World War II. The choice of transmission technology was established good practice rather than pioneering, but defensible for the distances envisaged and the dispersed availability of coalfields and port facilities.

the system requirements. Running costs of the preexisting stations were reduced as a result of merit order scheduling, and by 1938 overall grid savings from interconnection had risen to 11% of total payments for electricity. Reserve power capacity was cut from 40 to 10%, saving almost the same again on annual levelised capital costs. These annual savings of £5.5 million can be compared with the construction cost of £29 million, or a crude return of 18% before deducting operating costs of the CEB. Hannah (1979, p. 129, fn. 59) calculates that the real return to the grid was more than 6%, well above the cost of borrowing, excluding all postwar benefits. The CEB standardised on generating sets of 30 and 50 MW, with occasional larger sizes, such as the 100 and 105 MW sets at Battersea (the largest in Europe, though not in the world). Competitive innovation was fostered by leaving the design and building of power stations to the individual undertakings. By 1935, some stations had thermal efficiencies of 27%, comparable to best practice in the United States.

Outside London all but three of the towns with populations of more than 60,000 had municipally owned undertakings. Before grid trading, the municipalities accounted for two-thirds of sales and capacity, but by the later 1930s, under grid trading, this fell to 56%, suggesting that private companies were more efficient when open competition was possible.[4] The CEB paid municipal generators a price that allowed a return on capital equal to the cost of their borrowed capital and paid private companies a price that allowed the rather higher rate of return of 5 to 6.5%, depending on the average interest or dividend paid the previous year. The CEB thus imposed a price cap on sales from the undertakings to the grid and imposed strict controls on the charges undertakings could levy for other services.

After the 1926 Act, supply expanded rapidly – between 1929 and 1935 output of public supply undertakings increased by 70%, despite the Depression. Given the capital-intensive nature of electricity supply, this could not be financed entirely out of profits, and only an estimated 48% was so financed. There appeared to be no difficulty in raising capital for what was a prosperous and rapidly expanding regulated monopoly. Municipalities, which accounted for somewhat less than two-thirds of investment, had access to fixed-interest cheap loans raised through the Public Works Loans Board and, by calculating costs using rather conservative depreciation, were able to earn good rates of return and pay off their debt. Private companies lacked the security of the local tax base and had to pay slightly higher interest on their debt, but their shares stood at a premium in the Depression, for they were not tightly regulated and were regarded as secure investments.

---

[4] Foreman-Peck and Waterson (1985) found that the best municipalities and private companies were equally efficient but that there was a long "tail" of inefficient municipalities.

Regulation: Municipal undertakings were price-capped but at ineffectively high levels, and profit transfers to reduce local taxes were restricted to not more than 1.5% of outstanding debt by the 1926 Act. The fact that domestic consumers had a majority of votes meant that this limit was rarely binding. The pro-consumer attitude of municipalities was illustrated by price cutting, which occurred when they exercised their right to buy private companies after their 42-year franchise, and by the fact that for lighting loads (preeminently of concern to domestic consumers) municipal prices were on average only three-quarters the level set by private companies.

Private companies were also price-capped at increasingly irrelevant high levels and were subject to a form of profit regulation in which they could increase their dividends only if they reduced prices. This was ineffective, either because the prices were lowered to attract commercial customers anyway, or because firms could circumvent the constraint by issuing preference shares rather than paying dividends. When selling to the grid, they were rate-of-return regulated, but the private companies had ample opportunities for inflating their costs by borrowing money or purchasing current inputs at excessive rates from unregulated subsidiaries. Hannah (1979, p. 227) notes both that the commissioners were pressing for controls over such abuses and that the existence of regulation perhaps quietened public hostility to private exploitation and hence protected the regulated.

The conclusion is that during this period of rapid expansion and cost reduction (with the move to more economic scales and newer technologies) there was no problem of regulatory commitment. The autonomous and commercial nature of the CEB undoubtedly helped, but its success in reaching agreements with diverse interest groups, especially municipalities, was undoubtedly the result of the considerable cost savings that allowed opposition to be bought off. This period of development demonstrated the value of public enterprise in achieving coordination in the natural monopoly element (the grid and dispatch) while permitting a competitive and diverse generation business.

The failure to secure local coordination: If the CEB was a notable success, the hope that the numerous distribution companies would voluntarily agree to merge and coordinate their activities was a disappointing failure. Studies in the 1930s suggested that the potential gains from coordination of distribution might be as large as those secured by the grid itself, but although many in the industry recognised the advantages of amalgamation, vested interests and the political opposition to nationalisation prevented such progress before World War II. Many Conservative members believed that the CEB's wish to coordinate generation was a form of creeping nationalisation and as such to be resisted in principle. The Conservative approach was to attempt to restructure around the existing undertakings, but it was doomed to failure because of the opposition by smaller undertakings (who would be closed down or merged) and the difficulty in reconciling municipal and private owners. The debate was suspended during World War II, but around this time the original 42-year franchises were maturing, and the threat was that municipal ownership would be extended and would make subsequent amalgamation and coordination even more difficult. During the war, these franchises were put on ice, but after the war the incoming government was faced with the choice of either nationalisation to impose a sensible coordinated distribution system or increased fragmentation among municipalities, which seemed incapable of rational coordination. Public ownership at the national level was thus a superior alternative to public ownership at the municipal level. One might conclude that nationalisation was forced upon the industry by the initial franchising provisions and that the Conservative Party were happy to acquiesce in the forced reorganisation, although they might have been individually unwilling to underwrite nationalisation.

Postwar nationalisation

The 1930s had demonstrated the beneficial effects of public ownership on restructuring the electricity industry, and the failure of regulatory solutions for railways convinced many of the need for railway nationalisation. The standard model of a public sector corporation was the first such, the British Broadcasting Corporation, one that seemed to combine the high hopes of public service with operational success. Perhaps it is therefore not so surprising that the early postwar nationalisations of coal and electricity commanded considerable cross-party support (Foster, 1993).[5] Such support may have obscured the most serious defect of the programme, that there was no coherent policy objective that nationalisation was supposed to achieve, and hence no guidance on how best to structure the system of regulatory oversight once the industry had been transferred to public ownership.

This failure to specify objectives has been argued persuasively by Foster (1993) to have been the ultimate source of the failure of public ownership of the natural monopolies. A deeper explanation would be that public ownership inevitably allows the various interest groups a stage on which to influence outcomes and precludes the pursuit of any simple single objective. A further complication is that the Labour Party derives substantial political support from the trade unions, which in turn are dominated by the unions in the large nationalised industries such as coal, rail, and to a lesser extent, electricity. Changes in political power therefore change the balance of these interest groups, although until the 1980s such changes were not able to seriously weaken the

---

[5] Churchill had been sympathetic to coal nationalisation in 1919, while his grandson was still vigorously defending the miners against his party line in 1993.

power of the trade unions. Indeed, on one view, privatisation was a mechanism for weakening the trade unions and with them, the Labour Party, thereby entrenching the Conservative Party.

The constellation of interest groups in the ESI was strongly influenced by the technical characteristics of electricity. Fuel costs are roughly half total generation costs from nonnuclear generators, and because electricity is nonstorable, security of fuel supply is critical. Britain has always been heavily reliant on indigenous coal, and the interdependence of coal and electricity has been close. In 1960, 80% of electricity was generated by coal, and power stations took one-quarter of all coal mined. By 1990, over two-thirds of electricity was still generated from coal, but power generation now took 80% of the output of British Coal. Until the late 1970s, the obvious alternative fuel, oil, was imported. The 1956 Suez Crisis revealed the insecurity of oil supplies and was responsible for accelerating the ambitious and ill-fated nuclear construction programme. The oil shocks of the 1970s created further concerns about security and further entangled energy policy with foreign policy. According to Yergin (1992), the geopolitics of oil made this entanglement inevitable for any major oil-importing power such as Britain. The General Strike of 1926 and the miners' strikes of 1974 and 1984 demonstrated that indigenous fuel supply did not ensure security when it was supplied by a single nationalised industry selling to another. These strikes prompted attempts at diversification away from coal.

The electricity industry is also unusual in the number and strength of interest groups concerned with decisions within the industry. One-third of electricity is sold to major energy users taking more than 1 MW, and for some of these, the price of power is a key determinant of their international competitiveness. The coal industry is critically dependent on the ESI for its market, as are the turbine manufacturers and other suppliers. The electricity industry has been seen as a key player in strengthening Britain's industrial base and attempting to secure technological leadership, particularly in the nuclear industry. Finally, electricity is essential for every consumer in the country. As a result, policies affecting the electricity industry are inevitably highly politicised. Energy policy in large part has been policy toward the electricity industry and has primarily consisted in determining the fuel mix of generation and the finance of the investment required to secure that desired balance of fuel burned. Electricity prices and investment demands both have macroeconomic significance and have at various times been constrained by the government's fiscal position. Prices have been held down to slow inflation and investment curtailed to protect the budget, with adverse effects on the industry. Given the varying political importance of these objectives at different times, it is hard to see how specifying the pursuit of a simple objective such as "minimise the (social) costs of meeting demand" would have been feasible. Given that, it is hardly surprising that the regulatory framework failed the test of economic efficiency.

History and regulatory framework

The ESI was nationalised by the 1947 Electricity Act. This Act established a British Electricity Authority (BEA) and fourteen subordinate Area Electricity Boards to replace the Electricity Commissioners, the Central Electricity Board, and the 537 authorised undertakings that produced and distributed electricity. Electricity stock worth £341 million was issued to compensate the owners of the 180 companies involved, and the 357 local authorities shared a cash payment of £5 million "as compensation for severance of their electricity undertakings from their other activities" (Select Committee on Nationalised Industries [SCNI], 1963, A65). The new structure formally came into being on March 31, 1948. In 1952 the two Scottish Area Boards and generation were split off, and the remainder became the Central Electricity Authority (CEA).

In 1958 the structure was stabilised for the next 32 years with the creation of the Electricity Council and the Central Electricity Generating Board (CEGB), which took over generation and transmission in England and Wales. The CEGB sold practically all of its electricity to the 12 Area Boards under the terms of a Bulk Supply Tariff (BST). Each Area Board then distributed and sold this electricity to the consumers in its region, using its own tariffs. The Electricity Council comprised the chairmen of the thirteen boards, two other CEGB representatives, and up to six central members. Its duties were to advise the Minister and to help the industry coordinate its policies. It had no formal control over the industry, although its advice could influence the Minister, who did.

The following brief history of the regulatory framework demonstrates more than anything else the failure to appreciate the underlying tensions between the objectives of different parties. In such a case, what was needed from the government was a clear statement of policy, which would guide the design of regulation, provide appropriate incentives, and monitor performance. Instead of the government taking these strategic decisions and leaving detailed operation to the industry, the converse happened, with little strategic guidance and much detailed interference. Again, this may have been inevitable given the diversity of interest groups, the salience accorded to different objectives at different times, and the difficulty of devolving strategic decisions involving fuel security, but some of the less controversial issues to do with the efficiency of investment management could surely have been handled better with forethought.

When the electricity supply industry was nationalised, it was as a group of public corporations. The public corporation was designed to give "a combination of public ownership, public accountability, and business management for public ends" (Morrison, 1933, p. 149). Each Corporation would be controlled by a Board, appointed by a Minister. The Board was then responsible for the Corporation's actions, with duties laid down by the statutes establishing the Corporation, and with independence in their day-to-day operations. The Minister's residual powers were also laid down by statute; he or she could typically issue general directions to the Board and had to approve its investment and borrowing plans, but was unable to intervene in matters of detail. Herbert Morrison, who was Deputy Prime Minister and in overall charge of the nationalisation programme in the 1945–51 Labour Government, had expounded the philosophy behind a public corporation of this kind in 1933: "The Public Corporation must be no mere capitalist business, ... though it will ... be expected to pay its way. ... its Board and its officers must regard themselves as the high custodians of the public interest" (Morrison, 1933, pp. 156–7). "With the exception of the limited duties legally imposed upon him, the Minister will have no right to interfere with the work of the Board" (Morrison, 1933, p. 171).

This philosophy is clearly behind the 1947 Electricity Act, which laid down the BEA's duties. The Central Authority was allowed to borrow money with the consent of the Minister and the approval of the Treasury. Morrison had expected the Boards to be self-regulating, following their view of the public interest, taking account of the views of the Minister and of public debate, but largely independent. Although the Minister had to approve the industry's capital programme, this did not in practice involve detailed control over individual projects, but a more general discussion of the size of each programme and the amount of money required, though approval was affected by the government's overall macroeconomic stance. In 1956–7 and 1958–9, the industry's capital programmes were cut by 4.5% and by 11%, respectively, as part of more general public expenditure cuts.

The first step toward more detailed financial control came in 1958, when the Electricity Council's duties included advising the Minister on the industry's capital programme and auditing selected projects (SCNI, 1963, pp. 121–2, 127–8). The 1961 White Paper *The Financial and Economic Obligations of the Nationalised Industries* (Treasury, 1961) restated the Council's general financial objectives. Each industry was to be given a rate-of-return target or a self-financing ratio for its investment, in addition to its statutory obligation to break even.

A second White Paper, *Nationalised Industries: A Review of Economic and Financial Objectives* (Treasury, 1967), introduced a Test Discount Rate of 8% before tax, to be applied in the discounted cash flow analysis of all investment projects.[6] Projects that failed to produce a positive return at this discount rate could still be undertaken to meet statutory requirements (which thereby ex-

---

[6] It was raised to 10% in 1969, and replaced by a required rate of return of 5% in 1978, which was raised to 8% in 1989.

empted much of the electricity industry's investment) or if a social cost benefit analysis proved positive, although projects with high rates of return might
be deferred in the short term if there were real resource constraints.

The White Papers encouraged industries to use either short-run or long-run
marginal cost, depending upon their circumstances, and to avoid large changes
in prices if those would be required to track marginal costs exactly. The ESI
was one of the few nationalised industries to take this injunction seriously, perhaps because the capital-intensive nature of the industry allowed it to justify
low prices in the presence of excess capacity, which in turn stimulated demand
and thereby allowed them to justify future capital needs. In the absence of financial limits, the injunction to set prices at marginal cost arguably contributed to excessive investment.

The framework set out in the White Papers lost most of its relevance in the
early 1970s, when the government deliberately kept most nationalised industries' prices down in order to influence the rate of inflation. The electricity industry received special subsidies of £583 million between 1970 and 1976 in
compensation for keeping its prices down, although the industry calculated its
losses due to the price restraint as more than £1 billion (National Economic
Development Office [NEDO], 1976, pp. 77–8).[7] The financial target for
1969/70–73/4 was missed by a third, and no target was set for the next five
years. This policy of sacrificial restraint was lifted in 1975, when there was a
price increase of 38% (though costs rose 28%, and the Electricity Council had
asked for a greater increase). Further increases in later years allowed the financial position of the industry to improve.

The growing awareness that injunctions to set prices at marginal cost had
poor incentive properties was recognised in the 1976 White Paper *Cash Limits on Public Expenditure* (Treasury, 1976), which supplemented medium-term
expenditure plans, conducted in real terms, with binding (in theory) limits on
the expenditure of government departments in cash terms, to put greater pressure on costs. For the nationalised industries, the limits applied to their net external financing, or changes in their total borrowing over the year, since the
government was prepared to let them spend more if their receipts were high.

After the ad hoc instructions of the 1970s, a 1978 White paper, *The Nationalised Industries* (Treasury, 1978), attempted to reimpose a coherent system of control, with the emphasis more on financial than economic objectives.
Many projects had not been analyzed with the Test Discount Rate procedure
(for instance, because they were held to be necessary for security of supply),
which reduced the overall return to the nationalised industries' investment.

---

[7] The compensation was limited to the accounting losses incurred, whereas the Boards felt that
they should have been compensated for the lost revenue that they would have earned had prices
been set to achieve their financial target.

Each Board now had to show that its investment programmes, as a whole, could achieve a Required Rate of Return of 5%, and this requirement was to affect their pricing policy, scale of investment, and financial target, if necessary. Financial targets were reintroduced, and the industries were required to publish their performance against their financial target and against a range of other performance indicators. The Electricity Council Reports contained figures on prices and costs per kWh, employees per 1,000 customers, per GW of capacity (for the CEGB), and per GWh, for system load factor, for availability of the 500 MW and 660 MW generating sets, and for thermal efficiency. Marginal-cost pricing lost some of its importance, for the White Paper required only that "the main elements of an industry's price structure are sensibly related to the cost of supply and the market system" (para. 68). Marginal-cost principles were still used to justify the structure of the Bulk Supply Tariff, in particular, though even this was adjusted to meet financial targets.

Because the government owned the industry, it could not apply meaningful financial sanctions when targets were missed but might hope that external criticism and ministerial directives could rectify matters. The government very rarely used its powers to issue formal directions to the industry. The Boards tended to "accept the wishes of the Minister of Power as an instruction" (SCNI, 1963, q. 2312), and so there was no need for formal directives. This was perhaps fortunate for the Ministers, because "Parliament has laid down what, in relation to the nationalised industries, Ministers must do, and Ministers have been doing something else" (SCNI, 1963, p. 44). Specifically, the ministers had been intervening on detailed matters, rather than confining themselves to guidance on general policy.

Investment

The main constraints on the electricity supply industry's investment behaviour were its statutory duty to meet all reasonable demands for electricity and the need to obtain the Minister's approval for its programmes. The generation security standard used in the 1980s required the CEGB to hold enough spare plant to limit disconnections to four winter peaks per century and voltage reductions to 19. Until 1964, the planning margin was 14%, but it was raised to 17% in 1964, to 20% for the 1970–1 plan, and to 28% in 1976–7, which the Monopolies and Mergers Commission (MMC) argued was not based on a proper analysis of the costs and benefits of security (MMC, 1981, p. 4.70–1).

The required capital stock implied by the demand forecast and the security standard basically determined the level of investment that each Board would need. The CEGB did not calculate rates of return for individual projects within its integrated system, but it did check that any saving in running costs bought by higher capital costs would be worthwhile (SCNI, 1963, p. 133). The

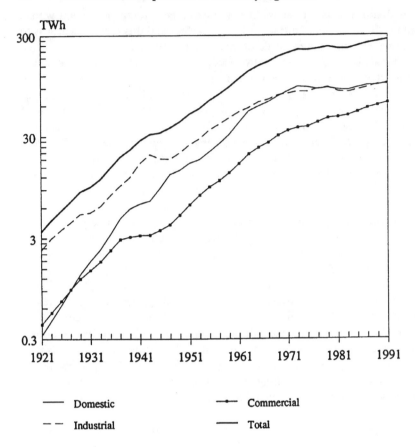

After 1981 scaled from U.K. data.
Source: From B. R. Mitchell, *British Historical Statistics,* 1988.

Figure 2-1. Electricity sales, 1921–1991, Great Britain

main effect of the rate of return required on the industry's investment was not upon the level of that investment but on the prices charged for electricity. The investment could earn an appropriate rate of return if the right price could be charged, and the price could be justified as reflecting the marginal cost of the investment required to meet demand. The forecast level of demand was assumed to be relatively invariant to price changes: if there had been a higher elasticity of demand, then an expensive investment programme might have reduced the level of the demand forecast and the amount of investment required. In these circumstances, the penalties for overinvestment would not be particularly severe, whereas underinvestment leading to power cuts would create much adverse publicity and would technically be an illegal breach of the industry's statutory duty. The incentives to overinvest are thus clear.

Figure 2-1 shows total demand and its three main components. Sales grew at 8.5% a year throughout the 1950s, but growth slowed to about 5% after the early 1960s and almost ceased for most of the 1970s. The key causes of the trend breaks in total demand were a sudden fall in the rate of growth of demand per domestic customer, probably in response to the growing penetration of gas for domestic central heating and its competition with electric space heating, and the decline in the rate of growth of industrial demand with the difficult period of the 1970s. One might conclude that although public ownership might have had a comparative advantage in mobilising investment to ensure coordinated expansion during the early period, the inflexibilities of a centrally planned CEGB were ill-placed to respond to the uncertainties in demand in the period after 1973, when investment was relatively less important.

Figure 2-2 compares forecasts and out-turns during the period of public ownership. It shows that until 1965 forecasts systematically underestimated demand, but with the change in trend growth in (peak) demand in that year, forecasts systematically overestimated demand for the following 20 years. These forecasts were made seven or eight years before the out-turn was known, so that errors may take a long time to be corrected.

Figure 2-3 shows the resulting evolution of investment in the ESI in real terms and shows the rapid build-up of investment in response to the early perceived acceleration of demand growth, as well as the move toward the more capital-intensive nuclear power stations in the period after 1956. In 1964 the government issued the National Plan, which required the industry to plan for a 4% growth rate for GDP. With the failure of demand growth to match forecasts, investment was eventually scaled back.

The level of demand in 1968–9 was 30% below the forecast level of 50 GW, which was perhaps fortunate, because capacity in that year was only 44.7 GW, 11 GW short of the planned amount. The backlog of capacity increased during 1969 and still stood at 5 GW of conventional plant and 3 GW of AGR capacity at the end of 1973. These delays can be traced back to an overreaction to earlier conservative investment choices. In the immediate postwar period, new orders were restricted to standardised 30 MW and 60 MW designs, which were relatively conservative but could be produced easily. These restrictions were lifted in 1950, though as late as 1953 over three-quarters of capacity ordered was to be 30 MW and 60 MW sets, the balance being 100 MW and 120 MW sets. This policy raised costs, because the 30 MW sets cost 40% more per kW than 120 MW sets and had a thermal efficiency of 25.5% compared to the 31% of the larger sets (Hannah, 1982, p. 114).

New managers for generation were appointed in 1954, and they had a policy of rapidly increasing plant sizes. Orders were successively placed for a 200

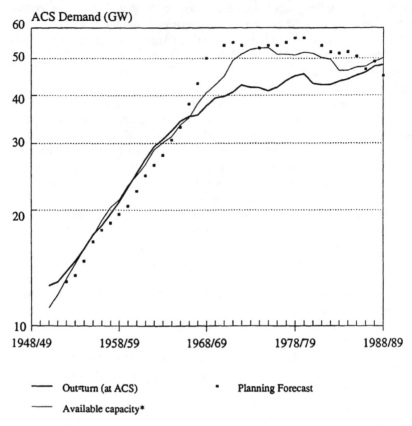

Figure 2-2. Demand forecasts and out-turns, 1950–1988

MW set, then 275 MW and 300 MW sets, and 550 MW "cross-compound" sets that linked two 275 MW sets. In each case the larger sizes were ordered before gaining operating experience of any in the series, and because only two or three sets of each size were ordered, there were no real opportunities to obtain economies of replication.[8] Slightly greater standardisation was achieved with the next size of plant, 350 MW, of which eight were ordered, and in 1960

---

[8] The same approach seems to have been followed in the United States (Gordon, 1992), where until World War II the approach followed was "design by experience." Rapid increases in forecast demand in the postwar period led to "design by extrapolation" where the lessons were learned after building many stations, rather than before. Increased temperatures and pressures resulted in stress corrosion cracking, with an increase in downtime of five times.

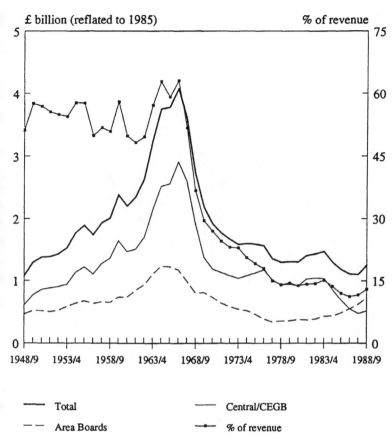

Figure 2-3. Capital investment (ESI, 1948–1989)

Source: Electricity Council.

the CEGB decided to concentrate on 500 MW sets. These were much larger than any then in use by the Board but had steam conditions similar to those of the 200 MW sets coming into operation. These larger sets were considered essential to meet forecast demand, given perceived difficulties in gaining planning permission for a larger number of smaller stations. By 1964, the CEGB had 33 of the 500 MW sets under construction, and it was realising that there were serious delays to its programme.

The move to a high rate of ordering proved too much for the manufacturers, who had not had the resources to increase output at this rate. The conservatism of the early 1950s had also meant that technical advances were being

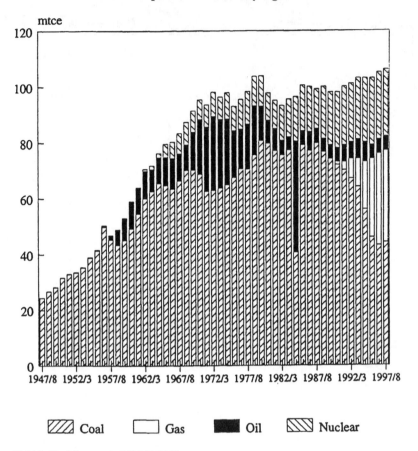

British Coal forecasts 1992/3–97/8.
Source: Trade & Industry Comm. (1993).

Figure 2-4. Fuel consumed by ESI (million tonnes coal equivalent)

introduced before there was experience of earlier generations of plant in use, and there was no chance to learn from mistakes. The overall station designs came from the CEGB's project teams, but the manufacturers were responsible for the components, and many components proved to have serious design faults. Many of the construction sites had unusually low productivity, sometimes due to poor management by the large number of subcontractors on each site. Altogether this period does not reflect well on British design, construction, and management, both in the public and private sectors, though some useful lessons were eventually learned from this experience, with resulting reforms in working practice.

Energy policy and the choice of fuel

Figure 2-4 shows the mix of fuels burnt by the industry since nationalisation. Almost all of the power stations inherited or under construction in 1948 were coal-fired. By 1954, the forecast demand for coal was higher than the National Coal Board's expected capacity, and the industry was faced with a choice between importing coal or building oil-fired stations (also using imported fuel). The CEA favoured the first option (Hannah, 1982, pp. 169–70), but the government wanted oil firing, anticipating falling oil prices and wishing to reduce dependence upon the National Union of Mineworkers. The CEA converted 14 stations from coal to oil, an investment that was handsomely justified by the fall in oil prices. By 1958, a coal surplus was anticipated, implying redundancies if additional markets could not be found. The CEGB was asked to reduce its oil burn and did so, despite the adverse economics.[9] As a result, fewer oil-fired stations were built in the period up to 1973 than the CEGB might otherwise have chosen, which may have been fortunate given the oil price rises of the 1970s.

The nuclear programme: The nuclear power decisions inspired by the government were less fortunate. In 1953, the government approved the construction of a reactor at Calder Hall, to produce electricity for the public supply system as a by-product. The reactor design was optimised for plutonium production for nuclear weapons. The 1955 White Paper *A Programme of Nuclear Power* (Ministry of Fuel and Power, 1955) announced a series of 12 power stations, totalling between 1,500 MW and 2,000 MW, to be built by 1965. The first four would be of the same Magnox design as Calder Hall, the next four were expected to be more advanced variants of it, and the final four might advance to liquid cooling. The Magnox design, named for the alloy used in its fuel cans, used natural uranium as fuel, a graphite reactor core for a moderator, and carbon dioxide gas as a coolant.

The White Paper argued that the first stations would have the same cost per kWh as conventional coal-fired stations and that the later stations could be expected to be cheaper, but that the programme did not stand or fall on these calculations alone. The cost estimates depended crucially on a "plutonium credit," which reduced the estimated net cost to 0.6 d/kWh, approximately the same as conventional power.[10] The figure quoted for the credit was variously between 0.3 d/kWh (CEGB figure [SCNI, 1963, A2]) and 0.17 d/kWh (AEA figure [SCNI, 1963, A81]). This was given to the plutonium produced in the reactors

---

[9] Coal-firing was cheaper on the coalfields, but oil stations cost the same on sites near coastal refineries. These calculations used market prices (including a tax on fuel oil), and would have given oil firing a clear advantage in resource cost terms (SCNI, 1963, pp. 346–52).

[10] 2.4 d (old pence) = 1 p (new pence) = £0.01.

on the assumption that it would be reused in fast breeder reactors in a later programme. The working party did not contain any CEA representatives (Hannah, 1982, p. 172), and the impending decline in the costs of conventional generation, the result of larger sets being developed, was not mentioned in the White Paper. The stations were to be built and partly designed by consortia formed between the existing boilermaking and generator firms. Four of these were created by early 1955 and a fifth in 1956, and their enthusiasm for nuclear power (and desire to win orders) made them campaign for a larger programme.

The Suez Crisis and the temporary oil embargo that followed it made the government fearful of an excessive reliance on imported oil and willing to contemplate a much larger nuclear investment. A committee was formed by the Ministry to consider this expansion, with proposals for 3.4 GW, 4.5 GW, and 6 GW programmes, to be built by the end of 1965. The largest programme (which was announced as a range of 5 to 6 GW) was chosen. It seems that strategic and political considerations were dominant, because Hannah (1982) observed that the CEA engineers argued for the smallest programme.

By the time the SCNI reported on the industry in 1963, the CEGB's first two nuclear power stations were operating, but the plutonium credit had been greatly reduced as uranium supplies became cheaper. This increased the cost of nuclear power while the larger size of conventional stations was reducing their costs. The CEGB estimated that nuclear electricity would cost 1 pence a unit, compared to 0.55 pence from modern conventional plants, although the differential would fall over time. Despite this, the CEGB was ordering approximately one station a year to keep the consortia occupied and available for the future – an example of strategic industrial policy with high costs to the CEGB (SCNI, 1963, p. 369). The CEGB eventually built 8 Magnox stations, which worked well but were an obsolescent technology using prewar turbine designs, with low temperatures and pressures and hence low thermal efficiency. It is estimated that the lifetime cost of the Magnox programme was 50% above that of supplying power from currently available alternative technology (Green, 1995).

The Atomic Energy Authority (AEA) continued its research programmes while the Magnox stations were under construction, and it soon concentrated on the Advanced Gas-cooled Reactor (AGR), which used the same combination of carbon dioxide for cooling and a graphite reactor core as did the Magnox stations. It was designed to operate at higher temperatures and pressures than the Magnox stations, so that efficient modern turbines could be used, giving higher thermal efficiencies. In 1958, the AEA began to build the Windscale prototype AGR, which had a capacity of 28 MW and performed well on completion in 1962. By then, the CEGB was attracted to the Canadian heavy-water reactor, the CANDU, but in December 1963 General Electric's Boiling Water Reactor (BWR) was announced to be the cheapest tender for a new station at

Oyster Creek in New Jersey. It was seen as a cost breakthrough, for its expected cost of 4 mills/kWh was significantly below previous estimates and less than the cost of a coal-fired station located near a mine.

Because the CEGB seems to have been pushing for an imported technology, the White Paper of April 1964 (Ministry of Power, 1964) required the CEGB to invite tenders for an AGR and for water-moderated reactors of proven design. In February 1965, the CEGB received full tenders for three AGRs, a Boiling Water Reactor (BWR), and a Pressurised Water Reactor (PWR), and two reactor-only tenders for PWRs. In July, the CEGB published an assessment of the Atomic Power Construction's (APC) AGR, which won the contract, and of the BWR, which was the runner-up (CEGB, 1965). The AGR's capital costs were higher, but its fuel and other costs appeared lower by a similar amount. The BWR was given a slightly higher total cost because it was designed to shut down for refueling, whereas the AGR was claimed to be able to refuel on-load (though this failed to materialise). The assessment also included data for the CEGB's latest coal-fired plant, Cottam, which was given a net effective cost of £9/kW, compared with £12.5/kW for the last Magnox plant at Wylfa, and £7.8/kW for the AGR. The unit generating costs, including capital charges, during the first years of their lives were given as 0.457 d for Dungeness B and 0.54 d for Cottam. These figures were taken as announcing the dawn of economic nuclear power, and the order for Dungeness B was to be followed by three others in England and one in Scotland.

The decision surprised the other two consortia because their own AGR tenders were significantly more expensive than their water reactors were. Atomic Power Construction, which was desperate for business, had based its design work upon a larger fuel element than that specified by the CEGB, though the change was accepted. The tender was awarded on the basis of a "sketched out design" and the process of filling in the detail "fully stretched" APC. The Nuclear Power Group had also asked for a similar specification change but had taken the CEGB's refusal at face value. They were given the order for the next AGR without a competition in recompense (Select Committee on Science and Technology, 1967, q. 524). This second AGR, Hinkley Point B, was therefore ordered in 1967 to a different design. The third consortium received the orders for stations at Hartlepool in 1968 and Heysham in 1970, following yet another design.[11]

By late 1968, serious problems were apparent at Dungeness B and at Hinkley Point. The Nuclear Installations Inspectorate (NII) required substantial modifications to the designs of Hartlepool and Heysham to meet new safety

---

[11] The Hartlepool station was the first to be sited near a coalfield, since the earlier projections of nuclear costs implied that coal-firing was cheaper for sites where transport costs were low. The choice of Hartlepool, which implied that nuclear power could compete everywhere, was seen to have great symbolic importance for the future of the coal industry and was strongly opposed by the NCB.

requirements. By 1980, the cost *overrun* in constant prices at Dungeness was estimated at 145%, at Hartlepool 140%, and at Heysham 62% (MMC, 1981, App. 25). These estimates were based on anticipated completion dates between 1981 and 1983; in fact, the reactors were not formally commissioned until 1989. All in all, the AGR programme was a financial and engineering disaster (see also Henney, 1991).

By 1973, the CEGB wanted to start work on another series of nuclear stations. The AGR was out of the question while none of the original stations were operating, and the CEGB 's choice was now the PWR. The SSEB, however, favoured the Steam Generating Heavy Water Reactor (SGHWR). A 100 MW prototype had been operating since 1968 at Winfrith, and because the design was based on a number of tubes rather than a single pressure vessel, it was felt to be easy to scale up. A Nuclear Power Advisory Board was asked for advice in 1973; it narrowed the choice to the PWR and the SGHWR but failed to decide between them. The government chose the SGHWR in 1974. By the middle of 1976, it was becoming clear that the SGHWR was not living up to its expectations, and orders could not yet be placed, while the AGRs at Hinkley Point and Hunterston[12] began to produce power. Walter Marshall, then Chief Scientist at the Department of Energy, found that a PWR would be able to meet U.K. safety standards, a finding confirmed by the NII in 1977. The government decided that the CEGB and the SSEB would each order one more AGR and that work would begin as soon as possible. In 1980 the Secretary of State for Energy endorsed the CEGB's advice for a 15 GW programme of PWR stations for the decade from 1982. However, the Energy Select Committee were unconvinced and questioned the CEGB's appraisal techniques (Energy Committee, 1981). These were investigated by the MMC and found "seriously defective and liable to mislead" (MMC, 1981, pp. 13, 14). The MMC's decision that the CEGB was operating against the public interest in this regard was a severe criticism for a public body.

A public enquiry into the CEGB's plan to build its first PWR at Sizewell opened in 1982, lasted a record 340 days, and cost £50 million to reach an answer subsequently shown by events to have been incorrect. By the end of the enquiry, the CEGB had scaled down its plans with lower estimates of future demand, and Sizewell was intended to be the first of a "small family" of four stations, totalling around 5 GW. The planning inspector eventually approved the application in 1987 (Layfield Report, 1987).

By that time, the privatisation of the ESI was being planned. The government's initial desire was to transfer all of the nuclear power stations to the private sector; to do this, they were to be grouped into a single generating company with around 60% of the conventional capacity to produce an organisation

---

[12] Built by TNPG for the SSEB, to a design similar to Hinkley Point B.

large enough to accept sizeable risks on construction costs and operating performance. The Energy Committee was concerned at the resulting duopolistic structure and expressed doubts about the costs of nuclear power (Energy Committee, 1988, pp. 56, 143–54).

These doubts were to be justified by events. When the electricity Bill was published in November 1988, it contained clauses setting up a fossil fuel levy, added to electricity prices to cover the difference between nuclear and conventional generating costs, and provided for payments of up to £2.5 billion for unanticipated increases in the costs of decommissioning power stations and reprocessing fuel. British Nuclear Fuels Ltd. (BNFL) was responsible for reprocessing the fuel from nuclear power stations and had held a cost-plus contract from the CEGB. With privatisation, a fixed-price contract would be required, and BNFL had to estimate its own future costs more accurately. This produced a large increase when decommissioning costs were recalculated, rising tenfold between 1985–6 and 1988–9 (Chesshire, 1991). These increases required additional provisions of £4 billion, and it became obvious that the Magnox stations could not be sold (Energy Committee, 1990, pp. 16–20). They were withdrawn from the privatisation in July 1989.

In the autumn, the CEGB provided new estimates of the prices that it would have to charge for electricity from PWRs using private sector accounting conventions (Energy Committee, 1990, pp. 25–32), showing a sharp increase (which could have been met from the fossil fuel levy), and also asked for government guarantees on the commercial and technical risks involved. The government was unwilling to give these "unprecedented guarantees," and so the PWR at Sizewell was withdrawn from privatisation in November 1989. The AGRs were also withdrawn, concentrating all the nuclear power stations in a new company, Nuclear Electric, which remained in the public sector. No new stations would be commenced before a review of nuclear power, to be held in 1994.

The Energy Committee's report on the affair attacked the Department of Energy and the CEGB for the time taken to produce "private sector" prices, and was "convinced that there has been a systematic bias in CEGB costings in favour of nuclear power." It criticised the Department of Energy for making "no attempt to obtain realistic costings from the CEGB until it was seeking to privatise nuclear power" (Energy Committee, 1990, p. 46).

Tariffs

Three central questions can be identified when discussing the tariffs used by the ESI under public ownership. First, how was the structure of individual tariffs determined? In particular, were there attempts to base prices upon marginal costs? Second, what happened to the average cost of electricity? Third, which groups paid more than the average, and which paid less?

The industry inherited a very large number of tariffs from its private and municipal predecessors, and their standardisation and simplification were one of the duties laid down in the nationalisation Act. Most of these tariffs charged separately for energy and for demand. Many of the inherited tariffs were "promotional," with final rates that barely covered the cost of buying power from generators, and some Area Boards were initially reluctant to raise their prices, despite excess demand. Financial targets introduced in 1961 compelled the Area Boards to raise prices. Separate day and night charges were introduced by one Board as early as 1952, and others followed in the early 1960s, when domestic storage heaters were introduced, improving the system load factor. More complicated tariffs, with maximum demand charges and several seasonal and time-of-day rates, were introduced for the larger industrial and commercial customers. The most complicated tariff was the bulk supply tariff (BST), on which the Area Boards purchased their power. In 1966, the CEGB announced that its 1967–8 BST would be based explicitly on marginal costs. In 1983, the Energy Act forced the Area Boards to buy electricity from other entrants at a rate equal to the avoidable cost, and the CEGB promptly altered the BST, changing some demand charges to lump sums and hence lowering the avoidable cost of CEGB power. Perhaps as a result, no entry occurred (Hammond, Helm, and Thompson, 1986), though the absence of long-term contracts from the Area Boards may have been a more important factor.

The overall level of prices can be seen in Figure 2-5, which has reflated all prices to 1985 levels, using the retail price index, and graphed them on a ratio or log scale.[13] At first sight, there is a steady decline to 1973–4, a sharp rise in the following 10 years, and a further decline to the end of the period. This does not reflect the industry's costs, for the decline in the early 1970s was caused by government-imposed price restraint, and the first part of the subsequent rise is a result of the end of this policy. For most of the postwar period, the decline in fuel costs (and the rise between 1973 and 1983) has been the main factor affecting prices.

Figure 2-5 also shows the relative prices paid by the main customer classes: industrial, commercial, and domestic. We might expect that the lobbying power of large industrial customers would keep their prices down and that Ministers would be wary of raising prices to domestic consumers, although their costs are likely to be the greatest. Commercial customers, who have neither votes nor lobbying power, faced the highest prices for 25 years, although their costs were almost certainly lower than those of (smaller) domestic customers. This differential declined over time and finally disappeared during the price rises after 1974–5. Those price rises were "tilted"

---

[13] If two series converge, the ratio of their prices is narrowing, so the log scale reveals the structure of relative prices well.

Pence/kWH Log Scale

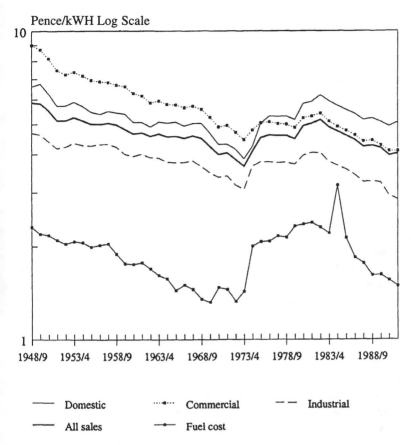

Source: Handbook Elec Supply Statistics.
Digest U.K. Energy Statistics.

Figure 2-5. Real electricity prices (constant 1985 prices)

away from smaller customers at the government's request, so that unit rates rather than standing charges were raised.

The average industrial price was the lowest of the three, in line with average costs, but some industrial customers received a particularly good deal in the 1980s. Load management schemes had been introduced to help the CEGB at a time when it had difficulty meeting peak demands, giving rebates on the capacity charges to large consumers who were willing to reduce demand at short notice. Indeed, the system load factor rose from 49% at the time of nationalisation to 60% in 1988–9, though not entirely for this reason. By the late 1970s, the

CEGB had excess capacity and little need for load management, but it continued and extended the schemes. In 1982, it introduced a "contracted consumer" scheme, and later the "qualifying industrial customer scheme" (QUICS), which reduced their prices still further to a level notionally based on the marginal cost of burning coal bought at world prices.[14] To jump ahead, when privatisation forced the industry to disaggregate its costs and to ensure that there was no discrimination between customers, the large users found that their prices rose significantly (even though still based upon world coal prices). Part of the explanation might be that the QUICS discounts were too generous, but part was that the privatised industry was pricing above short-run marginal cost.

Factor productivity and rates of return

The two key measures of the performance of the ESI during public ownership are the level of productivity achieved and the rate of return. The first is a physical measure of the efficiency with which the inputs of fuel, labour, and capital are combined to produce electricity. The latter depends on the prices of both inputs and outputs and is thus a measure of both financial and economic performance. Figure 2-6 shows the evolution of total factor productivity in the ESI during the period of public ownership. The graph clearly indicates a break in trend in 1973, as well as the hiccup caused by the delays and cost overruns of the mid-1960s.

The record is disappointing by comparison with U.K. industry as a whole, though it would be useful to make cross-country comparisons of the ESI. Gordon (1992) reports that labour productivity and fuel efficiency in U.S. generation actually declined from the end of the 1960s, particularly for new plant, as technological barriers were reached and environmental constraints began to have an impact, suggesting that the United Kingdom's experience may not be unique and may even seem favourable by comparison.

There is a problem of matching inputs and outputs when measuring productivity growth in industries with such long gestation periods as electricity, and the collapse of productivity growth in the 1960s can probably be ascribed to the delays in commissioning new, larger plant and the nuclear programme in particular. The general downward tendency over the period mirrors the fall in output growth rates and, apart from the productivity collapse of the 1960s already mentioned, also parallels the decline in investment. This would be

---

[14] This accords with good public finance practice, in which the subsidy to higher-priced British coal is financed by a tax on electricity consumers, that to be least distortionary should fall on final consumers rather than producers. Charging producers short-run marginal cost (i.e., not charging for capital in periods of excess supply) while basing consumer tariffs on LRMC or average cost is similarly defensible. What was not defensible was calculating the SRMC using the most efficient rather than the least efficient station.

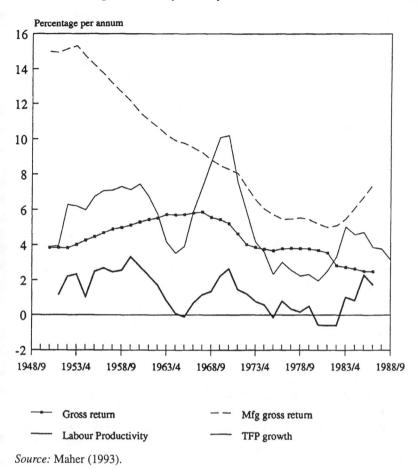

Source: Maher (1993).

Figure 2-6. Returns and productivity growth (five-year moving averages)

consistent with a view that relates productivity growth to the embodiment of new technology, which was rapid during the earlier period, but with the fall in demand growth and the maturing of steam technology was less important in the latter period.

Labour productivity has always risen more quickly than total factor productivity, because other factors were being substituted. Centralised wage bargaining kept basic hourly wage rates relatively low in the 1950s, and large-scale overtime working was used to raise earnings but lowered productivity. Despite various changes, manual workers' earnings were still below the average for manufacturing industry in 1970, and an overtime ban to support a pay claim caused the government to declare a state of emergency in December 1970. The ban was called off after a week, and the resulting Court of Inquiry (Wilberforce Inquiry, 1971) recommended a large increase. Since that action, workers in the industry have tended to be near the top of the "earnings league," and there has been very little further industrial action in the industry leading to disruptions in supply. The low growth of total factor productivity suggests an unwillingness to reduce surplus employment as demand growth collapsed and is consistent with the view that nationalised industries attach greater weight to employment than to the pursuit of profit. Privatisation subsequently revealed the ESI to have been significantly overmanned.

The second key measure of the industry's performance is the rate of return earned on its investment. There are two different ways in which this can be measured. The more reliable is to treat the period of public ownership as a single project, with an initial purchase cost (the value of inherited capital on nationalisation) and a final sales price (to the private sector on privatisation), with borrowing and repayments or dividends between. On that basis the real rate of return was 2.7% per annum.[15] The other approach is to measure the rate of return as the ratio of profits to capital. Annual figures can be produced but are very unstable. Figure 2-6 provides five-year moving (geometric) averages of gross profits divided by gross capital value.[16]

The rates of return in the ESI steadily rose in the first half of the period, though to rather low levels, and thereafter collapsed despite increasing pressures from the government to achieve target rates of return. Clearly, compared with the rest of U.K. industry, the ESI was earning an unsatisfactorily low rate of return. This was due partly to underpricing its output, partly to the excessive cost of generating plant, especially nuclear plant, partly to overmanning, and possibly partly through paying excessively high prices for British coal. A proper allocation of blame would require a comparison with the prices of inputs and outputs in other countries.

Assessment of the period of nationalisation

The main criticism that can be levelled against the publicly owned ESI was the excessive cost of investment, even discounting the overinvestment resulting from forecasting failures (which were common to many countries). The con-

---

[15] The sales proceeds of the nonnuclear part of the ESI were £11.46 billion (compared to a CCA value of £31.8 b including nuclear, and a market value shortly after the sales of £13.2 b). The CCA value would have given a rate of return of 4.3%, while the market value would have given a rate of 2.8%, with Nuclear Electric notionally included at zero (i.e., liabilities equal assets). For each £5 billion of terminal value, the rate of return increases by about 0.5%.

[16] Full details of the calculations are provided by Maher (1993).

sensus is that under the CEGB, power stations cost between 50 and 100% more than in other developed countries, took as much as twice as long to commission, and rarely achieved the economies of replication that a large buyer might reasonably have expected, instead being pressured by an industrial policy that aimed to keep alive an unreasonable number of internationally uncompetitive British firms.[17] The effects of this strategy can be seen in their least favourable light in the disaster of the AGR programme, discussed earlier and detailed in depressing detail in Layfield (1987). Jeffrey (1988) cites the cost for the AGRs as £2,446/kW actual capacity (at 1988 prices), which may be compared to 1992 CCGT costs of £350–500/kW capacity.

If investment costs were excessive, so were the costs of domestic coal, where the lack of international competition and the monopoly power of the National Coal Board (NCB), and even more of the miners, supported by successive governments denying the CEGB access to the international coal market, kept costs high and productivity low. In the years before 1973 the international coal market was arguably too thin to provide a plausible alternative to domestic coal, and the government certainly was willing to diversify into nuclear power. The reluctance to import fuel, the unwillingness to allow the much cheaper North Sea gas to be used in generation, and the failure to adequately restructure the NCB greatly increased the cost of power. The Department of Trade and Industry report (DTI, 1993, p. 95) states that "between 1979 and 1992 the Government has provided nearly £18 billion in assistance to the coal industry. ... the coal industry has also benefited to the extent of £1 billion a year over the past three years from the financial advantage conferred through the premium over market prices which the electricity generators have been paying for their coal supplies from British Coal."[18] To put these subsidies to British coal in perspective, if they are corrected to constant prices, they average 19% of the total sales revenue of the CEGB and successor generators over the period 1979 to 1992. More to the point, the fuel costs of the CEGB were raised by 5% of the CEGB's average selling price, so that electricity consumers were providing a subsidy to British Coal alongside the much greater subsidy provided by taxpayers.

[17] For example, see the evidence of Sir Alastair Frame and Michael Prior to the Sizewell Inquiry (Layfield, 1987; Prior, 1983). Thus the CEGB estimated that the cost of a coal alternative to Sizewell would be £664/kW (£1982) compared with an average for U.S. and European plants of £490/kW, or 136% of this average. But the CEGB's average cost overrun on coal-fired plant was 18% in real terms at this date, bringing the costs to more than 50% that of the average elsewhere.

[18] This claim seems exaggerated, and even if all British coal could have been replaced by imported coal (impossible given the port capacities), the extra transport costs of delivering imported coal to inland sites must be deducted. A closer estimate might be £900 million ignoring port constraints, or less than £200 million allowing for port constraints. Of course, had the CEGB always been free to import, the port capacities would have been increased earlier.

The case for privatisation

The 1979 Conservative Government had a variety of motives for privatisation, and one extremely telling argument for considering the privatisation of the electricity industry: Such industries operated under private ownership with apparent success in a number of European countries and certainly in the United States. There was a growing belief that the large nationalised industries, of which the CEGB was an excellent example, were inflexible, bureaucratic, secretive, and largely out of political control.[19] The government could audit them, commission studies, and subject them to the searching enquiries of the Parliamentary Select Committees, but it had few sanctions short of denying them access to investment funds, resisting requests to raise tariffs, or both. Such negative sanctions merely increased the inflexibility of the organisation and did little to promote an aggressive and competitive industry. Privatisation therefore held the considerable attraction of upsetting this very unsatisfactory politicoeconomic equilibrium, and for this to be successful, the industry had to be dismembered with the separate stages of the previously vertically integrated industry forced to operate in full public view in the marketplace rather than in the obscurity of committee rooms. As such, it was to be one of the most ambitious attempts anywhere to introduce competition into an industry normally considered to be a natural monopoly.

The privatisation of the English electricity industry

The British government published its proposals for privatising the Electricity Supply Industry of England and Wales in February 1988. The White Paper initially proposed that all the nuclear stations together with 60% of the conventional stations would be placed in one large company, National Power, with the rump of the conventional stations in PowerGen. Despite substantial financial support provided through a fossil fuel levy on conventional generation, nuclear power proved unsaleable, as detailed earlier. At a very late stage, all the CEGB's nuclear stations were withdrawn from the sale and transferred to Nuclear Electric, to remain in government ownership. The industrial logic for the duopoly of National Power and PowerGen had now disappeared, but there was no time for any further restructuring, given the government's timetable to accommodate a possible election in 1991. The revised proposals became law as the Electricity Act in July 1989.[20]

---

[19] Foster (1993, p. 114) cites Sir Geoffrey Howe's speech of July 1981 (when he was Chancellor of the Exchequer) as the critical recognition of the impotence of public control over nationalised industries.

[20] The Scottish nonnuclear electricity industry was subsequently privatised as two vertically integrated companies, while that of Northern Ireland was restructured and sold to four separately managed concerns. The chapter continues to confine attention to England and Wales.

Transmission was transferred as a regulated natural monopoly to the National Grid Company (NGC), so that the CEGB was divided into four companies (NGC, PowerGen, National Power, and Nuclear Electric), which were vested as public limited companies on March 31, 1990, at the same time as the 12 Area Boards, now to be known as the Regional Electricity Companies (RECs). The NGC was transferred to the joint ownership of the RECs, and the RECs were sold to the public in December 1990. Sixty percent of National Power and PowerGen were subsequently sold to the public in March 1991 and the remainder four years later.

The new structure introduced in March 1990 thus divided the process of electricity supply into four activities: generation, transmission, distribution, and supply. Generation accounts for around two-thirds of the industry's costs, transmission for 10%, distribution for 20%, and supply for the remaining 5%. Figure 2-7 shows the average cost breakdown (total costs divided by total sales) of electricity by activity and by cost category (capital, labour, and fuel and materials). Supply is further subdivided into sales to a franchise market of smaller customers, restricted to the local REC, and a nonfranchise market of large customers, which can be served by any company acting as a private, or second-tier, supplier. The right-hand part of Figure 2-7 shows how the price and cost breakdown differ as between large customers (often on base load, with lower average energy prices charged by the generator) and domestic customers with a lower load factor of around 50% and hence a higher proportion of energy bought at peak prices. Transmission and distribution costs also differ by category of customer as shown.

The privatisation of the English ESI marked a decisive change in the government's approach, for it was the first public utility to be broken up before sale with the specific intention of introducing competition into the industry. British Telecom (now BT) was sold as a single entity, though its tiny privately owned rival, Mercury, was granted a temporary statutory duopoly position. British Gas was sold as a vertically integrated monopoly, subject to regulation in the franchise (essentially domestic) market, though not in the nonfranchise or commercial market, on the assumption that British Gas would face adequate competition from rival fuels. The high-pressure National Transmission System was required to act as a common carrier, and British Gas was required to quote for the costs of transmission on request. Later, the Office of Fair Trading would rule that British Gas had to publish tariffs for the nonfranchise market to prevent the price discrimination previously systemic.

Earlier attempts to enforce common carriage provisions on the national grid to permit entry by new generators had failed to encourage a single entrant, and the government concluded that competition in the ESI would re-

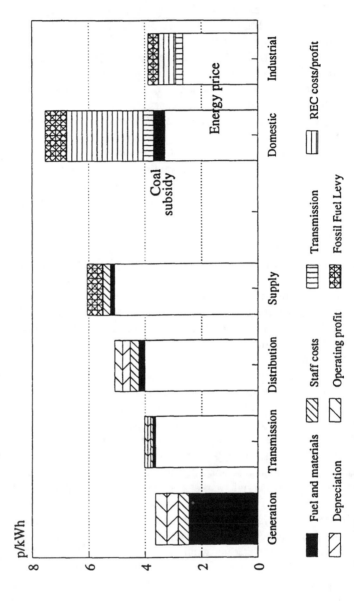

Source: Company Accounts.

Figure 2-7. The breakdown of electricity prices by function and by customer

quire the dismemberment of the CEGB.[21] Transmission and distribution were recognised to be natural monopolies, to be subject to regulation by the Office of Electricity Regulation (Offer), but the government argued that there was no natural monopoly in generation providing there was freedom of entry. This was guaranteed, and the generators were therefore not subject to detailed regulation but to the threat of competition from new entrants, as well as actual competition from one another.[22] The market setting for this competition was to be the bulk electricity supply market, which was set up as a spot market (more accurately, a "day ahead" market) for the dispatch and pricing of electricity.

This spot market, or "pool," is the most radical part of the 1990 reforms. Every morning, generators must declare which of their generating sets will be available the next day and announce prices for each set. A start-up price and no-load price should reflect the fixed costs of being ready to generate, and up to three incremental prices can be charged for successive tranches of MWh generated. At the same time, all suppliers submit estimates of the demand at each of the grid supply points from which they take power, for each half-hour of the following day. The NGC then runs a computer plant-scheduling programme that aims to minimise system generating costs over the next day in terms of the prices bid. The output of this programme is known as the unconstrained schedule, for it ignores all transmission constraints. These constraints would force some sets (typically in the South) to operate at times when their bid prices are higher than those of sets elsewhere that cannot transmit their electricity to consumers and must not operate. It is revised as necessary for changes in the availability of plant that are known in advance.

The interconnectors with Scotland and France and the pumped storage plants owned by NGC are treated similarly to conventional generators, but they also inform the schedulers of the price at which they are willing to buy

---

[21] Similar problems were encountered with the common carriage provisions for gas, where British Gas was initially very slow in quoting transmission charges and was subsequently ordered to publish and justify (illustrative) transmission tariffs. The allowed rate of return on the transmission business was felt so onerous by British Gas that in 1992 it submitted itself to an enquiry by the Monopolies and Mergers Commission (MMC), despite the possibility that the industry might be vertically dismembered. This was indeed the MMC's recommendation, but it was not implemented by the government, which preferred a faster end to British Gas's exclusive franchise, proposed for 1998. Regulating common carriage on a network in a vertically integrated industry is evidently not simple and is discussed later.

[22] They remained subject to general competition policy and remain vulnerable to a reference to the MMC as having a statutorily defined monopoly of more than 25% of the market. The two generators have been the subject of a number of investigations by the Director General of Electricity Supply, who has never concealed his hostility to the market power wielded by National Power and PowerGen. See, for example, Offer (1992a and 1992b).

power (or, in the case of NGC pumped storage, the time at which they will buy), rather than to generate it. Typically, the pumped storage plant will continue to generate at peaks, when the price is high, and refill the reservoirs during the nighttime periods of cheap electricity.

The price for each half-hour is calculated on the basis of the revised unconstrained schedule. During troughs in demand (known as Table B periods), when it is cheaper to operate some large plants on part-load than to let them cool down and reheat when demand rises, the System Marginal Price (SMP) is equal to the incremental price (for one extra MWh) of the most expensive plant running. For most of the time, plant must be started to meet extra demand. During these Table A periods, the SMP includes the cost of starting the marginal plant and its no-load price, spread over the output it produces during that period of operation, in addition to its incremental price of running.

Generators receive the SMP for each unit they are scheduled to generate during a period, and a capacity element for each unit of capacity that is available to generate, whether or not it is called upon. The capacity element is given by $LOLP \times [VOLL - \max (SMP, \text{the set's bid price})]$, where LOLP is the Loss of Load Probability, the risk that demand will exceed capacity, and VOLL is the Value of Lost Load, which is set administratively to reflect the cost of demand exceeding supply. For sets in operation, SMP exceeds their bid price, and the sum of SMP and the capacity element, which gives the pool purchase price, or PPP, is simply $SMP \times (1 - LOLP) + VOLL \times LOLP$. All companies buying electricity from the pool pay a pool selling price, or PSP, for their metered demand, raised by a factor equal to the average transmission losses in each half-hour.[23] During the Table B periods, with spare plant running, the pool selling price is equal to the pool purchase price, whereas in Table A periods, when demand is higher, the pool selling price includes an uplift that covers a variety of other payments made to generators.

Some of these payments are for essential ancillary services, such as the provision of reactive power to keep the transmission system stable. Others reflect the fact that the revised unconstrained schedule, on which the payments are based, is not the actual operating schedule. Transmission constraints and unexpected changes in demand and plant availability mean that some sets will be run when they were not due to run in the unconstrained schedule. They are paid at their bid prices, which exceed the SMP (since they would have been operating under the unconstrained schedule if their bids were lower). Other sets will be unable to operate because of transmission or other constraints, and they must buy back at their bid price the power

---

[23] Second-tier suppliers' demands, metered at their customers' premises, are further raised to account for distribution losses, by factors agreed with the REC whose system they use.

that they had sold in the unconstrained schedule.[24] This will be lower than the SMP, so that they effectively receive a "lost profit" payment as compensation for the effect of the transmission constraint. Finally, the capacity payments to generators who are not called upon, and payments for providing reserve, must be financed. The uplift is set so as to recover all of these costs on a daily basis and was initially allocated to all consumers, rather than to the grid (to provide it with appropriate incentives for reducing their cost), to consumers responsible for constraining on more expensive plants, or both. As a result of an enquiry, a share of these costs was subsequently allocated to NGC, as later described in the section titled "Effects of privatisation on investment efficiency."

Pool prices may vary by a factor of 3:1 over the course of the day, and peaks eight times the normal level have been observed on occasions, sometimes as a result of failures in the scheduling programme, GOAL. These spikes have been the subject of Offer enquiries (Offer, 1991, 1993b). If demand rises relative to declared capacity, the Loss of Load Probability can rise dramatically. Most of the time, however, LOLP has been negligible, though on one occasion, one of the generators benefited substantially by declaring capacity unavailable the day before and redeclaring it available on the day, after a high capacity value had been calculated. This was investigated as an abuse (Offer, 1991), and new rules designed to prevent this kind of manipulation were agreed, though as later described, the generators have been successful in gaming the transmission constraints to increase profits (via increased uplift payments). Both generators have established teams of expert modellers to devise profitable market strategies in the best traditions of financial markets, and it would be realistic to accept that if the spot market can be legally and profitably manipulated, then this will occur. How serious this is will depend on the competitiveness of the market, the extent of transmission constraints (which can create local monopoly positions), and the ability and willingness of NGC to devise contracts to reduce the manipulability of the constraints.

At vesting, the generators and suppliers were provided with contracts that hedged against the pool price, and as they matured over the next three years, they could be renewed. The normal contract is a Contract for Differences, under which a generator receives, in addition to the normal pool price for any sales, a sum equal to the difference between the specified strike price and the pool price, multiplied by the specified number of units

---

[24] Hunt and Shuttleworth (1993) use this concept of buying back electricity, in a paper that breaks the pool into three parts: a forward market (the unconstrained schedule produced the day ahead), an option market (the availability payments for generators who do not generate in the unconstrained schedule), and a spot market in which generators who supply more or less than is in the schedule sell or buy back the difference, at a price depending on the circumstances.

contracted.[25] The effect is as though the generator had sold electricity forward at the strike price while the supplier had purchased forward at this same strike price, which thus provides a hedge for both parties while ensuring that the pool price serves its role of dispatching stations in the correct merit order. These vesting contracts were of critical importance both in making firm the forecast revenues and profits needed to sell the companies and in explaining the subsequent performance of the pool, discussed in the next subsection. In addition to these contracts for electricity, the generators were provided with three-year contracts for fixed tonnages from British coal at indexed prices well above international prices. The time at which these contracts were due to expire was graphically described as the "cliff-edge," and its consequences are discussed next.

Does the new system work?

The system of pool settlement appears to operate reasonably well, and the experience to date is an impressive technical success. Substantial entry has been induced, with an extra 11.2 GW of CCGT plant by 1996[26] (compared to total capacity of about 60 GW). This entry was facilitated by long-term contracts at prices that compared favourably with the vesting contract prices, though these were substantially higher than pool prices. These pool prices were still below medium-run avoidable costs and long-run average costs up to 1992 (Offer, 1992b). Pool spot prices in the first three years after privatisation were primarily influenced by the existence of the contracts of varying lengths between the generators and RECs that were put in place at privatisation. Because these cover over 90% of expected sales, the incentives on the generators, who also have take-or-pay contracts with British Coal, are to bid in at almost short-run marginal avoided cost, essentially the cost of the fuel burned. For British Coal, the opportunity cost is below import parity, for large stocks have developed during the period in which the generators are locked into their coal contracts, but after April 1993 the generators expected to be free to reduce their purchases from British Coal, to run down a large part of these stocks, and to be free to import coal. This would explain the early experience in which pool prices were below the estimated marginal fuel cost derived from average

---

[25] In addition to Contracts for Differences there is a market for Electricity Forward Agreements (EFAs), which allow the main components of electricity price uncertainty (such as the spot price between certain weekday hours, or the capacity charge) to be hedged on a short-term basis. This differs from a classic futures market primarily in its lower liquidity and the resulting difficulty in pricing and liquidating specific EFAs.

[26] This figure is for plant existing or under construction in early 1994. The National Grid Company has been informed of plans for another 12 GW by 1999, although much may not be built (NGC, 1994).

British coal prices (Green, 1991).[27] As some of the contracts have matured, pool prices have risen, though coal costs have fallen (Offer, 1992b).

Green and Newbery (1992a) built a model of the spot market in which the two fossil generators (who absorb all the variations in supply) bid in a supply function to the grid dispatcher the day before. The supply function specifies the number of MW capacity available at each price and is chosen to be the profit-maximising supply function, given a prediction of the supply function bid in by the other duopolist, an estimate of demand and its variation over the day ahead, and the running costs of its generating sets. An equilibrium is a pair of supply functions such that each duopolist is content with its choice, given the actual choice of its rival. Green and Newbery calibrated the model to estimated marginal generation costs and found that there was a continuum of possible supply function equilibria, ranked by their profitability. The most profitable equilibrium would be the natural choice for the duopolists if there were no threat of entry and no existing contracts limiting market power, and would result in prices well above operating costs and large deadweight losses. Had the fossil stations been divided among five instead of two companies and if collusion could be deterred (by the threat of entry), then competition would have almost completely eliminated these deadweight losses.

If, on the other hand, entry cannot be deterred except by reducing prices, then the most profitable long-run strategy for the duopolists would be to choose equilibria with lower prices to ensure less entry, and hence less spare capacity. However, with only two large incumbents, it is not possible to reach an equilibrium with sufficiently low prices to avoid all spare capacity unless the incumbents sign supply contracts, and the main inefficiency arises from excess entry, with prices closer to the competitive level, but considerable unnecessary investment expenditure. Had the industry been more competitive to begin and had the threat of entry been credible, making it unattractive to collude in raising prices, then less entry would be induced and less inefficient excess investment incurred.

The best outcome would be to make the market for long-term contracts for electricity supply contestable, perhaps by requiring the RECs to seek tenders for long-term supply contracts for some fraction of their market, thus making the threat of entry credible and of low financial risk. Faced with such a credible threat, the incumbents would then be motivated to offer slightly more favourable long-term electricity supply contracts. If the contract price is determined by the price at which entry would be attractive, then the incumbents have no incentive to manipulate the pool price in order to affect the long-term contract price, and the only benefit of restricting supply to the pool would be to affect the price at which their residual, uncontracted output is sold. The larg-

---

[27] At one point, pool prices fell to zero, so anxious were the generators to burn coal.

er is the fraction of output sold under long-term contracts, the smaller is the output that enjoys the benefit of manipulated pool prices, and the less would be the incentive to raise prices above marginal cost. In the limit, as the level of contracts approaches the average level of production, their best bidding strategy would be to bid in generating sets at marginal cost, as they were supposed to do under public ownership.

By 1992, a market for long-term electricity supply contracts began to emerge very rapidly in the "dash for gas." The RECs signed long-term contracts with "independent" power producers (the IPPs), who planned to enter the industry by contracting for turnkey high-efficiency, combined-cycle gas turbine (CCGT) generator sets. These can be rapidly installed at modest scale (350 to 650 MW). The independents, all of whom are part-owned by the RECs (and hence hardly independent), have been able to sign long-term contracts for gas supply,[28] and their contracts with the RECs contain the same indexation clauses, effectively completely hedging the spot price risk. By late 1992, the RECs and the incumbent generators had signed gas contracts for 8.7 GW of CCGT plant, which would displace about 25 million tonnes of coal, compared to the 1992 coal burn of 60 million tonnes. The impact this had on the negotiations for new coal supply contracts between British Coal and the generators was considerable and led British Coal in October 1992 to announce a massive closure programme.

The impact on the market for coal is discussed later, but the question to be addressed here is whether the RECs acted within the terms of their licence to purchase economically in signing long-term contracts for the CCGT generators. Offer (1992c, 1993a) examined the contracts between the RECs and the IPPs and compared them with the offers made during 1992 by the main generators, and concluded that the evidence did not suggest that the RECs breached their economic purchasing licence conditions. On that basis, the Director General of Electricity Supply did not need to disallow the cost passthrough to the franchise market.

This does not mean that the costs of new CCGT sets are necessarily less than the costs of existing coal-fired conventional stations. The problem in comparing costs is complicated by a number of factors. First, British coal is substantially more expensive than imported coal, and much depends on the basis for the comparison. Second, Britain is a signatory to the EC Large Combustion Plant Directive that mandates reductions in sulphur dioxide emissions,

---

[28] In some cases these are take-or-pay, thus lowering the opportunity cost of gas to its resale value. In addition, the contracts are normally for delivery to the station, and if resold, would incur transmission costs from the station to the final customer, even when the customer might be nearer to the source of original gas supply (and hence would lower rather than raise gas transmission costs). The effect is to further depress the resale value and hence lower the avoidable generating costs.

with target dates in 1998 and 2003. The emissions limits for each of the two main generators in each year have been laid down in British law and impose constraints on the amount of British coal (with moderately high sulphur) that may be burned without flue gas desulphurisation (FGD). It has been claimed that the costs of the new CCGT sets will be above the average cost of efficient coal-fired conventional stations with access to imported coal (or British coal at import parity prices) even if FGD is required. The House of Commons Energy Committee (in late 1991) estimated that even with gas at the low price of 20 p per therm, new CCGT stations have a supply price of 2.64 p/kWh, slightly less than the 2.73 p for running costs of existing large inland coal-fired stations burning British coal with FGD, but above that of 2.19 p using imported coal and FGD.[29] British Coal was, by late 1992, offering to lower the contract price of its coal to a level competitive with imported coal at inland sites by 1996, but the incumbent generators clearly felt under no commercial pressure to lower their electricity contracts much, if anything, below the prices offered by the IPPs, particularly as the price of gas had been increased sharply in 1992 to ration demands.

The incumbents appear to have been somewhat surprised by the extent of entry and may have failed to appreciate the commercial (and political) attractions to the RECs of attracting entry from other suppliers. From the RECs' point of view, the prospect of earning profits on the nonregulated generation activities that they could underwrite by offering long-term contracts at prices that could be passed straight through into the franchise (regulated) market may have been tempting, though they had to be careful not to violate their licence obligation to purchase economically, lest the regulator prevent them from passing the costs of purchases through to the franchise customers. The political attraction of reducing their dependence on the former CEGB, with whom they had had a long and subservient relationship, may have been an additional factor. The economic argument of reducing their dependence on suppliers with such dominant market power at no obvious cost penalty was also important, as was the risk-reducing or portfolio argument of selecting suppliers whose supplies were less vulnerable to any proposed EC carbon tax.

On their part, the incumbents have expressed righteous indignation that the RECs were allowed to sign contracts in which they alleged there was a clear conflict of interest between their duty to purchase economically and their wish to earn unregulated profits. The incumbents may have expected the RECs not to offer long-term contracts to potential entrants, in which case the risk of entry would have been sufficiently large to have deterred all but a few, and the

---

[29] Energy Committee (1992, Vol. I, para. 50–1) notes that new CCGTs are certainly cheaper than *new* coal-fired stations but are not obviously cheaper than existing base-load (i.e., efficient) coal-fired stations.

need to deter entry by signing away their market power with long-term contracts would have been much diminished. Only when they realised that the RECs would be allowed to sign such contracts have they belatedly responded and lowered the prices of their contracts (and the confidentiality surrounding the contracts makes it hard for outside observers to assess the extent of their response).

This situation poses a fascinating regulatory dilemma. On the one hand, if the incumbents are protected against the threat of entry, they are unlikely to behave very competitively when bidding in the pool. On the other hand, if the RECs have no financial interest in encouraging entry, they would have little incentive to sign long-term contracts because they are allowed to pass on the purchase cost of electricity in the franchise market and have no compelling need to offer long-term contracts to nonfranchise customers, rather than one-year hedges. It is clearly desirable that potential entrants be able to secure long-term contracts before making the entry decision, and it is also desirable that these be at prices no higher than the long-run average pool prices. The dilemma consists of reconciling these two objectives. The resolution is for the Director General of Electricity Supply (DGES) to monitor the contracts to ensure that they satisfy licence condition 5 (to purchase economically),[30] and to encourage the RECs to solicit open tenders for long-term contracts.

It remains an open question whether it would have been better to have created a more competitive generating industry by dividing the fossil-fueled plant among five equal-sized firms, or whether it is better to have two large incumbents who must actively compete on a contestable long-term contract market. An ESI of many smaller firms might have been able to develop systems of collusion if protected from the threat of entry, and if not, might have behaved like the volatile commodity markets of capital-intensive goods such as metals. Such instability would have been unacceptable and would either have precipitated bankruptcy and merger, restoring the equilibrium concentrated form or, more probably, would have led to regulation and a structure closer to some continental forms. Whether the system of regulation and vertical disintegration leads to an inefficient choice of entry and investment given the present duopoly and an embryonic contracts market will be addressed shortly. The House of Commons Energy Committee was certainly concerned on this account (Energy Committee, 1992, paras. 51–8).

The issue of excessive entry surfaced again dramatically in the autumn of 1992, during the later stages of the renegotiation of coal contracts between National Power, PowerGen, and British Coal. Given the prices that National Power and PowerGen were willing to offer and the volumes they were prepared to take at these prices, British Coal suddenly declared that it would need

---

[30] As reported in Offer (1992c).

to reduce the number of pits from 50 to 19 (with an expected redundancy of 30,000 miners), and announced the immediate closure of the first 10 pits on October 13, 1992. Although the possibility of closures of this scale had been widely discussed in the Rothschild Report of 1991, and in the evidence to the Energy Committee, published earlier in 1992, the speed and scale of the announced closures and the resulting public and Parliamentary response clearly caught the government unprepared. After initially arguing that such decisions were purely the response to market forces and that intervention in the privately owned ESI was inappropriate, the Department of Trade and Industry[31] embarked on an enquiry into the matter, while the House of Commons Trade and Industry Committee also prepared a report.

Both reports were published before the final coal contracts had to be renewed on March 31, 1993 (Trade and Industry Committee, 1992, 1993; DTI, 1993), and both recommended that British Coal be subsidized to enable it to compete with imported black fuels (oil, Orimulsion, and coal) and that Orimulsion be subject to the hydrocarbon oil duty. The DTI White Paper goes to considerable lengths to uphold the principles behind privatisation and the independence of the regulator. It states that "The Government's energy policy therefore centres on the creation of competitive markets" (DTI, 1993, p. 3). As part of that strategy, bids have been invited for each of British Coal's five regions, while a few pits that the Corporation wished to close have been leased to private companies. Most of the pits threatened in October 1992 were in fact closed over the following two years. The generators signed five-year contracts similar to those proposed the previous October, and the corresponding electricity contracts were shared amongst the RECs on the basis of their franchise demands, less their commitments to buy from CCGTs.

The issue of contestability has thus been overlain by issues of fuel choice and the fate of the U.K. coal industry. Arguably, the main legacy of the privatisation of the ESI will be a forced resolution of U.K. energy policy, particularly as it concerns the state-owned industries of coal and nuclear power, with further consequences for another state-owned industry, British Rail.

Effects of privatisation on investment efficiency

Efficiency has a number of different dimensions, all of which have been affected by privatisation. In the short run, the main question is whether power is transmitted to its final destination at least cost, that is, whether stations are run in correct merit order and operated efficiently. In the medium run, is the industry using the right inputs (of fuel and labour) in the right amounts? In the long run, are the right amounts of investment undertaken at least cost, using

---

[31] Which had taken over the responsibilities of the previous Department of Energy.

the best technology, and in the correct place? One might expect that the main potential benefit to be derived from restructuring the capital-intensive ESI and changing the system of incentives and regulation lies in improvements in investment efficiency rather than in current operating efficiency, and this is considered first here.

It is hard to make fair comparisons with the previous regime, because CCGT stations lend themselves to rapid construction and subcontracting, unlike the earlier CEGB stations. As noted earlier, though, investment costs under the CEGB were excessive and not adequately exposed to competitive pressures. The main argument for expecting improved investment efficiency is that a privatised industry is likely to introduce proven technology more quickly while avoiding the temptation to invent the next-generation technology (such as AGRs). For a modest-sized industrial economy like Britain, adopting tried and proven technology probably makes sound economic sense.[32] The main argument that privatisation saved investment costs is that it halted the programme for a further 6 GW of PWR stations intended to follow Sizewell B, whereas the counter-argument is that a considerable part of the 10 GW of CCGT was ordered prematurely, for they will not all be needed to meet the sulphur limits until the latter part of the decade.

Under the CEGB, investment decisions were taken to minimise the expected present discounted cost of meeting the forecast demand for the foreseeable future, and they involved decisions of the choice of size and type of power station, its location, and additions to the national grid. The new system is that any generator or potential supplier has freedom to choose the type of power station and its location.

In order to encourage suppliers to provide an adequate security margin to deal with unexpected variations in demand or supply (the sudden unavailability of stations), the NGC calculates the loss of load probability (LOLP) and the DGES specifies the value of lost load (VOLL). Generators available to supply, even if not dispatched, receive a payment equal to LOLP × [VOLL − Max(SMP, bid price)]. The VOLL was set at £2/kWh in 1990 (rising with inflation), and typical bid prices are 2 p/kWh, so that LOLP of 1% would typically double the payment made to the generator. The intention is that if demand rises relative to capacity, so will LOLP, and generators will anticipate higher returns to having capacity available. This will induce extra investment. The problem is that LOLP is highly sensitive to the relation between demand and supply. A small excess in capacity drives LOLP to zero, whereas small shortfalls beyond the point at which LOLP is positive rapidly increase the return. This problem may be alleviated by the existence of a forward market in

---

[32] CCGTs, developed from high-efficiency aircraft turbines, had already been proven by large turbine manufacturers. See, for example, Larsen and Williams (1986).

the capacity charge (VOLL × LOLP), which enables generators to offer insurance to customers against having to pay the capacity charge, and in equilibrium the rewards for this insurance or hedge should be the average cost of additional capacity.

There is the further question whether this is the correct way in which to decentralise investment decisions. If generators bid in at only marginal operating cost, roughly constant up to full capacity, then VOLL × LOLP is required to cover the capacity costs. But even if the industry were competitive, so that no generator has the market power to raise prices above the level of his competitors without losing his market, the appropriate equilibrium concept is one in supply *functions* or supply schedules, not in a single price per generator. Newbery (1992) argues that the system marginal price would rise above operating costs as the industry reached full capacity output, and the equilibrium level of capacity would be such that the average price covered total average costs, without the need for the capacity charge. In an imperfectly competitive industry, the opportunities for raising prices above operating cost is greater, and the current worry is that there is too much entry and hence capacity, rather than too little.

Decisions on location are now decentralised, but generators are encouraged to discuss their plans with the NGC as early as possible, and they will have to negotiate a connection agreement that may include the costs of reinforcing the grid to accept the new load. The NGC publishes each year a seven-year forecast showing the capacity expansions firmly committed and those under consideration, together with its plan for grid investments. The cost of delivering power to consumers depends quite sensitively on the location of power stations, because the grid is constrained in the loads that it can transmit at various critical points. Grid capacity expansions are expensive, as is moving electricity over long distances. At the moment, there is an excess supply of electricity in the North and an excess demand for electricity in the South, resulting in substantial North–South flows of up to 10 GW. The grid provides crude signals to encourage generators to locate in areas where power is needed by differentiating the price of access to the grid in different areas.

The whole system of setting tariffs for the grid was admitted to be unsatisfactory upon privatisation and was reviewed in 1992. The NGC published a consultative document for its Transmission Use-of-System Charges Review (NGC, 1992), in which it admitted that its existing charges failed to give the correct signals for the location of new stations. By the time of the review, some 15 to 20 GW of new capacity had signed use-of-system agreements (i.e., about one-third of the total system capacity), so its review had the air of shutting the stable door after the horse had bolted. On strict efficiency grounds, several contributors to that review (e.g., Green and Newbery, 1992b) argued that the connection charges for new stations should be made on a "deep connection"

basis, in which the new station pays all the extra costs that its presence causes the system to incur (in terms of strengthening the system elsewhere). These
charges would be computed for each node in the transmission system, and announced. There would still remain the problem that the signals for capacity expansion (VOLL × LOLP) and capacity location are highly sensitive to the size
of the capacity provided at the location. As a result, the present system of pricing may not be adequate and might better be supplemented by assignable long-
term contracts for supply within a specific area.

Even if the grid devised a correct set of price signals to induce generators to
locate in the correct places, there remained the problem of ensuring that NGC
constructs the most efficient transmission system. Here the initial regulatory
regime provided no incentive for cost-reducing grid investments, for NGC's
total revenues depend largely on the peak Average Cold Spell (ACS) system demand,[33] while its contractual obligations are only to ensure system stability, not
its optimality. There was no mechanism to induce NGC to find the cost-minimising combination of paying generators to remain on the system to relieve capacity constraints, inducing consumers to reduce demands by load management
in constrained areas, or investing to relax transmission constraints. In response
to concern from the regulator and others, NGC has now agreed on an incentive
mechanism by which it gets part of the benefit if uplift payments are below a
target level and pays part of the excess if they are higher.

There are other problems involving the "constrained on" stations that are
called upon to meet demand when transmission constraints are binding and are
then paid any price that they ask, the subject of an Offer report (1992a). PowerGen was criticised for raising the prices of stations behind temporary constraints to make profits that the regulator felt to be excessive. In contrast, National Power argued that the returns earned by its station at Fawley were not
sufficient to cover the overhead costs of maintaining the station available,
even bidding in at a high price, given the small number of hours during which
Fawley was required. They would prefer a contract providing a fixed payment
to cover the costs of availability in return for bidding at marginal cost. Similar problems affect the open-cycle gas turbine stations required for peak lop-
ping, which are required very few hours per year and do not recover their costs
even at bid prices of 16 p/kWh. Again, the NGC is considering contracts to
provide these stations on standby. They would then fill much the same function as the pumped storage system currently owned and operated by the NGC.

It could be argued that the final equilibrium will be a comprehensive set of
contracts that will virtually reinstate the vertically integrated nature of control

---

[33] Charges for use-of-system and existing connections are based on the forecast of ACS demand
and, after the first regulatory review, must decrease in real terms at 3% per year (i.e., RPI –
3%), to reduce the excessively high NGC profits. New connections are charged to yield a rate
of return on the assets involved.

of the previous industry. If so, the old barriers to entry may re-emerge, and little may have been gained from the restructuring. Against this, one could argue that the main advantage of the restructuring is to make explicit the costs of meeting the variety of demands made upon the present system and to raise questions as to whether they are currently being satisfied at least cost. For example, many hospitals and large firms keep standby generators as insurance against power loss. If these generators can be centrally dispatched, subject to an overriding priority allocated to the owner, the amount of spare capacity required for security could be reduced with considerable cost-savings.

Operating efficiency

The evidence on operating efficiency is mixed. Green and Newbery (1992a) suggest that the size of the two privatised generators gave them the ability to bid at prices well above marginal cost, with potentially serious deadweight losses as a result. A contestable contract market might force the generators to keep contract prices down to the long-run marginal cost of entrants. Competitive pool prices would be above this level when there was a shortage of capacity, promoting entry, but should be much lower when there is excess capacity. That was the position during the early 1990s, and the regulator determined that pool prices were too high during 1993 (Offer, 1994). Using the threat of referring National Power and PowerGen to the MMC, he obtained a promise that they would aim to keep pool prices at a time-weighted average of 2.4 p/kWh during 1994 and 1995. By the end of that period, further entry should make the base-load market very competitive, but to increase competition in the rest of the merit order, the companies have agreed to use their "best endeavours" to sell or otherwise dispose of 6 GW of plant. This structural remedy may be enough to keep pool prices close to competitive levels over the long term, while the cap provides some benefits to industrial consumers over the short term. Ironically, the main loser from the cap is Nuclear Electric, because the other companies had already sold much of their output on long-term contracts at prices unaffected by the cap.

One of the effects of privatisation has been to make explicit the old system of cross-subsidy that was supposed not to happen under state ownership. The Large Industrial Consumers (LICs), notably those whose electricity costs were a high fraction of sales revenue and who exported in competitive markets (preeminently the chemical, steel, and pulp and paper industries) complained in the past that they were handicapped by unreasonably high electricity prices resulting from the high cost of British coal. In addition, the CEGB had excess capacity through the 1970s and 1980s, so the deal struck allowed the LICs to buy electricity notionally generated with coal purchased at import parity prices at a generation cost set equal to short-run marginal cost. The LICs effectively avoided paying for the capital cost of generation through the load management schemes. Doubtless much the same was true of their continental competitors, and on short-run economic efficiency arguments their case was sound. It was probably also the case that the system of implicit regulation under state ownership gave the CEGB an incentive to overinvest, for the costs of shortages were perceived to be very high (power cuts being perceived as both politically damaging and professionally incompetent), and the costs of excess capacity were borne by the Treasury, not the consumer, under the logic of short-run marginal cost (SRMC) pricing. As a result, the LICs could enjoy an equilibrium in which they rarely had to make any contribution to the capital cost of generation. Not surprisingly, they now resent the passing of this regime.

Clearly that is not a sustainable equilibrium in a privatised ESI, where the generators have to cover their capital costs. If the industry were sufficiently competitive for the generators to sell at prices below long-run average cost (LRAC) in periods of excess supply, they would need to be able to charge above LRAC in periods of tight demand. Industrial customers who wished to buy at low pool prices when there was excess supply would face high prices when there was a shortage of capacity. Perhaps the mechanism would be that as demand was forecast to tighten, so generators would succeed in persuading customers to sign long-term contracts that covered the required capital costs, rather than facing the unpredictability of the now important VOLL × LOLP payments.

Incentives for cost reduction: Pricing is only one aspect of efficiency, and reducing the costs of generation is a more important component. There is evidence that individual power stations have greater incentives to achieve improved efficiency, and that they have done so. The effect of privatisation on the generators is that they have nearly halved their staff in the first three years, as well as closing research laboratories. There are clearly strong incentives to reduce the cost of fuel, and this has primarily affected British Coal, as discussed earlier. The enthusiasm with which the generators have experimented with Orimulsion as a coal substitute for use in oil-fired stations is another sign. The same drive for increased efficiency is, however, also observed in the commercialised but still state-owned nuclear industry, whose performance can now be measured in the competitive market. In contrast, the RECs and NGC have been rather slower to reduce employment. It may be that this is because they were not as badly overmanned as the generators to start with, but an alternative view – that companies that are privatised without an increase in competition take longer to adjust to "private sector" standards – would be consistent with the experience from other utility privatisations in the United Kingdom.

There are strong incentives to prematurely retire the older, labour-intensive, coal-fired stations operating infrequently, in part because this will reduce "excess" capacity and improve the prospects for raising bid prices into the pool.

The Director General of Electricity Supply has properly insisted that stations scheduled for closure should be subject to review to see if they should be offered for sale, to ensure that closure takes place when justified at current or projected prices rather than as an attempt to raise prices by restricting supply.[34] Given the uncertainties about the future supply of coal and the terms under which it will be available, demand for such stations may not be very strong.

The merit order and the grid: The final worry is that the old merit order is compromised at two stages. Green and Newbery (1992a) suggest that the merit order could be compromised by the asymmetry in the size of the two privatised generators that gives the larger an incentive to bid in at a relatively higher margin over marginal cost, though the larger generator may also have a greater incentive to appear not to be manipulating the market, possibly offsetting this incentive.[35] There may be distortions even with "competitive" bidding, when generators bid at their avoidable costs, if take-or-pay fuel contracts mean that avoidable costs are below true marginal costs.

The present system of charging for grid services does not properly relate energy charges to energy losses, and therefore it prejudices the true merit order. Power losses increase as the square of the current, and hence the marginal cost of using the grid is an increasing function of the load on the grid between any two points. Under the existing system, all generators are paid the same pool purchase price, no matter where they are located, even though the difference in transmission losses between stations could amount to over 10% of the bid price (NGC, 1994, Table 8.1). It is somewhat ironic that in their efficiency audit (MMC, 1981) the Monopolies and Mergers Commission criticised the CEGB for failing to adequately allow for transmission losses in computing the merit order. The CEGB made the necessary changes, but these have been sacrificed in the interest of producing a workable pool charging system on a short timescale. Green (1994) shows that overall costs could be reduced by £2 million a year if the NGC took transmission losses into account. This could create winners and losers on a large scale (stations in the North would generate less and might have to pay transmission charges), and so the privatised industry is likely to resist the reintroduction of such charges, although welfare would have been greater if they had never been abolished.

Lessons for regulating network industries

The experience of regulating network industries like the ESI (as well as British Gas and BT) highlights the importance of one of the issues that need to be ad-

---

[34] This may have perverse effects on whether and which stations to retire, if they might be purchased by a competitor.

[35] This certainly appears to be consistent with behaviour in the first year's operation.

dressed in designing the appropriate regulatory framework for any network industry. That issue is the choice between two alternative models for its structure. In the first, production (i.e., generation) and the network (i.e., the grid) can be retained as a vertically integrated monopoly, perhaps with provisions for common carriage and access to a fringe of smaller producers. The other model is one of vertical separation, with the objective of ensuring competition in those stages of the industry that do not suffer from natural monopoly, retaining regulation for the natural monopoly elements.

There are advantages and drawbacks in either choice. If the industry remains vertically integrated, regulation can be confined to a price cap on the basket of final products, and the industry is free to choose the most efficient organisation of production and distribution. If the industry is vertically disintegrated, the network must be subject to separate regulation. The evidence from the NGC is that it is difficult to get the transmission prices right, particularly because marginal-cost pricing will not cover total costs. In such cases, price discrimination is typically preferable to uniform pricing, but it is difficult to regulate adequately. Compared to a vertically integrated industry, the outcome is likely to be one in which intermediate transactions are less efficient. In the case of the NGC, the main inefficiencies were that the merit order failed to properly account for transmission costs and that the locational decisions by new generators were inappropriate.

The advantage of vertical disintegration is the competitive pressure when entry is feasible, and the resulting gains in efficiency may offset the transactions inefficiencies of the network. Vertical disintegration hinders cross-subsidisation and makes pricing more transparent. This in turn has lead to a close scrutiny of the value of such services as reliability, security, and national self-sufficiency. It is difficult to see how else the existing and often unsatisfactory politico-economic equilibrium of various interests will be adequately changed without such a radical step, though privatisation without restructuring will go someway toward changing the balance of commercial and socio-political interests.

The inefficiencies of the Fossil Fuel Levy

British nuclear power is not competitive with either coal or gas, given current safety standards and commercially accounted costs of decommissioning and disposal, if it has to meet capital costs at commercial rates of interest. On vesting, Nuclear Electric inherited liabilities of reprocessing, radioactive waste management, and decommissioning estimated at £9.3 billion. These were to be met by the Fossil Fuel Levy, payable on sales of all leviable, that is, fossil-generated, electricity, which should collect £9.1 billion by its terminal date in 1998. (Both figures at 1992–3 prices. See Trade and Industry Committee, 1993, paras. 120–30.) In 1992, the levy was 11% of the sales price to final consumers, and the subsidy gave Nuclear Electric almost half its revenue. This has the rather odd consequence that power supplied over interconnector from France receives the price inclusive of the levy (i.e., 11% higher than fossil-fueled stations in England and Wales), even if at the margin Electricité de France (EdF) is generating electricity from fossil-fueled stations. This perverse subsidy of the French amounting to £95 million in 1992 is an unintended by-product of the particular way of protecting the British Treasury.

The logical alternative would have been to write off the accumulated liabilities for decommissioning and associated reprocessing, on the principle that such sums should have been notionally set aside by the government during the earlier operation of the nuclear power stations remaining in state ownership. These past investment mistakes are regrettable bygones, and their financial legacy should not be allowed to distort current generation decisions through the levy. The government has refused to remove the FFL, even for large consumers, on the illogical ground that this would involve an unwarranted *subsidy*. But the FFL is not a cost, it is a device to recover revenue for the Treasury, and it is good tax practice to exempt all producers, not just large producers, from such taxes. Changing the structure of the FFL might also save the £95 million transferred to EdF each year.

Conclusions

The effects of privatisation have been to gradually make the high costs of British coal and nuclear power explicit, as the contracts fall due for replacement and the actors are driven by market prices and explicit taxes. The wide diversity of conflicting interests involved – British Coal, the miners, large energy-intensive industries, the incumbent generators, the independent power producers, the oil and gas companies, nuclear power, the RECs, the Treasury, the Department of the Environment, the European Commission, and the GATT – ensure that any deviation from market solutions (as well as unsatisfactory or controversial market solutions) must be debated in public, rather than being settled in the secrecy of Civil Service meetings. Although this is not necessarily a guarantee of reaching a better solution (the recent nuclear programme was approved by the most expensive public enquiry in history), the erosion of market forces on bureaucratically induced costs appears so far to have been beneficial.

The rest of the world should be grateful that Britain has undertaken the experiment of privatisation and restructuring the ESI. One obvious benefit may be the discovery of potential cost-reducing changes in operating practice. Once these have been identified, it is possible that well-regulated state-owned enterprises could introduce administrative and regulatory reforms to achieve the benefits at lower cost, though the history of careful reports and recommendations in Britain suggests that good advice is not sufficient. The deeper question is whether privatisation and deintegration are needed to actually secure these gains. Public ownership has at least the advantage of making possible far-reaching structural reforms that become difficult if not impossible once the industry is privately owned, so there is an option value on public ownership. More to the point, there may be only one chance to restructure if privatisation is planned, so it is important to get it right.

The other question is whether the gains of privatisation offset the costs. The private costs of uncertainty, risk, and the unpredictability of future regulatory regimes might be expected to raise the price of delivered electricity in Britain. On the other hand, there should be greater pressure to cut costs, raise factor productivity, and increase the rate of profit, thereby improving the allocation of resources between electricity and other goods. The contrast between the generators and the RECs shows that competition can be at least as important as privatisation in creating pressure for efficiency. The regulator of the monopoly parts of the industry will have to act as an alternative source of pressure for efficiency – this will be easier when there are many companies and yardstick comparisons are possible. The main problem is that of coordination and the possibly larger costs of ensuring the required coordination through markets and contracts rather than internal negotiation within a vertically integrated industry.

Another potential benefit to Britain will be the restructuring of the coal industry and its rapid privatisation. The main benefit to Europe might be to cause the European Commission to query the extensive subsidisation of German and Spanish coal mines that are kept operating at costs higher than those of closed British pits at a time when reducing carbon dioxide emissions makes coal subsidies seem peculiarly inappropriate. The rethinking of the nuclear programme is not peculiar to Britain, and it may well be that when the time comes to increase the share of nuclear electricity, the privatised British structure will be less well suited than state-owned systems. It will, for example, be hard to demonstrate that state-owned nuclear power is not being subsidised in competition with privately owned fossil fuel electricity in Britain, and there are likely to be endless wrangles about the appropriate cost of capital and of reprocessing services to the nuclear industry if such a move is contemplated.

It may be that Britain was lucky in deciding to privatise at the moment at which the right technology (CCGT) and adequate gas supplies became available. In such cases the concern over a possible bias toward short-term investment may not be too serious. Certainly, recent environmental concerns, first with acid rain, and more recently with greenhouse gases, suggest that a move to gas was probably inevitable, and matches the capabilities of a privately financed electricity industry well.

REFERENCES

CEGB. *An Appraisal of the Technical and Economic Aspects of Dungeness B Nuclear Power Station.* London: CEGB, 1965.

Chesshire, J. *Electricity Privatisation and Nuclear Power.* Mimeo, Science Policy Research Unit. Sussex: University of Sussex, 1991.

Digest of UK Energy Statistics, annually. London: HMSO.

DTI. *The Prospects for Coal: Conclusions of the Government's Coal Review,* Cm 2235. London: HMSO, 1993.

Energy Committee. *First Report from the Select Committee on Energy: The Government's Statement on the New Nuclear Power Programme,* HC 114 of 1980/1. London: HMSO, 1981.

Third Report: The Structure, Regulation and Economic Consequences of Electricity in the Private Sector, HC 307 of 1988/9. London: HMSO, 1988.

Fourth Report: The Cost of Nuclear Power, HC 205 of 1989/90. London: HMSO, 1990.

Second Report on the Consequences of Electricity Privatisation. London: House of Commons Energy Committee, 1992.

Foreman-Peck, J., and M. Waterson. "The Comparative Efficiency of Public and Private Enterprise in Britain: Electricity Generation Between the World Wars." *Economic Journal,* 95, Supplement (1985): 83–95.

Foster, C. D. *Privatization, Public Ownership and the Regulation of Natural Monopoly.* London: Basil Blackwell, 1993.

Gordon, Robert. "Forward into the Past: Productivity Retrogression in the Electric Generating Industry." NBER Working Paper No. 3988 (1992).

Green, R. J. "Bidding in the Electricity Pool." Paper presented to Office of Electricity Regulation seminar on pool prices, October 1991.

"Do Electricity Transmission Networks Need Optimal Spot Prices?" Mimeo, DAE, Cambridge, U.K.: 1994.

"The Cost of Nuclear Power Compared with Alternatives to the Magnox Programme." Mimeo, DAE, Cambridge, U.K.: 1995.

Green, R. J., and D. M. Newbery. "Competition in the British Electricity Spot Market." *Journal of Political Economy* 100 (1992a): 929–53.

"Comments on NGC's Use of System Charging Proposals." Mimeo, DAE, Cambridge, UK (1992b).

Hammond, E., D. Helm, and D. Thompson. "Competition in Electricity Supply: Has the Energy Act Failed?" *Fiscal Studies* (1986): 11–33.

Hannah, L. *Electricity before Nationalisation.* London: MacMillan, 1979.

Engineers, Managers and Politicians: The First Fifteen years of Nationalised Electricity Supply in Britain. London: Macmillan, 1982.

Handbook of Electricity Supply Statistics, annually. London: Electricity Council.

Henney, Alex. *The Economic Failure of Nuclear Power in Britain.* London: Greenpeace, 1991.

Hunt, S., and G. Shuttleworth. "Forward, Option and Spot Markets in the UK Power Pool." *Utilities Policy* 3 (1993): 2–8.

Jeffrey, J. W. *Proof of Evidence to Hinkley Point C Public Inquiry, Hinkley Point C – A Dangerous, Unnecessary and Uneconomic Source of Power,* September (1988).

Larsen, E. D., and R. H. Williams. "Steam-Injected Gas Turbines." Contributed paper by the Gas Turbine Division of the American Society of Mechanical Engineers for presentation at the 31st International Gas Turbine Conference, Düsseldorf, June 8–12, 1986. Paper 86–GT–47.

Layfield, Frank. *Sizewell B Public Inquiry.* Report by Sir Frank Layfield, Department of Energy, 1987.

Maher, M. "Total Factor Productivity and Rates of Return in the English ESI." 1993.

Ministry of Fuel and Power. *A Programme of Nuclear Power,* Cmnd 9389. London: HMSO, 1955.

Ministry of Power. *The Second Nuclear Power Programme,* Cmnd 2335. London: HMSO, 1964.

Mitchell, B. R. *British Historical Statistics.* Cambridge, U.K.: Cambridge University Press, 1988.

Monopolies and Mergers Commission (MMC). *Central Electricity Generating Board: A Report of the Operation of the Board of Its System for the Generation and Supply of Electricity in Bulk,* HC 315. London: HMSO, 1981.

Morrison, H. *Socialisation and Transport.* London: Constable, 1933.

National Economic Development Office. *A Study of Nationalised Industries.* London: NEDO, 1976.

Newbery, D. M. "Capacity-constrained Supply Function Equilibria: Competition and Entry in the Electricity Spot Market." Mimeo, DAE, Cambridge, U.K., 1992.

NGC. *Transmission Use of System Charges Review; Proposed Investment Cost Related Pricing for Use of System,* National Grid Company, 30 June 1992.

Seven Year Statement for the Years 1994/5 to 2000/1, National Grid Company plc, March (1994).

Offer. *Report on Pool Price Inquiry,* Office of Electricity Regulation, Birmingham. December (1991).

Report on Constrained-on Plant, Office of Electricity Regulation, Birmingham, October (1992a).

Review of Pool Prices, Office of Electricity Regulation, Birmingham, December (1992b).

Review of Economic Purchasing, Office of Electricity Regulation, Birmingham, December (1992c).

Review of Economic Purchasing: Further Statement, Office of Electricity Regulation, Birmingham, February (1993a).

Pool Price Statement, July 1993, Office of Electricity Regulation, Birmingham, July (1993b).

Decision on a Monopolies and Mergers Commission Reference, Office of Electricity Regulation, Birmingham, February (1994).

Prior, M. *Sizewell B Power Station Public Inquiry, Aspects Concerning Fossil Fuels, Proof of Evidence.* Town and Country Planning Association, September (1983).

Select Committee on Nationalised Industries. *Report from the Select Committee on Nationalised Industries: The Electricity Supply Industry,* HC 236 of 1962/3. London: HMSO, 1963.

Select Committee on Science and Technology. *Report from the Select Committee on Science and Technology: United Kingdom Nuclear Reactor Programme,* HC 381–XVII of 1966/67. London: HMSO, 1967.

Short, R. P. "The Role of Public Enterprises: An International Statistical Comparison." In *Public Enterprises in Mixed Economies: Some MacroEconomic Aspects,* edited by R. Floyd, C. Gary, and R. Short. Washington, D.C.: IMF, 1984.

Trade and Industry Committee. *British Energy Policy and the Market for Coal,* Memoranda of Evidence, Vols I and II, House of Commons HC 326. London: HMSO, 1992.

British Energy Policy and the Market for Coal, Report, House of Commons HC 237. London: HMSO, 1993.

Treasury. *The Financial and Economic Obligations of the Nationalised Industries,* Cmnd 1337. London: HMSO, 1961.

Nationalised Industries: A Review of Economic and Financial Objectives, Cmnd 3437. London, HMSO, 1967.

Cash Limits on Public Expenditure, Cmnd 6440. London: HMSO, 1976.

The Nationalised Industries, Cmnd 7131. London: HMSO, 1978.

Wilberforce Inquiry. *Report of a Court of Inquiry into a Dispute Between Parties Represented on the National Joint Industrial Council for the Electricity Supply Industry,* Cmnd 4594. London: HMSO, 1971.

Williams, T. "No Combination Without Regulation." *Annals* 32 (1908).

Yergin, D. *The Prize: The Epic Quest for Oil, Money and Power.* New York: Simon & Schuster, 1992.

CHAPTER 3

How should it be done?
Electricity regulation in Argentina,
Brazil, Uruguay, and Chile

Pablo T. Spiller
University of California, Berkeley
Luis Viana Martorell
Montevideo, Uruguay

Introduction

The privatization drive in developing countries has reached the electricity sector. In Argentina, Brazil, Jamaica, Malaysia, Mexico, Pakistan, Uruguay, and Turkey, just to name a few, private sector participation in the provision of electricity is currently directly promoted or is being considered by government officials. Although there is much interest in promoting private sector participation, however, few of those countries can show major private sector investments in the electricity sector.[1]

The combination of government interest in private sector participation with the lack of actual private sector response, however, is in sharp contrast to the

The research for this paper was conducted as part of a research project on the Regulation of Electricity in the Southern Cone of South America. This research project was supported, in part, by a grant to CERES from the University of California Universitywide Energy Research Group. Project members were Carlos Givogri and Mario Damonte (Argentina), Adriano Pires (Brazil), Bruno Philippi (Chile), S. Antmann and Luis Viana Martorell (Uruguay), and Pablo Spiller (coordinator). This paper provides a synthesis of the four country studies that form the body of the project. Spiller would like to thank the University of California Energy Research Group at Berkeley for providing the right intellectual environment and the facilities to complete this project. We would like to thank participants at the CERES Workshop on Electricity Regulation in the Southern Cone, Montevideo, May 17, 1991, in particular Ing. S. Antmann, Mario Damonte, Bruno Philippi, and Adriano Pires, and Richard Gilbert for helpful comments and suggestions.

[1] For example, Pakistan and Turkey have so far unsuccessfully tried to develop large (1,000 MW+) projects and build operate and transfer projects (BOTs). Mexico, on the other hand, has just started a smaller electricity operation BOO (build, operate, and own) project. Jamaica has called for private participation in its long-term investment plan, without much success so far. The remaining countries in that list, however, have yet to implement any privatization process.

drastic transformation of the electricity sector that occurred in Chile, where in less than a decade the sector moved from being government owned to private provision and ownership, not only of generation but of transmission and distribution facilities as well. Not only has Chile been successful in transferring ownership from the government to private hands, but it has also promoted large private investments in all areas, with current investment projects by private electricity firms amounting to close to US $2 billion.

We claim in this paper that such a contrast is not mere coincidence. Instead, Chile's success is based on a drastic transformation of its regulatory structure and institutions, a transformation that occurred *before* privatization took place. Most of the countries trying to promote private sector privatization have an extremely ad hoc regulatory system, which not only generates very large inefficiencies but also lacks the assurances of fair play that private investors naturally would require. As a consequence, countries promoting Build Operate and Own or Build Operate and Transfer generation projects find that potential private investors require substantial governmental guarantees (e.g., repayment guarantees for the external debt, minimum purchase requirements, exchange rate convertibility guarantees), which seem to allocate most of the risks to the government.[2]

If, as in the Chilean example, these countries would attempt first to reform their regulatory structure and institutions, then private sector participation could be expected to proceed at a more rapid pace, notwithstanding their macroeconomic problems.

In this chapter we compare the regulatory structures and their efficiency implications in four countries of the Southern Cone of South America – Argentina, Brazil, Chile, and Uruguay – and derive implications for future regulatory reform.

The political economy of public provision of private goods[3]

Electricity, as well as water, telephones and other traditional public services, is provided in most developing countries by publicly owned corporations.[4] To a large extent, this is not totally unexpected, because these industries are characterized, at least at their distribution level, by highly specific assets and relatively large economies of scale. As a consequence, in the absence of safe-

---

[2] See, for example, Lecat (nd), for a discussion of this type of problem.

[3] Much of this section is taken from Spiller and Levy (1991).

[4] There has been a recent trend toward privatization of telephone systems in developing countries (e.g., Argentina, Jamaica, Mexico). The Philippines, on the other hand, has always had a private telephone sector. Other countries (e.g., Argentina, Malaysia) are considering privatizing electricity and water services as well.

guarding institutions that assure that specific assets would not be expropriated by the local governments, either outright or through administrative procedures, private investors would be unwilling to undertake those capital commitments. These safeguarding institutions can take many different forms. See Spiller and Levy (1991) for a lengthy discussion of this issue.

Safeguarding institutions and private investment: First, the existence of a well-functioning judicial system with respect for property rights can serve as an institution that could to a large extent deter such expropriation. Thus, countries with well-developed and functioning judicial systems, like Costa Rica or Chile, can use to some extent access to the judiciary as a safeguard of the interests of private investors and, more generally, of the original regulatory intent. In this sense, it is interesting to note that Chile's regulation of electricity rates has a conflict resolution process that provides private companies access to the judiciary should the administration attempt changes without changing the law (Bernstein, 1986). Countries like Brazil, where the judiciary system is not reliable, may have to use alternative methods to safeguard the interests of private investors (Rosen, 1984).

Second, a similar function can be performed by properly functioning independent regulatory institutions that are not subject to much influence by the polity. Many developing, and some developed countries as well, have regulatory bodies that are also producing bodies. For example, until the latest administrative reforms, the Mexican SCT (Ministry of Communications and Transport) had a monopoly on airline reservation services, as well as of private lines communications, whereas Telmex, the public telephone company that is currently in the process of privatization, had the monopoly for local and long-distance services except cellular (World Bank, 1990). Similarly, the Uruguayan telephone company is currently the institution that regulates all telecommunications issues (Perez Montero, 1990). The blending of regulatory and production activities tends to insulate the regulatory body from the legislature because the agency does not need legislative support to obtain funding. Because the regulatory body has independent financing, the identity of the decision makers in the regulatory body becomes crucial, creating strong incentives for party membership to be a critical condition for appointments at the high levels of the regulatory body, with its possible detrimental effect on administrative quality.[5]

Third, a high sectorial growth rate, as well as in the economy at large, could also provide assurances to private investors. If the government would expropriate the assets of the incumbent firm, the government would then have to undertake by itself further future expansions, for the government's loss of rep-

---

[5] That is, the president will not appoint a person to the regulatory body unless he is reasonably assured of that person's political tendencies.

utation would deter other private firms from entering the sector (or other sectors where the government would like to see private investments). Our emphasis on growth in the sector as a substitute for safeguarding institutions is quite different from the observation that economic growth and the level of government intervention in the economy seem to be negatively correlated. See, for example, North and Thomas (1973), Olson (1982), Murphy, Shleifer, and Vishny (1990). We are looking at reforms in a given sector of the economy. If the sector is growing, say because of particular demand factors, but the economy is stagnant, then opportunistic behavior will be costly to the government. If, instead, the sector is a declining one but the economy is growing rapidly, then, because not much more investment will be required in that sector in the future, the incentives for opportunistic behavior by the government are exacerbated.

In general, then, in economies where the incentives for administrative expropriation are high, regulatory reform in sectors (like the electricity sector) where the efficient technology requires large sunk investments will not attract efficient levels of private investment, unless new safeguarding institutions are created that will protect investments.

Fourth, private investment may not be forthcoming even in the presence of a sensible regulatory structure if the coalition that instituted the original regulation cannot deter others from modifying the regulatory system toward their own interests. The higher the likelihood that the relative power of interest groups changes, the higher the likelihood that regulations will change accordingly. Furthermore, because one of the costs of deviating from the stated regulatory policy is the loss in reputation that the government faces, a party in government with a low probability of remaining in, or regaining, power, may find it more politically profitable to deviate from previously stated regulatory purposes than one that has a longer horizon. The latter will internalize the loss of reputation and hence will tend to deviate only under more extreme circumstances. Political stability, then, reduces the need to develop special safeguarding institutions. Countries with a strong tradition of stability of party governance, as in Mexico, or where the same political parties alternate in power, as in Costa Rica, may use more easily administrated procedures, for the political parties in power will internalize the costs of changing policies, thus reducing regulatory stability. Political parties' policy stability also encourages regulatory stability. A relevant feature of party organization in this respect is the extent of control that the political parties can exercise over their legislators. Thus, the higher the power of parties, the more stable policies will tend to be over time, and hence, the lower the need for safeguarding institutions (Spiller and Levy, 1991).

Fifth, the division of regulatory responsibilities among state and federal organizations can be helpful in restricting the ability of governments to administratively expropriate industry-specific assets. As long as federal regulations restrict what states can actually do, then although a particular state may want to administratively expropriate assets, its ability may be restricted by federal regulations. In such cases, for administrative expropriation to occur, both levels of government have to be aligned, a situation less likely than if the political composition of the country involved just one level of government.[6] Furthermore, state and federal competition may allow a firm facing adverse conditions in one state to move part of its business to a neighboring state without necessarily relocating its assets. This could, for example, be the case for electricity generation when a company facing a local regulatory body setting prices well below long-run costs may find it profitable to contract with a nearby state and wheel its electricity rather than sell it to the local transmission or distribution company. The threat of such a move may reduce the pricing ability of the local government.[7]

Political instability and government ownership of large sunk costs in domestic production sectors: In economies where neither political instability nor government ownership is present, then public sector ownership may become the default mode. If the country has neither stable politics nor an independent judiciary, is not growing rapidly, and has no tradition of independent and professional regulatory agencies, then private sector investment in sectors with large economies of scale and sunk investments producing mostly for the local market are excessively risky and will not be forthcoming. Because lower prices will provide substantial political support, governments will find it politically advantageous to expropriate the sunk investments of the private firms. This expropriation may take the form of setting maximum prices that do not compensate for future (and past) investments. Private investors, then, anticipate that such development will not invest and that future investments will have to be undertaken by the government itself.

If we compare the four countries of the region, we find that until the mid-1950s Chile and Uruguay were characterized by relatively stable politics, strong party control, and a reasonably working judiciary. Neither, though, experienced dramatic economic growth. In the late 1960s and early 1970s, though, political stability started to fade in both countries. In 1930 Chile's electricity sector was in private hands, but by 1970 the government held 90% of the generation and 80% of the distribution.[8] Uruguay, on the other hand, has had full government control for more than 60 years, with a single public company providing all public electricity services. Argentina, on the other hand, has

---

[6] On the economic and political implications of federalism, see Rose-Ackerman (1981) and references therein.

[7] The local government may try to prohibit the company from selling out of state. This policy, though, may conflict with federal statutes.

[8] The nationalization of CHILECTRA was undertaken before the socialist period.

had an unstable political structure since the 1940s and has not had strong economic growth, but it has had strong provincial (vs. federal) institutions. Although some private utilities have existed (mostly as cooperatives), until the recent privatization they have not been very important. Finally, Brazil, although not having an efficiently working judiciary, has had one of the largest rates of growth in South America. This may explain the important role that private utilities had until they were acquired in the 1970s (like the Light Co., which provided electricity to Rio de Janeiro). In the 1970s, though, political instability may have reduced the incentives for private investment, triggering the movement toward full government ownership of the sector.

Government ownership may have been the default mode in at least three out of the four countries we consider here.[9] Government ownership may, then, reflect the workings of long term economic and political features such as political instability, weak judiciary and regulatory institutions, and slow economic growth. In those circumstances, short-term considerations take center stage over long-term ones. For example, Cukierman, Edwards, and Tabellini (1992) and Edwards and Tabellini (1991a and 1991b) provide conditions under which politically unstable governments (what they call myopic governments) tend to "rely more heavily on the inflation tax," as a way of financing their expanding deficits (Edwards and Tabellini, 1991b).

Political instability not only triggers government ownership but also government interference with the pricing and investment policies of the sector.[10] In particular, because investments in electricity provide benefits only in the future, political instability implies that current governments will tend to delay investments and that their investments will tend to be of shorter lead time. As a consequence, countries characterized by unstable politics will not only have chronic electricity shortages, but also their electric park will be inefficient, with larger emphasis being given to smaller, lower initial capital investment plants (e.g., emphasis on smaller thermal plants).[11] Similarly, because politically unstable governments will find it profitable to provide subsidies to their constituencies directly through preferential electricity pricing, we should observe that this type of country will not only have relatively low prices in general but that prices will differ substantially by end use, with residential prices being particularly subsidized. The relatively low electricity prices and the in-

---

[9] We do not necessarily include Chile in that set for two reasons. First, until the beginning of the government of Dr. Allende, there were private electricity companies. Second, even though the public ownership of electric companies lasted beyond the government of Dr. Allende, the latter did not last long and public ownership has been reversed since then.

[10] In a sense, that was the direct reason why private ownership failed in the first place.

[11] Unstable politics have to be differentiated from unstable governments. Unstable politics capture changes in the political leadership from the governing party (or group) to an opposition party, rather than just minor changes in head of government or in cabinet composition. See Edwards and Tabellini (1991b) for further discussion of this issue.

Table 3-1. *Argentina: Electricity generation by type and ownership (in GWh, 1987)*

Company	Thermal	T. Gas	Diesel	Hydro	Nuclear	Total
Federal						
SEGBA	8,106.8	339.0				8,445.8
AyEE	5,251.2	1,793.4	116.2	5,718.4		12,879.2
CNEA					6,464.8	6,464.8
CIMSG				7,657.3		7,657.3
HIDRONOR				7,480.9		7,480.9
Provincial						
EPEC	980.0	614.5	7.2	406.1		2,095.8
DEBA	1,376.9	324.2	26.1			1,727.2
EMSE				398.0		398.0
EMSA	81.7	172.7	53.9	2.6		310.9
OPESTAFE		10.5	87.8			98.4
OPESALTA		30.2	4.6	34.8		69.6
SPSE			57.1			57.1
DPEC			37.2			37.2
DPE			26.5			26.5
APELP				26.1		26.1
SECHEP			11.2			11.2
EPER			8.2			8.2
SESLEP				7.3		7.3
DECA				3.1		3.1
OTHERS		12.5	132.7	4.0		149.2
Municipal[a]		66.1	62.4	1.1		129.6
Cooperatives						
RIO GRANDE		57.8				59.8
EL DORADO			15.3			15.3
SC DE BARILOCHE		8.3	4.3			12.6
VENDADO TUERTO			5.1			5.1
COMODORO RIVADAVIA			3.2			3.2
RIO PICO				0.6		0.6
CONCORDIA			0.5			0.5
TREVELIN				0.3		0.3
PERITO MORENO				0.2		0.2
OTHERS			34.0			34.0
TOTAL	15,804.6	3,363.1	631.4	21,019.8	6,464.8	48,083.7
SHARE (IN %)	32.9	7.0	1.3	45.4	13.4	100.0

[a]One company.
Source: Givogri and Damonte (1991).

efficient generating park imply that this type of country may have to introduce quantity restrictions to avoid the collapse of the system.

On the other hand, because most voters live in large cities, we should observe a subsidy toward large towns. In countries where the electricity is mostly based on hydroelectric plants, such cross-subsidy could be achieved through uniform pricing across the country. Large hydroelectric plants are usually far away from the larger towns, but although the surrounding agricultural areas and smaller towns may be closer to the source of electricity, they will have to pay prices equal to those paid by the more distant large towns. Uniform prices are usually proposed as a way to subsidize small cities, because their average costs of distribution and transmission are usually higher than those of larger towns.

Finally, because electricity prices, as well as those of other publicly provided goods, are controlled by the government, politically unstable governments will tend to manipulate the prices of publicly provided goods, including electricity, to try to reduce inflationary expectations, even at the expense of larger future deficits. Future larger deficits may have to be taken care of by a future opposition government, while reducing current inflation may help the current government.

To summarize, in countries characterized by unstable politics, weak judiciary and regulatory institutions, and slow growth, government ownership may become the default organizational mode of the electricity sector. Unstable politics also implies that the pricing and investment policies of the publicly owned electricity companies will be determined by redistributional and macroeconomic concerns. As a consequence, average electricity prices may not cover long-run costs, and residential prices may be heavily subsidized. Furthermore, countries characterized by politically unstable governments will tend to show chronic electricity shortages and inefficient generating (as well as transmission and distribution) plants.

In the following section we discuss the characteristics of the electricity sectors in Argentina, Brazil, and Uruguay. In two later sections we explore the main characteristics of Chile's electricity sector and compare the performance of Chile and the other three countries, and provide general comments on prospects for regulatory reform in the Southern Cone.

The regulatory and institutional structure of the electricity sector in Argentina, Brazil, and Uruguay, and its effects: Or how not to do it

The regulatory and institutional structure:[12] Argentina (until 1992), Brazil, and Uruguay have shared similar regulatory structures: first, the sector is

---

[12] Since the research for this chapter was finalized (June 1992), the government of Argentina has undertaken a wholesale restructure of the electricity sector. This restructure has involved a drastic regulatory reform similar, to some extent, to the Chilean regulatory approach. We do not deal here with the recent privatization and restructuring process in Argentina. We analyze the period up to the end of 1991. Interested readers are referred to Perez-Arriaga (1994).

Table 3-2. *Brazil: Installed capacity of utilities (by energy source and ownership) (1989)*

Type	Public		Private	
	No.	MW	No.	MW
Hydro	238	43,491.2	49	116.0
Thermal (coal)	5	1,040.0	0	0.0
Thermal (fuel oil)	12	1,842.1	0	0.0
Thermal (nuclear)	1	657.0	0	0.0
Thermal (others)	3	15.9	0	0.0
Diesel	270	546.1	2	1.2
Gas turbines[a]	7	660.7	0	0.0

[a]Mostly diesel; natural gas was not used for generation before 1988.
Source: Pires and Braga (1991).

based on publicly owned enterprises (in the case of Uruguay, a single one). Private sector participation in the electricity market, although it may not be legally prohibited, is for all purposes nonexistent. For 1987, for example, in Brazil there were 25 very small private utilities (Pires and Braga, 1991), but they were mostly concentrated on distribution, owning 50 generating plants with 0.02% of total installed capacity (see Table 3-8). Private investment in self-generation was quite important, representing close to 8% of installed capacity and 5% of actual generation (see Table 3-11).

Similarly, in Argentina until 1992, most of the generation was done by federal and state companies (see Table 3-1), whereas self-producers generated in 1987 around 8% of total generation (Givogri and Damonte, 1991).[13] Self-producers in Argentina and Uruguay, however, are not necessarily interconnected to the national grid. In Uruguay, for example, the current electricity law requires the public company to operate and maintain all domestic plants that are interconnected to the grid, including those mainly used for self-generation (Antmann and Viana, 1991). Because of this requirement, the public company has not interconnected the private self-generating plants. In any case, though, self-generating capacity has remained a small percentage of overall capacity (see Table 3-9).

Second, the regulatory structure in all three countries is not transparent. Tariffs, for example, are set by a Cabinet decision, even though there may exist, in the books, a governmental agency in charge of the determination of electricity policy. For example, in Argentina the Ministry of Public Works and

[13] In Chile, self-production amounts to 24% of total electricity generation. Its rate of growth is slower than that of the interconnected systems.

Services, through the office of the Deputy Secretary of Energy, was supposed to control the electricity sector's planning, licensing, tariffs, and development, but in fact tariffs and investment programs were controlled by the Ministry of Economics. Furthermore, in 1991 the Deputy Secretary of Public Enterprises (SEP) of the Ministry of Economics took the power to control operative aspects of the public electric companies. There was a separate federal agency in charge of harmonizing the regulatory and tariff structures of the different public enterprises (the Federal Commission of Electric Energy, CFEE). This agency, however, was not able to achieve any of its mandated objectives. The pricing of electricity, though, did not have to follow a particular scheme, either at the wholesale or at the retail level. In particular, the Electric Energy Law of September 1960 does not stipulate a methodology to compute tariffs or a particular regulatory system. Furthermore, in its treatment of return on capital it is extremely confusing, for it uses different and contradictory terms like "Reinvestment Fund," "Reserve Fund," "Amortization," "Interests on Capital," "Interests and financial expenses in issuing debt." See Givogri and Damonte (1991, para. 1.03). It specifies, though, that the regulatory regime for *each* license has to be developed separately (Givogri and Damonte, 1991). In that way, for example the license of HIDRONOR, a 2,770 MW hydroelectric company to provide service to the northern region, requires HIDRONOR to sell its surplus energy only to the National Integrated System (SIN) at prices that should provide HIDRONOR with a guaranteed return of 8% over the capital base. If the operating profit does not cover the 8%, then either a direct federal contribution has to take place, or the federal government may reduce HIDRONOR's capital base by increasing the portion of "excluded capital." The federal government, though, has to compensate HIDRONOR for the reduction in its capital base (see Givogri and Damonte, 1991, para. 1.04).

In Uruguay there is no separate agency, and the prices and investment plans of the electricity company (UTE) have to be approved by the Office of Planning and Budget of the Presidency, and tariffs are set by the executive power, with substantial intervention by the Ministry of Economics and Finance (Antmann and Viana, 1991). In Brazil several agencies determine basic investment and tariff policies. Although in principle the National Department of Waters and Electric Power (DNAEE) is responsible for setting prices and contractual conditions, in fact the Secretariat of Plan (SEPLAN) controls investment programs and intervenes in the determination of electricity prices (Pires and Braga, 1991).

Because the three countries have had during the past 20 years relatively high inflation, there has been a definite tendency to use the Cabinet's ability to manipulate electricity prices (as well as those of most other public services) as part of anti-inflationary programs. This, for example, has implied that during their bouts of hyperinflation, real electricity prices have fallen drastically in both Brazil and Argentina, only to be drastically increased later on. See

Figure 3-1. Argentina: Electricity prices [average at wholesale (in US$/MWh)]

Table 3-3. *Argentina: Evolution of average final users' prices (in UScents/kWh)*

Year	Industry	Residential	Commercial
1972	1.68	2.44	2.63
1973	2.19	3.42	5.62
1974	3.08	4.06	7.81
1975	1.83	1.82	4.25
1976	1.87	1.72	3.32
1977	3.46	3.22	6.41
1978	4.63	5.06	8.69
1979	4.17	7.23	9.58
1980	6.01	13.22	15.65
1981	3.36	10.31	9.86
1982	2.20	4.78	2.20
1983	3.33	4.45	5.89
1984	4.01	4.87	6.69
1985	4.05	4.98	6.78
1986	4.17	5.30	7.32
1987	4.28	5.77	6.52
1988	4.20	7.52	10.54
1989	4.18	4.73	9.15
1990	6.76	7.27	14.05

Source: OLADE, various issues.

Table 3-4. *Brazil: Average prices per category (in UScents/kWh)*

Year	Industrial	Residential	Commercial
1972	1.49	3.88	4.02
1973	1.80	4.80	4.42
1974	1.90	5.20	4.81
1975	2.30	6.00	5.00
1976	2.20	5.80	4.79
1977	2.30	5.80	4.86
1978	2.50	5.80	4.77
1979	2.50	5.70	3.89
1980	2.50	5.70	4.57
1981	3.60	5.70	4.75
1982	3.40	5.30	4.95
1983	2.30	3.70	2.82
1984	2.30	3.40	2.69
1985	2.20	3.00	3.28
1986	2.40	3.10	4.59
1987	3.40	5.00	3.98
1988	4.90	6.00	9.03
1989	4.10	4.50	11.84
1990	4.40	5.80	8.06

Source: OLADE, various issues.

Figure 3-1 for the evolution of Argentina's wholesale prices, and Tables 3-3 and 3-4 for the evolution of electricity prices for final users in Argentina and Brazil.

In Uruguay, since inflation has been relatively more steady during the last decade, electricity prices have tended to be adjusted every quarter, with substantial less variation over time than in its two neighbors. Nevertheless, in Uruguay, during macro-economic adjustment periods nominal electricity prices have been kept relatively constant so as to affect inflationary expectations and/or reduce current inflation rates (see Table 3-5).

Third, in the three countries, the public electricity companies' investment decisions are substantially controlled by the central government. In particular, long-term investments were curtailed during periods of macroeconomic adjustment, as well as during periods of political instability.[14] Tables 3-6 through 3-9 provide the extent of investment in capacity for the three countries.

[14] We define as unstable political periods those during which the party (or group) in government is in danger of being replaced, either because of losing the coming elections, or by some other means.

Table 3-5. *Uruguay: Average electricity prices (in US$/kWh)*[a]

Year	Residential	Industrial	Commercial	Total[b]
1972	0.019	0.014	0.050	
1973	0.028	0.022	0.053	
1974	0.041	0.028	0.079	
1975				
1976	0.040	0.027	0.066	
1977	0.053	0.030	0.063	
1978	0.047	0.033	0.074	
1979	0.055	0.040	0.083	
1980	0.079	0.057	0.113	0.0760
1981	0.078	0.054	0.122	0.0752
1982	0.074	0.052	0.115	0.0721
1983	0.053	0.036	0.080	0.0507
1984	0.053	0.036	0.079	0.0505
1985	0.048	0.036	0.073	0.0472
1986	0.059	0.043	0.085	0.0569
1987	0.063	0.048	0.088	0.0615
1988	—	—	—	0.0674
1989	0.066	0.057	0.090	0.0665

[a]Average totals available only after 1980.
[b]Includes municipal lighting and electric transport.
Source: Data after 1980 from Antmann and Viana (1991); data prior to 1980 from OLADE, various issues.

The mixing of politics with tariff setting and investment plans is particularly important given the fact that all three countries have abundant hydroelectric potential. These investments, though, are larger and require longer gestation lags than the smaller and simpler thermal plants. As a consequence, investments may not follow proper economic calculus, nor may they be properly timed.

For example, whereas during the 1970s the Brazilian government financed approximately 20% of the sector's investment, during the first half of the 1980s the government financed not more than 5%, forcing the sector to increase its leverage to finance the investments that were currently under way, and to postpone or retard investment (see Table 3-10). In particular, if the Brazilian electricity park in 1989 is divided by installation date, we find that 9% (or 4,524 MW) of all installed capacity was installed before 1960, 16.5% (7,994.8 MW) was installed between 1961 and 1970, 48% (23,328.7 MW) between 1971 and 1980 and only 26% (12,522.7 MW) was installed between 1981 and 1989

Table 3-6. *Argentina: Installed capacity trends (in MW)*

				Utilities				
Year	Hydro	Fuel oil	Gas oil	Diesel	Nuclear	Total	Self-gen-eration	Grand Total
1970	584	3,134	393	750		4,861	1,830	6,691
1971	687	3,250	575	771		5,283	1,828	7,111
1972	691	3,431	713	775		5,610	1,776	7,386
1973	1,308	3,501	920	768		6,497	1,848	8,345
1974	1,508	3,507	1,121	752	340	7,228	1,910	9,138
1975	1,506	3,459	1,229	747	340	7,281	1,949	9,230
1976	1,721	3,769	1,254	768	370	7,882	1,903	9,785
1977	1,919	3,768	1,277	773	370	8,107	1,943	10,050
1978	2,920	3,821	1,367	771	370	9,249	1,938	11,187
1979	3,145	3,913	1,468	775	370	9,571	1,927	11,498
1980	3,601	3,818	1,514	783	370	10,086	1,931	12,017
1981	4,161	3,974	1,703	786	370	10,994	1,950	12,944
1982	4,628	3,964	1,773	789	370	11,524	1,956	13,480
1983	4,815	4,401	1,898	465	1,018	12,897	1,949	14,846
1984	5,355	4,233	1,985	733	1,018	13,324	1,967	15,291
1985	5,967	4,387	1,897	725	1,018	13,994	1,964	15,958
1986	6,192	4,387	1.965	715	1,018	14,277	1,952	16,229
1987	6,567	4,409	1,969	719	1,018	14,682	1,908	16,590
1988	6,567	4,454	1,955	703	1,018	14,697	1,833	16,530
1989	6,473	4,750	1,990	982	1,018	15,213	1,842	17,055
1990	6,477	4,874	1,937	980	1,018	15,286	1,800	17,086

Source: OLADE, various issues.

(Table 3-7). The Brazilian electric park is almost totally hydroelectric. Hydro comprises today 90% of installed capacity (Table 3-8), 95% of actual generation (Table 3-11),[15] and more than 90% of the capacity that was added during the 1970s and 1980s (Table 3-7). Also, newer units are on average bigger than older ones – the average plant in the 1980s was 140 MW compared to 70 MW for older plants. Finally, most generation comes from larger plants, three-quarters of existing capacity coming from plants with more than 1 GW of installed capacity, whereas five-sixths of all plants have between 30 and 50 MW but in total comprise just 4% of total installed capacity (see Table 3-12).

Similarly, in Uruguay, out of the 1,563 MW of currently installed capacity, 228 MW were installed before 1959, 227 from 1959 to 1973, and 1,108 from

---

[15] Self-producers, though, are mostly thermal (80%).

Table 3-7. *Brazil: Installed capacity by initial operating date (1989)*

	Before 1960		1961–70		1971–80		Post 1980	
Type	No.	MW	No.	MW	No.	MW	No.	MW
Hydro	177	3,930.5	46	6,512.3	45	21,815.6	19	11,348.8
Thermal								
(coal)	1	20.0	3	574.0	1	446.0	0	0.0
Thermal								
(fuel oil)	3	538.0	5	751.9	4	552.2	0	0.0
Thermal								
(nuclear)	0	0.0	0	0.0	0	0.0	1	57.0
Thermal								
(others)	0	0.0	0	0.0	0	0.0	3	15.9
Diesel	14	35.5	31	146.6	156	252.4	71	112.8
Gas turbines[a]	0	0.0	1	10.0	2	262.5	4	388.2
Total	195	4,524.0	86	7,994.8	208	23,328.7	98	12,522.7

[a]Natural gas was not used for generation before 1988.
Source: Pires and Braga (1991).

1973 to 1982, with no further investments in public generating capacity since then (see Table 3-9). The 1,108 MW installed after 1973 include two hydro-electric plants, Constitucion with 330 MW and the Binational Salto Grande project with Argentina, of whose total installed capacity Uruguay takes an increasing share during the years. For 1991 that share corresponds to 630 MW; by 1995 it will increase to 895 MW (Antmann and Viana, 1991).[16] The years 1959 to 1973 represent the most unstable political period in Uruguay since World War II. The traditionally minority party ascended to power for the first time in 1959, albeit for only one presidential period. This unstable period ended in 1973 with the military coup. It is striking that from 1959 to 1973 there were three years in which consumption restrictions were introduced (1959, 1965, 1972), half of all postwar restrictions (Antmann and Viana, 1991). Although the Uruguayan system is based on hydroelectric generation,[17] it is subject to large variations in water stocks because its ability to retain water for future years is very limited.[18] For example, although at regular water lev-

[16] The 1108-MW capacity addition represents gross investments, without considering down rating of old facilities.
[17] Currently, 71% of the capacity is hydro. The proportion is expected to increase to 75%, with the additional capacity coming from the Salto Grande project.
[18] First, although the Rincon del Bonete dam is the system's only water reserve, it has very little storage capacity. Second, the different water systems, the Uruguay and Rio Negro rivers, have highly correlated water flows. As a consequence, the Uruguayan hydroelectric system has to be complemented with substantial thermal capacity.

Table 3-8. *Brazil: Installed capacity trend*

Generators	Utilities								Self		
Year	Hydro (%)	Coal (%)	Fuel (%)	Nuclear (%)	Other (%)	Diesel (%)	Gas (%)	Total (GW)	Hydro (%)	Thermal (%)	Total (GW)
1970	83.9	2.4	9.9		0.1	3.7		10.29	37.4	62.6	0.95
1975	86.4	2.7	8.0			2.9		18.48	18.4	81.6	2.72
1980	88.6	2.5	6.1			2.8		30.57	19.5	80.5	2.91
1985	89.0	1.8	5.0	1.7		2.5		39.78	19.0	81.0	3.29
1987	89.2	2.2	4.5	1.6		2.5		40.94	19.0	81.0	3.29

Source: Pires and Braga (1991).

els the average annual electricity generation by the hydroelectric group is around 2,700 GWh/year, in dry years it may only reach a fifth of that amount (Antmann and Viana, 1991, p. 9). As a consequence, social marginal costs fluctuate drastically over the years (and even during different months of a given year), implying that the optimal pricing scheme would have to be quite flexible. Dry years would require substantial price increases to reduce consumption; to shift consumption away from peak consumption periods, such pricing schemes would seldom be introduced during periods of political instability. The introduction of quantity restrictions to avoid the collapse of the system would then be required.[19]

Finally, Argentina, clearly the most politically unstable country of the three, is the one with the lowest share of hydroelectric installed capacity, but highest in nuclear.[20] During 1987 hydroelectric plants generated 45.4%, whereas nuclear plants generated 13.4% of the total system output (48,083 GWh) (see Table 3-1). Their shares of total installed capacity (12,802 MW) are 46% and 8%, respectively (see Givogri and Damonte, 1991).

The effects

Public ownership, nontransparent regulatory systems, and direct intervention by the administration on the pricing and investment decisions of the electric companies, coupled with relatively unstable political regimes, have produced in the three countries relatively similar pricing policies. First, average tariffs have traditionally been below long-run average costs; second, tariffs discriminate by end-use; and third, there is an attempt to have uniform pricing across regions.

---

[19] Because 50% of the Uruguayan consumption is residential, restricting that sector's consumption is usually enough to maintain the system's integrity.

[20] For example, since 1976 Argentina had five changes of government, while Brazil and Uruguay had two, and Chile had only one.

Table 3-9. *Uruguay: Installed capacity trends (in MW)*

	Public service						Grand
Year	Hydro	Fuel oil	Gas oil	Diesel	Total	Self-generation	total
1970	236	208	31	55	530	29	559
1971	236	208	31	57	532	29	561
1972	236	208	31	59	534	29	563
1973	236	208	31	55	530	45	575
1974	236	208	31	55	530	45	575
1975	236	333	31	55	655	35	695
1976	236	333	31	60	660	35	695
1977	236	333	31	60	660	35	700
1978	236	333	31	60	660	40	700
1979	281	333	31	60	705	40	745
1980	371	333	31	60	795	40	835
1981	461	333	55	55	904	40	940
1982	881	333	55	55	1,324	40	1,364
1983	881	333	55	31	1,300	40	1,340
1984	881	313	55	31	1,280	40	1,320
1985	881	313	55	31	1,280	40	1,320
1986	1,039	313	55	31	1,438	40	1,478
1987	1,039	313	55	31	1,438	40	1,478
1988	1,039	313	55	31	1,438	40	1,478
1989	1,196	313	55	31	1,595	40	1,635
1990	1,196	313	55	31	1,595	40	1,635

Source: OLADE, various issues.

Average revenues vs. average costs: Average revenue has fallen over time in the three countries. In Argentina, for example, average (nominal) wholesale electricity prices were around 30 US$/MWh at the end of 1982. They dropped to 25 US$/MWh by 1985, to less than 20 US$/MWh by 1987, and were around 15 US$/MWh by 1989 (see Figure 3-1). A similar trend developed in Brazil, where, although at nominal prices industrial rates doubled from 1975 to 1990 (see Table 3-4), at constant prices a very different outlook appears. Indeed, at constant 1985 US$, average industrial tariffs were 46 US$/MWh in 1975, 33.36 US$/MWh in 1980, 17.26 US$/MWh in 1985, and 24.29 US$/MWh in 1987 (see Table 3-4).

For Uruguay, a similar trend occurred, with average residential tariff being 7.9 US$/MWh in 1980, 4.8 US$/MWh in 1985, and 6.6 US$/MWh in 1987 (see Table 3-4).

Average revenue in the three countries, however, has been systematically below average long-run marginal cost. For example, according to Givogri and

Table 3-10. *Brazil: Financing of capacity additions (in percentages)*

Year/period	Domestic	Foreign	Gov't	Own resources
1970	25.7	17.3	23.4	33.6
1975	15.1	18.0	19.4	47.5
1980	22.1	30.1	5.3	42.5
1985	35.1	29.3	1.6	34.0
1986	16.5	38.0	12.5	33.0
1987–91[a]				43.3–44.3

[a]Projection.
Source: Pires and Braga (1991).

Damonte (1991), the average long-run marginal cost in Argentina for the 1980s was approximately 38 US$/MWh at the 500 kV level, well above the average revenue for the period. See Table 3-13 for a description of the relation between economic costs and retail prices for different types of consumers in 1990. This created a substantial subsidy to the final users (and to the distributing companies). On the other hand, it reduced the incentives for the generating companies to invest and to maintain their generating facilities. With prices at such a low level as in 1989, generating companies may have chosen even not to produce. Thus, during 1988, 50% of the system's plants were supposedly out of commission because of repairs.[21] The situation for the final user is similar. For example, at the lowest residential tariff block, the tariff (including taxes) only covers 8% of the long-run average cost, whereas most of the residential customers' tariffs do not cover 50% of their average costs. Finally, industrial users pay between 80 and 100% of the average costs (see Table 3-13). It is not clear from the available evidence whether the distributing companies or the final users actually capture the subsidy implied by the low wholesale tariff. The distribution companies do not seem to transfer that subsidy to industrial users, but they seem to do so for residential customers.

In Brazil operating costs have been between 50 and 60% of operating revenues. Financial costs, on the other hand, have been from 100 to 150% of operating revenues. Thus, again, average revenues do not cover average costs (see Table 3-14). They also do not cover average long run marginal costs, which in 1989 were computed to be 71 US$/MWh, while the average billed power price was only 46.69 US$/MWh (Pires and Braga, 1991).

Finally, in Uruguay, except for the lowest consumption residential group (less than 50 kWh/month), average tariffs cover peak short-run marginal cost

---

[21] That year the generation problem was exacerbated because of low water levels and because of repairs at the two nuclear plants. As a consequence, a deficit of 1,500 GWh developed (Givogri and Damonte, 1991).

Table 3-11. *Brazil: Electricity generation trend*

Generators	Utilities								Self		
Year	Hydro (%)	Coal (%)	Fuel (%)	Nuclear (%)	Other (%)	Diesel (%)	Gas (%)	Total (TWh)	Hydro (%)	Thermal (%)	Total (TWh)
1970	91.4	2.9	4.8		0.1	0.8		42.03	37.7	62.7	3.71
1975	95.3	2.0	2.2			0.5		73.87	37.5	81.6	5.07
1980	96.2	1.9	1.2			0.7		131.04	33.2	80.5	8.44
1985	95.1	1.8	0.6	1.8		0.6		184.36	36.4	63.6	8.37
1987	94.7	1.9	1.7	0.5		1.3		192.28	34.8	65.2	10.07

Source: Pires and Braga (1991).

Table 3-12. Brazil: Utilities' installed capacity by source and size: 1989, in MW

Plant type	Below 50		50<=200		200<=500		500<=1000		>1000	
	No.	MW	No.	MW	No.	MW	No.	MW	No.	MW
Hydro	229	1,239.9	21	2,368.0	18	6,725.3	3	2,504.0	16	30,770.0
Coal	2	40.0	1	72.0	2	928.0	0	0.0	0	0.0
Fuel oil	6	151.9	3	328.2	2	762.0	1	600.0	0	0.0
Nuclear	0	0.0	0	0.0	0	0.0	1	657	0	0.0
Other thermal	3	15.9	0	0.0	0	0.0	0	0.0	0	0.0
Diesel	271	493.0	1	54.3	0	0.0	0	0.0	0	0.0
Gas turbines	1	10.0	6	650.7	0	0.0	0	0.0	0	0.0

Source: Pires and Braga (1991).

Table 3-13. *Argentina: Relation of retail prices to economic costs of electricity (in mills of US$/kWh; 1990)*

Consumer type	Average cost US$/MWh	Tariff US$/MWh	Tariff/cost
Residential			
Monthly usage (kWh)			
50	130.2	10.4	0.08
120	114.0	12.1	0.11
250	101.7	50.9	0.50
500	91.3	96.0	1.05
Industrial (less than 50 kW)			
Monthly usage (kWh)			
6,500	101.0	89.6	0.89
8,100	90.4	89.2	0.99
9,800	82.2	88.9	1.08
12,000	75.4	88.7	1.18
General			
Monthly usage (kWh)			
50	113.9	44.8	0.39
120	100.8	76.0	0.75
250	90.8	90.2	0.99
500	82.4	102.2	1.24

(none covers, though, the peak during summer months), but residential tariffs do not seem to cover the average long-run marginal costs of 1986. Industrial and commercial tariffs seem to cover average long-run marginal costs (see Tables 3-15 and 3-16). This computation, based on an analysis by Monchek and Marrero (1986), however, does not let us answer whether they would also cover the long-run marginal costs of peak, rather than simply average, long-run marginal cost. Monchek and Marrero (1986) find that excluding government offices and enterprises, the residential sector has a subsidy of 19% of its costs, whereas the industrial and commercial sectors are taxed at 12.2% and 31%, respectively.

Price distortions: Discrimination among final users: The three countries have prices that discriminate among the nature of the final users. For example, Uruguayan tariffs consider three types of final users: commercial, industrial, and residential. A commercial user that consumes less than 1,000 kWh per month pays a fixed monthly charge of US$ 6.14 and US$ 0.075/kWh. A user defined as industrial with similar consumption patterns would pay a similar

Table 3-14. *Brazil: Ratio of operating and financial costs to operating revenue (%)*

Year	Operating costs to revenues	Financial costs to revenues
1985	49.3	153.8
1986	55.9	128.3
1987	59.1	123.9
1988	55.0	60.1
1990	52.1	97.7

Source: Pires and Braga (1991).

fixed charge and US$ 0.074/kWh. A residential consumer with a monthly consumption of more than 500 kWh per month would pay a fixed charge of only US$ 1.82 and a variable charge of US$ 0.10/kWh (see Table 3-15).

In 1991 Argentina had a very large number of final users' categories, with each distribution company having its own set of categories (Givogri and Damonte, 1991). See Table 3-17 for the average prices charged by each company. In Brazil, on the other hand, there is a single, but quite large, set of categories for all distribution companies that is determined by the central government (Pires and Braga, 1991).

Price distortions: Uniform prices across regions: In the three countries there has been a policy of common prices for all regions of the country. In Brazil and Uruguay that policy actually means that the same type of customer pays the same price in all localities, but that has not been the case in Argentina, where the policy of uniform prices that was intended with the Federal Pact of 1989 actually implied an increase in price disparities.

Brazil's strict uniform pricing policy was instituted in 1974, implying that final user prices are independent of costs. Although in principle it was supposed to help the poor regions of the North and Northeast, the structure of costs has meant that the main beneficiaries of this policy are the richer regions of the South and Southeast/Central West. To understand this paradox, it has to be remembered that most of Brazil's generating capacity is hydroelectric and that most of the hydroelectric plants are in the remote North and Amazon regions. For that reason, transmission costs and different energy sources become very important in determining long-run marginal costs to the South and Southeast/Central West. For example, Pires and Braga (1991) compute that whereas the average long-run marginal cost for the North/Northeast is 59.02 US$/MWh, for the Southeast/Central West it is 75.53 US$/MWh, and for the South it is

Table 3-15. *Uruguay: Tariff rates (1990)*

Customer/consumption (kWh)	Monthly charge ($US)	Variable charge (UScents/kWh)
Commercial		
<1,000	6.14	7.5
1,001–5,000	6.14	8.5
5,001+	30.41	8.6
Industrial		
<5,000	6.14	7.4
5,001–10,000	30.41	7.4
10,001–50,000	30.41	6.5
50,001+	30.41	5.8
Residential		
1–50	0.97	4.2
51–200	1.82	7.0
201–300	1.82	9.3
301–500	1.82	9.3
501–1,000	1.82	9.3
1,000+	1.82	10.0

Source: Antmann and Viana (1991).

82.25 US$/MWh (see Tables 3-18 and 3-19). These discrepancies are even more exaggerated if we look at the different categories of users (small- vs. large-voltage users). For example, whereas high- and medium-voltage users' average long-run marginal costs in the North/Northeast are 44.91 US$/MWh, for the Southeast/Central West and South these costs are 57.35 and 64.03 US$/MWh, respectively. Residential users' average long-run marginal costs for these regions are 84.47, 110.11, and 107.40 US$/MWh, respectively. Even though all regions' final prices are below long-run marginal costs, because of the size of Brazil and the different regional electricity sources, the policy of uniform prices brings about substantial interregional cross-subsidies. For example, for 1989 the ratio of the average billed power price to the average long-run marginal cost was 79.1% for the North and Northeast regions, 61.8% for the Southeast/Central region, and only 56.8% for the South. As a consequence, the subsidies that each region receives amounts to US$ 98 million, US$ 382 million, US$ 3,893 million, and US$ 995 million for the North, Northeast, Southeast/Central West and South, respectively (see Tables 3-18 and 3-19).[22]

---

[22] These figures should be considered tentative because no adjustment was made for different modalities of consumption across regions.

Table 3-16. *Uruguay: Short-run marginal costs (1990: US$/kWh)*

Month	Average	Peak	Trough	Off-peak
Jan/Mar	0.0770	0.1454	0.0653	0.0458
Apr/Jun	0.0358	0.0369	0.0355	0.0355
Jul/Sept	0.0383	0.0458	0.0364	0.0355
Oct/Dec	0.0282	0.0285	0.0281	0.0281
Average	0.045			

Source: Antmann and Viana (1991).

The Brazilian system of uniform tariffs implies that different public service companies will have very different margins, with some having positive and others having negative margins. As a consequence, a Global Guarantee Reserve (RGG) was introduced that takes surplus revenues from low-cost utilities and transfers those to high-cost ones (Pires and Braga, 1991).[23]

In Uruguay the system of uniform prices implies that users located in the city of Montevideo, which is farthest away from the main sources of electricity supply (Salto Grande in northern Uruguay and the area of the Negro River in central Uruguay), pay the same price as those located in relatively large cities in northern and central Uruguay (e.g., Salto, Paysandu) where transmission costs would be substantially smaller. In fact, it could well be that the incremental cost that these cities impose on the transmission system could be negligible, because the main transmission lines toward Montevideo could easily accommodate their own demands (Antmann and Viana, 1991).

In Argentina, the Federal Pact of 1989 was introduced with the explicit purpose of making electricity tariffs uniform across regions (see Givogri and Damonte, 1991, para. 1.05). This was going to be achieved through the following method: First, all energy was to be sold to the system at its generating cost and bought at the average cost, multiplied by a factor that was supposed to compensate for the different distribution costs across the local distributing companies.[24] As a consequence, efficient distributing systems were taxed and forced to buy at the average cost of the generating system, eliminating incentives for entering into individual long-term contracts with generating plants. Furthermore, because in principle generating plants receive their individual cost, there are no incentives to reduce cost at the generating

---

[23] When tariffs fell below operating costs, associated utilities with surplus suspended those transfers which aggravated the situation of the high cost utilities, as well as of ELETROBRAS (Pires and Braga, 1991).

[24] This system is similar to that of the Brazilian Global Guarantee Reserve.

Table 3-17. *Argentina: Prices by final users (in mill US$/kWh)*

	Residential		Industrial			
			Low voltage		High voltage	
Jurisdiction	Nov. 89	May 90	Nov. 89	May 90	Nov. 89	May 90
Argentine interconnected system						
GBA (SEGBA)	9.1	59.7	66.6	142.4	35.8	75.4
Cordoba (EPEC)	20.1	63.5	84.9	159.3	50.7	75.2
Buenos Aires (DEBA)	48.1	81.5	55.6	213.3	25.6	116.8
San Luis	39.9	40.3	71.9	104.8	41.4	60.2
Interconnected to AyEE						
Tucuman	9.3	67.2	41.2	102.3	31.4	78.2
Chaco	21.0	40.1	60.6	103.7	45.0	77.1
Salta	29.7	67.7	42.1	129.2	35.2	112.3
Jujuy	25.7	40.6	44.0	69.5	34.7	51.4
Mendoza	12.4	26.8	46.7	78.3	34.8	58.6
San Juan	24.3	98.0	36.8	117.2	23.5	69.5
Corrientes	25.4	42.6	40.8	63.1	29.2	49.0
Entre Rios	25.2	56.2	72.5	116.0	38.9	59.2
Santa Fe	20.3	62.7	63.0	136.2	49.0	106.0
Others[a]						
Misiones (EMSA)	24.2	66.5	47.4	123.5	42.3	110.1
Neuquén (EPEN)	9.1	22.2	44.4	87.4	26.8	47.5
Average tariff	22.9	55.7	54.6	116.4	36.3	77.5
Highest tariff	48.1	98.0	84.9	213.3	50.7	116.8
Lowest tariff	9.1	22.2	36.8	63.1	23.5	47.5
Standard deviation	10.6	19.7	14.1	36.8	8.0	23.7

[a]Misiones is an isolated system, and Neuquén has a special tariff approved by the legislation creating HIDRONOR.
Source: Givogri and Damonte (1991).

level (recall, though, that these wholesale prices may not cover costs, as we discussed earlier).

The regulatory and institutional structure of the electricity sector in Chile and its effects

The regulatory and institutional structure: In 1978 the Chilean government started a drastic restructuring of the electricity sector, concerning both the nature of the regulatory process and of its ownership structure. Concerning the

Table 3-18. *Brazil: Long-run marginal costs by region (1989 in US$ per MWh)*

Codes	Description	Brazil	North/NE[a]	SE/CW[a]	South
A1	230 Kv or more	44.75	36.28	48.37	45.65
A2	138 Kv to 88 Kv	48.40	—	52.08	52.39
A3	69 Kv to 20 Kv	50.90	39.15	54.81	54.33
A4	13.8 Kv to 2.8 Kv	63.99	62.48	64.60	68.52
Average A group		54.32	44.91	57.35	64.03
B1	All residential	98.95	84.47	110.11	107.40
B2	Rural	123.67	119.98	137.34	136.77
B3	Other users	96.30	95.51	100.65	99.75
B4	Public lighting	96.40	84.48	95.64	95.49
Average B group		99.45	89.18	107.63	105.48
All voltage levels		71.25	59.02	75.53	82.25

[a]NE = Northeast, SE = Southeast, CW = Center/West.
[b]Only interconnected systems.
[c]Brazil = average LRMC for the country as a whole.
Source: Pires and Braga (1991).

tariff determination process, before 1980 tariffs were based on a rate of return method.[25] Today regulated tariffs are determined on long-run marginal-cost principles, with rates for large customers (and wholesale rates as well) being determined in the open market.[26] Before 1978 the government had direct say on electricity tariffs, but current tariffs are now set by a mechanism that does not allow short-run government interference with the determination of rates.

Concerning ownership and structure of the sector, in 1978 the electric system was based on two publicly owned integrated companies, ENDESA and CHILECTRA. Today there are 11 power generating companies, 21 elec-

[25] Until 1980, electricity companies were regulated by a tariff commission composed of representatives from government, the firms, and the consumers. The tariff commission would set maximum annual revenues that were to provide each company with at least 10% return on its "profit assets." Profit assets were computed as the company's annually revalued assets. The companies, which were vertically integrated and mostly public, could design their own tariff structure, subject to the maximum annual revenue. Electricity prices were substantially distorted during the 1971–74 period when they were frozen under high inflationary circumstances (Bernstein, 1988).

[26] We discuss later in more detail the workings of the current tariff determination process.

Table 3-19. *Brazil: Interconnected system marginal costs and economic transfers (1989 in US$/MWh)*

Region	Consumption GWh/yr	BPP[a]	LRMC	BPP/LRMC	Transfers US$ millions[b]
Brazil	202	46.49	71.25	0.655	5,368
North	8	46.49	59.02	0.791	98
Northeast	31	46.69	59.02	0.791	382
SE/CW	135	46.69	75.53	0.618	3,893
South	28	46.69	82.25	0.568	995

[a]BPP = Billed power price.
[b]Interconnected system only.
Source: Pires and Braga (1991).

tricity distribution companies, and two integrated companies, many of those being traded in the Chilean stock exchange (Philippi, 1991). The average daily trading of 11 electricity companies amounts to 45% of the value of all stock transactions in the Chilean stock exchange, with ENDESA accounting for 18.5% of that value and ENERSIS for 7.3% (see Table 3-20). Table 3-21 presents the distribution of ownership across the population for the largest companies.

This drastic restructuring of the sector was achieved by separating generation and transmission from local electricity distribution. For example, the distribution side of ENDESA was broken into several distribution companies, each with coherent geographic and economic units, and they were subsequently privatized. Similarly, CHILECTRA was broken into three units, one of generating and two of distribution. See Tables 3-22 and 3-23 showing the main generating and distributing companies, and whether they used to be part of ENDESA or CHILECTRA. Table 3-22 shows that in the CIS ENDESA controls more than 50% of total capacity. Nevertheless, the extent of divestment of ENDESA's generating capacity has been quite large. Table 3-23 shows the size distribution of the distributing companies. As we will see later, the distributing companies are regulated according to their density. CHILECTRA Metro, though, is the only one classified as "high density" because it serves more than 1 million customers. The remaining distributing companies are classified as either "medium density" (17 companies) or "low density" (seven companies with fewer than 20,000 customers). Tables 3-22 and 3-23 also show the extent of concentration in both generation and distribution that characterized the pre-1980s regime. The divestment of the larger companies was done

Table 3-20. *Chile: Electric utilities' stock transactions (first semester 1991)*

Utility	US$ Millions	Share of total (in percentage)
CHILECTRA	15.3	2.3
CHILGENER	89.1	13.2
CHILQUINTA	2.0	0.3
COLBUN	5.6	0.8
EDELMAG	0.3	0.0
EDELNOR	2.4	0.4
ELECDA	0.9	0.1
ELECTRICID	4.6	0.7
ELIQSA	0.7	0.1
EMELAT	1.2	0.2
EMELSA	2.8	0.4
ENDESA	125.0	18.5
ENERSIS	49.8	7.3
PILMAIQUEN	9.2	1.4

Source: Philippi (1991).

through sales to the public at large, whereas the smaller units (less than 50 MW) were sold directly through public auctions (Philippi, 1988).

The restructuring process has been quite successful. Electricity prices are closely related to long-run marginal costs, private investment is taking place in all areas of activity (including hydroelectric plants), and as we just saw, electricity companies are widely held and are daily traded in the local stock exchange. The market is very dynamic, with contracts among generating, transmission, and distribution companies and their consumers taking new and varied forms. For example, generation and distribution companies have recently started to invest in transmission lines. The regulatory system has sustained without much problems the financial crisis of the early 1980s and has been shown to be resilient to government and interest group pressures. The fact that the major electricity companies are widely held among small investors and pension plans may have also contributed to the stability of the regulatory system. For example, in 1989 two-thirds of ENDESA's stocks were held by small investors (Philippi, 1991).

Much of the success of this restructuring process is based on the nature of the regulatory regime developed following the creation of the National Energy Commission (CNE) in 1978.

Table 3-21. *Chile: Ownership of main electricity companies (in %; December 1990)*

Ownership	ENDESA[a]	CHIL-GENER	COLBUN	CHIL-ECTRA Metropol.[b]	CHIL-ECTRA V region
General public	38.8	8.2	1.3	—	—
Pension funds	26.3	31.1	0.0	29.0	17.0
Employees	3.3	1.5	0.0	28.3	—
Foreign funds	7.3	9.4	0.0	—	0.0
State	0.0	0.0	97.4	0.0	0.0
Others[c]	24.3	49.7	1.3	42.7	83.0
Total	100	100	100	100	100
Total shareholders	51,833	1,403	864	4,751	1,738

[a]Pehuenche, SA is owned by ENDESA (95.4%).
[b]CHILECTRA Metropolitana is owned by ENERSIS.
[c]Includes other legally established companies.

The regulatory regime: The regulatory structure is quite transparent.[27] The CNE is the basic regulatory institution in the electricity field. It has the responsibility for developing and coordinating investment plans, policies, and regulation for the sector. The CNE is a decentralized organism directly under the Office of the Presidency. It is formed by a council of seven ministers and an Executive Secretary. The staff of the Executive Secretary numbers 20 individuals, and its budget is approved yearly by the Minister of Finance (Philippi, 1991).

The CNE has two basic functions. First, the CNE determines the regulated prices (which have to be approved by the Minister of Economics). As we shall see later, the approval of the Minister of Economics, however, can be denied only for price adjustments that do not come from the specified automatic adjustment clause. Thus, the administration can interfere with only major retail (or toll) price realignments. Even then, though, the proposed prices have to satisfy the legislative mandate, providing firms with a recourse to the courts if the proposed prices seem to be too much below or above long-run marginal costs.

---

[27] For a detailed description of Chile's regulatory system, see Comisión Nacional de Energía (1989). For a technical description of the pricing methodology, see Philippi (1988) and Bernstein (November 1986). For a discussion of the movement toward marginal cost pricing and the problems involved, see Bernstein (1986), Philippi (1988), and Philippi (1991).

Table 3-22. *Chile: Power supply companies (1991)*

System	Ownership	Installed capacity (in MW)		
		Thermal	Hydro	Total
Norte Grande Interconnected System				
EDELNOR	S[a]	86.0	10.2	96.2
CODELCO	S[c]	471.0	0.0	471.0
Self-generators		132.2	0.3	132.5
Subtotal		689.2	10.5	699.7
Central Interconnected System				
ENDESA	P	349.4	1,602.7	1,952.1
CHILGENER	P[b]	511.5	245.1	756.6
PEHUENCHE	P[d]	0.0	500.0	500.0
COLBUN	S[a]	0.0	490.0	490.0
PULLINQUE	P[a]	0.0	48.6	48.6
PILMAIQUEN	P[a]	0.0	35.0	35.0
Others	[e]	0.0	66.3	66.3
Self-generators		226.6	84.6	311.2
Subtotal		1,087.5	3,072.3	4,159.8
Aysen Isolated System				
EDELAYSEN	S[a]	0.0	10.4	10.4
Self-generators		2.0	3.7	5.7
Subtotal		2.0	14.1	16.1
Punta Arenas Isolated System				
EDELMAG	P[a]	45.6	0.0	45.6
Self-generators		47.4	0.6	48.0
Subtotal		93.0	0.6	93.6
Total		1,871.7	3,097.5	4,969.2

[a]Previously owned by ENDESA.
[b]Previously owned by CHILECTRA.
[c]Self-generator.
[d]Previously owned by CORFO, now owned by ENDESA.
[e]Includes 3 small companies.
S: CORFO (state)-controlled company.
P: Private company.

A second role of the CNE is to guarantee the coordination of the several independent generation, transmission, and distribution companies in the interconnected systems (the Interconnected Central System, ICS, and the Norte Grande Interconnected System, NGIS).

Table 3-23. *Chile: Electricity distribution companies (1991)*

System	Ownership	Customers (in 1,000)	Capacity (MW)	Energy (GWh)
Norte Grande Interconnected System				
EDELNOR	S[a]	140	96	139
Central Interconnected System				
CHILECTRA Metro	P[b]	1,106	902	4,741
CGEI	P	365	217	1,138
CHILECTRA Region V	P[b]	285	213	1,119
SAESA	P[a]	114	62	328
EMEC	P[a]	110	55	289
FRONTEL	P[a]	107	35	184
CONAFE	P	94	52	271
EMEL	P[a]	91	37	195
ELECDA	P[a]	84	36	187
EMELAT	P[a]	46	36	187
EMELARI	P[a]	39	17	90
ELIQSA	P	35	17	90
EE DEL SUR	P	16	6	29
EE PTE ALTO	P	14	5	26
CE LITORAL	P	13	3	14
Others		12	4	22
Total		2,531	1,699	8,932
Aysen Isolated System				
EDELAYSEN	S[a]	14	8	148
Punta Arenas Isolated System				
EDELMAG	P[a]	36	46	72

[a]Previously owned by ENDESA.
[b]Previously owned by CHILECTRA.
P: Private company.
S: State-owned company (CORFO).
Source: Comisión Nacional de Energía, and Philippi (1991); installed MW has been estimated with a D.6 load factor, 1988 energy values.

Prices are based on two concepts: First, in the absence of strong economies of scale, competition at the generation level should bring wholesale prices (at the "center of gravity" of the system) close to the system's long-run marginal costs (including marginal power and energy costs). Thus, large users (those with installed capacity above 2,000 kW) have been allowed to negotiate freely with the generating companies to obtain the type of service they would like.[28] Negotiation may involve interruptable or not, peak or off-peak service. It may also involve partial joint investments in dedicated (or public) transmission lines. To provide for a competitive wholesale electricity market, wheeling charges have been regulated by the CNE.

Second, electricity distribution tends to be characterized by large economies of scale. As a consequence, the CNE regulates maximum retail tariffs. Maximum retail tariffs are designed to approximate long-run marginal costs. They are composed of three parts: (1) long-run marginal energy and power costs; (2) long-run marginal transmission costs; and (3) value of distribution added.

To compute marginal energy costs, the CNE has designed a relatively simple dynamic programming model that takes into account the dependency of Chile's electricity system on the current and on forecast hydrological conditions. In 1990 generation amounted to 18,000 GWh, of which 60% was hydraulic and 40% thermal. Although current hydroelectric installed capacity is just 3,000 MW, CNE (1989) estimates the hydroelectric potential to be 28,000 MW. The hydroelectric generating system consists of run-of-the-river plants, some reservoirs with limited regulating capacity, and several power stations associated with the Laja Lake that has an interannual regulatory capacity of about one-third of the annual consumption. As a consequence, the level of Laja Lake is crucial in determining the operating costs of the system. Furthermore, because of the significant regulating capacity in the reservoir, the marginal cost of energy tends to be relatively constant over the day and during weeks. It fluctuates during the year, though, when hydrological conditions change (Philippi, 1991; Bernstein, 1986). The simplicity of the program can be seen by the fact that to analyze one year of data it requires half a minute of CPU time in a Digital Dec 10 computer (Bernstein, 1986). The marginal power charge represents the marginal expansion cost of the system to accommodate an increase in peak demand. Since peak generation is done through reservoir or gas turbine power stations, the CNE uses the cost of installing a 50 MW gas turbine as the cost of peak power development (Philippi, 1991).

The CNE regulated energy and power prices are used for two purposes. First, energy (and power) sold to distribution is at CNE's levels. Second, they form part of the maximum retail price that distribution companies can charge. Although such a system provides the generating companies with investment incentives, because they can predict relatively well the prices they will get

[28] In April 1980 contracts with large clients were deregulated, with a floor of 4,000 kW of installed capacity. In 1982 the floor was reduced to 2,000 kW.

from selling to the distribution companies, it reduces the incentives for the distribution companies to search for the lowest-cost electricity supplier. Observe, however, that because the regulated prices are adjusted automatically whenever they differ by more than 10% of competitive wholesale prices, the inefficiency of such a system is relatively minor.

Regulated transmission costs are based on the relative location of the distribution company vis-à-vis the center of the system, which is Santiago, on the capacity of the distribution system, and on whether the flow is to or from Santiago.[29] The sum of transmission costs and energy and power costs are called *node prices,* because they are the prices at which transactions between generating and distribution companies take place.[30] The node charges computed by the CNE are adjusted every six months (April and October) in such a way that they equal the average of the anticipated marginal costs over the following three years (Bernstein, 1986). These charges are computed using indexing formulas that depend on fuel costs, equipment costs, dam levels, exchange rates, and so on. These formulas would operate automatically if the energy or power charges increase by more than 10% (Philippi, 1991). The node charges, however, are not allowed to differ by more than 10% of the competitive wholesale prices.

Finally, the regulated distribution costs are derived from a typical system efficiently adjusted to the size of the locality in question. Actually, the CNE uses only three types of distribution size: high, medium, and low distribution density. See Table 3-23 for a list of the various distribution companies. The value added of distribution is not related to energy supplied but, rather, to the power supplied. Thus, only energy losses are considered distribution costs. Furthermore, for each customer, distribution value added is allowed to depend on only three factors: administrative costs (including invoicing and customer service), power demand costs at peak time (this includes expanding the distribution system, as well as buying from the generating system one additional peak kW), and finally, the costs of losses associated with energy distribution. Thus, retail prices are derived from four components, each of which is based on relatively easy to compute formulas, none based on actual operating costs of the distribution companies. As a consequence, the distribution companies have strong incentives to reduce their own costs so as to increase their own profitability. The value added of distribution is recomputed every four years (Philippi, 1991)

A second role of the CNE is to guarantee the coordination of the several independent generation, transmission, and distribution companies in the inter-

[29] Regulated transmission costs have to be differentiated from the wheeling charges that are used in competitive wholesale transactions.

[30] The term *nodes* comes from the fact that the transmission costs are computed up to the relevant node (i.e., substation) in the integrated system.

connected systems. This objective involves two aspects. First, to assure that there is an efficient dispatch the CNE developed a set of rules to be followed by the Economic Load Dispatch Center (ELDC) (created in 1985) of each interconnected system. These rules apply to all companies operating in interconnected systems with over 100 MW installed capacity, selling at least 10% to the public grid, and with installed capacity of more than 2% of the system (Philippi, 1991). The ELDC plans the electricity system's operation for both the long and short term as well as the daily operations. It also estimates marginal costs, which are used to settle the daily accounts among the generating companies. For example, companies that have contracts to supply but who are not called upon, have to compensate those that have actually provided the electricity. Second, the CNE oversees the investment programs of the generating companies. Observe that investment programs are crucial for the tariff setting process to work, for it assumes that the system is constantly in long-run equilibrium. Investments in transmission are undertaken mostly by the main transmission company. Because there is free entry into transmission and interconnection is required, should the transmission company not invest, users might find it profitable to enter into transmission. Apart from the regulated wheeling charges, transmission owners receive payments based on the difference between marginal costs and node prices (CNE, 1991). As ownership in the sector has become increasingly private, CNE's role in promoting investment has become less important over time (Philippi, 1991).

The evolution of the sector: Chile's electricity sector has had a continuous expansion during the past 50 years. See Table 3-24 for the composition of current electricity generation and Tables 3-25 and 3-26 for the evolution of capacity and generation since 1940.

Initially self-generation accounted for two-thirds of total power generation capacity and generation, but by 1990 the share of self-generation fell to one-quarter of both capacity and generation, as the public service companies expanded their capacity, doubling the capacity every decade from 1940 to 1960, and growing at a slightly slower pace during the 1970s and 1980s. Most of the generation is hydroelectric, with self-generators also using hydro power (see Table 3-24).

The largest consumption sector has traditionally been industry and mining, accounting today for 70% of all consumption. To a large extent the importance of mining may also explain the role of self-generators in both total capacity and generation (see Table 3-27). The degree of electrification is quite high, with 97.9% of urban households and 62.0% of rural households being connected to electricity (the average penetration rate is then 91.4%) (CNE, 1989).

The current regulatory and pricing policy, designed by the NEC in late 1979, has been in force since 1980 but was formalized into a new electricity

Table 3-24. *Chile: Electricity generation (1988, in GWh)*

Company	Hydro	Thermal	Total
The Interconnected Central System			
Public Service			
ENDESA	6,907.8	511.9	7,419.7
CHILGENER	445.4	1,764.8	2,210.2
COLBUN	2,510.8	—	2,510.8
Others	802.1	0.1	802.2
Self-generators	17.9	0.1	17.0
Total pub. ser.	10,684.0	2,276.9	12,960.9
Self-generation	674.1	625.3	1,299.4
Total generation	11,358.1	2,902.2	14,260.3
The Interconnected Norte Grande System			
Public Service			
EDELNOR	69.2	65.8	135.0
Self-generators	—	296.0	296.0
Total pub. ser.	69.2	361.8	431.0
Self-generation	—	1,577.5	1,577.5
Total generation	69.2	1,939.3	2,008.5

Source: Comisión Nacional de Energía (1989).

law in 1982. Until then, though, electricity prices were based on the electricity law of 1931, with the amendments of 1959. The 1959 amendments provided for a maximum rate of return on fixed assets of 10%, and they introduced the automatic revaluation of fixed assets. From 1959 on, electricity prices were determined by a Tariff Commission, composed of representatives of the President, the enterprises, and consumers and headed by the Director of the Office of Electric Services. During the 1960s, though, the companies seldom reached the maximum allowed rate of return. The sector's financial situation deteriorated substantially during the period from 1970 to 1973, because no price adjustments were allowed even in the face of hyperinflation. From 1974 to 1979, attempts were made to improve the financial situation of the companies. This process culminated with the creation of the CNE and the development in 1979 of the current regulatory regime. Since then, electricity prices, in US$, have remained relatively stable, falling during the early part of the 1980s and increasing at the end (see Table 3-28).

Table 3-25. *Chile: Power generation capacity (MW)*

Year	Public Service	Self-generation	Power generation capacity
1940	179	308	487
1945	202	355	557
1950	390	385	775
1955	541	451	992
1960	600	543	1,143
1965	887	566	1,453
1970	145	686	2,143
1975	1,879	741	2,620
1980	2,212	728	2,940
1985	3,094	873	3,967
1990[a]	3,341	968	4,309

[a]In 1991, a 660 MW hydroelectric power plant was added.
Source: Philippi (1991).

The effects: The regulatory system that was implemented in the early 1980s has produced an electricity system that is based on the following principles: Prices should be close to long-run marginal costs, prices should not vary by end use, and prices should depend on the nature of the location.

The off-winter average retail tariff in 1988 was approximately 0.08 US$/kWh,[31] whereas the average node energy price in Santiago at the 220 V level was 0.032 US$/kWh, and the peak power node charge was 3.6 US$/kWh (Philippi, 1991).[32] As Table 3-29 suggests, though, customers have substantial choices among different types of tariffs, some including interruptable supply, off-peak usage, as well as maximum monthly readings. That prices are close to marginal costs can furthermore be seen from the high voltage tariff AT2 (which will be used by industrial and commercial users). The energy charge is 0.0396 US$/kWh, whereas the peak demand charge with partly peak-hour use is 3.93 US$/kW. The energy charge is almost identical to the energy node charge, as is the peak power charge (see Tables 3-29 through 3-33).

That prices also vary substantially across locations can be seen in Tables 3-30 and 3-31. Table 3-30 shows the average prices that ENDESA charged to public service distribution companies and to large private customers in 1986.

---

[31] Tariff BT1, which has a fixed monthly charge of US$ 0.87 per month (World Bank, 1988).
[32] The BT1 tariff has a winter charge of 0.16 US$/kWh, because winter is the peak consumption period. See Philippi (1991) for a fascinating discussion of the introduction of the winter tariff.

Table 3-26. *Chile: Electricity generation (GWh)*

Year	Public Service	Self-generation	Total generation
1940	588	1,365	1,953
1945	694	1,933	2,627
1950	1,159	1,784	2,943
1955	1,850	2,016	3,866
1960	2,342	2,250	4,592
1965	3,597	2,534	6,131
1970	5,042	2,508	7,550
1975	6,358	2,374	8,732
1980	8,833	2,919	11,752
1985	10,978	3,062	14,040
1990	14,017	4,354	18,371

Source: Philippi (1991).

First, we observe that large users get either the node peak-power price or slightly above that, whereas the energy charges for large users is 1 or 2% higher than that charged to the distribution companies. Thus, large users' prices are indeed close to marginal costs. Second, there is substantial variation across regions. Geographical price distributions can further be seen by comparing different locations and types of tariffs to the levels in Valparaíso, which is the load center of Chile. As can be seen, even in the Central Interconnected System there are substantial differences across locations. These differences arise from the workings of the transmission prices (see Table 3-31). Because large users' prices are competitive, it suggests that CNE's computation of marginal transmission costs may actually reflect their true value.

Even though prices seem to be close to marginal costs, that has not stopped the private electricity firms from making reasonable profits. ENDESA, for example, except for 1985 has had positive profits, with the average yearly profit level since 1983 amounting to US$ 71 million on less than 1,700 MW of installed capacity (in 1989) (see Table 3-32).

The regulatory system has also promoted large investments by private electricity companies. Currently, ENDESA, PEHUENCHE, and CHILGENER have six investment projects (five of those involving hydroelectric plants) for a total of US$ 1,830 million. These projects will add 1,429 MW of installed capacity over the next five years. This additional capacity represents an increase of a third of the industry's 1989 installed capacity (see Table 3-33). In 1989 the installed capacity of private firms was 2,902 MW, while that of public generating companies was only 586 MW (Philippi, 1991).

Table 3-27. *Chile: Electricity consumption by sector (in GWh)*

Year	Commercial and residential	Others[a]	Industry and mining	System consumption[b]	Total
1970	1,299	682	4,335	1,235	6,253
1975	1,808	831	4,691	1,405	6,927
1980	2,424	931	6,414	1,982	9,327
1985	2,837	1,214	7,486	2,502	11,202
1990	3,736	1,530	10,211	2,895	14,636

[a]Others include public and municipal consumption, public lighting, public transport, and irrigation.
[b]System consumption includes losses and consumption in transformation centers.
Source: Philippi (1991).

Summary: To summarize, Chilean regulatory and institutional changes of the late 1970s and 1980s has dramatically changed the nature of the sector. It has brought prices closer to marginal costs, while at the same time providing incentives for firms to invest in the three basic segments of the sector.

Final comments

The Chilean electricity system differs drastically from those extant in Argentina, Brazil, and Uruguay in the early 1990s. Whereas the latter three countries had public ownership, noncompensatory tariffs, and tariffs unrelated to marginal costs, the Chilean system was based on competitive markets and on a regulatory system based on legislation that attempts to replicate marginal cost pricing. The prices of electricity in Argentina and Brazil have been very volatile over time, but that has not been the case in Chile, where prices have had a slow downward trend. Whereas Argentina, Brazil, and Uruguay had important investment bottlenecks (particularly in distribution), that was not the case in Chile, where investment by generating, transmission, and distribution companies has been systematically strong. Argentina, Brazil, and Uruguay have had policies of regional uniformity, but Chile's marginal cost policy has implied regional price dispersion. Finally, whereas tariffs in Argentina, Brazil, and Uruguay discriminated among users depending on the nature of their use, that was not the case in Chile, where customers could choose among different tariff structures.

These differences are not random. They reflect basic differences in the countries' regulatory systems. Chile's regulatory system is based on very specific legislation that guarantees substantial independence from the political

Table 3-28. *Chile: Average electrical energy prices**
Central Interconnected System (US cents/kWh)

Year	Node price[a]	Residential tariff (100 kWh)	Public lighting[b]	Small industry[c]	Large industry[d,e,f]	Agriculture[e]
1972		1.93			0.72	
1973		1.52			0.65	
1974		1.53			0.61	
1975		2.54			1.21	
1976		3.04			1.70	
1977		4.61			2.91	
1978		4.53			3.05	
1979		6.28			4.26	
1980		8.96			5.11	
Apr 81	4.41	11.70	9.35	10.12	6.31	5.00
Oct 81	4.74	12.24	9.85	10.67	6.68	5.15
Apr 82	4.74	12.25	9.87	10.69	6.68	5.16
Oct 82	3.59	8.80	7.55	7.55	5.52	4.02
Apr 83	3.60	7.59	6.55	6.55	4.87	3.41
Oct 83	3.52	7.45	6.45	6.45	1.78	3.37
Apr 84	3.41	7.37	6.32	6.32	4.67	3.18
Oct 84	3.20	6.18	5.28	5.31	3.84	2.65
Apr 85	2.90	6.70	5.61	5.79	3.97	2.82
Oct 85	2.76	6.40	5.37	5.56	3.78	2.74
Apr 86	2.86	6.53	5.52	5.70	3.91	2.90
Oct 86	2.75	6.48	5.44	5.62	3.81	2.83
Apr 87	2.85	6.58	5.55	5.73	3.93	2.95
Oct 87	3.14	7.06	6.01	6.19	4.29	3.29
Apr 88	3.35	7.34	6.28	6.45	4.53	3.59
Oct 88	3.62	8.23	7.28	7.60	4.78	3.97
Apr 89	3.92	8.78	7.84	8.19	5.18	4.33
Oct 89	4.13	9.24	8.25	8.62	5.45	4.56
Apr 90	4.39	9.84	8.79	9.18	5.80	4.85
Oct 90	3.92	8.77	7.83	8.18	5.17	4.32

*Since prices do not discriminate by user, this table reflects the most advantageous tariff choice per time of customer.
[a]Load factor (LF) = 0.6; voltage level 220 kV.
[b]LF = 0.457, low voltage.
[c]LF = 0.274, low voltage.
[d]LF = 0.548, high voltage.
[e]Hourly tariff, high voltage.
[f]Series until 1980 may not be comparable with post 1980.
Source: Prices until 1980 from OLADE, various issues; from 1981 on Philippi (1991).

Table 3-29. *Chile: Typical electricity tariffs charged by distribution companies 1986–1988, in US$)*

Tariff	ELDENOR (Regions I & II) (12/86)			CHILECTRA Metropolitana (Santiago) (6/88)			
	Fixed charge month	Demand charge max kW month	Energy charge kWh	Fixed charge month	Demand charge max kW month	Energy charge kWh	Winter surcharge kWh
BT1 Metered							
up to 90 kWh/month	0.73	—	0.088	0.87	—	0.08	.16
over 90 kWh/month	1.08	—	0.102	0.87	—	0.08	.16
BT2 Monthly Contracted							
without peak limits	1.08	10.51	0.058	0.87	10.0	0.046	—
partly peak usage	1.08	7.00	0.058	0.87	6.43	0.046	—
B3 Monthly Maximum							
without peak limits	1.72	10.51	0.058	1.61	10.0	0.046	—
partly peak usage	1.72	7.00	0.58	1.61	6.43	0.046	—
AT2 High Voltage with Monthly Contracted							
without peak limits	1.08	6.74	0.051	0.87	6.08	0.0396	—
partly peak usage	1.08	4.34	0.051	0.87	3.93	0.0396	—
AT3 Monthly Maximum							
without peak limits	1.72	6.74	0.051	1.61	6.08	0.0396	—
partly peak usage	1.72	4.34	0.051	1.61	3.93	0.0396	—
AT4 Off-Peak Tariff	2.52	—	0.051	2.41	—	0.0396	—
Plus off-peak demand	—	0.95	—	—	0.76	—	—
Plus peak demand	—	5.79	—	—	5.31	—	—

Source: World Bank (1988).

process, but prices and investments in the three other countries have been determined at the Cabinet level. As a consequence, although politics has plagued the electricity systems of Argentina, Brazil, and Uruguay, that has not been the case in Chile, where prices have moved almost independently of politics.

Argentina has now privatized its electricity system. The privatization and regulatory restructuring of the current administration resembles the Chilean electricity law, in that it creates a competitive wholesale market and regulates transmission and distribution. There are two important differences between the Chilean and the Argentinean regulatory reform processes. First, Chile's restructuring of the sector was more measured. It started with a regulatory re-

Table 3-30. *Chile: Typical tariffs charged by ENDESA for high voltage customers (December 1986; US$1 = Ch$195)*

Location	Voltage	Demand charge Ch$/kW max/month	Energy charge Ch$/kWh
Public Distribution Companies			
Taltal	110	965.50	6.78
Diego de Almagro	220	768.7	5.4
San Isidro, Alto Jahuel	220	620.3	4.01
Rancagua	154	571.1	3.91
Temuco	154	571.10	3.91
Valdivia	66	557.3	3.14
Osorno	66	592.7	3.15
Puerto Elviar	23	1,537.30	6.97
Large Users			
Diego de Almagro	220	816.4	5.51
San Isidro, Alto Jahuel	220	620.3	4.09
Rancagua	154	571.1	3.99
Valdivia	66	557.3	3.21
Osorno	66	592.7	3.21

Note: Delivery points are ENDESA's substations. Additional charges may apply for other delivery points. Tariffs do not include value added of 20%. *Source:* World Bank (1988), Annex 15.

form that forced the state-owned enterprises to behave according to the new regulatory rules. The second stage was privatization. Furthermore, the privatization was done at a relatively slow pace, to the point that there still are public generating companies (the distribution companies are all private, though). Second, Chile's electricity companies are widely owned by both employees and the public at large (a large portion through institutional investors). As a consequence, there is strong political support for maintaining the financial viability of the companies. Furthermore, the electricity law is such that should the companies and the administration differ radically on major price readjustments, there is a process for conflict resolution that limits administrative discretion. On the other hand, Argentina's centralized decision making in the hands of the administration reduces to a large extent the credibility of any regulatory legal statute, raising questions about the credibility of Argentina's current reform.

Table 3-31. *Chile: Electricity prices geographical price dispersion**

System	Node price[a]	Residential tariff (100 kWh)	Public lighting[b]	Small industry[c]	Large industry[d]	Agri-culture[e]
Norte Grande Interconnected System						
Antofagasta	176	122	128	134	139	136
Central Interconnected System						
La Serena	122	110	111	111	115	114
Valparaíso	100	100	100	100	100	100
Santiago	100	95	102	104	96	92
Concepción	91	92	85	86	87	89
Puerto Montt	79	86	86	88	83	79
Aysen Isolated System						
Aysen	175	145	134	136	148	142
Punta Arenas Isolated System						
Punta Arenas	77	79	77	80	72	56

*Since prices do not discriminate by user, this table reflects the most advantageous tariff choice per time of customer.
[a]Load factor (LF) = 0.6; voltage level 220 kV.
[b]LF = 0.457, low voltage.
[c]LF = 0.274, low voltage.
[d]LF = 0.548, high voltage.
[e]Hourly tariff, high voltage.
Source: Philippi (1991).

Brazil and Uruguay may, to some extent, be better positioned to adopt the Chilean regulatory system. Perhaps it would be easier for Uruguay, for its interconnection with Argentina makes for a very easy implementation of a competitive wholesale market. Brazil, similarly, with its size and multiple generating plants could naturally form a competitive wholesale market.[33] Because of the size of its system, though, the divestiture process should take longer. The privatization of Brazil's huge electricity sector, if done properly, could overnight provide political support for an efficient regulatory scheme. Furthermore, both Brazil's and Uruguay's divided governments limit to some extent the ability of the administration to undertake major changes in the interpretation of the statute without triggering a judicial review.

[33] Observe that the Chilean system would fail if there were no competition in generation, because estimates of marginal costs are based on current and expected capacity.

Table 3-32. *Chile: Profitability of ENDESA (in US$ millions)*

Year	Profits
1983	101
1984	33
1985	−65
1986	50
1987	62
1988	179
1989	106
1990	104

Source: Philippi (1991).

Table 3-33. *Chile: Energy projects under construction (1991)*

Company/project	Capacity	(US$ millions)	Projected date
CHILGENER			
Hydro: Alfalfal	160 MW	US$ 300	1991 (I SEM)
Thermal	150 MW	US$ 200	1996 (II SEM)
ENDESA			
Hydro: Canutillar	144 MW	US$ 280	1991 (I SEM)
Hydro: Pangue	400 MW	US$ 400	1996 (I SEM)
PEHUENCHE			
Hydro: Pehuenche	500 MW	US$ 500	1991 (I SEM)
Hydro: Curillinque	75 MW	US$ 150	1994 (II SEM)

Source: Philippi (1991).

It is clear, though, that Chile's success and the other countries' failure is not based on particular energy endowments (all are mostly hydro-based) or macroeconomic difficulties (Uruguay's economy was relatively stable during the decade) but, rather, that they are based on a basic difference in their regulatory and political institutions. Changing those institutions should be at the core of future structural reforms.

REFERENCES

Antmann, S., and L. Viana Martorell. "Los Efectos Económicos de la Regulación del Sistema Eléctrico: La Experiencia Uruguaya." CERES, Montevideo (May 1991), prepared for presentation at the CERES Workshop on Electricity Regulation in the Southern Cone, Montevideo, May 17, 1991.

Bernstein L. "Marginal Cost Pricing of Electric Power in Chile: Conceptual, Methodological and Practical Aspects." National Energy Commission (November 1986).

Comisión Nacional de Energía (CNE). *The Energy Sector in Chile* (1989).

Cukierman, A., S. Edwards, and G. Tabellini. "Seignorage and Political Instability." *American Economic Review* (1992).

Edwards, S., and G. Tabellini, "Political Instability, Political Weakness and Inflation: An Empirical Analysis," NBER (May 1991a).

"Explaining Fiscal Policies and Inflation in Developing Countries." *Journal of International Money and Finance* (1991b).

Givogri, A. C., and M. C. Damonte. "El Marco Regulatorio y La Asignación de Recursos en el Sector de la Energía Eléctrica." (October 1990), prepared for presentation at the CERES Workshop on Electricity Regulation in the Southern Cone, Montevideo, May 17, 1991.

Lecat, J–J. "An Overview of BOT Projects Proposed in Turkey," nd.

Monchek, E., and N. Marrero. "Nueva Estructura Tarifaria Basada en Costos Marginales." Mimeo, 1986.

Murphy, K. M., A. Shleifer, and R. W. Vishny. "The Allocation of Talent: Implications for Growth." Mimeo, 1990.

North, D. C., and R. P. Thomas. *The Rise of the Western World: A New Economic History.* Cambridge, U.K.: Cambridge University Press, 1973.

Olson, M. *The Rise and Decline of Nations.* New Haven: Yale University Press, 1982.

Perez-Arriaga, Ignacio. "The Organization and Operation of the Electricity Supply Industry in Argentina." London: Energy Economic Engineering Ltd., 1994.

Perez Montero Gotusso, G. "El Monopolio de las Telecomunicaciones en el Uruguay: Costos y Alternativas de Reordenamiento," CERES, Uruguay, 1990.

Philippi, B. "Estrategia Energética Chilena y la Organización del Sector." (1988).

"The Chilean Electric Power Sector in the Last Decade: The Design and Implementation of a New Policy." Universidad Catolica de Chile (1991), prepared for presentation at the CERES Workshop on Electricity Regulation in the Southern Cone, Montevideo, May 17, 1991.

Pires Rodrigues, A., and F. Braga Monteiro. "Electricity System in Brazil." Prepared for presentation at the CERES Workshop on Electricity Regulation in the Southern Cone, Montevideo, May 17, 1991.

Rose-Ackerman, S. "Does Federalism Matter? Political Choice in a Federal Republic." *Journal of Political Economy* (1981).

Rosen, K. S. "Brazil's Legal Culture: The *Jeito* Revisited." *Florida International Law Journal* (1984).

Spiller, P. T., and B. Levy. "Regulation, Institutions and Economic Efficiency: Promoting Regulatory Reform and Private Sector Participation in Developing Countries." Urbana: University of Illinois, 1991.

World Bank. "Chile Energy Sector Review." August 1, 1988.

"Mexico, Road Transport and Telecommunications Sector Adjustment Project: Telecommunications Sector Technical Report," Vol II (1990).

CHAPTER 4

From club-regulation to market competition in the Scandinavian electricity supply industry

Lennart Hjalmarsson
Gothenburg University

Introduction

In an international comparison the price level of electricity (net of taxes) is very low in Scandinavia, in particular in Norway and Sweden. One obvious reason is the large share of hydro power in all countries except Denmark. This is not the only reason, however. Well-functioning electricity markets are, in my view, another one.

The most important features of the Scandinavian model of the electricity supply industry are the following. Although the share of public ownership is large, the share of private ownership is also substantial. The formal, government-enforced regulations have historically been fairly weak. Instead, the industry is to a large extent characterised by publicly owned dominant firm leadership, self-enforced club-regulation, and yardstick competition. The Scandinavian countries are highly cooperative societies, and the development of the electric power sector is mainly the result of negotiations, cooperation, coordination, and self-enforced regulation among the major market agents. This holds, for example, for power exchange, transmission services, reserve capacity, and the like. In particular, there has been a close coordination of planning for long-term capacity expansion among the main power companies and at the same time an established pattern of "gentlemanly competition" for market shares in the short run. An important

I am indebted to Ann Veiderpass for research assistance and to Jorgen Bjorndalen, Nils Henrik von der Fehr, Einar Hope, and Rolf Wiedswang for valuable comments. Financial support from the Sydkraft Research Foundation, HSFR, Nordic Economic Research Council, and the Gothenburg School of Economics Foundation is gratefully acknowledged.

126

objective of this study is to explain the functioning and performance of this type of club-regulated market.

A decade of regulatory evolution in public utilities all over the world has not passed without impact on electricity market policy in Scandinavia. The countries are in different stages of a deregulation process, with the same ultimate objective to achieve a competitive electricity market.

In this study, I will concentrate on the Swedish and to some extent the Norwegian electricity markets with less space devoted to Finland and Denmark. Finland is quite similar to Sweden, and Denmark is less interesting from a regulatory point of view. Except for a brief survey of its system, Iceland will be kept outside this study. Most statistics are taken from official sources. Even if most statistics are from about 1990, not much has changed since then in Scandinavia, either in physical quantities or in constant dollar cost figures. Energy is measured in TWh, GWh, or KWh and capacity in MW or KW (1 TWh = 1000 GWh). All monetary values will be given in US$ or US¢ and in local currency (Swedish SEK, SEK 1 = 100 ore or Norwegian NOK; the exchange rates are approximately SEK 8 = US$ 1, NOK 7 = US$ 1, and SEK 12 = £ 1).

Historical background and evolution of the Scandinavian system: The Swedish case

Brief history of the origins of the system

The present ownership and regulatory structure of the Scandinavian electricity market are to a large extent the outcome of a historical evolution that has been fairly similar in all Scandinavian countries. Here, I choose Sweden as the example (Vattenfall, 1984).

The first electric steam power plants, fueled with oil and coal, were built for lighting purposes in Swedish towns in the 1870s. In the 1880s, the first hydro power plants were established. These plants were usually built by private companies where there had previously been directly driven machinery for grain mills, saw mills, hammers, and so on.

The first commercial private power company to produce and distribute electricity on a large scale was established in 1894 for the exploitation of hydro power. Between 1898 and 1906 several independent private power companies were established, among them the presently second-largest power company in Sweden, Sydkraft.

During the first decades of this century, consumption of electricity was largely limited to bulk consumers (industry) and to urban areas. In the latter, electric power plants were built and managed, by and large, by municipalities. The actual beginning of the government's involvement in power supply was the 1906 Parliamentary Resolution to develop the Trollhätte water falls. However, it was not before 1909 when Trollhätte's board was converted into the Swedish State Power Board, Vattenfall, that the administration of all the state's hydroelectric power resources were more fully coordinated.

In rural areas, a large number of local cooperatives were formed during the first decade of this century, but the expansion of the retail distribution network went slowly up until World War I. Toward the end of the war, when paraffin and coal were in very short supply, the need to speed up the introduction of electricity became more obvious, and Vattenfall took a leading role in this process.

The problem of financing the capital-intensive exploitation of hydro power was solved in various ways. Sometimes large retail distributors, like cities, became shareholders in the generating companies. Private corporations in the forest and steel industries mostly generated their own capital from their own profits and shareholders. The development of distribution cooperatives was of the utmost importance to the financing of a rapid development of electricity distribution in rural areas. In general, there were no government subsidies because the state had its own power company, Vattenfall. This company borrowed directly from the state and had to pay an interest equal to the government bond rate and, in addition, write off the investments at replacement value. This probably meant a somewhat lower cost of capital (net of taxes) than for the rest of the industry. On the other hand, Vattenfall had the main system responsibility. On balance, the official objective has been to get competition "on equal terms" in electricity production.

Early regulation and the evolution of the mixed private/public system

In 1896 Parliament initiated legislation concerning concessions for power lines and property rights of water falls. This early establishment of property rights linked to the ownership of land and the access to land for power lines determined, to a large extent, both the evolution of a mixed private/public electricity market and the regulatory structure. Because many water falls were owned by (or subsequently bought by) large corporations in the forest-based and mining-based industries, a combination of heavy industry and electricity production became typical for Sweden, and so also for Norway and Finland. In Denmark, lacking both heavy industry and hydro resources, the municipalities took the lead in the development of electrification both as generators and distributors.

In 1902 Sweden got its first comprehensive legislation of the electricity industry by the first version of the Electricity Act, the aim of which was to regulate electricity distribution. In addition to safety rules, this act regulated and still regulates the following aspects:

- Obligation to supply based on area concessions.
- Reasonable prices.
- Structural efficiency.

Concerning generation and national grid transmission, no formal regulation was imposed. Instead, Vattenfall became the price leader and club chairman of the industry. Largely, the development of generation and transmission was based on self-enforced club-regulation without much direct interference from the government except indirectly through its state-owned producer and club chairman, Vattenfall.

Nationalisation or heavy-handed regulation of the electricity supply industry never became a very important issue. It was sometimes discussed in Parliament, particularly during World War II, when a committee was appointed to review this issue. However, the mixed ownership structure in general and the combination of heavy industry and electricity generation in particular were effective barriers to nationalisation. Moreover, the efficient club regulation of the industry did not motivate any direct government regulation. From a financing point of view, the government also preferred that money for investments in the electricity supply industry be generated outside the state budget.

The development of the Scandinavian system since World War II

From rapid expansion of hydro resources to nuclear power

World War II meant that for the first part of the 1940s Sweden was largely unable to import or export. As during World War I, there was a shortage of fuel, and this was an added incentive to develop domestic hydroelectricity (Vattenfall, 1984). Therefore, a rapid expansion of hydro capacity took place in the 1940s and 1950s.

Because hydro power was the least-cost energy source, the exploitation of hydro totally dominated capacity expansion until the 1960s. This was the case in all the Scandinavian countries except Denmark, which had to use coal and oil. Due to increasing environmental concern (river preservation movements) in combination with less unexploited potential of hydro capacity, alternative sources of electricity production got increasing attention.

In the 1960s, with Germany and Denmark as models, there was an increased interest in district heating and combined power and heating plants. Several municipalities in Denmark, Finland, and Sweden developed district heating cogeneration systems based on oil, coal, trash, and biomass or peat. Industrial cogeneration plants were also built in Sweden and Finland.

In general, the expected utilisation time of district heating cogeneration units amounts to about 4,000 hours per year, and the addition to the total generation capacity was marginal, except in Finland. For base-load production, Norway stayed with hydro, Finland expanded into coal, oil, and nuclear, and Sweden concentrated on nuclear power.

Thus, a large-scale nuclear power expansion program was worked out in Sweden, and the end result of that program, completed in 1985, was 12 reactors (9 Swedish ASEA boiling water reactors [BWRs] and 3 U.S. Westinghouse pressurized water reactors [PWRs]) at four sites and with a mixture of public and private ownership.

Before commercial nuclear power was introduced, a government financed R&D program had come to its end in Sweden (Wittrock and Lindstrom, 1984). The background was the shortage of fuel during World War II and a growing concern about an increasing dependence on imported oil. The objective was to develop a heavy-water nuclear power technology based on very large domestic (but low grade) uranium deposits ("the Swedish road"). The program became a failure: A small reactor for district heating (Agesta) was completed after huge cost overruns, and a nuclear power plant was completed (Marviken), but as a result of safety reasons, the latter was never taken into operation and later converted into an oil-fired plant. Even if this program generated spillover effects to the private ASEA (now ASEA–Brown Boveri, ABB) company, it must be considered an economic disaster.

Parallel with this program, ASEA developed its own light-water BWR technology. In 1965 it got its first reactor order (OI) from a group of private Swedish power companies. This was the start of commercial nuclear power in Sweden. Because of this technology choice, state-owned Vattenfall decided to spread the risks, and after a first BWR reactor order it chose the PWR technology, ordering three reactors from Westinghouse. Because the ASEA BWR technology proved to be the most successful one, ASEA got all future reactor orders in Sweden. In Finland a group of private companies chose two ASEA BWR reactors, whereas the state-owned Imatran Voima (IVO) chose two Soviet PWR reactors.

It may seem peculiar that a state owned enterprise (SOE) would choose to buy from abroad whereas the private investor-owned utilities would buy from a domestic producer, but this is just an illustration of the free-trade tradition in Scandinavia. According to the public procurement acts, state-owned enterprises or agencies are not permitted to favour domestic producers.

Development of the national grids and spot markets

In elongated countries like Sweden, Norway, and Finland, with the majority of their population in the South and its major share of exploitable hydro resources in the North, the transmission network became of vital importance at an early stage. As early as 1938, all regions in Sweden were connected to the national transmission system, which consisted of 130 kV and 200 kV transmission lines running in the north-south direction.

Most lines were built by Vattenfall, and after recommendations from Parliament in 1946, Vattenfall got the main responsibility for future planning and operation of the national grid, although in practice the grid was run by a club of large wheelers. The first formal grid agreement between Vattenfall and the wheelers was reached in 1949. The exploitation of the vast hydro resources in the northern part of Sweden in the 1940s and 1950s necessitated the construction of a large high-voltage (400 kV) transmission system with several parallel lines from north to south. The ensuing construction of a few large nuclear plants led to a further development of a strong transmission system between these plants and the main load centers. As discussed later, the *real time dispatch* of the system, *frequency and voltage regulation,* and the like were also regulated by the grid agreement.

To enhance the efficient use of existing capacity (*merit order dispatch*), the Swedish government before World War II urged the power companies to cooperate in a *power pool* or, rather, short-term *power exchange.* Gradually, a system of bilateral power exchange developed both within Sweden and between Sweden and the other Scandinavian countries. A pool club, separate from the grid club, was instituted. To be eligible as a pool member a company had to meet certain *reserve capacity requirements.* On the other hand, there was a price cap in the pool so that an emergency situation would not be too costly for a company. Similar cooperation developed in the other countries, although the Norwegian solution was a large pool in the form of a spot market.

The development of retail distribution

Most towns and cities formed their own utilities or companies for retail distribution, but the electrification of rural areas was generally handled by distribution cooperatives. The result was a very large number of small and fairly inefficient distributors in the Swedish countryside in the mid-1940s. According to the Electricity Act, structural efficiency is a main target for regulation. Among the important means to achieve this are the rules for concessions.

To obtain or retain the concession to distribute electricity in an area, a distributor has to prove its economic, technical, and administrative ability to perform efficient operation. Moreover, concession is not granted if the geographical area is too small. An extensive rationalisation has for a long time taken place, either through voluntary mergers or takeovers or (more seldom) through concession-based enforcement. The number of distribution companies has been reduced from approximately 2,000 in the mid-1950s to the present 300.

Innovations

Because Sweden has been the host country for some of the world's largest companies in production of electrical equipment (ASEA now ABB), in drilling (Atlas Copco), and in special steel for drilling (Sandvik), it is natural that several innovations have been first introduced in the Swedish electricity system. Important examples are the development of large turbines for hydro power and the construction of tunnels and dams. The Swedish ASEA nuclear power reactor design has also proved very successful.

However, some of the most important innovations have been in transmission. The first 130 kV line in Europe was built in Sweden in 1921, and the very first 400 kV AC line in the world was finished in 1952, connecting a large hydro plant in the North with southern Sweden. The first large-scale commercial DC link was built in 1954, connecting the Swedish island Gotland in the Baltic Sea with the mainland.

Swedish ASEA has in cooperation with Vattenfall taken a leading role in the development and introduction of capacitors for reactive-power compensation, increasing the capacity of active-power generation and reducing losses in the transmission system. This technology, developed in the early 1970s, is now used worldwide.

Alternative technologies and energy conservation

As a result of the low electricity price level, taxes included, alternative technologies such as wind power and gas-combined cycles have not been able to compete with hydro and nuclear-based electricity generation. However, Denmark is an exception with a large-scale wind turbine program and an electricity production share of wind power of 2%. Except from that source, only in cogeneration for district heating or steam production, alternative fossil fuels have become commercial in some municipalities and industries in Scandinavia. Some municipal utilities burn trash, biomass, and peat in their cogeneration and heating plants.

Since the mid-1970s, energy conservation measures have been a very important element in the energy policies. The most important policy measures have been subsidies for retrofitting of existing buildings and building codes for new buildings. In addition, large resources have been spent on research and development of alternative technologies for electricity production and heating, substituting capital and fuel for electricity (Wittrock and Lindstrom, 1984). Again, like the nuclear power R&D program, the result has been meagre. The only energy-saving technology that has become a success in Sweden is the heat pump, especially (large ones) for district heating. In 1990, 12 TWh was generated by heat pumps in Sweden out of a total production for district heating of 40 TWh.

Table 4-1. *Ownership of generation in 1990*

Country	Sweden		Norway		Finland		Denmark	
	Gener-ation[a]	Dis-tribu-tion[b]	Gener-ation[a]	Dis-tribu-tion[b]	Gener-ation[a]	Dis-tribu-tion[b]	Gener-ation[a]	Dis tribu-tion[b]
State	55	11	25	0	46	0	0	0
Munici-palities/ Counties/ Co-ops	20	66	38	80–90	18	75	100	100
Private	25	23	38	10–20	36	25	0	0

[a]Percentage share of electricity generation.
[b]Percentage share of customers.
Source: NUTEK (1991).

A brief survey of the Scandinavian electricity systems

General features

As a result of the ownership pattern of hydro sites, both private and public firms were involved in the exploitation of Scandinavian hydro resources. Because of resource-based comparative advantages in mining, steel, and forest-based industries, a close integration of heavy industry and electricity generation became typical for Finland, Norway, and Sweden.

Except for Denmark, there is one large dominating state-owned producer of wholesale electricity to large industrial firms and retail distributors; see Table 4-9 for a comparison of European company sizes. The dominating SOEs have also – until deregulation started – been the owners of most of the national grids, although in Finland there is a parallel grid owned by a private company. In all the Scandinavian countries municipalities dominate retail distribution. Table 4-1 shows the ownership structure in generation and distribution. See Wiedswang (1992) for a brief survey of the Scandinavian electricity markets.

In distribution as well as in generation, mixed ownership of single companies is frequent, especially in Sweden. Therefore, the distinctions between private, municipally owned, and state-owned assets are not as clear-cut as Table 4-1 may indicate.

Concerning the degree of vertical integration, there are fairly large differences between the countries, but in general the systems are mixed. Almost all power companies have some retail distribution, but except for some cities, few distribution companies are completely vertically integrated. Because of the complicated structure, it is rather difficult to find out the exact degree of vertical integration. In Sweden about 25 to 30% of total consumption is sold by the generators to end-consumers within their own distribution areas.

Sweden

The Swedish State Power Board (Vattenfall) generates about 50% of Swedish electricity (76 TWh in 1993). About 10 large generators produce more than 90% of the electricity that is supplied to retail customers by about 300 distributors, serving a population of 8 million people. The dominating sources are nuclear and hydro. Although most generating companies own retail distribution and some large retail distributors also generate all or large shares of their electricity, most retail distributors are independent buyers of electricity. The generation and transmission part of the industry has been ruled by a club of the 10 to 15 largest producers with a joint market share exceeding 80%, although formally, Vattenfall has been the sole owner of the grid. All large power producers using the national grid have long-term wheeling contracts. Since 1992 the national grid has been owned by an independent SOE, Svenska kraftnät (SwedeGrid).

Norway

The Norwegian electricity market is characterised by a large number of small generators and retail distributors. Norway is unique in the sense that more than 99% of generation is based on hydro. Approximately 600 generators have a capacity exceeding 10 MW, and of those, 73 exceed 100 MW. In Norway, Statkraft generates approximately 25 to 35 TWh per year representing 25 to 30% of the Norwegian total of about 100 to 110 TWh per year. The hydro reservoir capacity is 80 TWh. Because of variation in precipitation, the difference in power production between dry and wet years exceeds 30 TWh.

The electricity sector includes about 230 distribution utilities that provide electricity at retail, serving a population of 4 million, and 63 production and wholesale power companies of which 24 produce more than one GWh per year. Only Statkraft and Norsk Hydro produce more than 10 TWh per year. The 34 largest producers generate 96% of total output. Approximately one-half of the domestic/commercial market is served by 25 vertically integrated utilities, whereas most other distribution utilities are more or less tied into a long-term relationship with a wholesale power company.

Concerning ownership structure, about 75% of the total generation and distribution capacity is owned by public entities (state, county, and municipal). Most of the distribution companies are municipal or intermunicipal companies. Before deregulation, Statkraft owned 80% of the high-voltage transmission network.

A characteristic feature of the Norwegian system has been its power pool, the Norwegian Power Pool (NPP or Samkjöringen), with more than 70 members. The spot market for "occasional power" operated by the NPP has been the primary mechanism for short-run coordination and optimisation of the Norwegian system. This organisational setup greatly facilitated the deregulation of the Norwegian electricity market.

From 1992 a new state-owned company, Statnett (Norwegian Grid Company), has been given the responsibility for operation of the high-voltage grid and international power exchange. From 1993 a subsidiary of Statnett, Statnett Marked, has also taken over the operation of the power pool and organised a set of short-term markets for electricity; see "The development of the Norwegian reform," pages 171–4.

A special feature of the deregulated Norwegian electricity market is the rapid entry of power brokers and traders into the market. By the beginning of 1993, about 10 trading companies had been established. Some 50 people are presently employed in these functions.

Finland

In Finland, private industry has a market share in electricity generation of about 40%, the state has approximately 40%, and the municipalities have about 20%. The state-owned Imatran Voima (IVO) is the largest generator with 40% of the electricity production and approximately 45% of the wholesale market. Production comes mainly from nuclear, cogeneration, and hydro, but Finland also has a large net import of electricity (see Table 4-3). Imatran Voima owns most of the central grid. However, a private company, Teollisander Voime (TVS), owned by Finnish industry, has built parallel transmission links in the southwest part of the country. The Finnish club is fairly large and involves 60 companies; all are producers with at least 2 MW generation. The short-term coordination (real time dispatch and merit order dispatch) is based on a club contract (STYV–84). This contract regulates, for example, the rules for frequency and voltage regulation and the coordination of annual maintenance of power plants. Merit order dispatch is achieved through a bilateral power exchange with pricing based on the split-saving principle. Both IVO and TVS are involved in direct power exchange; all other companies exchange power with either IVO or TVS.

The distribution sector contains 130 utilities. The 35 largest of these supply approximately 75% of the consumers. Retail distribution is dominated by municipally owned utilities. Many of these have their own cogeneration–district heating activities.

Table 4-2. *The composition of the Scandinavian electricity generation (GWh) in 1990*

Type of generation in GWh	Sweden	Norway	Finland	Denmark	Iceland	NORDEL
Hydro power	71,459	121,137	10,823	27	4,159	207,605
Wind power	4	—	—	515	—	519
Geothermal power	—	—	—	—	283	283
Nuclear power	65,250	—	18,581	—	—	8,831
Back-pressure: District heating	2,070	—	8,587	—	—	10,657
Back-pressure: Industry	3,070	221	7,744	360	—	11,395
Condense, conventional	252	116	6,426	22,993	—	29,787
Gas turbine, diesel, etc.	52	127	11	—	174	364
Total generation	142,157	121,601	51,718	23,895	4,447	343,818

Source: NORDEL (1990).

Denmark

The Danish electricity industry structure is quite different from the rest of Scandinavia. First, there is no state ownership. All assets are owned directly or indirectly by retail distributors that in turn are owned by municipalities or cooperatives. Second, because of geographical conditions, the industry is separated into two independent systems. In the two separate geographical areas, the utilities have formed central coordinating boards, ELSAM for the Juteland peninsula and the island Fyn (seven utilities) and Elkraft for the rest of Denmark (three utilities). These boards operate the generation and transmission systems and export and import, and they also own the transmission grid. Third, generation is entirely based on conventional thermal and wind power. Twelve power companies generate 99% of the electricity in 19 thermal plants, all larger than 25 MW.

Iceland

In Iceland, with a population of only 250,000 people, electricity production is dominated by one large company, Landsvirkjun, which generates more than

90% of total output and owns the high-voltage transmission system. It is jointly owned by the state (50%) and two municipalities (50%). All utilities are either owned by the state or municipalities or are jointly owned by these. There are 16 retail distribution companies, all of which buy at least some share of their power supply from independent generators. Of the two largest distributors, one (Reykjaviks Elverk) is municipally owned, and the other (Statens Elverker) is owned by the state. So far the Icelandic electricity market is separated from that of other countries. Generation consists of hydro, approximately 95%, and geothermal, approximately 5%.

Iceland has a large potential for hydro power generation – about five times its present production. Recently, Landsvirkjun has commissioned a study of the possibility of laying a 1,000 km undersea power cable between Iceland and Britain. The length of such a link is five times the length of any existing high voltage direct current (HVDC) undersea cable. The longest one present (Fennoskan), between Sweden and Finland in the Baltic sea, is 200 km.

The composition of the Scandinavian (including Iceland) electricity production in 1990 is presented in Table 4-2.

Because the years 1989 and 1990 were "wet years" (i.e., characterised by an unusually good precipitation), the hydro production figures in Table 4-2 exceed the figures for an average year. During normal years the Swedish hydro production is only 63 TWh and the Norwegian 108 TWh. Correspondingly, the normal average-year nuclear power production in Sweden is 71 TWh.

Regulatory institutions

Brief history of legal precedents for regulation in Sweden

In 1902 Sweden got the first version of the Electricity Act. This act comprises the most important rules and regulations governing the electricity market in general and electricity distribution in particular.

The 1902 Electricity Act, "Act (1902:71) comprising certain regulations concerning electricity plants" constitutes the most significant legal restriction in the Swedish electricity market. The Act has been amended and revised several times. Work on a revised act is currently going on. The purpose of this current revision is to enhance competition in the electricity market.

Description of regulatory system up to recent past

Entry: The formal regulation by law of power generation is primarily affected by the Environmental Protection Act and the Water Conservation Act. The 1902 Electricity Act deals solely with safety aspects and imposes no environmental restrictions upon the establishing of new production plants. The Act is limited to entry into electricity distribution. Entry into generation in Scandinavia is primarily a problem of meeting environmental standards.

In Swedish retail distribution there are two types of entry conditions, *line concession* and *area concession*. The first concession applies to a line with a primarily predetermined distance and location (line concession), and the second to a system of lines within a certain area (area concession).

Concessions for commercial distribution are granted only to those who from a "general point of view" are found suitable to undertake operations of this type. Concessions are granted for only a specific duration. Normally, the maximum is 40 years, although concessions for 60 years may be granted when special circumstances render this desirable.

Obligation to supply: The Act stipulates that the holder of an area concession for commercial distribution is *obliged to supply* electricity to all those in the area requiring it for normal consumption, unless particular reasons for exemptions exist. However, this obligation does not (after 1977) include cases where electricity is intended to be used for heating buildings in an area where district heating or natural gas is or will be distributed and cases where heating cannot be provided more advantageously by means of electricity than by means of the already existing system in the area.

Price regulation: The holder of a concession is furthermore obliged to submit to a regulation of price and other conditions for the supply or transmission of electricity. Questions concerning price regulations are dealt with by an authority designated by the government. However, as will be discussed later, this type of price regulation has had a small impact on the electricity price level.

Mergers and acquisitions: Concerning the acquisition of electric distribution systems and so on, the Act stipulates, for example, that systems intended for commercial local distribution of electricity for which concessions are required may not without permission by the government (i.e., the National Industrial Board) be acquired through purchase, exchange, or donation.

The National Industrial Board deals with most matters pertaining to the Act, such as concessions to draw or use electric power lines and permissions to transfer such concessions, obligations to supply electricity, changes of boundaries for area concessions, rescinding of concession, and the like.

The working of the regulatory system

The legal framework has been important for the working of the electricity market in its creation of barriers to entry and obligation to supply in retail distribution. On the other hand, the nonlegal aspects are of larger importance when it comes to the functioning of the electricity supply industry as a whole.

Until recently, the concepts *regulation* or *deregulation* hardly existed in the Scandinavian vocabulary and even less so in connection with the electricity supply industry. This reflects reality in the sense that formal price, rate of return, or cost of service regulation has never been imposed on that industry in Scandinavia. Among the two major regimes for electricity markets, regulated private ownership and public enterprise, Scandinavia falls somewhere in between with its club-regulated markets.

On the regulatory side, the key notions have been *self-regulation, price leadership,* and *yardstick competition.* In generation, Vattenfall in Sweden, Statkraft in Norway, and Imatran Voima in Finland have been the market leaders and trendsetters for tariffs and rules. Here I will concentrate on Sweden.

Club regulation

Most public service obligations (e.g., concerning merit order dispatch, real-time dispatch, frequency and voltage regulation, and reserve capacity) have been solved through the club organisations, especially the grid clubs and the pool clubs. To avoid free-rider problems, membership in these clubs has been tied to obligations to share the costs of system responsibility. In Sweden, frequency and voltage regulation has been linked to grid club membership, whereas reserve capacity obligations have been linked to pool membership.

Real-time dispatch and merit order dispatch: In all countries the clubs of large producers have had the system responsibility. In general, the dominating state-owned producer, Vattenfall in Sweden, IVO in Finland, and Statkraft in Norway, has acted as chairman of the club, although in Norway the power pool has also had an important role. To achieve a reliable real-time dispatch and an efficient merit order dispatch of plants and efficient coordination of hydro resources, the club organisations have been of utmost importance. See the next section, "Coordination of supply and the efficient use of hydro power."

As an example, in Sweden Vattenfall has been responsible for the operations management, including permanent monitoring of load distribution, voltage regulation, and relay settings. The Nordic countries have jointly determined *criteria for the stability of the grid* and for *voltage and frequency regulation.* Using these criteria, and after consideration by the National Grid Committee, Vattenfall determined the required momentary disruption reserve capacity in Sweden.

Grid services: The high-voltage transmission system has formally been owned and operated by the state-owned producers, but in reality all decisions have been made by the club of wheelers whose members have covered the costs of the transmission system on the basis of agreed-on principles.

Coordination of capacity expansion and maintenance: Countrywide and Scandinavian-wide coordination of capacity expansion in generation and transmission has also been very important. Within each country producers' associations have coordinated investments in generation and transmission (capacity, timing, and technology). Among the countries there is a Nordel organisation, with the main power producers in Scandinavia as members, that performs the coordinating role. This coordination has been important for the efficient exploitation of scale economies (see next section).

There is also a close coordination of power plant maintenance, especially the scheduling of annual maintenance of nuclear power plants. Because to a large extent the same service crews are used by all nuclear plants, such a coordination is necessary. Moreover, with a large nuclear generation share, the timing of maintenance becomes an important optimisation problem for the entire system as well as for the individual companies.

Reserve capacity: The driving mechanism behind capacity expansion in Scandinavia has been the reserve capacity requirements imposed on the club members. In general, these requirements have been settled in the power exchange or power pool agreements.

International trade: Either the club chairmen have had an export–import monopoly (Norway) or a dominating position in international electricity trade together with one or a few other club members (Sweden, Finland, Denmark).

Pricing: In Sweden pricing in the wholesale market for bulk power has been indirectly regulated through state ownership of Vattenfall. Its formal objective has been to break even subject to depreciation on replacement values and a rate of interest on loans from the government at the bond rate level, according to the general rules for SOEs. This has established Vattenfall as a price leader, and yardstick competition has created a downward price pressure on the private generators.

Electricity distribution has been indirectly rate-of-return regulated in the following way. In the Swedish law for municipal activities up to the recent past, there has been a general rule that municipal activities are not permitted to earn any profits. This also holds for electricity distribution. Because urban municipalities in general have rather favourable geographical conditions for electricity distribution, they can attain relatively low electricity prices. Yardstick competition puts a pressure on rural (mostly private) distributors to set a price level that does not deviate too much from that of the surrounding service areas. In addition, if a distributor is not regarded as efficient enough, it will not get its concession renewed and its service area will be merged with an adjacent one.

As noted earlier, there is also a legal form of price regulation in the Electricity Act. With reference to the Act, consumers can complain about the electricity price to the price regulation board at the National Industrial Board. Approximately 25 cases per year are handled by the Board. Most of these cases are solved through intermediation. The major impact of this institution has been to prevent price discrimination among consumer groups. The impact on the average electricity price level has probably been of minor importance in comparison with the municipality law.

In general, the decentralised structure of the Scandinavian electricity market has created an established pattern of "gentlemanly competition" for market shares in the short run (in combination with coordination of the capacity expansion path). Moreover, competition from other energy sources has been important. Especially in Norway and Sweden, electric heating of buildings has gained a large market share. Competition from municipal and industrial cogeneration has been of some importance in Sweden and Norway, mostly as a potential threat. The successful exploitation of large-scale hydro and nuclear power has effectively hampered the profitability of cogeneration.

Coordination of supply and the efficient use of hydro power

Real-time dispatch and merit order dispatch

All power systems have to cope with the problem of maintaining reliable electricity supply on a continuous real-time basis while coping with random fluctuations in load, and especially with random outages of generation and transmission plants. At the same time, they must achieve a high degree of overall system cost minimisation through merit order dispatch of plants. This problem is particularly acute in hydro systems, for which random inflow variations can be quite large, even when measured over a period of years. Two aspects are especially important. First, coordination is particularly important as a means of pooling risk in hydro-dominated systems and has resulted in a substantial reduction in the reserve margins that each individual power company, or region, must provide for. The development of long-term storage reservoirs opens up the possibility of storing water from one period to another in order to ameliorate the effect of random inflow variations. However, it also complicates the management of the power system. Second, in river systems, as in Sweden, with several owners of hydro plants in the same river system, coordination of the waterflow and use of the various plants is necessary. Therefore, for every large river system in Sweden with multiownership there exists a so-called *regulation company* that is in charge of the efficient use and coordination of the various plants along the river. These companies also perform the economic calculations of the distribution of costs and revenues among the plants.

In a mixed hydro-thermal system various power producers have various types of plants with large differences in variable costs, and differences among supply curves will arise. Considerable variations among the various power producers may also exist with regard to demand. This means that the equilibrium prices may vary considerably among utilities regarded in isolation. During periods of more than sufficient precipitation, firms with a large share of hydro electricity in their systems may have a very low expected equilibrium price, or *power value* as it is often called, at the same time that a firm with a large share of thermal power may have a very high expected power value. Without coordination mechanisms aimed at merit order dispatch, huge economic losses would arise in a disintegrated system. Thus, the differences in power values early led to the creation of markets for the exchange of power (usually called power pool operation) among electricity producers in Scandinavia within as well as between the different countries. It started already in 1915 with power exchange between Denmark and Sweden. As mentioned, there are two types of institutional setups in Scandinavia, namely, the Swedish, Finnish, Danish, and Inter-Nordic (Nordel) bilateral power exchange markets and the Norwegian spot market for occasional power. However, it should be emphasised that there are no central centers for merit order dispatch in Scandinavia. All dispatch is handled by the individual power companies. Merit order is achieved through voluntary exchange. Here I will concentrate on the Swedish, Norwegian, and Inter-Scandinavian (Nordel) market.

The Swedish power exchange

The Swedish power exchange is run by a pool club. The Pooled Operations Group consists of two main blocks: Vattenfall and the KGS group. Several other power utilities are indirectly associated with theses two blocks (Larsson, Wiklund, and Alfors, 1989).

Unlike the Norwegian spot market power pool with many agents, the Swedish power exchange system has a simple structure with few (at present six) participants and pool members (11 utilities of which five belong to KGS). It is based on bilateral trade and a multilevel or multistage optimisation. The potential for mutual beneficial exchange of power among the companies included in the two blocks, KGS and Vattenfall, are exhausted before any exchange of temporary power between KGS and Vattenfall or between Sweden and other countries takes place.

Pricing in this market is based on the so-called *split-savings principle*. Firms with either a surplus or a shortage of power notify a power pool control centre of their relevant marginal costs. The centre sets a mean price that consists of the average of the buying firm's marginal cost and the selling firm's marginal cost. The mean price is called the power pool's *marginal price*. In addition to this principle, certain qualifications imply that the seller's profit is limited by a price ceiling. This is motivated by reasons of fairness: Large differences in marginal values often occur when the buyer has difficulties (e.g., through malfunctions in units), and consequently it has been considered fair to impose a limit on the purchase price. The wholesale market for exchange of temporary power is characterised by extensive cooperation and information exchange between the parties involved and the pricing follows long established rules. The system is transparent and cheating seems to be very rare.

Only one other company exchanges power bilaterally with Vattenfall, whereas five exchange power within KGS. All six pool members also have transmission rights in the high-voltage grid. To be eligible for pool membership, a company must on average cover its own demand by own-generation, be large enough to profitably gain from pooling, and have enough *reserve capacity*. This last requirement is another aspect of the self-enforced club regulation.

The Norwegian power pool and the coordination of hydro power

Unlike Sweden, Norway has for more than 20 years had an established spot market for occasional power operated by the Norwegian Power Pool (NPP, or Samkjöringen) (Larsen, 1986). Although the NPP quite recently was merged with the grid company, Statnett, its functions are still to a large extent the same. See the section titled "The development of the Norwegian reform."

This market was cleared weekly, with participants declaring buy and sell bids for five load segments within the week. The NPP then compared these bids, derived supply and demand schedules, and from the intersection of these determined a pool price that cleared the market. In principle this defined the production and load schedules for the next week, although adjustments had to be made to accommodate real-time fluctuations in demand, inflow, and unit availability. If circumstances differed too much from those assumed at the beginning of a week, it could become necessary to clear the market again during the week. If it became apparent that transmission capacity between various parts of the system was likely to be constrained, the system was divided into two or more subpools, each with its own market-clearing price.

Neither the bids made nor the schedules produced were legally binding. The NPP did not directly control the plant of any of its members and had no legal right to direct them to generate, at least under normal circumstances. Thus, this market-clearing mechanism was effective only because the NPP members were prepared to cooperate and to honour the indicative commitments made. From a deregulation perspective, this market is interesting. It represents an organisational and institutional arrangement that could easily be extended to a market-based system.

Until the merger with Statnett in 1993, the NPP was a voluntary association involving all significant power producers in Norway and some major consumers who were in a position to trade contractual power. Its objective was to achieve "efficient use of electrical power stations, transfers and exchange of electrical energy." Eligibility for NPP membership required an annual production of at least 100 GWh and included all 63 companies that met this condition, but all together 77 agents were active in the market.

Members of the NPP were required to be able to cover their load with a reserve margin accepted by NPP. This cover could come from their own facilities or from long-term contracts with other power companies.

The other Scandinavian (Nordel) countries were not directly represented in this spot market. Instead, Statkraft until 1992 operated an export/import monopoly in which electricity was traded at a price based on the average of the pool prices in the two countries.

Hydro reservoir coordination: Another major mechanism for informal coordination of hydro resources in Norway is provided by the use of a common suite of water-value estimation models developed by the cooperative EFI research institute and adopted in various customised forms by the NPP, Statkraft, and other major participants in the market.

In principle, the spot market clearing process should provide very good price signals to coordinate the short-term operation of any production system, hydro or thermal. But it does not directly help a reservoir manager to decide how to balance production across time. In order to do this, the manager must make some kind of forecast of the likely value of reservoir releases, or equivalently in this environment, of the spot price of electricity, over a planning horizon that may be several years long, depending on the regulation capacity of the reservoir.

Ideally, such a forecast could be derived from a market in electricity futures, but in no country does such a market seem to have developed to the point at which it is considered to give a reliable indication of prices for reservoir management purposes. In the absence of such a market, reservoir managers are forced to rely on projections of market behaviour based on past observations. Given such a forecast, reservoir managers must employ some form of optimisation technique to determine the optimal release pattern or, equivalently, the "expected marginal water value." Models based on stochastic dynamic programming for this purpose and similar techniques have since been adopted in several other countries. The Scandinavian countries have been in the forefront of developments in this area.

For modelling purposes, in Norway 500 reservoirs are aggregated into 12 equivalent regional reservoirs. Each of these equivalent reservoirs is then optimised in turn, using stochastic dynamic programming, assuming a representation of expected market conditions. The results are then aggregated to the national level in a process similar to the market clearing actually operated by the NPP. If this implies significant changes to the assumptions under which the single reservoir submodels were optimised, another iteration of the model is required.

The EFI, which developed this modeling system, is cooperatively funded by the industry, and the models are made available to the NPP and to a number of power companies, including Statkraft. Each company is then free to run its version of the model, incorporating a detailed representation of its own system, with a less detailed representation of the rest of the system, about which it has less accurate data.

Statkraft: Statkraft itself, as the largest generator, has also (until recently) taken some responsibility for coordination, as was required in its terms of reference. However, it has never been such a dominant player in the market as Vattenfall in Sweden. Clearly, some generator is required to adjust output in order to balance supply and demand in the short term when the NPP's market-clearing mechanism does not act with sufficient precision. Any NPP member could be called upon to play this balancing role, but it was often carried out by Statkraft in practice. Although the NPP could not compel Statkraft to adjust its output, Statkraft has seen this role as a natural part of its "national interest" functions. Statkraft also has the advantage of controlling a large share of the major controllable plants suited to this role and of being in a position to monitor the requirements of the national system itself.

Nordel power exchange

Just as there are important differences within countries with regard to the structure of the production systems, the differences are large among the Nordic countries (see Table 4-2).

Traditionally, the systems have been energy dimensioned in Norway and Sweden but capacity dimensioned in Denmark and Finland. This implies that the main problem in the Swedish and the Norwegian systems has been to maintain the energy production throughout the year while, at the production level, there has always been sufficient capacity to meet the demand during peak-load periods. The opposite situation is found in Denmark and Finland (and now also in Sweden), where the main problem is to meet the maximum electricity demand at a certain point in time, whereas meeting the annual demand for energy does not pose a problem.

Norway with its pure hydro system has had an electricity surplus at low variable costs during most years. This surplus could be used as temporary power domestically or exported to the neighbouring countries. As a result of the low variable costs, this type of energy is highly competitive; to the extent allowed by the transmission links, this kind of energy is always used before thermal power in the Scandinavian electricity system.

Denmark has a pure thermal power system dimensioned to cover electricity consumption during peak-load periods. Because the marginal costs in the Danish system often are relatively high, Denmark is usually a large net electricity importer, covering about 25% of its consumption by import.

Sweden and Finland have combined systems including hydro as well as thermal power. The Swedish thermal power mainly consists of nuclear power produced at relatively low variable costs. Periodically, nuclear power is highly competitive in the Scandinavian electricity market. It may, for instance, be used to build up the Norwegian reservoirs during periods of low catchment. The share of nuclear power in the Finnish thermal power production is smaller. Within the Nordic system the greatest importance of Finnish thermal power, like that of Denmark, is experienced during dry years in Norway and Sweden.

These differences in the systems render electricity trade most advantageous, partly because of a short-term optimisation, which means that the demand for electricity at any given point in time is met through the power plants with the lowest variable costs, and partly because the cooperation among the power producers results in a reduction in the individual countries' reserve capacity requirements.

The extent of the electricity trade between the Scandinavian countries varies considerably from year to year, whereas the precipitation and the availability of nuclear power to a large extent determines who is a net importer and who is a net exporter. The electricity trade in 1990 is shown in Table 4-3.

In recent years Sweden has exported large amounts of electricity to Denmark and Finland, and, at the same time, it has imported large amounts from Norway.

Because of the hydro production in Norway, 1990 was a record year for Scandinavian power trade. The total trade amounted to approximately 32 TWh, about 9% of total Nordel production of approximately 344 TWh. Table 4-3 also shows that Norway was the largest net exporter (16% of its own gross consumption) and Denmark the largest net importer (23% of its own consumption). A substantial trade took place between Finland and the Soviet Union and some between Denmark and The Federal Republic of Germany.

Pricing mechanism: The principles for the inter-Scandinavian trade of temporary power are quite similar to those governing Swedish internal exchange

Table 4-3. *The trade of electricity among the Scandinavian countries in 1990*

Import from/ Export to	Denmark	Finland	Norway	Sweden	Nordel	Others	Total 1990
Denmark	—	0	7	220	227	2,681	2,908
Finland	0	—	2	361	363	—	363
Norway	3,958	114	—	12,329	16,401	—	16,401
Sweden	7,922	6,356	399	—	14,677	—	14,677
Nordel countries	11,880	6,470	408	12,910	31,668	2,681	
Other countries	93	4,617	0	0	—		

Source: NORDEL.

(i.e., the principle of split-saving is used in pricing, except now for trade with Norway). The main part of the electricity trade takes place as so-called temporary exchanges, whereas a smaller part is traded within firm power contract agreements.

For trade with the competitive Norwegian market, a bid system has now replaced split-saving. The market is administered by Statnett. Demand and supply from abroad take the form of price–quantity combination bids, which are fed into the domestic markets. See "The development of the Norwegian reform," and Hope, Rud, and Singh (1993) for a description.

Gains from trade: The profits from the exchanges have been estimated at approximately 20% of the turnover of each party involved. The annual amounts are, therefore, quite substantial (Alfors, 1980; Caputo and Mulligan, 1985).

The national grids and transmission pricing

In this section I will present three tariff structures of transmission pricing. They correspond to three market organisations: the Swedish transmission club with exclusive membership, the late Norwegian Power Pool organisation with a large number of members, and the present deregulated Norwegian spot market with open TPA (third-party access).

Concerning pricing of transmission services, transmission of electricity is characterised by considerable economies of scale ex ante in capacity expansion and indivisibilities and sunk cost ex post in existing networks. These characteristics create the classical conflict among optimal pricing, optimal investment, and revenue targets that are well-known from public economics and economic welfare theory. The under-recovery-of-costs problem seems to be very severe in transmission pricing. Simulations indicate that with perfect short-run marginal-cost pricing only 30 to 40% of capital costs will be recovered.

What makes transmission pricing still more complicated is the network property. This means that we cannot regard the transmission system as one single channel for electricity but must recognise the network characteristics. A network will in reality almost always be in disequilibrium in the sense that the degree of bottlenecks varies in real time between various parts of the system. There is no single shadow price that can be used as a basis for pricing but a whole time and space structure of expected shadow prices. Moreover, in an electricity network the electricity flows are quite different from the contract flows. Thus, the short-run marginal costs are not related to the geographical distance between the input point and the output point but to the entire load pattern of the system. Another feature is that marginal losses are approximately twice the average losses (i.e., the loss function is quadratic).

The conclusion from this discussion is that there are complicated trade-offs in transmission pricing between long-run, more distance-related costs and short-run, less distance-related costs. Even if the loss function is quadratic, there is a serious problem in covering capital costs. High fixed fees create barriers to entry, whereas markups on marginal costs create pricing distortions. Different outcomes of these trade-offs are well illustrated by transmission pricing in Sweden and Norway.

Sweden: The Swedish solution has been a short-run zero-price for a single transaction within a long-term subscription of wheeling capacity. Until recently, the Swedish transmission system has worked like a club, with Vattenfall as the club chairman and formal owner of the grid. Membership fees, in the form of subscription fees (SEK/MWkm), have been an important tariff element. These subscription fees have been distance-related in the sense that *distance has been measured to a load center* in Sweden. In addition there have been a MW connection fee and a MW fee on thermal power stations larger than 150 MW. All these tariff elements are of a long-run subscription nature, whereas the short-run marginal cost of a single transaction has been zero. The use of excess capacity in the grid has been determined by the owner, Vattenfall. The losses have been provided directly by the wheelers through a provision to feed a markup of electricity into the grid corresponding to the annual average losses for a wheeler.

This tariff structure in Sweden reflects the stable club arrangements. Work is presently going on within SwedeGrid on the future pricing of transmission services compatible with a more competitive electricity market with open entry and TPA.

Norway: The Norwegian solution with a large and less stable club has been a short-run, distance-related transmission fee. The following tariff structure was valid until 1992.

Transmission fees consisted of the following elements:

- A general MWhkm fee used when the distance is measured between input points and output points. For each user an average weighted length of transmission was calculated.
- A privilege of transmission MW fee.
- Use time in winter period, 3,600 hs.
- Average transmission length in km reflecting the losses (recently 2.5% per 100 km).

These elements were weighted together to form a transmission fee, as follows:

- An exchange fee, which was a subscription fee for transmission of unpreferential power when there was vacant transmission capacity. It was levied as a percentage of the annual average value of the exchange of temporary power with the power pool.
- A connection fee based on the average-year production of power stations. This was charged per MWh.

In 1992 a new and preliminary tariff structure, more consistent with a competitive market, was implemented in Norway by Statnett. The main elements in this three-part tariff are the following:

- Energy fee:
  - A marginal loss fee that varies by hour as a product of a loss factor and the pool price according to the following:
    - potential peak periods during winter: 5.1% of spot price.
    - potential trough periods during winter: 2.8% of spot price.
    - summer: 0.7% of spot price.
- Capacity fee:
  - a capacity fee in kW (NOK 60/kW (US$ 8), 1992) measured at the winter peak. This element is a revenue residual.
  - a capacity fee in kW for transports through bottlenecks in the grid. The fee corresponds to the price difference in the spot market between the two sides of the bottleneck. Capacity here refers to the capacity supplied to the power pool.
  - a capacity expansion fee levied in connection with substantial changes in the grid.
- Connection fee:
  - a connection fee in kW (NOK 5/kW (US 70 cents), 1992) based on noninterruptible peak power consumption.

It is interesting to note that all distance-related fees are removed and that there has been the introduction of a marginal-loss fee.

Electricity markets, pricing principles, and tariff structures

The electricity markets

Because of the disintegrated structure of the Scandinavian electricity markets there is one market for high-voltage electricity between generators and intermediary bulk consumers such as retail distributors and large industries, and one for low-voltage electricity between retail distributors and final consumers such as households, small firms, and the like. The classification of consumers into industrial, commercial, and residential is not used in Scandinavia.

Pricing principles

Since there is no price regulation in Scandinavia, the utilities are free to set their own prices. (There is, however, a possibility for consumers to complain about prices and other terms of conditions.) To get more uniform and economically efficient pricing, changes in tariffs have been based on a lot of committee work within the industry and recommendations from utilities' associations (SOU, 1981:69).

The basic principle behind electricity pricing in Scandinavia has been marginal-cost pricing (tariff structure) under a revenue or rate-of-return constraint (tariff level) for the state and municipally owned utilities. The tariff structure in principle reflects variations in production costs and transmission and distribution costs, but the tariff level has been determined by a revenue target. In general in Scandinavia, important tariff elements (i.e., the energy charge and the peak load charge) have been determined by short-run marginal costs, whereas the tariff level is determined by revenue or rate-of-return targets, the capacity charge, and the fixed charge adjusted for this latter purpose.

High-voltage tariffs

In general, the high-voltage tariffs consist of a fixed fee, a contractual demand charge, a peak load charge, and an energy charge that is both seasonally and time-of-day differentiated. The dominating firm has traditionally been acting as a price leader in the high-voltage bulk power market. Until recently, all bulk consumers have been offered open and public nondiscriminatory tariffs. Therefore, price differences mainly reflect location, voltage level, and load profile.

One distinguishing feature of the Norwegian electricity market is the importance of the electricity-intensive industries (aluminum, ferro-silicium, etc.),

Table 4-4. *The structure of Swedish electricity retail distribution in 1989*

Type of distributor	Cooperative	Private company	Municipal utility	Municipal company	State-owned company
Electricity purchase, ore/kWh	22.6	21.0	21.1	20.2	21.0
Total costs, ore/kWh	35.2	31.9	30.3	29.7	34.2
Sale price, ore/kWh	35.4	32.9	31.2	30.8	35.0
Average size, number of customers	3,234	21,068	16,169	23,543	13,609
Distribution line per customer, km	125	225	62	76	121

Source: NUTEK (1991).

which consume about 30% of the Norwegian total. To a large extent these industries have been subsidised by low electricity prices at long-term contracts, although there is now a trend toward decreasing subsidies. In Norway, Statkraft supplies a relatively high proportion of the electricity-intensive industries because it has been instructed by the Parliament to supply certain projects at prices that are not commercially viable.

Low-voltage tariffs

The main difference between high- and low-voltage tariffs is a more complicated tariff structure and often a longer contract period in the former case. The low-voltage tariffs, at least for small consumers, are fairly simple with only a subscription charge and an energy charge that may be both seasonally and time-of-day differentiated. (The tariff structure for large low-voltage consumers is similar to that of the high-voltage tariff structure.)

The basic principle is that every customer category is billed in accordance with their averaged marginal costs during a certain period. Thus, differences in transmission costs between high and low voltages, between northern and southern Sweden, and between urban and rural areas are the main causes of the differences in the levels of energy charges and subscription charges applied to various customer categories; tariff equalization within distribution areas (e.g., between urban and surrounding rural areas) is generally applied by electricity distributors. The structure of Swedish retail distribution is illustrated by Table 4-4.

Because most cooperatives are located in the countryside, the bulk power price to these customers is somewhat higher than for the other distributors closer to the national grid. The average price to industry in 1989 was 19.4 ore/kWh (2.5 c/kWh), about 8% lower than the average price to retail distributors. This price difference is not an indication of price discrimination among different consumer groups in the Swedish electricity market. Because the load profile in industry is more even than in retail distribution and the heavy industry is concentrated to the northern part of Sweden, the average price to industry should be lower than to retail distributors.

The length of distribution lines per customer illustrates the large differences between municipal-urban and rural distribution. In spite of having the most sparse distribution, the average costs of private companies are not much higher than those of municipal distributors.

Demand-side management

Because there is no formal price regulation, only imperfections in the existing tariffs may motivate demand-side management measures in addition to energy policy objectives of the government. In general, the existing tariffs for firm power do not provide incentives for reducing demand at the peak load of the system. Moreover, hydro-based systems get a large variation between years in low-cost hydro supply. Traditionally in Scandinavia, the large variation in precipitation has provided incentives for nonpriority deliveries in the form of special contracts for *interruptible, temporary,* or *occasional* power. In general, there is no guaranteed delivery period for this type of electricity. Compared to contracts for firm power, no peak-load charge and in some contracts no demand charge is levied on this type of power.

The most important market for temporary power is the large number of electrical boilers that are used, for example, for district heating or central heating (which in Sweden is approximately 10% of generation capacity). These boilers make extensive regulation possible. Together with the export and import of electricity they constitute a buffer when, for example, nuclear power units experience sudden stoppages.

Other kinds of demand-side management are fairly recent phenomena of limited importance in practice but discussed a lot in Scandinavia.

Investment behaviour and dynamic efficiency

Rate of growth of demand: From excess demand to excess supply

Between 1912, when the production of official electricity statistics started, and the mid-1970s, electricity consumption increased on the average by about 7%

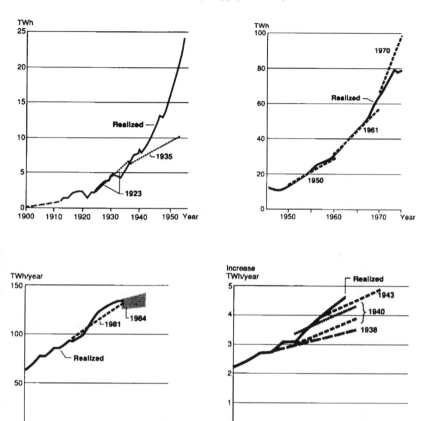

Figure 4-1. An illustration of the history of official electricity demand forecasting in Sweden.
Source: Vattenfall.

per year. Against this background, one should not be surprised if this period to a large extent was characterised by excess demand expressed in terms of narrow reserve margins in the system and periods of electricity rationing or electricity use restrictions as in 1941–3, 1947–8, 1955, and 1959. Up to the mid-1970s, the history of electricity demand forecasting in Sweden is also one of underestimation (see Figure 4-1).

As in many other countries, the future Swedish demand for electricity was largely overestimated after 1970. However, it is difficult to detect any noticeable excess capacity (see Table 4-5). These reserve margins may seem very high but are quite normal for large hydro systems. Moreover, bottlenecks in

Table 4-5. *Capacity, generation, and reserve margins in Sweden, 1960–1990*

Year	Capacity, MW	Peak demand, MW	Capacity reserve margin, %	Electricity production, TWh	Capacity use, %
1960	6,918			34.7	57
1965	11,953			49.1	47
1966	12,228	8,564	43	50.7	47
1967	13,302	9,430	41	53.8	46
1968	13,722	9,767	40	56.2	47
1969	14,799	9,588	54	58.1	45
1970	15,307	11,067	43	60.1	45
1971	16,118	10,580	52	66.6	47
1972	17,744	12,055	47	71.7	46
1973	19,465	12,254	59	78.1	46
1974	20,768	13,337	58	75.1	41
1975	23,135	14,700	57	80.6	40
1976	24,445	16,100	52	86.4	40
1977	25,108	15,700	60	90.0	41
1978	26,091	16,800	55	92.9	41
1979	26,227	18,300	43	95.2	41
1980	28,873	18,300	58	96.7	38
1981	29,919	20,300	47	103.3	39
1982	31,275	19,900	57	100.1	37
1983	31,316	21,500	46	109.4	40
1984	31,433	21,300	48	123.8	45
1985	33,636	24,700	36	137.1	47
1986	34,173	23,900	43	138.7	46
1987	34,263	26,200	31	146.6	49
1988	34,532	25,100	38	146.2	48
1989	34,590	25,800	34	143.1	47
1990	33,677	23,300	45	147.1	50

Source: Vattenfall.

the transmission system between northern and southern Sweden also increase the optimal reserve margin. As a result of the large variations in winter temperatures between years, the capacity reserve margin varies a lot. At the record-high peak load in 1987, the actual effective reserve margin was less than 10% compared to the calculated 31% in Table 4-5.

Concerning the energy reserve margin, there is a clear indication of excess capacity. The capacity use (defined as the ratio between observed production and potential production if all capacity had been used 8,760 hours per year) fell between 1973 and 1974 and did not reach the 1973 level until 1985. For a further evaluation of the reserve margins, see the later section titled "Capacity expansion and timing of investments."

The exploitation of scale economies

Because many technologies for electricity generation and transmission are characterised by considerable economies of scale ex ante in capacity choice, and because the Scandinavian countries are small, an important question is whether the existing market structure has made an efficient use of economies of scale possible in generation, transmission, and distribution.

An efficient exploitation of scale economies is mainly a long-run issue. In the short run (i.e., in the operation and capacity use of existing plants and equipment), the total capacity use of the entire production system is characterised by decreasing returns to scale (increasing merit order marginal costs) and the same holds for transmission (marginal losses = twice average losses).

As a production process, generation is fairly similar to heavy industry production, whereas distribution is more similar to light industry. In generation, productivity growth is extremely dependent on lumpy investments in capital equipment, whereas in distribution productivity growth is mostly dependent on the efficient use of labour (i.e., management). Therefore, *dynamic efficiency* is the main concern in electricity generation (and transmission), whereas in retail distribution *productive and managerial efficiency* are the main concerns.

Exploitation of scale economies in generation: As for generation, the possibilities of using economies of scale in capacity expansion are a function of technology, market size, and growth. An interesting question is whether the present market structure and size distribution of power companies in Scandinavia are rational or if *scale efficiency* gains could have been achieved through a different organisation.

In the case of hydro and cogeneration, the optimal size is determined mainly by exogenous factors such as the geographical site, the environmental aspects, and the demand for steam and heat. (There is also a trade-off between the length of water tunnels and the size of hydro plants, depending on the price of electricity.) There is no indication of suboptimal sizes in these technologies in Scandinavia. The same holds for fossil-fueled condenser units.

Concerning nuclear power, when optimal sizes are fairly large compared to the size of the market, a full exploitation of economies of scale in both Sweden and Finland has been achieved through coordination of capacity expansion and shared ownership among the power companies. Whereas half of the Swedish nuclear units (at two sites) are entirely owned by single power companies (Vattenfall and Sydkraft, respectively), more than half of the capacity is jointly owned by two companies with Vattenfall and Sydkraft as principal owners, respectively, in combination with a large number of other power companies. As mentioned earlier, a typical feature has also been the coordination of timing of large projects in combination with the swapping of electricity over time. Thus, the size and horizontal structure of the Scandinavian market does not seem to have caused any barriers to the use of economies of scale in generation.

Economies of scale in transmission: The degree of economies of scale in (Norwegian) transmission has been investigated by Johnsen (1992) on the basis of a generalised Leontief cost function. He obtained an elasticity of scale of 1.3 (i.e., a cost scale factor of 0.77). A similar result was obtained by Schreiner and Strom (1983). The results indicate the importance of an efficient exploitation of scale economies in transmission.

The central coordination of grid expansion in all countries and the sole ownership of most of the national grids (except in Finland) should lead to a fairly efficient expansion of high-voltage transmission. The lack of coordination in Finland has resulted in parallel lines built by a group of private producers, TVS. However, the degree of inefficiency caused by this investment is probably small. The two grid owners have been urged by the government to coordinate the operation and future expansion of the two grids, and the principles and rules for that have now been accepted by the Finnish association of power producers.

Scale efficiency in retail distribution: Although traditionally, most empirical studies have indicated substantial economies of scale in retail distribution, the scale effect may have been confounded with the density effect. *Returns to density* measures the economies of increasing the amount of electricity supplied when the network is held constant. *Returns to scale* measures the combined economies of increasing the amount of electricity supplied and the network.

A priori, one would expect economies of scale in electricity distribution to be less pronounced and to a large extent to depend on geographical factors. The investment process is gradual, and capital equipment is to some extent mobile, although for physical reasons the pure transmission of electricity reveals economies of scale. More recent estimates of *economies of scale* jointly with *economies of density* indicate that, although economies of density are very important, economies of scale are not that important.

Salvanes and Tjotta (1990) find no evidence of economies of scale for a large output range of Norwegian distributors, including the mean sample distributor (approximately 20,000 customers served) but important economies of density. For rather small distributors, however, the elasticity of scale exceeds one; for example, for distributors serving approximately 5,000 customers the elasticity of scale is 1.04. In a panel study Kumbhakar and Hjalmarsson (1994) found substantial scale economies at the beginning of the 1970s in Swedish retail distribution but approximately constant returns to scale around 1990. This may be a result of the process of mergers and takeovers that reduced the number of small distributors substantially during a 20-year period.

In all Scandinavian countries the number of retail distributors is large, and in all countries there are concerted efforts to increase the size of distribution areas and decrease the number of small (and usually financially weak) distributors. This is a slow and gradual process mainly for two reasons. First, distribution concessions are given for a long period (in Sweden normally 40 years), and it is rare that a distributor loses its concession due to "misbehaviour" during the concession period. Second, rural retail distribution is maintenance-intensive and regarded as less profitable. Therefore, small rural distribution areas are not very attractive for takeovers and mergers. In spite of that, the number of small distributors has decreased in all countries – for example, in Sweden from about 1,000 at the beginning of the 1950s to fewer than 300 in 1994.

Capacity expansion and timing of investments

Both in Sweden and in Norway there have been strong tendencies toward an overexpansion of the system. This seems to be a smaller problem in Denmark and Finland, which have large import shares. Therefore, I will discuss the investment criteria applied in capacity expansion in Norway and Sweden.

Investment criteria and capital use efficiency in Sweden: The Swedish power industry's investment criteria have been based on Kraftsam's criteria for optimal dimensioning of reserve capacity. (Kraftsam has been a central planning board for the club of producers, responsible for demand forecasting and other similar tasks.) The power industry, when making investment appraisals, has used a standard technique consisting of a cost-minimising model. The investment criterion comprises two capacity requirements which imply that the demand for energy and power is satisfied to the degree of certainty considered economically motivated with respect to the probability of various possible events.

In a critical review of these criteria, Andersson and Taylor (1992a, 1992b, and 1992c) find that the so-called combined investment criterion used in the Swedish power industry is economically justified. However, they object to the way in which the dimensioning of the energy reserves is carried out. The alternative method of calculation used by the authors leads to the conclusion that the approach applied results in an overdimensioned system. A reserve margin of 11 or 12%, instead of the one at that time of 16%, is more justified according to this analysis. In physical terms this means a difference of approximately 4 to 5% TWh annual production, depending on the cost concept used.

In addition, the authors point to two additional factors that tend to favour an overdimensioned system. One of these is the requirement for a certain minimum reserve that applies to individual members of the pool club. Accordingly, each of these firms must maintain a certain energy reserve but with a certain reduction that results from the internal "statistical energy criteria." The other factor that may contribute to a reserve capacity that is more than optimal is the fact that the Swedish energy reserve has been determined without regard to the energy exchange among the Scandinavian countries.

Andersson and Taylor (1992b) have also studied the conditions regarding optimal production capacity reserves. According to their result, the Swedish power industry should maintain a total power reserve capacity of 2,300MW (approximately 10%) – that is, an increase of approximately 1,300 MW compared to the conditions present at that time. Their calculations, however, do not include the capacity reserve that Sweden holds in the systems of the neighbouring countries through the Scandinavian power pool operations (i.e., the import potential). This potential is approximately 3,000 MW, but it is unclear how large a proportion may be included as part of the Swedish reserve capacity.

The main conclusion from this review of investment criteria in Sweden is that there has been a tendency to oversupply. This tendency may have become stronger during the 1980s, especially in the case of Vattenfall (see the section titled "Reasons for deregulation").

In Sweden, hydro development has also been part of regional policy. Most hydro projects developed parallel with the expansion of nuclear power have been very costly, nonprofitable, and mainly motivated for regional employment reasons. In some cases Vattenfall has got the permission to write off these investments immediately, whereas private companies have used their investment funds, causing a reduction in user cost of capital of approximately 40%.

Investment criteria in Norway: There seems to be a general opinion among Norwegian economists that their electricity production system has been constantly overexpanded. This opinion is also supported by several economic analyses and by the following observations.

A first observation is that pool prices appear to be systematically lower than they should be. On average, one would expect the market clearing prices in an unconstrained market to equal the long-run marginal cost of expansion, which in turn should equal the average cost of long-term contracts, at least when adjusted for risk. But according to data, the marginal expansion cost is currently around 30 ore/kWh (4 c/kWh). Current median spot prices are around 8 ore/kWh (1 c/kWh) and are expected to rise to only 15 ore/kWh (2 c/kWh) in the year 2000.

It also turns out that average pool prices have been consistently below the official wholesale contract prices for many years. Thus, it seems highly likely that they have also been consistently below marginal expansion costs over a similar period. Obviously, Norwegian power companies appear to have been investing too much in their own capacity, rather than relying on the market, with the net result being a national surplus of generating capacity. This situation results from a combination of the following factors:

- The requirement that the NPP should each be 95% self-sufficient in a critically dry year and the way in which reservoir managers apparently have interpreted this requirement as constraining reservoir management, as well as long-term development requirements.
- The fact that reservoir managers typically face an implicit reward structure that effectively penalises extreme events, such as spilling and especially running out of water, much more heavily than overall increases in cost.
- The fact that the ultimate consumers, who may be more sensitive to costs, have not been directly represented in the market and that the regional power companies, which theoretically represent them, have not been subject to competitive pressure to keep costs down.
- The natural desire of power companies, and particularly engineering departments within power companies, to continue to expand what has historically been their core business, that of building and operating power stations, rather than wheeling and dealing in a market.
- The natural desire of regionally based power companies to pursue projects that are seen to enhance the development of their own regions, even when cheaper power is available from the pool.
- A transmission pricing system that encouraged local construction by penalising long-distance transmission in a way that did not reflect the actual costs involved.
- Uncertainty about the future of nuclear power in Sweden created expectations about a large future market for Norwegian electricity.

Thus, there are potential gains of dynamic efficiency from the deregulation of the Norwegian electricity market. However, there may be obstacles along the deregulated path. One of the first decisions of the reorganised and corporatised Statkraft was to stop a major investment project in the northern part of Norway. This project would have added capacity to a sector already characterised by excess capacity. After being exposed to considerable political pressure from regional interests, the government intervened, however, and asked Statkraft to proceed with the project. Statkraft complied with the request because it was compensated economically by the government.

Optimal timing of capacity expansion and sequence of projects: Given a portfolio of exploitable hydro sites, the sequence and timing of exploitation are of great importance and still of relevance in Norway. In theory, the Norwegian Electricity Council (NVE) has had overall responsibility for coordination of the sector. In principle, one could imagine a central agency such as the NVE playing a strong coordination role with respect to new investment. But in practice, NVE actually maintained a much looser oversight of new investment and did not attempt to ensure that projects were developed in strict order of incremental cost. According to Rinde and Strom (1983, p. 144), "The official plans seem to select the projects almost randomly with a weak tendency of choosing an expensive project before a cheap one."

There are several explanations for this. One is that large hydro projects with relatively low costs may be environmentally damaging and take much time to get licensed in political bodies. Another reason is that in Norway the local authorities have a decisive influence on the selection and timing of hydro projects, and there is only a weak countrywide coordination. The large regional autonomy has prevented a functioning market for hydro sites to arise. In general, the environmental restrictions have determined the exploitation of hydro power in Sweden. Typical for Sweden has been the exploitation of entire river systems, although a few have been left totally unexploited.

Concerning the time path of thermal investments, a typical feature in Sweden has been the coordination of timing of large projects by Kraftsam in combination with swapping of electricity over time. After settling the time path of capacity expansion between two involved companies, the power company with the first large investment typically has lent power to the company with the later investment; when the second unit has come into operation the electricity debt is paid back. However, in the case of the last two nuclear power reactors, both unintentionally came into operation in 1985. The reason for this was political – one reactor was delayed because of the turmoil about the future of nuclear power in Sweden.

Transmission and distribution investments: Concerning transmission, there is no indication of underinvestment in transmission links, except in a few cases for limited periods, and then due to politico-environmental restrictions. Critics have, rather, argued that the transmission system is too reliable. On the other hand, elongated countries with large distances between production and load centers and a large nuclear capacity require strong transmission systems. The institutional club structure also seems efficient. In retail distribution there are no strong indications of either overinvestment or underinvestment except in a few rural areas with financially weak retail distributors.

Cost overruns

Large cost overruns in the electricity sector have been fairly rare in Scandinavia. That holds in particular for large conventional thermal or nuclear power projects. My own review of Vattenfall's investment projects between 1978 and 1988 revealed that only a few projects exceeded the expected investment costs. In those few cases two reasons dominated: (1) The project had been enlarged and some extra work done that had not been included in the investment appraisal; (2) in a few hydro projects, typically the quality of the rock had been worse than expected, so expensive concrete injection was required.

A more systematic investigation was performed by Segelod (1986), who also compared ex ante investment calculations with the realised costs ex post for a large number of Vattenfall's projects. This study suggests that it is relatively unusual for large projects to exceed costs to any extent but that greater variations between ex ante and ex post cost estimates are found in small projects. He found, however, a tendency to underestimate the costs of projects with long gestation lags (e.g., hydro power stations and large power line projects).

Nuclear power has been a most successful technology in Scandinavia. The deviation between expected and realised investment costs has typically been small and for the last two units, very small. Even if the cost of nuclear power still is low, there has been a fairly large increase in investment costs between the first reactors and the last ones. (Certain aspects of this cost escalation have been analysed by Jagren (1983), who has made a special study of the rate of construction concerning the building of one of the two last reactors (O III) compared to an earlier one (O II).)

The success of nuclear power

In comparison with many other countries, and with the United States in particular, the costs of nuclear power have been very low in Sweden and Finland. The most important reasons are probably the following:

- A successful choice of reactor technology.
- Efficient management during construction and operation as well as short (about 5 years for the most recent and largest units) construction periods.
- An efficient nuclear safety regulation and an efficient licensing process.

These three factors are important explanations of the good performance of the Scandinavian reactors shown in Table 4-6.

Another indication of the competitiveness of nuclear power in Scandinavia is a comparison with large-scale hydro. The most recent nuclear reactors came into operation in 1985, two 1,100 MW units. Construction started in 1980. The investment costs are known and almost exactly the same for both units, of which one was chosen for comparison. The development of the electricity price between 1985 and 1990 is also known. For comparison, I assume that

Table 4-6. *Energy availability (%) of the Swedish and Finnish nuclear power plants, 1985, 1990, 1991*

Plant	Type	Net capacity		Energy availability		
		MW	Vintage	1985	1990	1991
Swedish:						
Barsebäck 1	BWR	602	1975	87.9	95.2	90.5
Barsebäck 2	BWR	595	1977	97.1	88.2	94.3
Forsmark 1	BWR	970	1980	85.9	88.1	90.8
Forsmark 2	BWR	946	1981	87.9	91.2	90.7
Forsmark 3	BWR	1,060	1985	95.9	92.2	94.4
Oskarshamn I	BWR	440	1972	73.1	64.9	89.3
Oskarshamn II	BWR	595	1974	87.7	88.5	83.8
Oskarshamn III	BWR	1,060	1985	92.3	85.5	91.5
Ringhals 1	BWR	750	1976	85.1	77.6	85.0
Ringhals 2	PWR	800	1975	74.1	71.5	88.7
Ringhals 3	PWR	915	1981	84.4	76.5	79.7
Ringhals 4	PWR	915	1983	87.1	90.7	90.6
Average Sweden				86.6	84.2	89.1
Finnish:						
Loviisa I	PWR	445	1977	93.3	85.1	87.1
Loviisa II	PWR	445	1980	92.9	84.8	89.2
Olkiluoto I	BWR	710	1979	91.2	95.5	95.4
Olkiluoto II	BWR	710	1980	88.3	93.0	93.1
Average Finland				91.4	89.6	91.2

Source: Annual reports.

three different hypothetical hydro plants came into operation in 1985 after a construction period of three years. The investment costs are picked from an official committee report (SOU, 1983:49). From this report I chose one large-scale low-cost (SEK 3/kWh) river project from one of the largest rivers not exploited (the Pite River), one medium-cost (SEK 4/kWh) project from a smaller river (the Flarkån), and one high-cost (SEK 5/kWh) project, from another river (the Råne River).

Given actual production in nuclear and potential production in the hydro projects had these been realised, the income stream generated up to 1990 is given. Then I assumed the same real electricity price as in 1990 to hold for the future and plotted the present value profiles of the projects as shown in Figure

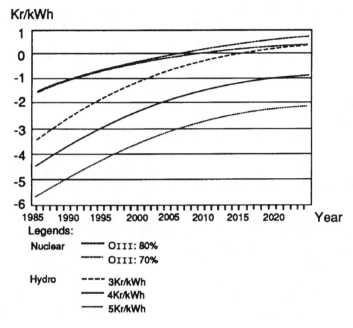

Figure 4-2. A comparison of nuclear power with hydro power

4-2. In the case of nuclear I assume either 70% or 80% availability, and in the case of hydro I chose the official estimates of average year production.

The illustration shows that only nuclear and the cheapest hydro project will realise a positive present value during their expected lifetime and, moreover, that the nuclear power plant breaks even earlier than the hydro project. Here I have used a very low real discount rate of 4%. A higher one will further increase the distance between nuclear and hydro and so will a higher availability in nuclear.

Allocative efficiency: Welfare losses from inefficient pricing

The market for bulk power

The most obvious inefficiency in Scandinavian electricity pricing has been the extensive variation in electricity prices in Norway (net of distribution costs) in general and the subsidised prices to the electricity-intensive industries in Norway in particular. According to Bye and Strom (1987), the electricity-intensive industry paid less than half the price it should had it not been subsidised. The amounts of electricity consumed at these low prices amount to about 30 TWh per year. A recent estimate of the allocative losses of this price dispersion is NOK 5 billion (US$ 700 million) per year (Bye and Johnsen, 1991). In addition to this price variation, there has been a substantial deviation between short-run marginal costs and the average tariff level.

In Sweden allocative efficiency has been more satisfactory. First, the degree of price discrimination has been very small. Second, the deviation between short-run marginal costs and the average tariff level has been smaller than in Norway. The results from numerical simulations of a market model suggest that the present price level is about 10 to 15% higher than the perfect competition solution. However, it is about 20% lower than the Cournot–Nash solution.

In spite of a high market concentration in Sweden, the high capacity use in plants with low production costs also suggests that the power utilities have not been able to take full advantage of their market power. The substantial addition of new nuclear power capacity in the mid-1980s has led to a falling real price of high-voltage electricity in spite of the higher costs of the last reactors brought into operation and considerable cash-flow deficits during the first years of operation. To exploit the potential market power and reach a Cournot–Nash equilibrium would mean that Vattenfall had to reduce its capacity use in nuclear power production. This would, of course, be politically impossible.

According to Hjalmarsson and Veiderpass (1988), the profitability of the largest Swedish power utilities has on average been somewhat lower than that of all larger Swedish firms. (The variations between the utilities and over time are, however, considerable.) The power utilities do not appear to have used their potential market power to attain a return above the Swedish industry average. This conclusion is supported by the stock price development for the companies registered with the stock exchange (Sydkraft and Gullspang): To match the development of the general stock index during the period 1982 through March 1986, the price of these shares would have to be doubled (see also SOU, 1991:8).

The market for low-voltage power

The efficiency of pricing in retail distribution probably varies a lot, although there is little concrete evidence in the form of systematic investigations. However, there is a considerable degree of variation in price levels among various retailers. To some extent this variation reflects differences in productive efficiency, to some extent differences in costs of own-power generation. In Sweden, in some municipalities there are indications of substantial cross-subsidisation from electricity distribution to electricity generation and district heating.

Productive efficiency and X-efficiency

In a recent study by Hjalmarsson and Veiderpass (1992a) for Swedish retail distribution the following conclusions emerge:

- The level of *technical efficiency* in terms of distances from the best practice production frontier (measured by Farrell measures) is rather low (i.e., there is a large efficiency variation across distributors) and, consequently, there is a large potential productivity increase.
- There is a high level of *scale efficiency* in urban service areas but a lower level of *scale efficiency* in rural areas and especially in cooperatives, which in general are very small.

Therefore, the general conclusion is that *technical efficiency* is the main problem in urban and *scale efficiency* a problem in rural electricity distribution, particularly for the cooperatives.

According to the same study, the *structural efficiency* in retail distribution in Sweden is fairly low. The ratio between potential amount of resources required had all distributors been at the best-practice frontier and the observed amount of inputs actually used was 70% in 1989. Kittelsen (1992) reports an even lower figure for Norway: a structural efficiency just over 50%.

Kumbhakar and Hjalmarsson (1994) found that private distributors are significantly more efficient than municipally owned ones. Interviews with managers of distribution companies confirm that, due to the lack of cost pressure, overstaffing is a typical feature in municipal electricity distribution. The lack of competition and private benchmarks of urban (municipal) distribution costs indicate a modest cost pressure. Furthermore, the boards of directors are generally politically appointed (but not directly elected) and represent political parties whose objectives may not be cost minimisation but different types of energy policy measures. Municipal companies are probably less politicised than municipal utilities are. Because of the higher distribution costs, however, one should expect a high pressure on rural distribution to reach an efficiency level that makes it possible to obtain a price level that does not deviate too much from surrounding urban areas. This kind of yardstick competition seems to be important in Sweden.

Productivity growth and price development

Rate of total factor productivity (TFP) growth since World War II

Electricity generation: Regarding productivity growth in generation, few investigations have been made. According to Grufman (1978), electricity-saving technical change in Swedish hydro production from 1950 to 1973 amounted to

0.5% per year compared to a rate of labour saving advance of 7.2%. The reason for the low rate of electricity saving advance is that in hydro the existing potential is very small because hydro plants are normally close to the upper physical bounds. In terms of a Solow residual, the annual change in total factor productivity was estimated to be 0.8% for the period 1950–60 and 3.1% for the period 1960–74.

Electricity transmission and distribution: Because of the vertical integration of transmission and generation, no studies have been performed of productivity change in transmission. Productivity change in distribution is addressed in Hjalmarsson and Veiderpass (1992b). The analysis is based on a four-output–four-input DEA (Data Envelopment Analysis) model, and the rate of TFP growth is measured by a Laspeyre version of a Malmquist index.

According to the results, productivity growth was rapid, on average 5% per year between 1970 and 1986. Compared with most manufacturing sectors in Sweden this is a fairly rapid rate of productivity growth. A decomposition into two subperiods, 1970–8 and 1978–86, revealed a dramatic fall in productivity growth between 1978 and 1979. The development of TFP was rapid during the first subperiod, on average 6% per year, but it decreased substantially during the second subperiod to an average 2.5% per year.

What, then, is the main reason for this rapid rate of productivity growth during the first period and the drop during the second period? The figures for partial labour productivity suggest that the returns to network density (i.e., the economies of increasing the amount of electricity supplied when the network is held constant) are a most important source of productivity growth. (This is also confirmed by the results from a two-output model with the amount of electricity received as output. On the other hand, in a two-output model with the number of high-voltage and low-voltage customers as output, productivity growth is negative.)

The low productivity growth rate during the second subperiod, 1978–86, is, however, not explained by a reduction of the amount of electricity consumed by the average consumer during the second period. The growth rate has been about the same during both periods. Instead, there are indications of overstaffing. The partial labour productivity in terms of the number of customers served dropped significantly. On average, these partial labour productivities are on a significantly higher level throughout the first subperiod. Although this is hard to prove, the main reason for the sudden shift in labour productivity between 1978 and 1979 probably is the government regulation that forced the municipalities to adopt so-called *municipal energy planning*. This is also indicated by the differences in productivity change between rural and urban areas between the two subperiods. Municipal energy planning is of less relevance for rural areas.

Table 4-7. *The development of real electricity prices: 1950–1990. Ore/kWh in 1990 price level. Nominal prices (net of consumption taxes) deflated by CPI. (1 cent = 8 ore)*

Year	Industry 30–50 GWh/year	Average annual change, %	Residential 10 MWh/year	Average annual change, %
1950			94.0	
1955	35.7		89.3	−1.0
1960	42.6	3.5	104.6	3.2
1965	28.8	−7.8	75.0	−6.7
1970	23.7	−3.9	55.4	−6.1
1975	33.2	6.7	61.6	2.1
1980	25.2	−5.5	56.2	−1.8
1985	20.9	−3.7	52.7	−1.3
1990	20.0	−0.9	44.2	−3.5

Source: Official statistics.

Price development

Because the degree of competition and regulation in the market has been about the same during the entire history of electricity, the development of the wholesale price level should also reflect the development of generating costs, whereas the difference between wholesale prices and retail prices should reflect the development of distribution costs.

The development of the industrial and the retail electricity prices from 1950 to 1990 (in 1990 prices, deflated by CPI) is shown in Table 4-7. It should be noted that the industrial price contains some transmission and distribution costs in addition to a tax on old hydro plants and that it consequently may not be regarded as an exact reflection of the production costs.

The price increase between 1970 and 1975 resulted from the oil price hike. Because of a smaller electricity input cost share in residential distribution (about 70%) compared to high-voltage distribution (90%), the price increase was lower for households than for industry. After 1975 expensive fossil fuels were substituted for by cheap nuclear power, leading to a decreasing real price of electricity.

A cross-country comparison is given in Figure 4-3. It shows the 1983 average price of high-voltage electricity for industrial use in various countries. The black part of the staples shows the range of variation for some countries.

In an international perspective, the Scandinavian industrial electricity prices are very low in Norway (although there is a substantial amount of price discrimination) and Sweden, but somewhat higher in Finland and substantial-

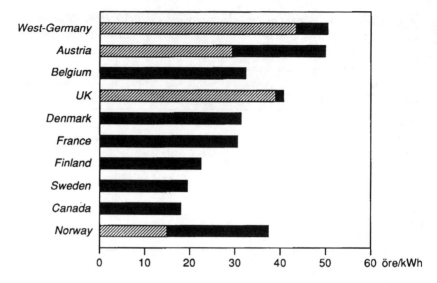

Figure 4-3. A cross-country comparison of electricity prices. The 1983 average price of high voltage electricity for industrial use in various countries. (*Source:* Unipede and Vattenfall.)

ly higher in Denmark (although on par with France). A similar picture is presented in Table 4-8, which shows the average electricity price in a selected number of countries. There are three major and a few minor reasons for this pattern, as follows:

- Norway in particular, but also Sweden and to some extent Finland, are countries that are naturally well suited for large-scale hydro electricity production. They enjoy cost advantages because large-scale hydro has been expanded at low costs. Because hydro power can be regulated, it also constitutes an excellent complement to other types of electricity production and, thus, further contributes to a lowering of system average costs. Hydro power is unique because it is suitable both for base-load and peak-load production.

- Swedish and Finnish power companies have been extremely successful in nuclear power production, and they have achieved a very high availability and low construction costs as well as operating costs.

- The public procurement process has been efficient. One of the most productivity-enhancing rules in the Swedish public sector is the Public Procurement Act, which determines the conditions and rules for procurement to the public sector, including publicly owned enterprises in electricity, telecommunications, and the like. According to this

Table 4-8. *The average electricity price in 1990 in pence/kWh*

Country	Price, p/kWh	Country	Price, p/kWh
Germany	6.17	Netherlands	3.68
Italy	5.27	Finland	3.60
Belgium	4.65	Norway	3.57
Ireland	4.57	Sweden	2.99
United Kingdom	4.50	Australia	2.91
United States	4.10	Canada	2.73
France	3.84		

Source: NUS International Price Survey, 1990 and Power in Europe, June 1990.

Act, public procurement should rest on competition among suppliers, and it is not permitted to favour domestic suppliers. Scandinavian firms must compete on equal terms with international firms. This Act is based on the fact that the welfare of a small country results from efficient use of comparative advantages and specialisation on a few products in international markets. The importance of this Act for public-sector efficiency and consumer welfare can hardly be exaggerated. In my opinion, a main reason for the (in an international comparison) very low price levels in telecommunications and electricity markets is this Act.

- As for capital-intensive projects, the level of the discount rate is of great importance to the rate of capacity expansion. In general, investments in electricity generation have been regarded as low-risk projects, and investment projects have generally been realised at fairly low real discount rates, normally in the range of 4 to 8%. Neither have there been any serious problems associated with financing. When written off, old hydro power plants are good cash cows for new investments. Because of their high degree of self-financing, the well-established Scandinavian power utilities have evened out their capital costs over time.

- In spite of small market shares for most of the power companies, except for the state-owned ones, economies of scale have been efficiently exploited by an extensive coordination and cooperation both among the private companies as well as between the state-owned and the private companies.

- The multi-firm structure in the electricity market has created benchmarks for yardstick competition that has promoted good management skills and internal efficiency, especially in generation. Without any formal price or rate-of-return regulation, there have been strong incentives for low-cost production.

Regulatory reforms

A policy discussion of the main weaknesses in regulation as practiced from post–World War II to the recent past may start with the conclusions drawn from the section titled "Capacity expansion and timing of investments."

Reasons for deregulation

The efficiency review discussed in that section indicates that there is scope for efficiency improvements of different kinds in different parts of the Scandinavian electricity supply industry. According to that review, there has been a strong tendency toward overexpansion of the Norwegian production system and a weaker tendency toward overexpansion of the Swedish production system. Thus, there are potential dynamic efficiency gains to be had from a deregulation.

The indirect type of regulation of SOEs also seems to work less efficiently today. This tendency may have become stronger during the 1980s, especially in the case of Vattenfall. In particular, there has been a trend toward less efficient use of capital. Up to the beginning of the 1980s, Vattenfall was in reality a large construction company investing its profits in new plants and equipment to meet a rapid growth in electricity demand. When demand growth decreases or stops in such a capital-intensive industry, the profits show up, turning the firms into cash cows. Private companies have several real or financial investment options for their increasing profits, but the options of an SOE are much more limited in scope: Either plough back the profits into new investments or let the owner (i.e., the state) reap the profits of past investments. A large SOE with a weak owner and dominated by investment-prone engineers has a strong position in the regulatory game with the government.

In this case the owner has been weak because formally Vattenfall belongs to the soft Ministry of Industry and not to the hard Ministry of Finance – and the former has turned out to have somewhat other objectives than the latter – for example, an active energy policy – and such objectives are usually expensive. As a result, the opportunity cost of capital in Vattenfall has been very low, resulting in too much investment, particularly in high-cost hydro power and R&D activities during the past 10 to 15 years, in addition to less successful (and also government-induced) diversifications into oil and natural gas businesses. Thus, from a dynamic efficiency point of view the regulatory system works much less efficiently than before.

Moreover, in retail distribution productivity growth has been slow during the past decade, and there is a large dispersion in productive efficiency among the retail distributors. Therefore, a fairly large potential for productivity improvements exists. With increased competition, one should expect a rapid productivity growth in retail distribution.

More competition will also increase the allocative efficiency at the high-voltage as well as at the low-voltage level. To a large extent this just means a redistribution of profits from generators and distributors to end-consumers. In Norway, as a result of the large price dispersion, one would expect a more uniform price structure and a substantially higher allocative efficiency after deregulation.

The development of the Norwegian reform

A prerequisite for deregulation in Norway was a new electricity act or Energy Law (law of production, transformation, sale, and distribution of energy) valid from January 1, 1991. Before that, the NVE (the Norwegian Electricity Council, a government agency) had proposed that the objective should be to create an electricity market consisting of approximately 20 vertically integrated utilities (Ot.prp.nr 43, 1989–90). However, these objectives were turned around during the preparation process, and the new Act recommended a more competitive electricity market. (For a survey and evaluation of the Norwegian deregulation, see Hope, Rud, and Singh (1993). This section is mainly built on their report.) The deregulation process can be summarised in the following way:

- A first step in the deregulation process was to separate the high-voltage transmission systems from Statkraft in Norway. Statnett is the SOE in charge of the national grid.
- The principle of common carriage and TPA has been established for all networks – national, regional, and local. Area concessions to grid owners are combined with an obligation to connect to the national grid and supply power to the area but not to block supplies from other agents through the grid. In principle, a household can buy power directly in the spot market for its own consumption.
- Vertically integrated companies have to ring-fence generation from distribution through separate divisions with a stated intention that the divisions are to be allowed to operate as independent entities in the market. Some distribution companies have been corporatised although so far without being privatised.
- The generation and distribution companies are no longer obliged to have a long-term contract coverage in relation to their obligation to supply power.

- Statkraft has been reorganised and corporatised, now being a pure generating company without any public obligations or system responsibility.
- A set of markets has been established or is in the process of becoming operational. These markets are administered by Statnett Market, a subsidiary of Statnett.
- Several new agents have already entered the market as independent brokers and traders.
- Foreign trade in power has been reorganised.
- Finally, a new regulatory regime has been established. The NVE has got a new role concentrating on competition policy issues in cooperation with the Norwegian Price and Cartel Board (Prisdirektoratet).

Barriers to entry: The market participants sign a contract, stipulating certain conditions, with Statnett Market. The barriers to entry are low and of the following type:

- An agent has to provide metering equipment so that quantities of electricity fed into the system or taken out of the system can be measured. The spot market is cleared every hour, so the agents must be able to measure power flows on an hourly basis.
- An agent has to pay transaction charges to Statnett Market: an entry charge of NOK 50,000 (US\$ 7,000) and an annual charge of NOK 15,000 (US\$ 2,000) gives access to all markets. In addition there is also a volume charge of NOK 1,2/GWh (US\$ 0.17/GWh).
- In order to trade power, a trading concession issued by the NVE is needed, but there is free entry for brokers.

The price formation mechanism used for all markets is basically the same as the one earlier described for the Norwegian Power Pool, but now with Statnett Market as the market clearing institution. In the reformed system there are the following three organised power markets:

- the spot market
- the regulation market
- the contract market

The spot market: The spot market is now being called the *daily market* because it is cleared daily. The market is basically an extension and refinement of the former market for occasional power described earlier. It is open to all potential agents. This market is now cleared on an hourly basis, but normally only six "price sections" are being issued per day (and four during the week-ends). The market participants declare their supply and demand in the form of a number of price–quantity combinations for each price section of the day. Statnett Market aggregates this information to market demand and supply curves and thereby determines the market clearing price for each price section. Deviations from contracted volumes are settled over the *regulation market*.

The regulation market: Whereas the *daily market* is the mechanism for *merit order dispatch,* the *regulation market* is directly tied to the *real time system dispatch.* Because electricity is not a storable commodity or service, the real-time coordination of the system, with permanent monitoring of load distribution, voltage, and frequency variations, is crucial for a high reliability. Spinning reserves for voltage and frequency regulation must always be available on short notice and of a volume so that even the largest generating units, when it is required, can be taken out of operation immediately.

Before deregulation, this coordination function was handled by the Norwegian Power Pool. When a generator was asked to increase its production above its planned output during a time segment, it could later be reimbursed according to the short-run marginal price or get the power back with a markup of 25%.

Since deregulation, no company has any specific system responsibility. Therefore, a market for the supply of reserve capacity is required. The real-time dispatch of the Norwegian system has been transferred to Statnett Market, which has created a market for backup capacity – the regulation market. Some of the largest generators, including Statkraft, are active in this market. The regulation market is operated on an hourly basis and based on price–quantity combination bids from the generators. From these bids Statnett Market picks the cheapest ones required for the regulation of the power flows.

Under many circumstances (e.g., sudden failures), there is a need for instantaneous regulation of the power flows. The system dispatcher must then have the authority to intervene directly, shut down generators, close transmission lines, and call upon spinning reserves. Statnett is presumed to do this in a cost-minimising way. The economic settlements are about the same as for the regulation market.

The futures market: One of the most interesting aspects of the Norwegian reform is the attempt to introduce a futures market for electricity – and it is still an attempt. It began to operate in the fall of 1992. This market is called *the weekly market,* since the week is the time-unit for contracts. The following two types of contracts are being traded in this market:

- A contract for *base-load power* traded for physical deliveries. It has a flat-load profile over the week.

- A contract for *day power* traded for physical deliveries during daytime (7:00 A.M. to 10:00 P.M.) from Monday to Friday. It has a flat-load profile during these hours.

Statnett Market has also tried to organise and administer a market for trading in these contracts, and it is the counterpart in all contracts. The contracts are not standardised with respect to volume. Contracts are traded once a week with the same pricing mechanism as for the spot market. However, a second-hand market for these contracts is not yet established. A committee has been appointed to work out proposals for a reorganisation of the market, formalising trading procedures, standardisation, security systems, and so on. For details, see Hope, Rud, and Singh (1993).

Forward contracts: The volumes of electricity traded in regulation, spot, and weekly markets account for only a small fraction of the total turnover of electricity in Norway. Forward contracts of a long-term bilateral nature still dominate the electricity market.

With these sets of markets and contracts – regulation, hourly, weekly, and long-term – all variation in demand for power should be satisfied.

Efficiency gains: The economic impact of the regulatory reform is discussed by Hope, Rud, and Singh (1993), whose main conclusions are the following:

- Generally, the real electricity prices have fallen but not necessarily as a consequence of the market reform. The reform coincided with a number of important circumstances on both the demand and supply side, such as mild winters, high precipitation, recession in electricity-intensive industries, and additions to capacity as a consequence of earlier investment decisions.
- Competition in generation and distribution has definitely benefitted the end-consumers in the form of increased consumer surplus.
- Competition has led to a higher degree of price uniformity in the end-use of electricity, but still there is considerable price dispersion. Obviously, further efficiency gains can be expected from increased competition in retail distribution.
- As expected, electricity prices have become more volatile. Before, this short-run price volatility was absorbed by the generators.

The rapid (two years) transition in Norway from a traditionally highly centralised and technologically oriented electricity supply industry to a market-based system has been quite dramatic. There has been a growing opposition from people within the electricity industry advocating corrective policy measures. So far, the Norwegian government and the Parliament have (with a few exceptions) resisted such demands.

The proposed Swedish and Finnish reforms

Compared to the Norwegian reform, the Swedish one is lagging behind. A decision by the Parliament to establish a deregulated market from 1995 was postponed at least a year by the new government that took over in the fall of 1994. The result so far can be summarised in the following way:

- Vattenfall has been corporatised and may in the future be privatised.
- The national grid has been separated from Vattenfall and transferred into a separate state-owned organisation, Svenska Kraftnät (Swede-Grid), independent of generators and distributors. However, its future organisation and scope of activities are not yet settled. Important issues presently under review are transmission pricing, the organisation of the power exchange or spot market for electricity, and to what extent new transmission lines between Sweden and other countries should be owned by SwedeGrid. According to its general terms of reference, SwedeGrid should enhance competition in the electricity market, within Sweden as well as between Sweden and surrounding countries.
- In the (now postponed) parliamentary decision, free entry (i.e., third-party access to all grids and networks) is established. Strict ring-fencing of distribution services from marketing of electricity in the sense that separate corporations are required. There is no formal price regulation, but distribution services should be based on "reasonable" prices. A new *Competition Law,* consistent with the European Common Market rules, will also further enhance competition in the electricity market.

The main reason for the postponement was that the new government wanted to further investigate the impact on small rural consumers and the impact on the potential phaseout of nuclear power in a free electricity market.

The main impact of the expected reform has already been a stronger competition in the bulk supply market, and lower prices. Recent negotiations for new contracts between large (or newly formed regional coalitions of) retail distributors and large industrial companies on the one hand and generators on the other show that the process toward lower electricity prices has already started. The generators were forced to deviate from their previously announced bulk supply tariffs. Expectations about a more competitive electricity market have already shown some of its potential. Some distributors have established cooperation with U.K. or Norwegian distributors. Several contracts have also been closed that presuppose third-party access.

Finland is moving in the same direction as Sweden. A new electricity act has been accepted by the Parliament in 1995, which is rather similar to the proposed Swedish act. This act removes all barriers to entry into the electricity market. The main effect so far is that Swedish Vattenfall has taken a substantial share of the Finnish market (5 Twh) from the dominating Finnish generator, Imatran Voima.

Denmark, finally, is also considering some steps in the same direction as Sweden and Finland, but the deregulation issue is still at the discussion stage.

REFERENCES IN ENGLISH

Andersson, R., and L. Taylor. "The Social Cost of Unsupplied Electricity." In *Studies in the Economics of Electricity and Heating,* edited by Andersson, Bohman, and Taylor. Swedish Council for Building Research, 1992a.

"Dimensioning Reserves of Electrical Production Capacity." In *Studies in the Economics of Electricity and Heating,* edited by Andersson, Bohman, and Taylor. Swedish Council for Building Research, 1992b.

"The Investment Criteria of the Swedish Electrical Industry." In *Studies in the Economics of Electricity and Heating,* edited by Andersson, Bohman, and Taylor. Swedish Council for Building Research, 1992c.

Bjerkholt, O., Longva, S., Olsen, Ö., and S. Strom, eds. "Analysis of Supply and Demand of Electricity in the Norwegian Economy." *Samfunnsökonomiske studier* 53, Statistics Norway, Oslo, 1983.

Caputo, M., and Mulligan, J. "Electric-Power Generation and Power-Pool Efficiency." Working paper, University of Delaware, 1985.

Hjalmarsson, L., and A. Veiderpass. "The Swedish Electricity Market. A Survey of Market Behaviour and Mode of Functioning." Department of Economics, University of Gothenburg, 1988.

"Efficiency and Ownership in Swedish Electricity Distribution." *Jounal of Productivity Analysis* (1992a): 7–24.

"Productivity in Swedish Electricity Retail Distribution." *Scandinavian Journal of Economics* (1992b): 193–205.

Hope, E., Rud, L., and B. Singh. "Market for Electricity: Economic Reform of the Norwegian Electricity Industry." SNF, Working paper, Oslo, 1993:12.

Kittelsen, S. "Stepwise DEA: Choosing Variables for Measuring Technical Efficiency in Norwegian Electricity Distribution." Working paper, SNF, Oslo, 1992.

Kumbhakar, S., and L. Hjalmarsson. "Relative Performance of Public and Private Ownership in Swedish Electricity Retail Distribution, 1970–1990." Working paper, Goteborg University, September 1994.

Larsen, O. *Power Transmission in a Multiowned Power System: The Central Grid System in Norway.* Oslo: Samkjöringen, 1986.

Larsson, S., Wiklund, L., and G. Alfors. *Operations Management in the Interconnected Nordic System.* Stockholm: Vattenfall, 1989.

Rinde, J., and S. Strom. "Cost Structure of Electricity Production." In "Analysis of Supply and Demand of Electricity in the Norwegian Economy," edited by O. Bjerkholt et al. *Samfunnsökonomiske studier* 53, Statistics Norway, Oslo, 1983.

Salvanes, K. G., and S. Tjotta. "Cost Differences in Electricity Distribution: Economies of Scale and Economies of Density in the Norwegian Electricity Distribution Industry." Working paper, Center for Applied Research, Bergen, Norway, 1990.

Schreiner, A., and S. Strom. "Transmission and distribution of electricity." In "Analysis of Supply and Demand of Electricity in the Norwegian Economy," edited by O. Bjerkholt et al. *Samfunnsøkonomiske studier* 53, Statistics Norway, Oslo, 1983.
Swedish Power Association: Annual Report 1990.
Sydkraft: Annual Report 1990.
Vattenfall: Annual Report 1990.

REFERENCES IN SCANDINAVIAN LANGUAGES

Alfors, G. "De dagliga nordiska kraftaffärerna." Nordel, 1980.
Bye, T., og T. A. Johnsen: Effektivisering av kraftmarkedet. Rapporter fra Statistisk Sentralbyrå 91/13, Oslo, 1991.
Bye, T., og S. Ström: Kraftpriser og kraftforbruk. *Sosialøkonomen* nr 4 (1987).
Grufman, A. Teknisk utveckling och produktivitet i energiomvand lingssektorn. Stockholm: IUI, 1978.
Jagren, L. OIII–Organisation, kostnader och säkerhet: En studie av produktivitetsutvecklingen i ett stort anläggningsprojekt. Stockholm: IUI, 1983.
Johnsen, T. A. Resursbruk og produksjon i kraftsektoren. Statistisk Sentralbyrå. Oslo: 1992.
Nordel: Årsberättelse, 1990.
NUTEK: Elmarknad I förändring. Från monopol till konkurrens. B 1991:6.
Segelod, E. Kalkylering och avvikelser. Liber Förlag, 1986.
SOU 1981:69. Pris på Energi.
SOU 1991:8. Beskattning av kraftföretag.
SOU 1993:68. Elkonkurrens med nätmonopol.
SPK 1979:26. Produktion och distribution av elektrisk kraft.
Svenska kraftnät: Handelsplats för el, 1993.
Vattenfall under 75 år, 1909–1984. Stockholm: Statens Vattenfallsverk, 1984.
Vattenfall: Stamnätet. Svensk Elförsörjnings Energipulsåder, Preliminär version. Januari 1985.
Wittrock, B. och Lindström, L. De stora programmens tid.Akademilitteratur, Stockholm, 1984.
Wiedswang, R. Elforsyningens organisasjon i de nordiske land. *Samkjöringen* (1992).

Table 4-9. *The biggest European power companies in 1989*

Company	Country	1989-sale, TWh	1989-sale, ECU	Employees, number
EdF	France	304.0	20,432	122,300
ENEL	Italy	220.5	12,719	111,000
National Power	United Kingdom	123.8	5,941	16,000
RWE	Germany	120.6	8,197	23,521
Vattenfall	Sweden	77.3	2,480	10,390
PowerGen	United Kingdom	76.5	3.875	9,430
Electrabel	Belgium	64.7	—	17,149
Preussen Elektra	Germany	51.1	2,957	6,676
Endesa Group	Spain	47.2	3,509	15,678
Nuclear Electric	United Kingdom	42.5	3,038	14,415
TEK	Turkey	36.8	800	68,310
Statkraft	Norway	36.4	1,192	1,544
Bayerwork	Germany	32.6	1,787	3,240
Imatra Voima	Finland	28.8	883	4,100
PPC	Greece	28.4	1,855	30,900
VEW	Germany	27.3	2,099	7,400
Sydkraft	Sweden	25.7	901	2,843
OEW	Austria	23.4	1,124	5,586
Hidrola	Spain	23.4	1,980	6,662
Iberduero	Spain	23.0	2,071	7,477
Scottish Power	United Kingdom	22.3	484	12,008
EDP	Portugal	19.3	1,470	22,816
Badenwerke	Germany	18.0	1,309	3,625
EPON	Netherlands	17.7	666	1,497
Energieversorg, Schwaben	Germany	17.6	1,441	4,775
Union Fenosa	Spain	16.0	1,559	6,205
Veba Kraftwerke	Germany	15.9	913	3,219
EPZ	Netherlands	13.8	1,605	1,523
Elkraft	Denmark	12.5	542	267
Oster Donau-kraftwerke	Austria	12.3	1,048	1,290
Teollisanden Voima	Finland	11.5	294	50
ESB	Ireland	11.2	1,173	10,904

CHAPTER 5

Competition and institutional change in U.S. electric power regulation

Richard J. Gilbert and Edward P. Kahn
University of California Energy Institute

Part I. Historical background and evolution of the U.S. electric power sector

Brief history of the origins of the system

The U.S. electricity system has been, and continues to be, a patchwork of state and federal regulations in a system with private, municipal, and other government ownership. In this section we give a brief survey of the origin and early history of the activities of the public and private sectors.

Private sector activities

The nineteenth-century origins of the U.S. electricity system involved substantial technological rivalry between incompatible systems (Hughes, 1983). The technical configuration first promoted by Edison and his associates and used in the famous Pearl Street Station (1882) was based on direct current (dc). Westinghouse and others, starting later and with less financial backing, promoted alternating current (ac) primarily to achieve longer transmission and distribution distances. The technical advantage of ac was due to the comparative ease of transforming voltage to levels high enough that resistance losses from transmission were small. The dc technology was not able to achieve high-voltage transformation for decades. Therefore, in the early development of the electricity industry, each technology had natural market niches. The dc systems prevailed in dense urban areas, where they supplied lighting and power for electric railways (traction); the ac systems dominated smaller cities and towns, where their advantage in transmission over longer distances was clear.

By the early 1890s, an interface technology, the rotary converter, made it possible to blend the two technologies into a single coherent system. Eventually ac systems dominated because of their advantage in transmission. In the

179

shorter run, hybrid systems could be operated using the interface technology, and therefore scale economies associated with mergers became possible (David and Bunn, 1988).

The system economies of large-scale transmission began to be exploited in the period just before World War I. A significant step in this direction was taken with the experiments of Samuel Insull, former secretary to Edison and builder of the Commonwealth Edison Company, in Northern Illinois during the period from 1910 to 1912 (MacDonald, 1962). By linking together separate systems, load diversity improved the efficiency of power production. Small plants could be shut down and only the most productive equipment used. This saved fuel and maintenance costs, which more than offset the extra costs of transmission lines. Thus, geographic economies allowed for both lower rates and increased profits compared to more isolated operations. This example of pervasive network economies drove the early growth of the large-scale electric utility beyond the confines of major metropolitan areas.

Scale economies could be exploited systematically only in a political regime that was stable enough to make raising capital feasible. The early history of competition in electricity was frequently destructive. Many private firms failed financially and were taken over by government entities. These seldom realized the scale economies that the larger private firms demonstrated. But the private firms faced a constant threat of franchise revocation by local political authorities. The political structure of state regulation with well-defined long-term franchises began with the first commissions established in Wisconsin in 1906 and New York in 1907. By the 1920s over half the states had adopted this framework. Therefore, natural monopoly conditions could be exploited without undue political disruption.

With favorable conditions for growth, financing expansion became a key constraint. Electricity is a very capital-intensive industry. Retained earnings were insufficient to finance market expansion. The need for external finance became critical. Insull was an innovator in this area as well as in technology. He pioneered the mass sale of common stock to customers during the 1920s and the broadening of debt markets beyond the New York financial community (MacDonald, 1962). At the same time, equipment vendors also acquired a significant quantity of securities from utilities as payment for goods and services. Utilities proliferated securities through holding companies, some of which were controlled by vendors such as General Electric.

Government ownership

Throughout the history of the U.S. electricity system there has been competition among various forms of ownership. The investor–ownership model became predominant but not without several different kinds of government ownership achieving niche roles.

The federal government has played a significant, but always limited, role in electric power. Federal authority functions principally at the wholesale level. Constitutional authority over interstate commerce evolved into an apparatus of federal regulation covering most wholesale transactions, including those occurring between parties strictly located within one single state. Moreover, the federal government has ownership rights over most hydroelectric resources. The Federal Water Power Act of 1920 (P.L. 66–280) codified federal powers. This Act established the Federal Power Commission (which became the Federal Energy Regulatory Commission) to issue licenses for nonfederal hydroelectric development and to regulate prices for wholesale transactions. It also embodied the principle of preferential allocation of surplus federal power sales to municipalities.

In the 1930s the federal government encouraged the growth of rural electricity service by subsidizing the formation of rural electric cooperatives. The Rural Electrification Administration (REA) provides loans, federal power preference, and tax exemption to electric power organizations in rural areas and small towns. The REA coops are also exempt from state and federal regulation. This initiative contributed to growth in the proportion of farm homes with electricity, which rose to 35% in 1941 from a level less than one-third of this in 1932 (Census, 1975).

The value of the federal power preference grew with the expansion of Bureau of Reclamation dams in the western states. In 1936, the Hoover Dam began generating. Grand Coulee, the largest dam in the United States, was completed in 1941. The U.S. Army Corps of Engineers built flood control dams, producing additional power for preference customers. Under the Tennessee Valley Authority Act of 1933 (P.L. 73–17), the federal government supplied power to municipalities and rural cooperatives in the region. Hydroelectric construction by the federal government continued during World War II and slowed only during the 1950s with a change in public policy and a lack of new major sites.

Municipal ownership of utilities seldom evolved into large systems. As cities grew, they typically gravitated into the domain of the investor-owned sector. Two prominent exceptions are Seattle and Los Angeles. In both cases, the early growth of the system was facilitated by the development of regional hydroelectric resources either under direct municipal control or later as preference customers of federal projects. Municipal ownership had long provided a competitive constraint on the prices of private utilities. This constraint was limited by the municipality's opportunities to realize scale economies, which were largely determined by its geographical boundaries.

Regulatory institutions

Origin and evolution of the investor-owned model

The regulatory structure governing the investor-owned segment of the U.S. electricity system involves three basic features: (1) geographically distinct franchise monopolies operated by vertically integrated firms, (2) price regulation intended to limit monopoly profits, and (3) the obligation to serve customers. Administrative agencies of state government typically determine franchise boundaries, control prices, and enforce service conditions.

There is considerable ambiguity about the origins of regulation. The system of state regulatory agencies was promoted by investor-owned firms as a reform of the political corruption that dominated the purely local franchising process. However, was its fundamental purpose the control of monopoly power, or was it a mechanism to facilitate raising capital? Jarrell (1978) analyzed the characteristics of firms in states that were among the first to preempt local franchise regulation and impose statewide regulation of privately owned utilities. He found that utilities in these states tended to have lower profits and prices than firms in states that were late to adopt statewide regulation. Following the implementation of statewide regulation, the firms in early adopting states tended to have larger increases in prices and profits than did the firms in late adopting states. Furthermore, when regulated prices declined during the 1920s, the rate of decline was slower for electric utilities governed by statewide regulation.

Statewide regulation thus appears to have been more of a pro-producer policy than one designed to limit excessive prices. However, one cannot conclude from this evidence that the introduction of statewide regulation harmed consumers. By failing to restrict entry into municipal franchises, local governments may have been trading short-run benefits of competition against incentives for utilities to invest and exploit economies of scale. Clearly, the sale of securities to finance electric power system expansion grew substantially in parallel with the growth of regulation, and this expansion resulted in large productivity gains (Scattergood et al., 1948). Hence, by adopting a more pro-producer regulatory policy, states may have contributed to the growth of the industry and ultimately to lower prices.

Throughout the first decades of regulation, most administrative issues involved accounting and service standards, and the issuing of securities. Growth in demand and capacity was financed by sales of common stock and bonds. Frequently, firms were assembled into holding companies that could be controlled by rather small percentages of stock. The holding companies were able to generate significant revenues from the operating companies through service

Table 5-1. *Structure of the U.S. electricity industry, 1989*

	Retail sales (thousand GWh)	Generation (thousand GWh)	Surplus (deficit) (thousand GWh)	Number of utilities	Capacity (GW)
Investor-owned	2,032	2,192	160	265	523
Publicly owned	372	246	(126)	1,994	71
Cooperative	190	123	(67)	956	25
Federal	53	224	171	10	65

contracts of various kinds. With the financial collapse of the 1930s, this system came under severe stress. Revenue from the operating companies for services declined significantly, and holding company stock prices fell considerably. The system of holding companies was reorganized under federal legislation that rationalized the structure but made subsequent consolidation of the industry more difficult.

The price deflation of the 1930s stimulated reductions in utility prices at the instigation of state commissions. Previously, utilities initiated the rate review process and determined the timing and magnitude of price reductions that were justified by productivity increases. When state agencies initiated the price reduction process, it was motivated by the perception that there were substantial excess profits (Wainwright, 1961). This shift in political initiative raised the question of defining the appropriate profit standard, which was resolved only by federal adjudication. The Hope Natural Gas and Bluefield cases set the standard of "just and reasonable" profits as the norm for regulated industries (see Bonbright, 1961).

Balance between public and private sectors

Throughout the postwar period the struggle between government ownership and the investor-owned segment continued. The issue reached the level of national political debate in the presidential election of 1940, when the Republican party nominated Wendell Wilkie, a vigorous opponent of government ownership, whose business career was associated with a large multistate holding company. The defeat of Wilkie did not end the debate. The election of Eisenhower in 1952 signaled the end of expansion of the federal system. Projects started previously were completed in the 1950s, and subsequent development stopped in the following decade. The public and cooperative segment continued to expand. The configuration of ownership structure in 1989 is illustrated in Table 5-1, which shows the dominant role of investor-owned firms. The small size of municipal and cooperative utilities is evident from either the average level of sales or capacity per utility. In terms of capacity, the average investor-owned firm in 1989 had 1,973 MW, compared to 36 MW per publicly owned utility and 26 MW per cooperative. A similar disproportion is evident by comparing average sales.

The magnitude of the federal hydroelectric subsidy to publicly owned and cooperative firms can also be estimated from these data. The total generation of these two sectors is 369 billion kWh, and their total combined sales is 562 billion kWh. The gap must be made up by purchases either from low-cost federal generation or higher-cost wholesale supply from investor-owned firms. The federal sector shows an excess of production over retail sales of 171 billion kWh. This power is sold at an average cost of 1.6 ¢/kWh to the publicly owned and cooperative segments (Energy Information Administration, 1991a). This is at least 4 ¢/kWh less than the open-market cost for long-term firm power supply. Therefore, the transfer payment is about $7 billion, or roughly 20% of the combined revenue of the publicly owned and cooperative segments.

Description of the electricity system since World War II

Fuel use

The dominant fuel used for power generation in the United States is coal. Limited hydroelectric resources and growing concern about environmental impacts of coal-fired power plants led to an expansion of alternative fuels. The two main alternatives were nuclear and petroleum-based fuels. The first sizable contribution from nuclear power occurred in the late 1960s. In the fast growth period of the 1950s and early 1960s, a large fraction of incremental capacity was fired by oil and natural gas. By 1970, before nuclear plants became a significant factor, oil and gas generation represented around 40% of all production (Edison Electric Institute, 1979).

The expanded use of oil and gas fuel for power generation was economic until the oil price shocks of the 1970s. During this decade fuel-related costs increased dramatically, making the need for substitutes apparent. Unfortunately, the principal solid-fuel technologies, coal and nuclear, encountered substantial siting and construction delays just when they were needed most. By the early 1980s, projects based on these fuels came into operation and substantially reduced the share of oil- and gas-fired generation. By 1989 only 15% of the fuel mix was oil and gas. However, the costs of most of the coal and nuclear plants were much higher than originally anticipated, and

Table 5-2. *Capacity and generation by fuel type, 1989*

	Capacity (MW)	Capacity (%)	Generation (GWh)	Generation (%)
Coal	296,614	43.3	1,553,061	55.8
Oil-steam	50,967	7.4	151,111	5.4
Oil-turbine	27,018	3.9	7,207	0.3
Gas-steam	94,150	13.8	245,057	8.8
Gas-turbine	22,994	3.4	21,542	0.8
Hydroelectric	90,467	13.2	265,063	9.5
Nuclear	98,161	14.3	529,355	19.0
Other	4,248	0.6	11,309	0.4
Total	684,619	100.0	2,784,304	100.0

with the fall in world oil and gas prices starting in 1986, the shift to solid fuels was probably excessive (Table 5-2).

Technological change

Throughout most of the post–World War II period, there was substantial technological improvement in the electricity system. The size and efficiency of generating units increased. The capacity of transmission lines increased; higher voltages reduced losses and allowed longer lines. These trends marked continuation of previous experience. The broad outlines of these developments are summarized in Joskow (1987). We briefly highlight particular details. In the postwar period, coal-fired steam turbines experienced falling capacity costs and increasing operating efficiencies until about 1965. Subsequently, the real cost of capacity approximately doubled and operating efficiency did not change. The capacity cost increases were a result largely of more stringent environmental regulation, but declining construction productivity and increased construction time also contributed. The data show that utilities with more experience in building complex coal plants achieved lower costs, which suggests that overall efficiency would have been better if a small number of more experienced firms had had a more dominant role. Finally, Joskow argues that the pursuit of scale economies "overshot" in coal generation, particularly regarding the "super-critical" boiler technology. These plants ended up having higher unit costs of production than did smaller scale subcritical boilers, mainly because of poor operating reliability.

Commercial nuclear power was introduced to the electric power industry after substantial intervention by the federal government. The federal role supported private development of this technology under the Atomic Energy Act of 1954 (P.L. 83–703). The Price–Anderson Act (P.L. 85–256) limited private liability in the event of catastrophic accident, thereby facilitating private investment. The federal government continued to support the nuclear industry with a substantial R&D effort throughout the postwar period. The economic promise of nuclear power did not materialize despite these efforts. Construction costs exceeded estimates by substantial amounts, although again there was a large variance. A few firms performed particularly well with regard to cost; several smaller utilities had disastrous experiences managing such complex projects.

Important technological developments occurred in the gas-turbine segment of the industry (Williams and Larson, 1989). The traditional use of this technology was for peaking operation, where its low capital costs and high operating costs made it ideal for limited service. With the emergence of the private power market in the 1980s, a new generation of more efficient turbines began to be used in base-load cogeneration applications. Further improvements led to highly efficient combined cycle plants that have both modest capital costs and relatively low operating costs. Because of the efficiency of combustion and the use of natural gas, these plants have relatively limited environmental impacts. Another advantage of the new gas-turbine technology was its greater flexibility with respect to planning. Construction and installation times are much shorter than for solid-fuel generation, and the units come in smaller sizes (25–200 MW) compared to the 1,000 MW size that was typical in the 1970s for coal and nuclear plants. Both of these features make it easier to adjust capacity to changes in expectations with regard to demand and relative fuel cost.

Retail rate structures

Rate setting in the postwar period has been dominated by the traditional rate-of-return model, in which prices for electricity are set at levels sufficient to cover total costs. This "revenue requirements" approach has begun to yield to rate mechanisms that provide incentives for efficient production, but this shift has occurred only recently and as of the date of this writing most utility revenues are cost-based. It is common for the revenue requirement to be determined by two separate kinds of hearings, one oriented to fuel costs and one oriented to all nonfuel costs. This distinction originated in the 1970s as a response to the price shocks in the world oil market, and what are generally known as "fuel cost adjustment" hearings have remained a permanent feature of the administrative process. Issues in a fuel adjustment hearing involve the utility's efforts to minimize operating costs by efficient fuel contracting and maximizing the opportunities for wholesale purchase. We discuss the wholesale markets further on pages 189–90. The nonfuel portion of electricity revenue requirements includes overhead and administrative costs, certain kinds of operation and maintenance costs, and the fixed costs of capital investment.

Once issues associated with determining the appropriate level of these costs have been resolved, the rate-making process involves several steps designed to allocate them to customer classes and collect the allocated costs through tariff design. The institutional practice of rate-making has traditionally been oriented to accounting issues, and relatively little attention has been devoted to marginal costs. Occasionally, economists are appointed to regulatory commissions, and then more emphasis on marginal cost may occur. An interesting account of such a case is given in Anderson (1981), which describes the tenure of Alfred Kahn on the New York Public Service Commission.

The main function of marginal costs in rate-making lies in defining time-of-use rates for large commercial and industrial customers. A time-of-use rate is an approximate representation of systematic variations in short-run marginal cost. Usually, these rates have two or three diurnal time periods and two seasonal components that result in four to six different prices for energy during the year. The goal is to embody the peak/off-peak distinction into prices for those customers whose consumption is large enough to justify the extra metering cost. Usually such customers are also large enough so that they also have demand-metering.

Before turning to the current structure of prices, it is useful to review the long-term historical trends. These are summarized in Table 5-3 which shows average nominal prices per kWh for residential customers and for all customers sampled over five-year intervals from 1930 to 1990, and the average rate of change of real prices between the sample intervals.

Table 5-3 shows the striking long-term decline in electricity prices, reflecting the productivity growth characterizing the industry up until the 1965 to 1970 period. The rate of decline was greater for residential rates than for all customers because, in part, residential prices started at much higher levels. The gap between residential and nonresidential rates in the early 1900s is consistent with profit-maximizing behavior, which would have required low prices to induce industrial consumers to switch to electric power. Prior to World War II, average residential rates were about twice the average rate for all customers (which of course includes residential customers). The price increases, starting in the 1970–5 period, were distributed less to residential customers than to other customer classes. When real electricity rates peaked around 1985, the average residential rate was less than 10% above the system average.

Although the rate-making process is supposed to produce prices that are not discriminatory and are based on costs, there are clearly exceptions to these principles. Some states have explicit subsidy policies aimed usually at low-income residential customers, sometimes at all residential customers. More

Table 5-3. *Average electricity prices, 1930 to 1990*

Year	Residential rate (¢/kWh)	Residential rate (1982¢/ kWh)	Average annual percentage change	All customers rate (¢/kWh)	All customers rate (1982¢/ kWh)	Average annual percentage change
1930	6.0	38.6	—	2.7	17.2	—
1935	5.0	37.3	−0.7	2.4	18.4	+1.4
1940	3.8	27.8	−5.8	2.0	14.9	−4.1
1945	3.5	18.1	−8.2	1.7	9.2	−9.2
1950	2.9	11.4	−8.9	1.7	7.2	−4.9
1955	2.7	9.3	−4.1	1.7	5.8	−4.0
1960	2.5	7.6	−3.9	1.6	5.2	−2.3
1965	2.3	6.4	−3.2	1.6	4.8	−1.6
1970	2.1	4.9	−5.2	1.6	3.9	−4.1
1975	3.2	5.4	+1.9	2.7	4.9	+4.7
1980	5.1	6.0	+2.0	4.5	5.4	+2.2
1985	7.4	6.7	+2.2	6.5	6.1	+2.2
1990	7.8	5.9	−2.5	6.6	5.1	−3.5

often, subsidies are implicit. Agricultural customers frequently pay low prices that are difficult to justify on a cost basis. Economic development arguments are sometimes used to rationalize low prices to specific industries, or to specific geographic regions. Table 5-4 summarizes average electricity costs for 1989 by customer type for the four main ownership structures. This table shows the different rate policies and average costs of the investor-owned segment, the publicly owned segment, cooperatives, and the federal government. Because government-owned utilities pay no taxes and have no equity capital, their rates should be lower than those of investor-owned firms. There are also significant operating subsidies from the federal sector to the municipal and cooperative segments. As Table 5-1 indicated, federal power sales to ultimate customers are small. Most federal sales are preferential allocations of hydroelectric generation at very low cost. This explains why the average rate for federal power is lower than all rates to end-use customer classes.

Table 5-4 also indicates a tendency toward price discrimination against commercial customers. For both publicly owned and federal rates, these customers pay the highest prices. For investor-owned and cooperative firms, residential rates are somewhat higher than commercial rates. The differentials, however, are too small to be based entirely on cost. The typically higher voltages and higher load density of commercial as opposed to residential cus-

Table 5-4. *Average revenue (¢per kWh) by class of ownership and by sector,* *1989*

	Residential	Commercial	Industrial	Average
Investor-owned	8.0	7.3	4.7	6.6
Publicly owned	6.3	6.4	4.7	5.8
Cooperative	7.4	7.2	5.0	6.9
Federal	5.5	5.7	4.0	3.6
Average	7.6	7.2	4.7	6.5

tomers would suggest bigger price spreads. In all likelihood, the commercial customers' rates are more determined by their relative bargaining weakness compared to the political power of residential customers. Industrial customers wield economic power because they can shift production to regions with lower costs, and in some cases, they can generate their own power requirements.

Wholesale markets

There is a substantial amount of wholesale trade among electric utilities. It is organized into two kinds of markets – one for firm power and one for short-term economy exchanges. Firm power transactions are usually between adjacent utilities where transmission interconnections are direct. The term *firm* means that the seller has an obligation to deliver that can be breached only under a limited set of circumstances, usually involving the reliability of his system, and not including opportunity costs. The buyer of firm power treats it operationally as if it were his own unit. It contributes toward his reliability objectives in the short and intermediate term and is part of his resource plan. At the other extreme, economy exchanges are often contracted only on an hourly basis. They imply no commitment from the seller and cannot be relied upon by the buyer to meet reliability goals.

In practice, there is gradation between these two types of transactions. Some economy transactions may go on for weeks or even months at a time. Some firm exchanges may last for only one year. A common pricing distinction involves the payment of fixed capacity or demand charges. When these are paid, they usually imply the no-interruptibility condition, and therefore define a "firm" relationship. As a practical matter, however, when there is excess supply, interruptibility is moot and economy transactions may essentially be equivalent to firm. One additional reason economy transactions may not qualify as firm is that delivery from seller to buyer may require transmission service from an intervening utility (called "wheeling"). Traditionally, only limited wheeling has occurred, and in most cases such arrangements are interruptible. Under such circumstances, the energy transaction cannot be firm.

In contrast to retail sales, which are regulated at the state level, all wholesale transactions are regulated by the U.S. Federal Energy Regulatory Commission (FERC). The justification for federal regulation is that wholesale transactions occur in an interconnected grid and arguably fall under federal jurisdiction for interstate commerce. The FERC regulation focuses on reasonable pricing rules, and in practice FERC regulation of wholesale transactions has been much weaker than state regulation of retail sales (Tenenbaum and Henderson, 1991). Typically, FERC has allowed utilities to price nonfirm trades on the basis of "split the savings" and to price firm trades on embedded cost. The FERC normally exempts transactions conducted under formal arrangements, which are known as power pools because the terms and conditions of trade in these cases are defined by rules that are reviewed by the FERC. The term *power pool* covers a variety of institutional arrangements but essentially refers to an organized exchange in which trade is either directed (in the most centralized case) or at least coordinated among the members (FERC, 1981).

Statistics on the magnitude of wholesale markets and their composition are complex. Accounting practices are not standardized. Estimates of the size of "economy energy" transactions range from roughly 10% of sales in the New York Power Pool, to about 1% of sales for the Western Systems Power Pool (Strategic Decisions Group, 1991). At the other extreme, the total amount of purchased power (or alternatively, "Sales for Resale") reported by EIA at the national level is 35 to 37% of all production (Energy Information Administrations, EIA, 1991a). The larger figure includes the full spectrum of transactions including sales from private producers to utilities (about 3.5% of production), wholesale firm sales from investor-owned utilities to government-owned utilities, wholesale firm sales from government entities to public and private utilities (at least 6% of production), and the whole range of firm and nonfirm trade among investor-owned firms.

Investment behavior

Mismatches between supply and demand were particularly severe during the 1970s and 1980s as the size of generating units grew and construction lead time lengthened. At first, the issue was potential capacity deficiencies. During the 1970s, the requirements for environmental review of power plant construction became much greater than they had been previously. The Supreme Court ruled in 1971 that nuclear power plant proposals needed environmental impact reports before they could receive construction permits. This caused considerable delay between planning and construction. Repeated changes in safety requirements, particularly following the accident at Three Mile Island in 1979, lengthened construction and added to its cost. The oil price shock of 1973–4 made the economics of coal and nuclear power projects more attractive, but the contemporaneous rate increases also reduced demand growth. By the late 1970s, short-run marginal costs were high, reserve margins were low, and the backlog of large-scale construction projects was substantial.

This process began to reverse itself in the 1980s. Oil prices began a gradual decline. A severe economic recession reduced demand growth. Utilities began to cancel plans for capacity expansion. In the 1972 to 1974 period utilities ordered 107 nuclear plants. Between 1975 and 1978, 38 were canceled and another 48 were canceled in the 1979 to 1982 period (EIA, 1983). Despite these efforts to adjust supply, there was substantial excess capacity during the mid-1980s. The cost disallowances described briefly in the next section were based in part upon excess capacity considerations.

Table 5-5 shows the capacity balance for the period from 1966 to 1990. Reserve margin is used as the best single summary statistic measuring the adequacy of capacity relative to demand. A conventional industry rule of thumb for reserve margin (measured as the percentage of capacity above peak demand) is 20%. This is often related to some probabilistic measure of outage risk, but the appropriate outage risk level is usually specified by convention, rather than by economic criteria. The Table 5-5 data are at the aggregate national level. The noncoincident peak means just the sum of the highest demands, regardless of when during the year it occurred. As such, these data conceal regional variations, and probably understate effective reserves because of potential capacity sharing when peak loads occur at different times. Table 5-5 clearly shows the excess capacity period from 1974 to 1989.

For most of its history, the electric utility industry has had the greatest demand for investment capital of any U.S. industry. The tendency to invest large sums of capital has been attributed to the form of regulation, which provides earnings in proportion to investment cost. Averch and Johnson (1962) argued that rate-of-return regulation leads to an inefficient use of capital. When the regulator sets the allowed rate-of-return above the cost of capital, the utility will use more capital than if it were unregulated and will choose an inefficiently high capital/labor ratio for its level of output. Most tests of the Averch–Johnson hypothesis, based on data before 1973, have demonstrated a bias toward capital (see, for example, Courville, 1974). However, this could be explained by other factors, such as risk-averse behavior by managers.

After 1973 the applicability of the Averch–Johnson analysis to utility behavior and the relevance of its assumptions are questionable. Between 1973 and the mid-1980s, electric utilities probably earned less than the cost of capital. Yet the inertia of their investment program was so great that their demand for capital (even net of canceled projects) remained at historically high levels. After the 1970s projects for generation of power were complete, and cost dis-

Table 5-5. *Aggregate capacity, peak demand, and reserve margins*

Year	Capability (million kW)	Noncoincident peak	Reserve margin (percentage)
1966	241	204	18.1
1967	259	214	21.0
1968	280	239	17.2
1969	301	258	16.7
1970	328	275	19.3
1971	354	293	20.8
1972	383	320	19.7
1973	417	345	20.9
1974	444	349	27.2
1975	479	356	34.6
1976	499	371	34.5
1977	517	395	30.9
1978	546	408	33.8
1979	557	409	36.2
1980	570	437	30.4
1981	595	439	35.5
1982	593	420	41.2
1983	596	447	33.3
1984	615	459	34.0
1985	645	470	37.2
1986	649	480	35.2
1987	648	497	30.4
1988	675	529	27.6
1989	681	523	30.2
1990	685	558	22.7

allowances began to occur, utility management began to adopt a "capital aversion" strategy. In many areas excess capacity eliminated the need for new investment. In those segments where investment was required, the opposite of the Averch–Johnson behavior seems to have occurred, with only the most minimal capital investment taking place. This consists of either a decision to purchase capacity from others, or investment in low-cost combustion turbines rather than more capital-intensive base-load facilities. It is unclear whether this is a long-term phenomenon or only a transient phase. For the most part, the financial condition of investor-owned utilities has improved in the past few years. The allowed return may now be higher than the cost of capital (the necessary condition for Averch–Johnson behavior). This would argue for a return to more standard behavior.

Table 5-6. *Construction expenses of investor-owned utilities (billions of 1982 dollars)*

Year	Total construction	Generation	Transmission	Distribution
1973	31.0	17.4	3.9	7.3
1974	31.8	18.7	3.9	6.7
1975	27.3	17.0	3.0	5.2
1976	29.2	19.1	2.9	4.7
1977	32.2	21.8	2.6	5.1
1978	33.8	22.7	2.4	5.5
1979	34.7	23.7	2.7	5.6
1980	33.0	22.4	2.7	5.3
1981	32.7	22.3	2.4	4.9
1982	35.3	25.3	2.2	4.8
1983	37.3	24.0	2.2	4.8
1984	31.0	22.2	2.0	5.5
1985	28.0	19.3	1.6	6.0
1986	25.7	16.3	1.5	6.3
1987	21.7	12.3	1.8	6.3
1988	18.0	8.2	1.6	6.8
1989	18.3	7.8	2.0	6.9
1990	17.0	6.6	1.8	6.8

Table 5-6 gives aggregate data on the capital expenditures of the investor-owned segment from 1973 to 1990. The tremendous inertia of the commitment to nuclear power is indicated by comparing these data with those of Table 5-5. At the very time when price-induced declines in demand were increasing excess capacity, the capital budget of the industry was escalating substantially.

The Table 5-6 data are also interesting in the more recent period. The rapid decline in investment in the generation sector explains most of the decline in total construction. The only offsetting effect is an increase in distribution system investment, which increased by 40% from 1982 to 1990. These data suggest that although the vertically integrated firms are losing control of the generation segment (see Part III), they are relatively free to shift investment attention to the distribution segment, which is free from competitive pressures. There is no incentive to increase transmission investment because it would inevitably end up strengthening the competitive position of independent generators seeking wider markets.

Political economy of regulation

Dominance of the investor-owned model

There has always been, and continues to be, a great variety of organizational forms in the U.S. electric utility industry. Within this variety, however, the investor-owned firm, subject to state regulation, emerged as the dominant model and remains so today. Unlike most other industrial countries, the U.S. electricity industry has never been nationalized. It is not entirely clear why this is the case. Clearly, the strong judicial system in the United States and the constitutional commitment to the enforcement of property rights prevents conversion of private property to public use without fair compensation. Yet nationalization of electric power has occurred in other countries with strong property rights (such as the United Kingdom and France). Two hypotheses suggest themselves, however: (1) geographical diffusion (the "wide-open-spaces" theory), and (2) the relative lack of devastating destruction (the "no-land-wars" theory).

The geographical argument has both a technological and an institutional dimension. A nationalized industry will be operated in some sense as a single system. Whether this means "single area dispatch" or a national grid in some literal sense is unclear. But a nationalized system will have a central locus of decisionmaking that can be expected to be in the political capital of the nation state. The determination of standards and practices will emanate from such a center, with relatively little input from provincial interests. The U.S. history of localism in political decisionmaking is not consistent with a national scale model. Political struggles over the balance of power in the federal system are endemic in U.S. history.

Typically, it is national crises that have accelerated the gathering of political power in the national government. Indeed, the economic problems of the 1930s did have this effect to a certain degree in the United States. The federal role in hydroelectric power development grew to be an important force starting in the 1930s, as indicated earlier. But even these activities had a distinctly regional flavor to them. Where federal agencies were created for power development and marketing, they were dedicated to regional economic development mandates. The municipal preference for federal power helped to improve the competitive position of public utilities vis-à-vis investor-owned firms. But by propping up these small entities, the federal government was curtailing the consolidation of the industry into larger and larger units.

Consolidation did occur in the investor-owned segment of the industry, but there was less than could be justified on the basis of economies of scale. Table 5-7 shows the number of firms operating in certain individual states during the period from 1938 to 1968, as well as national totals. The rate of consolidation appeared to have slowed after the 1950s. Christensen and Green (1976), using

Table 5-7. *Number of investor-owned firms*

State	1938	1948	1958	1968
California	8	7	5	3
Illinois	16	16	9	8
Massachusetts	43	36	25	16
New Jersey	5	7	6	5
New York	22	19	14	8
Ohio	15	13	11	8
Pennsylvania	22	21	18	12
National total	412	321	265	236

data from the 1970s estimate a statistical model indicating that economies of scale at the firm level were not completely exploited until firms reach a capacity of 4,000 MW. Joskow and Schmalensee (1983) raise questions about the validity of such estimates, but still accept the notion that unexploited scale economies are prevalent at the firm level (as opposed to the plant level). The source of these firm level economies has not been clearly identified, but appears to lie in multi-plant coordination to meet demand fluctuations. Accepting the notion that firm level economies exist at least up to the level of 4,000 MW implies that most U.S. electric utilities are too small.

Productivity stagnation and its consequences

The U.S. regulatory system functioned smoothly during the post–World War II period as long as productivity increases continued. When these stagnated and began to reverse themselves in the 1970s and early 1980s, the system came under strain. The regulatory response to these conditions was a variety of experiments. We give here a brief overview of these experiments, some of which will be examined in more detail later.

The locus of productivity problems in electricity was in new generating capacity. Initially, the problem had its origin in the increased stringency of environmental regulation. The Clean Air Act and the requirements of the National Environmental Policy Act raised the cost of new power plants by requiring extensive review of the impact of new facilities and imposing mitigation costs. Increasingly stringent environmental regulation also affected nuclear power. Following the Three Mile Island accident of 1979, increased safety regulation required considerable extra work on a large number of plants under construction. The high interest rates during this period, slow growth, and management inefficiency also had negative impacts on construction costs. When plants entered commercial operation in the early 1980s, their nominal dollar costs were frequently five to ten times higher than original estimates.

Standard regulatory practice in the United States defers including new plant costs in rates until commercial operation. Then, the costs are placed into "rate base" and become part of the total cost of service to be recovered in rates. A crucial step in this process is the determination that the costs were prudently incurred and that the projects are "used and useful." The large costs of nuclear power projects focused more attention on these questions than they had previously received. State commissions refused to accept all costs. Disallowances in the range of 10 to 40% became frequent during the 1983–7 period. The total disallowance has been estimated at $10 billion (Oak Ridge National Laboratories, 1987, 1989). Sometimes the rationale for disallowance was "imprudence"; sometimes it was excess capacity. In the latter case, the utility would eventually recover some of the costs as demand increased.

The disallowance experience (which was not confined to nuclear plants) created strong incentive effects. Utilities that were punished financially had a disincentive for investment. Regulators, disappointed with the performance of firms, developed a more activist stance regarding alternative resource strategies. A number of state jurisdictions implemented performance incentive schemes for base-load power plants. Joskow and Schmalensee (1986) found that these were the dominant type of incentive mechanisms adopted in the U.S. electricity industry. The productivity of capital-intensive base-load power plants depends considerably on their level of output. Through a system of rewards and penalties, regulators hoped to induce good performance and lower overall cost. The effect of these incentives is doubtful. Berg and Jeong (1991) studied these programs and found that a measure of cost inefficiency is a good predictor of the agency's decision to adopt incentive mechanisms. Unfortunately, they found that firm efficiency does not improve as a result of these mechanisms. Presumably such results, if correct, occur because the incentive is limited to only part of a firm's behavior and not all of it.

The search for alternatives

More substantial discipline can be imposed on the firm through various forms of competition. There has always been a certain amount of interfuel competition, but it is usually limited to certain demand segments. The residential space heating and water heating are two such segments; industrial demand is another. In many precision applications, electricity is winning market share. Frequently, interfuel competition involves pricing strategies that push prices closer to marginal costs. The regulatory rationale for these prices, however, seldom invokes economic efficiency arguments but instead focuses on the desirability of retaining customers to contribute to system overhead costs.

Yardstick and franchise competition among regulated utilities play even more limited roles. There are cases when utilities compete for customers where franchise boundaries are loose or indistinct. Commonly, this competition is based upon price. Similarly, government-owned utilities of various kinds compete with investor-owned firms by offering lower prices. The economic performance of government-owned utilities is quite variable. When they are well managed, endowed with low-cost resources, or both, they can offer distinct advantages. In other cases, poor management and inefficiencies have led to their eventual absorption by investor-owned utilities. Studies of the relative efficiency of government-owned versus investor-owned electric utilities have detected no significant differences (Atkinson and Halvorsen, 1986).

By far the greatest competitive pressure comes from bypass in its various forms and from private power generation. These two forms of competition have several points of overlap and some distinct differences. The main form of bypass is self-generation by industrial firms. This usually takes advantage of opportunities that are not available to the utility. The two primary sources of efficiency are the use of waste fuels and cogeneration (i.e., useful application of industrial process heat produced jointly with electric power). Bypass can also occur if a customer can get delivery over the transmission network of power produced by someone other than the franchised utility. Transmission service of this kind is generally unavailable for ultimate customers but can be obtained by publicly owned utilities. Thus, municipalities may bypass investor-owned firms and get their former supplier to transmit the power supplied by a competing firm.

Frequently, industrial firms that seek the self-generation alternative find it economic to invest in facilities that have substantially greater capacity than the on-site requirements. In this case, the extra capacity is sold to the franchised utility under the Public Utilities Regulatory Policies Act (PURPA) rules. The economic opportunity depends critically on the prices and other terms offered for wholesale power, which are strongly influenced by the regulatory commission. By making the terms attractive, the regulator can encourage alternate, competitive suppliers that will take some of the native supply market away from the franchised utility (see Part II).

Regulation also can affect the market position of the utility by mandating demand-side policies. These interventions, primarily emphasizing conservation and load management technologies, became increasingly common in the latter half of the 1980s under the general heading of "least-cost utility planning." The basic perception here was that conservation represented the least social-cost approach to meeting the demand for electricity services but that market failures were limiting its role. Therefore, utility regulation should intervene to address this concern (Krause and Eto, 1988).

Demand-side interventions come in a wide variety of forms and with a multiplicity of objectives. Load management is typically a set of activities directed at reducing consumption for relatively brief periods of time when systemwide demand is at or near its peak levels. This can be done by using hardware devices aimed at specific end-uses, or more broadly with rate incentives to customers who select their own curtailment procedures. Conservation programs have potentially larger impacts on the utility because they affect a bigger fraction of sales. It is not in the utility's financial interest to pursue conservation activities unless the avoided cost of reduced sales exceeds the lost revenue. Although this may occur near times of peak load (thus making load management attractive), it is less likely for the broad spectrum of conservation opportunities. Thus regulators need to motivate utilities to pursue conservation though incentive mechanisms if these policies are to be pursued. Evaluating particular utility interventions on the demand-side can be extremely difficult. Sometimes, these programs are economic (Train and Ignelzi, 1987), but in other cases the costs of conservation have greatly exceeded the cost of supply (Joskow and Marron, 1993). As the range and scope of these efforts increases and becomes more varied (see Nadel, 1991), it will be more difficult to assess meaningfully the claims made on behalf of these efforts.

The political economy of deregulation

The first steps toward deregulation in the United States, the passage of the PURPA legislation and its implementation, were taken as a response to the problems of the nuclear power industry. Vigorous growth of the private power industry created constituencies that lobbied for the expansion of this sector at the expense of the investor-owned firms. This process eventually contributed to the passage of the Energy Policy Act of 1992 (discussed at greater length in Part III), which substantially expanded the rights of these producers.

These transformations were constrained to occur with no major disruption to existing stakeholders. Asset write-downs were limited, bankruptcies few. The contrast with drastic government intervention in other countries, however, is remarkable. Nationalization as a remedy of last resort is virtually absent from political discussion of the problems and solutions proposed for the electricity sector. The highly fragmented industry structure makes any kind of nationalization a formidable political and administrative task. It also limits the ability to achieve rapid, large-scale privatization.

Appraisal of economic performance

Because retail rates deviate from marginal costs, the electricity system in the United States is less efficient than it could be, given its existing capital stock.

Gilbert and Henly (1991) have estimated the welfare losses from inefficient pricing for Northern California. They find that annual losses amount to about 7% of costs for the conditions that they examine. If these results were scaled up to the level of the U.S. industry as a whole, then welfare losses would be about $12 billion annually.

It is interesting to compare the magnitude of this efficiency loss to productive inefficiencies in the firm. These can be measured in a variety of ways. One approach would be to focus on excessive employment. It is widely believed that utilities in developing countries use an excessive amount of unproductive labor. Similar assertions have been made about the situation in industrialized countries. As a rough approximation, we can estimate that the amount of employment in the U.S. electricity industry could be reduced by as much as 20% with no decline in service quality. Total employment in the industry is approximately 600,000 (Energy Information Administration, 1995). We estimate that the total wage bill is approximately $30 billion. Therefore, efficiency gains from streamlined labor practices would be about $6 billion annually.

A third area in which economic performance might improve is in the efficiency of investment. Experience with competitive bidding for electric generating capacity suggests that cost efficiencies are possible in that segment. Estimates of cost reductions compared to the behavior of regulated firms indicate benefits of 10 to 15% (Kahn, 1991). For a steady-state capital requirement of about $30 billion per year for generation, the potential efficiencies from competition in the new-capacity segment of electricity generation are about $3 to $4.5 billion annually.

Part II. Competitive bidding and independent power

Introduction

The creation of an unregulated independent power industry in the United States began incrementally and without explicit central policy design as a result of a number of separate legal, regulatory, and economic changes. The major watershed event was the passage of the Public Utilities Regulatory Policies Act (PURPA) of 1978, which created a class of private suppliers, called Qualifying Facilities (QFs) that were exempt from profit regulation and entitled to sell their output to franchised utilities. In some states, the terms of purchase were so attractive that development of QF capacity overwhelmed expectations. In response, utilities and regulators sought mechanisms to ration the supply efficiently. The result was a competitive bidding process for long-term power sales contracts. This mechanism has proved to be so sufficiently flexible and attractive to both buyers and sellers that it has been broadened to include new classes of suppliers: first, Independent Power Producers (IPPs), and more recently Exempt Wholesale Generators (EWGs). Together these new entrants are expected to sustain a significant share of the market for new generating capacity. In this part we describe the background and development of the private power industry and characterize its current state.

The Public Utilities Regulatory Policies Act of 1978

PURPA opened the door to competitively supplied power in the United States, but with considerable restrictions. Under PURPA, a Qualifying Facility could have production capacity of no more than 50 MW, unless it used either renewable fuels or cogeneration, the combined production of useful heat and power in a single process. Although PURPA legislation set a general framework for QF development, implementation was delegated to state regulatory commissions. FERC was mandated to write rules that state commissions had to follow in their deliberations. The two irreducible requirements of the legislation and FERC rules were the obligation placed upon utilities to purchase QF output and the avoided-cost concept as the guide to determining the purchase price. In this section we review these issues.

The primary obligation PURPA placed on utilities was the requirement to purchase QF output. Absent such an obligation, private suppliers had little or no bargaining power with the utility. Prior to PURPA, some utilities did purchase a minor amount of private power, principally from industrial self-generators selling excess production. PURPA required that all utilities create a tariff under which they would purchase from QFs (tariffs were also required for backup and related services from the utility). The FERC rules also allowed for long-term purchase contracts between utilities and QFs but did not require these.

In practice, the difference between tariff and contract turned out to be decisive. Private investors were reluctant to support projects whose revenue was based on revisable tariffs. Because many projects were financed on a "standalone" basis, long-term pricing certainty was necessary to support the project's credit (Kahn, 1988, Ch. 6). In states where regulators were sympathetic to QF development, utilities were encouraged or required to make available long-term contracts. These contracts typically had standard language that defined mutual relationships explicitly or at least substantially narrowed the room for negotiation. The availability of standard contracts frequently made all the difference with regard to development. For example, the staff of the New Jersey Board of Public Utilities found that when only tariffs were offered, the response was minimal. When long-term contracts were offered, the response was substantial (New Jersey Board of Public Utilities, 1986).

The need for long-term contracts to stimulate investment in private power probably results from the immobility of generating assets. The obligation to purchase is limited to the utility serving the region in which the QF is located. Transmission access has been quite limited, so QFs have very little ability to seek other buyers. Wholesale transactions are generally limited to interutility exchanges. Therefore, because the utility is a monopsony buyer and can potentially limit or manipulate the purchase price for QF output, the seller needs a long-term contract with fixed prices to limit opportunism.

PURPA defined the pricing rule in both the long and short run by using the notion of avoided cost. The fundamental idea underlying the avoided-cost concept was that ratepayers should be indifferent to QF purchases. This meant that any economic rent accruing from QF efficiency would flow to the private producers, not to utility ratepayers. State implementation of the avoided-cost concept focused on the substantial practical problems of estimating what constituted ratepayer indifference.

The distinction between the costs of avoided energy and avoided capacity is basic. The former is appropriately measured by considering the operations and dispatch of the power system (see, for example, Jabbour, 1986). The latter is essentially a reliability issue; capacity costs are incurred to reduce the probability that shortages will occur. Where utilities had excess capacity, avoided costs were predominantly associated with energy. Where utilities had capacity requirements, both terms had to be considered, commonly in a framework that examined a wide range of options in generation technology. In practice, utilities and state commissions negotiated estimates of avoided cost. The boundaries of these negotiations could be broad, requiring compromises between precision and ease of estimations.

Seen broadly, the avoided-cost dialogue is part of the "cost unbundling" process in which the underlying cost structure of the firm gets examined with increasing sophistication and depth. Cost unbundling is common in regulated industries under competitive pressure (Bailey, 1986). What is different in this case is that a competitive fringe of firms audits the costs of the incumbent by litigation in regulatory proceedings. The advantage of this arrangement is that the regulatory process can compel disclosure that otherwise would not occur. The disadvantage is that the competitors are seeking economic rents in their use of the regulatory process, so their auditing function is not necessarily unbiased.

Competitive bidding for private power

Competitive bidding for long-term contracts emerged as a successor to the "first-come/first-served" rationing mechanism associated with standard offers. The bid evaluation process requires complex trade-offs. Proposed projects differ by their fuel type, level of development, location in the transmission network, environmental effects, and operational flexibility, as well as price. Because it is difficult to compare all these attributes with a common metric, it is inevitable that qualitative judgment will play a role in the evaluation process.

Competitive bidding brought product differentiation to the independent power market. One important dimension for this involved operational flexibility. The PURPA obligation to purchase QF power meant that all such production was "must take" in nature. A number of factors, however, led to increasing operational problems on power systems, especially during off-peak periods. The fundamental problem is an excess of inflexible generation at these times, relative to demand (Le, et al., 1991). Thus, the demand for more flexible operation became great, and utilities began to require this in their requests for bids. Analytic problems associated with bid evaluation in this setting are described in Kahn, Marnay, and Berman (1992).

One of the principal motivations for competitive bidding is to lower the cost of power. Although evidence is fragmentary, there is reason to believe that prices are coming down. Table 5-8 from Comnes, Belden, and Kahn (1995) shows for a small sample of projects that prices are getting lower over time. These data are not without ambiguity and require some discussion. Furthermore, there is a variety of nonprice terms that affect the overall value of the projects. The nonprice terms involve either operational flexibilities or contractual performance requirements. Broadly speaking, the more recent projects offer the utilities more operating freedom and stricter contract terms. Kahn (1991) gives an account of the trend toward stricter contract terms. A brief explanation of the Table 5-8 data should make clear the extent to which clear conclusions are possible.

The data given in Table 5-8 are denominated in levelized nominal 1994$ over the contract term which is at least 20 years in length. This sample represents roughly one-sixth of the private power projects that entered service during the 1990–3 period, but most of that was based on standard offer contracts. This sample represents at least half of the projects acquired by some kind of competitive process. Within this sample, the coal-fired projects are an average 2.4¢/kWh, or 35%, more expensive than the gas-fired projects. In quantity terms, gas clearly dominates the market.

Broadly speaking, the coal-fired projects represent avoided cost expectations that were higher than subsequent developments proved to be justified. The dominance of gas-fired generation was due to both falling commodity costs for fuel and the rapid introduction of highly efficient combined cycle technology based on advanced combustion turbines. This technology has relatively modest capital costs and thermal efficiencies that exceed 45% (Beck, 1993).

Table 5-8. *Prices of private power projects*

Fuel type	Project name	Contract capacity (MW)	Capacity $/kW-yr	20-Year levelized prices	
				Energy $/kWh	Total 80% cf $/kWh
Coal	Indiantown Cogen	300	351	0.035	0.085
	Chambers (Carneys Point)	184	324	0.042	0.088
	Crown Vista	100	523	0.029	0.104
Average			400	0.035	0.092
Gas	Hermiston	409	181	0.020	0.045
	Independence	740	43	0.049	0.055
	Hopewell Cogen	248	150	0.035	0.056
	Richmond Power Ent./				
	SJE Cogen	210	145	0.036	0.057
	Doswell	600	171	0.033	0.057
	North Las Vegas	45	199	0.030	0.058
	Spanaway (Pierce Co., Wa.)	240			0.060
	Gordonsville/				
	Turbo Power I and II	100	128	0.045	0.064
	Panda	165	160	0.042	0.065
	Brooklyn Navy Yard Central	90	254	0.031	0.067
	Tiger Bay	217	299	0.028	0.070
	Blue Mountain Power	150	338	0.022	0.070
	Wallkill	95	269	0.034	0.072
	Brooklyn Navy Yard B	40	277	0.036	0.075
	Brooklyn Navy Yard A	40	278	0.036	0.076
	Linden	594	266	0.041	0.079
	Pedricktown	106	234	0.050	0.083
	Holtsville	136	251	0.050	0.085
	Dartmouth, Mass.	68	405	0.028	0.085
	Enron	83	520	0.020	0.094
Average			240	0.035	0.069
Peaker	Hartwell	303	90	0.038	0.051
	Commonwealth Atlantic	312	68	0.052	0.061
Average			79	0.045	0.056
Wind	Franklin & Somerset Co., ME	20			0.056*

*36% cf

These data are not conclusive. The number of cases reviewed is small. The productivity gains reflected in Table 5-8 may be generic to the industry, rather than a result of the superior performance of the private producers. Even if this latter hypothesis is correct, however, some of the stimulus for these gains can be attributed to competitive pressure.

Private power production offers incentives for technical innovation that are absent from rate-of-return regulation. Under the fixed-price formulas contained in private power contracts, any cost-reducing technology adopted by the supplier adds to profit. The private producer also takes the risk that the innovation adopted will not perform as expected. Regulated firms, on the other hand, must pass through to ratepayers all production economies realized through innovation. The economies do not contribute to profit. When the outcome of adopting new technology is not favorable, the regulated firm may also be denied cost recovery by the regulator (Zimmerman, 1988). These incentives may combine to bias the regulated firm away from risky new technology, while leaving the private firm neutral.

There was a significant record of new technology adoption by the private power industry during the 1980s. The first steam-injected gas turbine (STIG) was installed by a California paper mill subject to stringent requirements for air pollution control (Kolp and Moeller, 1988). The adoption of circulating fluidized bed (CFB) coal combustion was also substantially more widespread in the private power section than among regulated or government-owned utilities (Grahame, 1990). In the area of renewable energy, the solar thermal technology of Luz International was commercialized through private power contracts. Although none of this evidence conclusively proves that more innovation will occur under private power than under a regime of regulation, it is clearly suggestive.

The emergence of federal competition policy

Although the private power segment of the U.S. electricity market was almost nonexistent before 1980, by 1991 independent power producers accounted for 8.8% of all electricity sales. Regional differences in policy and resource opportunities contributed to a large variation in private power development across states. In 1991, private power accounted for 25% of sales in California, 20% in Texas, and 27% in Louisiana (Energy Information Administration, 1993). The unexpectedly large developments following PURPA stimulated a dialogue on the role of competition in electricity generation. This dialogue emerged in 1988 when FERC issued three Notices of Proposed Rulemaking (NOPRs) that addressed the commission's perceptions of appropriate reforms of the PURPA framework. Although these did not result in any explicit rule changes, they signaled a new interest in competitive mechanisms.

The FERC subsequently approved a number of wholesale transactions based on market prices that involved non-QF suppliers. The precise characterization of when a transaction qualifies for such pricing was subject to case law definition (Tenenbaum and Henderson, 1991). The FERC's activity in merger cases also showed a strong concern for competitive effects. As a condition for approving the merger of Pacific Power and Light with Utah Power and Light, specific transmission access conditions were required for third-party sellers.

In 1992, the policy agenda shifted to the legislative arena. The Energy Policy Act created a new class of private producers as part of a change in federal regulation under the Securities and Exchange Commission. The transmission access questions were also addressed in this legislation but in ways that will take time to assess.[1]

Part III. Alternative regulatory futures

Introduction

In this part we outline the generic options for regulatory policy in light of the political economy in which the electric power sector operates. We distinguish three principal alternative regulatory futures, each of which has a number of variations on the primary theme. The principal axis along which we differentiate is the role and scope of competition.

The *first* option we explore amounts to suppressing the competitive segment in generation and reverting to the traditional structure of vertically integrated franchise monopolies with rate-of-return regulation. We sketch the diagnosis on which this option is based and assess the forces that are likely to oppose this solution. The *second* option is a continuation of the current regulatory situation that has promoted more competition in generation but with only minor changes in the vertically integrated utility structure. There are problems facing this alternative. The regulator must have a strategy to "manage" the coexistence of competitive suppliers with the traditional regulated firm. Two important parts of this task are determining the incremental market share for new capacity and management of the transmission network. The *third* option is a movement toward a more radical restructuring model represented by the privatized British electricity system. The U.S. policy economy poses substantial barriers to such a movement, but it is not impossible and may represent a potentially more stable configuration than the managed-competition alternatives.

---

[1] The 1992 Energy Policy Act also addressed incentives for the development of alternative sources of electricity, which PURPA had exempted from the capacity limit for QFs. Under Title XII of the new Act, the U.S. government will pay producers of electricity from certain renewable resources a "production incentive payment" or provide tax credits. This subsidy, coupled with technological improvement, is apt to rekindle the market for renewable electric generation.

Option 1: Putting the competition genie back in the bottle

The competitive segment of the generation market is not viewed favorably by all participants in the U.S. electricity sector. The "unbundling" of generation from transmission and distribution, which has been the main channel for new entry into the industry, is not without cost. Extracting the private information about transmission costs can be very difficult and may not be worthwhile unless the benefits of competition are sufficiently great (Gilbert and Riordan, 1992; Baldick and Kahn (1993). Critics of deregulated generation assert that the apparent success of private producers was due to special regulatory treatment rather than to economic superiority. In many regions of the United States, the emergence of the private power industry is closely tied with the productivity problems of the vertically integrated firms. If these problems are viewed as transitory and solvable, then the basic traditional structure of franchised monopoly may be salvaged and revived.

The policy focus of this discussion is the role of prudence reviews. The proponents of a revitalized form of vertical integration argue that "rolling review" of utility construction projects can provide both flexibility to changing circumstances and regulatory oversight. The basic idea is that utility construction projects are reviewed periodically during their gestation. Once a certain stage of construction has been approved, there will be no further retrospective review. In this version of the regulatory compact, the firm recovers all costs that have been declared prudent but may cancel projects deemed uneconomic upon agreement with the regulator (Steinmeier, 1991).

It is hard to imagine such a system working easily. Although it would certainly protect the financial interests of the utility, it might not serve the consumer interest. The decision to declare a project uneconomic after substantial sums have been invested is politically difficult. The uncertainties surrounding any such decision are apt to produce a reluctant inertia. Ultimately, there is no competitive test for what defines an economic project.

The rolling review approach to the preservation of vertical integration as a regulated monopoly also runs into stubborn political and economic realities that threaten its viability. The private power segment has shown an ability to reduce prices to consumers and to promote technological innovation. This industry is also well represented politically and so is capable of defending its market so long as its economic claims are sustainable. Moreover, the Energy Policy Act of 1992 mandates more open access by independent power producers to transmission markets, and thus essentially bars a return to a less competitive era.

The importance of Option 1 lies in the vertical integration issue. The stark contrast drawn between complete vertical integration and its total absence is considerably overdrawn by proponents of this option. Nonetheless, there are very real questions about the role of utilities in the generation market where a competitive segment also exists. The next two options address these questions more positively.

Option 2: "Managed" competition

The U.S. electricity system is moving de facto toward a mixed system in which wholesale competition is balanced by some unclearly defined role for the traditional firm. The principal question is how the regulator will handle two structural issues: the market share in generation for the IOUs and the regulation of the distribution segment.

Allocation of market share in the generation segment

Competitive bidding for long-term contracts is the fundamental mechanism through which independent producers are entering the wholesale electricity business. The main regulatory policy question is whether this will result in a slow liquidation of the IOU role in generation. Regulatory policy amounts to deciding if and how IOUs continue to invest in generation. There are two basic alternatives: (1) explicit allocation on a case by case basis, or (2) bidding rules that allow IOU participation in the competitive process. Each of the alternatives for preserving an IOU share in the market for new generation presents its problems.

Explicit allocation may be arbitrary and subject to political manipulation. The case for it depends upon the utility having some unique asset or capability that is unavailable or more costly if acquired from independent producers. The best case of this kind involves the repowering of old powerplants. There are many aging facilities in the industry's capital stock. These plants frequently have desirable infrastructure features, including access to fuel delivery and favorable location in the transmission network. The incremental costs of adding new generation at these sites can be low compared to construction at new sites.

The case against explicit allocation is a case in favor of a bidding regime in which the utility offers projects that compete with those proposed by private developers. The problem with such a bidding arrangement is that it introduces potential biases in selection criteria. Electricity may be a fairly homogeneous product at the end-use, but power projects are quite differentiated in their features. A bid evaluation system must weigh these features against one another. The greater knowledge of value possessed by the firm makes it difficult for the regulator to know whether the bid evaluation criteria have been slanted to favor the utility project. Whatever might be gained potentially by including utility projects within the universe of bidders can be easily lost by distortion of the evaluation criteria. An important example of this problem lies in evaluating the impacts of transmission systems.

For large geographically diverse utilities such as Pacific Gas and Electric Company, Southern California Edison Company, and American Electric Power, the problems facing private suppliers are limited to negotiating with the monopsony buyer only over the terms for interconnecting with the utility transmission network. Even in this case, problems can arise when system reinforcements are necessary. Given the scale economies that are ubiquitous in transmission capacity, a reinforcement investment will typically be larger than the demands associated with individual project interconnection requirements. In this setting, conflicts over cost allocation are likely. Requiring utilities to make binding estimates of transmission interconnection costs before bidding takes place, as proposed by Pacific Gas and Electric (Shirmohammadi and Thomas, 1991), may limit opportunistic bargaining over cost allocation. However, this would not solve the problem of limited information about utility interconnection and transmission costs. With private information, utilities may earn excessive profits, or countervailing regulatory restrictions may be inefficient (Gilbert and Riordan, 1995).

The basic regulatory problem in the wholesale segment is that the utility is competing with private suppliers, yet still must act as the agent for consumer interest. These two goals can come into conflict. The locus of these conflicts frequently lies in management of the transmission system. Monopoly control of transmission can be used to put independent producers at a competitive disadvantage. Access conditions for these producers that are too liberal, however, may harm the distribution system's customers by inducing inefficient dispatch. Once again, the regulator must try to manage this conflict in the face of very little information.

Distribution system regulation

The regulatory problems in the retail distribution segment also involve questions of multiple goals. Distribution of electricity is generally assumed to be a natural monopoly and subject to franchise regulation. This raises important issues of efficient pricing and marketing of electricity, demand-side management (DSM), and investment in the distribution grid. The recent trend toward the promotion of utility DSM programs arises out of a perception that end-use efficiency is a desirable social goal that is underprovided by normal market forces. At the same time, the distribution segment of the business is not subject to much competitive pressure, so may become inefficient. The ability of regulators to encourage efficiency and promote social objectives (e.g., DSM) will be the central challenge of any future regulatory scheme. There are three generic alternatives: (1) traditional rate-of-return regulation, (2) rate-of-return regulation supplemented with targeted incentives, and (3) some form of comprehensive incentive regulation, such as yardstick mechanisms or price caps. We briefly discuss these alternatives.

Traditional rate-of-return regulation: The "business as usual" approach to regulation of the distribution segment assumes that there are no serious efficiency problems and no social goal agenda such as DSM. If the regulator does perceive such problems and goals, then the traditional approach is unlikely to be very effective.

One can already observe a shift in the investment behavior of investor-owned utilities in response to their declining market share in generation. Table 5-6 in Part I shows a rapid growth in investment in the distribution segment. Although this may be the result of long-delayed real needs in that segment, it is also possible that it is just Averch–Johnson type behavior in a protected market.

Regulation supplemented with targeted incentives: More recent trends in distribution system regulation involve targeted incentives. The principal arena in which this is occurring involves conservation and other DSM activities (Gilbert and Stoft, 1992). It may also be important in the generation business, if the utility must purchase capacity from independent suppliers, that there should be some incentives for efficient purchasing. There has been discussion of this question but virtually no concrete activity along these lines.

The main practical issues facing the targeted incentives approach are calibration of the appropriate incentive levels and finding reasonable measures of performance. It is easy to produce agreement that incentives are useful, but it is much harder to find an amount of money that is adequate to induce desirable but not excessive behavior. Similarly, the measurement of desirable performance can pose challenges. When are good outcomes due to luck or clever manipulation of the incentive scheme, rather than to efficient behavior?

If incentive mechanisms spread over a wide range of utility activity, they may begin to interact with one another. Even if that does not occur, there will still be questions of balance among the various mechanisms. Such issues motivate a broader approach to incentives, where behavioral targets are replaced by comprehensive measures of performance.

Comprehensive incentive regulation: The logical extension of targeted incentives is a regime based on a comprehensive incentive mechanism. The price-cap approach is used widely in Britain to regulate price in the natural gas, telecommunications, water, and electricity industries. Price-cap regulation uses an external price index adjusted by exogenous estimates reflecting anticipated changes in productivity and other factors (Littlechild and Beesley, 1989).

Applying a price-cap approach to electric utilities would fail to account for conservation and DSM activities. These can often raise the price of utility service, while lowering total social costs. Therefore, an alternative approach to comprehensive incentive regulation is necessary if DSM is to be incorporated into the mechanism. Suggestions along this line have been made, but as yet this approach has not been implemented.

Option 3: "Radical" restructuring: British model applied in the piecemeal American fashion

The privatization of the British electric power system implemented radical changes in regulatory policy. The British system is almost completely vertically de-integrated. Wholesale generators sell to the grid at prices that are determined in a national spot market. Regional electric distribution companies purchase their power requirements from the grid, also at spot prices. Thus, all transactions take place through the grid at market-determined prices, although nearly all buyers and sellers hedge these prices by engaging in fixed-price, long-term contracts.

Forming a centralized transmission/dispatch pooling entity in the United States would require a regional aggregation of systems. Absent a broad government mandate, such an organization would be a voluntary association led by large firms or regional government entities, at least at the start. Thus, the marriage of the transmission assets of Southern California Edison, Pacific Gas and Electric, Bonneville Power Administration, and Pacificorp, for example, would be necessary for the creation of a meaningful Pacific Coast Pool. Collecting the individually small transmission assets of a few scattered entities would not create a marketplace for wholesale electric power.

Existing generation would be transferred from rate-of-return regulation to competitive status. In the absence of large efficiency gains made possible from the transfer, the likely consequences are either that shareholders would be forced to take a loss or that distribution customers would end up paying higher prices for power from assets that they used to own. The former outcome would be resisted by utility management and the latter by regulators. Given the incentives faced by both shareholders and ratepayers, it is reasonable to expect that firms will seek to move assets out of the regulated domain as much for loss minimization as for expectations of realizing large profits.

The restructuring of the British system was the result of an executive order and was imposed over an extremely short period by American regulatory standards. In the United States, firmly embedded private property rights and a political tradition that encourages stable regulatory policies essentially prohibit the "bang-bang" restructuring approach implemented in England. If major restructuring were to be achieved in the United States, it would have to be approximated through slow and partial steps and it would apply incompletely. The highly fragmented industry structure in the United States makes full-scale rapid change virtually impossible.

Transmission – the strategic asset

Private power production will probably remain a significant feature of the generation mix. There is considerable uncertainty, however, over how large a share it may sustain. A study conducted for the Electric Power Research Institute (EPRI) projects a market share of about 30 to 45% for private producers in the next decade range (Resource Development Corporation, 1990). Representatives of the private power industry typically forecast a larger share. Much will depend upon the regulatory climate at both the state and federal levels, particularly with regard to the conditions of transmission access. For example, some potential sellers in the 1988 Virginia Power RFP were forced to drop their projects, even after their preliminary selection by the utility, because of lack of transmission from their West Virginia sites.

The alternative regulatory futures that we have characterized are chiefly distinguished by the extent to which vertical integration remains a feature of the U.S. electricity system, which in turn depends on regulatory policy with respect to the ownership of and access to transmission. Although transmission represents typically only about 10% of the delivered cost of electricity, it is a strategic asset. Wholesale trade occurs through the transmission network. More important, transmission access is the key to asset mobility for new generation capacity. The long-term contractual mechanism characteristic of private power development is a product of the limited transmission access regime in which these projects arise. If private producers had better access to the transmission system and could potentially sell to many customers, perhaps they could attract capital without the necessity of long-term contracts.

The principal area for feasible structural change is the wholesale market. The Energy Policy Act (EPAct) of 1992 has opened the door to significant change in wholesale competition by greatly extending the powers of the Federal Energy Regulatory Commission to mandate transmission access. Prior to this Act, the FERC was prevented from mandating transmission access that interfered with existing competitive relationships. This has now changed. The EPAct gives the FERC authority to mandate transmission access if the following pertain:

1. Voluntary negotiations have been conducted by the requesting entity and transmission owner for 60 days.
2. The order would be in the public interest.

3. Reliability of all utility systems affected by the order would be maintained.
4. Third-party wheeling is not subsidized by the utility's existing customers.

If the FERC has the objective of promoting wholesale transmission access, it appears that it will now have broad power to do so. The powers do not extend to transmission access at the retail level. There is substantial controversy in the United States over the issue of competition for end-use customers. Although some erosion of the franchised monopoly in distribution is likely to occur, for the most part there is a resistance to introducing retail competition on a wide scale, as is scheduled to occur in the British electric power market. For these reasons, the following scenarios presume that expanded transmission access will be necessary for wholesale, but not necessarily retail, transactions.

Alternative transmission proposals

In this section we outline four generic approaches to the organization of transmission transactions. These represent a range from current practices to reform proposals sponsored by government agencies or academics. We match each proposal against the three alternative regulatory futures sketched previously. Not every proposal fits coherently with each of these futures. Finally, we rate these proposals against several threshold conditions that each should satisfy and against certain barriers to implementation.

Business as usual: The historic form of transmission access in the United States has been to allow the owners of transmission facilities to decide upon terms and conditions without regulatory interference. This policy has not resulted in much third-party access to transmission. There has been, however, a fair amount of joint ownership of facilities. Because economies of scale are substantial in transmission capacity, projects built in the past 30 years have had an increasing amount of shared ownership. The pattern of shared ownership in new generating stations has also facilitated sharing in transmission.

In some cases, the voluntary approach has resulted in a reasonable level of trade, at least among franchised utilities. This occurs where many potential participants all have access to a particularly well-situated central location. One such "marketplace" is the Palo Verde switchyard adjacent to a large nuclear facility in central Arizona. Here buyers (primarily located in Southern California) transact with sellers (from Colorado, Utah, New Mexico, and Arizona), primarily for nonfirm energy sales at prices that are close to production costs. Such markets are relatively rare, in part because of the widespread presence of reciprocal voluntary arrangements described later.

The system of private ownership gives strong incentives for efficient transactions because utilities are in a position to appropriate benefits. The main exception to this is the externality problem of loop flow (also called *unintended power flow*). The electrical properties of the transmission network may result in unintended impacts affecting third parties who are not involved in particular exchanges. This externality is difficult to price and interferes with arranging transactions. Loop flow also interferes with incentives for investment in new transmission facilities under a system of private ownership, because investment may have uncompensated negative or positive impacts on other parties.

In principle, the "business as usual" policy might apply in either Option 1 or 2, for it does not depend upon the utility's share of generation. In practice, however, it is questionable whether this policy can be maintained any longer in the U.S. industry. The EPAct requires utilities to provide transmission services to third parties. The new law supersedes previous limitations on regulatory authority that restricted such services if they would have interfered with existing competitive arrangements. Thus, we must conclude that "business as usual" in transmission services is no longer feasible for any of the regulatory options.

It is possible that the access provisions of the Energy Policy Act could be eased in geographical regions where the underlying competitive conditions in wholesale markets are quite strong. In these situations a loose form of voluntary access may be sufficient to satisfy the requirements of the new legislation. In most cases, however, voluntary cooperation will need more explicit mechanisms, such as those discussed in the next subsection.

Regional transmission groups – reciprocal voluntary arrangements: There is a long tradition of reciprocal voluntary transmission arrangements in segments of the U.S. electricity industry. In its most elaborated form, these arrangements underlie the fully integrated power pools that operate principally in the Northeastern region. For a pooling arrangement to work, the members must be able to exchange power freely over the combined network of transmission facilities. When the pool does central dispatch of the combined generation resources, fully reciprocal use of the combined transmission network occurs.

There are looser pooling arrangements that do not involve central dispatch. In these, some form of reciprocal transmission arrangement is also necessary, but the mutual commitment is less than in the fully integrated case. "Loose" pools commonly operate a kind of brokerage service, where parties post willingness-to-buy and willingness-to-sell offers, but transactions occur through bilateral arrangement. Power pooling institutions in the United States are surveyed in FERC (1981).

The limiting cases of reciprocity are bilateral agreements to exchange transmission services and emergency support involving commitments among many participants in a transmission network. In the latter case, the agreements are only for extraordinary circumstances where reliability is involved. Such arrangements are nearly ubiquitous. Typically, the prices charged for emergency support are higher than the prices charged for routine firm and nonfirm transmission services.

In principle, reciprocal voluntary arrangements might operate in either Option 1 or 2. The requirements of the Energy Policy Act for offering transmission service might be accommodated within the framework of regional transmission groups (RTGs) that provide for reciprocal arrangements. These arrangements would be voluntary, although it is likely that they would be constrained by a constitution governing the policies of the group. There is considerable uncertainty about how and under what conditions concerning access to facilities such accommodation might or might not be achieved. One proposal would be for an RTG to develop a cost approach for transmission access that would be based on the avoided-cost principles that govern prices for qualifying facilities. This would require the following elements.

A transmission resource plan (TRP): The correct cost for transmission access is the incremental cost that a user imposes on a system. This requires an assessment of the impact that a user's demand for access would have on the current cost-minimizing plan for constructing and maintaining adequate transmission capacity to meet the needs of its members. This, in turn, requires the development of a resource plan that is accepted by the RTG members.

A cost model for the TRP: The preferred TRP would depend on the needs of the group members and on the costs of satisfying those needs. This requires the development of a transmission costing model. Such a model would compute the total present-value cost of building and maintaining a desired transmission configuration. Given the economies of scale and interdependencies of transmission costs, it is unlikely that an algorithm could be devised that would choose the optimal plan for the members' needs. Instead, several scenarios would have to be specified, and the RTG would have to narrow the search down to those plans that are most cost-effective. Finding the optimal scenario would be an iterative process. Iteration would be necessary to investigate the cost consequences of different plans. An additional complication is that users' demands for transmission services depend on their costs. Therefore, the optimal resource plan would have to be an iterated process so that demands would be consistent with the cost of the resources made available.

The incremental cost of additional demand for transmission services: If a transmission system has adequate capacity to meet all demand in the foreseeable future, the *economic* cost of transmission is only the cost of line losses and other operating costs that are directly attributable to a user's demands. If the system does not have adequate capacity, the economic cost of transmission includes the present-value of additional investment that must be incurred in order to provide the service. This is the same principle that governs the determination of avoided generation costs. The avoided energy cost is the utility's marginal operating cost. The avoided capacity cost is the present-value of the additional investment that the utility would avoid if it had another unit of capacity on the system. The latter depends not only on the cost of capacity but also on the timing of the investments that would be required to maintain adequate system reliability.

To estimate a transmission user's capacity cost, it would be necessary to evaluate the change that the user's demand imposes on the present-value cost of meeting all users' transmission needs. Although the principle is identical to the principle of avoided generation capacity costs, this is a more complicated calculation because the cost is likely to depend on the size and the location of the transmission user's demands. Qualitatively, if T is a vector of all the transmission services that are anticipated in the RTG's optimal resource plan, and if t_{ij} is transmission demand of an individual user, the capacity cost of the transmission service is

$$c(t_{ij}) = C(T + t_{ij}) - C(T),$$

where $C(\cdot)$ is the cost of the optimal resource plan corresponding to the desired services.

Allocating fixed costs: The foregoing discussion focuses on allocating costs that are incremental to the use of transmission services. Any realistic transmission proposal would have to deal with allocating the fixed costs of transmission as well – costs that are not sensitive to demand. An RTG could have wide latitude to allocate these costs among its members. There could be a cost for joining the group, a fixed charge for each transmission service (postage-stamp pricing), or nonlinear charges. These charges are not determined with the objective of allocating scarce transmission resources to their highest-value uses but, rather, to spread the fixed costs of the network.

The RTG could use a variety of measures to allocate capacity in the short run. One possibility would be the use of node pricing (to be discussed shortly). Another would be to use the avoided cost-based prices and to rely on administrative measures to deal with congested paths. However, it is unlikely that pricing would be effective as the primary instrument to allocate transmission access, coordinate its use, and plan for new resources. The bulk power grid is technically complex. It can be reasonably argued that even its current owners do not fully understand apparently simple concepts such as "capacity." Recent studies in the power engineering literature indicate the difficulty of planning in a competitive environment (Adamson et al., 1991; McCalley et al., 1991). An advantage of the RTG is that it would not be limited solely to prices as a means for allocating transmission resources. The RTG could specify conditions for access, consistent with the provisions of the Energy Policy Act. The extra flexibility to use nonprice conditions for access could lead to increased efficiency.

Centrally mandated prices: Regulatory control of transmission access at the federal level is consistent with Options 2 and 3. It is less relevant to the traditional vertically integrated utility structure of Option 1. The political pressure for mandatory access arises from both the independent power sector and the generation-deficient municipal utilities. A regime of mandatory access would look rather different in each of the options, depending upon how the federal mandate was implemented. The key variable determining the variations is the treatment of opportunity costs in the pricing of mandated transactions.

A centralized determination of the cost of transmission services has the problem that it is difficult to account for individual circumstances. The FERC has recognized that transmission services provided by a utility for third parties have opportunity costs. Moving from the principle of recognizing these costs to the practice of estimating their magnitude for pricing purposes is a substantial step. At one extreme, a liberal view of lost opportunities can result in very high estimates of an appropriate transmission price. The practical result of such estimates may be very little in the way of actual transactions. This kind of approach may result in substantial limits for third-party users. Without the ability to have low-cost access to the network, market share for the utilities is maintained.

At the opposite extreme, a verifiable standard for identifying opportunity costs may be so strict as to deny their reality in practice. A compromise solution that would recognize opportunity costs, yet allow access, would be to price access at long-run incremental cost (LRIC). Yet LRIC for firm transmission would be too high in many circumstances. The actual cost that a transmission user imposes on a system may be much less than the cost of expanding the system to satisfy that user's demand. In other situations, LRIC may be less than the true cost that a user imposes on the system. For example, LRIC might not account for siting constraints and delays that add to the cost of providing transmission services. LRIC also fails to provide users with the right signals for expansion of the network.

Another approach using centrally mandated prices would be to set a price cap, perhaps at LRIC, and allow utilities to negotiate lower prices when the market allows (see Einhorn, 1990). Although this would make regulation more flexible, it would not solve the basic problem of asymmetric information about transmission costs. The greatest potential for efficient application of a price-cap approach to the pricing of transmission access would be in geographical regions where competition is already relatively strong, as evidenced by many buyers and sellers that can access a high-voltage transmission bus. The Palo Verde switchyard in Arizona is an example, but this is more the exception than the rule in the United States.

Prices that are mandated centrally by the FERC would amount to a de facto open access system with no limits on the parties seeking to make transactions. It is difficult to imagine exactly how such a system would work in the absence of a centralized grid authority that would apply some kind of rationing method through either a price or a nonprice mechanism.

Geographical spot pricing (node pricing): The proposal for node pricing is a version of the spot pricing theory of transmission cost pricing developed by Caramanis, Bohn, and Schweppe (1986), Schweppe et al. (1988), and more fully articulated by Hogan (1992). When an electric power network is efficiently dispatched, the marginal value of transmission between any two points in the system is equal to the difference in the cost of generation at those points. The costs of generation at two points in the system may differ because there are line losses in moving power from one point to another or because transmission capacity constraints impose a congestion cost. The generation cost difference is a natural choice for the price of transmission services. At these prices, a generator should supply power to the grid if, and only if, the marginal cost of the generator plus the price of transmission to the destination is less than the marginal cost of generation at the destination.

One of the main virtues of node pricing is that it is able to deal with the troublesome problem of loop flow. In the Hogan proposal, generation is dispatched efficiently conditional on transmission constraints. Implicit prices for transmission between node i and node j are determined ex post and are equal to the differences between the costs of generation at the two nodes. If unintended power flows (loop flows) cause congestion on a transmission path, the implicit transmission price is increased. This occurs either because congestion limits the capacity on the transmission path, so that the difference in nodal generation costs increases, or because congestion leads to increased line losses, or both. Each user of transmission has to pay for the right to send power across a desired path. Provided all users subscribe to the principle of node pricing for transmission, unintended flows are properly priced because the node prices reflect the true cost, including unintended flows, of sending power across any path, whether or not that path is the physical circuit used for sending power from one node to another.

The main difference between the Schweppe version of node pricing and the Hogan version involves timing and information. Schweppe envisioned true spot markets. In the case of electricity this could mean a substantial degree of fluctuation and large informational burdens, for the relevant spot price would vary from minute to minute. Other commodity markets settle trades over much longer intervals. In natural gas, for example, the spot interval is one month. Furthermore, because of real-time network interdependencies, the true spot price is in some sense the result of dispatchers' decisions that are easier to report ex post than to forecast or communicate instantaneously. Therefore, Hogan proposes that the system be operated in the current fashion by a number of loosely coordinated control centers and that node prices be computed ex post assuming the dispatch is efficient.

Efficient dispatching is an important element of node pricing. Without efficient dispatch, generation costs at each node would not correspond to the marginal value of power, and the transmission prices would be meaningless as a measure of social value. Efficient dispatch does not mean that prices must be determined in a perfectly competitive market. Monopoly owners of transmission services may dispatch their resources efficiently. If their internal marginal generation costs were public knowledge, they could be used as the basis for transmission prices. Unfortunately, if internal values are private knowledge, a monopolist could misrepresent them in a way that would codify monopolistic pricing.

Consider a transmission monopolist who serves demand at point D, owns a line from point O to point D, and owns a generating resource with a marginal cost m at point O. Suppose the line has no losses or capacity constraints. Let p^m be the monopoly price at point D ($p^m = m \div [1 - 1/\eta]$, where η is the magnitude of the elasticity of demand at D). The monopolist's internal marginal value of power is m at both ends of the transmission line. However, suppose the monopolist could misrepresent that the internal value at point D is p^m. Node pricing would result in a cost of transmission equal to $p^m - m$, which merely would serve to sustain the transmission owner's monopoly. Of course, this inefficiency would be mitigated if the monopolist's power to misrepresent values were limited, perhaps as a result of auditing of actual transmission operations.

A second problem with node pricing is that it does not necessarily provide efficient signals for the expansion of a transmission network. Economies of scale and cost complementarities in a transmission network suggest that local prices may be a poor signal of the most desirable way to expand the network, although this is a subject for further study.

Hogan suggests that his version of node pricing is compatible with the existing institutional structure and therefore would apply to our Option 2 as a basis for pricing transmission to private producers. There is some reason to question this assertion. Implementing node pricing requires an initial definition and allocation of capacity rights. When transmission owners have private information about the network and this forms the basis of market power, it is doubtful whether a truly unbiased capacity definition and allocation process

Table 5-9. *Feasibility of transmission policies in alternative regulatory futures*

	Transmission policies			
	Business as usual	Regional transmission groups	Centrally mandated prices	Node pricing
Option 1: Vertically integrated IOUs	NA	Y	NA	NA
Option 2: Mixed VI, IOUs, and competition	NA	Y	Y	NA[a]
Option 3: Spot markets	NA	NA	Y	Y

[a]Applicable only with considerable difficulty in assigning capacity rights.

would or could occur. It is difficult enough without private information to define capacity in an electricity transmission network. When private information is ubiquitous, the prospects are dim. Therefore, it is best to think of Hogan's node pricing as applicable primarily to our Option 3, where spot markets are the dominant institution and market power issues are a less large consideration. In this kind of more competitive setting, the assumptions of Hogan's node pricing are more consistent with the institutional structure.

Summary: Table 5-9 summarizes the feasibility of each transmission proposal with respect to the regulatory-policy–industrial-structure options that we have outlined. In the next section we consider how the transmission policy alternatives might perform with respect to important economic criteria.

Policy evaluation

The feasibility of a transmission policy in a particular regulatory regime says nothing about its desirability. In this subsection we examine more closely the performance (or potential performance) of the transmission proposals with respect to important economic criteria. The criteria we consider are: (1) efficient dispatch, (2) reliability, (3) choice of service quality, and (4) incentives for efficient investment.

Efficient dispatch: The existing institutions in the United States provide for reasonable efficiency in the use of generating resources. This is accomplished in the "business as usual" scenario by central dispatching of units within a utility's control area. Regional transmission groups could preserve centralized dispatching, as demonstrated by the operations of existing power pools. Node pricing implicitly assumes centralized dispatching. Without efficient dispatch, node prices are unreliable indicators of transmission costs.

Clumsy regulatory intervention may have more potential to cause harm than improvement in the use of existing assets. The mandated access policy carries the greatest risk in this regard. If mandated access results in a pattern of generation that displaces efficient production with inefficient production, then it is not clear whether the net effect is positive.

Reliability: The existing bulk power system was built with reliability objectives in mind. As wholesale trade has increased, there has been a growing perception among power engineers that the safety margin has declined. To a large degree, reliability in the bulk power system is a coordination problem. The interconnectedness of the network means that many real-time actions are required to control or contain disturbances that may originate locally but that propagate throughout the system. Although new technology is increasingly available to improve response time and automate coordinated response, this is offset by increasing the number of entities involved in managing or using the network.

The transmission policies are differentiated along this dimension in much the same way as they are with regard to efficient dispatch. Existing institutions, either "business as usual" or regional transmission groups, are capable of maintaining a high level of reliability. Mandated access could cause some stresses by overloading particular links or failing to require sufficient emergency coordination obligations. Node pricing should result in high levels of reliability because centralized dispatching is assumed.

Choice of service quality: Transmission services can be differentiated according to several characteristics. These include the extent to which the service is firm, the probability of forced outages, the voltage level (and whether transmission is ac or dc), and the location of the service (point-to-point vs. area-wide). Users of transmission services value these characteristics differently, and proposals that allow choice in service qualities are likely to make better use of scarce transmission resources.

Both "business as usual" and regional transmission groups permit the design of pricing alternatives for transmission services with different qualities. In node pricing, each holder of a transmission capacity right is entitled to firm service over a contract path. Thus, all services are "notionally firm" in the node pricing methodology. This is a disadvantage of this costing proposal, because it does not allow purchasers of transmission rights to elect different qualities of service.

Centrally mandated prices are unlikely to provide for choices in service quality. If prices are based on the costs of transmission upgrades, the implied service quality would be firm. Under these conditions, transmission access would be required to be purchased on a firm basis when buyers might prefer a lower-cost nonfirm service.

Efficient investment: This criterion speaks to the long-run evolution of the electricity market. Transmission capacity is, by and large, a scarce resource. Any policy must encourage efficient expansion of the system. Existing institutions have been moderately successful at this process but not enormously. With respect to incentives for new investment, the main difficulty with the "business as usual" approach has been incomplete coordination among transmission owners who are affected by expansion decisions.

Most of the reform proposals promise to do worse instead of better. Centrally mandated prices are likely to lead to inefficient investment in the network. If buyers of transmission services have the right to force expansion when service is not available, the result may be too much expansion or expansion at the wrong place or time and in the wrong amount. If transmission owners are not obligated to expand, centrally determined prices that allow the owner only to break even could result in too little investment. Owners of the assets would not achieve any substantial benefit from such investments and could suffer competitive losses by strengthening the position of others.

Node pricing would promise efficient signals for new investment only if the transmission cost function is well behaved (i.e., concave). Unfortunately, there is every reason to believe that this is not the case (see, for example, Baldick and Kahn, 1993).

The regional transmission group allows a forum for the evaluation of alternative options to expand the network in a cost-efficient manner. Although private interests will attempt to promote a transmission resource plan that minimizes their individual costs, this strategizing can be checked through administrative oversight. Although RTGs may encounter strategizing behavior by members that would distort investment decisions, they may improve on "business as usual" by resolving impacts on neighboring transmission systems. Both the costs of strategizing and the ability to internalize transmission impacts depend on the judicious choice of the size of the regional transmission group and on the conditions for membership.

Summary: We summarize this discussion in Table 5-10, where we rate the policy alternative by high performance (H), medium (M), or low (L). Consistent with the requirements of the Energy Policy Act of 1992, all the policy options assume a system of open access to wholesale generators. This is a significant departure for the "business as usual" option. It is included primarily as a benchmark against which the other options may be evaluated.

Table 5-10. *Rating transmission proposals on key criteria*

	Criteria			
	Efficient Dispatch	Reliability	Choice of service quality	Efficient investment
Businss as usual	H	H	H	M
Regional transmission groups	H	H	H	M-H
Centrally mandated prices	M	M	L	L
Node pricing[a]	H	H	L	L

[a]Assumes central dispatching.

The value of competition in regulated industries

In this section we look broadly at the value of competition in regulated industries, where the focus of competition policy should lie in this industry, what guidelines the regulator should observe, and what sort of an institution the regulated firm becomes under a regime in which competition is mixed with regulation.

Independent producers as auditors

Recent theory on regulation consistently raises the theme of imperfect information. The Principal–Agent theory casts the regulated firm in the role of an agent that is acting on behalf of a social regulatory principal. The principal is nominally in charge of the agent but can monitor the agent's behavior to only a limited degree (Baron and Besanko, 1984; Laffont and Tirole, 1986). In such a setting, the competitive fringe can become a valuable auditing tool for the regulator by helping to uncover the true costs of the regulated firm.

This framework is particularly relevant to private power, where the avoided-cost concept provides a natural opportunity to observe the cost structure of the regulated firm. Private producers have a strong economic incentive to discover the costs of the regulated firm, because these costs become the basis on which they will be paid. Avoided cost also provides a framework in which to pursue more general regulatory goals. Thus, the tendency of regulators to use avoided costs for other regulatory functions (such as evaluating demand-side programs) indicates these costs' importance as a cost-revelation process. The intricate computer simulation modeling used in the California regulatory process also facilitates the unbundling process, whereby the different aspects of cost of service become better-defined and measurable. Presumably, it is the profit motive of the private producers that makes them a superior auditor of the regulated firm. By contrast, the regulatory agency itself is weaker, less capable, and less motivated than the private producers are.

In practice, the audit function will occur in two distinct settings. Private producers being paid on some kind of short-run marginal-cost or avoided-cost basis will focus attention primarily on the operational characteristics of the regulated firm. If the regulated firm is operating an overly constrained system, so that plants must be run even if the power is not needed, then marginal and avoided costs will be low compared to a more optimal configuration. Many operating constraints limit power system flexibility – in particular the off-peak "minimum load" problem is fairly widespread (Le et al., 1991). Private producers being paid avoided cost are in a position to propose changes in operating procedures that will lower total costs and raise their own payments.

The other setting in which the private producers may serve the audit function involves long-run capacity acquisition. Here, too, the regulated firm must defend either its selection method, or its results, or both to the regulatory commission. The private producers have the opportunity to participate in adjudication of this kind and try to influence the process in a direction beneficial to their interests.

The auditing function of the private producers is not a shortcut to eliminate all regulatory oversight. The self-interested positions adopted by private producers in adjudication do not necessarily reveal the truth. Although they can frequently shed light on inefficient operating practices or planning procedures, positive recommendations will necessarily involve strategic goals. Private producers will always see in any situation substantial avoided costs, the demand for more power, and the corresponding higher costs of acquiring it. Regulatory scrutiny must extend to these claims as well.

The usefulness of the paradigm of competitor as auditor for understanding the role of private power depends upon the ultimate market share. What if the competitive fringe can expand its control of the market and become the dominant source of supply? Then the audit function will ultimately be replaced by market forces acting to control supplier behavior. This outcome is fairly remote at the current stage of development. Moreover, it will be very difficult to determine for quite some time what the ultimate prospects may be for the fully competitive outcome. These uncertainties motivate our discussion of the next issue.

Can the wholesale power market be competitive?

If the answer to this question is yes, then regulation of bulk power supplies will ultimately wither away. If the answer is no, then regulators will have to decide whether protecting the independent private power sector is worthwhile to preserve the benefits of the auditing function that we have described and the increased potential for technological innovation.

A major factor affecting this decision is the role of unregulated utility affiliates. At least 40 investor-owned utilities have formed affiliated or subsidiary companies that now participate in the private power market (Resource Development Corporation, 1990). There is a potential for abusive self-dealing under these circumstances that has already been identified. One well-publicized case of this kind involves Southern California Edison (SCE) and its affiliate Mission Energy. Mission Energy is a 50% partner in the Kern River Cogeneration Company (KRCC), a large QF that sells power to SCE. The California Public Utilities Commission (CPUC) found that the contract between KRCC and SCE was overpriced. The difficulty involved contract clauses that essentially allowed nonfirm power delivery conditions, while paying prices that were intended for firm capacity. The CPUC disallowed the collection of the difference between the nonfirm value and the contract capacity price, which amounted to $48 million with interest (CPUC, 1990).

Concerns similar to those in the Mission Energy–KRCC–SCE case may follow from an increasingly dominant role of utility affiliates in the private power market. There may be a danger of reciprocal dealing, where the affiliates of two regional utilities and their corresponding regulated cousins agree to collude with one another. Regulated firm A may contract exclusively, or preferentially, with the affiliate of firm B, and regulated firm B deals exclusively, or preferentially, with the affiliate of A. Other forms of collusion are also possible.

It is useful to inquire about the forces that would produce a private power industry structure dominated by unregulated utility affiliates. Several trends favor market domination by affiliated producers. On the cost side, competitive bidding for long-term contracts has effectively raised entry barriers against small firms. Preparing proposals in response to RFPs can involve expensive site acquisition and engineering investments. An interesting empirical study of competitive bidding in Maine showed the utility placing substantial emphasis in its evaluation on "project viability" factors such as site control (Eastman-Perl, 1991). Utility affiliates all appear to be well capitalized, because they are financed largely by retained earnings from the regulated side. Furthermore, the affiliates may be willing to settle for lower returns than other competitors. Finally, utilities as buyers are likely to be better disposed to proposals from utility affiliates because of "cultural affinities." The affiliated firm is likely to "speak the same language" as the purchasing utility. This means using similar terminology, having a reputation for reliability from the parent firm, and possibly relying on subsidized services from the parent firm.

The extent to which utility affiliates dominate the private power market will be limited by new entry from large industrial firms. Oil and chemical companies with an interest in coal gasification technology are one class of potential new entrant. Texaco and Dow Chemical are already active in this area, and Shell Oil is also a participant in a large-scale project in Europe. Another potential class of entrant is the international trading company. Mitsubishi has already sponsored one large IPP, the 600 MW Doswell project in Virginia.

What if new entry does not materialize, and utility affiliates absorb or drive out other firms? Then, the regulator will be faced with the proposition of supporting private power through unregulated utility affiliates, or giving up on the experiment in the long run. Furthermore, the Energy Policy Act of 1992 may weaken the ability of regulators to monitor unregulated utility affiliates. In that case, we may end up with the worst of all possible worlds: collusive behavior and no real competition. In this setting, the benefits of nominal competition may turn out to be quite illusory.

Regulatory policy in an IPP regime

Will the growing market share for independent power production diminish the role of regulation in electricity markets? A case can be made for the expansion of regulation in a more competitive industry. There is a strong trend toward greater regulation that is motivated largely by interest in demand-side management (DSM) activities. Beyond regulatory emphasis on DSM, there is also a trend in some states toward a greater role for the regulator in planning and managerial decisionmaking with respect to conventional generation. This approach is exemplified by the Wisconsin Public Service Commission through its advance planning process. The California Public Utilities Commission and the Nevada Public Service Commission also engage in the exercise of detailed planning. Utilities, as well as regulators, have expressed support for this approach, because it reduces the risk of cost disallowances for new investment.

Even when the regulator explicitly encourages competition and private power production, there can be a dominant role for the regulator. This is the paradigm envisioned by the FERC's "bidding NOPR," which postulated extensive regulatory review of bid evaluation criteria. To date, only California and Massachusetts have shown much enthusiasm for litigating and adjudicating the details of bid evaluation. In other states, the regulator has usually just reviewed the outcome of the competitive process. As an alternative, the regulator can set broad guidelines for bid evaluation, leaving the utility to implement a system of its own design that meets the guidelines. This is the solution adopted in New Jersey.

Regulation in a market with a competitive fringe will inevitably be complicated by conflicts among the objectives that the regulator is trying to achieve. Minimization of social cost can lead to outcomes very different from ratepayer cost minimization. These differences are common to DSM programs. They also arise in the private power sector through the definition and use of avoided cost concepts. Jurewitz (1990) points out a number of ways in which ratepayer cost minimization can come into conflict with social cost minimization when avoided costs become endogenous to the regulatory process. For example, in assessing the need for new generating capacity, is it reasonable to count the reduction in avoided cost payments as a benefit of new capacity? Jurewitz argues that because these are transfer payments, they should not be counted. Some regulators (e.g., in California) count such reductions as benefits, in which case social costs may be increased inefficiently by building too much capacity.

Environmental externalities are another important arena in which social and ratepayer cost minimization can lead to different decisions. Utility regulators are beginning to grapple with externality costs in planning and operations. There are substantial uncertainties associated with estimating these costs and a variety of ways in which they can be used in the planning and regulatory setting. Boundary issues also arise. Should state regulators address externality issues that lie beyond their domain of authority? What, for example, is the value of a renewable energy technology that offsets pollution in another state? Should a bidding system incorporate this effect, or will doing so contribute to an economic disadvantage for the local community?

The utility as the residual risk-taker

In a regime where private power plays a substantial role, the regulated utility will still retain its obligation to serve. Planning to meet that obligation, however, may become increasingly difficult. The demand for new capacity facing the utility is likely to become more uncertain. In addition to the ordinary uncertainties associated with end-user demand, the utility will face a resource availability uncertainty. Private power projects may fail at either the development stage or the operational stage. The former is probably more likely than the latter, but it is still too early to predict relative or absolute failure rates.

If the utility must fill an unanticipated capacity need, it may not be able to select a particularly efficient source of supply. Given the very short lead times facing the utility, about all that would be possible would be to purchase combustion turbines. If this type of capacity was, in fact, needed by the utility, there would be no loss. Alternatively, if a neighboring firm could sell excess capacity at a reasonable price, there would be little economic cost. These two possibilities cannot be expected to be generic, so the expected outcome would be some inefficiency. Moreover, contractual remedies do not appear, as yet, to offer much relief. Although private power contracts do have provisions for liquidated damages that address the premature termination contingency, the amount of money is relatively small. Mostly the damages are about $20/kW (Kahn, 1991), which is only about a third of the annual capacity deficiency charge of a large power pool, for example.

Concluding remarks

This chapter has reviewed the development of the U.S. electric power industry and described the directions of anticipated change. The U.S. industry is remarkable for its fragmented structure of generation and transmission and for its mix of private ownership and public power. Despite a ragtag mix of firms and regulatory authorities, the U.S. electricity industry has been able to exploit most of the efficiency advantages of vertical integration and, until the early 1970s, to achieve stunning productivity gains over time. Problems developed in the early 1970s with a combination of increasing environmental concerns, higher fossil fuel prices, cost overruns, and excess capacity from nuclear and large-scale coal construction programs. These adverse developments prompted a number of changes in the industry, exemplified by the Public Utilities Regulatory Policy Act of 1978. Although PURPA led the way for the introduction of private power into the U.S. industry, it was more a symptom of the underlying regulatory changes in this industry than the catalyst for change. Regulators were searching for new ways to meet anticipated electricity needs at lower costs and with less severe environmental impacts. Allowing independent power producers to bid for power supply contracts held promise to address the former concern. The independent projects have been smaller and thus easier to site, and the environmental impacts, although not necessarily less than those associated with utility projects, have been more diffuse and easier to overlook.

The Energy Policy Act of 1992 codified establishment of a viable independent power sector. The growth of this sector and its ultimate role in the U.S. electricity market is as yet unknown and will depend on many factors. The FERC will have to assert its authority to assure access to wholesale transmission. Regulators will have to cope with the challenges of managing a more competitive electric power market. The presence of unregulated suppliers may undermine the ability of regulators to subsidize preferred customer groups and undertake demand-side management programs whose costs may exceed the price of privately produced power. Finally, a complete unknown is the likelihood that increased competition in wholesale markets will spill over to competition at the retail level. If that happens, the traditional relationship of regulators as the providers of a relatively stable financial platform to encourage utility investment would evaporate, and the industry would have little in common with its present structure.

REFERENCES

Adamson, A., L. Garver, J. Maughn, P. Palmero, and W. Stillinger. "Summary of Panel: Long Term Impact of Third-Party Transmission Use." *IEEE Transactions on Power Systems* 6 (1991): 1183–8.

Anderson, D. *Regulatory Politics and Electric Utilities.* Boston: Auburn House, 1981.

Atkinson, S., and R. Halvorsen. "The Relative Efficiency of Public and Private Firms in a Regulated Environment: The Case of U.S. Electric Utilities." *Journal of Public Economics* (1986): 281–94.

Averch, H., and L. Johnson. "Behavior of the Firm Under Regulatory Constraint." *American Economic Review* 52 (1962): 1053–69.

Bailey, E. "Deregulation: Causes and Consequences." *Science* 234 (1986): 1211–16.

Baldick, R., and E. Kahn. "Network Costs and the Regulation of Wholesale Competition in Electric Power." *Journal of Regulatory Economics* (1993): 367–84.

Baron, D., and D. Besanko. "Regulation, Asymmetric Information and Auditing." *Rand Journal of Economics* (1984): 447–700.

Beck, R. W. and Associates. "Independent Engineer's Report, Independence Cogeneration Project." Appendix B to *Offering Circular $717,241,000 Sithe/Independence Funding Corporation.* New York: Salomon Brothers, 1993.

Berg, S., and J. Jeong. "An Evaluation of Incentive Regulation for Electric Utilities." *Journal of Regulatory Economics* (1991): 45–56.

Bonbright, J. *Principles of Public Utility Rates.* New York: Columbia University Press, 1961.

California Public Utilities Commission (CPUC), Decision No. 90–09–88, 1990.

Caramanis, M., R. Bohn, and F. Schweppe. "The Cost of Wheeling and Optimal Wheeling Rates." *IEEE Transactions on Power Systems* 1 (1986): 63–73.

Christensen, L., and W. Greene. "Economies of Scale in U.S. Electric Power Generation." *Journal of Political Economy* 84 (1976): 655–76.

Comnes, G., T. Belden, and E. Kahn. *The Price of Electricity from Private Power Producers Stage V: Expansion of Sample and Preliminary Statistical Analysis.* Berkeley, CA: Lawrence Berkeley Laboratory Report LBL-36054, 1995.

Courville, L. "Regulation and Efficiency in the Electric Utility Industry." *Bell Journal of Economics and Management Science* 5 (1974): 53–74.

David, P., and J. Bunn. "The Economics of Gateway Technologies and Network Evolution: Lessons from Electricity Supply History." *Information Economics and Policy* 3 (1988): 165–202.

Eastman-Perl, K. PhD thesis, Princeton University, 1991.

Edison Electric Institute (EEI). *Historical Statistics of the Electric Utility Industry Through 1970* (1975).

Statistical Yearbook of the Electric Utility Industry for 1978, 1979.

Einhorn, M. "Electricity Wheeling and Incentive Regulation." *Journal of Regulatory Economics* 2 (1990): 173–89.

Energy Information Administration (EIA). *Nuclear Plant Cancellations: Causes, Costs and Consequences.* DOE/EIA–0392, 1983.

Electric Power Annual 1989. DOE/EIA–0348(89), 1991a.

Electric Sales and Revenue 1989. DOE/EIA–0540(89), 1991b.

Electric Power Annual 1991. DOE/EIA–0348(91), 1993.

Federal Energy Regulatory Commission (FERC). *Power Pooling in the United States.* FERC–0049, 1981.

Transmission Task Force's Report to the Commission. *Electricity Transmission; Realities, Theory and Policy Alternatives.* 1989.

Financial Statistics of Major U.S. Investor-Owned Electric Utilities 1993, DOE/EIA-0437 (9311) 1995.

Gilbert, R., and J. Henly. "The Value of Rate Reform in a Competitive Electric Power Market." In *Regulatory Choices: A Perspective on Developments in Energy Policy,* edited by R. Gilbert. Berkeley: University of California Press, 1991.

Gilbert, R., and M. Riordan. "Regulating Complementary Products: Comparative Institutional Analysis." *RAND Journal of Economics* 26, 1995.

Gilbert, R., and S. Stoft. *A Review and Analysis of Electric Utility Conservation Incentives.* Universitywide Energy Research Group PWP–005, 1992.

Grahame, T. Memo to K. Kelly, U.S. Department of Energy, 1990.

Hogan, W. "Contract Networks for Electric Power Transmission." *Journal of Regulatory Economics* 4 (1992): 211–42.

Hughes, T. *Networks of Power: Electrification in Western Society 1880–1930.* Baltimore: Johns Hopkins University Press, 1983.

Jabbour, S. "The Short-Run Value of Non-Utility Generated Power." *IEEE Transactions on Energy Conversion* 1 (1986): 11–16.

Jarrell, G. "The Demand for State Regulation of the Electric Utility Industry." *Journal of Law and Economics* 21 (1978): 269–95.

Joskow, P. "Productivity Growth and Technical Change in the Generation of Electricity." *Energy Journal* 8 (1987): 17–38.

Joskow, P., and Marron, D. "What Does a Megawatt Really Cost? Evidence from Utility Conservation Programs." *Energy Journal* 13 (1993): 41–74.

Joskow, P., and R. Schmalensee. *Markets for Power: An Analysis of Electric Utility Deregulation.* Cambridge, MA: MIT Press, 1983.

"Incentive Regulation for Electric Utilities." *Yale Journal on Regulation* 4 (1986): 1–49.

Jurewitz, J. "When Avoided Cost Becomes an Endogenous Regulatory Variable." Rosemead: Southern California Edison, 1990.

Kahn, E. *Electric Utility Planning and Regulation.* Washington, DC: American Council for an Energy Efficient Economy, 1988.

"Risks in Independent Power Contracts: An Empirical Survey." *The Electricity Journal* 4 (1991): 30–45.

Kahn, E., C. Marnay, and D. Berman. "Evaluating Dispatchability Features in Competitive Bidding." *IEEE Transactions on Power Systems* 7 (1992): 1259–65.

Kolp, D., and D. Moeller. "World's First Full STIG LM5000 Installed at Simpson Paper Company." *Transactions of ASME Journal of Engineering for Gas Turbines and Power* 111 (1988): 200–10.

Krause, F., and J. Eto. "The Demand Side: Conceptual and Methodological Issues," Vol. 2 of *Least Cost Utility Planning, A Handbook for Public Utility Commissioners.* Berkeley, CA: Lawrence Berkeley Laboratory, 1988.

Laffont, J., and J. Tirole. "Using Cost Observation to Regulate Firms." *Journal of Political Economy* 94 (1986): 614–41.

Le, K., R. Jackups, J. Feinstein, H. Thompson, H. Wolf, E. Stein, A. Gorski, and J. Griffith. "Operational Aspects of Generation Cycling." *IEEE Transactions on Power Systems* 5 (1991): 1194–1203.

Littlechild, S., and M. Beesley. "The Regulation of Privatized Monopolies in the United Kingdom." *Rand Journal of Economics* 20 (1989): 454–72.

MacDonald, F. *Insull.* Chicago: University of Chicago Press, 1962.

McCalley, J., J. Dorsey, Z. Qu, J. Luini, and J. Filippi. "A New Methodology for Determining Transmission Capacity Margin in Electric Power Systems." *IEEE Transactions on Power Systems* 6 (1991): 944–51.

Nadel, S. "Electric Utility Conservation Programs: A Review of the Lessons Taught by a Decade of Program Experience." In *State of the Art of Energy Efficiency: Future Directions,* edited by E. Vine and D. Crawley. Washington, DC: American Council for an Energy-Efficient Economy, 1991.

New Jersey Board of Public Utilities. "Staff Assessment of PURPA Implementation 1981–1986." Trenton, NJ, 1986.

Oak Ridge National Laboratory (ORNL). *Prudence Issues Affecting the U.S. Electric Utility Industry.* Oak Ridge, TN, 1987.
    Prudence Issues Affecting the U.S. Electric Utility Industry: Update, 1987 and 1988 Activities. Oak Ridge, TN, 1989.

Resource Development Corporation (RDC). "Cogeneration and Independent Power Production: Market Insight and Outlook." EPRI CU–6964, 1990.

Scattergood, J., J. Bonbright, L. Brown, S. Ferguson, M. Lincoln, and P. Shoellkopf. *Electric Power and Government Policy.* New York: The Twentieth Century Fund, 1948.

Schweppe, F., M. Caramanis, R. Tabors, and R. Bohn. *Spot Pricing of Electricity.* Boston: Kluwer Academic Publishers, 1988.

Shirmohammadi, D., and C. Thomas. "Valuation of the Transmission Impact in a Resource Bidding Process." *IEEE Transactions on Power Systems* 5 (1991).

Steinmeier, W. "Prudence and Power Procurement: Will We Preclude Utility Ownership?" *The Electricity Journal* 4 (1991): 20–9.

Strategic Decisions Group. "Western Systems Power Pool Assessment, Final Report." Menlo Park, CA: 1991.

Tenenbaum, B., and S. Henderson. "Market Based Pricing of Wholesale Electric Services." *The Electricity Journal* 4 (1991): 30–45.

Train, K., and P. Ignelzi. "The Economic Value of Energy-Saving Investments by Commercial and Industrial Firms." *Energy* 12 (1987): 543–53.

U.S. Bureau of the Census. *Historical Statistics of the United States.* Washington, DC: U.S. Government Printing Office, 1975.

Wainwright, N. *History of the Philadelphia Electric Company 1881–1961.* Philadelphia: Electric Company, 1961.

Williams, R., and E. Larson. "Expanding Roles for Gas Turbines in Power Generation." In *Electricity: Efficient End-Use and New Generation Technologies, and Their Planning Implications,* edited by T. Johansson, B. Bodlund, and R. Williams. Lund, Sweden: Lund University Press, 1989.

Zimmerman, M. "Regulatory Treatment of Abandoned Property: Incentive Effects and Policy Issues." *Journal of Law and Economics* 31 (1988): 127–44.

CHAPTER 6

The Japanese electric utility industry

Peter Navarro
University of California, Irvine

A few small and undercapitalized private firms gave birth to Japan's electric utility industry a little more than a century ago. Although these companies initially supplied only lighting services to a few customers, the industry today has over 142,000 MW of generating capacity and is projected to supply Japan with nearly 228 GW (billion watts) of capacity in fiscal 2000.

Japan's ten privately owned electric companies enjoy a net worth of $924 Billion, relative freedom from regulation, and far-reaching, firm support from the government. However, today's industry faces the tightest supply–demand gap in recent memory and must develop 15,000 MW of new generating capacity each year, just to meet demand. This situation has been characterized as "urgent" in a country that imports over 80% of its energy requirements. Coupled with competition from other energy suppliers and public opposition to nuclear power, Japan's electric utilities are facing new and growing challenges.

The industry consolidates: 1880 to World War II

When Ichisuke Fujioka first proposed establishing an electric power company in the early 1880s, he found little financial backing. Because the government was concentrating on increasing industrial production, it was short on capital; it thus expected entrepreneurs to finance new ventures. Private businessmen, however, were reluctant to invest in what they considered to be a novelty. But with the help of senior government official Yasuzo Yamao, Fujioka found 64 aristocrats, businessmen with political affiliations, and wealthy merchants to invest in his company, Tokyo Electric Light Company (TELC–Tokyo Dento). TELC opened its doors for business in 1883 with initial capital of 200,000 yen (Japan Electric Power Information Center [JEPIC], 1988, p. 1). From these rather humble beginnings, TELC later became Tokyo Electric Power Company, the world's largest privately owned utility.

The author would like to acknowledge the research of Margaret Carmine and Wynne Cougill in the preparation of this chapter.

The demand for electricity

When it began operating, TELC did not have enough money to build a generating plant, so it instead installed self-generating facilities scattered in various areas of the city, as well as portable generators. The company used its generators to light the Yokosuka Shipyard, the Bank of Tokyo, the government printing office, and a spinning plant company (Ohsawa, 1985, pp. 3–4). By 1888, rising lighting demand enabled TELC to construct and operate a generating plant specifically to supply electricity to the "red light" district of Yoshiwara.

TELC's success in the government, commercial, and industrial sectors did not spread as rapidly to residential customers, who considered electricity to be both costly and dangerous. In 1888, a year after it began supplying power to the public, TELC powered only 138 lights. But the use of electric lamps began to spread rapidly in the next decade, primarily in the cities, and by 1892, TELC provided some 14,100 lights with electricity, even though gas and kerosene lamps were still more popular with the general public (JEPIC, 1988). By 1906, a total of 33 utilities were supplying electricity to 120,000 residential lights (Nihon Denki Kyokai, 1990, p. 6).

The use of electric lighting gained even more prominence when TELC was able to lower its rates by increasing its hydropower capacity and manufacturing a tungsten light bulb in 1976 through a technology tie-in between its Tokyo Denki subsidiary and General Electric. In that year, the number of lights leapfrogged to 780,000 (Ohsawa, 1985, p. 7).

The demand for electric power in addition to lighting began to spread in the last decade of the nineteenth century, owing to technological advances, the rapid development of modern industries, and the relative decline in the cost of electricity against such power sources as coal, causing many factories to switch from steam to electric power (Minami, 1987, pp. 153–7). The operation of the country's first electric railways in Kyoto in 1895, and increases in transmission voltage, which allowed power to be transmitted over longer distances, further boosted nonresidential demand. Electricity accounted for 36% of the country's total power consumption in 1907, and by 1918, industrial demand had surpassed lighting demand (Minami, 1987).

World War I brought a further expansion of Japan's markets, spurring the growth of its chemical and heavy industries and leading to a number of electric power shortages. However, the depression of the 1920s brought about a stagnation in electricity demand and consequent excess capacity. As a result, the nation's utilities began competing fiercely for customers (in some cases, more than one utility supplied electricity to the same customer) (JEPIC, 1988).

The 1930s saw these companies' fortunes rise again with economic recovery, when the amount of generation in the country doubled. Demand grew by leaps and bounds during this period, from 16.4 TWh in 1932 to 22.3 TWh (trillion watt hours) in 1935, when Japan became the world's fifth-largest generator of electricity, and to 27.1 TWh in 1937, a 65% increase over five years (JEPIC, 1988). With this demand growth, however, came shortages, especially in industrial districts. By 1940, electricity's share of the nation's total power consumption had reached 88% (Minami, 1987). By the end of World War II, electricity demand in Japan had climbed to 16,458 million kWh (Nagao, 1991).

Electricity supply

TELC's rise from a provider of small portable generators to a builder of power plants was nothing short of meteoric. It began its ambitious expansion by building the 25 kW coal-fired Nihonbashi power plant in 1887, the first such plant in Japan to supply electricity to the general public (Ohsawa, 1985). By 1908, it had built four more plants, bringing its total capacity to 945 kW. Scattering its small-scale thermal plants in numerous districts soon proved to be economically inefficient and difficult in densely populated Tokyo, so TELC built the country's first central station in 1895, the 2,400 kW Asakusa thermal generation plant.

As Japan's demand for electric power changed, so did its capacity mix. Copper mining and spinning interests began to develop self-generating hydropower capacity in 1890, and Kyoto City's Keage hydropower plant opened in 1891 and began to supply power to the public in 1894 (JEPIC, 1988). Following the establishment of this plant, a number of other small-scale hydropower plants were built in mountainous districts of Japan. By 1895, 24 electric power companies had thermal generation facilities, eight had hydropower facilities, and three had both types of facilities. Hydropower reached 31% of the country's total capacity by 1905. Six years later, the power capacity of hydro and thermal stations was roughly equal, but by 1911 hydroelectric capacity, with its relatively lower cost, had gained a 69% market share of Japan's generation (JEPIC, 1988). Hydropower became the nation's main source of electric power for industry in the 1920s, but it had to be supplemented by thermal (largely coal-fired) plants in the winter because Japan's hydro plants typically lacked storage facilities.

The industry's financial health

The introduction of the silver standard to Japan in the early 1890s brought great prosperity to the country. This stimulated investment in electric power companies, and many utilities started up in major cities (unlike most of Japan's industries, which first developed as joint public-private projects, its electric utilities were always private enterprises). This period saw great increases in demand, allowing utilities to lower their rates and increase their profits, which peaked in the 1910s (Ohsawa, 1985). By the mid-1920s, some of these utilities were even issuing foreign bonds.

A record 738 utilities were operating in Japan in 1925 (up from 116 in 1907) (Nishihiro, 1991). Most of these, however, were soon forced out of business as a result of cutthroat competition. By 1928, the five most powerful generating companies had consolidated their control of the industry: TELC, the Toho Electricity Company, the Daido Electricity Company, the Ujigawa Electricity Company, and the Nippon Electricity Company (Hein, 1990). These companies succeeded simply because they had more cash for expansion, which they raised by taking the risk of borrowing abroad, largely from Britain and the United States, making the electric utility industry the only industrial sector in Japan to rely heavily on foreign capital (Hein, 1990). The government provided the stimulus for their dependence in 1927 by waiving the legal limit on foreign borrowing and allowing utilities to issue corporate bonds equivalent to twice their existing debts. In 1931, it permitted utilities to enter into completely unsecured borrowing. By the end of that year, these five utilities owed ¥357 million abroad, or 16% of all foreign debt in Japan.

The 1930s revealed the quixotic nature of this overreliance on foreign capital when currency devaluations engorged the sector's foreign debt, the export of capital was prohibited in order to deal with the Great Depression, and competition among the five firms led to price wars (Hein, 1990). The industry leader TELC fell victim to this disaster and stopped paying dividends in 1932. The utilities soon accepted the leadership of the banks and agreed to share equipment under the auspices of a new industry organization, the Electric Power Federation (Denryoku Renmei), which served in part to subordinate the independent electric power entrepreneurs to the needs of the established *zaibatsu* groups (industrial and finance conglomerates formed in the late nineteenth century, which often enjoyed government patronage). The agreement to create this new federation included provisions that no major investments in new generating capacity could be made without consulting the banks. In late 1932, the Finance Ministry approved the industry's request for a state buy-out on foreign debt, and by March 1934, virtually all of the industry's foreign debt was cleared.

From the 1920s until the end of World War II, the electric power industry was closely associated with military production and was thus afforded financial protection by the government. For example, the government set low power rates for Hassoden, a state-controlled but privately owned "special corporation" established in 1938 to generate power. However, when Hassoden's costs exceeded its revenues, the government granted the company a subsidy. The industry depended on government subsidies because rates had been set low; 28% of Hassoden's receipts came from subsidies in 1944. However, the nine regional privately owned and stated-operated transmission and distribution firms established in 1941 did not receive any direct subsidies. (Government support was removed during the Occupation, forcing utilities to turn to the Reconstruction Finance Bank for loans to meet their current operating expenses.)

Regulation

When TELC and other electric power companies were established, there were no special regulations or government authorities to oversee them. They were instead supervised under police regulations, and prefectural authorities routinely granted the licenses utilities sought (Ohsawa, 1985). The government simply expected that the industry would police itself to maintain an orderly market.

Stricter regulations were not long in coming, however (Samuels, 1987). The burgeoning number of utilities being established around the nation and a fire at the just-opened Imperial Diet building in January 1891 served as the main catalysts for national regulations (the cause of the fire was unknown, but some believed it was accidentally caused by a short circuit). In July of that year, the organizational structure of the Ministry of Communications was revised, and it became the supervisory agency responsible for electric power. Two years later, the ministry assumed the prefectural governors' authority to issue licenses to private utilities, requiring these authorities to receive permission from the Ministry before granting a license to establish a power company.

The Regulation on the Electric Utility Industry of 1896 and its amendment in 1902 created the legal structure for the national regulation of electric utilities. These regulations required safety precautions for generators and electric railways, standardized transmission voltages, and centralized permit authority.

In 1909, electric power was first deemed of sufficient importance to warrant special supervision, and the Electric Bureau (Denki Kyoku) was set up within the Ministry of Communications (the administration of electric power remained in the hands of the Bureau until 1939). At the same time, the Ministry began seeking more general state controls and authorization to set rates in response to what the government and consumers considered the monopolistic pricing practices of Japan's utilities.

These and other moves began the shift from an emphasis on public safety to one stressing the protection and development of the industry (Nihon Denki Kyokai, 1990). The concept of public utility was soon introduced to the electric power industry, electric railways, and water services. Japan's first power law, the Electric Utility Industry Law, was implemented in 1911; it provided for government permission to open power plants, revocation of permission if a firm did not start up business within a specified term, and the common use of transmission lines (Kurihara et al., 1964). This law, which remained in effect until 1932, also provided for the regulation of the rates charged by utilities. During this period, utilities also continued to be supervised by the cities in which they provided power. The utilities signed a compensation agreement concerning their installation of electric wires and poles in places owned or supervised by the cities (e.g., parks, streets).

Energy policy became an important issue for the Japanese government during World War I. Previously, only a few members of the Diet had concerned themselves with energy policy. In March 1927, the government created the Temporary Council on the Electric Power Industry to deal with such issues as the nationalization of facilities, regional monopolies, and the creation of semigovernmental corporations.

In 1931 a revision of the Electric Utility Industry Law was submitted to the Diet. This law formally changed the legal character of the industry to one of "public utility." It recognized the authority of the Ministry of Communications over the industry, changed the rate system from one in which utilities notified the Ministry of rate changes to requiring the Ministry's permission, necessitated government permission for the merger of companies, obligated companies to submit financial reports, and proposed regulations pertaining to the government purchase of utilities as well as regulations that strengthened the role of electric power companies as public utilities. Recognizing that the cutthroat competition among electric companies had cost the state as well as the utilities dearly, the government adopted the revised law in 1932. Since then, electricity rates have been under government control.

In 1932, Denryoku Renmei, an electric power self-control association, began operations. Regional monopolies were recognized as embodied in this association. The banks and government closely supervised Denryoku Renmei, which was given the responsibility of allocating production, markets, and prices.

The end of the 1930s saw the industry enter a period of greater state control. The government had passed new laws requiring government permission for such things as rate decisions, plant development, and construction of transmission networks. The industry was effectively forced to act only in accordance with government wishes. The core of the state's control over the utilities was contained in the Electric Power Control Law and the Law for the Establishment of Japan Electric Power Generation and Transmission Company (Nippon Hassoden Kabushiki Gaisha, or Hassoden) (Hein, 1990). These two laws were designed to assure a sufficient supply of cheap electricity in order to expand military production capacity and to develop other industries such as metals and petrochemicals. In 1938, Hassoden, a state-controlled but privately owned "special corporation" (*tokushu gaisha*), which generated electricity and sold it to transmission and distribution companies, was created by forcibly consolidating 33 generation companies across Japan. This semigovernmental company enjoyed a virtual monopoly over all electric generation and transmission throughout the country.

In 1939, the state established the Electric Board (*Denki-cho*) to oversee the electric power industry, including Hassoden. A year later, it prepared the National Policy Guidelines for the Electric Utility Industry to cement its control over the utilities, stimulate the consolidation of power facilities under Hassoden, and encourage the development of hydroelectric power and the integration of the transformation network.

By 1941, approximately 600 electric power transmission and distribution companies nationwide were integrated into nine regional privately owned and state-operated firms known as Haiden (Hokkaido, Tohoku, Kanto, Chubu, Hokuriku, Kansai, Chugoku, Shikoku, and Kyushu power companies). These firms were placed under the supervision of the Ministry of Communications' Electric Power Bureau. As a result, during World War II, a giant, state-controlled electric utility (Hassoden) delivered power through these nine firms. The framework for exerting state control over the electric power industry was thus firmly in place.

The giant roars: 1945 to the present

Industry structure

Japan's electric power industry today is comprised of 10 vertically integrated ("common") electric utilities and 56 wholesale utilities that supply power to the common utilities. The 56 wholesale utilities include within their ranks 34 power-generating companies that are owned and operated by local governments. In addition to these are 20 joint-venture power companies established and owned by the utilities and their large power consumers.

The 10 common electric power companies (*ippan denki jigyosha*) have specific districts in which they hold a regional monopoly. They are Hokkaido Electric Power Company, Tohoku Electric Power Company, Tokyo Electric Power Company (TEPCO), Chubu Electric Power Company, Hokuriku Electric Power Company, Kansai Electric Power Company, Chugoku Electric Power Company, Shikoku Electric Power Company, Kyushu Electric Power Company, and Okinawa Electric Power Company. Each of these utilities is independently and privately owned, and their boards of directors are elected by shareholders. The first nine utilities were created in May 1951 when the country's electric power industry was reorganized; Okinawa Electric was created in May 1972 after Okinawa prefecture was returned to Japan from the United States.

During fiscal 1989, the 10 utilities supplied more than 613 TWh of electricity, accounting for approximately 90% of all the electric energy consumed in Japan (Ota, 1991). Tokyo, Kansai, and Chubu meet two-thirds of the country's electric power demand today (see Table 6-1).

Table 6-1. *The ten "common" electric power companies in Japan as of March 31, 1990*

	kWh Sales (million kWh)	Generating capacity (MW)	Capital stock (billion yen)	Total assets (billion yen)	Total revenues (billion yen)
Tokyo	204,452	43,338	657	10,644	4,101
Kansai	112,305	30,173	477	5,601	2,085
Chubu	93,668	21,375	362	4,265	1,712
Kyushu	51,013	13,300	235	3,039	1,073
Tohoku	49,769	10,058	247	2,294	1,086
Chugoku	39,498	9,219	182	2,142	822
Hokuriku	20,156	3,945	116	1,048	373
Hokkaido	19,245	4,876	113	1,347	453
Shikoku	18,749	5,423	146	1,078	401
Okinawa	4,443	902	7	153	98
Total	613,279	142,618	2,542	31,609	12,203

Source: Tokyo Electric Power Company, Inc. *Statistical Review of TEPCO.* Tokyo, 1990, p. 2.

The industry today is well capitalized and diversified. Nine electric power companies (all but Okinawa) had a total of 216 subsidiaries as of December 1, 1987 (JEPIC, 1988). Of these subsidiaries, 26 are electric power wholesalers and the rest are engaged in such activities as the production of electric equipment and appliances, the construction of electric facilities, computer service and software sales, and sales of electric appliances.

An example of the industry's financial clout is its venture into related business. When the Japanese telecommunications industry was deregulated in 1985, for example, these utilities began dealing with products like beepers and car phones. In the latter half of the 1980s, the nine electric utilities had either established, or provided capital to, approximately 40 telecommunications-related firms (Tomita, 1988). TEPCO, for example, has established almost 20 telecommunications-related companies since 1986.

The nine electric utilities have worked together to minimize generation and transmission costs since 1958, when they and the Electric Power Development Corporation, Ltd. (EPDC – Dengen Kaihatsu Gaisha), one of the wholesale utilities, established a coordination system that acts in the same way as the power pooling system in the United States (JEPIC, 1990). The system is designed to facilitate cooperation activities in a number of areas, including power plant construction and operation, transmission and other facilities, power exchange, and the introduction of new technologies. Over the years, this system has permitted the utilities to greatly improve their transmission links.

During fiscal 1990, for example, Japan's electric utilities exchanged 24.6 billion kWh, a 4% drop from the previous year (JEPIC, 1990). Of this amount, 24.7 million kWh represented planned power exchanges between two utilities; the rest was exchanged to meet daily supply–demand fluctuations.

Many of the 56 wholesale utilities, which do not have their own supply districts, are under either public or joint public-private management. With a few exceptions, the wholesale utilities play only a supplementary role in Japan's electric power industry. Their primary role is to help the retail sales of electricity by the common utilities through the wholesale supply of electricity to these utilities. It is not legal for the wholesale companies to sell electricity directly to general customers.

The EPDC, for example, is owned by the Japanese government and the utilities; like the common utilities, it is administered through the Ministry of International Trade and Industry (MITI). Created in 1952 as a part of a larger government policy to expand electric power capacity and lower costs, the EPDC has more autonomy than the ordinary government-spawned corporation (*kodan*) in Japan. However, the government does exercise control over the EPDC through stock holdings, budgetary arrangements, the appointment of personnel, and the placement of retired MITI officials in top company positions. The EPDC is responsible for the development and maintenance of a number of large-scale hydropower and coal-fired plants. The power generated by these facilities is sold to the common utilities at cost; the EPDC does not sell directly to consumers. The EPDC, "to the chagrin of most of the private companies," has also been the pioneer in the development of air quality control equipment and innovative technology for burning coal; its success has encouraged MITI to pressure TEPCO and other large utilities in central Japan to exert similar efforts (Gale, 1981).

The utility-controlled Japan Atomic Power Company (JAPC), another wholesale power-generating company, is supported financially by the electric utilities, the EPDC, and other enterprises. Its primary function is to develop nuclear power. The electric utilities "prevailed upon the government in 1957 to allow the creation" of JAPC to "foreclose EPDC's entry into the nuclear power generation business (as well as to spread the risk of introducing nuclear reactors)" (Gale, 1981).

According to Managing Director Hiroji Ota of Chubu Electric, the present structure of the electric power industry (Table 6-2) in Japan has been rated as highly successful (Ota, 1991). Through its efficient management system, the industry has been contributing to the improvement of service standards by both securing stability in energy supply and maintaining low energy prices. For ex-

Table 6-2. *Electric power industry in Japan, as of March 31, 1990*

	Common companies	Wholesale companies (municipal)[a]	Total
Number	10	56 (34)	66
Capital (million yen)	2,542,379	813,056 (401,606)	3,355,435
Hydropower plants			
Number	1,154	360 (235)	1,514
Maximum power output (1,000 kW)	26,593	9,729 (2,326)	36,322
Thermal plants			
Number	174 (4 geothermal)	22 (1)	196 (5 geothermal)
Maximum power output (1,000 kW)	89,527 (168 geothermal)	12,846 (13 geothermal)	102,373 (180 geothermal)
Nuclear plants			
Number	13	3	16
Maximum power Output (1,000 kW)	26,497	2,783	29,280
Total			
Number	1,341 (4 geothermal)	385 (1 geothermal)	1,726 (5 geothermal)
Maximum power output (1,000 kW)	142,618 (168 geothermal)	25,358 (13 geothermal)	167,976 (180 geothermal)

[a]Municipal companies, shown in parentheses, are involved in hydropower generation only.
Source: Nihon Denki Kyokai. *Anata no Shiritai Koto – Denki Jigyo ni Tsuite 43 no Shitsumon to To 1990* (43 Questions and Answers Concerning the Electric Industry 1990). Tokyo, 1990, pp. 16–17.

ample, the price differentials between the highest-price and lowest-price utilities was 2.25-fold in fiscal 1951; this figure was narrowed to 1.3 in fiscal 1989.

The supply–demand balance

August 1945 saw the elimination of Japan's wartime electricity loads. Soon after, its industrial production stagnated and the country experienced a power surplus (GHQ, Allied Powers, 1951). This short-lived situation changed by the second half of 1946, however, when shortages arose due to a lack of coal for thermal power generation and inadequate rainfall for hydropower generation. By August, the Japanese government began restricting the distribution of electric power to conserve the available supply for industry. Even this sector suffered, and in one particularly harsh month, the chemicals industry was able to procure less than half of the electricity it needed.

By March 1948, abundant rainfall and increased coal production again changed Japan's supply–demand balance, and power was plentiful for nearly two years. But the production of electricity could not keep up with demand by December 1949, when demand soared to 5.5 million kW, the highest level the nation had ever attained (GHQ, Allied Powers, 1951).

Electric power shortages proved to be one of the most serious barriers to Japan's economic development until the early 1960s. Although these shortages were initially largely caused by rising residential demand, industrial demand took the lead in 1950 with the outbreak of the Korean War. Power restrictions were again imposed on the economy in 1951 and 1952 and periodically throughout the decade. The industry was not able to meet demand again until 1962. For the nation's electric utilities, however, this meant a constant assured market, and industry leaders "knew that the faster they constructed new plants, the more electricity they could sell" (Hein, 1990).

The industry's fortunes changed again in the 1970s when demand from the energy-intensive industrial sector nosedived. Higher energy costs had choked off smokestack industries and encouraged a shift to the high-tech and service sectors. Moreover, energy conservation measures increased the efficiency of electricity use and contributed to the declining growth in consumption.

During the summer of 1990, Japan experienced an electricity supply shortfall that resulted in programmed brownouts in certain parts of the country – a rarity by Japanese standards ("Some Lessons ...," 1991). Although the country's utilities were able to meet demand, their aggregate reserve margins dropped from 11.3% in 1989 to just under 4% in 1990, against the desired 8 to 10% (Ohsawa, 1991). (Japan's reserve margin peaked at 24.9% in 1980 and had been in the double digits between 1974 and 1989. See Table 6.3).

Today, Japan faces the tightest electricity supply–demand gap in recent memory. During fiscal year 1990, its aggregate peak load reached 140,600 MW, a 15,000 MW increase over the previous year. According to Hiroji Ota, managing director of the Chubu Electric Power Company, Japan's current situation is "urgent" (Ota, 1991). A closer look at the history of Japan's voracious demand for electricity and its supply-side responses sheds some light on this phenomenon.

Demand: In 1955, Japan's demand for electricity was 1.5 times its demand in 1951 (Ohsawa, 1991). Demand began to increase sharply in the mid-1950s for all of the country's sectors, especially the residential sector, largely due to the

Table 6-3. *Japanese reserve ratios, 1965 to 1990 (in percentages)*

Year	Reserve ratio	Year	Reserve ratio	Year	Reserve ratio
1965	8.7	1974	17.2	1983	11.8
1966	9.3	1975	14.4	1984	10.5
1967	3.6	1976	15.3	1985	11.2
1968	7.4	1977	10.9	1986	13.3
1969	7.3	1978	12.2	1987	11.8
1970	3.4	1979	16.1	1988	10.8
1971	8.6	1980	24.9	1989	11.3
1972	6.4	1981	19.5	1990	4.0
1973	3.6	1982	19.2		

Source: Information provided by Etsuji Ohsawa, Central Research Institute of Electric Power Industry, 1991.

home appliance and television boom. Electricity consumption increased by 15% a year during this decade (Ohsawa, 1990).

The high economic growth experienced by Japan in the 1960s led to demand increases of 10.7% a year between 1961 and 1973 (JEPIC, 1988). By 1965, the nation's diffusion rate of electric lighting reached 99.93%, one of the highest levels in the world.

During the early 1970s, the demand for electricity paralleled GDP growth at a little under 4% per annum. However, demand fell 1.4% in fiscal 1974, the first negative growth the electric power industry had experienced since it was reorganized in 1951 (Ohsawa, 1985). Demand stagnated between 1979 and 1983 when GDP growth slowed and primary energy use declined by approximately 10% (International Energy Agency, 1985). This decline has been attributed to less intensive energy use by the industrial sector, technology advances, and energy-saving appliances.

However, this situation shifted again in 1983 when electricity demand reached 38% of the country's total energy demand (JEPIC, 1986). During fiscal year 1983, demand grew 6.4% and during fiscal 1984, 4.9% (Ohsawa, 1985).

New demands for electricity have been coming in recent years from the nonindustrial sector, which grew from about 28% of total electricity demand in fiscal year 1970 to 42.4% in 1984 (Ohsawa, 1990). This change stemmed from the diffusion of intelligent office buildings and office automation, the rise in demand for larger, better-equipped houses, and the increased use of air-conditioning. Although Japan's industrial sector has become less energy-inten-

Table 6-4. *Electricity demand outlook, FY 1988 to 2010 (percentage of total demand)*

Sector	Fiscal 1988 (actual)	Fiscal 2000	Fiscal 2010
Industry	58.2	51.3	46.7
Residential and commercial	41.8	48.7	53.3
Maximum demand (million kW)	121.45	172.50	221.0
Total demand (billion kWh)	672.3	927.0	1.8 trillion kWh

Source: Nihon Denki Kyokai (Demand–Supply Division of the Electric Power Industry Advisory Council). *Denki Jigyo no Genjo, 1990* (The Current Status of the Electric Power Industry, 1990). Interim Report. Tokyo, 1990, p. 34.

sive, its overall demand remains high as a result of factory automation for high-grade manufacturing, labor shortages, and other factors. The demand for air-conditioning, particularly in the summer, has caused a constant decline in Japan's annual load factor; it has been hovering around 60% in recent years, which is nearly 10% lower than it was 20 years ago (Ota, 1991).

Although the projections of Japan's future demand situation vary, they all point to enormous growth in demand. The Central Electric Power Council, a coordinating organization formed by the nine electric utilities and the Electric Power Development Company, forecasts a 3% average annual increase in demand over the next decade, with total demand reaching 791.3 billion kWh by fiscal 1999. August peak demand is expected to continue growing an average of 3.1% annually, reaching 165,500 MW by 1999 (JEPIC, 1990). Assuming an average annual GDP growth rate of 4% between 1990 and 1999, Dengen Kaihatsu Chosei Shingikai predicts that total energy demand in fiscal 1999 will reach 908.8 billion kWh (an average annual growth rate of 2.8%), that electricity demand will reach 822.5 billion kWh (an average annual growth rate of 2.7%), and that the August peak load will be 170.32 million kW (an average annual growth rate of 2.7%) (Nihon Denki Kyokai, 1990).

The electricity demands of Japan's residential customers are expected to continue growing at a high rate. By the year 2010, the combined demand of the residential and commercial sectors is expected to surpass that of the industrial sector (see Table 6-4). Japan's electricity demand is expected to grow consistently faster than its total energy demand between now and 2010. The Advisory Committee for Energy, an advisor to MITI, predicts that if Japan achieves 6% energy conservation in 2000 and 11.2% in 2010, its average annual growth rate for energy will be 1.2% between 2000 and 2010. According to the Electric Utility Industry Council, another advisory body for MITI, electricity demand is expected to grow at 2.8% annually between 1988 and 2000, and 1.6% per year between 2001 and 2010 (Ota, 1991). Many analysts, however, believe that these figures are too conservative. Actual demand growth for electricity in recent years has been well ahead of Japan's projections (5.8% and 7.4% in 1989 and 1990, respectively).

Supply: Laura Hein (1990, p. 28), writing on Japan's energy situation during the Occupation, stated that "the dearth of energy supplies posed one of the biggest problems of economic construction; the first postwar decade can be characterized accurately as one long energy crisis." Since 1951, however, Japan's electric power industry has bounced back with a vengeance, increasing its energy sales by 20-fold. The nine newly restructured utilities produced 30 TWh in 1951; by 1990, they sold 609 TWh, for an average annual growth rate of 8.2% ("Some Lessons ...," 1991).

Japan's supply mix has vacillated over the years with the introduction of technology advances, changing fuel prices, resource availability, and other factors. However, unlike many other nations, the sources of Japan's energy supplies have also changed as a result of the studied and forward-looking policy efforts of the government. According to Roger Gale (1981, pp. 86–7) of the Berkeley Institute of East Asian Studies, one of the wisdoms of Japan's policy for supplying energy is its medium-term perspective. "Not coincidentally, the span is measured at around 30 years, the expected lifetime of larger electric power plants. In contrast to the United States, where a workable distinction between the purportedly imminently achievable and the possible is now rigidly drawn, Japan has been able to avoid the discordant shifts in energy policy that are so common in the United States. Both countries have trouble contemplating the future, but Japan's goals have remained stable. Those goals include a diversification of energy sources by type and geography, a lid on oil consumption, increased reliance on nuclear power, and the medium-term use of liquified natural gas (LNG) and coal."

In the first postwar decade, the government's official policy was to develop hydroelectricity as the country's main power source and to use thermal plants as backup (Hein, 1990). But as the result of several events, hydroelectricity rapidly began falling from favor. First, most of the country's good hydroelectric sites had already been developed. Second, rapid progress in United States thermal power technology had improved efficiency and made large-scale thermal plants possible, thus sharply increasing these plants' economic efficiency (Public Utilities Dept., 1988). Coupled with falling fossil fuel prices and the facts that thermal generation is more stable than hydro and thermal plants are less costly and faster to build, the industry moved toward fossil fuels.

By 1955, with the passage of the Heavy Boiler Law, Japan's utilities were required to use coal. The power industry found this acceptable because utili-

ties were able to buy domestic coal cheaply. However, the newest electric turbines were oil-fired when the prices for oil fell below those of coal in 1958.
As a result, the utilities shifted toward cheap oil. In December 1959, the in-
fluential Arisawa Commission Report argued that domestic coal was a victim
of an international "energy revolution" and that Japan should change its energy policies and economic strategy to rely on imported oil (Hein, 1990). By that
time, the changeover from coal to oil was already in full swing, urged on by
the low price for oil.

Thermal power took the lead from hydroelectric power as Japan's dominant
energy source in the early 1960s (1961 for the nine utilities and 1963 for the
industry as a whole) (Public Utilities Department, 1988). The fuel consumption of Japan's thermal plants changed during this decade. Originally coal-
fired, these plants first moved to heavy oil and then to crude oil as a result of
pollution concerns and cost efficiency. By 1964, crude oil accounted for 15%
of the fuels used in thermal power generation (JEPIC, 1990).

TEPCO began importing liquified natural gas (LNG) in 1969, not as part of
a long-term strategy but simply because it seemed the quickest, cheapest way
to reduce air pollution in the midst of a growing environmental crisis. Liquified natural gas enjoyed the additional advantages of being available in 20-
year contracts and not requiring sophisticated technology to burn, thus providing Japan with an ideal medium-term way to diversify its energy sources.

Just as the first international energy crisis stunned the world in 1973,
Japan's dependence on thermal power was over 80%, and its dependence on
oil-related fuels for thermal power generation was 87% (Public Utilities Dept.,
1988). As a result, the electricity supply structure of Japan suffered a major
blow.

The oil crisis years, ironically, saw the near-demise of coal use in Japan.
TEPCO's use of coal had peaked in 1965, but it stopped burning this fuel after
1973. The environmental effects of coal burning, labor disputes, mining accidents, and the exhaustion of the most efficient mines all contributed to the
abrupt drop-off in coal burning. By the mid-1970s, only Kyushu Electric and
Hokkaido Electric were burning coal, relying almost entirely on the coal
mined on the two islands that comprise their service territories.

The late 1970s and early 1980s saw a utility industry that was concerned
about supply instability, surging oil prices, and the imposition of stringent antipollution measures. During this period, Japan experienced significant growth
in the use of nuclear power and imported natural gas for electricity generation.
By the early 1980s, LNG supplied about the same amount of electric power as
TEPCO's six nuclear reactors, even though the decision to import LNG was
made 15 to 20 years after the company made the commitment to "go nuclear."

Today, oil still plays a significant role in the generation of thermal power to
provide peak-load power, but its role in total generation has declined to around

Table 6-5. *Current sources of thermal power generation fuels, Japan*

Fuel	Sources
Coal	Australia (70%), People's Republic of China, South Africa, Canada, United States
Oil	United Arab Emirates, Saudi Arabia, Iran, People's Republic of China
LNG	Indonesia, Brunei, Malaysia, United Arab Emirates, United States
Uranium	Canada, United Kingdom, Australia, Niger, United States

Source: Nihon Denki Kyokai. *Anata no Shiritai Koto: Denki Jigyo ni Tsuite no 43 no Shitsumon to To 1990* (43 Questions and Answers Concerning the Electric Power Industry 1990). Tokyo, 1990, p. 53.

29%. Oil has been displaced by two other controversial energy sources, LNG and nuclear power, whereas coal use is again on the rise (see Table 6-5).

One of Japan's attempts to wean itself from oil is being accomplished through its substitution with another scarce commodity, LNG. The volatility of this fuel produced fierce opposition to its importation into the United States and other nations, and by the 1980s, Japan was one of only a few countries that import LNG for power generation. Nonetheless, it is still pursuing a "no holds barred" LNG import policy, which has turned Japan into the world's largest consumer of LNG (Gale, 1981). In 1990, Japan imported 47.9 billion cubic meters of LNG; France, the second-largest importer, took 9.3 billion cubic meters in that year (British Petroleum Company, 1991). Public hearings on the construction of new LNG storage terminals in the Tokyo Bay area and the Inland Sea have provoked only minor protests. In addition, the siting of LNG-fired power plants, all of which are in congested areas, has not been subjected to the long delays that Japanese utilities have experienced in constructing other types of power plants in rural areas. As a result, the use of LNG has risen more rapidly than that of nuclear power. Japan obtains its LNG supply through inflexible take-or-pay agreements, and the country's utilities are now negotiating to amend this clause with their suppliers (JEPIC, 1990).

Japan contracts for 210,000 short tons of natural uranium from Canada, the United Kingdom, Australia, Niger, and the United States. The United States supplies Japan with 3,000 tons SWU of enriched uranium each year, and European consortiums are under contract to supply 16,000 tons SWU by the year 2000 (JEPIC, 1990). In addition, a private complex for enrichment, spent fuel reprocessing, and a low-level waste repository is being built in Rakkasho, Aomori Prefecture. Japan also has a reprocessing plant in Ibaraki Prefecture and contracts with private concerns to reprocess spent fuel. As a result of these measures, the electric power industry has secured sufficient supplies of natural and enriched uranium to operate its nuclear power plants into at least the mid-1990s.

Given the scarcity of land in Japan, the heightening antinuclear feelings in the country (due in large part to Japan's unfortunate position as the only country that has been attacked by nuclear bombs), and the looming possibility of seismic disturbances such as volcanic eruptions, Japanese electric utilities continue to encounter difficulties in finding new sites for additional nuclear capacity. Despite these obstacles, nuclear development has a high profile in the Japanese government's long-term supply plans. According to Managing Director Ota of Chubu Electric, MITI's 1990 projection of future electricity demand in Japan "puts stress on nuclear power development from the standpoint of energy security and the reduction of carbon dioxide emissions. In fiscal 2000, the nuclear capacity is scheduled to be 50,000 MW against an actual 28,700 MW in fiscal 1988 ... and in 2010 it is expected to be 72,000 MW. This is a drastic and challenging plan to increase capacity by 150 percent in the next two decades" (Ota, 1991).

Roger Gale (1981, pp. 101–2) found that, "It is MITI, using the successful example of the Electric Power Development Company's (EPDC) pioneering development of new technologies for burning coal, that is in the vanguard of the movement to use coal," not the utilities, which are only reluctantly returning to coal. The EPDC's experience suggests that coal-fired plants can meet Japan's rigid clean-air standards and are not opposed by a large portion of the population, unlike nuclear power. For years, MITI had pushed Japan's power industry to move more quickly to coal. The utilities, however, remained unexcited about this fuel, sensing they were being pushed into the coal importing business by MITI. Only when MITI hinted in 1979 that it would help EPDC finance the acquisition of large reserves of Australian coal and encouraged them to secure minority shareholdings in a number of companies did the utilities band together to establish the Japan Coal Development Company, a coordinating body that helps utilities secure long-term contracts for coal. According to Gale, "Although Japanese utilities are capable of moving with great haste, as exemplified by their aggressive LNG acquisitions, they are also capable of moving with glacial slowness when they are not attuned to MITI's desires" (1981, pp. 103–5). Many Japanese decisionmakers, however, are now questioning whether the importation of large amounts of United States and Australian coal will strengthen Japan's security or only worsen economic antagonisms and strain bilateral relations (Gale, 1981, p. 104).

Japan currently imports more than 80% of its energy requirements; according to Hiroji Ota (1991), managing director of the Chubu Electric Power Company, this represents "Japan's fundamental vulnerability." Japan's electric utilities rely on the trading companies to manage their foreign business affairs (Gale, 1981). Because these utilities are in the market for such large amounts

Table 6-6. *Electricity in Japan, fiscal 1951–1989 (100 million kWh)*

		1951	1965	1975	1985	1988	1989
Hydro	Utilities	331	701	793	812	886	905
power	Self-generation	40	51	66	68	73	73
	Total	371	752	859	879	959	978
Thermal	Utilities	71	975	3,096	3,638	4,005	4,323
power	Self-generation	31	175	551	607	786	858
	Total	102	1,150	3,648	4,244	4,972	5,181
Nuclear	Utilities	—	—	251	1,590	1,776	1,819
power	Self-generation	—	—	—	6	10	10
	Total	—	—	251	1,596	1,787	1,829
Total	Utilities	403	1,676	4,140	6,039	6,668	7,047
	Self-generation	71	226	618	680	870	941
	Total	474	1,903	4,758	6,720	7,537	7,988

Source: Nihon Denki Kyokai. *Anata no Shiritai Koto: Denki Jigyo ni Tsuite no 43 no Shitsumon to To 1990* (43 Questions and Answers Concerning the Electric Power Industry 1990). Tokyo, 1990, p. 42.

of uranium, LNG, coal, and oil, it is perceived that the trading companies tend to spend a disproportionate amount of time attending to the utilities' affairs. Electric utilities are now beginning to edge out Japan's oil companies as primary purchasers of energy from abroad.

For fiscal year 1989 (April 1989 to March 1990), the fuel consumption of Japan's thermal power plants totaled 97,580,000 kl (heavy-oil equivalent), a 7.1% increase over the previous year (Nihon Denki Kyokai, 1990a). Use of coal, heavy oil, crude oil, and LNG increased by 3.8, 13.1, 7.4, and 6.6%, respectively. The consumption mix of these utilities was heavy oil 23.6%, crude oil 18.4%, coal 15.5%, LNG 34.4%, and other fuels 8.1% (Nihon Denki Kyokai, 1990a). Together, Japan's nuclear power plants generated 181.9 billion kWh (41 million kl) in fiscal 1989 (Nihon Denki Kyokai, 1990a).

Japan's electric power industry has adopted a new policy to purchase electricity at fair prices from independent power producers such as self-generators or from local governments that have generators combined with refuse incinerators. The country's self-generators produced only 7.1 billion kWh in 1951, but their production reached 94.1 billion kWh in 1989 (see Table 6-6).

The Electric Utility Industry Council projects that Japan's supply capability will be 227.7 GW in fiscal 2000 and 267.0 GW in fiscal 2010 (Ota, 1991). Its generating capacity is expected to increase by 58,390 MW in the 1990s (JEPIC, 1990). Nuclear power will account for 32% of this growth, with gen-

Table 6-7. *Fuel sources for electricity generation, FY 1988 to 2010 (in percentages)*

Fuel	Fiscal 1988 (actual)	Fiscal 2000	Fiscal 2010
Oil, etc.	29.2	17.0	10.0
Geothermal	0.2	1.0	2.0
Hydropower	13.1	11.0	11.0
LNG	21.2	20.0	18.0
Coal	9.5	16.0	15.0
Nuclear power	26.6	35.0	43.0
Methanol	0.0	0.0	0.3
Wind, solar, etc.	0.0	0.3	2.0
Total supply (billion kWh)	666.8	946.0	1109.0

Source: Nihon Denki Kyokai (Demand–Supply Division of the Electric Power Industry Advisory Council). *Denki Jigyo no Genjo, 1990* (The Current Status of the Electric Power Industry, 1990). Interim Report. Tokyo, 1990, p. 36.

erating capacity reaching 48,140 MW. Thermal power plants, mainly coal-fired and LNG-fired, will contribute 55% of the increase. As a result, the share of oil-fired facilities in electricity generation will be reduced from 29% to 10% by 2010 (Table 6-7).

Within a decade, Japan's peak-load supply capability is expected to increase 31.7% to 181,527 MW (JEPIC, 1990). Of this total, the shares of peak hydroelectric, thermal, and nuclear supply capabilities will be 19%, 61.1%, and 19.9%, respectively. The industry's reserve margin will be approximately 9.7% by the year 2000.

According to Hiroji Ota, managing director of the Chubu Electric Power Company, Japan must develop 15,000 MW of generating capacity each year in order to meet projected demand (Ota, 1991). Investment in new electric power supply facilities will require that private companies spend about $96 billion between 1991 and 1993 to provide this power. These funds must be raised commercially.

The electric utility industry's financial health

During the Occupation, the Japanese government removed its financial support from the country's electric utilities, and many power companies were unable to adjust their finances. As a result, they found their deficits rising and their credit declining. Local banks were soon reluctant to provide more money to the power companies. The utilities then turned to the Reconstruction Finance Bank for loans that were used to meet their current operating expenses (loans granted to the industry accounted for about 16% of all the Bank's loans to industrial enterprises during this period).

The electric power industry was a major beneficiary of the many tax, tariff, and depreciation exemptions enjoyed by Japanese industry in the 1950s (Hein, 1990). It soon became a "key industry" in order to become eligible for maximum aid. In addition, the Japanese government used a number of ad hoc methods to help certain favored industries (electric power clearly being one of these) to accumulate capital. For instance, in 1955 the Ministry of Finance allowed the electric utilities to convert their short-term loans into long-term debts in a special one-time move. This allowed the utilities to transform $140 million worth of loans from private financial institutions into company debentures (at 8.5% interest for five years). They also received loans from the World Bank, which served as a key force in their reconstruction efforts.

After 1954, the "maker's credit" system became the primary method of financing new power plants and later was important in the development of nuclear power. Under this system, United States companies borrowed funds from the United States Export–Import Bank and allowed the Japanese utilities to buy new machinery from them on credit. The Japan Development Bank stood as the guarantor for these loans.

During the mid-1970s, operation and maintenance costs for utilities rose dramatically (for example, as a percentage of total plant costs, O&M costs for PWR and BWR nuclear power plants increased from 8.4% per year in 1973 to 17.1% per year by 1985) (Uchiyama, 1988). The major causes of these increases were rising capital charges resulting from a reduction in the operating rate of plants and other facilities, increased fuel costs, especially for LNG, and increases in the costs to carry on business (e.g., salaries). In response, utilities implemented rigorous cost controls, such as cutting maintenance cost and facility expansion and reducing the unit cost and volume of new construction.

During the late 1970s and early 1980s, the electric utility industry suffered another financial deterioration as a direct result of a number of exogenous factors, including oil price escalation, abrupt and radical changes in the exchange rate, and inflation following the two oil crises. In response, the utilities sought major rate increases in 1974, 1976, and 1980 (as the yen climbed and oil prices dropped beginning in late 1985, the utilities tentatively lowered their rates on two occasions) (JEPIC, 1988). As a result, their financial performance improved from 1982 onward. Japan's utilities, which together incurred losses of nearly ¥5 billion in 1979, saw their fortunes rise in 1984, when they recorded profits of ¥23.4 billion. During this period, their net worth increased from *minus* ¥108 billion to ¥924 billion (see Table 6-8).

Table 6-8. *Financial data on electric utilities in Japan, 1979 and 1984*

	1979	1984
Ratio of net worth to net profit	13.4%	15.2%
Net profit (1 billion yen)	−108	924
Net worth (1 billion yen)	2,264	3,943
Ratio of profits to net worth	−4.8%	23.4%
Business profits (1 billion yen)	616	2,155
Total liabilities and net worth (1 billion yen)	16,941	25,989
Ratio of business profit to total liabilities and net worth	3.4%	8.3%
Leverage ratio	6.5%	5.6%

Source: Tomita, Teruhiro. "Simulation Analysis with a Financial Model of Japanese Electric Utilities." *CRIEPI-EPRI Workshop on Energy Analysis.* CRIEPI Report 1987. Tokyo: Central Research Institute of Electric Power Industry, 1987, p. 159.

Japan's electric utilities still face financial difficulties due to such exogenous factors. To deal with these problems, they have been promoting both cost reduction and the diversification of power sources (Tomita, 1987). Today, the burden of capital costs for electric source diversification has become the greatest straining factor for utility management, and its reduction has become a task of increasing importance.

The Japanese government provides capital to the electric utility and other industries to promote particular national policy goals. For example, through the Japan National Oil Company, MITI provides loans and guarantees to the oil industry for off-shore exploration. For electric utilities, these loans are designed to reduce Japan's dependence on oil imports and to stabilize electricity prices by financing coal conversion, conservation, and nuclear power development (Japan Development Bank, 1984). The loan program is administered by the Japan Development Bank (JDB), which typically lends at interest rates 200 basis points below market (Bronte, 1984). The electric utility industry accounts for 45% (¥3.5 trillion) of JDB's total outstanding loans, making it the bank's single largest beneficiary. These loans convey an annual subsidy of approximately ¥70 billion.

"The voracious appetite for new capital in the utility industry dwarfs the demands of any other industry in Japan" (Gale, 1981, p. 86). At approximately $5 billion, TEPCO's capital spending plan for fiscal 1980 was the largest such budget for any company in Japan and the largest of any private utility in the world (Gale, 1981, pp. 91–2). In terms of capital, six of Japan's 10 "common" utilities rank among the 25 largest companies in the country, some of them ahead of such giants as Hitachi and Toyota (see Table 6-9).

Table 6-9. *The 25 largest Japanese companies ranked by capital (excluding banking companies) as of March 31, 1990 (in ¥100 million)*

Company	Capital	Company	Capital
Nippon Telephone & Telegram	7,800.0	Fujitsu	2,161.9
Tokyo Electric Power	6,571.1	Kobe Steel	2,127.1
Kansai Electric Power	4,771.9	Sumitomo Metal Industries	2,040.4
Nippon Steel	4,188.5	Nissan Motors	2,021.6
Chubu Electric Power	3,615.8	Marubeni	1,896.1
Sony	2,780.4	Japan Air Lines	1,882.9
Toshiba	2,617.2	Toyota Motors	1,873.2
Mitsubishi Heavy Industries	2,596.0	Matsushita Electronic Industrial	1,849.4
Hitachi	2,469.1	Chugoku Electric Power	1,822.8
Tohoku Electric Power	2,468.1	Nomura Securities	1,807.1
Kawasaki Steel	2,396.3	NEC	1,753.5
Kyushu Electric Power	2,353.5	C. Itoh	1,742.3
Nippon Kokan	2,335.1		

Source: Chugoku Electric Power Company, Inc. *Annual Report, 1990.* Hiroshima, 1990, p. 9.

*Economies of scale:*Seishi Madono and Yasuo Nakanishi (1989) of the Central Research Institute of Electric Power Industry (CRIEPI) employed a variable-cost function and a static equilibrium model to measure the optimal capital stock level (slightly less than the actual capital stock) for utilities, and then used that level to compute the economies of scale for Japan's nine electric utilities between 1981 and 1985. These researchers found that the actual stock levels are excessive in capacity for most of the firms and that the firms react on the short-run cost curve. They did not conclude that the Averch–Johnson effect (that utilities have a tendency to invest in ways that inflate the rate base) was the cause of this phenomenon. Nakanishi and Madono also found that although economies of scale existed in the short run (ranging between −0.372 and 0.820) and resulted from excess capacity, they did not exist in the long run (ranging from −0.0924 to −0.0646).

Nariyasu Itoh and Yasuo Nakanishi (1988) of CRIEPI measured the scale economy (defined as a proportion of the rate of increase in the amount of electricity with respect to the rate of increase in cost) for these utilities between 1961 and 1985. They found that scale economies decreased at the aggregate firm level (generation, transmission, distribution, etc.), from 0.785 in 1961 to 0.164 in 1985. At the aggregate generation level, however, they found that these economies have all but disappeared (from 0.809 in 1966 to −0.150 in

Table 6-10. *Economies of scale, 1961 to 1985*

	Aggregate		Large firms		Medium firms	
Year	Firm level	Generation level	Firm level	Generation level	Firm level	Generation level
1961	0.785	—	—	—	—	—
1963	0.831	—	0.558	0.331	—	0.265
1966	0.806	0.809	0.451	0.231	—	0.267
1970	0.745	0.427	0.296	0.081	0.969	0.214
1975	0.285	−0.030	0.212	−0.057	0.534	−0.109
1980	0.048	−0.231	0.127	−0.196	0.213	−0.254
1984	0.135	−0.150	0.048	−0.261	0.340	−0.123
1985	0.164		0.040		0.343	

Source: Itoh, Nariyasu and Yasuo Nakanishi. *Denki Jigyo ni Okeru Kibo no Keizaisei* (Economies of Scale in Japanese Electric Utilities). CRIEPI Report No. Y807107. Tokyo: Economic Research Center, Central Research Institute of Electric Power Industry, July 1988, p. 7.

1984). Their results were similar for both individual large and medium-sized utilities (see Table 6-10).

   In another study, Teruhiro Tomita (1990) calculated the average scale elasticity of the nine utilities between 1978 and 1987 (Table 6-11). He found that all but Tokyo Electric, Chubu Electric, Chugoku Electric, and Kansai Electric had elasticities above 1.

Industry efficiency: A 1990 study by Teruhiro Tomita analyzed the efficiency of the electric power industry in Japan, using total-factor productivity analysis induced by a translog cost function (Tomita, 1990, pp. 1–12). This technique attempts to measure an industry's productivity by measuring all of its factors of production (e.g., employees, material, capital). Tomita found that total factor productivity averaged −0.01456 for the nine utilities for the period from 1979 to 1987, against a technology growth rate of −0.0527. Tomita pointed out that the technology growth rate of the smaller-scale utilities is more negative, in the −2 to −3% range. He concluded that this is the cause of the negative total-factor productivity growth rate for the industry as a whole. Tomita also stressed that the total-factor productivity growth rate has worsened in recent years; for 1979 to 1984, it was −1.42% for the nine utilities, but for 1985–7, it dropped to −1.62%.

   In another study, Nariyasu Itoh (1988) compared the electricity rates and cost structure of Japan's electric utilities with those of utilities in other coun-

Table 6-11. *Average scale elasticity of nine utilities, 1978–1987*

Tokyo Electric	0.879	Tohoku Electric	1.028
Chubu Electric	0.959	Shikoku Electric	1.080
Kansai Electric	0.924	Kyushu Electric	1.008
Chugoku Electric	0.050	Hokkaido Electric	1.091
Hokuriku Electric	1.136		

Source: Tomita, Teruhiro. "Denki Jigyo no Seisansei Bunseki" (Total Factor Productivity Analysis of Japanese Electric Power Industry). *Information and Communication Studies,* vol. 9, 1990, p. 6.

tries. He also compared total-factor productivity, labor productivity, thermal efficiency, and other factors. He found that Japan's productivity was lower than the levels in other countries, concluding that this reflects factors such as the strictness of regulations in Japan, and citing a need to reexamine factors concerning regulations, including the Averch–Johnson effect.

Investment behavior and diversification: According to Etsuji Ohsawa, advisor to CRIEPI, the basic issue for Japan's electric power industry is the establishment and maintenance of a stable electrical supply structure (Ohsawa, 1991). With this in mind, Ohsawa stated, the industry independently makes decisions on investment in facilities. Thus, it is thought that regulations do not affect the investment behaviors of Japan's electric utilities.

Takashi Nagao of the Japan Electric Power Information Center holds a slightly different view, observing that the investment behavior of the utilities is influenced by rates. According to Nagao (1991), MITI does not approve tariff revisions until it understands the need for capital expenditures or demand forecasts. Because it takes a great deal of time for the utilities to gather the necessary justification for a proposed rate increase and for MITI to approve it, the electric power companies must generally use the same tariffs for several years, and their profits begin to decline. Under such circumstances, the utilities are discouraged from investing, and after new tariffs are approved, they are encouraged.

Teruhiro Tomita (1988) observed that the Japanese electric power industry is extremely cautious concerning its investment in new power facilities, and as a result, one can see a tendency to "overengineer." Although Japan's electric utilities may be somewhat reluctant to invest in new power facilities, they have openly embraced investments in diversification. In recent years, the electric power companies have been making moves to participate in other energy and nonenergy industries, and nonelectric power companies (e.g., gas utilities) have been doing the same with the electric power industry (Tomita, 1988b).

One area in which utilities have been focusing is district heating services that use waste heat from large cities. In 1989, TEPCO began the operation of its first commercial district heating service, which uses water discharged into a river in the Hakozaki area of Tokyo (JEPIC, 1990). In April 1989, it completed a district heating system in the Makuhari area, which is a newly developed city center accommodating a conference center, office buildings, and residential units.

Japan's electric power companies gained entry into the telecommunications field with the enactment of the Telecommunications Industry Law of April 1985 (JEPIC, 1988). In August 1986, the mobile telecommunications industry in Japan was deregulated, giving the utilities further opportunities for market entry. The following examples provide but a brief illustration of the enthusiasm with which Japan's electric power companies are entering this field.

Chubu Telecommunications Co., Ltd., a subsidiary of Chubu Electric Power Company (1990), operates a private-line service for corporations in four prefectures. A semiaffiliate, Chubu Telemessage, Inc., is expanding its pocket-pager service. Car telephone and portable telephone services are run by Nippon Idou Tsushin Corporation, and cable television services are mainly handled by Chuden Construction Company, Inc., another subsidiary of Chubu Electric, which currently serves 2,896 families in the Nagoya area.

In March 1986, TEPCO (1990) established Tokyo Telecommunications Network Company. Its several general trading companies provide industrial-use facsimile, data transmission, and public telephone services. TEPCO has also entered into such other new ventures as mobile telecommunications, international value-added network (VAN) systems, and cable television. TEPCO Cable TV was established in November 1989.

During fiscal 1990, Kyushu Electric Power Company (1990) established Kyushu Telemessage Company, Ltd. to market pocket-paging systems, and Kyushu Telecommunication Network Co., Ltd. to deal in car phones.

In 1989, Shikoku Information & Telecommunication Network Co., Inc., a subsidiary of Shikoku Electric Power Company (1990), began a fixed telecommunications business as a common carrier, providing telephone and data communication services. The utility is also involved in the mobile telecommunications business through the joint management of Shikoku Cellular Telephone Company, a portable and car telephone company established in April 1989, and pocket-pager companies in Shikoku's four prefectures. In January 1990, the Shikoku Electric group and NGK Insulators jointly established Techno-Success Co., an electric equipment manufacturing company.

As of March 31, 1990, Kansai Electric Power Company (1990) had equity participation of 20% or more in 38 corporations, including general contracting, electric equipment and apparatus manufacturing, architectural engineering, and consulting services. Kansai's stated goal is that the new businesses it operates will "have grown to account for half of the entire Kansai Electric group's business" by 2030 (Kansai, 1990).

When an electric power company diversifies, it can do so by either directly undertaking the new business or by investing in corporations that operate the new business. Provisions in Article 12 of the Electric Utility Industry Law of 1964 cover the engagement of an electric utility in other business activities (JEPIC, 1988). Under this law, a utility must secure approval from the Minister of MITI before engaging in another business. To obtain the Minister's approval, the diversification of utility business must not conflict with the public interest, the utilities must refrain from exercising monopoly power (areas to be entered should be such that new markets are created by the participation of the utilities), and cross-subsidization should be avoided. On the whole, however, the Japanese government regards utility diversification as using the electric power companies' assets and to respond to social needs. Investing in a new business is also covered under this law, which does not treat a utility's investment activity as a business activity to be approved but as an item to be reported to the Minister after such an activity has taken place.

Japan's electric utilities are supported in these efforts by CRIEPI (1990), which is currently investigating realistic strategies for the industry's diversification. CRIEPI's aim is for a power company to contribute to the economy not only as an electric power supplier but also as a major regional industry in order to strengthen the electric power company's business foundation in the face of growing competition. CRIEPI has identified urban planning development as the new diversification business for Japan's electric utility companies.

Competition: Since the 1970s, the Japanese energy industry has entered a period of increasing competition, stemming from deregulation and drastic changes in both the nation's energy demand structure and the technological systems for energy supply (e.g., decentralized power-generating units such as cogeneration, which might undermine the economies of scale in power service). These new technical systems have paved the way for the participation of gas utilities, oil companies, and other energy suppliers in the electric service market. Such new systems are said to be "challenging the principle by which the licensed electric utilities can claim the need for regional monopolies" (JEPIC, 1988).

The cases of self-generation and utility bypass illustrate the intense competition Japan's electric utility industry is facing from other energy suppliers. Today, self-generation in Japan is not regulated in principle, except for the maintenance of generating equipment. Although most self-generators produce electricity only for their own demand, some companies also serve the loads of nearby related companies. Industrial self-generators represented about 9% of the country's total installed capacity and 10.6% of the total electric energy generated in Japan in 1987. There are only a few self-generating facilities in the country for residential and commercial uses, which provide only about 0.05% of the country's total installed capacity (JEPIC, 1988). Many of these systems are used for office buildings. In the past few years, however, the oil industry has begun to open up a new market in the residential and commercial sectors for self-generation, using sales promotions stressing the particularly high thermal efficiency of cogeneration facilities that use gas turbines, gas engines, or diesel fuel.

Competition with other types of energy supply companies is expected to increase in coming years as the liberalization and deregulation process continues in the electric utility industry. Such competition is significantly influenced by prices, and market shares depend largely on the development of techniques for energy use. As a result, efforts to cut the cost of energy production are becoming increasingly important for Japan's electric utilities, and there is growing competition in the development of new techniques for energy use such as thermal storage-type heat pumps.

Regulation of the electric utility industry

Several regulatory changes designed to weaken the enormous powers of Japan's electric utilities were implemented after World War II. In 1946, the government revised the Electric Utility Industry Law again, this time to separate the electric railway industry from the electric power industry, to allow the determination of electricity rates by the "competent" Minister (at that time, the Minister of Communications), and to require utilities to obtain permission from the Minister on various issues (Public Utility Department, 1988).

The Law for the Elimination of Excessive Concentration of Electric Power, directed at breaking up monopolistic enterprises, was applied to Hassoden and the electricity companies in 1948 (JEPIC, 1990). Until 1951 when the nine vertically integrated utilities were established, the reorganization of the electric power industry elicited strong debate among government officials and fervent opposition from the utilities. As Richard Samuels (1987) succinctly states, "No sector of the Japanese political economy offers more sustained evidence of private resistance to state intervention than electric power."

The electric utility industry was placed under the supervision of the Electric Power Bureau of the Ministry of International Trade and Industry (MITI) when the ministry was established in 1949 (Johnson, 1982). All the bureaus in charge of energy (including the Electric Power Bureau) were then grouped into one external bureau of MITI, the Resources Agency, in order to downplay their importance. This agency was abolished in 1952. (It was reestablished in 1973, when energy policy once again became a matter of urgency, as the Agency of Natural Resources and Energy.) According to one observer, "All of these internal MITI arrangements were intended to reorient it away from MCI's [the Ministry of Commerce and Industry] emphasis on internal control and priority production and toward international trade and the promotion of exports" (Johnson, 1982, p. 192).

In late 1950, the Electric Utility Industry Law and the Electric Power Control Law were abolished and the industry was reorganized under the Electric Utility Industry Reorganization Order and the Public Utilities Order (JEPIC, 1990). Based on these orders, the Public Utility Commission (PUC), an independent administrative body, was established in December 1950 to oversee the electric and gas companies.

With the outbreak of the Korean War, officials of SCAP (Supreme Commander of the Allied Powers) stepped up their pressure on the Japanese to accept the privatization of the electric power industry. The government at last divested itself of its holdings in the industry in May 1951, selling its generating facilities to nine public stock companies. Nippon Hassoden was abolished, and the public stock companies became Japan's nine privately owned electric companies, each of which enjoyed a regional monopoly.

At the end of the Occupation in August 1952, the PUC was abolished. It had been opposed by both the liberal party, which attacked the PUC for granting rate increases too quickly, and the general public, who perceived it as aiding, rather than regulating, the industry. In the PUC's stead came the Public Utilities Bureau, which was established as part of MITI. According to Richard Samuels (1987, p. 161), the PUC had been one of the "most powerful, peculiar, and short-lived (19 months) organs in the history of Japanese public administration." The jurisdiction over the nine utilities was thus transferred back to MITI.

The demise of the PUC, the transfer of jurisdiction over the nine utilities back to MITI, and the creation of the Electric Power Development Company (EPDC) in 1958 as a close affiliate of both MITI and the utilities brought the power companies under tighter government oversight. The establishment of EPDC in particular returned the government to the power generation business, albeit on a limited basis. Although the government again had more policy control over the industry, the utilities themselves were also more powerful than they were before the war, and Japan's electric power company officials did not seriously fear the recurrence of state control.

In 1962, the Electric Utility Industry Advisory Council (also known as the Electric Industry Advisory Council) was created as an advisory body for MITI. It is in charge of deliberating issues of concern to the industry, such as government regulations, industry goals, and safety systems. The Council wields considerable influence. Its work was taken into consideration by the Diet when it passed the current Electric Utility Industry Law, which became effective in 1965, and it also has a strong voice in the determination of rate increases.

The 1960s witnessed the passage of a number of environmental laws. The Basic Law for Environmental Pollution Control of 1967, the Air Pollution Control Law and Noise Control Law of 1968, and the Water Pollution Control Law of 1969 mandated that power stations operate under a strict set of regulations concerning pollution.

The MITI established the Agency of Natural Resources and Energy in 1973 to integrate the ministry's polices in this area. Also, recognizing the need to encourage public acceptance of new power plant construction projects, the government passed three laws in 1974 to provide tax benefits to local communities located near construction sites (JEPIC, 1990).

The oil crisis of 1979 acted as a catalyst to increase Japan's determination to lessen its dependence on imported oil. The Law for Promoting Development and Introduction of Alternative Energies to Oil was implemented in May 1980 in accordance with the International Energy Agency's resolution that advised against the construction of new oil-burning thermal plants and promoted the use of coal (JEPIC, 1990).

Regulatory institutions: Today, the Ministry of International Trade and Industry is virtually the only body through which Japan's electric power utilities are supervised (Gale, 1981, p. 95). This ministry oversees utility construction plans, rates, and certain safety and environmental issues. Besides regulating the utilities, however, it also promotes them, especially their nuclear power plant programs. The MITI assists the utilities in supporting national objectives through systems of loans and tax credits as well as through active advertising and conservation campaigns and joint government–electricity sector enterprises such as the Electric Power Development Company. Although MITI "wields considerable legislative and extra-legal clout" over certain industries such as the domestic oil companies, it is "more of an arbiter between the electric power utilities and the contending interests of other industries and the consumer, rather than the regulator" (Gale, 1981, pp. 85–6).

Within MITI, the Public Utilities Department under the Agency of Natural Resources and Energy oversees the country's electric power industry and the city gas industry. This agency also supervises a number of councils, among which it distributes authority for deliberation on issues such as rates, siting, forecasting, and fuel choice.

The several industry–government councils have been set up to regulate or provide assistance to the electric utility system, or both. The most important of these is the Electric Power Industry Advisory Council, which attempts to balance utility and consumer interests, and makes public policy recommendations. Other such councils include the Electric Power Resources Investigation Advisory Council, which plays a key role in siting power plants; the Central Electric Power Council, which coordinates industry views before bringing them before formal government councils; and at least three advisory councils to the nuclear power industry.

Tokyo Electric Power Company (TEPCO) provides an illustration of the degree of cooperation between MITI and the utilities, as well as its own immense influence. Within TEPCO's service territory are 31% of Japan's population and 35% of its industry, giving it enormous economic and political influence. Roger Gale (1981, p. 94) has found that "what most distinguishes TEPCO from its American cousins – because of its size – is its relative autonomy and freedom from regulations. The MITI does not allow TEPCO to do as it pleases, but it does guarantee it a broad freedom *from* unwanted regulatory controls" (Gale, 1981, p. 94). TEPCO is perceived as exercising suzerainty over Japan's other electric utilities and wields powerful influence in the formulation of national energy policy. "Through the Federation of Electric Power Companies (Denki Jigyo Rengokai), TEPCO's influence over MITI, the trading companies, and other actors in the energy arena has become increasingly institutionalized" (Gale, 1981, p. 85).

Regulations governing the industry: The basic law governing Japan's electric utilities today is the Electric Utility Industry Law of 1964, which aims to facilitate the rational development of the industry in a safe manner, promote cooperation between regions, and protect consumer interest (International Energy Agency, 1985). Although recognizing that the regional power companies have a monopoly in supplying power to their respective service areas, the law stipulates that electricity be provided to all residents, that services be integrated over a wide area, and that facilities be safe. The law also features rules on the international coordination of utility matters.

Until recently, the law also prohibited the direct sale of surplus electricity to end-users by power sources other than the common utilities, except in the severely restricted case of "special supply." The MITI relaxed this restriction in November 1987; now, electricity created by self-generation may be sold to an end-user if the self-generation facility and end-user are located in the same building (Ohsawa, 1991). In practice, however, whether to allow for parallel operation is a matter that is often left to the individual electric utilities.

Two taxes are applied to electric power companies in addition to corporate income tax. The first is the Promotion of Power Resources Development Tax, which is applied to electricity sales and the proceeds of which are used for the promotion of electric power siting and electric power source diversification by the Japanese government. The other is the Electricity Tax, which is applied to electricity use and the proceeds of which accrue to the general revenue accounts of the municipal governments. These taxes compensate local governments for allowing the construction of power plants within or adjacent to their jurisdictions (Gale, 1981, p. 95).

The Law Regulating Nuclear Source Materials, Nuclear Fuel Materials, and Nuclear Reactors, as well as the Electric Utility Industry Law, stipulate that incidents and failures at nuclear plants be reported to MITI. These laws also give MITI responsibility for permitting nuclear plant establishment, approving detailed construction plans, approving safety regulations established by the electric power companies, safety analysis, regulatory inspection, and other aspects of nuclear plants.

Although Japan's electric utilities enjoy far more freedom from regulation than their counterparts in the United States, they do face fairly stringent pollution control requirements. When emissions from thermal power generation began to rise with increased oil consumption in the late 1960s, the government began to impose antipollution measures that required electric utilities to adopt high-quality fuels such as LNG to reduce emissions of sulfur oxides, nitrogen oxides, and particulates.

The Basic Law for Environmental Pollution Control of 1967 and the Air Pollution Control Law of 1968 provide for systematic countermeasures against pollution. The Basic Law sets ambient air quality standards for five kinds of pollutants; these standards are very strict compared with those of other OECD countries. The Air Pollution Control Law sets emission standards for areas of the country, standards for stack heights in the case of sulfur (SOx), and standards for the type and scale of facility in the case of nitrous oxide (NOx) and particulates. In areas where there are high concentrations of plants, area-wide total pollutant control standards are set with respect to NOx and SOx. In addition, the amount of radioactivity discharged from nuclear power stations is targeted so that people living nearby will receive a dose of less than one-hundredth of 500 millirems, a basic value determined by government regulation (Tokyo Electric Power Company, 1986).

A very distinctive feature of environmental administration in Japan is the existence of voluntary agreements made between the power companies and local government authorities outside the formal regulatory structure. These frequently supplement national regulations, setting target values for pollution prevention and clarifying the details of antipollution measures. Although they are frequently more strict than formal regulations and are not legally binding, the companies tend to take them seriously. These agreements place obligations on a utility to seek to prevent environmental pollution. They cover such topics as atmospheric pollutants; water quality; the prevention of noise, vibration, and offensive odors; waste processing; and liability for compensation.

Among the other pollution control measures Japan's electric utilities have undertaken are the desulfurization of heavy oil through mechanical means, moving from heavy oil to crude oil in the 1960s and 1970s, the adoption of higher stacks, and the use of electric precipitators to reduce particulate emissions. Today, Japan's electric power industry has almost fully reduced NOx and SOx, either by installing pollution control devices or by using low-sulfur crudes and LNG. (For example, clean-burning LNG is used primarily in power plants that serve main load centers such as the metropolitan areas of Tokyo and Osaka, where stringent pollution control measures exist.)

The construction of coal-fired power plants to supplement nuclear power facilities to carry base load in the 1990s and medium load in the long term has a high priority for Japan's electric power industry. The industry recognizes the benefits of coal, but it is also acutely aware of this fuel's drawbacks and the need to minimize its impact on the environment. It is thus currently working on carbon dioxide removal and coal use technologies (e.g., pressurized-fluidized bed combustion).

Plant siting has remained a volatile issue in Japan, where residents consider thermal power stations to be a major source of pollution and are deeply mistrustful of nuclear power plants. Because of the siting difficulties encountered by utility management, the government has enacted three laws to facilitate this activity. The Law on the Development of Areas Adjacent to Electric Power Generating Facilities, the Electric Power Development Promotion Law, and the Law on the Special Financial Measures for Promotion of Electric Power Development were enacted in 1974. Together, they form an incentive system of grants to local authorities who accept the siting of a power plant (Overseas Electrical Industry Survey Institute, 1982).

Retail rate structure

By the early 1950s, Japan's Public Utility Commission had approved two large rate increases. It also amended the rate structure to lower rates for industrial customers relative to those for households. Today, however, there is no explicit cross-subsidization among the country's different consuming sectors (Nishihiro, 1991).

Japan's utilities have not been granted many large rate increases in recent years. The overall rate of return for utilities was set at 8% when the rate base rule was adopted in 1960. When rates were revised in January 1988, the rate of return was reduced to 7.2% to reflect the lower interest rate at that time. The utilities file their proposed rate revisions and accompanying supporting data with MITI, which examines the data and holds public hearings for all interested parties before granting authorization for a revision.

Considering that the prices of productive factors (facilities, fuel, labor, etc.) in Japan are not internationally competitive, it is surprising that its electricity rates compare favorably with those of the United States and Western Europe. Roughly speaking, for residential electricity consumption, one hour's wage in the United States will purchase 71 kWh from Consolidated Edison, an hour's wage in Japan will buy 68 kWh from Chubu Electric, and an hour's wage in France will purchase 50 kWh from Electricité de France (Nagao, 1992).

Japan's electricity rates are based on three principles (International Energy Agency, 1985). The first is cost-based calculation, under which rates should reflect the proper cost of supplying electricity. This principle stipulates that rates be determined on the basis of the utility's total cost of service, which is calculated on the basis of forecasted costs for a certain future period. The second is fair return to the utilities; this fair rate is calculated as the "real and effective" value of property (rate base) multiplied by an appropriate number of customers. The third is the fair treatment of customers, meaning that rates should be applied without discrimination within various customer categories.

In general, electricity rates in Japan are composed of a minimum or demand charge that is applicable to every kW of a customer's contract power and an energy charge that varies according to the amount of electricity (kWh) consumed (JEPIC, 1990). In addition, there are two higher rates: a higher demand charge and a higher energy charge, which are applicable to additional demand and consumption (JEPIC, 1990). In the 1980 rate revision, a seasonal surcharge system was introduced in every service category except residential, in order to lessen the impact of summer peak loads and to further the concept of energy savings among consumers.

All of Japan's consuming sectors face progressive rate tariffs that respond to increasing average costs. (According to Etsuji Ohsawa [1991] of CRIEPI, the principal of marginal costs is used for research purposes only. However, there has been some discussion in recent years on whether the industry should introduce a rate structure that reflects marginal costs.) As a secondary effect, Japan's tariffs are also structured to encourage energy conservation. Since 1974, for example, a three-block inverted rate system has been used for residential service. Certain large-scale customers may on approval from MITI conclude a special supply contract with an electric power company at lower-than-normal rates on the condition that they can adjust their demand to terms stipulated in their contract or upon notification by the contracting power company (JEPIC, 1990).

The basic electricity rate systems: The following three rate systems form the basis of the Japanese electricity rate structure:

1. Flat rate. Under this system, electricity charges are determined according to the capacity of a customer's contract service installations, without regard to energy consumption. The rate is fixed in proportion to the wattage or volt-amperes of each contract service installation. A per-contract customer charge is collected in addition to lamp and

small appliance charges. This system is applicable only to those customers whose energy consumption is so small that it is not economical to install and read a meter for billing purposes.

2. Meter rate (minimum charge system). Under this system, customers are charged for their energy consumption only (kWh). Because the utility's fixed costs cannot be recovered under this system if there is little or no energy consumption, the utility imposes a fixed minimum charge up to a certain amount of electricity consumed.

3. Two-tier rate. This system is a combination of the flat rate and meter rate systems. Under the two-tier system, electricity charges consist of a demand charge (determined according to contract capacity, electric current, or demand in kW) and an energy charge, which increases in proportion to energy consumption. This system has been adopted for most of the country's contract categories.

In addition to these three basic systems are a number of distinctive rate systems, as follows:

First, since 1974, a three-block rate system has been in effect for the energy charge of certain residential consumers. Under this system, which is a kind of incremental rate system, energy consumption is divided into three blocks: (1) up to 120 kWh/month, the amount necessary to maintain a minimum standard of living and to which a relatively lower rate is applied; (2) 121 to 250 kWh/month, where the applicable rate is set at a level almost offsetting the average cost; and (3) over 250 kWh/month, where a rate is applied to promote energy conservation.

Second, Japan's electric utilities have offered a number of innovative electric service contracts in order to contribute to load leveling. These conservation-inducing contracts include a cut-rate contract for the use of electric water heaters at night, a seasonal price system for commercial and industrial consumers, a time-of-use contract for large industrial customers, and a time-of-day rate system for residential consumers.

A seasonal price system was introduced in 1980 to alleviate capacity strains during the summer (July through September). The summer rates are about 10% higher than the rate for other seasons to reflect the utilities' higher cost of service during the summer. All of Japan's utilities except Hokkaido Electric, whose peak loads occur during the winter, have adopted this price system. The seasonal system is applied to commercial consumers and to low-tension, high-tension, and extra-high-tension industrial power but not to lighting service. Japan's time-of-use system was implemented experimentally for high-tension Power B and extra-high-tension customers in 1988. Under this system, which is optional for the consumer, energy charges are differentiated according to time-of-use blocks fixed by the utilities. In November 1990, all 10 of Japan's utilities introduced a time-of-day rate system for residential customers. This system charges higher rates for energy consumption during the day hours and is applicable to consumers who can shift their appliance demands.

Third, Japan's load adjustment contract system allows customers to receive a reduction in their electricity bills in return for reducing their load. These contracts are formed to shift loads from daytime to nighttime throughout the year, to adjust loads during the summer, to interrupt loads when necessary (e.g., during power service disruptions, tight supply-demand situations), and to shift thermal loads (e.g., air-conditioning) from day to night. Because these contracts are more detailed than the general services contracts such as seasonal price contracts, they are subject to regulatory approval.

The allocation of fixed costs in pricing: The procedures for electricity rate determination are established in the "Guideline for Ratemaking of Retail Electricity Rates," which defines the utilities' revenue requirements as the total cost of service (the sum of depreciation, operating expenses, taxes, and the fair return) (JEPIC, 1989). After a utility determines its total cost of service, individual items are allocated into seven functional categories: hydropower generation, thermal power generation, nuclear power generation, transmission, substation (primary, secondary, distribution), distribution (high and low voltage), and sales (JEPIC, 1989). Items that cannot be classified into these categories are separated out as suspended costs.

The cost of each category is then divided into fixed and variable costs and allocated to one of four demand classes: lighting (residential and other small demand), low-tension (100–200 volts), high-tension (up to 600 volts), and extra-high-tension power (6,000 volts) on the basis of ratios that are derived from the utility's supply–demand plan. The differences in the costs required to supply electricity to each class are then reflected in the electricity rates.

Seven ratios form the basis for allocating these costs. These are the noncoincident class peak (NCP), which is the ratio of the maximum demand of each class on the day of the annual system peak; the summer peak responsibility (SPR) and winter peak responsibility (WPR), which are the ratio of the demand of each class during the days of these system peaks; energy generation (EG), which is the ratio of energy generated per year for the sales of each class; and the energy generated by hydropower, by thermal power, and by nuclear power, which are the ratios of the energy generated by year by these respective plants for the sales to each class. For each type of basic ratio of allocation, the sum of the ratios of the four demand classes must equal 100%.

The allocation of fixed costs falls into three categories: In the first, the sum of the fixed costs for the hydro, thermal, transmission, and primary and secondary substations is allocated to each demand class in proportion to the weighted ratio derived from the following formula:

$$\frac{(NCP) \times 2 + (SPR) \times 0.5 + (WPR) \times 0.5 + (EG) \times 1}{4} \qquad (1)$$

In the second, distributing substation and high-voltage distribution fixed costs are summed and allocated to the lighting, low-tension power, and high-tension power classes according to the weighted ratio obtained by the following formula:

$$\frac{(NCP) \times 2 + (EG) \times 1}{3} \qquad (2)$$

In the third, the fixed costs of low-voltage distribution are shared between the lighting and low-tension power classes on the basis of the weighted ratio (Equation 2).

Relationship of Japan's rates to Ramsey pricing: According to many scholars, there is no relationship between ratemaking in Japan and Ramsey pricing, which sets lower rates to price-elastic customers (e.g., large industrial customers who may choose to self-generate) (Itoh and Nakanishi, 1988). However, Ramsey pricing has been gaining attention in recent years, and proposals have been made to introduce such a pricing system into the rate structure in an attempt to better balance revenues and expenditures.

These proposals have arisen from the increase in self-generation and cogeneration in recent years, resulting in more intense competition in the electric power industry. There is concern that an increase in these two forms of generation will not only decrease the demand for electricity provided by utilities but will also invite rate increases, which would come about by increasing the utilities' fixed-cost burden on remaining consumers.

A CRIEPI study by Madono, Matsukawa, and Nakashima (1991) on Ramsey pricing found this system to be socially efficient. Their study examined the most appropriate pricing structure for both industrial and residential customers by using the actual electricity demand and cost structure of the nine utilities over the period from 1980 to 1988. These authors found that self-generation and cogeneration are socially inefficient when the benefits to those who receive electricity by these two means are lower than the costs incurred by the utilities and those who do not receive such electricity.

This study also estimated the price elasticities of demand for the Japanese industrial and residential sectors for 1980 through 1988 (Madono, Matsukawa, and Nakashima, 1991). They found that on average, for the nine Japanese utilities, the price elasticity of demand was -0.63 for the industrial sector and -0.37 for the residential sector. The authors concluded that because the elasticity of the industrial sector is much higher than that of the household sector, industrial customers would be more responsive to prices. (See Table 6-12.)

Table 6-12. *Energy–GNP elasticity coefficients in Japan, 1960–1989*

	1960–1973	1973–1979	1979–1988	1973–1988	1989
Annual average GNP growth rate	9.6%	3.9%	4.0%	3.9%	4.8%
Annual average growth rate in final energy consumption	11.4%	0.9%	0.8%	0.8%	3.4%
Elasticity coefficient growth rate in electric energy sales[a]	1.18	0.23	0.21	0.22	0.71
Annual average elasticity coefficient growth rate	11.6%	4.4%	2.7%	3.4%	5.8%
Elasticity coefficient[b]	1.20	1.13	0.68	0.86	1.21

[a]Elasticity coefficient = growth in final energy consumption (%)/GNP growth (%)
[b]Elasticity coefficient = growth in electricity energy sales (%)/GNP growth (%)
Source: Information provided by Takashi Nagao, Japan Electric Power Information Center, 1991.

This study also found that the marginal cost of supplying electricity to the household sector was higher than that for the industrial sector. The authors concluded that except for cases when household sector rates are above the existing levels by a wide margin, it is possible to set industrial sector rates lower than their current levels.

Looking to the future:
Technology advances and research and development

Judging by Japan's preeminence in many technological areas and considering the enormous supply–demand gap the nation is facing in the coming decades, it would be natural to presume that its utilities are in the forefront of developing electricity technology. Although Japan does have several research and development programs in this area, such efforts do not appear to be uppermost in the minds of the country's utility management.

In the 1950s, it was the practice of Japan's electric power companies to buy the first new plant of each type from abroad, copy or modify the technology, and then switch to manufacturing the units in Japan. This situation has not changed greatly in the past 40 years. The Tokyo Electric Power Company (TEPCO), for example, has customarily bought or licensed General Electric technology through Toshiba and Hitachi; Kansai Electric, TEPCO's "rival for influence," has been dealing primarily with Westinghouse through Mitsubishi. The utilities' "conservative attitude toward technology has long been a sore point with the Science and Technology Agency, which wants to promote indigenous technology" (Gale, 1981, p. 90).

Yohji Uchiyama (1988) of CRIEPI studied the effects of changes in the energy environment since the two oil crises on the research and development of new technology, particularly generation technology. He concluded that the slowing down in the growth of demand for electricity, sharp increases in construction costs resulting from inflation and other factors, and the decline in fuel prices have decreased the attractive features of new technology research and development. He found that R&D plans for some new technologies have been canceled and that others have no timetables. (Uchiyama found that the same effect is present for conventional technologies.) Teruhiro Tomita (1990), another researcher, found evidence to support this claim, citing the relatively low proportion of R&D in many utility budgets (e.g., a mere 1.6% of TEPCO's budget is devoted to R&D).

Although the private sector accounts for a much larger share of national research and development in Japan than in any other advanced industrial nation, most of the country's R&D efforts are government directed (Samuels, 1981). The electricity sector is one area in which government domination in R&D is great, largely because of the long lead times necessary to bring technologies to commercialization, the extremely high project costs, the "public goods" aspects of energy technologies, and the role of energy in the nation's security.

Prior to 1979, the public sector had a virtual monopoly on nuclear R&D, and the private sector dominated nonnuclear R&D, but the situation today has grown more fluid. With the changes accompanying the Alternative Energy Law of 1980, the government now is very much at the center of most nonnuclear research as well.

The Ministry of International Trade and Industry has been assuming an increasingly significant role in energy research and development since the first oil crisis (it had an energy R&D budget of only ¥400 million in 1973, rising to over ¥80 billion for fiscal 1980). According to Richard Samuels, "the vigor with which MITI has moved into energy R&D is a clear indication of the government's perception of the relationship between Japan's energy security and its national economic health. Japan's energy R&D programs, especially the growing number of those administered by MITI, are therefore at the cutting edge of Japanese industrial policy, and they continue in the Japanese pattern of placing the commercialization of technologies, whether domestically developed or licensed from abroad, at the forefront of industrial growth" (Samuels, 1981).

In Japan today, basic research in the electric power industry is consigned to universities or national research institutions. Research leading to practical applications is usually conducted under cooperative programs between utilities and equipment manufacturers, and evaluations and demonstrations for commercialization are conducted by the utilities themselves. In addition, each utility has a central research institution and a technology development division to promote and implement technology development programs.

Because of the time and expense involved in electricity technology development, the utilities jointly subsidize the Central Research Institute of Electric Power Industry (CRIEPI), which coordinates the R&D work conducted by the utilities in addition to conducting its own research in areas of common concern to the electric power companies. The CRIEPI investigates both new generation and supply technologies, as well as ways to use electricity more efficiently. In addition, the utilities organize committees of experts in the Central Electric Power Council and the Federation of Electric Power Companies for coordination and information exchange on their R&D programs.

Although Japan's utilities have made advances in transmission and thermal power technologies, it is in nuclear power, use of waste heat, technologies such as gas turbines and fuel cells, and alternative energy in which they are placing the bulk of their efforts. In addition to these technologies, the nation's electric power companies are experimenting with a number of techniques to conserve energy, such as peak shaving.

High-voltage transmission lines: Japan's first 275,000 volt transmission lines were constructed by Kansai Electric for its Shin Hokuriku Main Line in 1952. The introduction of these high-voltage lines increased the stability of the nation's electricity supply system and drastically reduced transmission losses and cost.

The first 500,000 volt line was completed by Tokyo Electric in 1966, and other utilities followed suit a few years later. By the end of 1989, the 10 utilities' transmission lines stretched over 83,000 km, twice the length of 1951 (JEPIC, 1990). The maximum transmission voltage is possessed by TEPCO (500 kV), which plans to introduce 1,000 kV lines within the next few years.

Thermal power: During the high-growth period for Japan's electric utilities in the 1980s, a number of major technological achievements were made at its oil-fired plants. The industry was able to increase steam pressure from 60 kg/cm^2 to 246 kg/cm^2, steam temperature from 450°C to 566°C, and unit generating capacity from 53 to 600 MW. Heat efficiency climbed from 32 to 38%. In addition, Japan commissioned its first combined-cycle thermal plant in 1985 (Ohsawa, 1985).

Nuclear power: By the mid-1950s, Japan began to look to the development of atomic power as an attractive long-term solution to its energy problem. Research and development on nuclear power generation began in 1954 with an annual government budget of ¥2.4 billion. The Atomic Energy Research Institute was established in November 1955, and the Atomic Energy Commission and Atomic Energy Bureau were created in 1956 to conduct R&D. In parallel, business groups organized into five consortia to develop nuclear energy, and the electric power companies also began internal research on atomic power, following the general technology purchasing patterns they had established with conventional power equipment. In order to build this industry rapidly, the government has provided these firms with tax breaks, permission to import technologies, and loans.

The Japan Atomic Power Company completed a Calder Hall type of gas-cooled reactor at Tokaimura, Ibaraki Prefecture, in 1966 (JEPIC, 1988). The company's boiling-water reactor began operations in March 1970, and soon after, Japan's electric utilities began to operate their own nuclear power plants. In November 1970, Kansai Electric Power Company began service at its 340 MW pressurized water reactor at Mihama, and TEPCO followed with its 466 MW boiling-water reactor in March 1971. The industry gained much know-how and experience during the development of these pioneering efforts. It gradually mastered the light-water reactor technology introduced from the United States; almost all of Japan's light-water reactor units are now manufactured locally.

The Science and Technology Agency is responsible for nuclear R&D, and MITI is responsible for virtually all other forms of energy R&D. However, MITI has been expanding vigorously, if not always successfully, the scope of its energy activities in the nuclear area. Because it is charged with regulating the electric utility industry, and because nuclear energy is almost entirely restricted to electric power generation in Japan, MITI has much to say about the country's nuclear option.

Japan is making a number of efforts to improve its nuclear technology. The quasi-governmental Power Reactor and Nuclear Fuel Development Corporation completed the first experimental 100 MW fast-breeder reactor in 1977 and is now undertaking work on the prototype 280 MW Monju reactor, which is scheduled for completion in the early 1990s. The CRIEPI is developing a system to store spent nuclear fuel in casks and other facilities and is conducting storage tests with the Electric Power Research Institute of the United States.

Because Japan must import all of its uranium, it faces problems of supply insecurity. The government is thus leading the effort to establish a complete nuclear fuel cycle by stressing the development of "domestic" technologies in the recovery of uranium from sea water, uranium enrichment, breeder reactor development, and fuel reprocessing. These moves have been hastened by the decline of support for nuclear power in the United States, resulting in construction delays for reprocessing plants and fast-breeder reactors there, and forcing Japan to rely increasingly on its own technological abilities (Gale,

1981, p. 90). Although Japan's private companies are "philosophically supportive" of an ambitious advanced nuclear program, they also appear reluctant to finance the development of new fuel-cycle technologies or to see them owned and managed by the government.

Although Japan has been dependent on the United States in the past for nuclear power plant construction technologies and equipment (often purchased from General Electric and Westinghouse), this situation has changed dramatically in recent years. Currently, about 90% of the materials used in Japan's nuclear plants are manufactured locally; only a small percentage is imported form the United States. According to Takashi Nagao of Chubu Electric, Japan continues to import from the United States because of licensing agreements between the two countries (Nagao, 1992). The Japanese rightly feel that their technology is very advanced now and that the country has no need for United States assistance in plant construction. They also consider their nuclear plants to be highly reliable, and Japanese officials are confident that the Three Mile Island type of incident will not be repeated in Japan.

Use of waste heat: In recent years, Japan's utilities have been focusing on district heating service by using waste heat from large cities. TEPCO began to operate the first commercial district heating service in 1989, using heat from water discharged into a river in the Hakozaki area of Tokyo. In 1990 it completed a district heating system in the Makuhari area, a newly developed city center. This system uses heat pumps and thermal storage tanks to recover heat from discharged water. Hokkaido Electric Power Company is also participating in the heat supply business, and Kansai Electric plans to supply heat to office buildings by recovering heat from a computer center complex.

New energy technologies: CRIEPI is now pursuing research and development on gas turbines that can burn gas at 1,300°C and create the smallest possible volume of NOx (CRIEPI, 1990). It is also pursuing projects in coal gasification, more efficient fuel cells, super-heating pumps, electric-powered automobiles, and electric cooking technologies, and is studying generation systems for storing compressed air energy.

Kyushu Electric Power Company (1990) is developing new types of batteries capable of storing electricity produced at off-peak periods and releasing it into the company's grids during periods of high demand. It has also developed a 1,000 kW zinc bromide pilot plant, which it hopes to make as efficient as pumping power plants. This company is also conducting R&D on superconducting magnets and high-speed input and output control technology. In addition, Kyushu recently achieved efficient and clean electricity generation with a new high-performance solid electrolyte fuel cell, one of the most efficient in the world. This type of cell, which the company is developing for commercial use, is capable of running on coal gas, LNG, or even waste heat.

TEPCO's Electric Energy Storage Project is currently developing a highly compact sodium-sulfur battery. The utility is also conducting research on superconducting technologies for power storage equipment, a surge-arresting insulator to prevent power failure from lightning strikes, an aseismic-base isolation technology that would minimize vibration in an earthquake, a high-performance XLPE cable suitable as an underground transmission line in the Tokyo metropolitan area, and a multihole tube propulsion construction method for underground conduit works. Its other research efforts include projects on various types of fuel cells and on the applications of heat-resistant ceramics (TEPCO, 1990).

Tohoku Electric Power Company (1985) has been working on a system to link photovoltaic generation with electric power systems, and on the use of low-loss transformers that use amorphous materials.

Alternative energy: According to Richard Samuels (1981), nowhere in the world is there greater incentive for the development of alternative energy resources than in Japan. Although the government has dominated nuclear R&D, the electric power industry has dominated R&D activities in solar, geothermal, wind, wave, biomass, and energy conservation.

Japan's Sunshine Project, established in 1974, tends to improve the country's vulnerable energy supply structure through the development of new energy technologies (Agency of Natural Resources and Energy, 1991). It has been conducting comprehensive R&D in solar energy (photovoltaics and solar heating and cooling), geothermal energy, coal liquefaction and gasification, hydrogen energy, and other renewable projects such as wind, biomass, and ocean power. The Moonlight Project, established in 1978, deals with R&D on energy conservation technology, including magnetohydrodynamic power generation technology, waste-heat technology, and advanced gas turbines.

The government and private sector have established the New Energy and Industrial Technology Development Organization (NEDO) to accelerate the development of new energy and energy conservation technology (Agency of Natural Resources and Energy, 1991). A hybrid combination of a public and private enterprise, NEDO plays a key role in the construction and operation of large-scale plants and is involved in such new energy R&D projects as photovoltaics, coal liquefaction and gasification, solar technologies, and the exploration and use of geothermal energy. It is also involved in mining financing, issuing energy development bonds, subsidizing prospecting, and guaranteeing bank loans for energy development. Thus, its efforts are as much financial as scientific.

Energy conservation: Japan achieved an estimated energy conservation gain of 36% in terms of a GNP unit between fiscal 1973 and 1988, largely due to the efforts of the industrial sector (Ota, 1991). As a result of its conservation efforts, Japan now leads the world in the efficient use of energy in many sectors, particularly industry. For example, considerable improvements have been made in such areas as decreased energy consumption per unit of product in such large energy consumers as steel, pulp, and paper mills, increased consumer appliance efficiency, and increased fuel efficiency for automobiles.

A number of Japan's electric utilities have been developing air-conditioning and heat systems that feature heat pumps that use underground water, solar heat, and heat storage that uses latent heat (Tohoku Electric Power Company, 1985). Its technology efforts on the supply side of energy conservation also include the development of high-efficiency, combined-cycle power generation.

In its Interim Report (June 1990), the Supply–Demand Division of the Electric Utility Industry Council listed the following as responses on the demand side of Japan's current electricity situation: increase the understanding of consumers with respect to supply and demand problems, develop new energy conservation measures, and promote further load leveling (Nihon Denki Kyokai, 1990). Although Japan's electric utilities have not been as aggressive as their United States counterparts in pursuing these measures, they are taking some steps in these directions.

The country's electric utilities have also been conducting large-scale public relations campaigns geared toward educating their customers on energy use. Although TEPCO has a conservation campaign, it apparently has not been compelled to initiate new conservation programs. Like other utilities, it lacks "a legislative mandate or effective regulatory pressure" to do so, unlike United States utilities (Gale, 1981, p. 94).

Japan has made numerous efforts to implement demand-side management over the past 40 years but through programs that did not offer rebates to consumers. Today, however, under the current rate system, certain large-scale consumers, on approval from MITI, can conclude a special supply contract with an electric power company at lower than normal rates on the condition that they adjust their demand to terms stipulated in the contract or to notification by the contracting power company (JEPIC, 1990). Japan is now considering the use of such methods in the residential sector.

Japan's electric power industry has made several efforts toward load leveling by offering a number of innovative electric service contracts, such as a cut-rate contract for using electric water heaters during night hours and time-of-use contracts for large industrial customers (JEPIC, 1990). In November 1990, the utilities introduced a time-of-day rate system for domestic consumers.

Aside from these measures, there does not appear to be much more room for energy savings in Japan than in the United States, partly because Japan has constantly made efforts to save energy, and most of its electric appliances are now designed to use energy more efficiently.

REFERENCES

Agency of Natural Resources and Energy, Ministry of International Trade and Industry. *Energy in Japan – Facts and Figures.* Tokyo, 1991.
British Petroleum Company. *BP Review of World Gas.* August 1991.
Bronte, Stephen. *Japanese Finance.* London: Euromoney Publications, 1984.
Central Research Institute of Electric Power Industry (CRIEPI). *Electric Power, Promise for Tomorrow.* Tokyo, 1990.
Gale, Roger W. "Tokyo Electric Power Company: Its Role in Shaping Japan's Coal and LNG Policy." *The Politics of Japan's Energy Strategy-Resources-Diplomacy, Security,* Ronald G. Morse, ed. Berkeley, California: Berkeley Institute of East Asian Studies, University of California at Berkeley, 1981.
General Headquarters (GHQ), Supreme Commander for the Allied Powers. *History of the Nonmilitary Activities of the Occupation of Japan: 1945 through March 1950. Vol. XV, Fuel and Power, Part B: Expansion and Reorganization of the Electric Power and Gas Industries,* 1951.
Hein, Laura E. *Fueling Growth: The Energy Revolution and Economic Policy in Postwar Japan.* Cambridge, Mass.: Harvard University Press, 1990.
International Energy Agency. *Electricity in IEA Countries – Issues and Outlook.* Paris: Organization for Economic Cooperation and Development (OECD)/International Energy Agency, 1985.
Itoh, Nariyasu. *Denki Ryokin, Hiyo Kozo no Kokusai Hikaku* (International Comparison of Electricity Rates and Cost Structure). CRIEPI Report No. Y87904. Tokyo: Economic Research Center, Central Research Institute of Electric Power Industry, October 1988.
Itoh, Nariyasu, and Yasuo Nakanishi. *Denki Jigyo ni okeru Kibo no Keizaisei* (Economies of Scale in Japanese Electric Utilities). CRIEPI Report No. Y87017. Tokyo: Economic Research Center, Central Research Institute of Electric Power Industry, July 1988.
Japan Development Bank (JDB). *Electric Power Industry and JDB's Loans.* Tokyo, Japan Development Bank, 1984.
Japan Electric Power Information Center, Inc. (JEPIC). *Marketing Activities in Japan.* Tokyo, 1986.
Deregulation of the Electric Power Industry in Japan. Tokyo, 1988.
History of the Electric Power Industry in Japan. Tokyo, 1988.
History of the Electric Power Industry in Japan. Tokyo, 1990.
Electric Power Industry in Japan 1990/91. 1990.
Electricity Rate Regulation in Japan. Tokyo, 1989.
Johnson, Chalmers. *MITI and the Japanese Miracle.* Stanford: Stanford University Press, 1982.
Kansai Electric Power Company, Inc. *Current Information 1990.* Osaka, 1990.
Kurihara, Toyo et al. *Gendai Nihon Sangyo Hattatsushi* (History of the Development of Modern Japanese Industries), Toyo Kurihara, ed. Tokyo: *Gendai Nihon Sangyo*

Hattatsushi Kenkyukai (Research Group for the History of the Development of Modern Japanese Industries), 1964, DD.

Kyushu Electric Power Company, Inc. *Annual Report 1990.* Fukuoka: Kyushu Electric Power Company, Inc., 1990.

Madono, Seishi, and Yasuo Nakanishi. *Static Equilibrium Model and Optimal Capital Stock: An Application to Japanese Electric Utilities.* CRIEPI Report No. EY 89002. Tokyo: Economic Research Center, Central Research Institute of Electric Power Industry, September 1989.

Madono, Seishi, Isamu Matsukawa, and Takako Nakashima. *Denki Jigyo ni okeru Ramsey Ryokin no Tekiyo* (Ramsey Pricing in Electric Power Industry: An Empirical Analysis of Optimal Pricing with Intermodal Competition). Tokyo: Economic Research Center, Central Research Institute of Electric Power Industry, April 1991. DD.

Minami, Ryoshin. *Power Revolution in the Industrialization of Japan: 1885–1940.* Economic Research Series No. 24, the Institute of Economic Research, Hitotsubashi University. Tokyo: Kinokuniya Company, Ltd. 1987.

Nagao, Chief Researcher, Takashi, Tokyo: Japan Electric Power Information Center, Inc., 1991.

Personal communication, Mr. Takashi Nagao, Manager, International Procurement Group, Purchasing and Materials Department, Chubu Electric Power Company, August 1992.

Nihon Denki Kyokai. *Anata no Shiritai Koto – Denki Jigyo ni Tsuite 43 no Shitsumon to To 1990* (43 Questions and Answers Concerning the Electric Power Industry 1990). Tokyo, 1990a.

Denki Jigyo no Genjo 1990 (The Current Status of the Electric Power Industry 1990). Tokyo, 1990b.

Nishihiro, Yasuteru, Manager, Research Division, General Planning Department, Tokyo Electric Power Company, Inc., 1991.

Ohsawa, Etsuji. *Nihon no Denki Jigyo No Kindaika: 1883–1985* (Modernization of the Japanese Electric Power Industry, 1883–1985). Tokyo: Central Research Institute of Electric Power Industry, 1985.

Electric Power, Promise for Tomorrow. Tokyo: Central Research Institute of Electric Power Industry, 1990.

Ota, Hiroji, Managing Director of Chubu Electric. *Japanese Electric Utility: The Challenge Ahead.* Speech delivered in London, Chatham House, May 16, 1991.

Overseas Electrical Industry Survey Institute Inc. *Electric Power Industry in Japan 1982.* Tokyo, 1982.

Public Utilities Department, Agency of Natural Resources and Energy, Ministry of International Trade and Industry. *Denki Jigyo-ho no Kaisetsu* (Explanation of the Electric Utility Industry Trade Law). Tokyo: Tsusho Sangyo Chosakai (Research Committee on International Trade), 1988.

Samuels, Richard J. *The Business of the Japanese State: Energy Markets in Comparative and Historical Perspective.* Ithaca and London: Cornell University Press, 1987.

"The Politics of Alternative Energy Research and Development in Japan." *The Politics of Japan's Energy Strategy-Resources-Development-Security,* Ronald G. Morse, ed. Berkeley, California: Berkeley Institute of East Asian Studies, University of California at Berkeley, 1981.

"Some Lessons from Japan on Conservation and Co-operation." *Power in Asia,* June 17, 1991.

Tohoku Electric Power Company, Inc. *Aiming at Research and Development of Future Technology in Electric Power Utilities.* Sendai, 1985.

Tokyo Electric Power Company, Inc. *Perspectives on Energy and the Environment.* Tokyo, 1986.

Towards Tomorrow's Technology. Tokyo, 1990.

Tomita, Teruhiro. "Simulation Analysis with a Financial Model of Japanese Electric Utilities." *CRIEPI-EPRI Workshop on Energy Analysis.* CRIEPI Report 1987. Tokyo: Central Research Institute of Electric Power Industry, 1987.

"Denki Jigyo no Keiei Takakuka Senryaku - Tokyo Denryoku to Seidoku RWE-sha to no Hikaku o Chushin to Shite" (Diversification Strategies of Electric Utilities – Comparative Study between TEPCO and RWE). *Information and Communication Studies 9,* 1988a.

"Denki Jigyo no Seisansei Bunseki" (Total Factor Productivity Analysis of Japanese Electric Power Industry). *Information and Communication Studies,* 11, 1990.

Uchiyama, Yohji. *Enerugi Josei to Denryoku Gijutsu Kaihatsu no Hensen* (Changes of Energy Situation in R&D Activities of Electric Power Technologies). CRIEPI Report No. Y88014. Tokyo: Economic Research Center, Central Research Institute of Electric Power Industry, November 1988.

CHAPTER 7

Regulation of the market for electricity in the Federal Republic of Germany

Jürgen Müller
Fachhochschule für Wirtschaft
Konrad Stahl
Universität Mannheim and Zentrum für Europäische
Wirtschaftsforschung, Mannheim

The current structure of the electricity sector in Germany: A brief description

The West German electric power industry consists of three major subsectors, namely, firms selling electricity to the public (public electricity supply), industrial plants generating for their own use, and electricity generated by the federal railway system.[1] The first and dominant subsector is public electricity supply. According to the energy law of 1935 (*Energiewirtschaftsgesetz* [EnWG]), public electricity supply encompasses all enterprises supplying electricity to third parties. The second and third subsectors include firms and the federal railway system, respectively, which satisfy their own energy demand entirely or partially and do not sell electricity to third parties.

Within the first sector, three groups of firms can be identified, namely:

- Nine vertically integrated firms controlling most of the power production and interregional high-voltage distribution. The firms differ substantially in size and scope, with the *Rheinisch-Westfälische Elektrizitätswerke* (RWE) dominating the rest. They are the only ones interacting with foreign suppliers.

We acknowledge very competent research assistance by Thomas Dietz, Stephanie Rosenkranz, and Stefan Arping, and comments by Michael Brand, Joel Dirlam, Richard Gilbert, and Manfred Horn. Günter Veigel of the Pfalzwerke AG Ludwigshafen contributed many details on regional energy distribution. Finally, M. R. Schmitt of the Rhineland Palatinate State Ministry of Economic Affairs has served as an extremely competent informant and discussant on regulatory practice.

[1] Unless indicated, our discussion focuses on the electricity sector in West Germany. The primary reason for this is the paucity of data on the East German energy sector.

Table 7-1. *Size distribution of electric power generation companies in 1992 (public supply, 658 firms)*

Size classes GWh	Number of firms			Net generation		
	Number	Percent	Cum. p.c.	GWh	Percent	Cum. p.
16,000 and more	8	1.2%		173,720	47.1%	
6,300–16,000	20	3.0%	4.3%	97,486	26.4%	73.5%
2,500–6,300	32	4.9%	9.1%	68,245	18.5%	92.0%
1,000–2,500	39	5.9%	15.0%	18,709	5.1%	97.1%
400–1,000	63	9.6%	24.6%	6,560	1.8%	98.9%
160–400	91	13.8%	38.4%	2,342	0.6%	99.5%
63–160	138	21.0%	59.4%	1,111	0.3%	99.8%
25–63	137	20.8%	80.2%	406	0.1%	99.9%
10–25	84	12.8%	93.0%	161	0.0%	100.0%
4–10	34	5.2%	98.2%	45	0.0%	100.0%
1.6–4	10	1.5%	99.7%	11	0.0%	100.0%
0.63–1.6	2	0.3%	100.0%	1	0.0%	100.0%
Total	658			368,797		

Former GDR not included.
Source: VDEW.

- About 40 regional distributors, which produce about 25% of their supply and serve about 28% of final demand.
- About 1,000 local distributors, which exclusively serve final demand.

In 1992, 98.9% of total electricity was generated by 24.6% of all power-producing enterprises.[2] Details on the size distribution of electricity-generating enterprises are shown in Table 7-1.

The larger firms are highly integrated in terms of ownership and long-term supply contracts, with the nine large power producers as the leading firms. They also form legally independent subsidiaries for power generation, thus creating advantageous tax situations and limiting the mother company's liability.

Investment by other sectors of the economy in electric power generation and distribution is very small. By contrast, the largest power-generating enterprises are also active in the market for energy at large, which effectively limits competition across the different forms of energy. For instance, RWE owns the *Rheinische Braunkohle AG* that in 1989 mined more than 95% of West

---

[2] The East German energy sector is not included in this calculation, as explained in footnote 1.

German lignite.[3] On the other hand, we observe little forward integration – that is, investment in enterprises with high electric energy demand or in those producing electric appliances.

The electric energy producing and distributing enterprises are owned in large portion by regional public authorities. In 1992, some 68.8% of the 606 enterprises distributing nearly all electricity were owned (to 95% and more) by public authorities; in 15% of these enterprises public ownership was between 25 and 95%; and only the remaining 16.2% were private companies with a share of public capital below 25%. Table 7-2 gives more details on the distribution of public ownership in 1992.

The large communities typically own their public utility. Privately owned enterprises are mainly active in thinly populated rural areas. Firms under mixed ownership are active in interregional distribution. This difference is most clearly shown in Table 7-2, where the areas and inhabitants served are compared across the different ownership forms.

Even in enterprises under mixed ownership, where the public authorities (such as municipalities or states) typically own the smaller portion of shares, they insure themselves the majority vote by double voting rights. Often, no voting rights are associated with privately owned shares.[4] Indeed, public authorities command over a majority vote in more than 83% of all enterprises accounting for 93% of demand. However, this apparently overwhelming public control is mediated by the fact that the interests involved are rarely homogenous.

History

The origins of the system

The initial impulse toward the establishment of the German electricity system came from the private sector in the early 1880s.[5] Rathenau and Siemens had founded the *German Edison Society for Applied Electro-Technology* (DEG), a private partnership constituting a key role in the evolution of the sector. Rathenau also started a partnership that in 1882 provided first a club and later a whole residential street with electric light.

The first publicly owned power plants were built in 1884–5. However, private supply continued to dominate, because the communities thought the electricity business to be much too risky, in addition to being an inconvenient com-

---

[3] However, a large East German lignite pit has recently been taken over by a multinational consortium, consisting of companies from the United Kingdom, the United States, and Canada. See the section titled "Postscript."

[4] For example, communities and consortia of communities own 30% of RWE's capital but control 60% of this company's voting rights.

[5] Most of this section is extracted from Gröner (1975).

Table 7-2. *Ownership patterns in the German electric power industry in 1992 (public supply, 606 firms)*

	Public ownership		Mixed ownership		Private ownership		Total
Number of firms	417	68.8%	91	15.0%	98	16.2%	606
Area served (km^2)	51,249	20.9%	171,588	70.1%	22,058	9.0%	244,895
Number of communities served	1,355	15.9%	6,355	74.7%	793	9.3%	8,503
Inhabitants (1,000)	25,918	40.1%	34,876	54.0%	3,761	5.8%	64,555
Gross generation (GWh)	50,035	12.5%	279,839	70.0%	69,641	17.4%	399,515
Gross sustainable generation (MW)	13,460	15.0%	59,146	65.9%	17,180	19.1%	89,786
Standard tariff distribution[a] (GWh)	53,826	37.4%	82,512	57.3%	7,742	5.4%	144,080
Special tariff distribution[b] (GWh)	74,859	33.3%	133,354	59.3%	16,777	7.5%	224,990
Total (GWh)	128,685	34.9%	215,866	58.5%	24,519	6.6%	369,070

[a]To household customers at regulated tariffs.
[b]To large customers at unregulated tariffs.
Former GDR not included.
Source: VDEW.

petitor to their gas utilities. Thus, the inability to finance expansion with private sector funds was the key constraint on the growth of the system.

Up to 1900 the electricity system developed mainly in the larger cities. During the following years, regional power stations were also built to serve the rural areas. Private capital started much of the activity. By 1900, all but one out of 25 regional stations were run by private enterprises. Eventually, the municipalities took over the electricity supply in the large cities, but the pioneer work was mostly done by cooperatives combining private and public capital.

Before World War I, most larger firms produced their own electric power, because that was much cheaper than public power supply. In 1913, self-generation still accounted for 81% of all electricity supply. Yet public utilities gained increasing importance as suppliers to small firms and households. Between 1900 and 1915, the production of electric energy doubled every four years. Most of it was for industrial use. In fact, between 1903 and 1909 the share of electricity used for lighting dropped from over 52 to 31%. At any rate, around the beginning of World War I some 4,000 companies that were mostly privately owned existed.

By the end of World War I, the distribution network had expanded to include the whole of Germany. Growing economies of scale in generating capacity, and long-distance transmission with low resistance loss had led to enormous structural changes because it was now possible to overcome long distances economically with high-voltage transmission lines. Many local power plants were no longer able to compete and had to close down production, surviving only on distribution activities. Nevertheless, power production continued to be largely local. Linkages between electricity suppliers existed but served only to satisfy emergency demands rather than to pool power generation.

Concentration in the electricity energy sector started in the early 1920s with the advent of more efficient long-distance transmission and growing generating capacity, often near cheap sources of primary energy. The cities had to decide whether or not to continue power production and distribution. The big cities continued, but the small ones left the market. Large private producers often merged with smaller public utilities, which then became minority owners in then mixed public-private enterprises. The same process took place in rural areas, up to then served by cooperatives, with a greater degree of concentration in production than in distribution.

At this time, some of the states were already active in organizing electricity distribution at the regional level, using regional rights of way, restricted access to state land, and expropriation possibilities as policy instruments. Baden and Saxony used regional distribution companies as countervailing power to large private producers. Bavaria created a mixed private-public enterprise at the state level. In 1919, Bavaria had set up its own generation and regional distribution system, relying mainly on water power developed by the state. The federal government also took a share in the company through its holding company *Vereinigte Industrie AG* (VIAG).

Other states encouraged the creation of regional public utilities with the leadership of the large city's power company. Some of the Prussian city utilities grew into large regional, vertically integrated companies, such as RWE, *Vereinigte Elektrizitätswerke Westfalen* (VEW), or *PreussenElektra*. The RWE, the largest of today's regional companies, originated as a private company in the highly populated and industrial Ruhr basin. Hugo Stinnes, its early owner and one of the important coal mine operators, was able to expand RWE's influence through a sequence of takeovers of city utilities. By 1906 RWE was the most important player in the region.

Some of the other communes feared the dominant influence of RWE and combined their utilities into a Westphalian electricity company, which later became the VEW. In 1908 the takeover and price war between the two companies ended by political intervention, with a demarcation agreement on their respective geographic areas of influence. In 1927, a similar demarcation agreement was signed between RWE and *PreussenElektra* in the North. Similarly in the Southwest, regional companies were formed, so that by 1930 the main features of today's industry structure were in place. It was dominated by nine regional operators that were responsible for operating the German high-voltage transmission network. Today, these nine companies are organized in the *Deutsche Verbundgesellschaft* (DVG), an institution serving to coordinate large-scale power production, energy wheeling, and international cooperation.

Early regulatory structure

At the communal level: Already early on, the cities regulated the utility's access by exclusive concession contracts and levied a tax on electricity (up to 20% of the utility's sales to private households, but less for industrial users), typically leaving the entrepreneurial risk to the private supplier. The standard contract lasted for 10 or more years.[6] This policy was supported by the early industrial entrepreneurs, for exclusive contracts would reduce the risk to investors and allow them to quickly recover their investment. The concession agreements with the community usually required the obligation to serve and often involved some control over electricity tariffs. This implied that the individual communities were also the regulators.

---

[6] In contrast to concession contracts typical for the gas lighting business, these contracts did not involve build, operate, and transfer (BOT) clauses involving network transfer to the communities after the amortization of the invested capital. Those would have led to significantly higher electricity tariffs.

As the importance of electricity became apparent, the states that regulated water and gas companies also took an active interest in the electricity sector, at least in issuing building and transit permits. The licensing of power plants started in Bavaria in 1912.

However, with rapid technological development in the industry, territorial restrictions and demarcation contracts hindered its implementation, resulting in massive overbuilding of small capacity plants.[7] Calculations showed that in 1913 the whole German market could have been served by some 100 existing big power plants with capacity of more than 5,000 kW each. But many of the 4,000 power plants remained in the market. As described before, the main objective of the early equipment suppliers was to stimulate the demand for electricity. But the DEG also wanted the market area of each utility to be secure and exclusive. Special clauses in the concession contracts led to a de facto equipment monopoly for installations also. Later, when the communities refused to accept that kind of restriction, other ways were found to limit competition. In fact, lack of competition and the high degree of vertical integration between DEG and Siemens were the main reasons for lack of technical progress in the electricity industry.[8]

At the state level: States with a lot of water-powered utilities, such as Saxony, Bavaria, and Baden, were the first to exercise some regulatory control in the electricity industry. This took many forms. Some states tried to restrict excessive municipal involvement because they thought it too risky. Saxony and Württemberg aimed toward controlling municipal utility expansion by supervising the emission of municipal bonds. Baden's specific aim was to prevent the creation of small inefficient communal power plants. Some states, such as Baden and Saxony, assisted communities in the negotiations with electricity companies, also in an effort to establish publicly controlled regional distribution companies as a countervailing power to private operators. This led to the current pattern of entry regulation at the state level (*Fachaufsicht*).

At the federal level: In 1911–12 the German empire was hopelessly in debt. The taxation of energy was considered one source of financing it. The federal government also planned a more centralized power regulation, up to a nationalization of the industry. However, with the advent of World War I, these plans

---

[7] Most power plants built in 1900 became obsolete after only 10 years, against a calculated lifetime of 30 years.

[8] The lack of competition also induced the persistence of excess capacity. Although in 1928 the capacity of cities and regions was about 90% higher than that of the large federal companies, the actual production level was about the same, indicating low capacity utilization in the former (Gröner, 1975).

Table 7-3. *Sector shares of total power generated*

	1950	1961	1972	1983	1987	1992[a]
Public electricity supply	60.3%	60.4%	71.5%	83.3%	85.8%	86.4%
Industrial self-generation	38.7%	38.2%	26.7%	15.1%	13.0%	12.3%
Railway electricity supply	1.0%	1.4%	1.8%	1.6%	1.2%	1.4%

[a]Former GDR not included.
Source: BMWi.

did not materialize against the opposition of the states, the owners of private power plants, and the large self-generating industries.

The next regulatory move started after World War I, again with an attempt to socialize the industry. But the corresponding legislation was never implemented, so that the mixed industry structure continued to stay in place. The law was eventually replaced by a centralized regulatory structure during the Nazi regime.[9] Investment control and licensing at the federal level started in 1934, complemented by price controls based on the energy law of 1935 (*Energiewirtschaftsgesetz* [EnWG]).

That law was implemented only after World War II, because in 1936 all electricity prices were frozen or regulated. Till today, the EnWG is the basis for intervention into the electric utility system.

Description of the electricity system from World War II to the present

Development of the subsectors

The role of public activities in electricity supply has expanded over time. Industrial electricity supply had a dominant share up to and including the 1920s. After 1930, public electricity supply took over. Table 7-3 shows the evolution of the shares of these two groups and of railway electricity supply since 1950, and the increasingly dominating role of public electricity supply.

In 1933, the public electricity supply sector included some 16,000 firms (which were of course not all under public ownership). The number of firms supplying public electricity drastically declined in the sequel. In 1955, only about 3,000 firms had survived. The number of firms declined further to some 1,400 in 1971 and to about 1,000 in 1987. During the same period, total power

---

[9] In attempts to centralize the industry under the Nazi regime, most of the centralization and co-ordination were achieved without changing the ownership and the structure, so that one could return after the war to the structure still present in West Germany.

Table 7-4. *Characterization of firm groups by type of ownership (public supply)*

Share of firms	Public ownership	Mixed ownership	Private ownership
1964	70.4%	9.4%	20.2%
1974	67.4%	11.8%	20.8%
1981	66.0%	15.2%	18.8%
1989[a]	66.3%	16.8%	16.9%
1992[a]	68.8%	15.0%	16.2%
Share of total power supplied			
1964	53.0%	44.0%	3.0%
1974	34.5%	61.8%	3.7%
1981	33.2%	63.2%	3.6%
1989[a]	33.1%	59.5%	7.4%
1992[a]	34.9%	58.5%	6.6%
Share of area served			
1964	54.2%	35.9%	9.9%
1974	23.3%	67.4%	9.3%
1981	20.9%	70.4%	8.7%
1989[a]	20.9%	69.7%	9.4%
1992[a]	20.9%	70.1%	9.0%
Share of costumers served			
1964	61.9%	33.1%	5.0%
1974	42.7%	52.1%	5.2%
1981	41.7%	53.3%	5.0%
1989[a]	40.6%	53.6%	5.8%
1992[a]	40.2%	54.0%	5.8%

[a]Former GDR not included.
Source: VDEW.

generated increased dramatically. It is interesting to observe that among the utilities, the concentration did not dramatically change over time. Whereas in 1964 the 61 largest (8% of all) enterprises generated 95.4% of all electric power, in 1992 the 32 largest enterprises (9.1%) produced some 92.0% of all electric power (see Table 7-1).

Table 7-4 shows that the structure of the electricity industry has substantially changed since World War II. The privately owned enterprises' market-

Table 7-5. *Investment in electric energy supply (in millions DM)*

| | Public electricity supply | | | |
	Generation	Transmission and distribution	Total	Industrial self-generation
1965	1,468	2,649	4,117	na
1970	1,422	3,463	4,885	466
1975	4,249	5,389	9,638	271
1980	2,743	6,082	8,825	378
1985	8,258	5,242	13,500	365
1989[a]	4,864	6,334	11,198	1,140
1991[a]	2,957	7,153	10,110	549

[a]Former GDR not included.
Source: BMWi.

shares in terms of both area served and power supplied remained remarkably stable over the years, but the shares controlled by mixed enterprises substantially increased relative to those in purely public ownership. The dramatic changes between 1964 and 1974 can be traced back both to strong growth of the firms in mixed ownership and to the partial privatization of two very large firms formerly under public ownership (VEBA and VEW).

Investment behavior

Investment in replacement and capacity expansion has increased over time, from DM3.5 billion in 1962 to DM11.2 billion in 1989 (i.e., nominally by 320%). However, its share of total revenues fell from 16.2% in 1976 to a mere 12.8% in 1987. Nevertheless, the capital intensity (measured as share of depreciation to sales) in the mid-1980s was still higher than that of manufacturing by an order of 2.5 (Kroll, 1990).

Table 7-5 demonstrates how investment was distributed between generation and transmission and distribution. Until 1981, more than 50% of investment went into transmission and distribution. This pattern abruptly changed effective 1982, with a higher share of investment devoted to power generation. More specifically, after the first oil crisis of 1973–5, investment in power generation had increased substantially, but it decreased thereafter. Only after the second oil crisis did priorities consistently change, and investment focused on a restructuring of the system of power plants toward mineral coal and nuclear energy as primary energy sources.

Table 7-6. *Shares of primary energy use in total power generation (public supply)*

	1950	1961	1972	1983	1989[a]	1992[a]
Water	26.6%	14.8%	5.3%	5.3%	4.5%	4.3%
Mineral coal	47.4%	45.8%	34.2%	32.5%	27.0%	29.4%
Lignite	24.2%	36.9%	31.6%	27.1%	20.8%	20.7%
Nuclear energy	0.0%	0.1%	4.6%	20.8%	39.3%	39.5%
Gas	0.2%	0.2%	9.2%	9.2%	6.0%	4.4%
Oil	0.6%	1.9%	11.9%	1.8%	1.4%	1.2%
Others	1.0%	0.3%	3.2%	3.3%	1.0%	0.6%
Gross generation (1,000 GWh)	26.8	75.2	196.5	310.9	377.6	399.6
Power generated per capita (MWh)	0.6	1.3	3.2	5.1	6.2	6.2

[a]Former GDR not included.
Source: VDEW.

This reorientation was complemented by a strong increase in investment toward environmental protection. The environment's share of investment in power production increased from 16% in 1983 to 70% in 1988, followed by a decrease to 61% in 1989 (Kroll, 1990). However, since the nominal price decrease for oil in 1985–6 and the finalization of the first wave of environmental protection projects, the share of investment in electric energy production has decreased continuously. At current forecasts, it will reach a level of about 40% of total investment by mid-1990. This forecasted investment pattern should dramatically change by the end of the 1990s with the replacement of depreciated mineral coal power plants and with the need to take care of nuclear waste. All of this reflects only the status in former West Germany. With the integration of East Germany, investment in both production and distribution has drastically increased. Current forecasts predict a short-run investment of about DM 30 to 40 bn. in the Federal Republic of Germany's (FRG's) new eastern states.

Fuel sources

In 1989, public electricity suppliers consumed some 33% of the total primary energy bill in former West Germany, as compared to 30% in 1983 and 24% in 1967. Table 7-6 surveys the evolution of the shares of primary energy use over time.

As in other countries, we observe a very steep increase in the share of nuclear energy used. However, the decrease in the use of mineral coal is not nearly as strong as we observe elsewhere, because of the very protected status of the national coal industry and other regulatory instruments. In particular, a politically induced long-term supply contract (*Jahrhundertvertrag*) between the (by now) state-owned or state-controlled mines and the public electricity suppliers resulted in the continued absorption of some 40 mio. tons of mineral coal per annum for power generation at a price of more than twice the world market price.[10] The *Jahrhundertvertrag* is also the reason for the relative decline in the use of lignite, despite its lower cost involved in electric power generation.

The declining share of water used for electric power generation is largely a result of the more than proportional increase in electric power demand relative to limited water resources. Concerning the use of oil and gas, we must remember that no permits were given during the 1980s for the construction of new power stations involving (imported) oil or gas as primary energy sources, so that the development of relative prices for these sources played a lesser role in the choice of fuel.

Evolution of demand

Both total energy consumed and energy consumed per head increased between 1950 and 1992 from 43 TWh and 900 kWh, respectively, to 408 TWh and 6,300 kWh, respectively – i.e., ninefold and sevenfold. The increase in consumption was interrupted only in 1975 and 1982 during the respective oil crises. However, the annual rates of increase in energy consumption did monotonically decline over time. From 1991 to 1992, there was even a small decrease of the total level (about 0.3%).

The historic increases in consumption vary across consumer groups. Over the past 40 years, the share of demand from manufacturing has declined from above 60% to about 47%, while the share of residential demand has increased by about the same order of magnitude. Nevertheless, with the exception of the two oil crises, total consumption from the manufacturing sector has increased over time.

The German energy law differentiates between consumer groups by two rate structures.[11] The first consumer group encompasses households and small businesses, which are subject to a standard tariff to be explained later. The second group consists of the so-called special customers, including both electric energy distributors as intermediaries and large firms as final consumers. In 1961, the first group absorbed about 30% and in 1992 about 38% of total energy. This increase largely resulted from increasing household demand that

---

[10] See the later section that describes the regulatory system.
[11] See also Table 7-2.

Table 7-7. *Average revenue (Pf per kWh) by consumer groups (public supply)*

	Standard tariff	In prices of 1960	Special tariff	In prices of 1960	All	In prices of 1960
1960	16.1	16.1	7.3	7.3	10.0	10.0
1965	14.3	12.4	7.5	6.5	10.0	8.7
1970	12.4	9.6	6.9	5.3	9.1	7.1
1975	15.9	9.2	9.4	5.5	12.2	7.1
1980	17.4	8.4	11.1	5.3	13.8	6.6
1985	22.7	9.0	14.7	5.8	18.1	7.2
1990[a]	23.6	8.8	15.0	5.6	18.4	6.8
1992[a]	23.8	8.2	15.0	5.2	18.5	6.4

[a]Former GDR not included.
Source: BMWi, Statistisches Bundesamt.

was counteracted to some extent by a transfer of the retailing sector from the former into the latter consumer group. Table 7-7 shows average revenues over time for the two customer groups.

We generally observe decreasing average revenues. In particular, the price index for standard tariff customers decreased by 51% between 1960 and 1992. The corresponding price decreases for the special tariff customers amounted to only 29%, resulting in an overall decrease of 36%. It is interesting to observe that this pressure toward price decreases was not uniform interregionally. A survey conducted on the pricing behavior between 1986 and 1991 of 50 representative public energy suppliers shows that only 36 had decreased their prices nominally (maximally by 13.7%), seven enterprises had kept their prices constant, and yet another seven had increased their prices up to a maximum of 7.7 percent. In fact, effective January 1, 1991, the maximal interregional difference in high-voltage energy prices amounted to 40.1%.

Table 7-8 surveys the evolution of household expenditures on electricity and the share of electricity expenditures on total disposable income. Whereas expenditures totally and nominally increased over time, the share of electricity expenditures increased only until the 1980s and decreased afterward.

Experiences with excess supply and demand

Total capacity as well as capacity per plant increased between 1950 and 1992, the former 13-fold and the latter 5.5-fold. Similarly, capacity per head of the population in West Germany increased from 1950 until 1992 by an order of magnitude of 10, from 138 to 1,390 W. Tables 7-9 and 7-10 give the relevant

Table 7-8. *Household electricity expenditures*

(in bn. DM)	1972	1983	1989	1992[a]
Electricity expenditures (a)	6.36	17.8	20.9	23.6
in prices of 1960	4.5	7.4	8.0	8.2
Disposable income (b)	528.2	1,069.2	1,384.5	1,648.8
in prices of 1960	370.5	443.1	529.0	569.7
(a)/(b)	1.2%	1.7%	1.5%	1.4%
Consumer Price Index	142.6	241.3	261.7	289.4
(1960 = 100)				

[a]Former GDR not included.
Source: BMWi, Statistisches Bundesamt

numbers. We observe a capacity use around 50% and a reserve capacity of below 20% in the public electricity supply sector.

Role of technological advance in the development of the electric power system

Economies of scale in generation and transmission: A more detailed look at the capacity figures shows that the share of power plants with capacity above 100 MW has increased over the past 40 years from 43 to 87%. However, as already observed, in the early days of the system, small power plants had not completely exited from the market. In fact, there was an absolute increase in the number of power plants after 1950 in each size class between 1 MW and 100 MW, namely from 276 to 626 in 1989.

The observed increase in average capacity is clearly explained by the increasing use of nuclear energy: Since 1975, nuclear power plants were the only ones constructed with capacity of more than 1,000 MW. In 1989, the nuclear power plants (3.2% of all plants) represented 27.8% of total capacity.

Economies of scale rose in power transmission also. Between 1975 and 1989, the total length of transmissions above and underground increased from 880,000 to 1,172,500 km. In 1983, 0.26 GWh/km of public electricity supply was flowing through these lines. The corresponding number for 1989 was 0.3 GWh/km, with the share of high-voltage transmissions (> 60 kV) remaining at 7%. The increase in transmission flow must thus be attributed to efficiency increases in the expansion of the low-voltage system (< 1 kV). Between 1975 and 1989, its share increased from 57.5 to 62%, whereas the share of the medium-voltage network (1 to 60 kV) decreased from 35.5 to 31%. Incidentally, in 1989 some 73% of the low-voltage network had been placed underground.

Table 7-9. *Capacity and average capacity utilization (public supply)*

	1950	1961	1972	1983	1989	1992[a]
Capacity (GW)	6.9	17.8	41.6	76.4	89.6	89.7
Index (1950 = 100)	100	258	603	1,107	1,299	1,299
Capacity per plant (MW)	24.7	48.6	89.6	140.4	143.1	136.3
Index(1950 = 100)	100	197	363	568	579	552
Average capacity utilization[b]	44.3%	48.2%	53.9%	46.5%	48.2%	50.9%

[a]Former GDR not included.
[b]= gross generation / (capacity * 8,760 h)
Source: BMWi, VDEW.

These figures slightly changed after unification. Eventually, after completion of the large replacement investment cycle, both generation and distribution technologies in East Germany will be of a much more recent vintage.

Behavior of costs over time: Only aggregate data on power generation and distribution costs are publicly available. Between 1975 and 1991, they show only moderate changes in cost shares, namely, an increase in materials costs from about 49 to 55% and a decrease in personnel costs by less than 3%. On the basis of calculations for a model utility, Schmitt (1989) shows that in the mid-1980s 56% of the total average costs of 18.2 pfennig/kWh were attributable to power generation; 13% to power transmission; and about 31% to power distribution (including transmissions losses and concession fees). About 70% of these costs (including capital depreciation and personnel costs) were fixed, and 30% variable. The latter varied between 2 pfennig/kWh for nuclear power plants and 13 pfennig/kWh for gas turbines, the former between a maximum of 450 DM/kW p.a. and the latter a minimum of 60 DM/kW p.a.

Among the largely fixed costs for transmission and distribution, about one-third were attributable to the high-voltage network; one-sixth to the medium-voltage network; and the remaining 50% to the low-voltage network, including stations, meters, and other household connection and distribution cost items. The costs of connecting households and agricultural plants were about 50% above the average common costs of power transmission and distribution, whereas manufacturing connection costs were about 80% below the common costs. On average, the connection costs for the special customers were 25% below this figure. In all, this implies that the share of common costs attributable to regular customers was higher by an order of magnitude of two than that attributable to special customers.

Table 7-10. *Capacity, demand, and reserve margin at the peak day of the year (public supply)*

	1975	1980	1985	1990	1992[a]
Available capacity (GW)	48.54	60.85	69.09	71.7	74.75
Non-coincident peak demand (GW)	42.01	48.55	56.92	58.98	59.34
Reserve margin	13.5%	20.2%	17.6%	17.7%	20.6%

[a]Former GDR not included.
Source: BMWi.

Unfortunately, the public electricity suppliers are not willing to give details on their cost structures. The European Commission intends to break this information barrier. In a first step, 60 large utilities will have to present their average costs of production, of import and export, and of the transmission and distribution of electric power. However, they will be allowed to employ idiosyncratic accounting figures, which again will curtail cost comparisons across enterprises and even across plants.

Power supply from renewable energies: Table 7-11 gives some evidence on the power supplied from renewable energies.

Thus, water power dominates with some 86% of the total power supplied from renewable energies in 1992. By contrast, power supplied from wind and sun amount to less than 0.1% in total. The most important explanatory factor for this is the production cost: For water-power plants, average production costs are calculated between 15 and 20 pfennig/kWh; for wind-power plants they are between 25 and 50 pfennig/kWh; for photovoltaic-power generation they amount to 2 to 6 DM/kWh. By contrast, production costs involving solid-waste combustion are calculated at about 10 to 12 pfennig/kWh. However, there are increasing political impediments against solid-waste combustion.

The number of plants generating electricity from renewable energy sources increased from 1989 to 1992 by almost 50%. In particular, the number of gas, sun, and wind plants increased by more than 210, 240, and even 770%, respectively. This is mainly a result of subsidy programs at the state and federal level.[12] However, compared to water the roles of sun, wind, and gas as energy sources for electricity generation continue to be very minor.

Grawe, Nitschke, and Wagner (1992) anticipate a continuing dominant use of water among the regenerative energies, complemented by solid-waste com-

---

[12] East Germany is included in the 1992 figure. However, renewable resources play only a very minor role in East Germany.

Table 7-11. *Public electricity supply from renewable energy sources*

1989	Number of plants	Share	Capacity (MW)	Share	Output (GWh)	Share
Water	605	79.5%	3,733.0	87.3%	15,726.0	89.0%
Solid waste combustion	29	3.8%	518.0	12.1%	1,877.0	10.6%
Sewage gas	8	1.1%	6.1	0.1%	28.6	0.2%
Deposit gas	23	3.0%	13.4	0.3%	41.9	0.2%
Wind	81	10.6%	4.9	0.1%	5.9	0.0%
Sun	15	2.0%	0.4	0.0%	0.1	0.0%
Total	761		4,275.8		17,679.5	

1992[a]	Number of plants	Share	Capacity (MW)	Share	Output (GWh)	Share
Water	660	86.7%	4,049.0	94.7%	15,154.0	85.7%
Solid waste combustion[b]	40	5.3%	550.0	12.9%	2,060.0	11.7%
Gas	66	8.7%	39.6	0.9%	139.4	0.8%
Wind	192	25.2%	36.3	0.8%	66.7	0.4%
Sun	115	15.1%	2.1	0.0%	1.0	0.0%
Total	1,073		4,677.0		17,421.1	

[a]Former GDR is included.
[b]Number of plants and capacity are estimated.
Source: Grawe et al. (1989), (1993).

bustion and deposit gas. Concerning the use of wind and sun, they predict a larger role resulting from subsidy programs. However, the output generated from wind and sun is so small compared to water, that they will continue to be of little importance.

During the 1980s, the federal government subsidized R&D on renewable energy use with about DM 200 mio. per annum. The development and use of renewable energies is also subsidized by general investment subsidies that were primarily absorbed toward additional use of water power, and by the pricing of privately supplied electric power from renewable resources to the public electricity network. During the second half of the 1980s, only about 1,500 GWh were supplied this way, amounting to merely 0.4% of total electricity supply to the public network. However, access was restricted, and prices then were set at very low levels. This was changed by law effective 1991 (see the next section titled "Regulatory institutions and regulatory system.")

Technical advance in cogeneration and energy conservation technologies:
The employment of energy conservation technologies has advanced rapidly
since World War II. Between 1970 and 1989 power cogeneration almost doubled, from 6,670 GWh to 12,940 GWh (*Bundesministerium für Wirtschaft,*
1989). However, its share in total electric power supply still remained at a very
low level of 3.5%.

Technical advances in electric power transmission resulted in substantially
decreased network losses. Whereas in 1950 these amounted to an estimated
15% of total energy transmitted, they decreased in 1961 to 8.8%, in 1972 to
6.4%, in 1983 to 5.5%, and finally in 1989 to 4.1%. This decrease is attributable in part to an increase in transmission voltage from 220 to 380 kV in the
interregional supply network; to both the quantitative and qualitative improvement in the transformer network; and to the reduction in the number of
voltage levels (Möning, 1975).

Structure of research and development in the
electric power industry

Most of the research and development relevant to the generation of electric
power is conducted in the electric power industry itself. A 1989 survey on financing R&D among the members of the VDEW suggests that of the sum total
of about DM 930 mio. of 1989 expenditures on R&D and demonstration
plants, some DM 752 mio., or 80.8%, resulted from internal financing of the
electric power industry (in particular of the nine large power generators); and
DM 201 mio., or 19.2%, were supplied from other sources. Expenditures on
the development of nuclear energy power dominated with 50%, followed by
those on energy-related research on environmental protection with about 15%,
and the development of new methods for heating and electric energy generation with about 12%.

Regulatory institutions and regulatory system

Today's regulatory structure is still based on the 1935 federal energy legislation (EnWG). Its explicit objective is to prevent economic harm as a consequence of competition, and it encourages cooperation among the electric
power suppliers. In particular, the exclusive territory concept is legalized
therein, resulting in so-called demarcation contracts between utilities about the
geographical areas they supply, both wholesale and retail. Thus, the locally
monopolistic structure that had emerged in the early part of the century was
sanctioned ex post. The energy sector is also explicitly exempted from the
most important regulations contained in the federal antitrust law (*Gesetz gegen*

Wettbewerbsbeschränkungen [GWB]). According to that law, regulatory efforts on the utilities should be geared toward mimicking competition (*Als-Ob-Wettbewerb*).

Given that exemption, we can divide regulatory intervention into that on investment behavior, including the entry and exit of firms; on the control of right of way; on prices; and on the abuse of dominant power (Gröner, 1984). The latter is institutionalized at the federal level, but the control of investment behavior is shared by the federal and the state governments, and the control of right of way and price regulation rest with the communities and the states, respectively. Although the asymmetric division of legal and factual responsibilities went unchallenged over a long period, it recently was severely strained when it came to the licensing of atomic power plants.

At the outset, it should be emphasized that the German regulatory system is formally rather tight, with the exception of the wholesale and the large-scale retail markets that go virtually uncontrolled. It remains to be discussed whether it is tight de facto. It is also rather conventional. In particular, none of its components contains aspects of incentive regulation.

Description of the regulatory system

Investment control: The primary legal basis for controlling investment in electric power plants is the Energy Law, complemented by land use and environmental protection legislation, as well as legislation on the use of atomic energy. Investment control is carried out at the state level through a licensing requirement for both new plants and capacity changes involving existing plants, as well as for their discontinuation. The regulatory authority cannot initiate projects on the basis of the energy law, but it can refuse a license if it is not deemed "in the interest of the general public." Its legal interpretation concentrates on ascertaining an efficient and uninterrupted flow of electric power supply. Thus, the regulatory authorities would not license any public power stations below 300 MW, a measure enacted in 1964 (and recently scrapped) to encourage the construction of larger and more efficient generating plants. Beyond this, there is little the regulatory authorities have done thus far toward controlling for the efficiency of investment in power generation or distribution.

A very important restriction to investment in the energy sector is § 4 EnWG, demanding permits on virtually all investment and disinvestment activities – in particular, for the construction, the expansion, and the closing of nuclear energy plants. These permits are issued by the states concerned. They are currently under intense pressure by environmentalists toward rigidly controlling investment activities, in particular investments in nuclear energy plants. Prominent examples for the exercise of restrictive policies are the shut-down of the high-temperature reactor in Hamm–Uentrop in 1990; that of the experimental megareactor in Kalkar after billions of investment subsidies by the federal government in 1991 before it even went to the network; and the still pending permit to start a conventional nuclear-technology-based reactor in Mülheim–Kährlich, where construction was finished as early as 1991.

Recent popular pressure against the continued use of nuclear energy has finally led to the closure of a very large and important public project, namely, the nuclear waste reprocessing plant in Wackersdorf. It also is likely to have induced an initiative by the top managements of the two largest energy concerns, RWE and VEBA, toward voluntary restraints on the further use of nuclear energy.

Another important political influence on investment behavior in the public electricity sector is public concern with the coal-mining industry, resulting in a subsidization of coal-fired plants and a restrictive issue of permits for the construction of oil and gas plants (Vogelsang, 1982).[13] By contrast, the use of atomic energy was heavily favored by substantial federal R&D subsidies.

In the aforementioned *Jahrhundertvertrag* of 1977 between the coal-mining and the electricity industries, it was determined that between 30 and 36 mio. tons of coal would be absorbed by coal-fired power plants within the following 10 years. That agreement was renewed in 1980. By then, the quantity to be absorbed was increased to 40 mio. tons per annum for the following 15 years. The coal-mining industry is guaranteed the annual absorption of coal at prices well above those of imported coal.[14] Instrumental in the political pressure resulting in this agreement was the coal-mining and energy union. In an addendum to the agreement arranged between the public electricity suppliers and that union, the expansion of nuclear energy use was conditioned on a sufficient absorption of coal in electric energy production. This addendum was instrumental in moderating the union's resistance against the expansion of electricity production based on nuclear energy.

The bulk of new construction involves the existing power suppliers. In fact, the energy law requires a special licensing procedure for new entrants into the electric power market. The regulator can (and does) prohibit the construction of a power plant by a new entrant in view of the public interest if the region to be served is already sufficiently supplied with electric power. There is also an exit control corresponding to the entry control. In principle, the right to serve an area can be waived if the company cannot guarantee the uninterrupted supply of

---

[13] The Electric Energy Production Law (*3. Verstromungsgesetz*) calls for restrictive licensing of both the construction and the capacity expansion of oil- and gas-fired plants, favoring coal as input and thus guaranteeing a certain degree of national independence on the cost of reduced efficiency. This law has recently been challenged, because it does not apply to the East German electricity sector.

[14] In 1993, costs were about DM 280 per ton, more than twice the price of imported coal; this adds about 7.5% to the average electricity bill.

power. Rather than a new company, a neighboring power supplier is allowed to enter in order to guarantee the continuing supply. These clauses effectively preserve the existing locally monopolistic structure of power supply and distribution.

Controlling the right of way: The right of way for establishing the distribution network depends by and large on the communities. By contrast, private proprietors must tolerate the power companies' activities. The communities decide whether they wish to assume power supply and distribution themselves or to license it out. In the latter case, they issue an exclusive concession contract guaranteeing the right of way across communal property and service to the community, usually for 25 or 50 years. The contract also involves the utility's annual concession payment, which can be quite sizeable.[15]

Price control: Regulation of electric utility prices is confined to low-voltage retailing (i.e., to about 50% of sales). It is specified at the federal level within general guidelines (*Bundestarifordnung* [BTO]). Its execution rests exclusively with the states in which the respective utility is located. For a utility supplying more than one state, the state housing its headquarters is responsible for its overall price control.

In line with the Energy Law, the regulation aims at securing an efficient and uninterrupted supply, which in the most recent revision of the guidelines includes an explicit concern with environmental protection. The guidelines specify that customers must be supplied at a cost-oriented price. More specifically, the guidelines allow for prices involving a fixed capacity and metering cost and a variable-cost component. Both capacity-cost and variable-cost components can vary by hour, day, or season. Thus, the regulation of household tariffs provides for both two-part and peak-load pricing that is based on the utility's cost structure.

Price regulation at the level of the individual states is based on the rate-of-return principle, and in particular on utility costs in the past and the current year, and estimated costs for the subsequent year. The cost specification follows federal guidelines specified for government procurement contracts (*Leitsätze für die Preisermittlung auf Grund von Selbstkosten* [LSP]). Tariffs are approved in the form of a price cap. There is no explicit provision for cost overruns. However, the utility is entitled to reapply at any time for a price increase that results from unexpected cost increases.[16] The utility must submit the relevant accounting and profit-and-loss statement, including their forecast of costs. The large utilities have to reveal their cost structure every year, the

---

[15] In 1993, it amounted to DM 2.6 bn. in West Germany alone.

[16] The reason cost overruns have been so important in the United States and in the United Kingdom is probably because regulation is much more stringent and sometimes does not allow the full allocation of a price increase. By contrast, there is considerable flexibility de facto in German price regulation.

smaller ones only every two years. The comparative compilation of cost structures in principle allows the state regulator to identify inefficient producers within the state and to disapprove proposed tariff increases.

However, the regulatory detail is neither uniform nor very transparent across states. Although regulation has become more systematized in the 1980s, significant differences in implementation continue to exist. A joint federal-state regulatory committee was created to obtain agreement at least on the general process and the form of price control. Northrhine–Westphalia, housing both by far the largest utility and the largest customers, has acted as leader in this process. There are now attempts to exchange data among the states and to unify cost accounting manuals and depreciation formulas. The database so enlarged should allow for more specific yardstick measures in the future. But at present, there are still large differences in the accounting practices used by each state.

The remaining most crucial differences are the following:

- Northrhine–Westphalia allows for an accelerated depreciation of assets (up to five years), whereas the other states require linear depreciation schedules.

- The allowed rate of return on capital differs. In some states, investment financed with retained earnings is treated differently from debt-financed investment. For example, in Bavaria the former is depreciated at the current (or replacement) value, whereas debt-financed capital is depreciated according to book value. Northrhine–Westphalia uses current value for all capital equipment, whereas Lower Saxony uses only book value. The issue is far from being settled. A court case on this has been pending in Bavaria for nine years.[17]

  In fact, Busse von Colbe (1987) shows that at least three different methods of asset evaluation are compatible with the LSP framework.[18] The federal government that could exert a stronger influence on this has also been reluctant to intervene, because it might involve an upward adjustment of some regulated prices.[19]

---

[17] The Bavarian regulators also claim a 5% per annum discount for technical progress on physical capital depreciated at its current replacement cost. This is also a point under litigation in the current court case.

[18] Busse von Colbe (1987, page 22) also argues that the LSP regulation refers to current replacement cost of capital and to 6.5% real. This should be independent of the financing structure of the company. For states using the net capital or "book value" principle, Busse von Colbe recommends that they should look at the financial structure of the firm.

[19] The unclear specifics in the regulatory framework, in as much as it relies on public procurement rules, are exemplified by the recent decision of the Defense Ministry that allows firms to recover an acceptable rate of return only on the book value of invested assets. This latest revision of the LSP has confused even further the situation in the electricity industry. There is currently an attempt to solve this problem by another joint state-federal committee.

A peculiar problem arises for replacement, or capacity generating investment. The investment costs appear only in the application for tariff increases if monetary costs to the utilities arise in terms of payment to third parties. Investment paid out of retained earnings is reflected only in changing the capital stock. Depreciation on such investments can be added to the cost base only when the investment is used. The utilities therefore tend to finance such investment with loans, even if retained earnings are available. Alternatively they generate a subsidiary, usually a leasing company, especially for this purpose.

- There are also diverging opinions about which costs are to be included in the rate base. For example, Northrhine–Westphalia allows for the inclusion of concession payments to the communes as costs, whereas all other states do not. There is also a disagreement on which taxes can be included.

- According to recommendations by the Federal Ministry of Economic Affairs, the real rate of return to be applied within LSP is 6.5%. However, the state of Northrhine–Westphalia uses instead the average yield for public bonds over the past months, which is generally lower. There is also the possibility of adding 3.5% real as an extra margin for risky investment, an option normally claimed by the industry.

In all, the critics of the regulatory system argue that only maximum prices are regulated. There is room for pricing flexibility that can be used in the pursuit of competition and must therefore also be controllable (Jüngst, 1990). This dispute was renewed with the 1990 revision of the BTO; price approval now also extends to the previously unregulated wholesale suppliers. This extension of regulation is disputed by the utilities on the grounds that the need for revealing wholesale price information is not covered by the EnWG.[20]

Controlling behavior: The primary institution controlling the abuse of dominant power is the federal antitrust authority (*Bundeskartellamt*), but in some instances the regulator is also the antitrust office of an individual state. Although the antitrust law (GWB) explicitly grants exceptions to utilities by allowing exclusive territories and therefore exclusive dealing, it allows for an intervention in case of an abuse of market power eventually resulting from these exceptions.

The antitrust authority can intervene in exclusive territory agreements between utilities if the agreements do not serve the efficient and secure supply objective but lead to a price increase (Monopolkommission, 1976). The bases for intervention are price variations across neighboring exclusive territories,

---

[20] A 1993 court ruling currently under appeal has ascertained the utilities' position. As a consequence, this issue will be taken up in the planned reform of the EnWG.

together with the expectation that the high-price territory could be served by the low-price utility. Gröner (1984) argues that the threat of such an efficiency comparison has had a small yet not immaterial proactive announcement effect. To some extent prices were reduced, and some utilities postponed applications for price increases.

However, regulatory efforts along these lines were curtailed by the Supreme Court, which ruled in 1972 that price differences could be justified by territory- (rather than firm-) specific differences in utilities' cost structures. This ruling necessitates a detailed price and structural comparison of the respective utilities to give proof of misconduct. In particular, it requires an almost undoable task, namely, the dissection of territory-specific and firm-specific cost components.

The 1990 reform of the antitrust law (GWB) was intended to sharpen this regulatory instrument again. Abuse of dominant power was defined as deviation from behavior expected under effective competition ("as-if-competition" clause). However, this again implies identifying groups of similarly (i.e., identically) structured utilities and comparing their cost structures. Abuse of dominant position could be assumed only if cost differences were large. Hence, Gröner (1984) argues that this reform has even weakened the case for intervention. Anyway, in addition, the intervention would be based on differences in tariffs controlled by the state regulators. This would not only cloud regulatory responsibilities but also curtail the allocative function assigned to the antitrust authorities.

Market competition as a regulatory influence

Three dimensions of market competition potentially affect the utilities' behavior: competition from other energy sources for particular electricity uses such as residential heating; competition for franchises between electric power suppliers at the wholesale level and between final distributors; and competition between power suppliers and vertically integrated self-generators.

Competition from other energy sources has become virtually negligible in Germany. The electric power industry in the 1960s and beginning 1970s had promoted electricity as the primary energy source for residential heating, but the decline in the real price for oil and (through the institutionalized pricing link) in that for natural gas has melted these efforts. Today, electricity is no longer a serious competitor in this market.

Up to now, there has been virtually no competition at the wholesale level. Because demarcation contracts were exempted from the antitrust law, the utilities have been protected from forced wheeling. This also has led to a very close interaction between electric power suppliers and distributors, either through ownership or through long-term supply contracts. Franchise competition at the retailing level was excluded by the exclusive territory principle. This in turn has reinforced very stable long-term supply contracts at the wholesale level.

There is practically no competition at the retail level. The current retail situation is typically characterized by a long-term (15 to 50 years) exclusive concession contract between a utility and the community. Beyond often substantial concession payments, the contract involves the utility's commitment to supply all final customers at uniform tariffs against the right to do so for the duration of the contract. However, large firms may negotiate a special deal with the utility. It was precisely to prevent this kind of cream skimming that demarcation contracts were introduced (Gröner, 1984). Thus, with a few exceptions, large users within the community are not able to purchase power from other producers if their power link has to cross the public right-of-way.

The Monopoly Commission (1976) has severely attacked the lack of franchise competition by arguing that exclusive franchise did not lead to more efficient energy production and distribution but to increased energy prices. By introducing yardstick competition, it also opted for more behavioral control of abuse of dominant market position.

Many franchise contracts have been discontinued during recent years especially between distributors serving large regions and large cities, with the cities taking over the utility's distribution facilities. The reason is that large distributors are forced to charge a territorially uniform price, which invariably induces cross-subsidization favoring countryside consumers. Thus, the utility's returns are above average in the larger municipalities, in which service can be provided at below-average cost. Regulatory practice implies, however, that prices do not vary within large regions even across utilities, so that the large municipalities can reap considerable profits by setting the utility's price well above the average cost of serving the community's custom. This reinforces the communities' incentives for this kind of cream skimming. It remains to be seen whether self-generation by the municipalities (e.g., by cogeneration) will further reinforce the fragmentation of concession areas.

Competition at both the wholesale and the retail levels will soon be under review, as the considerably more liberal EC antitrust law comes into effect. It remains to be seen whether this law will overrule national antitrust and competition legislation. However, another reform of the Germany antitrust law is planned for 1996. Plans are to enhance competition at both levels by encouraging power wheeling through better control over the abuse of dominant positions and by synchronizing the termination of demarcation and concession contracts. This will ease the adjustment of franchise and concession areas.

As has been shown, self-generation has always been important for large industrial firms and publicly owned transport utilities (especially the railroads). However, there has been some controversy about the role of self-generation as the system became more integrated and benefited from large-scale generating units. Self-generators were seen by the large utilities as an impediment to a fully integrated regional or national system. As a consequence, the utilities provided incentives against self-generation. In particular, conditions imposed on self-generators for supplying excess electricity into their distribution system were made quite unfavorable. The large utilities were willing to pay for only the amount of fuel saved rather than also including savings in capacity costs.

This policy was effectively challenged after the first and second oil crises. The fourth amendment to the antitrust law (§103 GWB) in 1980 deals specifically with this issue. It attempted to prevent restrictive practices toward industrial generation, but mainly with a view toward cogeneration.

This policy shift was enhanced by the 1987 agreement between the utility association (VDEW) and the association of industrial energy producers (VIK) that promotes interconnection through even more favorable conditions on entry, provision and prices for reserve capacity, and payment for supplies entering the system. In 1990 this voluntary agreement was replaced by a new law to help small generators and cogenerators (up to 5 MW). Utilities must now purchase solar-generated electricity at 90% of retail price and all other electricity up to 500 kW (mainly water-generated) at 75%; above 500 kW at 63% of retail price. The main argument used was that with a closer cooperation between self-generators and utilities, primary energy could be saved in line with the policy aims of the federal government. Water-power generators received a windfall gain as part of this regulation.

The main reason self-generation is viewed more positively now is the increasing political opposition to the building of new power plants. Self-generation provides extra long-term capacity. Thus, utilities no longer oppose self-generation but are willing to engage in serious discussions about possible collaboration up to joint ventures.

The potential for utility bypass is more difficult to assess. The most extreme example is the right the large chemical company BASF has obtained for wheeling its electricity from its coal-fired plant in the Ruhr area to its major industrial plant at Ludwigshafen. But in general wheeling is not widely accepted. This might change with the 1995 amendment of the antitrust law and increased efforts to support wheeling by the EC.

Demand management

Key examples of demand management are the early introduction of peak-load pricing and of interruptible tariffs. The small utilities were the first to introduce both in order not to lose the mobile customers or those located in the border areas of their territories to the larger vertically integrated suppliers. However, some of the larger utilities soon imitated them, in part to persuade industrial self-generators to give up their own generation attempts (Mitchell, Manning, and Acton, 1978). Another initiative arising during the 1960s and 1970s at a decentralized level was storage heating. This came about through favorable off-peak night tariffs and detailed customer advice. As discussed earlier, this initiative has lost importance during recent years.

As we have said, the utilities' initiatives for demand management have received regulatory support at the federal level, within the 1990 revision of the BTO. Large customers now enjoy additional tariff differentiation between summer and winter months, which further tends to flatten the load curve. However, the critics of this recent BTO reform criticize its main objective, namely, load filling, and in particular valley shifting and peak clipping, to the neglect of a reduction of energy consumption in general.

The discussion of least-cost planning has of course also reached Germany. The utilities are still somewhat skeptical about adopting it for the following reasons: First, they argue that the saving potential in the United States is much higher because the average consumption there is much larger. Second, load curves in Germany are already pretty flat because load management has a long tradition. Last, there is a large volume of excess capacity. Nevertheless, some states have pushed least-cost planning and offered specific programs.[21] These are often organized by advisory institutions set up for electricity customers in cooperation with both the utilities and electric appliance manufacturers. These programs also invite the purchase of energy-saving appliances and better insulation for housing.

However, the advocates of LCP claim that there is no incentive for its greater adoption. Because the regulatory structure emphasizes rate of return, utilities have little interest in this new policy. Also, the communities receiving concession payments proportional to electricity sales show little interest in it.

Incentives for utility research and development

Most of the R&D effort in the industry originates from the manufacturing sector for generation and transmission equipment. This results partly from the regulatory structure that does not allow for R&D expenses as a legitimate operating cost. An inquiry from the utilities showed R&D expenditures of only DM 0.75 bn. for 1989, and subsidies from third parties of DM 0.2 bn. (VDEW, 1989). Almost half of those were earmarked for research on nuclear power stations, and another third to environmental protection and to new methods for cogeneration.

---

[21] A first policy application was the tariff increase applied for by the municipal utility of Paderborn. The cost analysis by the states' regulators showed that this tariff increase was not justified. However, the utility was called upon spending excess returns on LCP initiatives.

Regulatory policies concerning utility diversification

There exists little if any regulatory policy on utility diversification, except for a restriction on cross-subsidization. As a consequence, the industry has diversified significantly over the years. Especially active have been the large unregulated wholesale suppliers. They have integrated backward vertically or moved to related areas (gasoline distribution, refining, chemical industry). Others have moved to resource and environmental protection such as recycling or environmental damage cleaning, for which there exists considerable demand, especially in East Germany.

Some distributors have exploited their right of way to move into joint cost operations such as the distribution of natural gas, or telecommunications. Others have diversified into completely nonrelated areas such as banking, insurance, management consulting, and so on. The effect is a fairly business-minded management culture that extends from these competitive areas to the regulated one. The only requirement imposed by the regulators is that these companies must be run as wholly independent subsidiaries.

Retail rate structure

Until the 1990 BTO reform, consumers faced the choice between two tariff options – one involving a small fixed cost and a high variable-cost component, and the other involving a high fixed-cost but a low variable-cost component. These options essentially amounted to a declining block-rate structure. The fixed components were allowed to vary with dwelling unit size, as suggested by a weak correlation to electricity consumption and thus the associated capacity cost.

However, it was difficult for households to find ex ante the right breakeven point between the two rates. The optional tariff thus resulted in higher revenues than a declining block-rate structure would have, where the utility would calculate the tariff each month and allocate it to the relevant tariff, thus allowing consumers to be better off. However, this policy was adopted by a large number of utilities. The BTO effective in 1990 no longer contains two required tariffs but allows for optional tariffs.

The old federal BTO regulation required identical (maximal) prices per kWh. As a consequence, price differences arose mainly though variations in the fixed-capacity charge. However, it was also possible for the states to claim an exemption from the uniform maximal tariff, and they increasingly made use of this. Thus, the original intention to harmonize tariffs for households and small industrial users across Germany was not successful. Initially, tariffs did become harmonized, but more and more states were taking advantage of the exemption so that the price spread was increasing over time. In addition, some states had started to encourage specific energy-saving initiatives by loading all price increases on to the variable component.

It thus became difficult for the regulators to evaluate requests for price increases unless they knew the load structure of each individual household or customer group. Schulz (1978) has therefore tried to group customers according to capacity utilization and then carried out price comparisons. For 43 utilities analyzed, he found that household customers faced price variations of 20% between the highest and the lowest cost utility. The actual price differences were probably larger because some small (higher cost) utilities were not included in his sample. For industrial customers he found price differences between 25% for small loads (about 3 MW) and 35% for larger loads (above 10 MW). Schulz found not only variations between states but also within states. The differences were not proportionate between industrial customers and household customers, indicating a potential for price discrimination.

Under the new BTO effective 1990, the utility must offer its tariffed customers at least one standard two-part tariff and an off-peak tariff. In the former, the fixed-cost component is now specifically capacity-related. It is determined on the basis of the household's peak demand during 96 hours specified in the tariff. Added is a specific metering cost. There is no regulation of the absolute magnitude of the capacity charge. In fact, it can be set to zero. The variable component is allowed to vary by time of day, week, or both. The regulation also requires a price cap, presumably for low-intensity users. The off-peak tariff applies to night-time consumption and includes an additional fixed charge to cover the added metering costs. The off-peak period is usually six to eight hours long. There are also special tariffs earmarked to low-demand seasons and appliances, which are used exclusively during these times.

The idea behind this recent BTO tariff reform was to replace the traditional declining block-rate structure by a tariff, which is related more to consumption and thus induces energy savings. There has been no detailed analysis of the resulting changes in consumption patterns. However, for the largest utilities in Northrhine–Westphalia about 67% of the revenues under the pre-1990 regulation were related to the marginal pricing component. The new BTO has significantly increased this share. Some utilities use tariffs, which are almost completely linear, with the remaining fixed portion allowing for the depreciation of the metering devices.

At any rate, the electric utilities association, VDEW, questions to what extent the new off-peak tariff will lead to a more balanced load curve. Already now the system-wide load curve is more or less balanced. Under very optimistic assumptions capacity requirements could be reduced by at most 2%.

Finally, there are individually designed unregulated contracts with large-scale, high-voltage customers. Typically, their prices are indexed on fuel prices. They may also contain interruptible service clauses.

Cost overruns by the utilities will typically lead to contract renegotiations. For instance, the unexpected extra environmental costs involved in use of nuclear energy were passed to the customers because some companies were able to add these costs to the price index. Other companies chose to add a special component to cover environmental costs.

Wholesale markets and energy swaps

It was emphasized before that wholesale markets for electric energy go virtually unregulated in Germany. Although the BTO that became effective in 1990 in principle allows regulators to oversee wholesale prices, they can intervene only if the supplier charges a wholesale price higher than the price charged to large-scale final customers. However, the latter are individualized and go uncontrolled. Thus, the regulator cannot relate these prices to the cost of energy production.[22]

The German energy law explicitly allows for coordination contracts among energy suppliers. Of particular importance are agreements concerning the joint use of reserve and peak-load capacities (i.e., power pooling between the individual electric power firms). Wholesale markets, national markets, and to some extent international energy swaps are coordinated by the *Deutsche Verbundgesellschaft,* a voluntary association of the nine largest suppliers of electric energy.

Coordination of energy production and wholesale distribution at the international level also takes place through the *Union pour la Coordination de la Production et du Transport de l'Electricité* (UCPTE), founded in 1951. The main task of the UCPTE is to guarantee energy availability by swaps in emergency cases, in particular power plant breakdowns. No intention exists to develop continuing transnational supply flows, but some countries are net importers during certain parts of the year, whereas others (like Switzerland, because of its favorable conditions for water power) are net exporters (Arndt, 1989).

In 1989, energy swaps between the FRG electric power system and the rest of the UCPTE members amounted to merely 5% of total electric energy supplied. Almost all of these were supplies among the national public electric energy systems. Virtually no electric energy transits borders within the industrial, or the railway self-generation system.

This situation will likely change if the proposals by the European Community for regulatory reform become law. Since 1989, the European Commission

---

[22] As mentioned before, this is subject to a court case pending between the state of Niedersachsen and PREUSSAG, the local electricity supplier. The energy suppliers argue that cost control at the production level is not covered by the EnWG. Among other features, this dispute instigated the EnWG reform currently under discussion.

has been discussing the new rules for a transfrontier energy distribution system on the basis of a common carrier principle (Arndt, 1989). A first step was taken with the EC's "Orientation Paper on the Transmission of Electricity Supplies in Large Networks" issued in 1990. The explicit objective was to reduce both investment and fuel costs via the employment of common carrier principles within the existing network.

However, the current discussion focuses exclusively on the high-voltage network involving, within Germany, only the interregionally active producers and wholesale distributors. There is no discussion of the involvement of large-scale final consumers or of the employment of the common carrier principle involving regional distributors.

Other initiatives by the European Commission concentrate on principles of information revelation that involve the determination of electric energy and gas prices for industrial consumption, and on the coordination of electric energy investment within the European Community.

Regulatory policy: Where does it stand, where should it move?

Controlling entry

The current system of territorial demarcation and concession contracts and the extensive vertical integration in the German electric power industry almost per se exclude competition for franchise areas. The payments for concession rights play an important role in this. This problem was to be removed with the 1990 revision of the antitrust law (GWB), by which concession contracts were limited to 20 years and had to expire simultaneously with the demarcation contracts. Furthermore, all contracts older than 20 years were to terminate in 1994.

So far, the effects of the reform have been disappointing, even though it has also changed the incentives of the communities to the extent that concession fees are no longer related to the utilities' annual turnover but to energy consumption. The communities have all used the opportunity provided by the abolition of old contracts to renegotiate concession fees to the maximum level. In fact, utilities themselves have offered to pay higher concession fees in order to maintain the privilege to supply their old franchise areas.

This outcome has in a way curtailed the intended increase in competition for franchise areas. In fact, only a few areas have changed hands. In addition, some 125 communities have used the option to take over the distribution system from the previous supplier. However, this did not result in new franchise areas but in a repartitioning of existing ones, for most of these cities were already active in distribution. Most were interested only in extending their franchise region to the new political boundaries, enlarged in the 1980s as a result of community reforms. At most 30 to 40 franchise areas have effectively changed hands but only by substituting the communities' own distribution systems for the licensed utilities.[23]

The other instruments of entry control available in Germany – the vetting of investment projects by the regional regulator – seem to be without much effect as well. Except for safety considerations in the nuclear power plants, where (political interpretations of) technical considerations blockaded entry at the plant level, all posted investments for new capacity have been allowed. The current excess capacity indicates the magnitude of the agency problem faced by state regulators in correctly assessing investment plans. After all, the regulators have only to react to proposals and cannot initiate changes in investment strategies.

Price control

Regulating retail prices suffers from the typical Averch–Johnson effect, because virtually all investments (covering about 50% of demand) can be added to the rate base. Again, the regional price regulators face an enormous agency problem. They are confronted with a large staff of specialists in the large utilities. Even the use of certified accountants helps little to obtain more accurate cost figures, for they are hired and paid by the utilities. It is therefore very difficult for the regulators to question cost figures. They are successful only in very flagrant cases. The utilities have also pursued ways to legally avoid regulative pressure – in particular through divesting their generating capacity to their own subsidiaries with which they have a leasing arrangement and which do not operate under price regulation because they supply under specialized contracts.

In essence, the utilities see the price regulation as a political bargaining process. Anticipating requests for confining a requested price increase, they may prepare their proposal for price increases to allow for a settlement at a lower price. The only way this system can work reasonably well is as a result of some degree of yardstick competition arising from price comparisons at the state level and by reports from large customers and consultants that provide additional tariff information. Finally, there is the bargaining power of large nonregulated customers, who may even threaten to use own-generation or cogeneration.

---

[23] As discussed earlier, this is a clear case of cream skimming. It is in the regulators' interest to keep tariff structures and levels within their supply area uniform. This induces in particular uniformity in the tariff structures between urbanized and rural areas. Since the communities enjoy much lower distribution costs within a high-density population, they obtain high surpluses that are typically used to subsidize other public activities of the cities, such as public transit.

Controlling behavior

The Federal Cartel Office can become active only on the basis of complaints filed by electric energy customers. Pursuing such complaints is difficult, because half of the electric energy supply is distributed under customer-specific contracts of which the antitrust office has no information (Immenga, 1982). It is thus very difficult to establish cost and return comparison as a basis for proving misconduct. Some enterprises rely on specialized outside consultants in this process, but the resulting yardstick comparison is likely to be of little effect. In the cases in which the cartel authorities have ordered an energy company to lower its prices, the courts usually did not support these orders. The main reason was that the antitrust authorities are not really able to differentiate between company-specific structural effects and abuse of monopoly position. This may change with the EnWG reform, which, if approved in the version currently under discussion, will allow regulators to obtain more detailed information on production costs.

Incentive regulation

Energy savings and better load management became added objectives in the 1990 BTO reform. We have seen that load management was already quite effective even before that. However, there are no explicit incentives for saving energy, except for the fact that now almost linear tariffs can be employed. In view of stagnating electricity markets, the utilities themselves have few incentives to be active in this direction.

Postscript: Electricity supply in the integrated East Germany

Soon after the fall of the Berlin Wall in 1989, discussions took place between the former GDR and West German utilities with the aim to take a financial stake in the East German power companies. A takeover race between large energy suppliers began, as a result of which the three dominant players (RWE, *PreussenElektra,* and *Bayernwerk*) agreed, in the so-called *Stromvertrag* in August 1990 (i.e., before unification), to take over the majority of the East German energy generation, transmission, and local distribution in a single joint venture. This agreement gave the three a majority stake in the *Vereinigte Energiewerke AG* (VEAG), the largest East German utility, which also controlled the region's high-voltage grid. The regional distribution companies were required to purchase 70% of their demand from the VEAG over the next 20 years.

Very soon thereafter the other large West German power-producing companies objected and threatened a public campaign unless they were involved. In addition, there was strong opposition from the Federal Cartel Office. A solution was found in 1993 allowing for minor participation of other large West German electricity suppliers. After a lengthy court case, the options of the cities to run their own utilities was also strengthened by giving them a chance to take over the local distribution, rather than just having a minority stake in the regional distribution companies.[24]

This policy move strengthened the position of the three largest West German utilities. This may change the status quo that has existed up to now, which has involved strictly separate spheres of influence among the nine major players of the national grid. The implications of this change may increase competition in the sector.[25]

The large electricity suppliers also used this chance to extend their activities to related energy fields. For example in the East German state of Thüringen, *Contigas,* a natural gas subsidiary of *Bayernwerk,* was allowed to enter into a joint venture. This implies joint ownership of competing energy sources in the same territory. This entry was even sanctioned by the Federal Cartel Office on the ground that it would create a stronger competitive position of gas vis-à-vis oil. In a later proposal, however, the Federal Cartel Office reversed its position (not its earlier decision) by denying any further cross-energy links within the East German states.

One important implication of the unification process and the opening up of Eastern Europe has therefore been a first move from a spheres of influence arrangement toward a more aggressive expansionist policy of some of the large utilities.[26] But in general, the integration of the two Germanys has reinforced the industry structure we have seen evolving in the former West Germany.

[24] Incidentally, during the negotiations about full sovereignty for Germany involving the two German governments and the four allied powers, *Electricité de France* (EDF) proposed to enter East Germany. However, the EDF proposal was later modified to allow EDF entry only to the extent to which EDF would allow entry of German utilities into France. So far, this option has not been realized.

[25] This option has not gone unnoticed abroad. When the *Treuhandanstalt* sold the East German lignite pits of *MIBRAG,* it had to choose between a subsidiary of RWE (and therefore the old industry structure) and a multinational consortium consisting of *Power Gen* of the United Kingdom, *NRG of Minneapolis* (a subsidiary of the Northern States Power Company) and *Morrison Knudson* (a mining company based in Idaho). But only by pressuring the VEAG to give them also an option to take a stake in a new power plant and a guaranteed long-term supply contract of 15 mio. tons per annum could this sale be concluded.

[26] Another issue raised in connection to East Germany's entry is the long-term use of lignite. Production was reduced from 300,000 tons in 1989 to about 116,000 tons by 1993.

REFERENCES

Arndt, H.-W.: "Common Carrier" bei Strom und Gas, *Recht der Internationalen Wirtschaft,* Beilage zu Heft 10 (1989): 1–34.

Averch, H., and L. Johnson: "Behavior of the Firm under Regulatory Constraints." *American Economic Review* 52 (1962): 1052–69.

Bundesministerium für Wirtschaft, BMWi (div. years): Die Elektrizitätswirtschaft in der Bundesrepublik Deutschland im Jahre x (annual reports).

Busse von Colbe, W.: Gutachten zur Bestimmung ausreichender Tarifanhebungen im Strompreis-Genehmigungsverfahren, ms. 1987.

Grawe, J., J. Nitschke, and E. Wagner: Nutzung erneuerbarer Energien durch die Elektrizitätswirtschaft. Stand 1988/89. *Elektrizitätswirtschaft* (1989): 1696–8.

Nutzung erneuerbarer Energien durch die Elektrizitätswirtschaft. Stand 1992. *Elektrizitätswirtschaft* (1993): 1511–5.

Gröner, H.: Die Ordnung der deutschen Elektrizitätswirtschaft. Baden-Baden: Nomos, 1975.

Elektrizitätsversorgung, in: Oberender, P. (ed.): Marktstruktur und Wettbewerb in der Bundesrepublik Deutschland. München: Vahlen, 1984, 87–138.

Immenga, U.: Strompreise zwischen Kartell- und Preisaufsicht unter besonderer Berücksichtigung des internen Kostenvergleichs zwischen Abnehmergruppen. Baden-Baden: Nomos, 1982.

Jüngst, R.: Zum Verhältnis von Kartell- und Preisaufsicht in der Elektrizitätsversorgung. *Zeitschrift für Energiewirtschaft* 2 (1990).

Kroll, G.: Die Investitionen und deren Finanzierung in der deutschen Elektrizitätsversorgung. *Elektrizitätswirtschaft* 89 (1990): 1019–22.

Mitchell, M., M. Manning, W. G., and J. P. Acton: *Peak Load Pricing, European Lessons for U.S. Energy Policy.* Cambridge, Mass: Ballinger Publishing Company, 1978.

Möning, W. Determinanten des Elektrizitätsangebots und Volkswirtschaftliche Kriterien zu seiner Beurteilung, 1975.

Monopolkommission: Mehr Wettbewerb ist möglich. Hauptgutachten 1973/1975. Baden-Baden: Nomos, 1976.

Schiffer, H.-W.: Energiemarkt Bundesrepublik Deutschland. Köln: TÜV Rheinland, 1988.

Schulz, W.: Ordnungsprobleme der Elektrizitätswirtschaft. München: 1978.

Schmitt, D. Kosten und Kostenstruktur in der Elektrizitätsversorgung der Bundesrepublik Deutschland. *Elektrizitätswirtschaft* 88 (1989): 1090–9.

Verein Deutscher Elektrizitätswerke, VDEW: VDEW Statistik, Teil 1 Leistung und Arbeit (annual reports). Frankfurt: Verlags- und Wirtschaftsgesellschaft der Elektrizitätswerke (div. years).

Vogelsang, I.: Anreizmechanismen zur Regulierung der Elektrizitätswirtschaft. Tübingen: 1982.

CHAPTER 8

The evolution of New Zealand's electricity supply structure

J. G. Culy
New Zealand Institute of Economic Research
E. G. Read
University of Canterbury
B. D. Wright
University of California at Berkeley

Introduction and summary

Given the original technological and economic dominance of large-scale hydro projects in New Zealand, the strong link of electricity with national and regional development in a sparsely settled country, and the leading role of government in economic development in general, initial direct public control of generation and transmission was a logical choice. Under this system, most of New Zealand's good hydro projects have now been developed.

By the 1970s discovery of coal, gas and geothermal resources, difficulties in achieving scale economies in a small country, and a concern with energy security resulted in a perceived coordination problem among various public authorities involved in supply and pricing. To improve energy supply performance within the public sector, electricity supply was placed under the control of the Ministry of Energy, which adopted a centrally coordinated energy planning structure. This reorganisation was consistent with the widespread intervention in the economy by the government of the time.

A subsequent general economic crisis resulted in election of a government that embraced a radical reorientation in policy toward privatisation. As just one element of this revolution in policy, wholesale supply was removed from political control and set up as an independent public corporation (the Electric-

The authors wish to thank the Electricity Corporation of New Zealand for assistance with data for this project, but the views expressed here are those of the authors, not of the Corporation, or of the authors' employers, or of any funding agency. We also thank Olivia Patterson for research assistance, Paul Winters for editorial assistance, and Emy Peterson and Ros Hogguer for preparation of the manuscript.

ity Corporation of New Zealand, or ECNZ) with commercial objectives. This move was conceived as the first step in a plan for privatisation of generation and deregulation of distribution that parallels the privatisation policies implemented in many other sectors of what had been an economy with unusually extensive government production.

Further stress in the privatisation plan has been impeded by difficulties in resolving several issues. These include the conditions of sale of ECNZ, the distribution of the proceeds, including the extent to which its value might be apportioned among consumers through sales of contracts or assets at concessional prices, and particularly the desirability of breaking up the corporation with several independent corporate entities.

An essential element of plans for privatisation is the market discipline anticipated from entry of competitive generators, which has become more feasible with the advent of smaller-scale, combined-cycle technology. Competitive entry will not occur, though, unless entrants are assured of long-term access to lines, market structures, ancillary services such as backup, and ultimately to customers. Thus, providing such access in a competitively neutral environment has been a major focus of policy to date. To this end ECNZ's high-voltage transmission activities were formed into a separate subsidiary and then into a separate public corporation, Trans Power. More recently, the Electricity Market Corporation (EMCO) has established an independent trading floor for contracts.

Initially, distribution and retailing remained in the hands of a large number of local public authorities, but this sector has now been deregulated. Many of the retail local authorities remain as public entities but with more commercial objectives and with distribution lines operating essentially as common carriers. About half of the load is now supplied by power companies that are at least partially privatised.

Experience with three quite distinct organisational forms in the wholesale sector offers insights regarding the economic merits of each. As a separate government department, the sector's quality of technological decisions, including innovations in geothermal and a direct current interisland link, and the delay, then rejection, of the nuclear option, appears very good overall. But inaccurate forecasting in the 1960s and 1970s resulted in substantial overinvestment, with a bias toward hydro that exacerbated the problem of fluctuations in water supply. However, similar forecasting errors were made elsewhere at that time by private sector organisations.

The difficulties experienced by the government in controlling and coordinating its own energy supply activities offers insights about the distinction between government ownership and public "control" that are important in assessing the merits of privatisation. When wholesale supply was placed under the Ministry of Energy, the limited success of centralised planning of public entities, even in this small island democracy with a tradition of honest public service and a simple, centralised parliamentary system, is a lesson in the limits of public performance in this area.

In its subsequent form as a state-owned enterprise, wholesale supply has achieved impressive economies of staffing and cost-cutting and improved pricing performance. These are attributable to improved managerial incentives and greater independence from constraints, in particular on labour management under this more independent structure, and a general diminution of previously strong labour power in New Zealand over this period of reform.

Past overbuilding has made provision of future capacity a less pressing consideration. At the same time it lengthens the interval before meaningful new competitive generation capacity can be expected to appear, requiring a greater regulatory role for the government in the short run. As a result, the industry has had the luxury of indulging in a protracted debate about the ideal form of wholesale market, while perpetuating a situation in which generation is theoretically deregulated but practically dominated by publicly owned agencies to the extent that the general public still believe that government is ultimately responsible. Meanwhile, the public's support for privatisation and deregulation has declined, and there are signs that political interference in wholesale markets is increasing, leading to fears of a relapse to the inefficiencies observed in previous regimes.

Thus, pressures for further movement toward the goal of privatisation, disciplined by competition rather than regulation, are motivated not by hopes of further economies but by the desire to make permanent what has been attained thus far. The prospects of this occurring are now considerably reduced, though, as the country enters a new phase of political uncertainty, with a proliferation of minor parties leading up to elections under a new proportional voting system. Ironically, the success of economic reform to date has reduced pressures for privatisation because a growing economy has removed the fiscal necessity for asset sales and focused public attention on the possibility of electricity shortages rather than on potential efficiency gains. At this stage it seems clear that government will have a continuing involvement in pricing in the natural monopoly sectors of transmission and distribution. It is highly likely that generation and retail will be at best oligopolistic in the long run, so that explicit or implicit government regulation of price and supply reliability may also become a permanent feature of the industry in spite of current efforts directed toward facilitating entry.

Historical, political, and economic context

The history of electric power in New Zealand reflects the natural endowments of the country and the political environment. It also reflects the fact that development of its electricity supply occurred in step with the development of its initial administrative and economic infrastructure as a country of recent settlement.[1]

The fact that hydro was the cheapest source of power made direct government involvement almost inevitable. Although there were pioneering private schemes to provide hydro power for gold mines, large-scale hydro development worldwide tended to come under government control, and New Zealand was certainly no exception. Damming major river systems has radical effects on the environment, property rights, communities, navigation, and economic activities. Additionally, because many hydro development opportunities occur at remote sites, investment in transmission infrastructure is necessary. Especially in a context in which the economic and administrative structure of the country was newly evolving, it might well have been difficult for private investors to negotiate with affected parties, secure property rights, and take on potential liabilities. Furthermore, the country is relatively small, making central control possible, and socialist ideals were in vogue when New Zealand was settled and developed, leading the New Zealand government to play a dominant role in the economy in general. A particular feature of the New Zealand experience was the concerted drive by the government, with support of the general public, toward development. This tendency toward state power production was reinforced by the belief that an integrated network, along with extensive reticulation, would be an engine of economic growth and social development – the benefits of which would be only partially captured by the power companies.

Accordingly, in the late 1800s, the government passed a series of acts that granted power to the state to establish lines of communication, put water from streams, lakes, and rivers under Crown agency control, and prevent private enterprise from constructing and maintaining electric lines for lighting purposes in public places. It also became illegal for local authorities to grant anyone the right to generate or use electricity as a motive power without obtaining special permission. The government began constructing its own hydroelectric stations after the turn of the century. Legislative actions formalised the financial role of the government and established requirements for funding hydroelectricity.

Under the Electric Power Board Acts of 1918 and 1925, local authorities were established to purchase a bulk supply of power from the state. The power board jurisdictions were defined so as to make urban communities subsidise the cost of reticulating to the local countryside. Because the system was not mandatory, several urban supply authorities refused to surrender their gener-

---

[1] More detailed discussions of certain aspects of this history may be found in Rennie (1989) and Jackson (1988).

ating and distribution systems, allowing these municipalities to retain control of their electricity departments and of any profits. These two types of Electricity Supply Authorities (ESAs) – the power boards and the municipal electricity departments – have persisted until the present.

Demand grew in the 1920s, slowed in the Depression, and then picked up before World War II. Coming out of the war, the New Zealand economy could be characterised as a small, dependent, primary producing, trading economy. It was almost entirely dependent on dairy and wool as exports and on one trading partner, the United Kingdom. The nation had developed a relatively centralised two-party political system with a single-chamber Parliament and a three-year electoral cycle, no written constitution, no separate states, and minimal involvement of local government in policy matters.

Favourable economic conditions in the 1950s and 1960s allowed New Zealand to gradually diversify its exports and maintain manufacturing share of the economy through protection, regulation, and government-sponsored energy projects. In this period of relative prosperity, New Zealand continued to develop what could be loosely called a "welfare state." The key features of this welfare state have been income support and subsidised housing for the needy, free education and health care, minimum wages, and compulsory unionism and centralised wage bargaining.

In addition to being the key provider of social services, the central government has also owned and run a whole range of traded services, including rail, air, building and construction, forestry, lands, electricity, oil, gas, coal, shipping, postal service, telecommunications, banking, insurance, and housing.

The period of strong economic growth in the 1950s and 1960s ended with the entry of New Zealand's major trading partner, the United Kingdom, into the EEC, and the first oil price shock, both in 1973. Since then New Zealand has struggled with a range of difficult economic problems. In the 1970s and 1980s the highly controlled and regulated economy was insufficiently flexible to respond adequately to the changing international conditions that confronted New Zealand.

It became clear by the early 1980s that significant structural reform was necessary. Reforms were undertaken abruptly and simultaneously by the newly elected Labour Government across a wide range of fronts.[2] The exchange rate was floated, international capital controls were lifted, import licenses removed, and tariffs reduced. At the same time a range of subsidies and market entry controls were removed. A radical shake-up of government trading departments and business was undertaken, which involved separa-

---

[2] These reforms are documented and discussed in Bollard and Buckle (1987) and Duncan and Bollard (1992).

tion of noncommercial activities, establishing many of them as State-Owned Enterprises (SOEs) but run as successful businesses without any special advantages or disadvantages. In some cases the government took the further step of privatisation. The proceeds of privatisation have been significant, amounting to $7.6 billion from 1988 through 1992. This is equivalent to an average of 3.6% of GDP in those five years, higher than for any other country.[3]

The reforms caused significant disruption, and were followed by a period of high unemployment and low growth. Inflation was brought under control, however, and levels of productivity increased substantially, particularly in the SOEs, which are now showing much higher profits. The economy is much more flexible and responsive and is now growing strongly, although unemployment is still relatively high.

Overview of state electricity supply (1945–1992)

Introduction

During the period from World War II to 1992, the basic structure of electricity generation and distribution remained largely unchanged. The ESAs continued to handle local distribution as local bodies (power boards) or under local body ownership (municipal electricity departments). Generation and bulk transmission were dominated by the state. But the nature of the state organisation for generation did change substantially over that time, and our discussion must differentiate three distinct phases, as follows:

- **The Departmental Phase (1945–1978):** Electricity was supplied by a separate government department initially called the State Hydro-Electric Department (SHD) and later renamed the New Zealand Electricity Department (NZED).
- **The Integrated Ministry Phase (1978–1987):** In this period the NZED became the Electricity Division (NZE) of the Ministry of Energy (MOE), and electricity planning and pricing formed part of an integrated energy plan.
- **The Corporatisation Phase (1987–present):** In this period the NZE became the Electricity Corporation of New Zealand Ltd. (ECNZ), a State-Owned Enterprise (SOE), which was expected to act in a normal commercial manner.

---

[3] The United Kingdom, for example, has received $44.4 billion, or an average of 1% of GDP, in those five years. See *The Economist,* June 19, 1993, p. 112.

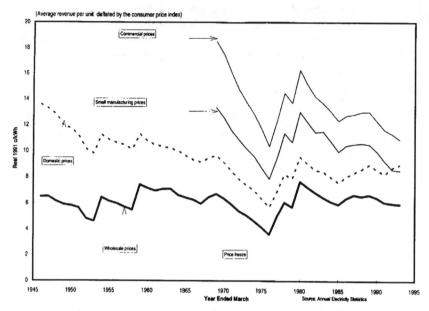

Figure 8-1. Average real electricity prices. *Source:* The New Zealand Institute of Economic Research based on data compiled from Annual Reports of the State Hydro Electric Department, New Zealand Electricity Department, The Ministry of Energy, The Electricity Corporation of New Zealand, Ltd., and the "Annual Statistics in Relation to the Electric Power Industry in New Zealand," Ministry of Commerce, Wellington.

Before examining each of these phases we will review electricity sector developments over the entire postwar period.

Price levels

Figure 8-1 shows the general trend in real electricity prices over the period 1946–91. It is notable that prices to the commercial and small manufacturing sectors were significantly higher than prices to households, implying a significant degree of cross-subsidisation that has persisted over time. A few very large energy-intensive manufacturers have special arrangements for low-cost electricity supply. The fluctuations in prices reflected fiscal or political factors, not electricity cost or supply and demand. It is also notable that despite the fluctuations, wholesale prices are now at about the same level in real terms as they were in the mid-1940s.

Demand growth

After World War II, shortages in labour and capital meant that supply could not keep pace with the burgeoning demand. Hence, demand restrictions were continued on and off until the 1960s.[4] The effects of these restrictions can be seen in Figure 8-2. Consumption grew at an average rate of 7 to 8% per annum between 1946 and 1960 and might well have had a 10% growth rate if it had not been for the restrictions. After 1960, with increasing modernisation, commercial and industrial took over from households as the strongest-growing component of demand. Major industrial developments occurred, or were promoted so that now industrial and commercial uses account for an unusually high 65% of total sales.

From 1960 to 1974, economic performance was generally good, and unrestricted electricity demand grew at about 8% per annum. After the first oil shock, New Zealand experienced electricity supply shortages caused by low hydro flows in 1974–1975. The shortages, combined with a change in attitude about electricity use, dropped growth in electricity consumption to 3 to 4% by mid-1970s. By the mid-1980s, the 10-year growth rate had steadied to around 2 to 3%.

The major components of electricity demand are illustrated in Figure 8-3. Increases in domestic demand were initially fueled by continual decreases in the price of electricity relative to coal and gas, and the falling real prices of electrical appliances. By the late 1970s and 1980s, the growth in household consumption leveled off in per capita terms, reflecting the saturation of appliance ownership, lower income growth, higher prices, and limited competition from natural gas. Electricity's share of the household delivered energy market was only 40% in 1960 but has now stabilised at around 85%.

The relationship between economic growth and electricity growth is illustrated in Figure 8-4. This shows electricity use following economic growth but at a higher level. During the 1950s and 1960s the differential between electricity and economic growth was around 4%. This differential dropped to 1% by 1974 and has remained at around that level.

Supply sources

Hydro power met 95% of total demand in 1945, dropping to 75% at present, but only around 1,200 MW of the remaining hydro potential is regarded as attractive for development. Geothermal power now accounts for about 7% of

---

[4] Restrictions occurred during periods of less than average hydro inflows.

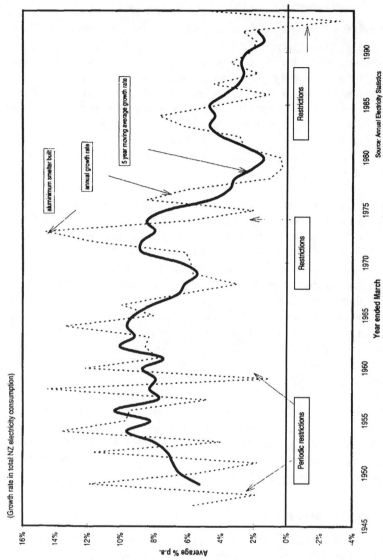

Figure 8-2. Growth in electricity consumption. *Source:* The New Zealand Institute of Economic Research based on data compiled from Annual Reports of the State Hydro Electric Department, New Zealand Electricity Department, The Ministry of Energy, The Electricity Corporation of New Zealand, Ltd., and the "Annual Statistics in Relation to the Electric Power Industry in New Zealand," Ministry of Commerce, Wellington.

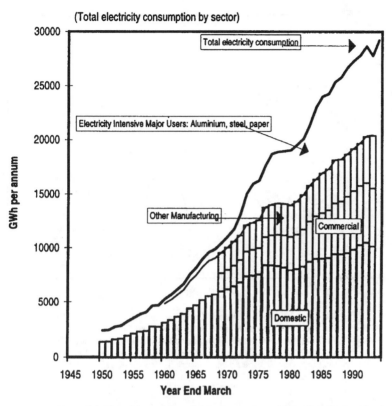

Figure 8-3. Electricity consumption by sector. *Source:* The New Zealand Institute of Economic Research based on data compiled from Annual Reports of the State Hydro Electric Department, New Zealand Electricity Department, The Ministry of Energy, The Electricity Corporation of New Zealand, Ltd., and the "Annual Statistics in Relation to the Electric Power Industry in New Zealand," Ministry of Commerce, Wellington.

total generation and probably has a similar economic potential for future development. Some wind developments are being pursued but are currently viable only where the economies of transmission make development attractive at particular sites.

Since the 1960s, natural gas has been piped to the main centres in the North Island and distributed to households and industry. The large off-shore Maui field has estimated remaining reserves of around 2,500 PJ, which should last until at least 2005 at expected consumption rates. New Zealand has substantial

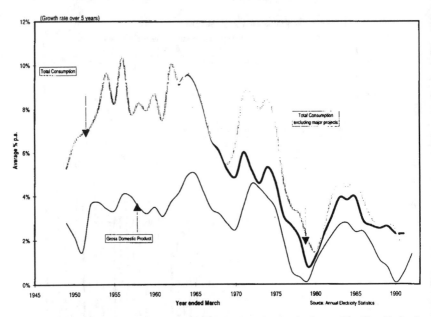

Figure 8-4. Electricity consumption and economic growth. *Source:* The New Zealand Institute of Economic Research based on data compiled from Annual Reports of the State Hydro Electric Department, New Zealand Electricity Department, The Ministry of Energy, The Electricity Corporation of New Zealand, Ltd., and the "Annual Statistics in Relation to the Electric Power Industry in New Zealand," Ministry of Commerce, Wellington.

coal reserves (well over 100 years at current thermal primary consumption rates), which could support coal-fired stations in the future. Several thermal stations have been built on the North Island to take advantage of the proximity of natural gas, coal, and also residual oil from New Zealand's only refinery at Marsden Point. These thermal stations account for around 20% of current electricity supply and fill an important backup role to cover for low hydro inflows.

Cost trends

Fuel costs: The trends in fuel prices are illustrated in Figure 8-5.[5] Until the late 1980s State Coal Mines produced around 65% of New Zealand's coal and

---

[5] The prices presented here do not necessarily represent national costs. The coal prices are average revenue earnings by the State Coal Mines until 1978, the Mines division of the Ministry of Energy between 1979 and 1987, and the Coalcorp. from 1987 to 1991. The gas prices are contract prices, including an energy resources levy.

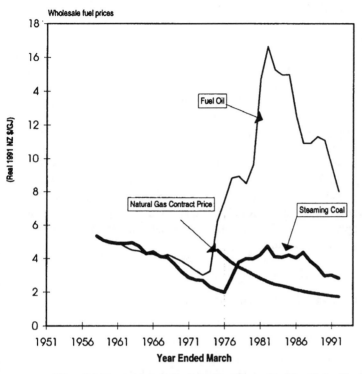

Figure 8-5. Trends in wholesale fuel prices. *Source:* The New Zealand Institute of Economic Research based on data compiled from Annual Reports of the State Hydro Electric Department, New Zealand Electricity Department, The Ministry of Energy, The Electricity Corporation of New Zealand, Ltd., and the "Annual Statistics in Relation to the Electric Power Industry in New Zealand," Ministry of Commerce, Wellington.

was the price setter for the industry, yet its prices did not always reflect costs or competitive conditions and it regularly ran at a loss. Coal prices are now determined by the competitive energy market. The price of heavy fuel oil reflects international oil price movements and the exchange rate. Natural gas prices have been governed by a long-term contractual agreement between the Crown and the developers of the Maui gas field. The Crown has subsequently sold gas under a long term contract to ECNZ. Prices are currently below wholesale coal prices.

Economies of scale: Trends in average cost reflect high fixed costs and economies in density (i.e., transmitting to more customers through the same infrastructure) rather than organisational economies of size. The latter appear to be significant but rather modest.

In the past there were almost certainly economies of scale based on the generation of individual plants, but these now seem less significant as a result of the development of combined-cycle technology. This is particularly fortunate for New Zealand. On a system-wide basis, taking into account the matching of supply with demand growth, and flexibility to respond to changing conditions, if larger conventional thermal plant were necessary to achieve low average cost, the prospects for cost reduction would be modest for a small and isolated country with relatively low growth rates. Although no combined-cycle plant has yet been built in New Zealand, it is expected that the next plant will use this technology. The availability of this technology has also made entry feasible for relatively small generators and presents new opportunities for structural reform options that would be unavailable if the prospective additions to supply were dominated by conventional sources such as hydro or large-scale thermal generation.

The Electricity Department phase (1945–1978)

Structure of the industry

In 1946 the State Hydro-electric Department (SHD) was formed as part of a postwar public sector reorganisation, with responsibility for the operation and maintenance of completed power schemes, including the installation of machinery and transforming equipment at the power site and the construction of transmission lines and main substations. It also took over the administration of acts relating to the supply and distribution of electrical energy and the electrical wiring of premises. This organisational structure persisted until 1978, but the SHD was renamed the New Zealand Electricity Department (NZED) in 1958 to reflect the introduction of thermal and geothermal plant. Within the department, long-distance transmission was entirely integrated with large-scale generation. The civil engineering aspects of power stations were normally designed and constructed by the MOW, while the SHD, and later NZED, normally took responsibility for the electrical engineering aspects, as well as operating the plant and selling at a wholesale level.

Local distribution, which was integrated with some small-scale generation, was under entirely separate control. Competition from other domestic energy sources (coal and wood) was not very significant. With the exception that the department served a few large users directly, all other consumers were served by ESAs, the organisation of which remained largely unaltered over the period. In 1945 there were 94 ESAs. Attempts to persuade supply authorities to merge into fewer, larger bodies had limited success. In 1991 New Zealand still had 55 ESAs. Major urban ESAs were often owned by local bodies that were significant customers in their own right, using electricity particularly for street lighting, water pumping, and public transport. Local distribution authorities were also frequently involved in the retailing of electrical appliances and also in general electrical contracting, but they were not dominant in either area. The NZED did not get involved in such activities.

Control and planning processes

Although supply authorities initially engaged in little formal planning or forecasting, by the late 1950s a formal body was created to compile demand forecasts. A committee of ESA, NZED, and MOW membership was also formed to consider New Zealand's power requirements and to publish recommendations for future development of power sources.

As a government department, NZED had little management autonomy or flexibility. All staff appointments, terms, and conditions were controlled by the State Services Commission (SSC). Virtually all investment and pricing decisions were taken by cabinet committees on the basis of advice from the relevant government departments. The control authorities, particularly the Treasury, had a major influence on the setting of expenditure budgets.

The control system was characterised by a detailed, inflexible, and restrictive emphasis on inputs. Monitoring emphasised adherence to detailed expenditure budgets rather than to the achievement of objectives or outcomes. This meant that important but unplanned or unexpected expenditure could not be undertaken, while at the same time unnecessary spending toward the end of the financial year was promoted.[6] On the other hand, there was really no formal review of the prudence of investments or the accuracy of estimates. Contractual relationships between NZED and the various government departments that supplied them were rather loose. Cost overruns were effectively absorbed into the government account.

Toward the end of the period, there was widespread public criticism of the overforecasting, overbuilding, and overruns that seemed to characterise power planning at that time. It was also argued that imprudent investments were disguised by attempting to sell blocks to new industries at low prices.

---

[6] This occurred because there was a widespread belief that expenditure budgets needed to be fully spent, otherwise they would be reduced in future years.

Rather than institute a formal regulatory review process, successive governments first created another control layer by incorporating the NZED into the MOE, then later moved in the reverse direction to corporatise the various parts of the MOE.

At the local level power boards have controlled their own expenses and set a wide variety of tariffs, subject only to the requirement that they make no profit. The MEDs were able to transfer profits to other local authority uses, although pressure was applied to limit this practice toward the end of the period.

Pricing policy

The basic thrust of government policy throughout this era seems to have been simple: to get power to the people at as low a price as possible. Electricity, and particularly hydroelectricity, was seen as a national resource to be exploited, not simply a commodity to be priced by the market and certainly not an activity that should be undertaken for profit. Hydro development was also a means of opening up areas that had previously been virtually uninhabited and were now viewed as a key resource for national development, particularly for industrialisation.

After World War II, supply and capital scarcity problems called for a reassessment of the structure of the wholesale Bulk Supply Tariff (BST), which was based entirely on maximum demand. In 1952, Treasury suggested that a portion of the capital expenditure should be funded from revenue and that the current tariff should be replaced by a two-part tariff comprising both an energy and a demand charge. The tariff structure remained, but a higher tariff was introduced and legislation passed stipulating the price charged should produce a 25 to 50% surplus, over operating expenses and charges, to contribute to future capital works.

In 1967 a five-year contract was drawn up, with 65% of revenue being derived from a single annual winter peak-demand charge and the remaining 35% from the energy charge. The capital contribution was initially set at 25% but was reset to the maximum 50% in response to an economic downturn later that year. Thus, wholesale prices increased as the economy slowed. As part of an anti-inflation policy, government charges, including electricity prices, were not allowed to adjust to the rampant inflation that followed the 1973 oil crisis, so that the real price of electricity fell significantly. By 1975 revenue from electricity sales was not even covering interest costs, let alone generating the 25 to 50% surplus for capital works. In 1976 the tariff was finally raised by 60% and the ratio of energy to demand charges became one to one. Rates increased again by 40% in 1977, 5% in 1978, and 40% in 1979.

But inflation was high at that time, and the real increase was only about 66% over the period.

At the retail level, supply authorities endeavoured to limit maximum demand by charging higher rates for peak-period supply and particularly by remote control of domestic water heating, which was a major load component. During the 1950s, domestic supply pricing was simplified, with one meter often being used for all domestic consumption, and a common price per unit consumed was charged regardless of the purpose of the supply, in a declining block pricing structure.[7] Incentives for ESAs to design tariffs and control arrangements to limit peak demand reduced as the energy component of the BST increased after 1967. But active demand-side management was, and still is, routinely practised by ESAs to limit peak loads.

A feature of retail pricing in New Zealand has been the way different classes of consumers have been given vastly different treatment. Generally there has been a cross-subsidy from business consumers[8] to domestic consumers, and generally a cross-subsidy from urban consumers to rural consumers. In 1959 nearly two-thirds of supply authorities charged domestic consumers less than the actual average cost of their consumption. This reflects the fact that the supply authorities were controlled by elected bodies.

Supply developments

After the war, it was forecast that the existing hydro construction programme would meet only 65% of the estimated unrestricted North Island demand by 1962–3, but there were no more easily exploitable hydroelectric resources. New thermal and geothermal plant were commissioned in 1958 and 1960, respectively, and in 1961, with the demand for electricity still growing strongly, the government approved an interisland link of 600 MW. The link was in operation by 1965, forming a truly integrated national grid for the first time and allowing South Island hydro resources to be exploited.[9]

All major developments during this period were undertaken by the government. The only major private sector initiative during this period was by a multinational, which proposed to build an aluminium smelter that would use power from a 700 MW hydro station that it would develop at Manapouri, in a national park. This proposal was extremely controversial, and the government

[7] Some users maintained a two-meter system. Previously multimeter systems were common, with different rates for different appliances, to promote their use, for example.

[8] The affected business consumers do not include the very large industrial consumers supplied directly by the government.

[9] On average, 20% of the North Island's requirements are met through the link, and occasionally it is reversed to supplement South Island supplies during periods of low inflows.

took over the private initiative in 1962, modifying the plans as a concession to environmental concerns. In many ways this scheme was a turning point for the sector, signalling that unlimited hydro development might no longer be environmentally acceptable.

In the 1960s domestic consumption increased rapidly as consumers switched to electricity for space heating and electrical appliances proliferated. Although growth tapered off around the end of that decade, planners continued to forecast demand growth in the vicinity of 7 to 8%, whereas it actually averaged only 6.4% over the following decade. Unfortunately, though, adverse hydraulic conditions in the early 1970s again resulted in the imposition of restrictions, a situation that had not been experienced for many years.[10] The oil crisis of 1973–4 heightened the impact of the shortage for the government was reluctant to use expensive oil-fired stations. The heightened concern with energy security led the 1976 Power Plan to see nuclear power as one of the main options for thermal generation beyond 1990. In 1978 a Royal Commission reported that a nuclear programme was viable, but there was considerable public opposition to nuclear power. By 1978 load forecasts were being revised downward, allowing a decision on the adoption of nuclear power to be deferred for 10 years, by which time it was realised that cheaper and more acceptable alternatives, principally the recently discovered offshore Maui gas field, were adequate to meet the anticipated demand growth.

Toward the end of the period, attitudes began to change significantly to include a much greater emphasis on conservation. Hydro schemes, which had previously been viewed as "improving" the landscape, started to be seen as having a negative impact on the natural environment, and the first oil crisis focused attention on the concept of energy conservation. Electricity began to be seen as a scarce resource, to be conserved and controlled in the context of an integrated national energy plan. Hence, the formation of the Ministry of Energy and of the planning processes now to be described.

The Ministry of Energy phase (1978–1987)

The role of the Ministry

When the first energy crisis focused attention on the energy sector, the policy objectives of the government ranged far beyond the simple goal of abundant, cheap power. Energy issues were highly politicised, with conflicting pressures

---

[10] Note that optimal investment and operational policy imply that such shortages should occur occasionally in an isolated hydro-dominated power system. Traditionally, the New Zealand system has been planned so that supply restrictions are expected once in every 20 years. But the general public invariably seem to interpret such occurrences as indicating an immediate need for more capacity, even in situations where the addition of such capacity would not actually decrease the probability of shortage unless the operating policy was also changed.

to reduce dependence on imported oil (at that time almost 100%), to create jobs and economic growth, to create a sustainable energy future based on conservation and renewable resources, to avoid nuclear power and limit development of hydroelectric resources for environmental reasons, and to balance regional development interests.

By the 1970s the New Zealand government had extensive direct interests in the energy sector that were administered through separate departments. Not only did the Electricity Department produce almost all electricity, but most of its inputs, including water, geothermal sources, coal, gas, oil, and a large share of power station construction, were produced or controlled by the state. The government also exercised enormous influence in the sector through direct negotiation with major industries, intervention in crisis situations, and manipulation of demand by means of price controls, subsidies, and taxes.

But state ownership did not equate with centralised control. Difficulties in coordinating the government's various agencies led to the formation of a single Ministry of Energy (MOE) in 1978. The NZED became New Zealand Electricity (NZE), one of the two major operating divisions in the Ministry,[11] but central policy and planning groups had overall responsibility for coordination of supply from all energy sources to meet all types of demand through an annual Energy Plan. The distribution sector was not affected by the formation of the MOE, but some rationalisation continued to occur.

The goal of the Energy Plan was to provide a management plan for at least the state-owned elements of the energy sector. At the retail level, oil had basically priced itself out of much of the nontransport market. With the development of the new Maui field, natural gas had became a much more significant competitor for domestic and industrial uses in the North Island. But a specific goal of the centralisation of control in the MOE was to eliminate "wasteful" competition between government agencies. It was felt that electricity and gas were planning to meet the same demand and that excess capacity would result in both sectors. Balancing tariffs so as to adjust market shares was an explicit part of the MOE's brief, although the actual degree of control achieved was not always great. The MOE was also responsible for fostering alternative energy sources and for conservation as ways of reducing electricity demand, and it sponsored a number of measures, including funding for research, development and demonstration, advertising and provision of information, mandatory insulation standards for houses, and subsidised loans for solar water heating.

---

[11] The other is the Mines Division (formerly State Coal Mines). The Ministry's coordination role also covered oil and gas, but the state's oil and gas interests were handled by separate State Corporations: Petrocorp; responsible for oil and gas exploration and development, and the Natural Gas Corporation (NGC), responsible for the natural gas distribution network.

Centralised control and policy formation

After considerable public debate, the basic pattern of centralised energy planning in New Zealand was set by the Energy Strategy document (Birch, 1979) and centered on a national Energy Plan that covered a 15-year horizon and was to be updated annually. By this time, electricity demand growth had fallen, with demand actually falling 0.4% in 1980. The second oil crisis appeared to confirm the wisdom of a major development programme, known as Think Big. The aim was to use gas to reduce New Zealand's dependence on imported liquid fuels, while creating jobs and boosting exports from energy-intensive industries based on electricity and gas. Thus, while development of a focused, comprehensive, and coordinated energy strategy was emphasised, and the importance of energy conservation stressed, the government was simultaneously endeavoring to sell cheap surplus power to major electricity projects as well as continuing with an active construction programme.

This apparently contradictory situation can be partially explained by the fact that there was a window of opportunity to develop electricity-intensive industries from the temporary surplus of electricity, available from hydro and "surplus" gas at low marginal costs.[12] Once the surplus was exploited, new supply would have to come from coal and/or hydro capacity at a higher marginal cost which, it was argued, should be signalled to users in their electricity prices in order to promote conservation. But much of the confusion can be attributed to the diversity of objectives promoted by political interests. Simultaneously the MOE was using construction to boost employment while promoting conservation to please environmentalists, and trying to protect an overvalued exchange rate by artificially subsidising exports and import substitution industries. Not surprisingly, the economics of most of these Think Big electricity proposals was rather dubious, and many did not proceed. However several did go ahead, including expansion of two existing smelters, electrification of the main trunk railway, and some pulp and paper projects. As a result, despite efficiency improvements in some sectors, New Zealand actually increased its energy-intensity ratio, with electricity intensity (GWh/GDP) in particular increasing by about 10% during this period.

In practice the centralisation of control extended only to obtaining a consensus agreement on an integrated plan coordinated by using national "shadow prices" and, hence, by implication, on the major projects for which government approval could be sought. The central planning group had no control

---

[12] It has been argued that the marginal cost of gas was negative. The offshore production platform did not have the technical capability to strip the condensate out and then re-inject the gas. The benefit from producing the valuable associated condensate flows more quickly outweighed the depletion-related opportunity cost of the gas.

over how the divisions operated and did not even formally monitor performance or cost overruns, for example.

Pricing

A significant rise in prices was posted in 1979 soon after formation of the Ministry. This may be seen as a long-overdue adjustment and necessary to increase revenues. But a surplus was already developing by the time the Ministry was formed, and revenue was being raised to pay for construction that was not actually required. The real price of electricity fell every year from 1980 until 1986, for price increases were held below the rate of inflation. In the 1984 Energy Plan, it was argued that electricity prices needed to be raised to give a reasonable return on investment, and that they should move toward long-run marginal cost (LRMC) to maximise total welfare by sending appropriate price signals to consumers. In 1985 the theoretical basis of pricing was subtly altered from LRMC to short-run marginal cost (SRMC), with LRMC taken to indicate the expected level of SRMC prices for a system in equilibrium.[13] However, price levels were still constrained by the requirements of the Electricity Act 1968 and by public resistance to price rises so that there was very little real movement.

At the retail level, pressure was gradually applied on ESAs to rationalise prices so as to better reflect costs and to reduce the use of MED profits to subsidise other activities. Some progress was made, particularly after the MOE threatened that it would supply major users directly unless ESAs brought their tariffs for those users into line with the BST.

Supply developments

After the price rises of 1970, the electricity sector had a major surplus of capacity. But this surplus capacity did not imply corresponding energy security because much of it was oil-fired and uneconomic at the new prices, whereas much of the gas was to be diverted to new petrochemical plants. Thus, major expansion of hydro, geothermal, and coal-fired capacity was being planned to replace oil and gas and to meet a projected additional demand from electricity-intensive industry of about 8,000 GWH, most of which never eventuated. Several of these planned developments were intended to provide work for construction teams; the developments, it was claimed, would be needed again as soon as "normal" growth resumed. Fortunately, they were gradually deferred, and most have now been shelved indefinitely.

---

[13] Note that the definition of SRMC often used in New Zealand included conservation and shortage elements as appropriate and might more properly be called the "market clearing price."

The Electricity Corporation phase (1987–present)

The pressure to change

By 1984 the New Zealand economy was becoming increasingly stressed, with debt levels rising. This resulted initially from a failure to adjust to the changed conditions of world agricultural trade, particularly the United Kingdom's entering the EEC. The situation was significantly exacerbated, though, by developments in the energy sector when the cost of imports rose substantially with the oil crises and New Zealand borrowed substantially to finance the Think Big investment programme, supposedly to rectify the situation. Soon, the world cost of capital rose and energy prices began to collapse. The government, which had always controlled import quotas and exchange rates, finally resorted to controlling wages, prices, and interest rates as well, leading to a crisis situation, a snap election, and a change of government.

A major programme of economic restructuring was initiated by the newly elected Labour Government, which embarked upon a policy of deregulation. The efficiency of almost every sphere of the economy was examined, with special attention being paid to those sectors under the direct control of the government. It was believed that traditional bureaucratic structures were inhibiting efficient allocation and use of resources, and that far-reaching structural changes, and particularly the commercialisation and possibly privatisation, of government trading activities, were necessary to rectify the situation.[14] The goal was to maximise the role of markets, establish commercial mechanisms, and regulate only as much as was necessary. Thus, electricity sector reform was just one element of an economy-wide revolution in attitudes toward the role of government, the scope of which was perhaps as wide as seen in any democratic nation in the 1980s.

Formation of the corporation

In 1987 the Electricity Division of the Ministry of Energy was restructured as the Electricity Corporation of New Zealand (ECNZ), a limited liability company with no statutory obligation to supply. Simultaneously, controls on entry into the generation and wholesaling of electricity were removed, creating, at least in theory, a competitive environment. As a State-Owned Enterprise (SOE), ECNZ was expected to make a commercial return on its assets. Under this new structure, for the first time management was separated from owner-

---

[14] This was provided for in the State Owned Enterprise (SOE) Act, 1986. In the same year, a new Commerce Act was passed to establish a Commerce Commission to act as a watchdog over mergers and anticompetitive practices, such as price-fixing and the use of a dominant position in a market to an unfair advantage.

ship. Government was distanced from the running of the business, although retaining ultimate control of the organisation, being the sole shareholder. The ECNZ is subject to all normal commercial law but also to some special accountability and control provisions under the SOE Act of 1986.

In 1988 ECNZ restructured itself into a corporate group and four trading units: Production, Marketing, Trans Power, and the PowerDesignBuild Group. Trans Power, which owns and manages the national transmission grid, and PowerDesignBuild, which offers consultancy and contracting services on a fully competitive basis, were established as subsidiary companies with their own boards. In the same year the Ministry of Works and Development was disestablished, and its commercial division, including the Power Engineering Division, became the Works and Development Services Corporation, another SOE.

The ECNZ has subsequently conducted several reviews and internal restructurings, reducing staff numbers directly employed from around 6,000 in 1987 to fewer than 3,200 by 1992.[15] To achieve an appropriate commercial debt–equity ratio, ECNZ was originally set up with a substantial debt owed to the government but with a requirement to raise its own finance to repay this debt over three years and to fund any capital expenditure.

Reorganisation of distribution

Reform of the electricity distribution sector proceeded in a similar direction but at a much slower pace, partly as a result of the complexities of dealing with such a large number of organisations, with some under local rather than central government ownership, and the remainder (the power boards) not actually being "owned" by anyone. During most of this period, ESAs still provided electricity to end consumers (apart from the few large customers supplied directly by ECNZ), but an Empowering Act in 1987 enabled them to adopt corporate structures with appointed directors replacing elected members, with the aim of making the ESAs more commercially oriented. In the same year they became liable to pay tax on any surplus after paying for bulk supply and other expenses. It was clearly understood that further change was inevitable, and that ESAs would be exposed to market forces in future and needed to plan accordingly. This policy resulted in significant internal restructuring, and several mergers.

The Energy Sector Reform Bill, passed in 1992, signalled a number of changes in the distribution of electricity, including the corporatisation of supply authorities and the removal of franchise areas, starting in 1993 with small

---

[15] These numbers are not strictly comparable, though, because many functions previously carried out by employees are now contracted out.

customers and extending to all customers in 1994. A "light-handed" regulatory regime has been adopted with key requirements being to "ring-fence" distribution activities (i.e., the "lines" business) and to adopt nondiscriminatory pricing for lines service, thus allowing retail wheeling so that energy retailing, as distinct from distribution, can become competitive. Apart from the general provisions of the Commerce Act relating to "abuse of a dominant position," an information disclosure regime has been adopted and the Minister retains the right to impose price controls for domestic users. Perhaps the most difficult issue to be resolved was the ownership of the ESAs, and particularly of the power boards, which had no initial owners, thus making it unclear to whom the proceeds of any sale might be distributed. Public attitudes to this issue illustrate the peculiar political problems associated with the electricity sector, at least in New Zealand, and are worth discussing.

Share sales were strongly resisted on the grounds that, if they were sold to consumers, this would be "paying again for the assets they have already paid for," and if not "the government" would be "selling the people's assets," even though mechanisms were proposed to return the proceeds from any sale to local communities. On the other hand, a proposal that shares should initially be given away to consumers was opposed by various groups on the grounds that many, especially poorer, households, receiving a parcel of shares with market value estimated to average around $1,400 per household, would most likely sell them. This would allow concentrated shareholdings to develop and effectively disenfranchising their descendants, who would lose their say in how the company was run. The implicit assumptions that widely dispersed community shareholdings would prove effective in disciplining management, that consumers do not know what is good for them, or that poor consumers have significant influence over local bodies are all highly debatable, but the selective application of this argument to electricity illustrates the special role this sector is seen to play in society. The issue of private ownership also tended to pit local bodies, who have always been seen by the people as "their representatives" and who stood to lose control of very substantial businesses, against the central Government, whereas commercialisation is viewed negatively by the members of the "green lobby," who see local noncommercial ownership as an opportunity to ensure that their own agendas achieve appropriate recognition.[16]

With the government's inability to sell its position on the share giveaway proposal, community trusts were set up for each ESA, and these trusts, in conjunction with the existing commercial directors and the Ministry of Energy, decided the future ownership structure of the ESA concerned. Many are still owned by local authorities or trusts, but privatisation, either through share

---

[16] It is instructive to note the parallel with health and education, both of which are dominated by articulate and well-organised professional elites who command respect in their local communities.

giveaways or sales, has occurred in several cases, representing 50% of ESA sales. Several energy companies are now listed on the stock exchange, and others allow trading through their own share registries.

Integration and competition

Formation of the ECNZ represented a very substantial reversal of the MOE philosophy of vertical integration backward from electricity into the fuel sectors. The ECNZ was left to negotiate new and fully commercial contracts for fuel supplies. In the case of gas, the result was that ECNZ effectively took over a share of the Crown's take-or-pay arrangements for Maui gas, but the new coal contract, negotiated with Coalcorp (formerly the Mines Division of the MOE) was for substantially lower quantities at a substantially lower price. Overall, the result was significantly lower fuel costs for electricity. Although ECNZ has continued previous direct supply arrangements, it does not integrate backward into gas supply, nor does it compete with the ESAs by seeking further direct sales or entering the distribution and retail sectors.

Within the electricity sector, long-distance transmission and real-time control of the system have been separated from large-scale generation, initially as a separate company, Trans Power, within ECNZ, but now as a separate SOE. This has been done to encourage potential competitors to ECNZ to enter the market without having to deal with ECNZ to obtain transmission access. Various reasons have been cited for lack of actual entry to this date, including ECNZ dominance of the energy market, the ancillary services[17] market, and the fuels market.[18] However, the basic reason seems to be that there is still a surplus of capacity and that, even though ECNZ is pricing power significantly above short-run marginal costs, this is still below entry costs. Beyond this surplus period, though, it seems unlikely that truly independent entry, as opposed to entry by major customers, will occur unless many of the uncertainties relating to the future of ECNZ, and of the sector generally, are resolved, for reasons discussed later in the section titled "The current status of the reform process."

Interfuel competition is now clearly a reality. The liquid fuels sector has been deregulated, the state's gas interests have been privatised, and Coalcorp (formerly the Mines Division) has been set up as an independent SOE, with the announced intention of privatisation in the near future. Thus, ECNZ Marketing has pursued an aggressive national advertising campaign and has worked with

---

[17] An independent would require access such as backup, frequency control, and reactive support.

[18] New Zealand is still largely dependent on the Maui field, the output of which is locked up in two major contracts held by ECNZ and by the privatised gas/petrochemicals corporation, which arguably has little incentive to promote electricity generation.

ESAs to target particular markets, with the result that electricity has increased its share of the nontransport energy market. Another ECNZ business unit is responsible for a franchised national chain of electrical appliance retailers and has successfully promoted technologies such as heat pumps and storage heaters. The PowerDesignBuild group is also expected to compete on equal terms with local and international contractors for work from ECNZ and Trans Power, and for any other work it can find, nationally or internationally.[19]

At the retail level, ESAs have been preparing to compete with one another for much of this period. Even before that competition became reality, there was a substantial realignment of retail rates to meet potential competitive threats, and there was a greater emphasis on meeting customer requirements. There is understandable public skepticism, though, about the effectiveness of competition to limit prices in the domestic retail market. Competition for energy trading to large customers is occurring, and this is likely to lead to low margins and back-to-back contracting in that area. This is putting an end to gross cross-subsidisation, forcing domestic prices to rise. Distributors' lines businesses retain strong natural monopoly features, and it is not at all clear that the ring-fencing and information disclosure provisions in the Act are strong enough to be effective in ensuring that outside competitors get truly equal access. The Commerce Commission has already received several complaints in that regard. It seems likely, then, that local retailers and distributors (the former ESAs) will have an effective monopoly franchise in their local domestic markets for some time. Several strategic alliances have already formed on a dispersed geographical basis, amalgamations have occurred, and more can be expected. Thus, the number of truly independent energy traders is now much smaller and may well reduce to three or four competing on a national basis. On the other hand, because these traders are no longer closely aligned to any particular local distribution network, the separated lines businesses may have no reason to discourage fairly open competition.

Regulation, control, and planning processes

The ECNZ is not subject to any electricity sector specific regulation, apart from the supply standards and safety regulations, which are now administered by the Ministry of Commerce. But it is now subject to the same antitrust and commercial legislation as the private sector, including the Commerce Act 1986, which among other things restricts anticompetitive behaviour or abuse of a dominant position and provides for the possibility of price control.

---

[19] Initially, ECNZ actually set up two competing organisations in this area because there was insufficient local competition. However, competitive pressures have increased, and these two organisations have now been brought together into one company.

"Resource Consents" must now be obtained under the Resource Management Act of 1991. The ECNZ must now renegotiate water rights for hydro plant and discharge permits for thermal and geothermal plant, as they come up for renewal, on the same basis as any other commercial operator. Initial experience is that some hydro capacity will be lost to environmental interests as a result. Land access, particularly for transmission lines, is another area in which the loss of Crown status is expected to add significant costs to the electricity sector. On the other hand, it may be argued, these environmental and other costs are not new but are simply made more explicit under the new, commercially separated regime. It is paradoxical that commercialisation has focused more attention on the true social cost of electricity sector developments and may enable a better trade-off to be made between these and other potential developments.

The SOE Act of 1986, under which ECNZ operates, provides for appointment of a Board of Directors, accountable to the Minister of Finance and a further responsible Minister – all of whom hold the shares in the company and are responsible to Parliament for performance. Under the Act each enterprise is required to compose a Statement of Corporate Intent, which in ECNZ's case includes a commitment to "take account of the pricing policies which might be pursued by a market competitor in a comparable situation."[20] The ECNZ conducts its affairs in a normal commercial fashion, through an internal business planning round, which is finally subject to Board approval. It treats commercially sensitive information as confidential and is not required to publish its long-term plans and forecasts. The last Energy Plan was published in 1985, and after a less thorough Energy Issues Paper in 1986, the publication of public planning documents of the kind published since the mid-1950s came to an end. The Ministry of Commerce has recently begun to publish energy sector forecasts again, although these are much less detailed than under the MOE.

Strenuous efforts were made to make ECNZ as much like a normal business as possible, but it has become increasingly clear that, at least so long as it is dominated by a single firm, the public and hence the government believe that the electricity sector should be paid particular attention. Thus, there have been two Parliamentary Commissions of inquiry into particular aspects of ECNZ's behaviour in recent years, both of which are explained further in the next section, "Appraisal of economic performance." One declined to regulate ECNZ's price, but ECNZ "chose" to withdraw its proposal to raise prices in real terms, after several years of falling prices. The other concluded that ECNZ had operated properly in maintaining security guidelines during a severe drought in 1992. But the very occurrence of such an inquiry made it clear that the public and the current government do not believe that such matters are an entirely commercial arrangement between ECNZ and its customers.

---

[20] "Statement of Corporate Intent" Year Ending March 1990.

Pricing

The four-part BST tariff remained in place until 1988, when it was replaced by flexible pricing options and individual agreements that ECNZ negotiates with supply authorities on an annual basis. The new pricing options have a complex structure varying with time of day, time of week, and time of year. These are reflected in a variety of retail rates, especially for large consumers. In some cases ECNZ cooperates with ESAs to offer temporary discounts on margins for loads under threat from other fuels or other economic pressures.

Separate energy and transmission components are in the tariffs. The transmission component consists of a demand charge, a fixed charge for connection assets, and a transmission service charge based on a 10-year rolling average of consumption. The latter is designed to recover the fixed costs of the transmission network from users with minimum economic distortion. Supply authorities can choose to have their full energy requirements met at fixed time-of-use (TOU) prices, but most contract for fixed quantities through a two-way hedging contract, with those who use less than their contracted quantities being credited for the difference, and those who use more being charged for the difference, at the spot prices. These spot prices reflect "actual" marginal costs of production as declared by ECNZ for each separate half-hour one week in advance.

These arrangements allow the supply authorities and their customers to benefit by shifting demand from periods of high-cost generation to periods of low-cost generation. They also provide significant commercial signals for co-ordination of a sectoral response to fluctuations between wet and dry years and strong incentives for ECNZ to maintain hydro reserves so as to reliably meet the fixed contracted quantities. Although it was not well understood initially, the spot price mechanism now appears to be working well. It survived a severe test in 1992, when an unprecedented drought forced spot prices up to over 15 ¢/kWh (against an average contract price of 4 to 5 ¢/kWh). The ECNZ paid out over $50 million to buy back contracted power during this shortage. This provided such strong incentives for energy saving that 10 to 15% savings were easily achieved through water heating restrictions of relatively low impact, efficiency improvements, fuel switching, and voluntary savings and negotiated reductions by major users. This compares with only 5 to 7% savings achieved without price signals in a similar crisis in 1974–5.

In 1991, after decreasing prices by 8% in real terms over the preceding four years, ECNZ proposed to increase the average wholesale price of electricity by about 2% in real terms and stated that a 20% rise would be required before any new stations would be economic, and that this should be expected over the next 10 years. In response to public pressure, a Parliamentary Select Committee Inquiry was set up, which concluded that the increase was not justified because the Corporation was making an adequate return on investment and that no supplier in an oversupplied competitive market could expect to raise prices to LRMC. It also considered that any price rise would have a detrimental effect on export competitiveness and on inflation. Some of these arguments are at best dubious, but it is interesting to note that the policy concerns of earlier years are still current. Although the Committee declined to rule against the rise, ECNZ eventually restrained its price rise to the inflation rate. The ECNZ's current contracts are on an annual basis only, though, and provide no long-term security. The ECNZ plans to issue longer-term contracts, and the price of these is still being debated by the industry, as discussed later in the section titled "The current status of the reform process."

Supply developments

Overexpansion had left New Zealand with excess capacity in electricity supply. The ECNZ was set up with purely commercial objectives, and until prices rise significantly does not see any reason to invest in new plant. Internally, the major thrust of ECNZ policy has been to reduce costs in order to improve returns on assets. This has involved reducing manning levels, with many stations now under remote control, and improving unit availability. The net effect has been an increase in system capability, despite the retirement or mothballing of some older and less efficient plant.[21]

Appraisal of economic performance

This section provides a broad quantitative review of the economic performance of the sector over the period since the war. Several aspects of economic performance are covered: capital and labour factor productivity, pricing and investment efficiency, and X-efficiency. This review is used later in the section titled "Policy discussion," which attempts to draw some broad qualitative conclusions about the differing incentives and relative strengths and weaknesses of the traditional "public supply" organisational structures as compared with the new "corporatised" commercial structures.

Factor productivity

Capital productivity: Figure 8-6 shows the trends in a simple measure of average gross capital productivity, defined as gross sector output (proxied by elec-

---

[21] Now that the period of surplus is drawing close, ECNZ is focusing on planning for a new combined cycle Clyde plant, while entering into negotiations aimed at having that plant developed by private interests.

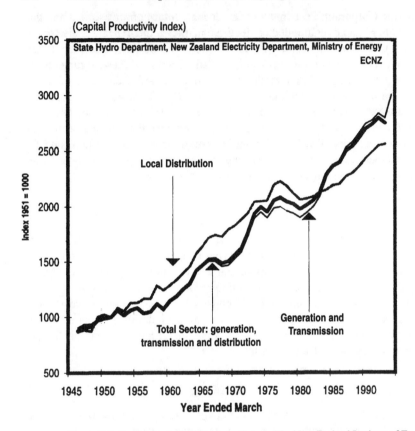

Figure 8-6. Capital productivity indices. *Source:* The New Zealand Institute of Economic Research based on data compiled from Annual Reports of the State Hydro Electric Department, New Zealand Electricity Department, The Ministry of Energy, The Electricity Corporation of New Zealand, Ltd., and the "Annual Statistics in Relation to the Electric Power Industry in New Zealand," Ministry of Commerce, Wellington.

tricity generation in GWh) per unit of capital stock.[22] In the figure, capital productivity shows a generally increasing trend over the period (around 2% per annum) reflecting the high fixed costs and economies of scale, particularly in distribution and transmission. This is most noticeable in the distribution sector

---

[22] The capital stock index is built up from the annual capital expenditure data and involves a number of rather arbitrary assumptions that need to be recognised when interpretation is attempted. The initial capital stock measure for 1945 is the real depreciated book value of the assets. A fixed depreciation rate of 3% is assumed. There is no adjustment for investment quality, and the distinction of capital formation from maintenance is often unclear.

during the period of strong demand growth prior to 1976. The slowdown in productivity growth from the mid-1970s to the mid-1980s reflects the investment expenditure in "surplus" capacity during the period. Likewise, the strong improvement (3.5% per annum) after 1985 simply reflects the slowdown in new construction and the increasing use of surplus assets constructed earlier. The overall capital productivity trend for generation reflects the changing mix of thermal versus hydro and geothermal, although the percentage of thermal has been relatively constant since 1960. By 1991 the capital productivity, as measured by this index, had reached around 1.3 kWh generated and delivered per dollar of capital invested, compared to 0.5 kWh in 1951. Nevertheless, with the benefit of hindsight, it is clear that a significant portion of the capital expenditure (several billion dollars) was wasted because of forecasting errors, cost overruns, delays in commissioning, and poor choice of investments.

Labour productivity: Figure 8-7 shows the number of employees in generation and transmission and in distribution, and Figure 8-8 shows the trends in labour productivity, measured in GWh per employee, for the whole industry and for distribution and generation/transmission separately, over the period 1951 to 1991. These measures of labour productivity suffer from a number of limitations that need to be recognised when temporal and international comparisons are attempted.[23]

In 1991, 2.4 MWh were generated and delivered for each employee in the industry, about five times the level in 1951, as indicated in the middle curve in Figure 8-8. All similar measures show a strong trend of increasing labour productivity, at around 3% per annum over the 45-year period since 1946. This trend reflects economies of larger throughput volume in transmission, distribution, and system operation, as well as technological improvements in control and management. It may also reflect some substitution between capital and labour.

After corporatisation, there was a very strong 90% improvement in productivity for generation and transmission. Although part of this productivity increase may be explained by a reduction in construction activity and increased

---

[23] These are average rather than marginal measures, and the number of full-time employees is only a proxy for the volume of labour input. Ideally, some measure of labour input in hours should be used. The measures also suffer from an aggregation problem in that all types of labour are treated as though they are homogeneous. Furthermore, the measures of output are gross rather than net. Purchases of intermediate inputs and services are included. This means that an increase in the use of intermediate inputs such as contract labour services will appear as higher productivity, even though there may have been no change in real productivity of labour. Conversely, some personnel involved in design and construction of new investments are included during the 1950s and 1960s, biasing down measured labour productivity in those decades.

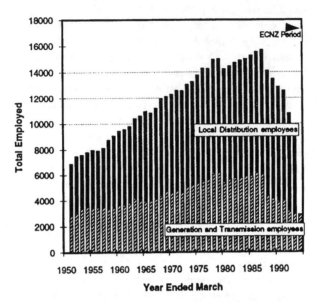

Figure 8-7. Generation, transmission and distribution: Number of employees. *Source:* The New Zealand Institute of Economic Research based on data compiled from Annual Reports of the State Hydro Electric Department, New Zealand Electricity Department, The Ministry of Energy, The Electricity Corporation of New Zealand, Ltd., and the "Annual Statistics in Relation to the Electric Power Industry in New Zealand," Ministry of Commerce, Wellington.

use of contractors instead of employed labour, it also reflects the impact of the rationalisation and improved efficiency achieved by the Electricity Corporation since it was established. For distribution, there is a noticeable, but not so dramatic, improvement in labour productivity since 1987, reflecting the more gradual introduction of commercial structures and incentives in that sector.

Pricing efficiency

Pricing efficiency and cost concepts: Data indicate a generation LRMC of around 6 ± 2 ¢/kWh in real 1991 terms. This would drop to around 5 ± 2 ¢/kWh if a 7% pretax (i.e., around 5% posttax) discount rate was used. Around 1 to 2 ¢/kWh should be added to this to account for the bulk transmission costs. Short-run marginal costs during the period of excess supply from the mid-1970s should reflect coal or gas prices at around 2 to 4 cents per unit, significantly lower than the LRMC. During periods of shortages, the SRMCs

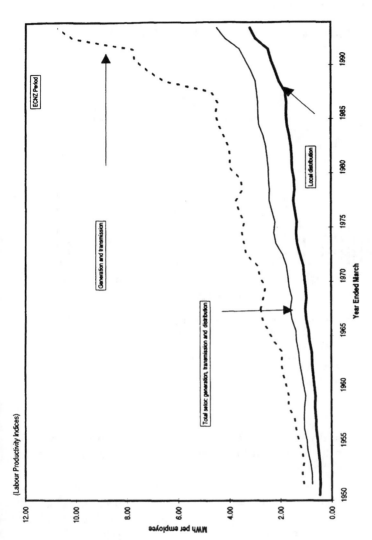

Figure 8-8. Labour Productivity. *Source*: The New Zealand Institute of Economic Research based on data compiled from Annual Reports of the State Hydro Electric Department, New Zealand Electricity Department, The Ministry of Energy, The Electricity Corporation of New Zealand, Ltd., and the "Annual Statistics in Relation to the Electric Power Industry in New Zealand," Ministry of Commerce, Wellington.

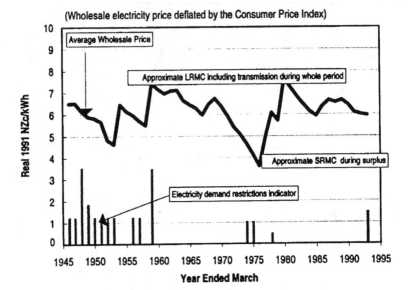

Figure 8-9. Average wholesale prices and marginal costs. *Source:* The New Zealand Institute of Economic Research based on data compiled from Annual Reports of the State Hydro Electric Department, New Zealand Electricity Department, The Ministry of Energy, The Electricity Corporation of New Zealand, Ltd., and the "Annual Statistics in Relation to the Electric Power Industry in New Zealand," Ministry of Commerce, Wellington.

should rise, typically above the LRMC level.[24] These indicative marginal costs are compared with average price levels (see Figure 8-9). See also the earlier discussion titled "Price levels."

The level of wholesale prices over the whole period approximately reflected LRMC, but there was substantial pricing inefficiency in various subperiods. After the war, the price level was 1 to 2 ¢/kWh below LRMC, and also below SRMC if this is interpreted to include the cost of the frequent restrictions that occurred during this period. Moreover the 4 ¢/kWh fall in real prices from 1969 to 1975 was not consistent with a period of relatively tight supply mar-

---

[24] This depends on how SRMC is defined. In a hydro-dominated system it is typically set by the "water value," or opportunity cost of water. If shortages are occurring or likely, this must be reflected in the water value and hence in the SRMC. Such SRMCs correspond to market clearing prices but not necessarily to pure "supply costs," as might be defined in a thermal system.

gins and restrictions. On the other hand, prices were around 2 ¢/kWh higher than the SRMC level experienced during the sustained period of surplus during the 1980s. However, the most significant and sustained price distortion over the period is cross-subsidy between domestic and small and medium-sized nondomestic users, at around a 2 ¢/kWh underpricing for domestic commercial customers, and a 2 ¢/kWh overpricing for nondomestic users.[25]

Cost of supply considerations would indicate that domestic prices should be considerably higher than nondomestic prices. For example, Ernst and Young in "Retail Electricity Tariffs," May 1990, report that the estimated differential between the cost of supply to domestic and nondomestic customers was over 20% for a sample of four ESAs. Domestic users do, however, receive a lower quality of supply in that their water heaters are generally subject to ripple control. It is clear, though, that even when this is taken into account, there remains a degree of cross-subsidy in the region of 20 to 30%. This gap has been reduced somewhat in recent years as ESAs have attempted to rebalance their tariffs. Some might argue that this cross-subsidy simply reflects recovery of the fixed distribution costs according to Ramsey pricing principles (i.e., that higher margins are charged to the least responsive customers). Econometric studies indicate that in New Zealand, domestic users are more price responsive than commercial and industrial users, at least in the short term. However, it is unlikely that even Ramsey pricing would give as high a level of cross-subsidy as has been observed in New Zealand over the past 40 years. How relative responsiveness will change as a result of institutional reforms is an interesting question.

Investment efficiency

It is very difficult to assess investment efficiency accurately because any after-the-fact analysis reflects unforeseeable random disturbances in a sample too small to allow us to distinguish their effects. Furthermore, the peak MW reserve margin is not a very useful measure in a hydro-dominated system in which peak loads have traditionally been managed to match transmission capacity.[26] Nevertheless it is possible to examine some of the elements of efficient investment practice: forecasting demand, estimating costs of alternative investments, choice of investment and timing, and project management.

---

[25] Overpricing has been much more significant than this for some users, such as commercial, in some parts of the country.

[26] A peak MW criterion was actually considered by planners but seldom, if ever, proved to be a binding constraint. An energy-planning margin was used in practice.

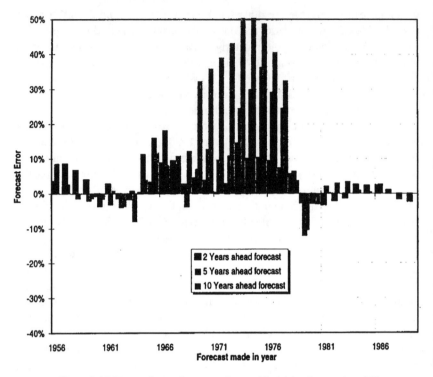

Figure 8-10. Forecasting performance. *Source:* Electricity Corporation of New Zealand, Ltd. (ECNZ), Wellington, NZ.

Forecasting accuracy: As may be seen from Figure 8-10, forecasting performance was relatively good in the 1950s and early 1960s. Of course, sales are easy to predict in a system that is capacity constrained. However, the forecasters failed to recognise until the end of the decade the drop in the growth rate trend that emerged in the early and mid-1970s. This resulted in significant overforecasting by up to 50% during the early and mid-1970s. Similar errors were made by private utilities in the United States in that period. The forecasting performance significantly improved from 1980, during the Ministry of Energy phase, and appears to have been sustained after corporatisation.

Cost estimation and project management: Accurate estimation of project costs is also important for investment efficiency. An after-the-fact-review of selected past power schemes, carried out by the Treasury in 1985, showed significant cost overruns and delays in commissioning of many of the schemes constructed in the 1960s, 1970s, and 1980s. The very high variations in the standardised cost of power[27] found for these projects partly reflects the inherent geological uncertainties in hydro and geothermal developments. However, it also reflects relatively poor project cost control and inadequate research and cost estimation before project commitment. It is clear that this performance was not good and that even a partial improvement promises national benefits of many tens of millions per annum, perhaps equivalent to around 3 to 5% of total wholesale electricity cost. It is difficult to assess performance since corporatisation, but the only major project committed in that period, the expansion of the HVDC link, was built approximately within budget and on time.

X-efficiency: The impact of corporatisation

Some idea of the level of X-inefficiency, or organisational slack, existing under the government department structure can be obtained by looking at the impact of corporatisation on NZE. This has been reported by ECNZ in its annual reports and elsewhere[28] and is fully discussed in Spicer et al. (1991) and Duncan and Bollard (1992).

Since corporatisation there has been considerable progress in reducing costs, particularly by reducing staff numbers, automating, contracting out competitively, and negotiating new fuel contracts. The improvements over the five years (1987–92) since corporatisation are as follows:

- Wholesale prices have been reduced by 8% in real terms.
- Unit operating costs (excluding fuel and capital-related costs) have been reduced by 13% in real terms.
- Sales volume has increased by 2.6% per annum (in an essentially static economy).
- Profits have increased from $262 million to over $400 million.
- The rate of return on equity has increased from 4 to 12%.
- Average plant availability increased from 73 to 91% for thermal, and from 87 to 95% for hydro.[29]

---

[27] This is the output price that would have covered the operating costs and provided a reasonable real return on the capital invested, over the economic life of the assets.

[28] These improvements were documented by ECNZ in their submission to the 1991 Select Committee of Inquiry into Electricity Pricing. They report improvements in plant availability from 84 to 91%, reductions in real unit operating costs of 22%, and increased profits from $141 million to $404 million.

[29] These measures differ from the results reported by ECNZ and Spicer et al. (1991) in the choice of the deflator used. The ECNZ used a consumer price index that included the effects of a 10% Goods and Services Tax, which was introduced in 1986 and later increased to 12.5% in 1991. The ECNZ, like most firms, reports its revenues and costs exclusive of GST, hence costs should be deflated by a price index that excludes GST. We have used such a price index.

- The number of employees (including PowerDesignBuild group wage workers) was reduced by about 47% from 6,000 to around 3,150.
- Productivity as measured by GWh/employee almost doubled from 4.5 to 8.5 GWH/employee.

These results need to be interpreted with caution. Comparisons are made difficult by the lack of proper accounting systems in the old MOE and possibly by the treatment of accounts to present a positive result. Reduction in staff numbers is also to a significant extent offset by contracting out, and some of the technical progress would have occurred anyway. Nevertheless, the results are impressive and do indicate that significant organisational slack had existed under the earlier structures. The cost of this X-inefficiency is estimated to be at least 10 to 15% of the total generation and transmission costs, excluding finance, tax and fuel – this is, around $50 million dollars per annum, or about 3% of total wholesale electricity prices. It is likely that similar levels of organisational slack have existed in the distribution sector, which is only now going through the process of corporatisation.

Policy discussion

Introduction

This section reviews the major achievements and failings of the generation and transmission sector. It draws on the authors' experience during the Ministry of Energy and Corporate phases to discuss that performance in relation to the differing incentives operating in the public service and commercial environments. Performance under a corporate structure is reviewed and related to the previous discussion, followed by a brief discussion of the distribution sector.

Performance in the department and MOE phases

Technological choices: The major technological decisions made by New Zealand during this period were the following:

- To prefer hydro to thermal development.
- To adopt HVDC technology at an early date.
- To develop geothermal power at an early date.
- To defer, and then abandon, nuclear developments.
- To await further developments with regard to wind and other alternatives.

In general, these decisions would probably be accepted as a good record of technical judgment,[30] even if it may seem surprising that New Zealand still has no combined-cycle plant.[31] In fact, however, the choice of hydro over thermal is actually quite debatable on both environmental and economic grounds.[32]

Why did successive governments prefer hydro even in the 1970s, when the record suggests it was known to be more expensive? It might be hypothesised that not only does hydro development attract government interest but that historically governments have preferred hydro development, perhaps because it is a visible symbol of national, and especially of regional, development. If it is true that greater government involvement is likely in hydro systems, we must be careful not to falsely conclude that the characteristics of such systems are a result of government involvement. In New Zealand's case hydro development was also preferred because of its high use of local labour and lower requirements for imported technology. This may be interpreted as a tacit acknowledgment that the exchange rate was overvalued[33] and raises the possibility that hydro may actually have been cheaper than thermal when evaluated at a realistic exchange rate. The bias toward hydro also points to a fundamental dilemma and national debate underlying power planning. From the early 1970s the Treasury insisted on a 10% (real pretax) discount rate for all economic studies. But the public frequently support options that correspond to discount rates more in the 4 to 7% range when asked about trading off hydro and thermal projects. It is not surprising that politicians, reflecting these views, tend to choose such options irrespective of "economic" analyses performed at 10%. Nor is it surprising that public investment consistently crowds out private in the sector. Thus, the debate about public versus private involvement revolves in part around a much wider debate about the relative merits of their respective discount rates.

[30] "Unexpected" geological problems were often experienced, but this seems to have been more the product of an approvals regime that encouraged the understatement of contingencies and that made it difficult to alter plans once political commitments had been made, rather than of poor technological choices as such.

[31] This can probably be explained by the fact that no new thermal capacity has been committed since 1975, because it has been apparent since then that gas supplies for electricity generation were likely to fall and that there was likely to be a surplus of generation capacity.

[32] The economics of geothermal generation have also been challenged, the major problem being the typically long delay between initial investigations of a large number of potential sources and the final proving of a "field" (i.e., a group of bores concentrated enough to support a significant generation station). The debate hinges crucially on the extent to which initial investigations can be justified as "research," rather than attributed to a particular development, and of course on the discount rate. It has also been suggested that a more flexible development programme, using smaller but less efficient plant, might be more economic. If geothermal development was not actually economic, this only reinforces the comments made about hydro.

[33] In fact this was made explicit by the use of a 10% foreign exchange weighting in later years.

Supply–demand balance: Because new supply options are often rather lumpy and inflexible compared with the load growth, it is intrinsically more difficult to avoid supply–demand mismatches in a small country. For a hydro-dominated system this difficulty is compounded by unreliability, coupled with very long lead times (typically four years from conception to approval and then eight years more to commissioning) and the need for integrated catchment development plans covering perhaps 20 years. It takes time to bring a workforce together and to build towns and roads to exploit hydro resources in a remote region, and it is then difficult to defer construction, mothball the town, and allow the workforce to disperse. Nor is it always environmentally acceptable to abandon a half-finished hydro project.

The early postwar shortages were probably the inevitable result of a sustained surge in demand that was not foreseen by the private or public sectors during the wartime years. It is questionable whether a private system would have closed the gap faster, especially given the government's advantage in overriding obstacles to hydro development, which was the dominant technological alternative at that time. Some shortages, especially in the early 1970s, were caused by low-probability hydrological events and were not necessarily indicative of poor planning, given the dominance of hydro technology. On the other hand, the bias toward hydro development clearly increased the system's and the economy's exposure to this additional, weather-related disturbance. It is doubtful whether these problems were appropriately recognised in evaluating hydro versus other, more flexible, technological alternatives, and it is virtually certain that developers in the private sector would have opted for development less dominated by hydro projects. Thus, although governments may do hydro better, better results may have been produced by private sector developers who would have produced a greater technological variety and a more resilient system.

Surpluses may also be attributed to inflexible construction programmes, and in New Zealand, this was compounded by the desire to maintain "workforce continuity" so as to preserve an appropriately skilled workforce in the country. This argument carries more force in a small isolated economy, but studies in the 1970s suggested that disbanding a hydro construction workforce and mothballing the infrastructure between projects would actually only add 15% to (real) costs, making it certainly cheaper to do so if a deferral exceeding two years, say, is expected. Nor could this argument really justify a supposed requirement to maintain *three* complete workforces in parallel. After it was recognised that a project was uneconomic, it tended to be slowed down but not halted. Politicians had made commitments to particular projects and would lose face if they were abandoned, and governments are understandably reluctant to abandon the regional infrastructure associated with hydro developments. Thus, we might expect governments to persist with construction rather longer, after surpluses become apparent, than an unregulated private firm would, and that regulated utilities might lie in between the two in this regard.[34]

Pricing: The foregoing discussion concentrates on the physical supply–demand balance. But the apparent lack of any connection between the supply–demand balance and pricing, and the related discrepancy between (marginal) costs and prices, are perhaps even more surprising from an economic perspective.

The historical data suggest that, contrary to rational economic policy, falling prices were associated with times of shortage and rising prices with times of surplus.[35] It would be tempting to interpret the supply–demand imbalances as solely reflecting the effect of such perverse pricing policies on demand. Indeed, price rises during the 1970s were seen as part of a general energy conservation package, even though there was actually a surplus of electricity. This pattern may also be partially explained by the fact that government revenue requirements were less pressing during times of high economic, and hence load, growth. In any case it seems clear that the structure failed to provide any real discipline on pricing, while giving politicians opportunity and incentives to manipulate it for reasons unrelated to the economics of the electricity sector.

A simple cost-plus regulatory regime solution might not have given superior dynamic demand side signals, because it would have had much the same effect, always moving prices in a direction opposite to that required to balance supply and demand. But a regime with regulated private firms would almost certainly have performed better in terms of disciplining supply-side investment and aligning prices with long-run average supply costs.[36]

The public service context

Political and managerial factors: Direct payoffs to individuals or companies are not generally considered to be a significant feature of political life in New

---

[34] However some observations from other countries including the United States make us cautious of the superiority of private-sector decisionmaking with respect to investments in capacity. A more systematic cross country investigation would seem to be a worthwhile research project.

[35] It should be noted, though, that the data relate only to the bulk supply tariff applicable to most sales. The government did seek to bring the market closer to equilibrium by selling bulk power to potential major users in the international market, at prices close to marginal cost, when surpluses became apparent.

[36] It may be observed, though, that no regime that requires prices (for incremental load) to be set more than a month in advance will be able to deal with the kind of random year-to-year fluctuation in supply–demand balance, and hence marginal cost, experienced in a hydro-dominated system. Recent experience suggests that such pricing flexibility can play a major role in reducing the impact of such hydrological variations.

Zealand, but no Minister could ever ignore the local and national electoral implications of each and every investment decision. Politicians naturally want to be seen to be doing something positive, and to foster feelings of national pride, irrespective of the actual value of the project. Major construction works, in particular hydro projects in the period before environmental concerns gathered force, were ideal for this purpose.

Management tend to pursue the interests of the professional group to which they belong, in this case engineering.[37] These interests largely coincide with those of the politicians in favouring large-scale construction projects and investment in high-technology equipment.[38] It seems unlikely that individual advisers could have been so successful in promoting their technological agendas in a purely commercial environment, and private sector interests, in the absence of regulatory guarantees, would probably not have been so bold (or foolhardy) as to pioneer development of geothermal power and the HVDC technology of the interisland link with no prospect or intention of selling the technology elsewhere. The fact that these particular developments are generally considered to have been successful, technically and economically, might be at least partly attributable to the merits of strong engineering influence within the departmental structure. On the other hand, some of the state's later high-technology investments in the energy sector, such as synthetic gasoline, although technically successful, were economic failures.[39]

Labour unions: Until recently, labour unions have been strong in New Zealand and have had a high national profile, negotiating national awards covering a high proportion of workers and frequently resorting to strike action. Although it is not clear that union leaders exerted any significant direct influence on government decisionmaking in relation to particular projects, it is clear that employment considerations were a very significant factor in the decision to go ahead with several major projects.

Union strength had even greater influence on day-to-day management decisions. In particular, the PSA (Public Service Association) covered most state employees, and union power in the electricity industry has traditionally been regarded as among the strongest in the country. As a result of constant negotiation with the State Services Commission, the Public Service Association was

---

[37] Note that departmental heads are professional, not political appointees, in the New Zealand public service. They generally remain in office for longer than the Ministers they serve, and may hold private or professional opinions quite different from those of the government.

[38] Although it should be said that, at least at times, professional departmental heads were in favour of restricting demand rather than committing sufficient resources to meet it.

[39] We might also suggest that the New Zealand Government was on much safer ground in pursuing developments in a sector with which it was familiar, in a controlled domestic market, than it was in attempting to develop a petrochemical industry from scratch in a volatile international environment.

governed by a complex set of rules.[40] Any infringement or variation on the rules became a very serious matter for both sides because what might appear to be a sensible solution to a local problem could set a precedent that would have to be applied over the whole state sector. Conversely, a dispute in another sector could affect work practices in electricity, and, in a major dispute covering the whole state sector, the electricity sector could become a convenient pressure point.

Perhaps the most striking aspect of this agreement, from a commercial point of view, was that it was virtually impossible to dismiss a public servant for any reason, making it difficult to downsize or disband a workforce and greatly reducing incentives for efficiency. Appointments had to be made on the basis of seniority, and most senior positions in the NZE were reserved for registered engineers.[41] Contracting out was subject to approval by the PSA, which vetted proposals to determine that employees of the contractors were employed under conditions similar to those of PSA members. Not surprisingly, the union assumed a powerful position, being consulted on a monthly basis by senior management.[42] It is clear that the union, or at least the public service structure, had a major negative impact on the sector by increasing manning levels, reducing efficiency, and further increasing costs by insisting on restrictive practices. The extent of these extra costs really became evident only after corporatisation, when major cost reductions were made largely by tackling these issues.

Planning processes and incentives: The iterative planning process adopted by the MOE was successful in identifying and reconciling major discrepancies between sectoral forecasts and plans, especially in reducing the tendency for sectoral interests, and electricity in particular, to overestimate their own market shares, and so attract funding for overinvestment.[43] Communication of the shadow price structure also helped to resolve persistent misunderstanding about the true cost of meeting the extremely variable fuel requirements of a hydro-dominated electricity sector, and so it improved prospects for effective coordination. Planning criteria were gradually refined during this period. At the beginning of this period, the electricity system was planned on the basis of

[40] Spicer et al. (1991) refer to "42 different occupational determinations and 50 agreements" (p. 43) with the PSA at the time of corporatisation.

[41] Some of these restrictions were gradually relaxed during the MOE phase in order to allow particular non-engineers to perform particular tasks for which they were obviously the best qualified.

[42] Spicer et al. (1991) go so far as to say that "the need to have agreement of the PSA before any substantive decisions could be made gave the PSA a role somewhat similar to that of a Board of Directors" (p. 43).

[43] A full discussion of the planning process and incentives during the Ministry of Energy phase and later is given in Read, Culy, and Gale (1992).

being able to meet the "high" energy load forecast plus a 7% planning margin, in a 1-in-25 Design Dry Year. By the end of the period, the criterion was to minimise the expected cost of supply and nonsupply combined, by matching the marginal value of each plant type in each island to its marginal cost.[44]

The fundamental flaw of this planning regime, though, was the fact that the traditional public sector structures often gave vague and conflicting objectives and inappropriate incentives for both analysts and decisionmakers. In particular there was a great deal of idealism but no allocation of ultimate accountability because the "shadow prices" remained exactly that, never being incorporated into any form of contract or binding agreement.

Performance of corporate structure

The improvements resulting from corporatisation, as documented in the previous section, are impressive, and similar progress, such as the development of a more sophisticated wholesale market, can be reported in other areas. To a large extent this improvement must be attributed to a deliberate reversal of many of the negative factors of the previous regime.

First and foremost, ECNZ now has a clear goal and clear accountabilities. Managers are employed under contracts that give them incentives to perform, and they have the power to manage their own business units without interference from outside bodies such as the SSC. Guaranteed employment, appeals, and rigid demarcation rules are a thing of the past. Contracting out is common, and internal contracts are frequently used to clarify objectives and relationships and to give incentives to managers. Contracts for fuel and construction, for instance, are now binding commitments with other commercial parties and must be taken seriously by both parties. When possible, competitive pressures are used to control costs, and managers are expected to innovate as necessary and to be accountable for their units' performance.

Managers are no longer required to be engineers, and when the new organisation was set up, all senior positions were open to competition from internal and external applicants. A similar approach was adopted at progressively lower levels. As a result, many of the senior management team that was appointed were nonengineers from outside the organisation, and they have driven a radical organisational cultural change down through the organisation. Management are free from union coverage, but this is still a major issue for lower-level staff, making it difficult to extend bonus schemes, for example, throughout the organisation. Although many employees still belong to the PSA, the union now has much less influence than it did. The kind of changes

---

[44] These marginal values were calculated as "option values," given the distribution of SRMC "spot prices."

that have been made, and particularly the downsizing that has been achieved, could never have occurred under the old arrangements. There were some industrial disruptions during the initial restructuring process but very few since 1990.

In principle, ECNZ is now largely free from political interference. Although the shareholding ministers do reserve the right to explicitly (and as a matter of public record) instruct the Board on certain matters, this has not occurred. It seems clear, though, that the threat of substantial interference is growing and that ECNZ is already having to take action to comply with the government's wishes in order to avoid formal intervention. This trend suggests that the SOE model, which has achieved impressive results to date, will not be sustainable in the long run. It seems unlikely that senior management will continue to pursue profitability aggressively in such a climate, and it is salutary to note that, although the Committee that reviewed the 1992 hydro crisis exonerated the Corporation, the Chief Executive and half the senior management team moved on to other positions, mainly in the private sector, within a few months. Prospects of continuing to attract high-calibre management from the private sector are poor so long as the job involves intense public criticism and the prospect of political interference.

Ironically, one aspect of the Corporation's performance that has attracted much criticism has been its vastly improved profitability. Even though, apart from a very small proportion paid in staff bonuses, that profit is all channelled back into public funds through taxes, dividends, and increased value, many of the public apparently still feel that it is somehow "wrong" to make a profit out of selling an essential service, or that it is "wrong" for an organisation to make profits out of assets "which the people have already paid for." In particular, there is a feeling that an organisation that is already profitable should not be allowed to raise prices or lay off staff.[45] Considerable resentment has also been expressed at commercially realistic remuneration packages now available to senior management.

Other criticisms relate to ECNZ's promotion of consumption, the narrowness of its objectives, and the way in which formerly public data are now treated as commercially sensitive.[46] It is true that decisionmaking is now more narrowly focused, based on a narrower database, and taking account of fewer factors. The old public service structure encouraged, in part, a spirit of cooperation across departmental boundaries in broad-minded scientific inquiry, which has certainly disappeared. On the other hand, the quality of the data "owned" by each business unit is generally far better now that their commer-

---

[45] Identical criticisms were made earlier of Telecom, but much less so now that it is privatised and experiencing significant competition.

[46] For example, under the old regime, there was a public list of every employee's status and salary, and technical data on station performance and fuel costs were freely available.

cial survival depends upon it, and the data incorporated into contracts between units, or between ECNZ and other corporate bodies, although less detailed than before, have generally been researched and challenged far more thoroughly. Objectives are also much clearer, leaving much less room for the kind of holistic approach desired by some but also much less room for the pursuit of unacknowledged personal agendas.

On balance, the data available to decisionmakers and the quality of decisionmaking have almost certainly improved. But much of the criticism of the lack of relevant data, which comes particularly from the environmental lobby, arises because adequate funding has not yet been found for the kind of analyses that should be done if the more adversarial approach to energy and environmental policy is to be effective. At present, there is a distinct informational and analytical asymmetry.

Concerns have been expressed about the "wasteful" duplication of expertise and analysis between business units, but this generally arises out of conscious choice and was seen to be economically justified by the managers concerned. Thus, it should be seen as a necessary part of the market process whereby issues of significance attract appropriate resources, and competing analyses contribute to determining the outcome.[47] There is no evidence that unwitting duplication occurs any more often in the new organisation than in the old, and the reduction in staff numbers may be taken as prima facie evidence that it occurs less.

Finally, the reduction in staff numbers and the emphasis on performance have substantially reduced the number of young engineers being trained, raising fears that at some future date there will be a shortage of qualified personnel familiar with the New Zealand system and that ECNZ will be vulnerable to loss of a very small group of experienced staff. This is a legitimate concern, and ECNZ is taking steps to address it. Similarly, with the dispersal of the Clyde workforce, New Zealand is now in the position long feared by earlier planners: of not having a team on hand locally to take on any new major projects. This is probably a lesser concern now that the New Zealand economy is more open and more competitive. But to some extent the impressive results to date would have to be attributed to the fact that the new management were able to use a stock of professional capital built up over many years.

Performance of the distribution sector

The distribution utilities have received little criticism from New Zealanders, but this probably reflects the fact that prices are dominated by the genera-

---

[47] It should be acknowledged, though, that the market may be temporarily out of equilibrium and that excessive decentralisation and duplication may well occur during restructuring.

tion/transmission sector, and that this provides a natural focus for the national media, rather than that this sector has exhibited superior performance. In fact studies suggest substantial variations in efficiency among utilities, even when accounting for differences such as population density. It is generally accepted that local body politics has not provided a good mechanism to monitor or control costs and has not led to efficiency. Retail pricing is a clear example. The voters were given cheap power at the expense of commercial and industrial users, whereas farmers were subsidised by urban users, and overinvestment in rural reticulation occurred. Performance of the "local hydro" policy of the 1970s is also clear. Almost all of the schemes built under this regime exceeded estimated costs, were of dubious quality, and were pursued primarily as a means of local development rather than economic viability.[48]

Electricity retailing is now competitive, and rapid progress has been made on reducing cross-subsidies and on increasing efficiency.[49] The new organisations also appear to be much more oriented toward meeting customers' needs. Although several have expressed interest in new generation ventures, the need to raise finance on the open market and to face competition in the local market should be sufficient to discipline any tendency toward rash investment, provided "ring-fencing" is adequately enforced to prevent losses from generation projects being cross-subsidised from the distribution business, which remains a local natural monopoly.

The current status of the reform process

The political context

When the economy-wide reform process was initiated in 1986, SOEs were set up with the clear intention that privatisation should eventually occur, to improve incentives for efficiency and to reduce public sector debt. The radical changes proposed were viewed with apprehension by the public, but there was a general air of optimism, for the share market and construction sectors boomed and the new policies seemed to have a positive impact. But it was unrealistic to expect that New Zealand's economic difficulties, which had built up over many years, would be quickly solved by restructuring. Over time, and particularly after the 1987 share market crash, a more realistic mood set in and

---

[48] Central government can be blamed, here, for encouraging that tendency with subsidised loans and inadequate scrutiny of proposals and cost control. On the other hand, many other local authorities successfully built and operated unsubsidised local hydro plant over the years. We are not aware of any systematic study on the economics of such ventures.

[49] There is some evidence that direct labour productivity has improved during the period, but it is not possible to tell if total productivity has improved. There is also anecdotal evidence of improved operating efficiencies of up to 20 to 30% in some cases.

support for the reforms became more precarious. Although reelected in 1987, Labour soon became divided over the reform process. The government was effectively paralysed coming into the 1990 election, and the National party returned to power in a record landslide.

Since then, the National Government has pursued policies very similar to those of its Labour predecessor, driven by the ongoing need to reduce government debt, by the realisation that reversing the direction of reform is not a realistic alternative, and by a generally favourable view of private enterprise. It is generally accepted, though, that those who support continued reform have gradually lost power to those who favour a traditional, centrist, pragmatic approach. Labour has reverted to a more centrist position, and the Alliance, a loose grouping of third parties who are critical of recent reforms and who broadly support a return to "more traditional New Zealand values," are expected to win a substantial block of seats in the next election, which will see a change to proportional representation. With a very small majority, and after its experience with the retail reform process described above, the government will be understandably reluctant to put forward any proposal that is not sure to receive fairly widespread support, and it cannot ignore the fact that large sections of the community are less than happy with the prospect of further reform. Furthermore, although the proceeds from asset sales would still help it to reduce the debt burden, this factor is much less critical now that the economy is growing and the government is operating in surplus.

Issues for wholesale sector reform

Because retail sector reform is now complete we concentrate here on the status of reforms in the wholesale sector. Despite the apparent success of the SOE model in the case of ECNZ, as discussed earlier in this chapter, the current political context is such that the direction and nature of future wholesale market reform is uncertain and controversial. There have now been three major studies of the sector: by the Electricity Task Force (1989) with representatives from the industry and from government; the industry-sponsored Wholesale Electricity Market Study (WEMS, 1992); and the more broadly based Wholesale Electricity Market Development Group (WEMDG, 1994). All have reached broadly similar conclusions with regard to the kind of market structures required, but none has proceeded to the point of action.[50] This is partly because successive governments have been increasingly reluctant to pursue privatisation, which would be the natural expectation in such a market, but also because the various parties within the industry have found it very difficult to agree on a reform package.

---

[50] WEMDG's recommendations, which are discussed later, are currently being considered by government.

In view of the stakes involved, it is not surprising that various parties have taken great interest in these issues. The problem is that the sector has evolved in the context of a social consensus that no longer exists and was never formalised, forcing the invention of transitional structures that preserve the positions of various stakeholders in the industry without imposing rigidities for any future market. Naturally, though, such arrangements tend to involve some form of averaging, causing approximately half of the industry to object to any particular proposal. This has been a major problem with Trans Power's pricing policy, for example.

In theory, it should be possible to establish a consensus on such issues, and both government and the industry have been strongly of the view that the industry should be left to do this and to establish structures on that basis. There are no mechanisms to enforce any such consensus within the industry, though, and it might be suggested that no resolution will be reached unless the government is prepared to at least set a deadline by which consensus must be reached, and to endorse the industry structures agreed to by the industry, by legislation if necessary.

Without such industry consensus, any government proceeding with reform will find itself exposed to criticism by one party or another. On the other hand, it has been argued that the single greatest hindrance to entry by independents is not fear of retaliation by ECNZ, as such, but uncertainty over government intentions. In particular, the greatest commercial threat must be that ECNZ might be required by government to keep prices down, or to subsidise the building of new capacity from profits on old capacity, not as an anticompetitive strategic move for purely commercial reasons but to meet government's social objectives. So long as the industry believes that the government will finally act to minimise political risk, each party has incentives to lobby for its individual advantage. For example, the same parties who want to see independent entry, also want low-priced power from existing assets. It is generally agreed, though, that, apart from resolving the political impasse, the key issues are as follows.

A neutral competitive environment: The advocates of further reform generally favour using competitive entry to keep contract prices close to entry costs, with the general sanctions against "exploitation of a dominant position" in the Commerce Act applying in the shorter term. Thus, all studies have recommended development of neutral market structures to facilitate efficient coordination, contract trading, and entry. One major component of this was the establishment of Trans Power as a separate SOE. It is not yet clear, though, that Trans Power will be allowed to implement pricing policies that will allow competition at various levels while still achieving the benefits of an appropriate degree of vertical integration, in an economic sense.

Fundamentally, the industry is characterised by large, expensive, inflexible, and long-lived investments in generation, in transmission, in distribution, and to a large extent in consumption. Furthermore, these investments are linked together into a network of interdependence, suggesting the need for strong vertical coordination. Traditionally, these problems have been solved by integrating transmission and generation into a single vertically integrated firm, covering a geographic region, with relatively minor cross-border transfers (if any) traded at SRMC-related prices and carried on link lines, the costs of which were shared by mutual agreement or covered by long-term contracts.

Trans Power has completed a substantial body of work on transmission pricing (Turner, 1989) and there is now a well-developed theoretical basis for pricing access to, and use of, the high-voltage network. Under this proposal the bulk of the network asset costs would be charged by way of long-term take-or-pay access contracts, or "capacity rights." These contracts would effectively provide the vertical integration necessary to allow the horizontally disintegrated sectoral structure to work. Anyone with an access contract would be free to wheel power across the network at relatively low SRMC-based transmission usage prices that can best be thought of as "nodal price differentials."

Under such a regime, dispatch and investment decisions will not be significantly distorted by second-order effects arising from the regional market power that particular parties may have in various parts of the grid. These principles are accepted with regard to new investment, but no such contracts are in place for existing assets. Thus, those parties who stand to gain from such second-order effects by building and operating local power stations that reduce use of the existing grid will almost certainly force Trans Power to adopt a pricing regime based on which charges vary more on the basis of net consumption, so that such projects are effectively credited with an artificial "benefit" resulting from a notional reduction in "optimised" line capacity, even though no such reduction or benefit will occur in reality. The consequent distortion of dispatch and investment is believed to be significant, although it is argued that there will be benefits in terms of increased competition.[51]

There has also been much debate about the form of contracts in the market. The ECNZ contracts are currently in the form of financial hedges referenced to a spot price which, it was envisaged, would eventually be set by a competitive market, as in the United Kingdom. This form of contract was strongly endorsed by the WEMS study, which put great emphasis on the need to establish a limited set of tradeable standardised instruments if liquidity was to be achieved in such a small market. The WEMDG, though, substantially reversed

---

[51] There certainly would be more independent power stations under such a regime, but the number which any particular customer has effective economic access to is actually reduced when variable transmission charges are increased in this way, thus strengthening local monopolies. This is clearly not the ideal way of reducing ECNZ's current dominance.

that recommendation by stressing the necessity of allowing parties to form whatever contracts they desired, whether "physical" or "financial," with or without reference to the pool. In the meantime, the industry itself has begun to implement some elements of a wholesale electricity market. In 1993, ECNZ and the ESA Association established the joint venture Electricity Market Company (EMCO). This company has made significant progress in the development of a secondary (financial) contract trading market and a metering and reconciliation agreement to enable trading within distribution networks.

Probably the greatest area of dispute has been over the extent to which it is necessary or desirable to breakup ECNZ, with some arguing that the current organisation is efficient. If entrants have access to all market services and structures on a neutral basis, and ECNZ is heavily contracted to reduce its market power, a contestable market exists and will become competitive in time. Others have argued for breakup into seven to eight equally sized firms, several of which would have only one power station in the small New Zealand market.

Analytically, a consensus could probably now be found for a heavily contracted "core" ECNZ consisting of the two major river systems and producing about half the load, and 2 to 53 smaller groups. But the political environment makes it increasingly unlikely that there will be radical moves in that direction. Thus, WEMS refrained from recommending wholesale breakup and/or privatisation in the belief that such actions were not realistic for the immediate future, instead recommending an initial trial market, involving semiindependent generation groups within ECNZ and any new entrants, with the hope and belief this would demonstrate that at least some of these organisations were ready for privatisation. Similarly, WEMDG recommended the reduction of ECNZ's dominance in the generation market by requiring it to do the following:

- Lease approximately 40% of its plant to independent operators within five years.
- Offer long-term contracts for a substantial portion of its remaining capacity.
- Sell sufficient gas for a 300 to 400 MW power plant to a third party.
- Refrain from building more than 50% of the new capacity required in the future.

At this stage, it remains to be seen if the New Zealand economy is large enough to sustain an unregulated competitive market in generation, even if the political obstacles can be overcome. If competition does not develop, then regulation may be the only option.

Protection of stakeholder positions: As the government has learned from its experiences with the retail sector, the consuming public has strong preferences that constrain the conditions of sale of public electricity supply assets. Economic efficiency, which has been the focus of most studies, has hardly featured at all in the public debate. Public distrust of the possibility of facing an unregulated privatised generator with an effective monopoly is understandable and legitimate, and they will demand strong assurances on both prices and supply security, whether by regulation or the promise of effective competition. Unfortunately, the public are understandably skeptical about the latter, since their experience to date has been of historically low subsidised domestic retail prices being raised while businesses reap the benefits of falling wholesale prices. The public are also concerned about loss of access to, or sovereignty over, "their" lakes and rivers. This is particularly true of the native Maori population and the conservation movement.[52]

Energy companies, which would benefit from a more competitive generation market and would like to acquire a stake in the generation industry, have adopted strong positions in favour of breakup and competitive entry, but they also want low-priced energy and transmission. Conversely, ECNZ initially favoured being privatised as a single unit, with the possibility of some individual power station sales, but when that prospect seemed improbable, tended to favour breakup and privatisation as preferable to regulation or reversion to direct state control. Finally, the government itself is a major stakeholder, not only as the body that will be held at least partially responsible if prices rise or security standards fall but also as owner of ECNZ.

Initially, a major motivation for the government to support privatisation was, rightly or wrongly, the size of the debt reduction that could be achieved by the sale. ECNZ is a major corporation, by New Zealand standards, and sale of such an asset would have a significant impact on public sector debt. But the valuation of such an entity in the absence of a market or even of cross-border competition or comparison depends largely on the prices that can be expected in the market.

In principle, it might be thought that the New Zealand public, being both shareholders and consumers, would be more or less indifferent on this issue, provided the value of ECNZ was captured in any sale process and remained more or less equitably distributed among New Zealanders. In fact, because the voting public pay most of the taxes and consume a much smaller proportion of the electricity, they might be expected to favour solutions with high electricity prices.

It seems, though, that New Zealanders do not see profits made by the government as "their" profits and would much rather see low electricity prices

---

[52] Particular Maori interests in water resources were recognised, but unspecified, by the Treaty of Waitangi in 1840. This treaty is now being treated seriously, and several large claims have been settled. But these can only be made against the Crown, so that privatisation could permanently alienate resources of both cultural and commercial significance.

than good return from "their" electricity investments. Indeed, there has been much criticism of ECNZ's increased profitability.[53] Others presumably do not trust the government to apportion the proceeds fairly or efficiently among tax reduction, loan repayment, and increased spending. Thus, various attempts have been made to provide a more visible mechanism by which the profits might be returned to the public.

It is generally agreed that contractual mechanisms provide a more suitable and flexible mechanism than regulation to protect stakeholder positions and can be used to facilitate, rather than inhibit, market development. Thus, one group advanced a proposal that concessionary contract allocations be redistributed annually among all consumers so as to ensure that future generations of New Zealanders got their "fair share" of the nation's "hydro heritage."[54] Similar contracts, without the elaborate rebalancing mechanisms, were incorporated into the WEMS proposal and have been the subject of subsequent industry negotiations.

The challenge is to find mechanisms to ensure that the benefits are passed on to consumers, rather than captured by retailers.[55] One proposal was to assign the concessional contracts to distributors, who would use the proceeds to reduce fixed line charges. A similar result was achieved, though, by agreeing to a rebalancing of transmission and energy contract charges, lowering the former and raising the latter nearer to entry costs, while providing an "expected price path"[56] for the next three to 15 years. This deal was conditional, though, on retailers and major customers taking up enough long-term energy contracts at these higher prices, and it remains to be seen if this will occur.

The WEMS also recommended that initially retailers be required to hold "capacity tickets" covering a fairly high proportion of their load, so as to provide the public and government with adequate assurance of supply security. A similar mechanism involving security hedges was proposed by WEMDG, but on a purely voluntary basis.[57]

---

[53] Judging from many comments, it seems likely that many actually believe that these profits accrue to ECNZ management – although the issue has certainly been confused by the practice of awarding bonuses, amounting to perhaps 0.1% of profits, to management.

[54] Given that the annual amounts involved would have amounted to about $100 per household, the relative popularity of such a proposal in a society that has now moved away from the principles of free access to education and health care is puzzling, but manifests the special value New Zealanders appear to place on hydro electricity.

[55] This is an issue because retailing has been fully deregulated.

[56] The average price can only be "expected," since it is proposed that the price of marginal supplies be determined by the market.

[57] A security hedge is a special tradeable contract that provides the holder with financial protection against spot prices exceeding the fuel cost of a thermal peaker (approximately 15 ¢/kWh) and special rights in the unlikely event that physical rationing is required.

Costs and benefits: Finally, government and the public need to be convinced that the benefits of further reform will outweigh the costs. Successive studies have found this hard to prove, particularly in view of the relatively large overheads required to establish sophisticated market mechanisms in such a small economy. Privatisation is not expected to provide further improvements in operational efficiency or coordination, both of which appear to be more than adequately furnished in the status quo, but to improve the environment for competitive investment and to prevent an otherwise inevitable regression of the ECNZ to the inefficiencies of its former self. Fears of such regression were encouraged by the perception that the Commissions of Inquiry into the industry in 1991, and again in 1992, were setting a pattern of increasing ad hoc government interference in the industry, and recreating some of the worst features of the precorporatisation phase, without even the checks and balances of public sector procedures. Obviously, the industry has not found it easy to convince government that this behaviour is imposing major costs on the economy.

On the downside, concern has arisen, particularly after recent experience of shortages, that a multitude of generators will encounter difficulties in coordinating their activities or that they may deliberately "play games" in ways that raise prices, increase costs, reduce energy efficiency, or cause outages. Studies confirm that such behaviour can be expected unless a fairly high level of contracting, breakup, or both is established and can impose costs on the economy by distorting economic dispatch. On the other hand, long-run prices will ultimately be disciplined by entry, and short-run gaming can be interpreted as legitimate market behaviour designed to establish an appropriate level of contracting in the market. It may also be suggested that attempts to interfere with the market by regulating against such gaming will be ultimately counterproductive.

The benefits of improved investment incentives may also be debated. It is widely believed that retailers will not be in a strong enough financial position to invest in plant or, equivalently, to buy long-term contracts to meet their customers' requirements, particularly for dry-year backup.[58] On the other hand, the environmental movement fears that too much plant will be built, and it has been suggested that 100 new schemes are currently under investigation. This debate has not been resolved, but a key factor is the extent to which the financial resources of the interested parties, and their need to hedge against risk, are directed to buying interests in the existing system rather than to new invest-

---

[58] Finally, it should be observed that the financial position of the new retail organisations is unclear. The distribution businesses have substantial assets, but unless the retailers are allowed to use the distributors' assets as collateral, which could be interpreted as breaching the ring-fencing provision, they may have difficulty in financing power station developments, or equivalently, buying long-term contracts. This has significant implications for the design of any wholesale market and for the government's fiscal position, which it intends to enhance by selling a share of the transmission business to the ESAs.

ment. Transmission pricing is another key factor. A move toward more recovery of fixed costs through variable charges, provides excessive encouragement for a proliferation of small generation plant near load centres, when that load could actually be met more efficiently by larger plant sited closer to fuel sources, using spare transmission capacity.

REFERENCES

Birch, W. F. "Energy Strategy," Wellington, N.Z.: New Zealand Government, 1979.
Bollard, A., and R. Buckle (eds). *Economic Liberalization in New Zealand.* London: Allen and Unwin, Port Nicholson Press, 1987.
Duncan, I., and A. Bollard. *Corporatisation and Privatization: Lessons from New Zealand.* Oxford, U.K.: Oxford University Press, 1992.
Electricity Task Force. "Structure Regulation and Ownership of the Electricity Industry." Wellington, N.Z.: Report to New Zealand Government, 1989.
Jackson, K. E. "Government and Enterprise: Early Days of Electricity Supply and Generation in New Zealand." *British Review of New Zealand Studies,* 1 (July 1988).
Ministry of Energy. "Energy Plan(s)." Wellington, N.Z.: New Zealand Government, 1980–6.
Read, E. G., J. G. Culy and S. J. Gale. "OR in Energy Planning for a Small Country." *European Journal of Operations Research,* 56 (1992): 237–48.
Rennie, N. "Power to the People: 100 Years of Public Supply in New Zealand." Wellington, N.Z.: Electricity Supply Association, 1989.
Sell, P., and G. Saha. "Retail Electricity Tariffs: The Impact of Commercialisation and Regulatory Changes." Wellington, N.Z.: Report to the Minister of Commerce and Energy, Ernst and Young, May 1990.
Spicer, B., R. Bowman, D. Emmanuel, and A. Hunt. *The Power to Manage.* Oxford, U.K.: Oxford University Press, 1991.
Turner, A. (ed). "Principles for Pricing Electricity Transmission." Wellington, N.Z.: Trans Power, 1989.
WEMS. "Towards a Competitive Wholesale Electricity Market." Wellington, N.Z.: Report to New Zealand Government, 1992.
WEMDG. "New Zealand Wholesale Electricity Market." Wellington, N.Z.: Report to New Zealand Government, 1944.

CHAPTER 9

Regulation of electric power in Canada

Leonard Waverman and Adonis Yatchew
University of Toronto

Introduction

The electricity grid in Canada is composed of generation facilities owned by 11 major companies organized primarily along provincial lines. Tables 9-1 and 9-2 provide data by province for 1993–94 on capacity and generation of energy by primary energy source.

The sources of power vary greatly across the provinces. In 1993, hydro generation represented 62% of electrical energy generated in Canada, hydro being near 100% in Quebec, Newfoundland, Manitoba, and British Columbia, 28% in Ontario, and less than 4% in Alberta. Nuclear facilities provided 17% of Canadian total electricity generated in 1993 but exist in only three provinces – New Brunswick and Quebec (35% and 3% respectively) and Ontario (52%). The choice of the nuclear option in Ontario is examined later. Conventional thermal generation represented 21% of Canadian sources.

The growth of electricity demand has over the years been highly correlated with the growth in gross domestic product, the two tracking each other fairly closely over the course of business cycles. Canadians are very intensive users of energy in general and electricity in particular. Climate and geography have been important contributing factors as has been the historically low price of electricity. The latter is not only a result of the availability of major hydraulic resources but also because public utilities, which dominate in Canada, do not pay corporate income taxes and are able to borrow at favourable rates. The real average price of electricity, which was 4.25 1991 Canadian ¢/kWh in 1970, increased during the mid-1970s as new facilities came on line, particularly nuclear facilities in Ontario. In 1991, the price of electricity was about 5.2 Canadian ¢/kWh – about 60% of which is attributable to generation, 15% to

From a paper presented at the American Economic Association meetings, Anaheim, California, January 6, 1993. © 1994 by Leonard Waverman and Adonis Yatchew. The authors would like to thank Anthony Frayne and Nicholas Sisto for assistance with data.

366

Table 9-1. *Generating capacity, winter 1993–1994 (MW)*

	Hydro	Steam	Nuclear	Internal combustion	Combustion turbine	Unspecified	Total
Newfoundland	6,597	507	—	73	192	—	7,369
Prince Edward Is.	—	65	—	10	39	—	114
Nova Scotia	390	1,708	—	—	222	—	2,320
New Brunswick	934	2,181	635	5	531	10	4,296
Quebec	28,955	625	675	56	886	67	31,264
Ontario	7,240	11,258	14,164	9	998	—	33,669
Manitoba	4,934	347	—	18	—	—	5,308
Saskatchewan	847	1,852	—	2	137	—	2,837
Alberta	819	6,945	—	46	465	11	8,286
British Columbia	10,687	550	—	69	151	167	11,624
Yukon	78	—	—	57	—	—	135
Northwest Terr.	48	—	—	170	26	—	244
Canada	61,538	26,038	15,474	514	3,646	255	107,466

Source: Electric Power Statistics, Capability and Load, 1993, Statistics Canada – Catalogue 57-204.

Table 9-2. *Energy made available, 1993 (GWh)*

	Newfoundland	Prince Edward Island	NovaScotia	New Brunswick	Quebec	Ontario
Hydro	39,193	—	884	3,057	150,048	40,693
Steam	1,581	52	8,787	6,751	36	22,123
Nuclear	—	—	—	5,323	4,807	78,498
Internal combustion	77	—	11	—	250	3
Combustion turbine	-2	7	33	23	25	2,072
Total	40,849	59	9,715	15,154	155,166	143,389
Receipts:						
United States	—	—	—	123	684	2,765
Provinces	—	731	255	1,518	30,192	1,579
Deliveries:						
Firm – United States	—	—	—	1,518	8,092	244
Firm – Provinces	29,942	—	—	359	1,129	7
Nonfirm – United States	—	—	—	359	4,916	6,913
Nonfirm – Provinces	—	—	41	668	1,003	217
Total available	10,907	790	9,929	13,891	170,902	140,352
Nonfirm deliveries within Province	—	—	—	—	100	—
Losses:						
United States	—	—	—	24	500	—
Provinces	552	—	—	62	70	—
Firm energy available	10,355	790	9,929	13,805	170,232	140,352

Source: Electric Power Statistics, Capability and Load, 1993, Statistics Canada – Catalogue 57-204.

Table 9-2 (cont.). Energy made available, 1993 (GWh)

	Manitoba	Saskatchewan	Alberta	British Columbia	Yukon	Northwest Territories	Canada
Hydro	26,891	4,051	1,808	53,174	289	260	320,348
Steam	241	11,099	44,261	6,224	—	—	101,155
Nuclear	—	—	—	—	—	—	88,628
Internal combustion	27	56	20	69	48	233	794
Combustion turbine	—	6	2,275	193	—	96	4,728
Total	27,159	15,212	48,364	59,660	337	589	515,653
Receipts:							
United States	196	147	2	3,633	—	—	7,550
Provinces	925	1,411	683	1,842	—	—	—
Deliveries:							
Firm – United States	3,466	—	—	1,889	—	—	15,209
Firm – Provinces	188	6	1	21	—	—	—
Nonfirm – United States	3,893	229	—	3,362	—	—	19,672
Nonfirm – Provinces	2,130	1,314	1,858	251	—	—	—
Total available	18,603	15,221	47,190	59,612	337	589	488,322
Nonfirm deliveries within Province	—	—	891	225	—	—	1,216
Losses:							
United States	611	—	—	148	—	—	1,283
Provinces	177	—	—	17	—	—	—
Firm energy available	17,815	15,221	46,299	59,222	337	589	485,823

Source: Electric Power Statistics, Capability and Load, 1993, Statistics Canada – Catalogue 57-204.

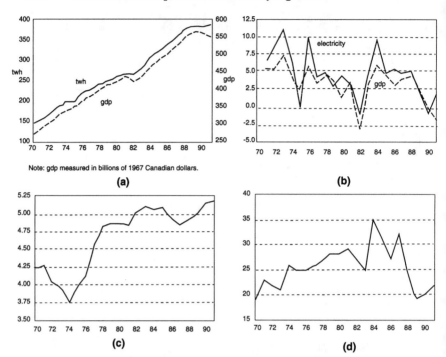

Note: gdp measured in billions of 1967 Canadian dollars.

(a)

(b)

(c)

(d)

Figure 9-1. (a) Electricity consumption vs. GDP – Canada; (b) change in electricity consumption vs. change in GDP (percentage); (c) real price of electricity – Canada (1991 Canadian ¢/kWh); (d) reserve margin – Canada (percentage). Sources of data: electricity consumption and price of electricity: National Energy Board (1990, pages 38–9); reserve margins, Energy Mines and Resources (1970–1992); Canadian GDP: *Short Term Economic Outlook, Fall Review,* Ontario Hydro, October 1992.

transmission, and 25% to distribution.[1] Reserve margins increased from 20% in 1970 to a peak of 35% in 1985 as projects, begun during a period of faster growth, came on line during a period of moderating load growth. Electricity demand, which was growing at 6% per year during the 1970s, slowed to 4% growth per year during the 1980s. See Figures 9-1 (a) to 9-1 (b).

The regulation of electricity in Canada is largely a provincial matter.[2] Under

---

[1] Adjusting for exchange rates prevailing at the time these figures correspond to 4 US ¢/kWh in 1970 and 4.5 US ¢/kWh in 1991.

[2] "Under the *Constitution Act,* legislative authority over management of national resources, and the generation, transmission, and distribution of electricity, rests primarily with the provinces. The provinces have jurisdiction over generating facilities within their borders and over intraprovincial transmission grids. This mandate of the National Energy Board (NEB) with regard to electricity supply is restricted under the *NEB Act* mainly to regulation of exports and to facilities related to international and designated interprovincial transmission lines." National Energy Board, *Inter-Utility Trade Review: Inter-Utility Cooperation,* 1992, p. i.

the *British North America Act* of 1867, the federal government has jurisdiction over interprovincial and international trade. However, the federal government has not attempted to exercise this jurisdiction over interprovincial electricity trade, nor has it attempted to coerce an interconnected electricity grid.[3] Federal jurisdiction over electricity exports relies on a 1907 Act – *The Exportation of Power and Fluids and Importation of Gas Act.* The National Energy Board (NEB) established in 1959 oversees electricity trade (as well as oil and natural gas) and certifies international transmission lines. Interprovincial transmission lines are not regulated by this Board "except in cases designated by the Governor-in-Council."[4] The amount of interprovincial transfers among Canadian provinces is low. In 1991 interprovincial transfers represented only 8% of primary and secondary supply. In 1974 the corresponding value was even lower. These values, although small, exaggerate interprovincial movements; 90% of interregional electricity movements are accounted for by shipments from Labrador to Quebec, the legacy of the 1960s contract to develop the Churchill Falls hydro project. Although the pattern of Canadian population density (80% of the population lives within 100 miles of the 2,700-mile-long U.S. border) helps to explain the lack of interprovincial transfers, a number of studies point to efficiency gains from greater coordination. The absence of federal authority is a prime reason for the minimal provincial interconnections.

It is thus provincial regulation that determines the operations of the Canadian electricity system. Table 9-3 provides information on the major electric utilities in Canada and the form of regulatory oversight. Two key features distinguish the Canadian system of electricity generation from that of the United States. First is the preponderance of publicly owned systems and second, the lack of statutory regulatory agency (SRA) supervision. In 1988, eight provincial publicly owned utilities accounted for 82% of total generated electricity (Nova Scotia Power was privatized in 1992). Of these eight major utilities, seven are totally vertically integrated.[5] The eighth – Ontario Hydro – which we deal with in detail, supplies wholesale power to over 300 municipally owned distribution utilities. Ontario Hydro is regulated in an unorthodox manner. Its new facilities needs are vetted by the provincial cabinet, and its rates are determined by the utility's board of directors after a public hearing before an SRA – the Ontario Energy Board, an agency that does not have the authority to set rates.

---

[3] The National Power Policy of 1963 encouraged connections between provinces as well as interconnections with the United States (see Economic Council of Canada, 1985, and NEB, 1992). In contrast telecommunications wholly within a province has been held to be a federal jurisdiction because the facilities can be used for interprovincial calling. This divergence between telecom and electricity is due to a difference in technologies, differences in the degree of interconnection, and the courts. A major telecom competitor, Unitel (formerly CNCP), sued for interconnection with the Alberta Government Telephone system in Alberta.

[4] See Ministry of Energy, Mines and Resources, Canada, 1988.

[5] In 1989 industrial companies produced 8% of Canadian electricity through self-generation.

Table 9-3. *Regulatory framework for the major electric utilities in Canada*

		Building new facilities						Rate setting	
	Ownership	Requirement	Costs	Debt issue	Environmental impact	Nuclear plants	Exports	Recmmded. by:	Approved by:
Newfoundland and Labrador Hydro Commission	Public			C	C		F	NFLD Pub. Utils. Bd.	C
Newfoundland Light and Power Company	Private						F		NFLD Pub. Utils. Bd.
Maritime Electric Company	Private	B	B	C	C		F		Pr. Edwd Is. PUC
Nova Scotia Power Corporation	Private			C	C	F	F		Bd. of Comm. of Pub. Utils. of Nova Scotia
New Brunswick Electric Power Commission	Public	C		C	C		F/C		C
Hydro-Quebec	Public			C	C	F	F/C		Prlmntry. Comm.
Ontario Hydro	Public	C		C	C	F	F/C	Ont. Engy. Bd.	Ont. Hydro Bd of Dirs.
Maintoba Hydro Electric Board	Public			C			F/B	Mntba Pub. Utils. Bd.	C
Saskatchewan Power Corporation	Public			C	C		F		Sask. Pub. Utils. Rev. Comm.
Alberta Power Limited	Private	B			C		F		Albta PUB
Transalta Utilities Corp.	Private	B			C				Albta PUB
British Columbia Hydro and Power Authority	Public	B	B	C	C		F/B		B.C. Utils. Comm.

C = Provincial Cabinet
B = Provincial Utilities Board
F = Federal Government

1 Regulated by the Atomic Energy Control Board
2 Regulated by the National Energy Board

In this chapter, we concentrate on the growth and regulation of the second largest Canadian electricity utility – Ontario Hydro. The reasons for this emphasis on examining one utility are the unique features both of Ontario Hydro's generation mix and of the regulatory mechanisms established over the decades.

In 1950 100% of Ontario Hydro's generation was from hydro sources (hence its name). In 1972 thermal-electric generation, principally from coal, represented 63% of Ontario Hydro's capacity. Ontario Hydro's commercial nuclear program, designed around the unique Canadian nuclear technology (heavy-water based), began as a 2060 MW facility (4 by 515 MW reactors) completed in 1974 (at Pickering). A second facility of 3076 MW (4 by 769 MW) came into service in 1979 (at Bruce). A third facility came into service at the Pickering site between 1983 and 1985 (2064 MW, 4 by 516 MW). A fourth facility (at the Bruce site) came on stream between 1984 and 1987 (3440 MW, 4 by 860 MW).[6] A fifth facility was brought into service during the early 1990s (Darlington, 3524 MW, 4 by 881 MW) and was subject to construction delays, cost overruns, and commissioning problems. Today, nuclear power represents over 50% of output in Ontario, by far the highest reliance on nuclear power in North America.

The regulation of rates and construction programs of Ontario Hydro has unique features. Ontario Hydro began in 1906 as a publicly owned transmission utility, connecting several private generating companies at Niagara Falls with a number of municipally owned distribution companies. Ontario Hydro bought out the private generators between 1914 and 1920 and expanded hydro capacity. The municipal distribution utilities, of which there are over 300, remain independent entities to this day. Ontario Hydro sets three rates – (1) the rate for wholesale power sold to the municipal distributors, (2) retail price schedules for electricity sold directly to rural customers, and (3) rates for large industrial customers tied to a transmission line. Retail rates for the vast majority of electricity users are set by the municipal distribution utilities and approved by Ontario Hydro.

Until 1974, no direct supervision of Ontario Hydro's rates (the wholesale rate and the retail rate schedules) existed. Beginning in 1974 (for the 1975 rate year), the Ontario Energy Board (OEB), which already set retail rates for natural gas distributors, was asked to examine Hydro's rates and make recommendations to Hydro and to the Ontario Provincial Cabinet. The OEB has no authority to set Ontario Hydro's rates and no authority over retail rates set by the municipal utilities, which in turn are regulated by Ontario Hydro. Municipal distributors, however, *are* responsible to their rate payers through elected commissions or through commissions appointed by locally elected officials.

---

[6] *Providing the Balance of Power,* Ontario Hydro's Demand Supply Plan Report, 1989, pp. 4–20.

In Ontario, regulatory supervision of the choice of technology, the amount of capacity, and the construction program is even more complex than rate setting. Numerous agencies are involved, both provincial and federal. However, no single supervisory or statutory regulatory agency is in charge. Instead, supervision of this crucial function rests on a standing committee and special committees of the provincial legislature, and ad hoc commissions set up to examine specific or general issues.

What explains this process and what are its impacts? The early expansion of public ownership was sold as "power at cost" and "power for the people." Public ownership per se was to ensure that the electricity producer acted in the public interest. We suggest that the theoretical economics literature can help to explain several characteristics of Ontario Hydro. In particular, the regulatory process in Ontario combined with asymmetric information, political uses of the firm, and a wage structure too compacted (in contrast to the suggestion made by Pint [1991]) contributed to overcapacity, emphasis on nuclear technology, and price shocks. The high reliance on nuclear power can be related to public ownership and political desires to base an industrial strategy and an economic development plan on the use of nuclear technology.

Cogeneration projects lag behind those in many U.S. jurisdictions. Demand-side management (DSM) was until recently to be promoted at a pace greater than that in the United States. We suggest that the nature of a publicly owned firm can help to explain these developments as well.

We also examine the current discussion to privatize Ontario Hydro and a number of alternatives – increased third-party access, and horizontal and vertical unbundling – whereby competition would be encouraged. However, an asset base of large nuclear plants, major hydro installations, aging thermal plants, and a set of smaller hydro and peaking plants does not make Ontario Hydro a difficult target for privatization.

Background and history

Early history of electricity in Canada

The rise of the electricity industry in Canada can be divided into two phases. The first phase started in 1880 and followed almost exactly the development of its U.S. counterpart.[7] In 1870 not a single horsepower of electricity was produced in Canada for lighting and manufacturing purposes, yet by 1880, 343 production units were in use. American investors and businessmen brought the new techniques to Canada. First arc and then incandescent lighting systems

---

[7] The Edison Electric Company was formed in the United States in 1878. In the same year, the American Electric and Illuminating Company, the first Canadian company in this sphere, was formed and a tiny generating plant was built in the retail business district of Montreal.

appeared in Canada, usually installed by the subsidiaries of American firms or by Canadian firms operating under license from the American patentees. Electric lighting systems were set up in smaller towns and villages. Around 1900, the introduction of larger-scale units and especially hydro stations made these small pioneer electrical works obsolete. The advent of the large hydroelectric station around the turn of the century rendered these pioneer electrical works obsolete. In Quebec, these enterprises were amalgamated into the Montreal Light, Heat and Power Company in the early years of the century, and into the Shawinigan Water and Power Company by World War I. Nevertheless, in Quebec some local enterprises escaped amalgamation. In Ontario, as will be detailed, economies of scale in the hydro development of the Niagara River led to a single firm.

Another factor was important in leading to the dominance of hydro power in this period. As electricity demand increased, so did dependence on coal from a foreign source – the United States. Ontario industry was experiencing a power shortage and increasing demand for cheap power in order to develop the manufacturing industries. Hard coal in Canada is found in the west in the Rocky Mountain foothills of Alberta, and in the east, in the Appalachian formations of Nova Scotia but not in Ontario. Neither source was economic for Ontario, even after the coming of railroads. As a result, Ontario became dependent on coal imported from Pennsylvania. In 1897 a two-month strike of 75,000 miners in Ohio, Pennsylvania, and West Virginia led to an American embargo against the export of coal to Canada. As a result, the price of coal in Ontario rose by a factor of three. A similar shock in the price of coal occurred in 1902.

From 1900 to 1940, hydro project facilities in Quebec and Ontario accounted for approximately 80% of the total capacity of water power in Canada. With large power developments at Niagara Falls in the early years of the century, Ontario became the leading province in hydroelectricity, but its margin over Quebec was never large. For the period from 1931 to 1940, the per-capita output of hydroelectric energy in Quebec was higher than in any other Canadian province. Quebec accounted for about 40% of the Canadian central electric station capacity in 1926 and more than half of the Canadian total of installed hydroelectric capacity in 1956. Today, Quebec accounts for 47% of Canada's hydro capacity and 29% of all capacity. Ontario has 31% of total Canadian capacity but provided slightly less energy in 1993 than did Quebec.

Early history of Ontario Hydro

Niagara Falls, one of the seven natural wonders of the world, was seen as early as 1881 as an important source of hydroelectric power. In that year the first generating station was established on the U.S. side and used in an electrolytic process for the manufacture of aluminum. The limiting factor in the first three decades was the inability to transport electricity over long distances. This was a greater problem in Ontario than in New York State because major users in the United States were at Buffalo only 20 miles away, whereas in Ontario the major potential users were in various towns and municipalities around the countryside, Toronto, by far the largest market, being 85 miles away. This geographic factor provides a partial explanation for the rise of public ownership in Ontario as contrasted to private ownership in New York State.

Development of the U.S. side of the Falls therefore preceded Canadian development. As a response to the uncontrolled development of the U.S. side, the Ontario legislature in 1885 passed an act "for the preservation of the natural scenery above Niagara Falls," which allowed for public control. In 1902 a group of municipalities endorsed a report that authorized municipal control over transmission as well as over the development of electrical energy itself. The report was introduced by the mayors of two of the largest communities in the province. Adam Beck from London, who became the principal driving force behind public ownership and the first chairman of Ontario Hydro, stated that the provincial government should be involved in "building and operating as a government work, a line for the transmission of electricity from Niagara Falls to the towns and cities" (Denison, 1960, p. 40). That same year saw passage of the *Power Bill,* which gave municipalities the right to acquire or construct works for the generation and distribution of electric or other power and energy.

In 1905 the new Conservative government issued an Order-In-Council, creating the Hydro-Electric Power Commission of the Province of Ontario with Adam Beck as chairman.

What is interesting for this analysis is that the Hydro-Electric Power Commission of Ontario reported to Chairman Beck and was not controlled to any significant degree. The first attempt at control was in 1911, when a bill was enacted to transfer control of the Hydro-Electric Commission to the Ontario Railways and Municipal Board. The bill never received a second reading. It remained on the order table, but nothing more was heard of it (Denison, 1960, p. 98).[8] Thus, Ontario Hydro remained unregulated by any public board. This does not mean that Ontario Hydro was autonomous because the legislature exercised ultimate authority.

Beck announced publicly that Ontario Hydro would not become a government department (Denison, 1960, p. 99). A key event that shaped the regula-

---

[8] Several reasons for the demise of this early attempt at regulation may be adduced. The municipalities feared strong provincial controls. The Liberal Party and a number of prominent members of the Conservative Party also were opposed to controls, fearing political manipulation.

tory environment was the establishment by Beck in February 1912 of the Ontario Municipal Electrical Association (OMEA), a body that is one of the predecessors of today's Municipal Electric Association. "One of the purposes of the new association was to make Hydro independent of political interference, and protect it from the inefficiency of political appointments, then not uncommon in Ontario" (Denison, 1960, pp. 99). The OMEA, whose members were the appointed delegates of the councils in Hydro municipalities, became a powerful lobby group.

It was not long before Ontario Hydro's regulatory authority was further broadened. Hydro was given the authority to regulate rates charged by municipal utilities, a feature that remains today, as well as to oversee their accounting practices and determine how they disposed of surplus earnings. In 1915, Hydro was empowered to perform all electrical inspections, again for the sake of consistency.

Private producers lobbied continuously to control the expansion of Ontario Hydro. In each case, public ownership won. "Power at Cost" became the rallying cry for public ownership. In 1917, following rapid growth in demand during World War I, Hydro was authorized to become a producer, purchased the Ontario Power Company's generating station at Niagara Falls (with a capacity of 135 MW) at a cost of $18.5 million, and at the same time embarked on the construction of a huge hydro facility.[9] In 1919, Ontario Hydro built what was at that time the world's largest hydro facility – 580,000 horsepower or 433 MW.[10] The total cost was $76 million – $20 million above estimates.

At the end of World War I, progress on the rural electrification program was considered unsatisfactory. The "Power at Cost" concept was seen as an impediment to this progress, in that customer density among the remote farms and hamlets was so low that those customers could not by themselves bear the cost of the required transmission line extensions.

Throughout the Depression, successive provincial governments found Ontario Hydro increasingly useful as a political tool. Rural Ontario still retained a considerable degree of political importance, and the provision of affordable electricity was viewed as one means of winning its support.

Following World War II, Hydro engaged in an ambitious program to convert all electrical appliances in a 12,000-square-mile area in southern Ontario from 25 cycle to 60 cycle power. Work began in 1949 and took 15 years, at an estimated cost of $170 million to Ontario Hydro and $21 million to municipalities (Denison, 1960, p. 239). The actual cost to Ontario Hydro for the complete conversion operation was $352 million.

---

[9] This was authorized by way of a plebiscite held New Years Day, 1917.
[10] One horsepower equals 746 watts.

Developments in Quebec

Quebec developments were different. Until the 1930s, the hydroelectric industry in Quebec had been allowed to develop in an environment of unfettered
private enterprise.

Social control by regulatory boards in Quebec had been minimal. A Public
Utilities Commission was set up in 1909, which was renamed the Quebec Public Service Commission in 1920. The body exercised general supervision over
electrical as well as all other utilities until 1934. In that year a Provincial Royal
Commission was appointed to study the electrical industry, probably in an attempt to slough off public discontent associated with the Depression, which in
part was taking the form of agitation for public ownership of electrical utilities. The commissioner advocated private ownership regulated by a permanent
electricity commission. Consequently, the Quebec Electricity Commission
was set up in December 1935 with very wide powers of inquiry and regulation
and the old Public Service Commission was deprived of its jurisdiction over
electrical utilities. This new commission (and its successors) collected statistical data and other information pertaining to the power companies, but its usefulness as an effective regulatory body has been very small, in part because it
immediately became subject to political forces. The Quebec Electricity Commission of 1935 was replaced by the Provincial Electricity Board in 1937,
which in turn was taken over in 1940 by a refurbished general utilities commission under the name of the Public Service Board.

In Quebec only a few municipally owned generating stations developed –
20 in 1921, 12 in 1928, and 16 in 1940 – but they were small and accounted
for only an insignificant fraction of the total electrical output of the province.
On occasion they were responsible for forcing rate reductions by the private
companies, but on the whole the municipal stations were only a minor nui-
sance to private enterprise.

In 1944, however, the situation changed drastically. In that year the provincial government set up the Quebec Hydro Electric Commission, which took
over ownership and operation of the Montreal Light, Heat, and Power Company. The issue was rates – the private firm refusing to lower announced rates.
In 1963 the private generators were "provincialized." The developments in
Ontario, the foreign (i.e., non-Francophone) control over electricity in Quebec
and the existence of vast hydro potential in the remote North led to a public
monopoly.

Impacts of regulatory forms in Ontario

Costs of generation and prices charged by Ontario Hydro followed three
major phases, each linked to the transition from one major technology to an-

other. From 1908 to 1950, the system was hydraulic. As the size of the utility increased, the unit cost of production and supply decreased, although the cheaper hydro sites were developed first. Short-run marginal costs were very low. Thus, a declining block-rate structure and promotional efforts were likely efficient. In the early 1950s, coal-fired stations were introduced. These had two effects. The first was to raise average electricity costs, initially by 10% (Royal Commission on Electric Power Planning, 1980, p. 35). The second was to make electricity prices in Ontario a function of fuel costs for the first time. By 1970, thermal generation (mainly coal-fired) accounted for 60% of Ontario Hydro's energy production. Coal costs fell throughout the 1960s as oil prices also fell. Ontario Hydro added generation constantly, but demand grew even more quickly as a function of rapid economic growth and price decreases for electricity. Ontario Hydro continued to promote electricity use, even for uses with intrinsically low-load factors. The construction of the TransCanada natural gas pipeline in 1956 and the expansion of natural gas distribution through the 1960s provided a new and major source of interfuel competition. Thus, Hydro developed special rates encouraging the use of electricity for home heating purposes, water heating, and even a special low tariff for all-electric houses.

Between 1970 and 1973, the cost of coal rose 16% in real terms and real oil prices doubled. The construction program featured nuclear power, a technology in which the capital costs were clearly uncertain but in which fuel costs played a relatively minor role. Yet, in the 1970 to 1974 period, average-cost rather than marginal-cost pricing made real electricity rates fall, not increase. Locked into huge nuclear projects as demand growth slowed, Ontario Hydro came under major pressure to raise rates; public regulation, absent in the entire previous history of Ontario Hydro, began to emerge.

During the 1970s, regulatory scrutiny of Ontario Hydro intensified. Task Force Hydro, a quasi-independent ad hoc review body, completed five reports during 1972 and 1973. Perhaps its most important recommendation was that Hydro become a Crown corporation with a board of directors.[11] In addition, the Task Force recommended that an independent tribunal be set up to review Hydro rate proposals and rate-setting practices. The tribunal had only the power to make recommendations rather than to direct Hydro to undertake specific actions. The Task Force endorsed nuclear power but recommended that Hydro engage in a greater degree of contracting out. In 1974, consistent with the recommendations of the Task Force, Hydro became a corporation with a

---

[11] Crown corporations are wholly owned federal or provincial organizations that enjoy a greater degree of freedom from direct political control than government departments. They are usually structured in a manner similar to private enterprises but are typically not subject to the same incentives and market forces.

board of directors. It did not, however, become a Crown corporation, leaving the question of ownership unanswered.

In 1974 the Ontario Energy Board was selected as the review tribunal that had been proposed by both the Task Force and the Advisory Committee. The Ontario Energy Board Act provided for recommendatory powers to the board. That same year the OEB held hearings into Hydro system expansion plans and advised the government not to authorize a number of proposed nuclear facilities. The OEB recommended that an outside report be prepared reviewing these issues and that the interests of the province might be better served by a thermal plant instead of Darlington.

The Select Committee of 1977–81 on Ontario Hydro Affairs was initiated to investigate a number of areas, including heavy-water plants under construction at Bruce, fuel contracts, and the need for future nuclear plants. During this period, major uranium contracts were being negotiated between Ontario Hydro and producers at Elliot Lake. The government argued that the contracts were in the public's best interest. The opposition held the opposite view.[12] In the end, Hydro entered into long-term cost-plus contracts with Rio Algom and Denison Mines. During the 1980s, the price of uranium plummeted as worldwide construction of nuclear plants ground to a halt. However, the price Ontario Hydro paid for uranium was decoupled from the world price. Thus, Hydro ended up overpaying for uranium supplies by hundred of millions of dollars during the 1980s.

By the early 1980s, 16 nuclear units were either in service or nearing completion at the Pickering and Bruce sites. Individual units were in the 515 to 860 MW range. In addition, construction of a fifth nuclear station consisting of four 881 MW units was in its early stages at the Darlington site. Demand growth, on the other hand, had fallen dramatically from 6 to about 3% per year. The Select Committee found that Hydro was overestimating load growth and a more appropriate planning number would be in the range of 2 to 3%. The need for the Darlington station was therefore in grave doubt, and the Select Committee recommended that Hydro cease letting contracts in connection with its construction until the government had made a positive determination that the project should proceed as planned. Nevertheless, the Committee acknowledged that the government might decide to continue with the project on the basis of other considerations such as provincial employment, continued sustenance of the nuclear industry, the replacement of less efficient fossil plants, and maintenance of a higher reserve margin in case of a sudden resurgence of load growth. Thus the Darlington project continued to limp along, with occasional delays and postponements and at ever-increasing cost.

---

[12] Indeed, the New Democratic Party held that Denison Mines' shares should have been bought out earlier when they were cheaper.

The electricity costing and pricing hearings held during the late 1970s reconfirmed average-cost pricing as the basis for rate setting. Marginal-cost pricing had been proposed based upon arguments of economic efficiency and as a way to reduce load growth. In the midst of the hearings, Hydro filed a new study indicating generation surpluses that would make marginal-cost pricing infeasible. The Board ultimately rejected marginal-cost pricing on the grounds that it would be too difficult to implement.

In 1980, after four years of investigations, the Porter Commission filed its final report. The Commission had investigated a broad number of areas and its recommendations were far-reaching. The Commission recommended the Hydro plan on the basis that load growth would not exceed 4% per year to the end of the century and that only one additional four-unit station after Darlington would be required over that time. (In fact, no additional stations have been built and the usefulness of Darlington is debatable.) It further recommended increased emphasis on conservation, greater study of health and safety issues related to nuclear power plants, and greater public participation in the hearing process.

In the mid-1980s, the Ontario government commissioned yet another study – the Nuclear Cost Inquiry. The study, submitted in January 1989, concluded that although Hydro's methodology for estimating the lifecycle costs of nuclear generation was appropriate, the final costs would likely be at the upper end of Hydro estimates. Noting the CANDU (Canadian Deuterium Uranium) reactors had been observed for only about half their expected lifetimes, the study indicated that operations, maintenance, and administration costs during the later years were likely being underestimated. The study also found that Hydro estimates of costs of alternatives (such as advanced fossil generation) had not received sufficient attention and recommended that Hydro give consideration to advanced coal-fired plants as alternatives to nuclear generation (Ontario Energy Board, 1975–94).

In 1987–88, the Hare Commission conducted a review of the safety of Hydro's nuclear reactors. It found that: "Ontario Hydro reactors are being operated safely and at high standards of technical performance. No significant adverse impact has been detected in either the work-force or the public. The risk of accidents serious enough to affect the public adversely can never be zero, but it is very remote" (*Providing the Balance of Power,* 1989, pp. 15–38).

From 1989 to 1992 Hydro underwent an aborted public review of a 25-year demand-supply plan, details of which follow.

Table 9-4 lists 17 major inquiries and legislative committee reports that have examined some aspect of Ontario Hydro's operations in the 1974–90 period. This would suggest a strict regulatory environment. In fact, we will give examples of important asymmetries in information between the firm and the supervisory organizations. Public ownership does not by itself induce com-

Table 9-4. *List of major special inquiry and legislative committee reports related to Ontario Hydro*

Year	Name of committee / title of report
1960	Royal Commission; Report on the Purchase of Lands by Hydro-Electric Power Commission of Ontario
1973	Select Committee on the Hydro Electric Power Commission of Ontario Hydro New Head Office Building (Hearings)
1973	Task Force Hydro (Committee on Government Productivity); Hydro in Ontario
1975	Ontario Environmental Hearing Board; Public Hearing on Ontario Hydro Bradley Georgetown 500 kv Transmission Line Right-of-Way between Point 33 near Colbeck and Point 95 near Limehouse
1976	Select Committee on inquiry into Hydro's Proposed Bulk Power Rates; A New Public Policy Direction for Ontario Hydro
1976–1980	Reports of the Royal Commission on Electricity Power Planning, Volumes 1–9
1980	Select Committee on Ontario Hydro Affairs; Final Report on the Safety of Ontario's Nuclear Reactors
1980	Select Committee on Ontario Hydro Affairs; Report on the Management of Nuclear Fuel Waste
1980	Select Committee on Ontario Hydro Affairs; Report on Proposed Uranium Contracts
1980	Select Committee on Ontario Hydro Affairs; Special Report on the Need for Electricity Capacity
1980	Select Committee on Ontario Hydro Affairs; Final Report on the Mining, Milling and Refining of Uranium in Ontario
1985	Select Committee on Energy; Report on Darlington Nuclear Generating Station
1986	Select Committee on Energy; Final Report on Toward a Balanced Electricity System
1987	Select Committee on Environment; Report on Acid Rain in Ontario
1989	Select Committee on Energy; Report on Ontario Hydro Draft Demand and Supply Planning Strategy
1990	Select Committee on Energy; Interim Report on Climate Change
1992	Environmental Assessment Board hearing into Ontario Hydro's 25-Year Demand/Supply Plan; no report

plete revelation of relevant information by managers. Furthermore, the regulatory/supervisory apparatus over Ontario Hydro does not minimize informational asymmetries. The use of Select Committees with changing membership and without a permanent secretariat does not ensure that full information is built up and passed on. The division of responsibilities between rates (the OEB) and capacity (Select Committees and more recently the Environmental Assessment Board) also reduces the buildup of coherent information outside the firm. We suggest that these information asymmetries were partially responsible for choices made by the firm.

Regulation of a public utility under asymmetric information

Economics literature

In the sections that follow we discuss various aspects of Ontario Hydro in the context of the economics literature on regulation. Under the Power Corporations Act, Ontario Hydro is required to provide power at cost. Since regulation is not of a classic rate-of-return type, there is no reason to expect the bias toward capital from the classical Averch–Johnson effect. On the contrary, Pint (1991) suggests that in the presence of asymmetric information, government-owned firms are likely to be biased toward labour as a factor of production. In the case of Hydro, a case could be made for the proposition that it is biased toward *both* capital and labour and away from fuel. The nuclear technology, which is Hydro's principal technology, employs both massive amounts of capital and a large complement of highly specialized nuclear engineers, operators, and technicians.[13]

Pint's further prediction, that government-owned firms are likely to offer steeper compensation profiles to managers than private forms do, is also not borne out at Hydro: All Hydro employees are paid a significant premium relative to the private sector, but there is a compression of salaries at the top end. We discuss staffing levels and compensation later.

Various objective functions have been proposed for the regulated firm. Such objective functions have included producer surplus, consumer surplus, and worker surplus as well as benefits accruing to government. See, for example, Baron and Myerson (1982), Besanko (1985), Laffont and Tirole (1986), and Pint (1991).

In Ontario, significant surplus accrues to the consumer by virtue of average-cost pricing based on historical value of assets. Ontario Hydro ostensibly does not collect any producer surplus. However, we will argue that significant surplus has been appropriated by Ontario Hydro's labour force through premium salaries, an excessive labour force, and various employment benefits, in particular a high degree of job security and very generous severance packages

---

[13] For example, in 1991, about 50% of Hydro's revenue requirement consisted of interest and depreciation, about 30% was operations, maintenance, and administration, and less than 20% corresponded to fuel costs.

(though, in recent restructuring, its labour force has been reduced by over 25%). We will also argue that provincial governments have appropriated benefits by using Hydro as part of an industrial strategy as well as by implementing a number of nontransparent transfers through Hydro.

Selection of nuclear technology

With over 50% of its generation coming from nuclear sources, Ontario Hydro is among the most nuclear-intensive utilities in the world. The origins of nuclear energy in Canada go back to World War II. In 1942 it was decided that most of the personnel working on nuclear technology in Britain would be moved to Canada. The work in Canada was part of a tripartite agreement among Canada, the United States, and Britain. Wartime research in Canada focused on the development and design of nuclear reactors. In 1945, a reactor at Chalk River, Canada, achieved criticality – the first time a nuclear reactor was operated outside the United States. In 1952 discussions were initiated between the federal government and Ontario Hydro on the feasibility of nuclear generation for commercial purposes. In 1953 Atomic Energy of Canada Limited (AECL) was established as a federal Crown corporation whose principal purpose was the development of nuclear energy. In 1962 a 20 MW demonstration reactor achieved criticality, and for the first time nuclear-generated electricity was fed into a commercial grid.

AECL considered and pursued various designs including boiling-water reactor designs similar to those developed in the United States. In the end, the CANDU design was selected, a design that was unique.

The adoption of nuclear power in Ontario was justified on a number of grounds. Most of the hydraulic sites had already been exploited. (In contrast, Quebec had major potential for hydraulic development and its participation in the nuclear program was limited.) Nuclear energy was being touted as "too cheap to meter." Canada and Ontario had substantial supplies of uranium, thus there would be no concern about fuel availability. And the development of a nuclear industry could form part of an industrial strategy – one that offered escape from the traditional image of Canadians as "hewers of wood and drawers of water."

But eventually the selection of a unique technology as well as overwhelming dependence upon it at Ontario Hydro would leave a legacy that would benefit Ontario Hydro management and employees. Whatever the original reasons for the technological decisions made by Hydro, the choices that were made served to increase the asymmetry of information between Hydro and the various committees, commissions, and boards that would oversee Hydro. As a result, none of these bodies was in a position to fully and independently assess

Table 9-5. *World lifetime average capability factors by reactor type*

Reactor type	Average lifetime capability factor (%)
CANDU – Ontario Hydro	73.3
CANDU – all	74.2
Pressurized water reactors	65.5
Boiling-water reactors	61.9
Gas-cooled reactors	45.8

Source: Environmental Assessment Board Hearings into Ontario Hydro's Demand Supply Plan, Exhibit 519, Nuclear Panel Overheads, page 27.

the validity of Hydro cost estimates. That is not to say there were no benchmarks for comparison – after all, costs of Hydro nuclear generation compared favourably with those in the United States and France. Furthermore, capability factors at Hydro compared favourably with those elsewhere (see Table 9-5). There were a number of reasons for this, including multiple-unit stations, standardized design, and on-line refuelling. However, the uniqueness of the technology severely hampered any detailed comparisons between Ontario Hydro's nuclear program and those elsewhere.

The momentum behind nuclear generation continued into the 1980s, when new nuclear construction had all but halted in the United States. Despite the fact that there were major problems with pressure tubes involving significant capital costs, Ontario Hydro filed requests for approval before the Environmental Assessment Board in 1989 that included as many as 10 additional nuclear reactors (*Providing the Balance of Power,* 1989, pp. 15–28). These requests were subsequently dropped (January 1992) in the face of looming excess capacity.

Worker surplus

Wages and salaries: There is substantial evidence that Ontario Hydro employees succeeded in obtaining and sustaining a substantial surplus of workers. That surplus has been evident in at least three areas: compensation, overstaffing, and job security.

Nuclear technology confers bargaining leverage on Hydro employees. Management will not operate the nuclear reactors in the event of a strike, and given the very large share of nuclear power in Ontario's generating capacity, such a strike would paralyse the province. Furthermore, labour's willingness to bring down reactors prior to a strike (as opposed to leaving them running) was not something that could be assumed but required agreement.[14]

Evidence presented at various rate hearings indicates that Hydro workers consistently receive wages and salaries that are about 10% higher than those in "reference communities." Furthermore, the attractiveness of jobs at Ontario Hydro is reinforced by the high application-to-hire ratio: over the period 1985 to 1990, there were typically 10 to 15 job applications for every person hired. Although Ontario Hydro management indicated its desire to narrow the wage differentials with comparable employee groups, there is no evidence that it succeeded in doing so during the course of the 1980s. Indeed, the approximate 10% premium paid by Hydro is consistent with broad findings of wage differentials in the public sector (see, for example, Freeman and Ichniowski, 1988, and Ehrenberg, 1979).

Staff levels: In the nuclear area, comparisons of Ontario Hydro staff levels to those at other utilities would suggest that Hydro is either much more efficient or grossly understaffed. Data from the Electric Utility Cost Group (EUCG), an international organization of major electric utilities, show that in 1986 Hydro employed one individual per 3 MW of nuclear capacity. The average for the EUCG was about 2.5 individuals per 3 MW of capacity.[15] Indeed, Hydro used such comparisons, combined with declining nuclear performance, to justify a massive nuclear hiring program during the late 1980s.

Since 1993, in response to internal cost pressures as well as a modest degree of external competitive pressure (Ontario Hydro remains a monopoly), management has been able to cut the regular staff complement by over 25%. In addition, nonregular and construction staff levels have been reduced by over 50%. Thus, although Ontario Hydro was able to sustain excess staff levels for an extended period – partly through the absence of regulation as well as the difficulty in assessing labour requirements of the nuclear technology – the realities of impending market pressures have had an impact. There is significant risk, however, to the continued viability of the nuclear technology given the much lower staff complements. Furthermore, safety issues could become more prominent in view of these changes as the nuclear units progress into the second half of their lifetimes.

Job security: There is also significant evidence that Hydro employees have benefited from considerable job security. During the period 1987 to 1991 involuntary job terminations averaged 42 per year. With staff levels averaging about 26,000 over this period, this would correspond to a termination rate of

---

[14] HR 19, transcript page 2562; Municipal Electric Association HR 19, Final Argument, page VI–11.
[15] Ontario Hydro Memorandum to the Board of Directors, May 16, 1988, p. 20.

less than 0.2% per year. Furthermore, Hydro has had a generous policy of continuity of employment that has included multiskilling to ensure employee flexibility, retraining, retirement incentives for those who choose to retire early, external placement, redeployment within the corporation, work sharing, educational leave, elaborate bumping provisions, wage maintenance provisions, moving expenses, limitations to turnover, limitations to the use of nonregular employees, mortgage assistance, and severance pay.[16] There is also evidence that the policy, at times, hindered Hydro from acquiring the most appropriate employees as its work programs change.[17]

In 1988 the Ontario Energy Board recommended reexamination of the continuity of employment policy and recommended that Hydro consider "dismissal of personnel who are found directly responsible for budgetary overruns without strong reasons or direct authorization from a superior."[18] Despite such utterances, little was done at Hydro until 1993 when quite suddenly Hydro found that it was overstaffed. The resulting terminations, however, should not be interpreted as evidence against the hypothesis of job security given the largely voluntary nature of the programs and the financial incentives to leave. (Incentive payments to employees under several major job termination programs averaged over $100,000 per person.)

Remuneration at the senior executive level: The one category of Ontario Hydro employees that is *not* overcompensated is at the most senior executive level. Although, overall, executive salary roll (ESR) staff receive remuneration above the reference community, the most senior executives are relatively underpaid. One recent study found that total compensation packages for this group were 35% below a comparison group consisting of comparable Canadian private sector employees. A second study, which did not adjust for the size of the corporations, found substantially smaller differentials.[19] Both studies concluded that an insufficient portion of the remuneration of senior executives was tied to performance.

From the point of view of the senior executives, it should be noted that because many of them have come through the ranks at Hydro, during which time their remuneration was significantly in excess of those at comparable institutions, the present value of their *lifetime* remuneration in all likelihood compares favourably with alternative career paths.

From the point of view of the corporation, the wisdom of such a policy is questionable. If one subscribes to the "specific human capital" model, where-

[16] HR 18, Ex. 6.4.12, 6.4.47, 6.1.13, p. 20, Municipal Electric Association (MEA) Final Argument, p. VI–22.
[17] HR 18, Ex 6.1.3, p. 13, Tr. p. 3075, MEA Final Argument, p. VI–24.
[18] OEB HR 17, Report of the Board, pp. 7/6, 7/10.
[19] HR 21, Ex 11.1.2, 11.2.1.

by employees at Hydro have limited mobility to jobs outside the corporation, then the current policy would not hinder the retention of the highest-quality employees at senior levels. On the other hand, if the human capital accumulated at Hydro has significant market value, then senior employees have considerable job mobility and there is significant risk that Hydro is not retaining senior staff best suited and qualified for making its most important decisions. In effect, there is a selection process through which the most gifted employees are also most likely to leave prior to reaching the most senior levels.

Benefits accruing to government through nontransparent transfers

As a quasi-governmental body subject to directives from the government, Hydro has engaged in a number of transfers and policies that it would otherwise not have engaged in as a private corporation.

Nuclear technology – construction and jobs: An argument can be made that the nuclear program was designed partly as an Ontario and partly as a Canadian industrial strategy. The fuel was indigenous to Ontario as well as other parts of Canada, and the technology was also indigenous to Canada. The CANDU heavy-water nuclear technology was Canadian, a product of Ontario R&D, employed many engineers and scientists, and was viewed as having exceptional export and spillover potential.

Table 9-6 provides data on Ontario Hydro's construction program as a percentage of total fixed investment in the province and as a percentage of government investment. In 1965 the construction program of Ontario Hydro (150 million 1965 dollars) was 17% of the government of Ontario's capital investment and 3.4% of all capital investment in Ontario. From 1975 to 1979, as the nuclear program was accelerating, Ontario Hydro's investment was 73% of the government's and 10% of all investment in the province. Ontario Hydro's capital program represented over 80% of all Ontario government investment between 1980 and 1984, and was still half in 1990.

During the early 1980s, declining growth in demand for electricity led an independent committee to conclude that continuation of construction of the Darlington Nuclear Generating Station was not desirable from a cost/benefit point of view. Nevertheless, the committee concluded that the government might decide to continue with the project because of the job implications.

Uranium: During the late 1970s, Ontario Hydro negotiated major long-term uranium supply contracts with the Rio Algom and Denison Mines operating in Elliot Lake, Ontario. The contracts were on a cost-plus basis, and Hydro provided large capital advances for mine development that were to be recovered

Table 9-6. *Relative size of Ontario Hydro capital spending*

Capital expenditures in Ontario ($ million)	1965	1970	1975	1978	1981	1984	1987	1990
Total public and private	4,378.3	6,927.5	12,920.3	15,570	22,788	24,826	44,046	53,817
Utilities[a]	689.9	1,334.1	2,930.6	2,972	4,936	5,435	6,155	8,810
Government and institutions	884.2	1,299.7	2,003.4	2,904	2,573	3,548	4,497	6,758
Ontario Hydro	150.0	511.0	1,442.0	1,537	2,144	2,624	2,524	3,544
Percentage of total	3.4	7.4	11.2	9.9	9.4	10.6	5.7	6.6
Percentage of utilities	21.7	38.3	49.2	51.7	43.4	48.3	41.0	40.2
Percentage of govt. and institutions	17.0	39.3	72.0	73.4	83.3	80.0	56.1	52.4

[a]Including outlays on heavy-water plants ($250 million in 1975, $254 million in 1978).
Sources: Statistics Canada and Ontario Hydro.

from future purchases. The only significant risk borne by the producers was that uranium prices might rise even more than expected during the lifetime of the contracts. Two of the major reasons for procurement of provincially located supplies were security of supply and job creation. When the bottom dropped out of the uranium market during the 1980s, Hydro was left with contracts requiring it to pay prices that were several times market rates. When the opportunity to cancel the contracts arose in the early 1990s, Hydro was instructed, through a government directive, to continue the contracts until 1996 in order to preserve a modest number of moribund mining jobs. The costs to Hydro of delaying termination plus the additional contributions required by the government to the Northern Ontario Heritage Fund totalled about $250 million.[20]

Rural subsidies: The Power Corporations Act requires that rural electricity rates not exceed urban rates by more than 15%. This has led to substantial subsidies over the years. In 1992, rural rate assistance was approximately $115 million. The total costs for distribution to the rural sector were $371 million. Thus, nonrural customers bear a substantial portion of the incremental distribution costs imposed by the rural sector.[21]

Debt guarantee fee: Since the late 1980s Ontario Hydro has been paying a fee to the provincial government in the amount of 0.5% of Hydro debt. The ostensible rationale is that because Hydro debt is guaranteed by the province, Hydro customers benefit from lower borrowing rates than would be justified on the economics of the enterprise. In the case of an investor-owned utility, the shareholders bear part of the burden of adverse financial outcomes. In Hydro's case, unanticipated increases in costs are borne by the customers through future rate increases – indeed, the provincial government has never been called upon to provide funds of its own as a result of poor financial performance on the part of Hydro. Thus, the debt guarantee fee is more in the nature of a tax than a payment for service. (It should be noted that Hydro pays no corporate income tax.)

Comments on nontransparent transfers: The essential problem with nontransparent transfers is that the public has a very limited ability to assess the desirability of such transfers. Electricity consumers are generally unaware that the prices they pay have imbedded in them additional costs not directly related to the production and delivery of the product they are acquiring. Government intervention in the activities of Ontario Hydro for purposes of social engineering obfuscates the decisions that the electorate ought to be making on a rational and informed basis. Unfortunately, it is generally in the interest of an

---

[20] HR 20 MEA Final Argument, pp. XI–7.
[21] HR 20, Submission on 1992 Rates, pp. 65, 68.

incumbent political party to try to reap the political benefits of redistributive actions without paying the political costs of raising the required taxes in an obvious fashion. To illustrate the point, if the government had announced that it would raise taxes by $250 million in order to finance the subsidy Elliot Lake (see above), the public response would have been far stronger.

Ontario Hydro debt and financial policy

Ontario Hydro's debt is guaranteed by the Province of Ontario.[22] This arrangement permits Hydro to operate with a much higher proportion of debt in its capital structure than a private sector utility can. Indeed, since 1975, Ontario Hydro's debt ratio has remained above 80%. In 1994 it exceeded 90%. By comparison, investor-owned utilities in the United States have debt ratios in the range of 45 to 60%. Despite this very high debt ratio, Ontario Hydro has typically retained the highest credit ratings awarded by rating agencies such as Standard and Poor's and Moody's. The reason, of course, is the provincial guarantee of its debt.[23]

Over the past several decades there has been a secular deterioration in Hydro's financial performance indicators, most importantly its debt ratio and its interest coverage ratio. This has coincided with the advent of the nuclear program and a less conservative approach to financial policy.

If one examines real electricity prices over the past several decades, one finds that from 1965 to 1975, the real price remains fairly stable, just above 4 ¢/kWh (measured in purchasing power of the year 1991). In the mid-1970s, there is a real increase of about 30% followed by another period of stability. In the early 1990s there is another real increase in excess of 20%. Each of the two periods of rate shock was anticipated, yet little was done to smooth the effects over a longer period.

Two key factors appear to provide a plausible explanation for this failure to adopt a proactive policy on rates and a willingness to permit the financial picture to deteriorate. First, democratically elected governments find it in their interest to optimize with respect to short-term objectives, and they therefore explicitly or implicitly discourage rate increases until it is absolutely necessary to institute them.[24] Second, higher electricity prices have generally not been in the interest of Ontario Hydro because they would discourage demand and therefore reduce the requirements for future supply.[25]

---

[22] Hydro debt comprises about 40% of total provincial liabilities.

[23] HR 19-II, Report of the Board.

[24] Reference letters from the Minister to Ontario Hydro have typically asked Hydro to keep rates as low as possible while remaining consistent with financial soundness.

[25] During the 1980s, Hydro had a policy of "no real rate increases." This coincided with a period when Hydro was preparing major requests for approval for additional facilities.

The confluence of the interests of the government and Ontario Hydro undoubtedly contributed to the failure to increase rates on a graduated basis and
to consistently delay the achievement of a sounder financial footing.[26] The key
implication for the regulation of Ontario Hydro is that at least from the point
of view of financial soundness and the smoothing of rate impacts it would be
desirable if Hydro rates were regulated by a body that is independent from the
government of the day. Perhaps the ineffectiveness of the current regulatory
relationship is best illustrated by the fact that the OEB was unable to prevent
or even smooth the rate shocks that occurred in the early 1990s.

Asymmetric information

A number of examples are consistent with or support the proposition that there
is significant asymmetry of information between Ontario Hydro and its quasi-
regulators. Four are presented here.

The first is operations, maintenance, and administration (OM&A) costs.
These constitute the single largest controllable component of Ontario Hydro
revenue requirement. During the decade of the 1980s, OM&A costs at Hydro
grew substantially more rapidly than did electricity production. One of the reasons for this was the shift in generation mix toward nuclear, which is both cap-
ital- and OM&A-intensive, with relatively low fuelling costs. During the same
period, Hydro systematically underestimated its OM&A costs.

For these reasons the OM&A budgets came under close scrutiny at the annual OEB rate hearings. Over the years, the Board has taken three approaches
to OM&A costs. One approach involved presentation and analysis of budgets
at very detailed levels and specific recommendations on where budgets should
be reduced. A second approach involved review by external consultants.[27] A
third approach consisted simply of across-the-board freezes or cuts in total
OM&A costs. The very fact that the OEB resorted to the third alternative is
consistent with asymmetry of information between the reviewer and the entity being reviewed. Indeed, Board reports are replete with references to the difficulties in assessing Hydro budgets.[28]

During the late 1980s, Hydro presented an urgent appeal for substantial
increases in OM&A expenditures in the nuclear area. There is evidence that

---

[26] There is also evidence that Hydro delayed cost recovery through less than conservative accounting policy. For example, for years, it was Hydro's policy to depreciate the heavy water
used in its nuclear program to the year 2040 (sic). Hydro's rationale was that the heavy water
would be used in future CANDU reactors. The book value of heavy water far exceeded its market value.

[27] Elsewhere, we have indicated that following the most recent external review, (which found that
Hydro was over-staffed by 10%), staff level increases *exceeded* those projected *prior* to the
review.

[28] Ontario Energy Board, Report of the Board, HR 17, p. 7/4, HR 18, pp. 107, 108, 313.

Hydro had indeed anticipated the expenditures – various *leading* indicators or precursors to nuclear performance were cited in evidence, many of which had been declining for some time. Indeed, the Atomic Energy Control Board, a federal agency, was threatening not to renew certain operating licenses. On the other hand, the OEB apparently had not anticipated the need for additional funds to be allocated or reallocated to this area and was evidently previously unaware of the importance of the kinds of statistical data provided by Hydro. It even stated, "Reliability, it appeared, could be used to sanction any amount of expense," a statement it surely would not have made had it been in a position to *independently* assess costs, reliability, and safety.[29]

A second area where there is evidence consistent with asymmetry of information is labour. As we have indicated, Ontario Hydro pays substantially higher wages than those paid in various comparison groups. Hydro management and professional staff, consisting primarily of engineers, receive compensation that is 10% higher than that which is paid in an elite group of 15 comparison firms and institutions. Furthermore, Hydro unions have used their control of nuclear technology to advantage in bargaining disputes.

Third, there is the overoptimism in financial forecasting exhibited by Ontario Hydro during the 1980s. Again, this served the interests of the government by forestalling higher rate increases, and it served Hydro interests by not discouraging demand growth. Nevertheless, a number of down-side risks to the forecasts were known by Hydro in advance – and yet neither the OEB nor anyone else was successful in persuading Hydro to use more conservative assumptions in its financial forecasting. Indeed, the Board stated: "The experience has been that Hydro seldom, if ever, overestimates its eventual costs, especially of construction, but also of operations."[30]

Furthermore, there is evidence that Hydro has delayed costs. At HR 17, the OEB indicated that heavy water inventories (which were being depreciated to the year 2040!) and advances associated with uranium contracts were overvalued on the books.[31] Hydro did not recognize the problem until 1992.

Ontario Hydro is one of the largest corporations in Canada, and it is controlled, as we have pointed out, by a changing and ad hoc set of instruments. A single regulatory agency would be more able, and would have the incentive, to gather information and to regulate on a consistent basis. This, of course, would require either divorce from political uses of the firm or explicit recognition of political policies and their costs.

---

[29] OEB, HR 17, Report of the Board, p. 7/21.
[30] OEB, HR 18, Report of the Board, p. 313.
[31] OEB, HR 17, Report of the Board, pp. 8/14, 9/7.

Recent industry developments

Future requirements and Ontario Hydro's demand–supply plan: In 1989, after a number of years of plan development, Ontario Hydro submitted its 25-year demand–supply plan to the Environmental Assessment Board. Under the plan, Hydro was requesting approval for the construction of 8000 MW of nuclear facilities, 4300 MW of fossil generation, 2000 MW of hydraulic, as well as a 1000 MW transmission line from Manitoba. The plan also proposed to implement 5570 MW of demand management programs and incorporate 2120 MW of nonutility generation by 2014, the end of the 25-year period (Environmental Assessment Board, 1990–1993). Hydro's planning philosophy was predicated upon seeking to meet not median projections of load growth but "upper" projections. The purpose was to seek approvals so that in the event of upper load growth, Hydro would be in a position to respond more quickly with supply-side options.

In the year following the filing of these proposals, the New Democratic Party was elected to power for the first time in Ontario. Shortly after his inauguration, the Premier announced a moratorium on future nuclear developments, appointed a new CEO for Ontario Hydro, and announced that the government would be proposing changes to legislation affecting Hydro.[32] The legislation would provide for fuel substitution programs as well as more direct control of the government over Hydro policies and expenditures.

By the beginning of 1992, Hydro had decided to defer approval requests for *any* major nuclear or fossil stations. There were three major reasons for this change. First, demand management program targets were increased substantially on the expectation that government policy would mandate higher efficiency standards and would allow Hydro to offer incentives for fuel substitution. Second, nonutility generation was forecast to increase dramatically as a result of lower forecasts of natural gas prices. Third, Hydro had changed its planning philosophy. Rather than planning to meet upper load growth, Hydro would plan around the median. This change in planning philosophy was justified on the basis of increases in uncertainty regarding future demand.

By the end of 1992, as a result of stagnating load growth, it became clear that Ontario Hydro would have significant excess capacity until the turn of the century, and in January 1993 Ontario Hydro withdrew all requests for approvals before the Environmental Assessment Board.

Nonutility generation: As of 1989, a modest portion of electricity in Ontario was generated from sources other than Ontario Hydro. Installed nonutility generation (NUG) capacity in that year was 1288 MW, of which only 26 MW

---

[32] This left-of-center party had a long-standing policy of opposing nuclear power.

were classified as purchase generation. The remaining 1262 MW were load displacement NUG. These sources produced about 5 twh of electricity, or 4% of the total generation in Ontario.

In 1989 the government released a policy paper that underscored its desire to encourage NUG in the province. It indicated that Hydro should seek to achieve a target of 1000 MW of purchase NUG by the year 1995 and 2000 MW by the year 2000. In hindsight, these were woefully low estimates of the potential for NUG supply in Ontario.

A number of factors have contributed to substantial NUG potential in Ontario. First, there has been until recently the continental decline in the price of natural gas. Natural gas comes to Ontario principally from the western provinces, travelling several thousand miles through the TransCanada Pipeline System. Pipeline capacity is being expanded so that there is a significant supply of natural gas. Second, Hydro rates have risen by 30% in nominal terms in recent years, thus increasing the price differential with natural gas and increasing the incentive for load displacement nonutility generation. Third, nonutility generators benefit from an accelerated write-off of capital costs. Fourth, nonutility generators do not have to go through the kind of extensive environmental assessment required of Hydro projects. Fifth, nonutility generators do not have the "obligation to serve" required of Ontario Hydro. Sixth, for small projects (up to 5 MW), Hydro has offered purchase rates above avoided costs. The premium has been designed to encourage projects with greater thermal efficiencies or environmentally friendly characteristics.

However, there are a number of factors that NUGs claim give Hydro an unfair advantage. First, Hydro does not pay the usual corporate income taxes. Second, Hydro benefits from the provincial guarantee of its debt, thus lowering its borrowing costs. Third, nuclear generation in particular benefits from a federal statute that limits the liability of the generator. Finally, Hydro has benefited over the years from research sponsored by government (for example, in the nuclear area) as well as land grants.

Currently in Ontario there is no informed agency authorized to regulate and adjudicate disputes between Hydro and the NUG sector. An important role for the regulator would be to ensure that a level playing field exists so that neither Hydro nor private producers are accorded undue advantage.

In early 1993, Hydro announced that it was contemplating further limitations on NUG development in view of its own capacity surplus as well as internal financial pressures. Hydro has calculated that proceeding with currently planned NUG purchases would add as much as 3% to rates and as a result is reconsidering current contracts.

Hydro is very concerned that major industrial users and municipal utilities will build their own generating sources, which would increase the excess capacity on the Hydro system. Because the preponderant portion of Hydro costs is fixed, this would drive up rates for other users and thereby further attenuate demand. As a result, Hydro is implementing low incentive rates to certain industrial users in order to discourage them from building their own generation or otherwise curtailing purchases of electricity. However, such an approach could be in violation of the power-at-cost principle embodied in the Power Corporations Act.

Hydro's decision to severely limit the purchase of nonutility generation is being contested by the Independent Power Producer Society of Ontario, an organization that represents nonutility generators. The organization has taken the position that retubing of the Bruce A nuclear station, which is to take place during the 1990s, is not cost-effective and should not proceed. If the four units at Bruce A were mothballed, the 3000 MW surplus would disappear, and future needs could be met more cost effectively by private natural gas generation and cogeneration. (Most recently, Hydro has decided not to proceed with retubing of one of the Bruce nuclear units.)

One of the arguments that has been advanced in support of the competitive fringe is that it plays an important audit function because it is in the interests of private producers to discover and reveal Ontario Hydro costs. The current debate in Ontario about the cost-effectiveness of retubing nuclear reactors provides an example of this function.

Demand-side management: Ontario Hydro is implementing a range of demand-side management programs (DSM). Programs with the largest impact on demand are those that attempt to improve electrical efficiency in lighting, heating, and motors. In addition, Hydro has a load-shifting program and a fuel substitution program, as well as special rates for interruptible loads.

The residential sector accounts for about 29% of electricity consumption in Ontario of which more than half is for space and water heating. An additional 38% is for lighting and appliances and only 6% is for air cooling. However, the residential load is weather sensitive and generally contributes significantly to the winter and summer peaks. The commercial sector accounts for 34% of electricity consumption in Ontario, about 40% of which is used for lighting and another 40% for motors and equipment. The largest electricity consuming sector is industry, which accounts for about 37% of electricity consumed in Ontario, of which over 70% is used to drive motors and run equipment.

In evaluating potential DSM programs, Hydro uses the "total resource cost test," also known as the "total customer cost test." In calculating this test, Hydro incorporates the present value of the incremental cost of capital, changes in customer fuel and operating costs, program administration costs, and delivery costs. The test attempts to minimize the total societal costs of producing a given service.

The total customer cost test is premised on the idea that there exist market imperfections or distortions preventing the market from allocating resources efficiently. These include environmental externalities, pricing at average instead of marginal costs, imperfect information, differing social and private discount rates, and principal – agent problems. In a number of jurisdictions in the United States, there is movement toward monetization of environmental externalities in an integrated resource planning process that compares supply-side options to demand-side options. Recently, Hydro has been considering moving toward accounting methods that incorporate valuation of externalities.

In Ontario, electricity is priced at average historical cost. When marginal or avoided costs exceed average costs, there is potential for increasing economic efficiency by providing financial incentives that would reduce electricity consumption through conservation or fuel substitution. Economic efficiency would limit the incentive to the *difference* between avoided costs and average costs. Ontario Hydro, on the other hand, has considered paying incentives up to the level of avoided costs,[33] though the level of the incentive would be ultimately determined by program penetration rates as well as the overall impact on rates.[34] In 1989, avoided costs were estimated to be about 3.7 Canadian ¢/kWh.[35] Since then, as a result of excess capacity, avoided costs are expected to be below 2 ¢/kWh for most of this decade.

Hydro DSM programs are divided into the following categories: energy efficiency improvement, fuel substitution, load shifting, and interruptible power. Energy efficiency improvement programs encompass a broad range of initiatives in the residential, commercial, and industrial sectors. Included are programs to increase lighting efficiency (e.g., through the use of compact fluorescent light bulbs), to improve thermal envelopes, and to enhance motor efficiency and efficiency of industrial processes.

Load-shifting programs rely principally on time-of-use pricing. In 1989, Hydro initiated time-differentiated rates for all large industrial customers in Ontario.[36] Time-of-use rates are also available to municipal utilities on an optional basis.

Hydro's recent target of 2866 MW in demand management by the year 2000 is substantial – comprising in excess of 10% of the system peak. By the year 2015, Hydro plans to achieve close to 5000 MW of DSM savings, which would be about 15% of the system peak (see Table 9-7).

---

[33] *Providing the Balance of Power,* Ontario Hydro, Demand/Supply Report, page 7-6.
[34] The latter being the 'rate impact measure' or 'no losers test.'
[35] *Providing the Balance Power,* Ontario Hydro, Demand/Supply Report, page 7-14.
[36] Hydro is contemplating performing a real time pricing experiment with its large customers, (HR 21, Main Submission, p. 79).

Table 9-7. *Ontario Hydro's demand-side management programs (MW)*

Year	Load shifting	Electrical efficiency improvements	Fuel substitution	Interruptible load	Total DSM	Total system peak
1991	150	293	8	652	1,103	22,625
1995	302	1,039	43	617	2,001	23,574
2000	600	1,389	237	640	2,866	25,562
2005	925	1,814	413	601	3,753	27,258
2010	1,125	2,134	566	640	4,465	29,350
2015	1,225	2,324	691	687	4,927	32,954

Source: Environmental Assessment Board Hearing into Ontario Hydro's Demand/Supply Plan, Exhibit 796, Attachment C, page 45; Attachment I, Table I-1-1.

The debate on industry restructuring: The flurry of privatization that has taken place around the globe has spawned a debate within Ontario as to the most desirable structure of the electricity industry. A number of alternatives have been aired, each with its advantages and disadvantages. The main impetus driving the debate has been declining performance of the utility, particularly with respect to nuclear generation, and a dramatically increasing debt load at a time of economic recession. A number of alternatives are available, including privatization; vertical unbundling and inducing competition among pieces of the still publicly owned firm; allowing increased NUGs and third-party access; and removing the constraints on wheeling. Regulatory reform is crucial in all these possibilities.

Figure 9-2 provides details on the present generating and distribution facilities in Ontario. The system consists of the East (the major portion) and West systems, interconnected by one 230 KV line. The major demand areas are around the southwestern tip of Lake Ontario. Note how major 500 KV transmission lines form a spine into the Toronto area. The system operates over long distances with few major demand nodes. There are 79 generating stations: 68 hydraulic, 5 nuclear, and 6 fossil-fuelled. The 68 hydraulic structures have a peak capacity of 6489 MW; three river sites account for 55% of this total (six on the Niagara River – 2005 MW; one on the St. Lawrence River – 740 MW; five on the Ottawa River – 846 MW). The five nuclear stations have a peak capacity of 14164 MW – 44% of system peak capacity (32.5 GW).

Schemes to privatize, unbundle, and increase intrafirm competition must begin with the reality of the facilities – generation, transmission, and distrib-

Figure 9-2. Map of Generation and Transmission Facilities in Ontario [Ontario Hydro Major Stations (greater than 100 MW capacity) and 500kV and 230kV Line Routes (mid 1989)].

ution. Complete privatization of Ontario Hydro generating facilities is unlikely. Over half of the energy generated by Hydro comes from nuclear sources. These systems account for 44% of system capacity, and such facilities are difficult to privatize, as recent experience in the United Kingdom underlines. (In the United Kingdom, nuclear power represents a much smaller share of capacity.)

Another 25% of current generation in Ontario is hydraulic, with major facilities at Niagara Falls and on two other river systems. Given the unique nature of this particular site and the history of Ontario Hydro, which began as the transmission utility connecting this site to municipal utilities, any attempt to privatize would be met with considerable public resistance. The water rentals now charged are low when compared to the opportunity cost of the water as determined by the price of alternative sources of electricity. Thus, the asset value of the hydro site is contingent on the water rentals charged. Privatizing hydro sites would be dependent on the stated intent of the owner of the water – the province – with respect to charges for water rentals. A continuation of low water rentals would mean high bids: the present value of the difference between the opportunity cost of water and the price. High water rental rates would result in low bids but higher annual yields in the future. Privatizing the Falls by transferring shares to the public at current water rental rates would produce the low cost firm by definition.

This leaves the fossil generation, much of which is aging or is being used in peaking mode. Furthermore, the use of fossil facilities is limited in Ontario by strict provincial caps on acid gas emissions. Because coal is the swing fuel in Ontario, output for this type of generation is the most volatile, leading to increased risk associated with the ownership of this asset.

A variety of alternatives exist for partial transfer of ownership, including public sale of shares in Ontario Hydro from which the proceeds would be used to reduce Hydro's $36 billion debt. Another option would be to transfer partial ownership of the generating utility to the municipal distributing utilities, which in any event have never relinquished their historic claims to ownership of Hydro. The municipal utilities have very little debt and would be in a position to shoulder a significant portion of the debt. The *quid pro quo* would likely be increased representation of Ontario Hydro's Board of Directors, and thus greater influence on the decisions taken by Hydro. However, it should be noted that any attempts to introduce private ownership should occur *after* the transmission grid and distribution facilities owned by Ontario Hydro are separated from generation. Otherwise, the creation of private property rights would severely hamper any future possibilities for vertical unbundling of the natural monopoly segments of the industry (transmission and distribution) from those that can benefit from competition (i.e., generation).

There are a number of scenarios that would contemplate a larger role for private generation and a competitive element in the electricity industry of Ontario. One would involve competition at the wholesale level. The transmission company would be separated from generation and would be responsible for purchasing power from any willing suppliers at the lowest possible cost. It would then sell it to distributors. A second scenario would involve permitting third party access (TPA) to the grid. Municipal utilities and large users could purchase their power as they pleased. Current market conditions – in particular, high costs at Hydro combined with low natural gas prices – would yield a strong response to either wholesale or retail competition. However, moving to wholesale rather than retail competition has a major advantage in that the latter is essentially irreversible. Again, private property rights (e.g., contractual agreements amongst private purchasers and sellers) would be difficult to reverse if a decision were made at some point in the future to move to wholesale competition.

In any event, a central problem that would need to be resolved would be the "stranded assets" that could be created as customers purchased from generators other than Hydro. A critical role for the regulator would be to determine appropriate transmission charges, which could include levies for assets that a former customer could be deemed to have stranded. The regulator would also resolve transmission disputes as well as conduct rate and capital expenditure reviews of Hydro. In the short run, competitors would serve a useful auditing function in reviewing Hydro costs. In the long run, there is potential for downward pressure on prices through competition and innovation. A second central issue deals with the obligation to serve (or to ensure that adequate supplies of power are available). In any system, there would be strong political pressure to ensure that this responsibility resides with *some* entity.

Recently, discussion has begun in the province on how intrafirm competition might be introduced. In its restructuring, Hydro has been divided administratively into transmission, fossil, hydraulic, nuclear, energy services, and international enterprise units. Could the generating facilities at Hydro be induced to compete against one another? The economics literature is not supportive of this idea because managers would have to be induced to take risks and thus would have to earn rewards or be punished. Unless new compensation schemes were introduced, providing unit managers with contingent claims, competition between units would not be real.

Summary

Public ownership and the form of regulation in Ontario have not avoided the problems that have plagued private electric utilities in the United States. Indeed, a cursory examination of rate changes between Ontario Hydro and average U.S. rates shows similar increases in the mid-1970s but for totally different reasons. United States utilities were to a substantial degree oil-based, and the rate jumps in the United States in the mid-1970s were due to exogenous increases in fuel price. In Ontario, the rate increase in the mid-1970s was endogenous – the result of bringing nuclear onstream. Similarly, U.S. utilities and Ontario Hydro faced the high interest rates of the 1980s. Again, rate increases were common to all. Ontario Hydro, however, saw substantial (30%) rate increases in the early 1990s, rate increases largely absent in the United States. The long lead times, large capital requirements, huge construction overruns of the nuclear program in Ontario, and lower-than-expected load growth created upward pressure on rates.

In earlier sections we described how Ontario Hydro developed as an integrated publicly owned monopoly from its inception as a transmission utility. The firm was able to avoid direct regulation and supervision by intense political lobbying. As the complexity of the electricity system grew, so did the complexities of the regulatory system. Today, Ontario Hydro is regulated by a wide variety of government departments, ad hoc parliamentary committees, special hearings established to review construction programs, and a statutory regulatory board that examines rates without the authority to set rates. In essence, Ontario Hydro is regulated by its board and by government cabinet. Retail rates, set by over 300 municipal utilities, are overseen by Hydro.

This process has allowed the government to use Ontario Hydro as an industrial policy tool. As long as rates were low, the nuclear and construction programs were not seriously questioned. However, the nuclear program is no longer a success – exports of the technology have not been successful, overcapacity is large, and problems are showing up in the technology itself. The regulatory process needs complete overhaul.

We would recommend that a single regulatory authority examine Ontario Hydro – its rates and construction programs – and that the process be public and that the regulator have final authority. We would recommend an increased role for NUGs and a complete analysis of the vertical and horizontal unbundling of options. It is clear that the government as owner could establish policy but should do so through the use of directives to the regulator rather than informal setting of goals and criteria.

Conclusions

We have cursorily examined electricity developments across Canada and have focused on two key features of Ontario Hydro history. The first is the choice of nuclear technology. The second is the nonstandard form of regulation to which Hydro has been subjected.

A number of factors help to explain the selection of the nuclear technology. In the 1950s, proponents of nuclear energy were predicting that it would generate electricity "too cheap to meter." But the selection of the nuclear technology in Ontario was also part of a governmental industrial strategy because it provided jobs, expanded a domestic technology, and used indigenous fuel. It is our contention that it also increased the information asymmetry and thereby made Hydro more difficult to regulate as well as providing Hydro employees with job security and higher wages. This occurred because the use of a unique technology made it difficult for the government to use benchmarks or comparable ratings. In addition, the use of select committees rather than a permanent statutory regulatory authority made information gathering and the buildup of expertise outside the firm difficult. Furthermore, the lumpy nature of the technology, with very heavy up-front costs, meant that once a project was started it became difficult to stop. Information asymmetries may have served the firm and the government well, neither necessarily wanting annual independent reviews of actions.

The regulatory history of Ontario Hydro is punctuated by demands from various outsiders for stronger control over Hydro, followed by reviews by government agencies, committees, and boards. While rates were falling, as they did for a good portion of the century, such an informal, if prosaic, regulatory relationship could be sustained. When rates rose dramatically in 1975, the Ontario Energy Board (OEB) was given review powers over annual rate increases. The public review process served the government interest because it allowed politicians to distance themselves to some degree from the rate increases. However, Hydro interests were also served – the OEB could recommend but not prescribe. And annual reviews generally excluded capital program decisions and expenditures (these were relegated to other forums that did not have the benefit of an accumulation of information over time). Nevertheless, at least the continuing reviews by the OEB provided for the accumulation of information in *some* outside agency regarding Hydro's activities, which could in time reduce the information asymmetries. Still, a decade later, it was evident that the OEB was not on a comparable informational footing with Ontario Hydro and that Hydro, partly because of the uniqueness of the nuclear technology, was able to legitimize the rate increases and staff level changes that it was proposing.

The odd regulatory relationship has most certainly not insulated Hydro from the vicissitudes of politics; if anything it has exacerbated the effects. Hydro has been an instrument of social policy; it has been required to engage in policies and programs that it would not have engaged in as a private corporation. The government has used it to redistribute income. That Hydro has been very susceptible to the government of the day is well illustrated by the fact that between 1989 and 1992 Hydro altered its position from one of requiring the construction of as many as 10 additional nuclear reactors to one of no major supply requirements and a dramatically increased emphasis on demand-side management. Although declining load growth played an important part in this change in position, government policy and legislation also had a critical effect.

The rate shocks that occurred in the early 1990s have again focused attention on control over Hydro and will likely change the regulation of Hydro. In our view, regulatory change should incorporate the following features. First, there are no longer dramatically increasing returns to scale present in the generation of electricity. This fact, combined with low natural gas prices has led to a burgeoning potential for nonutility generation in Ontario. An important role for the regulator would be to smooth the transition as the mix of private and public generation in Ontario changes.

Second, regulation by a body that is independent of the government would reduce the politicization of Hydro activities. In 1986 the Select Committee on Energy expressed concern regarding the lack of public input into Hydro's decision-making process and the need for greater accountability. Among its many recommendations were the following:

> The Ontario Energy Board should be empowered to hold bi-annual public review of Ontario Hydro's Resource Development Plan, and publish a public report with recommendations to Cabinet. (p. 65)

> The Ontario Energy Board Act should be amended to give the Board the powers to regulate electricity rates. (p. 75)[37]

The recently aborted review of Ontario Hydro's 25-year plan before the Environmental Assessment Board proved fruitless principally as a result of the difficulties in forecasting over such an extended period such variables as load growth, fuel prices, economic activity, natural conservation, private generation, and technological change. An incremental approach, with regular capital program reviews, as recommended by the Select Committee, is far preferable. Furthermore, such reviews should be conducted by the same agency so that the regulator can benefit from the accumulation of information and thereby mitigate, to some modest degree, the informational asymmetries. Whether the appropriate forum is the Environmental Assessment Board, the Ontario Energy Board, or a forum that includes representatives from both of these is yet to be determined. However this is resolved, the authority to regulate, not just to recommend, should be granted.

Third, the informational asymmetries between Hydro and the regulator will persist because of the nuclear technology. However, an increase in performance-based pay and an increased role for competitive forces would substantially offset this disadvantage.

REFERENCES

Baron, Dave P., and Roger B. Myerson. "Regulating a Monopolist with Unknown Costs." *Econometrica* 50 (1982): 911–30.

Barry, Leon. *An Evaluation of Strengthened Inter-Provincial Interconnections of Electric Power Systems.* IPACE Networks Study Group, 1978.

Besanko, D. "On the Use of Regulatory Requirement Information Under Imperfect Information." In M. Crew, ed., *Analyzing the Impact of Regulatory Change in Public Utilities.* Lexington Books, Lexington, Mass., 1985.

Denison, Merrill, *The People's Power: The History of Ontario Hydro.* Toronto: McClelland and Steward, 1960.

Economic Council of Canada (1985), various publications.

Ehrenberg, Ronald G. *The Regulatory Process and Labour Earnings.* New York: Academic Press, 1979.

Energy Mines and Resources (1970–1992). *Electric Power in Canada* (annual publication). Ottawa.

---

[37] See also OEB, Report of the Board, HR 17, page 3/12.

Environmental Assessment Board. Hearings into Ontario Hydro's 25-Year Demand/Supply Plan. Various reports and exhibits. 1990–93.

Fleming, Keith R. *Power at Cost: Ontario Hydro and Rural Electrification, 1911–1956.* Montreal: McGill–Queen's University Press, 1992.

Freeman, Richard B., and Casy Ichniowski. *When Public Sector Workers Unionize.* Chicago: National Bureau of Economic Research, University of Chicago Press, 1988.

Hirsh, Richard F. "Regulation and Technology in the Electric Utility Industry: A Historical Analysis of Interdependence and Change." In J. High, ed., *Regulation: Economic Theory and History.* Ann Arbor: University of Michigan Press, 1991.

Laffont, Jean-Jacques, and Jean Tirole. "Using Cost Observations to Regulate Firms." *Journal of Political Economy* 94 (1986): 614–41.

Ministry of Energy, Mines, and Resources. *Electricity.* Ottawa: 1988, p. 6.

National Energy Board. *Canadian Electric Utilities: Analysis of Generation and Trends.* 1990.

National Energy Board. *Inter-utility Trade Review: Inter-Utility Cooperation.* Ottawa: 1992.

Ontario Energy Board Hearings into Ontario Hydro rates. Various reports, final arguments and exhibits. 1975–1994.

Ontario Nuclear Safety Review. The Hare Commission Report. 1988.

Pint, Ellen M. "Nationalization vs. Regulation of Monopolies." *Journal of Public Economics* 44 (1991): 131–64.

Plewman, William R. *Adam Beck and Ontario Hydro.* Toronto: Ryerson Press, 1947.

Providing the Balance of Power. Ontario Hydro's Demand Supply Plan Report, Toronto, 1989.

Report of the *Ontario Nuclear Cost Inquiry.* 1989.

Royal Commission on Electric Power Planning. Various reports of the Porter Commission. 1976–1980.

CHAPTER 10

The French electricity industry

Jean-Jacques Laffont
Institut Universitaire de France
Director at IDEI, Toulose

Historical overview of electric industry in France: 1880–1946

Discovery and beginning use of electricity

France played an outstanding part in basic scientific and technical discoveries for industrial and domestic usage of electricity. However, industrial and commercial applications were long to come, compared to the United States, Germany, and Switzerland.

In August 1881, the First Exhibition of Electricity held in Paris revealed foreign competition's vitality in the scientific domain and the American and German significant lead in industrial and commercial applications. Convinced of the commercial interest of electric innovations, industrialists from those countries were rushing in a patent race.

French researchers were involved very early in hydroelectric industrial specialties: electrochemistry and electrometallurgy. The first French industrialists interested in electric power were paper manufacturers installed on the Alps rivers' banks. Using until then the mechanical power of running water (with watermills), and willing to improve their performance, they became the pioneers of hydroelectric industry in the Alps. However, their production was restricted to the needs of paper manufacturing.

Because of their huge electricity consumption, electrochemical and electrometallurgical industries started off the rise of the use of hydroelectricity in France. These two technologically advanced industries generated the first great hydroelectric installations in the Alps as early as 1890. They alone escaped foreign rule. Rapidly, electrochemical and electrometallurgical firms improved their knowledge in electricity production and transportation enough to be able to sell the energy surplus to nearby towns and villages (among them Lyon and Grenoble).

I thank Jocelyne Thomas for valuable research assistance.

406

A decisive step forward was taken at the end of the nineteenth century, when hydroelectric firms were set up for the sole purpose of selling electricity to cities' distribution companies, as in Lyon, Marseille, Saint-Etienne, Nice, and Nîmes, or to tramway companies. Two public uses of electricity then became widespread: lighting and transportation. At the same time, along the Seine and in the coal basins, thermal electricity was attempting, with very little success, to compete with steam engines in factories. Established for a long time in the whole country and requiring a very costly investment, steam engines were making the market inaccessible to new forms of energy. The steam machine fitted perfectly the factories designed for them, and very few industrialists could change their power supply and electrify their plants.

In the North of France, public electric lighting was first adopted in Rouen and Le Havre. In Paris, the burning of the Opera Comique caused by lighting gas in May 1887 decided the town council to switch to electricity. In 1889, Paris was divided into six sectors each conceded to a different distribution company. By then, many private persons and shops were already using generating sets of their own.

Actually, significant use of electric public power spread to only the very big factories and to other areas where it was a necessity – electrochemistry, electrometallurgy, tramways, the underground, telephone and telegraph companies – and less for urban lighting and small driving forces.

The era of competition: 1880–1905

By the end of the nineteenth century, between 1880 and 1890, French electricity production was characterized by the coexistence of two technologies: thermal and hydraulic.

Hydroelectricity: Hydroelectric power plants were built in the South of France, especially in the Alps. The production of electricity was not regulated. To build a dam and a power plant, the owners were required only to buy riverine rights from private owners. In such a situation, all the producers tended to set up on the rivers known to be profitable, which thereby became less and less so. The great number of producers generated a competitive sector, disorganized and inefficient, ignoring increasing returns (for instance, each firm used to set up parallel costly high-tension wires).

The first important company interested in hydroelectricity without any relation to chemical or metallurgic industries was the Société des Forces Motrices du Rhône. In 1893 it built a power station at Jonarge on the Rhône to supply electricity to the city of Lyon. This plant was the most powerful at this time: 16,000 horse power (gross power). Huge, very modern, it cost 40 million francs and produced three-phase current, with a voltage of 3,500 volts at 50 Hertz.

Thermal electricity: Thermal power plants were set in the North of France, along the Seine, near coal basins and waterways used to carry the coal. The thermal sector always remained tied to coal mines and lighting gas companies to benefit from their commercial network. The setup of a thermal station was even simpler and cheaper than that of a hydroelectric plant (about three times cheaper). No permit was needed. A potential producer only had to buy a piece of land large enough. The building was fast: two years, instead of four or six years for a hydroelectric plant. The fuel used was coal and coal gas, and because coal was rare and expensive in France (nearly a third of the national consumption was imported), production costs of thermal electricity were high.

The first thermal power plants were fitted out with low-power steam engines, but from 1900 steam turbines were gradually used. Either single-phase or two-phase alternative or direct current was produced, from 40 to 42 Hertz, with a voltage varying between 3,000 and 12,000 volts.

In the beginning, the entire electric sector – production, transportation, and distribution – was private and subject to very minor regulation.

Some firms were only transporters of the electric current; others combined transport with production, with distribution, or with both. The structure of the firm was generally related to the technology. In the North, where the production was essentially thermal, the producers often were distributors and transporters as well, whereas in the South most of the hydroelectric producers, being electrochemists or electrometallurgists, sold their surplus to distributor companies for lighting or to transportation companies for tramways and the underground.

The emergence of local public service: 1906–1914

The first regulatory action: The entire electric sector was competitive until passage of the June 15, 1906, law on the distribution of electricity that legally set up a partition of the country among distribution companies and thereby established local distribution monopolies. The law on distribution defined concessions of 40 to 50 years for electricity distribution. With authorizations for such long periods, the distributors were induced to set up durably and to invest for the long run.

The connection policy: It soon became clear that the lack of organization of the electric sector was prejudicial to its efficiency and economic growth. In particular, the physical disparities in standards for current (each producer had its own standard) made impossible any widespread network which was judged necessary by local authorities as well as by private managers. Their project of an interconnected network was supported by the connection policy, the main aims of which were to favor electrification of faraway regions and to avoid duplication of lines. The decision rapidly became successful; the transportation network was 19,500 km long in 1913, whereas it was only a few hundred kilometers long in 1900.

Price cap in stationary economy: The prices formerly differed greatly among regions because of the use of different technologies, of the transportation costs, and of a pricing based on quantity consumed and on customers' type (public, domestic, driving-force).

The first legal measures concerning electricity pricing were adopted by the decree of November 30, 1909, defining maximum prices. In a very stable monetary background (the franc had been stable since 1803), no price variation had been provided for. With the coming of war in 1914, the government was forced to change this regulation.

The postwar period and the necessity to restructure

Electricity: The national energy: World War I made everyone realize the importance of having a power supply guaranteed for the whole country, independent of foreign countries and rationally organized. Hydroelectric power being obviously the only primary power supply available in France, it was necessary to carry out the feasible hydroelectric projects of the Alps, the Pyrénées, and the Massif Central.

For industrial managers as well as for the government, hydroelectricity became the national energy supply. Immediately after the war, the State adopted measures to favor hydroelectricity producers, removing juridical difficulties and advancing funds. As a result of these actions, the fitting out of Pyrénées and Massif Central could begin.

Simultaneously, demand increased on account of postwar rebuilding needs, rural electrification, and railway expansion. The development of the hydroelectric industry led to the understanding of the main economic features of this sector: increasing returns to scale in production and distribution and in daily and annual consumption cycles. From this immediate postwar period dates the first economic research on electricity, essentially comparisons between thermal electric power and hydroelectric power. These works showed that "craft" time was over, that professionalism and efficiency were necessities and that postwar difficulties made electric industry a real public utility.

The emergence of new state–industry relationships: With the concept of public utility appeared the problem of the relations between the electroproducers and the state – juridically, politically, and financially. Benefitting from the impetus of wartime measures, the State made its authority felt on the new industry with a set of regulation laws.

The industrialists understood that the only way to escape from the government's rule was to come to an agreement among themselves. To negotiate with the government it became necessary to bring together the various members of the electric industry, particularly thermal and hydroelectric producers.

Regulation: By the Act on Hydroelectric Power of October 16, 1919, the State became the owner of the energy extracted from tides and rivers. The setup of hydroelectric power plant needed henceforward the granting of an authorization, and for a plant above 100,000 kW a law had to be voted. Furthermore, the plant had to be returned to the State after 30 years, making amortization relatively short.

The Act of July 11, 1922 concerning electricity transportation produced fast progress in the interconnection policy. By this act, the State was established as the only party allowed to build high-voltage transportation networks, "for a more complete and better spread use of electricity." The public networks could, however, be granted to associations of producers and distributors.

These two fundamental acts gave the State a powerful position in the electric industry for it became the potential owner of a part of production means (the entire hydroelectric sector) and of the whole high-voltage transportation network.

Restructuring: In the interwar years, the trend to integration was asserted by agreements (contracts) between firms, shareholdings, and consolidations. New managers coming from the "grandes ecoles" took the direction of the renewed firms, and producers' and distributors' trade unions began to take a more active part. The agreements were necessary to gradually restructure the whole network by reallocating transportation and distribution means, building large power plants, and benefitting from complementarities between thermal and hydroelectric technologies.

This trend to integration materialized in two steps: at the regional level in the 1920s and at the national level in the 1930s. During the first step the firms formed large regional companies: one for the region of Paris and the East of the Massif Central, one for the coal mines region, three in the Alps, one in the Pyrénées, and the last for the West of the Massif Central. The second step allowed the national extension of the electric network; the regional networks were connected in 1936. For this time, two great names shared the control of the French electric system (actually almost the whole energy system): Mercier, rather Parisian and of thermal technology, and Durand, rather provincial and of hydroelectric technology. Apart from these two dominating large firms there remained a fringe of small firms of little influence.

Pricing: After 1921, prices were regulated on the basis of the electric economic index defined precisely by the decree of June 28, 1921. The price-cap regulation used until then had caused a lot of problems during World War I because of its immutability in an inflationary situation. It was then decided to create an index that varied as a function of the price of coal and the level of wages in the electric industry, to reflect the economic situation. The index was calculated by adding or subtracting from the price of coal a number N, depending on wages in electricity industry: $\bar{p}_é = p_é \pm N\ (\omega_é)$.

But then generalized inflation imposed the adoption of another index that was less sensitive to price variations. The decree of September 13, 1934 set up a steadier index calculated from the price of coal used in the electric industry and from an average wage combining the wages in the electric sector and in 38 other male employments.

This index was almost not applied, for in June 1935 the government set up a deflationary policy, imposing the immediate decrease of electricity prices. Direct measures were adopted, limiting severely the freedom in pricing. The maximum price was fixed at 1.50 F/kWh in Paris, and 2.40 F/kWh in towns of fewer than 20,000 inhabitants. These emergency measures were then established by the decree of October 30, 1935, regulating the prices of electricity, the licence fees, and the conditions of consolidation for the distributors.

During the government of Front Populaire, another electric index was defined by the decree of April 11, 1937. All wages having been increased in 1936, they were removed from the calculation of the new index to avoid an artificial increase. The new index was composed of three terms with different coefficients for high and low voltage: the price of one ton of coal; the cost of labor per 1,000 kWh of electricity (replacing the average wage in electric industry), and the retail price index (to replace the average wage of male employments).

The tariff decree of August 18, 1938 imposed differentiated pricing and standard maximum prices. Three tariffs were set up: cooking pricing, off-peak hours pricing (at least for 3,350 hours a year and 8 hours a day), and multipart pricing (*tarif à tranches multiples*) for domestic use.

The price per kWh of electricity in France was one of the lowest in Europe: in 1938, the price of 1 kWh in low voltage for domestic lighting was 1.50 F to 2.00 F in France, against 3.50 F to 4.00 F in Switzerland, 5.50 F in London, and 6.00 F in Berlin.

The nationalization of the electric industry:
The birth of Electricité de France

The natural evolution of the electric industry shows a trend to integration and growing control by the State, with the aim toward a more rational activity. Just before World War II, the electric industry had become a duopoly, and the trend was completed in 1946, when the vote for electricity nationalization made this sector a State monopoly.

After the war, the nationalization of the electric industry was the wish of the entire profession: engineers, technicians, and some managers thought that only nationalization could solve its problems. The expense of restoring and developing the electric industry after the destruction of war was estimated at about 100 billion francs. Most thought that only the State could finance such an investment. It was planned to open up huge works to develop hydroelectricity in all the country and to exploit coal to reduce imports.

Efficiency of the French electric network could be achieved only under the direction of a single management. The shortage of raw materials prohibited any wasting. The engineers requested a rational industry: coordination of hydroelectric producers' activities, suppression of tolls on companies' frontiers, use of a minimum of lines. In a technical meaning, the nationalization was regarded as the most efficient way to conclude the electric industry standardization, still unfinished. The most general idea was that the gathering of dispersed and inefficient means could generate a prominent industrial power and promote research, two aims that the former companies could never reach acting individually.

Though the nationalization was desired by the political majority and supported by the trade unions, it took 18 months to adopt the final act, after a succession of political vicissitudes and the presentation of numerous projects.

A compromise was finally reached: a bill proposed by the Minister of Transports, presented to the Equipment Committee of the National Assembly, which accepted it. This bill proposed the creation of two companies, one for gas and one for electricity, and the nationalization of the production units owned by electrochemical and electrometallurgic industries. In return the distribution cooperatives (Régies), the small producers (those producing fewer than 12 million kWh), and the production units owned by the SNCF (railway) and Les Houillères (coal mines) escaped nationalization. The special case of the Compagnie Nationale du Rhône, a big hydroelectric producer set in the Alps, took very long to settle, and though its nationalization was planned, its manager's eloquence was convincing and allowed him to keep his firm.

The nationalization law was finally voted with an overwhelming majority: 491 votes against 59, and 23 abstentions. On April 8, 1946, Electricité de France (EDF) was born.

The electric industry since nationalization (1946)

The fuel sources

When it was founded, EDF wanted to favor hydroelectric production technology to limit energy dependency on foreign countries. Until 1963, electricity was produced in equal shares by thermal technology and by hydroelectric technology. Then, the thermal technology became prevailing – first with the use of oil, and second with the development of atomic power.

Table 10-1. *Shares of primary energy sources in EDF since 1960 (TWh = billion of kWh)*

Year	1960		1973		1983		1989	
	TWh	%	TWh	%	TWh	%	TWh	%
Oil	2.4	3.4	67.6	39	13.5	5	26.3	7
Coal	12.3	17	28.2	16	52.4	19	—	—
Hydroelectric	40.5	56	47.6	27	70.7	25	46.2	13
Nuclear	0.15	0.2	14.0	8	136.9	48	284.7	80
Others	16.9	23.4	17.2	10	10.1	3	—	—
Total production	72.3	100	174.6	100	283.6	100	357.2	100

The thermal technology of electricity production that used coal began after the war gradually to use oil. Before 1960, the share of electricity produced from oil remained moderate, with a peak of 22% in 1955 and a slack of 5% in 1959, when the Suez crisis produced a fear of rationing. Between 1966 and 1969, the price of oil decreased a lot, allowing the substitution of oil for coal in thermal electricity generation. From this moment, the oil producers became essential to the French economy: oil represented 15% of energy consumption in 1949, 31% in 1960, and 67% in 1973.

French energy dependency on OPEC countries (the main suppliers of France were all in the OPEC trust) was very high: 75% in 1974, instead of only 30% in 1954. This is why the oil crisis had such considerable consequences. Under these circumstances, in 1974 the decision was taken to speed up the nuclear program, which had been found to be too expensive as long as oil was cheap.

Due to nuclear power plants, oil consumption in the electric industry then began to decline, even though electricity production was increasing. The present annual consumption of refined oil for electricity production is about 1 million tons: 1.1 million tons in 1987, 0.9 million tons in 1988.

Today, nuclear power is highly dominant, supplying more than 80% of electricity consumption (see Table 10-1).

Study of demand

Rate of growth of electricity demand: In 1947, the Division of Studies and Research of EDF, fearing that investments deficiency would cause a structural electricity shortage, studied the evolution of consumption to try to foresee the future development of electricity demand. Estimations gave a consumption increasing twofold every 10 years, which corresponds to an average annual rate of growth of 7%. This result was confirmed until the energy crisis in 1974, allowing EDF to establish the law of consumption doubling in 10 years as the first basis of evaluation for investments.

Excess demand and rationing

After World War II, the needs for rebuilding, for network development, and for satisfaction of consumers' new requirements (from the end of the war the demand was growing again) caused supply for a long time to be a lot lower than demand. Numerous difficulties prevented the increase of production: After the war all the materials were missing, especially oil. The situation was even worsened by the dryness of the summer of 1949, which caused bad performance of the hydroelectric power plants. In such a situation, power cuts were unavoidable and frequent. For instance, in 1949 domestic customers were subjected to a weekly power cut.

In autumn 1949, to protect the network against overcharge accidents and to avoid domestic customers being too often deprived of electricity, EDF began to carry out industrial power cuts, requiring the firms to stop their activities momentarily.

In October 1949, the Ministry of Industry set up an official rationing scheme for the industry. The Frequency Alert Plan provided that when the frequency on the network became lower than 48.5 periods per second, indicating network overcharge, the industrial customers had to stop operating their plants, or at least part of them, within 24 hours.

This decision generated a 15% network relief, avoiding a general current cutoff by deferring some activities. Though it was unpopular among industry managers as well as among EDF managers, who considered the state intervention as an intrusion, this measure avoided any power cut from 1950 on.

It is noteworthy that the electricity shortage during EDF's first years, when supply could not satisfy demand, was caused not only by the lack of oil and the summer dryness, but also by the investment choices. EDF had invested particularly in hydroelectric power plants whose building delay is very long: the new hydroelectric power plants only began to produce in 1950. The experience of electricity cutoff decided the government to adopt measures guaranteeing a "minimum service required for public security" (decree of July 18, 1965).

Gradually, electricity distribution, transportation, and production structured itself to supply a demand growing exponentially. Actually it was necessary to wait until the launching of the first EDF nuclear program in 1971 to obtain a production satisfying most of the demand.

Yet, in December 1978, the accidental overcharge of the transportation network caused by a severe cold snap induced an important power failure. A new Electricity Minimum Service was set up then, adapted to new consumption conditions, and fixing new general instructions of network load shedding.

Excess supply: Globally, since nuclear power is preponderant in electricity production, that is to say since 1985, the national demand does not absorb all the energy produced. On the one hand EDF now exports electricity to bordering foreign countries, and on the other hand, has an active commercial policy (supply policy) aimed at the internal market.

The new technologies and their effects on the development of the electric power system

Nuclear power in France: France long ago chose atomic power. The country had very poor fossil fuel resources (only a little coal and natural gas) and had achieved before 1950 most of the feasible hydroelectric projects. Therefore, the exploitation of nuclear power plants rapidly proved to be a necessity if minimal independence in energy production was to be achieved.

Research and technical progress were diverted from conventional thermal technology toward nuclear technology, which benefitted from particularly important governmental efforts. As early as 1945, the creation of the CEA (*Commissariat à l'Energie Atomique,* Atomic Power Committee) fostered nuclear power development by the setting up of scientific, technical, and economic research structures.

The evolution of electronuclear power production can be described according to four main periods, as follows:

1952–1960: The first period, from 1952 to 1960, was the period of exploiting the first nuclear power plants, solely of Natural Uranium-Gas-Graphite (UNGG) technology. In such power plants, the reactor's fuel is natural uranium, the combustion moderator is graphite, and the cooling fluid a gas–air or carbon dioxide.

The first French nuclear reactors stem from the five years program on atomic power of July 24, 1952. Worked out both by the CEA and the government, the first project was composed of three reactors named G1, G2, and G3, built in Marcoule, in the South of France. The reactor G1, put into service in September 1956, generated a maximum power of 2.5 MWe but in energy regeneration only, because the reactor auxiliaries consumed more energy than the plant could generate.[1] Rather experimental, with an air cooling system, this reactor was definitively stopped in October 1968.

The reactors G2 and G3, cooled with carbon dioxide, are still operating. G2 was put into service in April 1959, G3 in April 1960, and their theoretical power is of 250 MWh, running the energy production units at the power of 40 MWe.

---

[1] MWe is the notation for net electric power, and MWh is the notation for theoretical electric power, not always fit for use.

The first EDF nuclear program was set in 1956 for the constructing of three reactors of the same type UNGG: Chinon 1, Chinon 2, and Chinon 3, also denoted EDF1, EDF2, and EDF3, in Chinon on the Loire side. The net electric power of Chinon 1 is 70 MWe, of Chinon 2, 210 MWe, and of Chinon 3, 400 MWe. EDF's purpose at this time was to perfect a program able to compete with thermal power plants that used fossil fuel.

1962–1969: The second period was a transitional period between 1962 and 1969. Building and operating of UNGG–type reactors was going on. Four blocks of 460 to 540 MWe were initiated between 1963 and 1966. These power plants showed a good performance, particularly compared to conventional thermal power plants, but the massive building abroad (and first in the United States) of reactors of another technology opened a new way. Two twin technologies were rapidly developing: the pressurised-water reactor (PWR) and the boiling-water reactor (BWR), of net electric power of 600 to 1300 MWe. The fuel of these reactors is enriched uranium, the moderator and coolant is ordinary water (river, lake, or sea).

1968–1974: The emergence of the water technologies was the beginning of a third period, a conversion period, that may be dated from 1968 to 1974. The building of graphite-gas technology power plants (UNGG) was definitively abandoned in 1969.

Henceforward, the new projects were of PWR technology, whose first realization, an 870 MWe power plant, was begun in 1968 at Tihange (Belgium) in cooperation with Belgium.

From 1974: The fourth period is characterized by the intensive development of PWR technology from 1974. The oil crisis gave strong incentives to speed up the nuclear program. Under such compulsion, EDF managed to start the works of as many as six blocks a year of nuclear reactors of power between 900 and 1,400 MWe.

With 52,600 MW of set-up power, nuclear power supplied 75% of the 387 billion kWh produced in France in 1989. The share of nuclear power reached 80% in EDF production in 1989 (that is to say, 286 TWh over 357 TWh produced by EDF).[2] As a comparison, in the same year the conventional thermal power stations supplied 12% of national production and 7% of EDF production.

The alternative production technologies: The electricity-generating alternative technologies such as geothermics, solar power, wind power, or tidal power, are not very much used in France. They are usually limited to domes-

---

[2] 1 TWh = 10^9 kWh, 1 MWh = 10^6 kWh

tic or local use, though ambitious projects have been studied, especially for solar power.

Geothermics cannot be used in continental France to produce electricity. The only experimental geothermal electric power plant was in the Island of Guadeloupe (Antilles).

Tidal power is exploited in the Gulf of Saint-Malo, at the mouth of the Rance. The tidal power station of the Rance was put into service in 1966. It is fitted out with 24 reversible turbines of 10 MW, and produces 500 million kWh per year. It is the only great station of this type in the world.

The use of wind energy to produce great quantities of electricity is not considered in France. In spite of several experiments in progress, the building of great wind generators of some hundreds or thousands of kW of power poses technical problems: height of mills, length and width of hatches necessary for a good performance. Their use remains geographically very limited; only low-power stations for isolated sites are worthwhile – for example, in agriculture (for instance, to pump water), for domestic use, and for lighthouses isolated out at sea (as with the forthcoming setting up of a 100 kW windpower station on the Isle of Ouessant).

With regard to solar power, two technologies are used, the most sophisticated of which is based on the use of photopiles, or photovoltaic cells, able to transform solar radiance into electricity. Composed of semiconducor materials such as silicium, they are very costly and their maximum rate of return is 20%. Though limited to domestic consumption, beacons, transmitters, and the like, their use is now widespread, especially in the South. The main problem associated with the use of photopiles is the storage of electricity for nonsunny periods.

The second technology, less frequently used, consists in using the sun radiations to heat a boiler running a turbine. This is the principle of the solar power plant, in which a field of mirrors reflects the sunbeams on a boiler set on the top of a tower. In France a large-scale experiment in this technology was realized in the Oriental Pyrénées, in the solar power plant Themis, composed of 201 mirrors of 53.7 m^2 each, for a maximum electric power of 2.5 MW.

Energy savings: The alarm given in 1974 by the first oil crisis induced rapid decisions for energy saving.

During the long period when oil was cheap and easily available, the French energy system had evolved toward preferential use of oil, imported from a few oil-producing countries, as primary energy supply. Too much specialization was the main weakness of French energy policy. The crisis was not unpredictable. Earlier, in the 1960s, French petroleum engineers, who were experts on the Oil Commission of the Plan, were said to be "terrified by the increase of fuel-oil national consumption." They were fully aware of the necessity to limit waste and to prepare for the future by investments in other sources of energy, but the low price of oil did not give much incentive to such efforts. So, nuclear power development plans stagnated as long as oil was cheap, with the result that the nuclear program was not yet operating when it became necessary. In the emergency the government defined a new energy policy to reduce French energy dependency on three points: to develop national energy supplies (mainly nuclear), to increase the number of oil-supplying countries to avoid delivery embargo, and to reduce energy consumption.

To achieve this last goal, an energy-saving policy was then started on the basis of two principles: to make the energy-wasting behavior change, and to modify materials for a better use of energy.

Immediate measures suppressed the two main causes of waste: high heating temperatures and high-speed driving. Then, the development of new technologies perfected the energy-saving program, first in the industry and second in domestic use (cars, household appliances).

To support and control the program of the energy-saving policy, the Energy Saving Agency was created in 1974. Its mission was to stimulate energy savings by proposing new measures, giving information and advice to users, and favoring new energy-saving technologies and the use of alternative energy supplies by the allocation of grants.

The AFME (*Agence Française pour la Maîtrise de l'Energie,* French Agency for Energy Control) has observed the energy savings realized in three periods since the first campaign for energy saving: 1974–8, the period of setting up and of great motivation; 1979–81, the period in which previous investments began to pay off; and last, 1982–7, the period of less emergency.

The total saving realized is evaluated in million tons fuel equivalent, depending on whether they result from an investment (equipment, for instance) or from behavior (such as heating control). The results are shown in Table 10-2.

Human resources

EDF staff: On December 31, 1989, EDF had 122,300 employees. During the year, 2,500 people were signed on, among them 300 for managerial staff. For comparison, in the same year, the private electric sector had 7,578 employees, of whom 617 were working for the *Compagnie Nationale du Rhône,* the biggest nonnationalized firm (see Table 10-3).

In 1989, 19% of EDF employees were women, and one agent over two was younger than 36.

Human resources have changed a lot since the beginning of EDF. In 1949, EDF had 74,174 employees and in 1983, 124,125 (a 67% growth). At

Table 10-2. *Energy savings by sector from 1974 to 1987 (Unit: million tons fuel equivalent)*

	Sector			
Periods	Industry and agriculture	Residential and tertiary	Transports	Total
1974–8				
Investment	2.5	1.5	1.2	5.2
Behavior	2.0	7.0	1.3	10.3
Total	4.5	8.5	2.5	15.5
1979–81				
Investment	3.1	3.5	1.3	7.9
Behavior	0.7	2.8	0.6	4.1
Total	3.8	6.3	1.9	12.0
1982–7				
Investment	3.5	7.1	4.1	14.7
Behavior	−1.3	−4.2	−2.0	−7.5
Total	2.2	2.9	2.2	7.2

the same time, production increased from 30.8 TWh to 368,175 TWh (an 870% growth).

The companywide specific manpower (that is to say, the number of employees over sales volume) decreased from 2,409 employees per billion kWh in 1949 to 463 per billion kWh in 1983.

The evolution of EDF staff qualification has been very important, as can be seen from Table 10-4. Between 1946 and 1989, the percentage of managerial staff multiplied by 3.2, and the percentage of control employees by 4.

Trade unionism: Since its creation, EDF has had a powerful union strength used to support the management against the authorities. Even if its power has decreased greatly by now, the action within the firm of the CGT (*Confédération Générale du Travail,* General Labor Confederency), the trade union close to the Communist Party, was for a long time a support for EDF. Already before World War II the nationalization of the electric industry was an aim of the CGT, and it can be said that EDF originated with the CGT. Général de Gaulle entrusted a communist minister, Marcel Paul, with preparing the Nationalization Law. Since EDF's birth, agents and managers have shown a united front to carry out the firm's mission.

In 1946 unionism was almost a CGT monopoly at EDF. Its most important task was the management of social work, and it was a difficult mission.

Table 10-3. *Countrywide EDF staff in 1989*

EDF staff 1989: 122,300	
Management	70,200
Equipment management	4,600
Research and studies management	2,700
Functional organizations	5,900
Production and transport management	38,900
Thermal production	24,700
Hydroelectric production	5,600
Transportation	7,000
Energy moving	1,200

The CCAS (*Caisse Centrale d'Activités Sociales,* Social Work Central Fund) had a budget of several billion francs.

In 1964 appeared a new trade union, the CFDT (*Confédération Française Démocratique du Travail,* French Democratic Labor Confederacy) competing directly with the CGT, which was blamed for its relationship with the Communist Party.

The CGT lost its monopoly, and though this outcome allowed a gain in democracy, it was the end of the social consensus in the firm, as was illustrated by the opposition between the CGT and the CFDT in the nuclear debate during the 1970s.

Today the CGT still is in the majority but with only a short lead. The CFDT is the second most important union. The managerial staff unions, gathered in the UNCM, are not very successful. It must be said that a lot of members of the managerial staff vote for the CGT or other workers' unions (for instance, in the 1984 elections, 22.5% of the managerial employees voted for the CGT and only 40.2% for the UNCM).

The only available election results date from May 1984. In that year, the elections of the employees' representatives at EDF's Board of Directors gave the following percentage of votes: CGT 51.5%, CFDT 20.8%, FO 15.2%, UNCM 8.3%, CFTC 4.2%. The very weak abstention vote (8.3% of voters in 1980) shows the commitment to unionism of EDF's employees.

Public and private ownership of electric industry

Countrywide, the state's monopoly consists of 85% of the generation, 100% of the transportation, and 95% of the distribution. In this section, we study the generation and distribution organizations that are not part of EDF's monopoly.

Table 10-4: *EDF staff qualification*

Qualification	1946	1973	1979	1989
Managerial staff and engineers	5%	11%	12.9%	16%
Control agents and technicians	12%	40%	45.4%	49%
Employees and workers	83%	49%	41.7%	35%

Generation: The Nationalization Law of 1946 and the following acts provided several exceptions to electric production nationalization. The nonnationalized producers are the following:

- Private plants whose average production was below 12 million kWh a year in 1942 and 1943.
- The production plants of installed power below 8,000 kWh.
- Private production plants aimed at self-consumption.
- Production means owned by the distribution cooperatives (Régies) and by joint-owned companies (partly private and partly public, Sociétés d'Economie Mixte) with a majority of public shares.
- Plants aimed at the use of the calorific power of urban waste.
- Production plants owned by the railway company SNCF and by the coal mines company *Les Houillères* (also called *Charbonnages de France*).
- The *Compagnie Nationale du Rhône* (Rhône National Company).

Autonomous electricity production is subject to a heavy constraint – it is forbidden to sell or to supply electricity to a third party. The producers who do not consume all the electricity they produce are connected to EDF's network, and EDF is bound to buy the private production by a decree of May 20,1955. The sales price is the long-term marginal cost, but the cost estimates are always the source of difficult debates.

The small producers: Small power plants are almost all hydroelectric plants. There are about 1,400 of them in France, producing less than 1% of national electric production. The original Nationalization Law of April 8, 1946 did not call for the nationalization of plants whose production was less than 12 million kWh per year and per production unit. Then, the "Armengaud" Law of August 2, 1949 put the limit at 8,000 kWh of installed power.

The administrative difficulties of setting up are important for small firms. Ten years at least are necessary to amortize the investment, and EDF's prices are too low for the viability of most of the micro-power plants.

For its part, EDF complains of the bad quality of electricity sold by small producers; they cannot supply during dry years, and in wet years EDF must buy needless electricity. Furthermore, frequency regulation of the current is totally a responsibility of EDF.

The self-consumers (self-generators): Some electricity-consuming industries prefer producing their own energy, following the example of the paper manufacturers who were pioneers of hydroelectric development. Generally, the firm absorbs all its production.

The distribution cooperatives: Régies and SICAE: Régies are cooperative distributors, and the SICAE (*Sociétés d'Intérêt Collectif Agricole d'Electricité,* Agricultural Collective Interest Electricity Companies) are semipublic rural distributors. They have kept the right to produce and distribute electricity out of EDF monopoly. They own all kinds of power plants, including nuclear plants. Their administrative features are detailed shortly in the subsection dedicated to electricity distribution.

Railway company SNCF: The SNCF is the French nationalized railway company. As is EDF, it is a state monopoly.

The nationalization law of the electric industry left to the SNCF and to its subsidiaries the ownership of their means of electricity production. They include hydroelectric power plants in the Pyrénées and the Massif Central inherited from former railway companies. SNCF's electric production amounts to about 1.7 TWh and covers one-third of its needs. The produced energy is absorbed by EDF, which transports it and regularizes its frequency before returning it at the entrance of railway substations.

SNCF and EDF are on good terms. Their relationship is based on a contract signed on November 16, 1970. The two firms cooperate on large-scale projects, like the equipment of the dam of Marèges on the Truyère, property of the SNCF. The EDF, which is financing the works, will in return dispose of electricity in peak-load periods.

Coal mines company: Les Houillères – Charbonnages de France: The coal-mining (private) monopoly owns 15 conventional thermal power plants, supplied with nonsaleable secondary charcoal products: pulverulent, mived, schlamm, residuals containing a lot of water (about 20%), and ashes (45%), all unusable otherwise. A third of the coal extracted in France is consumed this way, to produce 16.6 TWh (14.3% of conventional thermal electricity produced in France), among which 2 TWh only are used by the company. The remaining two thirds of extracted coal is sold to EDF, according to a contract. For instance, in 1980 the contract with EDF agreed for the sale of 12.7 TWh, more than 5% of French electricity production.

Given the scale of the coal mines, monopoly production of electricity, and the weight of the constraint of exclusive sale to EDF, the relationship between the two firms is full of conflict, the circumstances putting the coal producer in a weak position.

Compagnie Nationale du Rhône: The *Compagnie Nationale du Rhône* is an old electricity company set in the Alps, with a capital shared by private and public owners. At the beginning, the capital was equally shared between the private and public sectors: a quarter each to the City of Paris, to the Rhône Valley local organizations, to private electricity companies, and to the Paris–Lyon–Marseille Railway Company.

The company was born on May 27, 1933, as a consequence of the law of May 27, 1921, which favored works along the Rhône, from the Swiss borderline to the Mediterranean Sea, for three complementary purposes: exploitation of hydro-electric power, navigation, and irrigation. Electricity sales were to finance the two other projects. Edouard Herriot, one of the company founders and the manager, saved the firm from nationalization, owing to his eloquence. His main argument (which won) was that neither navigation nor irrigation fell within EDF competence. So the company was not nationalized, but it lost all distribution rights and, as were the other producers, was obliged to sell to EDF its electric production.

By now, the company's annual electricity production is about 16 TWh (less than 0.05% of French production in 1989). Simultaneously, the Rhône improvement works are going on. In 1981, works of connection between Lyon and Marseille-Fos, started in 1933, were at last achieved. Furthermore, a projected canal from the Rhine to the Rhône is still pending.

Distribution: Only 5% of electricity distribution remains out of EDF's monopoly, and yet the whole sector nearly missed not being nationalized at all. Actually, several projects excluded nationalization of distribution, two of them being proposed by the 1944 Liberation government.

Distribution was the most profitable part of the electric industry; distribution alone was enough to make comfortable profits. That is why the private companies were willing to keep it. But the Minister of Industrial Production, Marcel Paul, aware of distribution's profitability, imposed nationalization on it. It was only to satisfy the Socialists that he left out the electric cooperatives.

Out of the national monopoly can still be found the Régies (cooperatives) distribution networks, the SICAE (rural cooperatives) networks, the users' cooperatives, and the jointly owned companies with majority public capital (state or local organizations). Examples of jointly owned companies are the *Electricité de Strasbourg,* half of whose capital is owned by EDF, which bought it for the Strasbourg municipality, and the *Société Monégasque d'Electricité et de Gaz,* 12.5% of whose capital is owned by EDF by inheritance.

Table 10-5. *Production of electricity according to the type of producer in 1987 in GWh (million kWh)*

	Conventional thermal production	Nuclear thermal production	Hydroelectric production
EDF	13,055	248,256	66,087
Régies and SICAE	67	3,264	218
Charbonnages de France	15,017		
SNCF			1,377
Industrial power stations	9,024		1,036
Other producers			3,343
Total	37,163	251,520	72,061

Such organizations own their own power lines and exploit them. Five percent of low-voltage customers are supplied by Régies or SICAE, especially in the countryside. Set up by the Socialists in the interwar period, essentially in the countryside, the distribution cooperatives were of the highest importance for the supporters of decentralization and the power of local authorities.

The autonomous distributors were gathered in 1933 in the *Fédération Nationale des Collectivités Concédantes et Régies* (National Federation of Conceding Organizations and Cooperatives) to establish the power of small communal organizations owing to interdepartmental superunions. The Federation immediately obtained better prices and set up a pressure group at the National Assembly to get favourable laws – for instance, the 10% price decrease for low-voltage electricity in 1935, and the creation of the *Caisse de Compensation,* a compensation fund for the amortization of rural electrification expenses.

The Federation was relying on its numerous political and representative members – senators, deputies, ministers, county councillors. This is one good reason why all the organizations depending on the Federation could remain out of the nationalization. In its decisive intervention, the Federation's vice-president, Paul Ramadier, who also was rapporteur on the bill of nationalization, argued that cooperatives could stay apart for "they had organized the electricity distribution far away from profit seeking."

Due to its political basis, and in spite of its small dimension, the Federation went on playing an important part in the electric industry after nationalization. It gained a great reputation for being an "antiquated and cumbersome parasite," obstinate in defending its old position concerning the amortization fund of rural electrification expenses, the prices, and over all, the rights of local authorities.

The present management of rural networks is not satisfactory. It causes abnormal costs and works delays compared to what EDF could do. For economic reasons (too-low prices, heavy social contributions), the cooperatives gradually disappear and rural networks are recovered by EDF. Only the urban cooperatives survive well apart from EDF, for they generally make profits.

Horizontal and vertical integration

An original experience of partly horizontal integration: Gas: The gas industry is a State monopoly called GDF (Gaz de France), now partly managed jointly with EDF in the single firm EDF–GDF. The gas industry was nationalized along with the electricity industry by the same Law on the Nationalization of Electricity and Gas of April 8, 1946. The distribution, the staff management, and the general secretary are in common with EDF, but GDF is independent in production, transportation, and investments.

Concerning the staff, the joint management with EDF still poses problems for GDF, for all its employees (particularly for emergency interventions) should be electricians and gasmen. The joint management greatly simplified the tasks of meter reading and facturation and rapidly proved to be invaluable. By going beyond the competition between two power suppliers, economic rationality and complementarity prevailed.

Vertical integration: Within EDF, the electric sector is totally integrated – generation, transportation, and distribution. The vertical integration includes also the supply of primary energy in the case of hydroelectric power, for the water (or more precisely the water energy) is granted to EDF by the state.

The coal mines company *Les Houillères* is an example of vertical integration of primary energy supply and electricity production out of the state monopoly. The nonnationalized *Les Houillères* owns coal mines, extracts coal, and produces electricity in its own thermal power plants. The produced electricity is then either self-consumed or sold to EDF.

The plan contracts binding EDF and the French government, as described below, specify that EDF has no right to own electricity-consuming industries or industries producing electricity-consuming goods.

The main indicators of the industry

Tables 10-6 and 10-7 summarize the evolution of the main indicators of the French electric industry.

Table 10-6. Annex 1—Section2—Electric data from 1938 to 1972

	Before 1950			1948	1949	1950	1951	1952	1953
	1938	1946	1947						
Electricity production (TWh)									
Hydroelectricity[a]	10.3			14.7	11.0	16.1	21.0	22.2	21.0
Conventional and nuclear thermal electricity[b]	10.4			14.2	18.9	16.9	17.1	18.3	20.4
—among them nuclear power									
Total production	20.7			28.9	29.9	33.0	38.1	40.5	41.5
(INSEE)									
Electricity consumption (TWh)									
High-voltage consumption			17.9						
Low-voltage consumption			5.1						
Total consumption			23.0						
(INSEE)									
EDF income (MF)									
Average income per kWh (F/kWh)									
(EDF)									
Cost price of production, purchase, transport and distribution of electricity by EDF (MF)									
Thermal production: nuclear production, conventional production, or both									
Hydroelectric production									
Purchase of energy									
Transportation and energy moves									
Distribution									
Insert differences and charges[d]									
Total									
(EDF)									
Average cost price per kWh supplied[e] (centimes = 0.01 F)									
(EDF)									
Cost of thermal kWh[f] (centimes = 0.01 F)									
conventional									
nuclear									
(EDF)									
Electricity price index									
Annual average (basis 100 in 1970)					40.1	40.2	44.8	55.5	55.8
(INSEE)									
Average price according to voltage									
Price in FF per 100 kWh, before taxes									
High tension (5,000 to 220,000 volts)									
Low tension (220 to 380 volts)									
(EDF)									
Electricity average price index according to the tariff (basis 100 in 1983)									
Green Tariff B & C (big industry)									
Yellow Tariff & Green Tariff A (small and medium industry)									
Blue Tariff (domestic and professional use)									
(EDF)									
Transmission and distribution network (1,000 miles)									
length of 400,000 volt line									
length of 225,000 volt line									
length of 45,000 to 150,000 volt line									
length of up to 45,000 volt line									
Total length									
(EDF)									
EDF staff number				72,400		75,500			
Production per employee (1,000 kWh)				399		437			
(EDF)									
Total GNP (MF)									
current prices, evaluation basis 1971					84,918	99,568	125,251	146,055	151,030
current prices, evaluation basis 1980									
GNP per capita (FF)									
current prices, evaluation basis 1971					2,047	2,380	2,971	3,440	3,533
price 1970					6,568	7,000	7,365	7,564	7,761
current prices, evaluation basis 1980									
price 1980									
(INSEE)									

TWh = 10^9kWh.

MF = 10^6 FF.

[a]Including pumping up until 1965.

[b]Nuclear power is included until 1979.

[c]The difference between total consumption and sum of low- and high-voltage consumption is due to the losses on wires and to self-consumption (from 1987).

[d]From 1985 are added insert differences, charges on previous financial year, and extra financial contributions.

[e]Between 1960 and 1970 the average cost price is expressed in 1970 centimes, and later in current centimes.

[f]Evaluated for an annual use of 4,500 house of the average net installed power. Expressed in centimes of 1970 between 1960 and 1970, and then in current centimes.

	1950s						1960s								
	1954	1955	1956	1957	1958	1959	1960	1961	1962	1963	1964	1965	1966	1967	1968
	24.3	25.5	25.8	24.8	32.2	32.6	40.3	38.2	35.8	43.4	34.7	46.2	51.5	45.0	50.2
	21.3	24.1	28.0	32.6	29.4	31.9	31.8	38.3	47.3	44.8	59.1	55.0	54.4	66.5	67.6
													1.4	2.1	3.1
	45.6	49.6	53.8	57.4	61.6	64.5	72.1	76.5	83.1	88.2	93.8	101.2	105.9	111.5	117.8
				42.2										80.4	
				9.9										25.2	
				52.1										105.6	
							12.5	12.5	12.5	12.1	12.2	11.9	11.7	12.0	11.8
							7.18	6.8	6.5	6.3	6.2	6.1	6.0	5.6	5.4
	55.6	54.7	54.6	60.9	67.5	73.8	73.8	73.8	73.8	76.8	79.9	80.4	84.0	88.0	90.8
				80,300			85,200		88,500	90,000	91,050	92,100	93,150	94,200	95,100
				715			846		939	980	1,030	1,099	1,137	1,184	1,239
	159,950	171,394	188,802	212,717	245,679	267,228	296,506	323,459	361,164	404,881	449,157	483,488	523,416	565,389	614,517
	3,715	3,947	4,306	4,801	5,485	5,907	6,491	7,007	7,684	8,467	9,297	9,916	10,647	11,410	12,313
	8,078	8,414	8,762	9,133	9,258	9,390	9,966	10,405	10,901	11,287	11,901	12,354	12,893	13,391	13,861

Table 10-6 *(cont.). Annex 1 - Section 2 - Electric data from 1938 to 1972*

		1970s							
	1969	1970	1971	1972	1973	1974	1975	1976	1977
Electricity production (TWh)									
Hydroelectricity[a]	52.7	56.4	48.5	48.5	47.3	56.4	59.7	48.0	75.4
Conventional and nuclear thermal electricity[b]	78.6	83.9	100.3	114.8	127.2	123.6	118.4	146.2	126.3
– among them nuclear power	4.5	5.1	6.9	11.7	11.9	12.5	15.4	13.7	14.6
Total production	131.3	140.4	148.8	163.3	174.5	180.0	178.1	194.2	201.8
(INSEE)									
Electricity consumption (TWh)									
High-voltage consumption	91.0	97.2	86.6	91.7	99.4	119.6	113.7	122.3	125.9
Low-voltage consumption	30.2	32.9	33.9	38.0	42.7	48.5	54.6	60.6	66.1
Total consumption	121.2	130.1	126.1	138.6	149.7	168.1	168.3	182.9	192.0
(INSEE)									
EDF income (MF)		11,753	13,311	15,093	16,885	20,770	25,106	30,431	34,387
Average income per kWh (F/kWh)		0.0837	0.0895	0.0924	0.0968	0.1154	0.1410	0.1567	0.1704
(EDF)									
Cost price of production, purchase, transport and distribution of electricity by EDF (MF)									
Thermal production: nuclear production,						1,493	1,782	2,449	2,897
conventional production,									
or both	2,938	3,287	3,999	4,791	5,403	8,428	9,817	12,666	13,032
Hydroelectric production	1,782	1,890	2,174	2,226	2,373	2,489	2,798	3,154	3,356
Purchase of energy	619	700	904	864	1,029	1,698	1,808	2,435	2,552
Transportation and energy moves	871	977	1,062	1,195	1,295	1,505	1,800	2,188	2,411
Distribution	4,404	4,864	5,330	5,948	6,712	8,016	9,248	10,490	11,982
Insert differences and charges[d]									
Total	10,614	11,718	13,469	15,024	16,885	22,136	25,471	30,933	33,333
(EDF)									
Average cost price per kWh supplied[e] (centimes = 0.01 F)	10.6	10.5	11.6	11.4	12.1	15.1	17.2	19.3	19.8
(EDF)									
Cost of thermal kWh[f] (centimes = 0.01 F)									
conventional	4.95	4.75	5.23	6.40	6.49	8.57	10.39	10.09	10.42
nuclear						11.9	11.57	16.32	19.84
(EDF)									
Electricity price index Annual average (basis 100 in 1970)	96.2	100.0	104.7	109.1	113.8	132.8	143.4	162.2	174.0
(INSEE)									
Average price according to voltage Price in FF per 100 kWh, before taxes									
High tension (5,000 to 220,000 volts)						9.7	12.0	13.4	14.3
Low tension (220 to 380 volts)						23.3	25.2	27.2	29.0
(EDF)									
Electricity average price index according to the tariff (basis 100 in 1983)									
Green Tariff B & C (big industry)									
Yellow Tariff & Green Tariff A (small and medium industry)									
Blue Tariff (domestic and professional use)									
(EDF)									
Transmission and distribution network (1,000 miles)									
length of 400,000 volt line						3.7	3.9	3.9	4.2
length of 225,000 volt line						13.9	14.1	14.3	14.6
length of 45,000 to 150,000 volt line						26.6	26.4	26.7	27.0
length of up to 35,000 volt line						586.0	596.1	608.2	618.5
Total length						629.8	640.5	653.1	664.3
(EDF)									
EDF staff number	94,900	94,430	94,325	94,892	96,948	98,086	98,774	100,282	101,318
Production per employee (1,000 kWh)	1,384	1,487	1,578	1,721	1,800	1,835	1,803	1,936	1,992
(EDF)									
Total GNP (MF)									
current prices, evaluation basis 1971	700,689	782,560	872,433	981,115	1,114,200	1,278,302	1,452,319	1,677,973	1,884,585
current prices, evaluation basis 1980		793,519	884,186	987,947	1,129,835	1,302,978	1,467,884	1,700,553	1,917,803
GNP per capita (FF)									
current prices, evaluation basis 1971	13,925	15,413	17,023	18,977	21,378	24,367	27,552	31,715	35,461
price 1970	14,709	15,413	16,095	16,895	17,660	18,112	18,065	18,923	19,413
current prices, evaluation basis 1980		15,629	17,252	19,109	21,678	24,838	27,854	32,141	36,086
price 1980		39,961	41,481	42,942	44,916	46,011	45,675	47,424	48,732
(INSEE)									

TWh = 10^9 kWh.
MF = 10^6 FF.
[a]Including pumping up until 1965.
[b]Nuclear power is included until 1979.
[c]The difference between total consumption and the sum of low- and high-voltage consumption is due to the losses on wires and to self-consumption (from 1987).
[d]From 1985 are added insert differences, charges on the previous financial year, and extra financial contributions.
[e]Between 1960 and 1970 the average cost price is expressed in 1970 centimes, and later in current centimes.
[f]Evaluated for an annual use of 4,500 hours of the average net installed power. Expressed in centimes of 1970 between 1960 and 1970, and then in current centimes.

		1980s										1990s		
1978	1979	1980	1981	1982	1983	1984	1985	1986	1987	1988	1989	1990	1991	1992
67.8	65.2	68.9	71.5	70.0	63.7	64.8	60.9	61.3	72.0	71.9	50.2	57.0	60.6	66.3
148.7	164.5	176.7	191.6	195.3	212.9	242.3	265.2	281.8	288.7	295.0	337.2	343.1	372.4	363.8
27.0	36.2	57.9	99.6	103.1	136.9	181.7	213.1	241.4	251.5	260.2	288.7	297.9	316.1	
216.5	229.7	245.6	263.1	265.3	281.6	307.1	326.1	343.1	360.7	366.9	387.4	400.1	433.0	430.1
130.9	140.4	148.1	154.2	152.5	147.8	154.6	165.7	175.4	174.7	184.5	190.7	195.0	203.7	
73.1	78.9	81.9	86.9	91.2	99.3	106.6	111.1	118.0	114.0	113.0	124.0	127.9	132.0	
204.0	219.3	230.0	241.1	243.7	247.1	261.2	276.8	293.4	327.0[f]	333.0	340.7	349.5	364.2	371.2
39,947	48,591	61,675	72,622	87,256	100,898	119,188	131,475	127,232	132,461	136,275	144,868	153,021	167,881	174,060
0.1845	0.2115	0.2511	0.2760	0.3289	0.3583	0.3881	0.4032	0.3708	0.3672	0.3714	0.3739	0.3825	0.3877	0.4047
4,264	6,813	Data not available		Data not available	34,739	43,414	49,230	51,916	50,848	54,897	61,072	61,190	71,900	79,108
11,765					19,121	16,179	15,332	11,857	10,219	9,615	11,314	11,437	13,397	12,909
16,029	20,947		38,793											
3,619	4,352		6,033		8,040	8,928	9,461	8,970	10,640	10,941	10,982	11,290	10,550	9,148
3,144	4,110		1,113		5,270	6,450	6,536	8,271	7,651	7,180	8,531	7,957	7,461	6,068
2,744	3,246		4,946		7,228	8,272	9,617	9,647	10,325	11,209	12,494	13,981	15,120	16,855
14,241	15,936		21,762		29,060	32,090	35,059	36,028	35,923	40,014	39,539	39,897	41,618	45,581
							430	1,154	6,436	3,990	4,918	6,792	5,541	1,320
39,777	48,591	61,500	72,647	77,175	103,098	115,333	125,665	127,843	132,042	137,846	148,841	152,544	165,587	170,989
20.9	23.7	27.8	32.3	33.2	41.3	41.8	42.2	40.6	40.1	40.3	41.6	41.0	40.8	39.8
12.72	14.72	Data not available			38.09	45.09	53.35	66.67	70.56	70.28	45.27	43.92	36.66	
15.85	18.82				24.75	24.33	23.42	21.86	20.48	21.4	21.38	20.82	23.00	
187.6	209.1	251.3	278.8	360.5	405.7	442.5	461.4	457.5	455.0	412.1	412.1			
15.5	17.1	21.3	23.5	26.9	30.4									
30.5	33.3	40.1	44.0	50.9	55.7									
					100.0	97.0	93.2	84.7	79.5	77.0	74.9	75.6	71.5	
					100.0	98.5	97.0	90.0	86.5	84.0	82.1	81.7	80.4	
					100.0	102.0	98.5	92.0	88.0	85.2	85.1	87.6	83.2	
5.1	5.4	6.3	7.0	7.7	8.1									
14.7	15.0	15.2	15.3	15.0	15.3									
27.0	27.1	27.4	27.5	27.6	27.8									
618.5	644.4	650.3	660.1	677.7	679.9									
665.3	691.9	699.2	709.9	728.0	731.1									
103,829	106,611	108,800	112,800	121,813	123,216	123,689	124,526	124,300	123,800	122,625	122,300	119,900	119,200	118,181
2,085	2,155	2,257	2,332	2,178	2,285	2,483	2,619	2,770	2,914	2,992	3,168	3,337	3,632	3,639
2,141,079	2,442,312	2,769,317	3,110,606											
2,184,588	2,481,097	2,808,295	3,164,804	3,626,021	4,006,498	4,361,913	4,700,143	5,069,296	5,320,834	5,692,725	6,113,118			
40,114	45,560	51,378	57,410											
20,061	20,636	20,746	20,726											
40,891	46,284	52,121	58,411	66,556	73,207	79,384	85,193	91,513	95,647	101,867	108,851	114,426	118,609	
50,147	51,550	52,121	52,440	53,481	53,609	54,097	54,892	56,046	57,031	58,959	60,908	62,238	62,613	

Table 10-7. *EDF power capacity (annual production below capacity)*

	Dec. 31, 1989	Dec. 31, 1990	Dec. 31, 1991
Nuclear power capacity	50,900 MW	54,000 MW	55,400 MW
(nuclear electricity annual production)	*(284.7 TWh)*	*(293.88 TWh)*	*(312.62 TWh)*
Conventional thermal power capacity	16,200 MW	16,100 MW	16,000 MW
(conventional electricity annual production)	*(26.3 TWh)*	*(26.04 TWh)*	*(36.54 TWh)*
Hydroelectric power capacity	23,100 MW	23,200 MW	23,300 MW
(hydroelectric annual production)	*(46.2 TWh)*	*(52.08 TWh)*	*(56.84 TWh)*
Total capacity	90,200 MW	93,200 MW	94,700 MW
(Total annual production)	*(357.2 TWh)*	*(372 TWh)*	*(406 TWh)*

The plan contracts

Introduction

Since EDF's establishment in 1946, most of the French electric industry has been a public monopoly. The nationalization allowed the government to exert a direct and permanent control on the sector. The government got into the habit of authoritatively intervening in EDF's industrial policy and management, particularly for pricing and investment matters.

In 1971, the government and the firm decided to adopt a new way of cooperation: the plan contract. Several ministries are EDF's partners, generally the Ministry of Finance and the Ministry of Industry. Therefore, EDF became a public monopoly regulated "by contract." Under this plan, the EDF and the State sign a contract defining the objectives to be attained.

Four plan contracts followed after the first experiment in 1971 in spite of economic crises and energy industry difficulties. In the hard times, the contracts had to be adapted to the economic situation, and sometimes they were suddenly cancelled. The first contract was broken as a consequence of the oil shock in 1973. Nevertheless, EDF and the government were willing to keep this kind of relationship, for it gives the firm relative autonomy and helps the government to define aims, even if those aims are not always precise.

The following subsections provide some general remarks concerning the theory of natural monopoly regulation suggested by the analysis of plan contracts, and consider in detail State–EDF plan contracts according to their historical and economic evolution.

Monopoly regulation

The theory of natural monopoly regulation, essentially developed for private firms, takes into account the difficulties generated by the regulator's lack of information about the firm's characteristics. The firm knows its technology better than the regulator does and disposes of control variables (effort level, input allocation) that cannot be observed by the regulator. This informational advantage enables the firm to capture an informational rent that is costly to the regulator.

The optimal regulation amounts to a trade-off between a cost-plus type of regulation and a price-cap type of regulation. Cost-plus regulation makes possible the elimination of the monopoly's informational rent, but the monopoly has then no interest in minimizing its costs. Price-cap regulation gives to the firm good incentives to minimize costs, but it leaves to the monopoly large informational rents.

This theory opens numerous debates, both theoretical and applied. For instance, to what extent is it desirable to stimulate the monopoly by competition with substitutes of the monopoly's outputs? Which sector of the monopoly activity has to be opened to competition? (The latter is a question of liberalization.) Is price-cap regulation better than a rate-of-return regulation?

In Europe, and particularly in France, the natural monopolies often have been nationalized, as it is the case for electricity. Let us recall some advantages and failings of public ownership, as they are understood by economists. Shortcomings include the following:

- The absence of control of the managers' performance by the capital market.
- The absence of the discipline imposed by the bankruptcy process (soft budget constraint).
- The fear that the managers may have their specific investments in the firm expropriated by the State (lack of long-term commitment by the state).
- The multiplicity of purposes making control of the managers difficult.
- The effects of political pressure groups.

Among the nationalization advantages are the following:

- The possibility for the State to use nationalized firms to reach social goals different from profit maximization.
- The possibility of a centralized control eliminating conflicts between the shareholders and the regulator.

It is noteworthy that such arguments do not always distinguish between a regulated private firm and a public firm. The State intervenes in both cases;

only the property rights are different. Only a study in an incomplete contracts framework allows one to theorize about this distinction.

The study of the State–EDF contracts shows the importance of nonfulfillment of contracts and of financial constraints. The first issue is well known but difficult to handle. Nonfulfillment reflects either inability to conceive the future, or the complexity of costs induced by a complete specification of the contracts. In both cases, the instruments of analysis seem inadequate. The second issue concerning financial constraints is more easily handled. Why is the State not the banker of its regulated firms? How can financial constraints allow better control of the managers? To regulate public firms, what should the State substitute for the capital market as a means of controlling managers?

Also note the multiprincipal character of the State–firm relationship. There is not a single principal seeking the maximization of social welfare; there are several principals (the signatory ministries) pursuing different aims. The Ministry of Finance, as a shareholder, is concerned about its investment's financial performance and about the inflation rate, and it must be distinguished from the Ministry of Industry, which is concerned about industrial policy and the success of the electric industry. A realistic regulation model should take into account this duality.

Another remark concerns the time limitation of the state's commitment, the importance of renegotiation, and ratchet effects.

The emphasis put on marketing and price-independent consumption forecasts reveals the importance that the partners in the contract give to the dependence of demand on marketing efforts. It is an underestimated point of the theory of regulation that could, however, be handled with the same technique as information asymmetries on costs. Last, the role of the choice of products and of R&D is noteworthy and still little studied by the theory of regulation.

State–EDF plan contracts

The pioneer: The 1971 program contract: The first plan contract (1971–5) was the first attempt to formalize the relationship between the State and the firm EDF. It has two government representatives, being signed by both the Ministry of Finance and the Ministry of Industry. The contract is preceded by a letter from the two ministers enclosing elements not appearing in the contract itself. This letter explains that EDF is a State monopoly whose duty is to maximize social welfare through the choice of its pricing policy, its diversification of outputs, and its quality levels. Furthermore, EDF must give preference to French raw materials in order to help the industrial policy, the firm is not allowed to develop itself by vertical integration, its investments must have preliminary approval, and its management is to be rewarded a posteriori.

The three important objectives of the first plan contract are the decrease of costs, the optimal use of capital resources, and an efficient commercial policy.

Quantitative aims are set, most of them for the first two years only, as follows:

- The average growth of production on the period has to be 4.85%.
- The rate of return on assets must be at least 8% in 1971 and 8.3% in 1972.
- The rate of price increase must be below 1.85%.
- Constraints on absolute cash flow and cash flow per unit must be respected.

Furthermore, any new State contribution to the capital of the firm will be rewarded with an interest rate of 5%, and quantitative limits are set to shareholding by EDF in other firms. And last, if EDF surpasses the objectives, the firm will be free to use its additional resources (Article 16). Article 18 is particularly interesting: "Whatever the results of the present contract are, they cannot question the application of wage agreements signed between the firm's management and the staff's representatives." In the post-1968 period, the absence of profit-sharing incentives for employees is laid down as a principle.

The contract includes nothing precise about quality regulation of EDF's outputs. It is important to notice that the contract is written for a single environmental scenario: the GNP's rate of growth of 6%, a price rate of increase of 2%, and consumption of 200 Twh in 1975.

In other respects, Article 17 specifies that if in any year one of the objectives is not reached, the State can suspend the execution of the contract. If the circumstances change, EDF and the State will renegotiate. This reveals the lack of commitment on both sides, especially because the renegotiation procedure is not specified.

Referring to the literal concept of contract, this first program contract between the State and EDF cannot be regarded as a contract, for there is no real commitment and no penalty is specified.

But, in a way, the program contract allows some deviations from the expected circumstances, deviations adaptable and unquestionable enough to allow quasi-automatic readjustments extending the contract commitment domain. And even if penalties are not explicit, they are implicitly felt by the management. Each deviation from the contract can easily become a pretext for the State to authoritatively modify the management staff and, overall, the management's efforts to free itself from the State's tutelage could be questioned. Actually, the environment did not behave as forecast by the program contract, and in 1971 and 1972 important additional clauses had to be negotiated. In 1973, the oil shock severity led to the abandonment of the first program contract. Tables 10-8 to 10-11 illustrate the gaps between forecasts and realizations.

Table 10-8. *Rate of return (in percentages)*

	1971	1972	1973	1974
Provided end 1970	8	8.3	—	—
Provided end 1971	7.5	7.6	7.8	—
Provided end 1972	—	8.2	8.4	8.6

Table 10-9. *Cash flow (in percentages)*

	1971	1972	1973	1974
Provided end 1970	17.8	18.9	—	—
Provided end 1971	15.8	15.5	14.5	—
Provided end 1972	—	20.0	19.1	19.0

Table 10-10. *Investment program (in million francs)*

	1971	1972	1973	1974
Provided end 1970	5,070	5,790	—	—
Provided end 1971	5,125	5,923	6,254	—
Provided end 1972	—	5,920	6,400	6,900

Table 10-11. *Used price growth expectations (in percentages)*

	1971	1972	1973	1974	1975
end 1970	2.5	2.5	2.5	2.5	2.5
end 1971	5.2	3.9	2.5	—	—
end 1972	5.5	5.2	2.5	—	—

The second plan contract: An illusion of contract: In 1984, EDF signs a new contract for the period 1985–9, but with the Ministry of Industry only. Two essential goals are fixed: to decrease production and distribution costs, and to sell at best the electricity produced by a very efficient nuclear program. In the second plan contract, the concern for quality appears clearly, and diverse quality measures are studied. A single quantitative quality measure is finally adopted: the connections must be done in less than two weeks. General pricing principles are stated: uniformity of low-voltage tariffs in the whole country, absence of discrimination, incentives to use long-run contracts and optional contracts. Again, quantitative sales objectives, independent from prices, are stated: from 370 to 390 Twh in 1990.

Except for pricing, the second plan contract shows the same shortcomings as the first: the statement of a set of quantitative objectives provided for a single, very precise environment. The objectives are 5% growth rate of prices, dollar at 8 F, 38 hours working week, particular prices of coal and oil, fixed interest rates. The new objectives are the following:

- The average production cost of electricity must decrease by 3%.
- The price of electricity must obey a price cap set at the price index, minus 1%.
- A self-financing constraint of 48% is imposed on the investments, which are always controlled by the State.

To such quantitative aims, remarkable by their weak commitment value, are added many nonverifiable qualitative obligations concerning social policy, R&D policy, and industrial policy. The EDF is even asked to contribute to the authorities' actions in favour of developing countries (Article 13).

Even if the awareness of the quality issue and the use of a price-cap tariff are improvements, this second plan contract appears rather like a regress compared to the first one – by the absence of the main participant, the Ministry of Finance, with which pricing is negotiated, and by the multiplication of objectives, which makes the control of management even more difficult.

As with the first program contract, the forecasts were wrong, but it seems that no additional clause existed, confirming the poor reality of the contract.

The third plan contract: EDF (relative) emancipation: The third plan contract, signed for the period 1989–92, is a real improvement as a contract. It is signed by EDF with the Ministry of Economy, the Ministry of Finance and Budget, and the Ministry of Industry and Territory Planning.

The contract returns to a progressive gain of autonomy for EDF by adopting a pluriannual investment program and by specifying commitments independent from the economic situation. "Only particularly favorable or unfavorable economic conditions could lead to a revision of the clauses of the contract," specifically according to Article 10: GNP average rate of growth of the period exceeding 3.5% or below 1.5%.

An important change with respect to the other contracts is the requirement to set up profit-sharing schemes for EDF's employees. Thus, the state intervenes in the firm's internal regulation in a way opposite to the first program contract (Article 18).

The second plan contract price-cap scheme is reinforced by being tied to a rate of decrease of electricity real prices of 1.5% instead of 1%. It is a price cap on the average rate of growth of the period. However, a sentence from Article 2 makes questionable the firm's real autonomy about its pricing policy. It reads: "The Firm and the Authorities set as an objective the average decrease of price of 1.5% per year in real terms."

The financial objectives include a 20 billion franc decrease of the debt in addition to the investment program. The firm is getting more autonomy for the intertemporal planning of its investments. It is, however, noteworthy that these investments are quality-improving investments; nothing is said about production investments in this period of excess capacity.

Quality is now the forefront issue, after having been delayed during the years of nuclear development. A great number of quality indicators are set up in order to easily compare the French results to international standards. However, there is no quantitative commitment, except to "reduce by half the number of worst supplied customers" between 1988 and 1992.

A greater freedom is left to EDF to extend the scope if its interests (Article 5), in agreement with the European concern for the absence of cross-subsidies provided from the main activity.

Article 3 shows the desire to consider the state to be an ordinary shareholder. It states: "The interest rate will be of 5%. The State payment will be complemented by a dividend determined according to the firm's results." Article 3 is very vague, for nothing defines the allocation of this dividend. What is the freedom of the firm's managers in such a case?

Another weakness rests in Article 9, which is about an annual follow-up of the contract execution by the authorities, even though there is no annual commitment in this contract, for all the quantitative commitments are in average on the whole period.

The 1989–92 plan contract was successful insofar as its objectives of price, of debt decrease, and of investment were reached. These results led to the renewal of the plan contract in 1993, with some new features essentially tied to the evolution of environmental concerns.

The 1993–1996 plan contract: The fourth plan contract defines new general objectives, as follows.

The first one is to reach a very low debt around year 2005, when it will be time to renew the nuclear power plants. Then, the absolute priority of security in nuclear power plants is recalled. The carrying out of quality improvement, the development of electricity-efficient uses (least-cost planning), a new effort toward protecting the environment, and the internationalization of the activities are also brought up.

The need for an incentive management of labor is emphasized in a context of guaranteed employment and of long-run management of human resources. The State's concern for employment still appears but in a way compatible with an always greater competitiveness of EDF.

The contract specifies precise quantitative commitments to be respected, unless particularly favorable or unfavorable environmental modification would result.

The debt must decrease by 40 billion francs in the duration of the contract, and measures are adopted for the debt decrease objective not to be disturbed by the setup of holdings created to manage EDF's international activities. The average price cap on the period is fixed at 1.25% below the growth rate of prices.

Article 3 seems to depart from the balanced-budget principle by introducing an additional payment to the State beyond the service of the debt. As a shareholder, the State seems willing to share the profits that could be generated by the new incentive policy.

Numerous quality measures are considered, some of them by sampling consumers. The average duration of service breaks for all consumers must decrease by 20% during the contract period. Experiments will be made in establishing a procedure for consumers' compensation.

Investment is still defined jointly by the State and EDF (144 billion francs), essentially allocated to the distribution of electricity, but the firm is free to plan its investments within the period.

The new concern for the environment is shown by the commitment of 4.5 billion francs to bury electric lines and of 3 billion francs to reduce pollution in thermal production (the objective is a decrease by 50% of SO^2 emissions and 25% of NO emissions).

The international activity of EDF is formalized by the statement of the principle of disallowing cross-subsidies from national accounts to foreign accounts. To facilitate the application of this principle, a specific holding called EDF International is established.

The commercial policy includes least-cost planning and pricing improvements with the spreading of a new domestic peak-load pricing through use of the blue-white-red option tariffs among 300,000 subscribers. (For a detailed analysis of these tariffs, see pages 455–456).

A great R&D program is defined but without precise qualifications. The State trusts the firm to guarantee its future competitiveness. Nevertheless, the State introduces the need for an agreement for long-term delivery contracts. It wants to keep the control of EDF's expansion, lest EDF be tempted to become the electricity supplier for Europe. Four ministers have signed the fourth plan contract, causing a certain stabilization in the State–EDF contracts.

This historical perspective shows how State–EDF relationships have been dealt with by use of contracts in periods in which there were no major developments (hydroelectric or nuclear) when the importance of investments led to a strict ministerial control. The evolution of contracts illustrates the possibility of innovation in the regulation of public firms. The future will tell us whether the relative decentralization of decisions allowed by the plan contracts will resist the great new wave of investments starting in 2005.

EDF pricing

Introduction: Institutional principles and marginal-cost pricing

Because of its public interest role, EDF is subject to institutional constraints defined by the nationalization law and those of the program or plan contracts. Its pricing policy must achieve budget balance, equity among consumers, and economic efficiency.

Budget balance: Budget balance was one of the earliest constraints imposed on the nationalized company EDF: Electricity had to become a public, national, and rapidly financially autonomous industry. Above all, the government was unwilling to provide for the needs of a public firm with a chronic deficit. On the other hand, budget balance does not allow for net profits: any surplus must just cover the debt. This requirement imposes on EDF the need to adjust very precisely the relationship between the cost of resources and the operating and investment expenses. This adjustment is made essentially by pricing.

Equity: The constraint of equity among consumers is another issue of the nationalization law. The principle of equity demands that each consumer pay what it costs to supply electricity to that consumer. This cost corresponds to the producer's long-term marginal cost.

Logically, equity implies personalized prices, for the costs supported by the producer can be different from one consumer to another. In practice, except for some important customers actually treated individually, it would be too costly to charge personalized prices. Price equalizations are therefore made. The consumers are aggregated in groups that pay an average price. Furthermore, price equalizations are required by the government for social redistribution goals; geographical price equalizations are imposed on all the domestic customers of low-voltage electricity, for example.

Economic efficiency: Economists in the EDF have wished to give the firm the best pricing possible – optimal pricing. In theory, the optimum is implemented when price equals marginal cost: each consumer has to pay for electricity supply the exact amount it costs the community to serve that consumer.

Resulting from theoretical and experimental research conducted by former companies before nationalization, marginal-cost pricing has become traditional for EDF. Applied since the establishment of EDF, it has never met serious opposition. Optimal pricing must take into account the institutional constraint of budget balance, but in the short run, marginal-cost pricing generally does not provide budget balance. In the case of increasing returns to scale, as it is for EDF, marginal-cost pricing leads to losses. This gap has to be made up by the use of "peages."

With a personalized pricing founded on marginal cost, all the consumers know the social cost of their consumption, they know that their invoice will take into account good decisions as well as wasteful behavior, and they can modify their consumption accordingly. Marginal-cost pricing gives to the consumers appropriate incentives for their choices in consumption and investment.

Marginal-cost pricing is limited by the need for price equalization and by the management costs of sophisticated pricing formulas. Another restriction on the practice of optimal pricing comes from the public firm obedience to the State, though it is juridically protected by a plan contract. Economic policies are the main reason for charging prices different from long-term marginal cost. Tariff manipulations are not rare in case of necessity. The oil crisis of 1974 required such manipulation in the electricity industry.

Price determination

EDF's pricing follows a logical process, the starting point of which is the observation of both consumption and costs. Owing to the regularity of the consumption patterns observed, EDF's pricing division was rapidly able to define a price schedule according to the similarity of consumption patterns, and therefore to the similarity of induced costs. The marginal cost in a given tariff period so defined showed, however, some remaining heterogeneity that was generated by diversity in load use in the period. The heterogeneous marginal cost of each tariff period was then approximated by a menu of two-part tariffs, which became the basis of EDF's two-part pricing. Later, the emergence of stochastic peak-load periods suggested the use of real-time pricing schemes, a step toward spot pricing.

Study of the demand and definition of tariff periods: Knowledge of demand is essential for the electric producer to solve two simultaneous problems: (1) short-run optimal management of existing production plants (starting the different technologies as and when required, stopping for maintenance), and (2) long-run adjustment in capacity and structure of means of production, transportation, and distribution, to the evolution of demand investment policy.

The study of the annual electric consumption uses a graph called the "power monotone," which gives the position of each of the 8,760 hours of the year in descending order of power demanded for each hour (see Figure 10-1). In particular, the power monotone exhibits the number of hours when consumption is significantly above average – the peak it is necessary to know about to be able to adjust production. Electricity being a nonstorable good, it is necessary to be able to make immediate adjustments in both production and consumption.

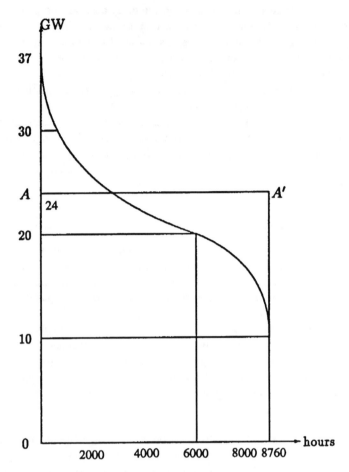

Figure 10-1. Example of power monotone

The power monotone shows how long consumption exceeds a given power but does not show at what time. Peak-load (and off-peak) position and height are given by the load curves, describing electricity consumption chronologically (see Figure 10-2).

These curves confirm the intuition of the existence of a daily cycle of consumption (two peaks, one at about 12:00 noon, and another at about 8:00 P.M., slack at night), a weekly cycle (consumption higher during the weekdays than on Sunday), and an annual cycle tied to the seasons (a much higher consumption in winter than in summer). These cycles depend on the main uses of electric power (lighting, heating, industrial uses) and on lasting structural phenomena such as labor organization and seasons.

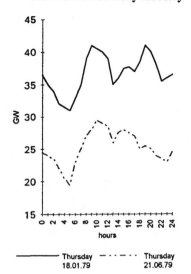

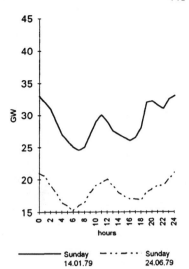

—— Thursday 18.01.79	— · — · · Thursday 21.06.79
—— Sunday 14.01.79	— · — · · Sunday 24.06.79

Annual Consumption Evolution

Average consumption in working days

— · — · · true values   —— values for normal temperature conditions

Figure 10-2. Daily load curves and annual consumption evolution in 1979

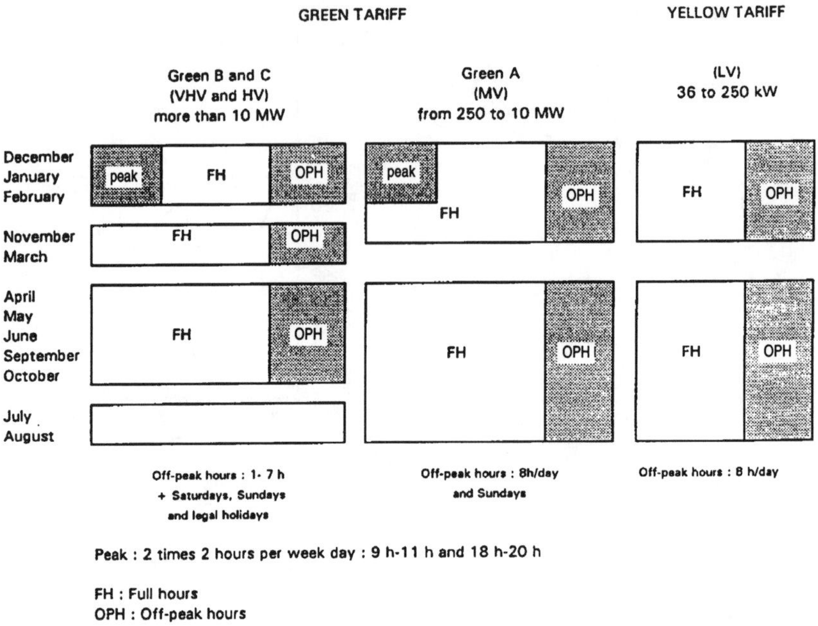

Figure 10-3. Horoseasonal structure of green and yellow tariffs

The relative stability of the consumption cycles leads to the derivation of a price schedule. The 8,760 hours of the year are divided into sets of identical electricity consumption. These sets of hours form the foundation of the horoseasonal pricing charged by EDF. See Figure 10-3, which shows horoseasonal structure of green and yellow tariffs.

The horoseasonal periods are defined so as to have the following characteristics:

- Marginal costs relatively homogeneous within each period.
- Meter and management costs generated by a more sophisticated pricing (one period more) not higher than benefits.
- An incentive scheme leading each consumer to choose the price corresponding to EDF's cost for that consumer.

Marginal costs and technological choices: Because EDF's pricing is based on the long-term marginal cost (or development marginal cost), let us first notice the difference between short- and long-term marginal costs:

- The short-term marginal cost of a supply is the additional cost of production, transportation, and distribution that results from any additional supply, with fixed production capacity.
- The long-term marginal cost of a supply is the additional cost of production, transportation, and distribution that results from any additional supply for a given year when this demand is far enough ahead in time for the electric power producer to be able to modify capacities.

Calculation of short-term marginal cost: The short-term marginal cost is the sum of an operating cost that depends on technical characteristics of the power stations (fuel, performance) and a failure cost that depends on the risk of not being able to provide the demanded energy.

Operating costs of power plants with various technologies differ. EDF's own production units are very diverse in size and technology. A main parameter affecting costs is power plant adaptability, which is defined by the time needed to start production and the ability to vary the power.

Let us examine briefly the characteristics of the various technologies available to EDF.

Hydroelectric power plants differ according to their water storage capacity and therefore, their potential energy production is affected by the following:

- The lake storage basins can keep a whole season's water, sometimes a whole year's.
- The lock storage basins storage capacity does not exceed a day.
- The downstream stations cannot actually keep stores.
- The pumping-up stations, where high basins are filled by pumping water up from low basins when electricity is cheap (at night, for instance). This water is then turbined in peak-load periods when electricity is expensive.

For all hydroelectric plants, investment cost is very high and operating cost very low. Adaptable and fast to run (almost instantaneously), they are very useful in peak-load periods. Against them are two weaknesses: their geographical limitation and their sensitivity to the weather.

Thermal power plants in EDF production are of three types as follows:

- Nuclear power plants need very costly investments, but the production cost is low. Production is not adaptable; starting is slow and power cannot vary.
- Oil- or coal-fired thermal power plants (or conventional power plants) have lower initial investment costs but production costs are quite high because of the fuel price. It is a moderately adaptable technology. The starting time is short, and it is possible to adjust the amount of power produced.

■ Gas turbine technology is cheap in investment and very expensive in use. Because it is highly adaptable, its use is reserved for peak-load periods. Starting is immediate, and power is produced at request.

The EDF coordinates the use of its heterogeneous set of power plants to satisfy demand constantly and at the lowest price. In the short run, this is achieved by starting the various plants in increasing order of operating cost, without consideration for investment cost: first hydroelectric power stations, then nuclear, then conventional thermal, until the demand is satisfied. The great adaptability of hydroelectric plants makes it better to keep them for peak-load use, when they are a lot cheaper than gas turbines.

Failure cost: Failure (an excess demand situation) can happen either if demand grows in an unpredictable way (very cold weather) or if supply falls (breakdown of means of production, transport, or distribution). There are two steps in a failure. The first step is characterized by the starting of the costliest power stations, the overcharge of transportation and distribution networks, the drop in voltage, uncommon imports, and the use of disabled production units. In this stage, demand is still satisfied, but the producer sustains exceptional costs of production: the beginning of the failure cost. In the second step of the failure, demand cannot be satisfied any more, and there is cutoff. It is only at this stage that customers support the failure. By then the failure cost becomes difficult to evaluate, for failure cost represents the social damage due to the cutoff.

Calculation of long-term marginal cost: When we envision changes of production capacity, pricing must be based on long-term marginal cost, as it is for EDF.

The necessary modification of capacity is made by anticipating by one year an investment already provided for the next year. The cost of this modification in investment planning is the anticipation cost.

The long-term marginal cost is the sum of the operating cost (according to the technology as detailed earlier) and the anticipation cost. For a given technology, the anticipation cost is the sum of the following three items:

■ The unit investment cost, multiplied by the rate of discount given by the commissioner of the plan expressing the intertemporal social cost of public funds.
■ The first year amortization of the added capacity.
■ The operating fixed cost of the new equipment for the first year.

Equality property of short-term and long-term marginal costs: When the whole sector – production, transportation, and distribution – is optimal, short-term marginal cost and long-term marginal cost are equal. This is a general property of optimal systems, verified when indivisibilities are negligible. Given the scale of the French electric industry, one can regard a unit investment as small when it is compared to the whole system. Because of this, at the optimum, it is equivalent to calculate long-term or short-term marginal cost, and it is equivalent to base the pricing on long-term or short-term marginal cost.

Technological choice, marginal cost, and price schedules: Production outlets of the same technology create the same marginal cost for the producer. The obvious relationship between technology and marginal cost allows us to use the technology to define the price schedules.

Let us consider a simplified case in which three technologies are available (see Figure 10-4).

- A basic technology, nuclear power, providing most of the demand, up to the power of k_3 GW. The marginal cost curve C^3 of this technology reflects its high cost investment and its very low operation cost.
- A peak-load technology, gas turbines, which are highly adaptable. They can provide up to the power of k_1 GW. Their marginal cost curve C^1 shows low investment cost and high operating cost.
- An intermediate technology, conventional (oil or coal) thermal, with medium capacity and operating costs, relaying nuclear power when it itself is not sufficient. Suppose conventional power can provide up to the power of k_2 GW, with a marginal cost function represented by C^2.

The upper part of Figure 10-4 shows the marginal costs of each technology i: $C^i = C_d^i + hC_f^i$ with C_d^i the (marginal) development cost of technology i; C_f^i the (marginal) operating cost of technology i; h the length of use (hours).

As long as demand is below k_3 GW, nuclear power is enough to satisfy it. This period of basic demand (8,760 hours $-H_2$) corresponds in EDF to 300 days, so 7,200 hours a year.

When power demand is over k_3 GW (but stays under $k_2 + k_3$), it is necessary to start the oil- and coal-fired stations, in addition to nuclear plants. This technological combination can provide up to the power of $k_3 + k_2$. If energy demand exceeds $(k_3 + k_2)$ GW, it is a peak-load demand, and gas turbines are added. Above $(k_3 + k_2 + k_1)$ GW, the electric system cannot supply all the demanded power, and there is failure.

Price determination from marginal costs

Marginal-cost heterogeneity in a single tariff period: Marginal costs of a tariff period remain heterogeneous according to the power demanded and the time of use of this power. For this reason it is useful to discriminate among the various consumption patterns within each tariff period.

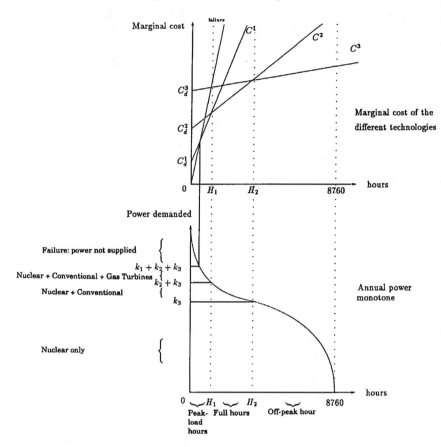

C^1 : marginal cost of gas turbines
C^2 : marginal cost of conventional thermal power plants
C^3 : marginal cost of nuclear power plant

Figure 10-4.

The pair power/time of use is often described usefully by a single variable, the load factor, varying in [0, 1]. The load factor is the ratio of the average power to the maximum power. It gives a measure of the capacity use in a period. The higher the load factor is, the more fully energy is used. A small load factor reveals great consumption irregularities, as does the existence of high peaks. The load factor grows as the load curve gets flat and marginal cost decreases. A high marginal cost is associated with a low load factor; irregular supplies require relatively more fixed-capacity costs.

marginal cost price

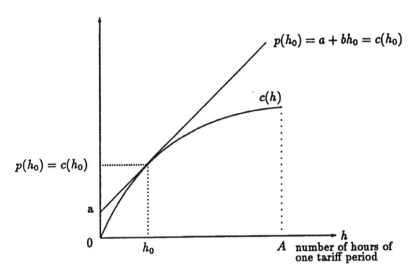

Figure 10-5.

Approximation of marginal cost in a tariff period by a menu of two-part tariffs: For a given tariff period, empirical observations show that the marginal cost is an increasing, concave function of the time of use h. During this tariff period, for a consumption of time h_0, the optimal price is the straight line $p(h_0)$. Price equals marginal cost (see Figure 10-5).

For longer use, $h_1 > h_0$, the optimal price is the straight line $p'(h_1) = a' + b'h_1$ such that $p'(h_1) = c(h_1)$ (see Figure 10-6). This price, different from the short-use price, permits the long-use consumers to self-select the proper tariff.

Actually, it would be more expensive for consumers of time of use h_1, to pay $p(h_1)$ than $p'(h_1)$, and conversely, it would be more expensive for consumers of time of use h_0 to pay the price defined for long use: $p'(h_0) > p(h_0)$. The definition of a price for short use and a price for long use reflects the difference in marginal cost between these two periods of use.

Faced with a menu of two-part tariffs, the consumers choose the more suitable price according to their pattern of use (see Figure 10-7). The EDF has defined the following four ranges of time of use:

- Short-use pricing
- General pricing
- Long-use pricing
- Very long-use pricing

marginal cost price

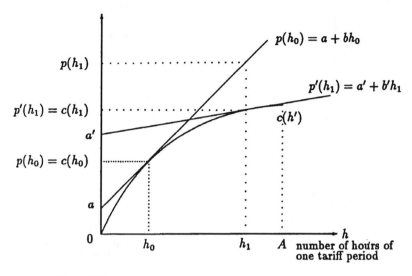

Figure 10-6.

Calculation of the two-part tariff: The two-part tariff charged (per unit of subscribed power) for a given type of consumption, of use duration h_0, takes the form $a + bh_0$ where a is the price of power and b is the price of energy (kWh). At the optimum, this price equals the development marginal cost of this particular type of consumption.

The marginal cost consists of two terms: a variable term corresponding to the fuel marginal cost depending on the time of use h, and a fixed term corresponding to the development marginal cost depending on the peak responsibility $f(h)$.

$$c(h) = \underbrace{\alpha h}_{\text{combustible}} + \underbrace{\beta f(h)}_{\text{development}}$$

For a consumption of time h_0, at the optimum:

$$p(h_0) = c(h_0)$$

$$a + bh_0 = \alpha h_0 + \beta f(h_0)$$

with

$$b = \frac{dc}{dh}(h_0) = \alpha + \beta \frac{df}{dh}(h_0) \quad \text{(slope of marginal cost)}$$

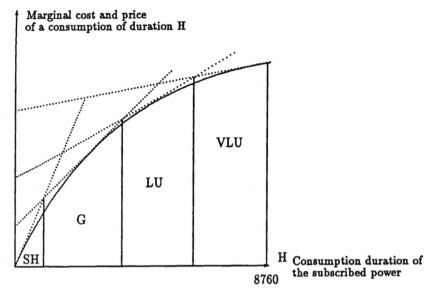

Figure 10-7. Menu of two-part tariffs

hence

$$a = \beta f(h_0) - \beta h_0 \frac{df}{dh} (h_0)$$

so the optimal pricing for a consumption of time of use h_0 is:

$$p(h_0) = a + b h_0$$

with

$$
\begin{cases}
p(h_0 = c(h_0) \\
a = \beta f(h_0) - \beta h_0 \dfrac{df}{dh} (h_0) \\
b = \alpha + \beta \dfrac{df}{dh} (h_0)
\end{cases}
$$

Peak-load pricing and stochastic demand: Because in peak-load days the cost of electricity is the highest, it is important to decrease consumption during this time by charging a specific peak-load tariff.

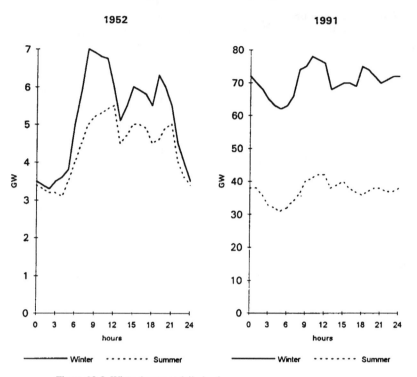

Figure 10-8. Winter/summer daily load curves

Peak-load demand tendencies: The demand tends to move in three main ways: regular increase of global consumption, smoothing of everyday consumption, and strengthening of seasonality in the direction of growing winter demand. The two last tendencies are the cause for a drastic change of the load curves and of the location of peaks. Influenced by price signals, everyday demand becomes more homogeneous: Off-peak consumption grows, peak-load consumption decreases, the load curves are smoothed. Changes in way of life and labor organization produce a decrease of activity and a consequent reduction in electricity demand in summer and on Saturday. Last, the development of electric heating has caused an important concentration of electricity demand in winter, especially on the coldest days, linking electricity consumption to a stochastic weather parameter (see Figure 10-8).

The emergence of peak loads caused by heating has created a pricing scheme that takes into account the random characteristics of demand that result from changes in the weather.

EDF pricing response to stochastic peak loads: Optional tariffs: To take into account the random weather parameters of the marginal cost, EDF proposes a specific pricing in real time in which periods move according to the climate. The advantage of movable-periods pricing is that it permits the producer to make the price equal with the actually observed marginal cost, instead of the expected marginal cost, as with fixed-periods pricing. The obstacle to pricing in real time is the adaptability of both producer and consumers. The producer has to be able to announce an unpredictable peak load and its cost, in real time or on a very short notice, and the consumers have to be able to respond by immediately adapting their consumption. That is the reason EDF prefers to charge pricing in real time in an optional way, to be chosen only by customers adaptable enough to offset meter and setting costs. On the other hand, EDF offers simple options to enable most customers to make rapid adjustments in consumption when peaks occur.

Consumers now have the following three pricing options:

- The EJP option (Option Effacement Jours de Pointe) for the relief of level of consumption on peak days.
- The tariff-adaptable option for only the most important consumers.
- The BWR (blue-white-red) option, which is set for low-voltage domestic customers.

Toward spot pricing? Spot pricing reflects cost with almost perfect accuracy, for it consists in announcing and charging at every moment the instantaneous marginal cost of the production system. This ideal is not easy to carry out, for it creates problems that are difficult to overcome, and it risks disturbing incentives for consumers' investment choices. Faced with such difficulties, EDF has opted for a progressive policy of pricing in real time. Deliberately simple, the EJP option appeals to many consumers who gradually get accustomed to this type of price signal.

Demand response to pricing: Designed for a given demand, this pricing has induced consumers to make changes in their consumption, especially peak-load and off-peak consumption, and in return pricing had to adapt to these changes. After 35 years of long-term marginal-cost pricing, the use of electricity is better distributed and more homogeneous. Peak-load production is therefore cheaper.

Figure 10-9 shows the flattening of the French daily load curve between 1952 and 1975. The four curves represent the hourly average reduced power of working days in the third week of January for the four years 1952, 1957, 1965, and 1975. The hourly reduced power (ratio of power over hourly mean power) permits a better comparison among the curves, for it neutralizes global consumption growth.

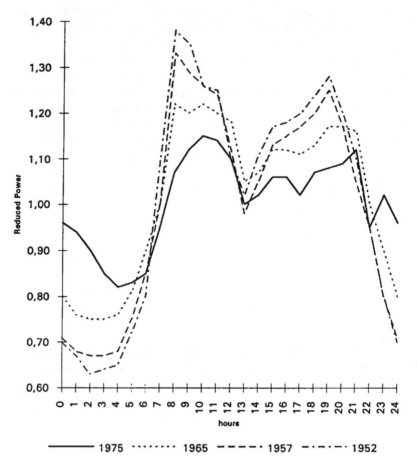

Figure 10-9. Load curve evolution (reduced power) from 1952 to 1975

Description of the French tariff system

The three main tariffs: Customers of EDF have been divided according to the marginal cost they cause to the electric production system into five large groups of nearly homogeneous consumption. The five customer groups correspond to five tariff groups and are distributed among three main tariffs: the green, the yellow, and the blue. The green tariff is further divided into three parts: green tariff A, B, and C.

Green tariff and yellow tariff: The green tariff is the pioneer of EDF's long-term marginal-cost pricing, having been set up in 1957. It concerns the most important customers, for industrial and professional uses, in medium, high, and very high voltage. The yellow tariff has been charged since 1984 to smaller industrial and service industry customers which are supplied in low voltage.

From the yellow tariff to green tariffs A, B, and C, consumption is growing in power, tension, and energy, the marginal cost is decreasing and the prices are showing an increasing fixed premium (power price) and a decreasing energy price. Horoseasonal partitions of these four tariffs are of increasing complexity, as can be seen from Figure 10-3, page 442. Actually, the greater the consumption is, the more profitable is a sophisticated pricing, for meter and setting costs become negligible with respect to the gains obtained from consumption adaptation.

The EDF's annual report lists users of the green tariff B and C and users of the yellow and green A tariffs.

- B and C green tariffs: The customers are 875 industrials supplied with high voltage (tariff B) and very high voltage (tariff C), for powers over 10 MW. They accounted for 21% of sales in 1989 and a consumption of 88 billion kWh. These two tariffs are the most complex, having eight horoseasonal tariff periods. The green tariff C is the only regionalized tariff charged by EDF, with six tariff zones.
- Green A and yellow tariffs: These tariffs apply to medium supplies to small industries, collectivities, services, trades, and big individual consumers. They represented 250,000 customers, 25% of sales, in 1989 and a consumption of 100 billion kWh. The green tariff A characteristics are a medium voltage between 250 kW and 10 MW, with five horoseasonal pricing periods.

Created in 1984 for low-voltage important supplies, the yellow tariff provides power between 36 and 250 kW, with four horoseasonal pricing periods. Most of this information is summed up in Tables 10-12 and 10-13.

Blue tariff: Resulting from the universal tariff set by EDF in 1965, the blue tariff is for domestic supplies in low voltage of power under 36 kW. The marginal cost of such supplies is very high, for it includes transportation, transformation, marketing, setting up of electricity meters on site, individual meter reading, and invoicing for 27 million customers. That is why the blue tariff is the most expensive pricing.

The basic blue tariff is the simplest of all EDF tariffs, for it includes only one period, one price for all of France. However, since the first days of the universal tariff in 1965, a price option that reflects off-peak hours has been proposed: eight off-peak hours a day, generally at night, beginning between 10:00 P.M. and 11:30 P.M. This option has rapidly become successful, with almost 8 million customers (almost a third of blue tariff users).

Table 10-12. *Customers and sales of EDF tariffs in 1989*

	Number of customers	% of sales	Volume of sales (in billion kWh)	Absolute value of sales (in billion francs 1989)	Average income by kWh (in centimes) 1989)
Blue tariff	27,000,000	48	116 tWh	$74,1.10^9$ F	62.6 c
Yellow tariff and green A tariff	250,000	26	110 tWh	$40,5.10^9$ F	39.8 c
Green tariff B and C	875	21	88 tWh	29.10^9 F	23.7 c

For low-voltage customers, tariff signals are neither as sophisticated nor as efficient as those for industrial customers. There are many reasons: hetero-geneity among consumers, simplicity of meter equipment, a reputation for less rationing of supply to the domestic consumer, and the obligation of price equalization, for example.

The EDF supplies 27 million consumers (23.6 million households) with the blue tariff. The blue tariff represented 48% of EDF sales in 1989, with a con-sumption of 116 billion kWh, for 74.1 billion francs.

Customer distribution among the tariffs – blue, yellow, or green – depends on the power subscribed to by the consumer. The choice of power determines the subscription fee to be paid by the consumer as the cost of access to this power.

The choice of voltage is left to the EDF, which decides according to tech-nical criteria.

Optimal tariffs in real time: Options in real time permit the pricing to be ex post efficient in spite of the occurrence of random events (especially climatic) by adapting the price instantaneously to the state of the world.

EJP option: Option for the relief of consumption on peak days: Set in 1982, this option was the first EDF experiment of pricing in real time. Its aim is to reduce (or to withdraw) electricity consumption during the costliest days of the year, that is to say, the coldest.

The peak period of the EJP option lasts 18 hours a day, 22 days a year, be-tween November 1 and March 31, for a total of 400 hours. Peak-load days are determined in real time by EDF, which gives customers at least half an hour notice. The other hours of the year remain distributed among the fixed tariff periods of the specific tariff applying to each consumer.

Table 10-13. *PLDE option customers*

	Number of customers of PLDE option	Percentage of customers of each tariff	Relief of subscribed power (MW)
Green tariff C	34	40	1,100
Green tariff B	80	25	650
Green tariff A	3,100	2.5	1,100
Yellow tariff	1,450	2.5	85

This option is now available for all customers, for every voltage, but it is logically more successful among the biggest customers. In 1990, the power relieved by customers on moveable peak-load days reached 2 GW (3% of the national peak). Table 10-13 shows the industrial and professional subscribers of the EJP option during the winter of 1988–9 and their results in this period.

Green tariff adaptable option: This option applies only to the great industrial customers already covered by the green tariff. Experimented since 1984 and set up in 1987, it is a generalization of the movable-period pricing to all the tariff periods. The year is distributed in movable weeks of three types: 24 weeks of movable off-peak season, which is the cheapest; 19 weeks of movable midseason, which is of middle price; and nine weeks of movable winter, which is of high price. The movable 22 days of peak load of the previous EJP option are superimposed on this scheme to define the earliest period, which occurs during movable winter weeks or movable midseason weeks. Table 10-14 shows the number of green tariff customers that have chosen this option.

BWR option from blue tariff (blue-white-red option): Now experimented within three cities (Clermont-Ferrand, Mulhouse, and Saint-Etienne) by 500 customers, the BWR option allows pricing in real time for domestic customers who use low voltage with the blue tariff.

The BWR option tariff includes six movable periods, distributed in three types of day and two types of hour. There are 300 very cheap blue days in the mild season, 43 middle-priced white days in midseason, and 22 high-priced red days in winter, coinciding with the movable peak load of the EJP option. Every day there are peak and off-peak hours: six off-peak hours in red days, and eight off-peak hours in both blue and white days (see Table 10-15). Customers are informed of the change of tariff period color by a visual signal.

The current experiment shows that it is in the interest of several kinds of consumers to adopt this option. Every adaptation, even in lighting, reduces the

Table 10-14. *Adaptable option customers*

	Number of customers	Percentage of customers of each tariff
Green tariff C	12	15
Green tariff B	41	15
Green tariff A	100	ε

Table 10-15. *Blue-white-red option tariff structure*

Off-peak hours 6h	Red D. O-P. H	White days Off-peak hours	Blue days Off-peak hours	8 off-peak hours
Full hours 18h	Red days Full hours	White days Full hours	Blue days Full hours	16 full hours
	22 red days	43 white days	300 blue days	

payment owned by the consumer. Prices are so constructed that without any adaptation, annual expenses are equivalent with or without subscription to BWR option.

REFERENCES

"1880–1980 Un siècle d'électricité dans le monde." Textes réunis et édités par Fabienne Cardot. PUF, Paris, 1986.

"La France des électriciens: 1880–1980." Sous la direction de Fabienne Cardot. PUF, Paris, 1986.

"Histoire de l'électricité en France: 1881–1918." Tome 1. Sous la direction de F. Caron et F. Cardot. Fayard, Paris, 1991.

"Cent ans d'électricité dans les lois." J. C. Colli. *Bulletin d'Histoire de l'Electricité,* numéro spécial. Association pour l'Histoire de l'Electricité en France, Paris, 1986.

"Chronique de 30 années d'équipement nucléaire à Electricité de France." Georges Lamiral. Association pour l'Histoire de l'Electricité en France, Paris, 1989.

"La tarification de l'électricité en France." Lionel Monier. *Economica,* Paris, 1987.

"Vingt-cinq ans d'économie électrique: Investissements, coûts marginaux et tarifs, études." G. Morlat et F. Bessiere. Dunod, Paris, 1971.

"Panorama de l'histoire de l'électricité en France dans la première moitié du XXe siècle." Henri Morsel, in "Un siècle d'électricité dans le monde." PUF, Paris, 1987.

"Histoire(s) de l'EDF." J. F. Picard, A. Beltran, M. Bungener. Dunod, Paris, 1985.

"Electricité de France, Entreprise nationale industrielle et commerciale." *Notes et Etudes Documentaires, n° 4575–76, 10 juin 1980, La Documentation Française.*

CHAPTER 11

The Yugoslav electric power industry

Srboljub Antic
Institute of Social Sciences, Belgrade, Yugoslavia

Introduction

Yugoslavia came into existence after World War I, uniting two independent states (Serbia and Montenegro) and parts of Austria–Hungary consisting of South Slav populations (Slovenia, Bosnia–Hercegovina, and Croatia). Differences in the level of development among the regions were very large, including the extent of electrification. Territory in Istria, acquired following World War II, was relatively advanced with respect to electric power. By the end of the 1980s there were almost no differences in the level of electrification, though not in consumption of electric power, among the republics. Strengthening of the republics vis-à-vis the federation, however, along with unresolved political, national, and religious questions, led to division of the country in 1991. The analysis that follows attempts to show how the industry managed to achieve a remarkable record in spite of adverse conditions.

Growth of the electric power industry before World War II

Installations for generating electricity in what later became Yugoslavia appeared near the end of the nineteenth century. The first power station began operations in the Croatian town of Duga Resa in 1884, followed in 1888 by Slovenia (Litija), Bosnia–Hercegovina (Zenica), and Serbia (Belgrade) in 1892. The first three of these were made for industrial purposes, whereas the Belgrade station satisfied municipal needs. The Belgrade station had a capacity of 440 kW, and its generators were powered by three steam engines. Very quickly thereafter power stations were built in Zagreb, Ljubljana, and other

In the course of two years during which this chapter was in preparation, I have been fortunate to have the assistance of Professor Joel Dirlam (Rhode Island University) and Professor Pavle Vasic (Institute of Social Sciences), who gave me many useful comments and with whom I discussed various problems concerning this chapter. All remaining errors are, of course, my own responsibility.

large cities. They supplied direct current and relied on oil or high-quality coal for fuel. The first alternating current was supplied by a station built in 1899 on the river Djetina at Uzice in Serbia.

The growth in manufacturing led to the construction of isolated industrial units that generated current for individual factories, most frequently textiles, and for mines. The central power central stations in towns provided for municipal needs (public lighting, pumping water, powering tramways) and household lighting. On account of consumption characteristics, most of these power stations operated only at night. The industrial and municipal features of electrification prevailed until the end of World War I. Sources of electric power were predominantly thermal, with only a few hydropower units being built.

In the period between the first and second world wars, electrification of towns gradually expanded from the center to broader surrounding areas. Current was distributed through networks of 220 and 400 volts. In places where there were neighboring towns, distribution lines were linked, creating small regional systems. More important, electric systems were not organized because the power stations supplied only a relatively small area. There were rather large differences in output among regions. Of the total output of 1,173 GWh in 1939, Macedonia accounted for 9 GWh, and Montenegro only 1 GWh. The low level of development of the electric power industry is indicated by an average output per capita of only 72 kWh in 1939.

Most of the 1,229 installations listed for 1939 were privately owned (Statistical Yearbook of Yugoslavia, Kingdom of Yugoslavia, State Statistical Service, Belgrade, 1941). Under public ownership were chiefly those power stations providing public lighting. Industrial units were completely in private hands. Funds for expansion came from two sources: the profits of private firms, and municipal budgets. Of total output in 1939, industrial use accounted for 76.9%, residential use (mainly lighting) 7.4%, public lighting 1.9%, and line loss 13.8%.

The creation of small regional systems in the period between the two wars stimulated the establishment of transmission interconnections. The voltage level was not uniform, ranging from 3 to 50 KV, and the transmission lines were fragmented.

Electrification of rural areas began in this interwar period. Although the statistics are incomplete and relatively unreliable, it is certain that the progress of rural electrification was extremely slow, which can be deduced from the very low average per-capita consumption.

Government bodies intervened in electric power only by extending certain legal privileges but did not function as important investors. Concessions assured the exclusive right of municipal enterprises, joint stock companies, or private owners to distribute and sell electric energy in a specified territory. Tariff structure was not prescribed but depended on the individual firm. The dominant feature was a flat rate for energy consumption, although there were block rates for residences in big cities, and large industrial firms had step rates or quantity and time limitations. Electric power distributors attempted aggressively to increase consumption, and adopted rate structures that would stimulate expenditure on additional use.

The limited regulatory experience prior to World War II had nothing to offer authorities subsequent to 1945. A socialist economy, diametrically the contrary in its fundamentals to the previous system, established its own regulatory institutions.

The economic system of Yugoslavia

Although usually classified and self-identified as a socialist country, postwar Yugoslavia's economy differed in important respects from that of other countries of East Europe. Only during the years 1945–52 did a centralized command economy function in Yugoslavia. In the constitution of 1950, and by subsequent amendments, Yugoslavia adopted a system of self-management that in principle was to convey a large degree of autonomy on all productive units, although the units were not set up as profit-making enterprises. The new system represented a divergence from the majority point of view that socialism required centralized planning and decisionmaking. The processes of capital formation and investment, however, still remained largely within the jurisdiction of the central government. Only with the adoption of a new constitution in 1963, which led to economic reforms culminating in 1965, were key decisions left to the self-managed business enterprises.

The 1965 reform embodied also a radical turn toward the establishment of a market economy that would determine commodity prices, allocate income among workers, and guide participation in international trade. After a few years, however, the attempt to associate self-management with free markets had to be jettisoned. Ostensibly this policy reversal was the result of developments held to be incompatible with socialist ideology: unemployment, transfer of enterprise decisionmaking power from workers to managers and technical experts, failure of some firms, and the appearance of a rudimentary capital market.

As was so often the case in Yugoslavia, several years went by before the official policy change was fully realized in enterprise organization, behavior, and financial accounts. Self-management was modified by the 1974 constitution and later legislation to emphasize the concept of social property, with no title holder. Whereas previously the assets of a firm were supposed to be held in trust for society, rather than being the property of the workers, ambiguity now went so far as practically to annihilate the firm as a managerial unit. Economic and financial decisions were now supposed to be made not by the management of an enterprise. Rather, the crucial decisions were lodged at a much lower level in a new institution, the basic organization of associated workers (OOUR), whose goal was to maximize not net profits but "income." "Income" corresponded most closely to profits plus wages in a private-ownership market economy. And the market was to consist of self-management contracts and agreements between producers and consumers. At the republic level, self-management interest associations (RSIZs) were formed to coordinate the agreements and pricing. In the electric power industry, for example, RSIZs purchased electricity for distributors and other consumers and took on additional functions, including investment (see the section titled "Regulatory institutions and policies").

According to Yugoslav socialist theory, only living, or current, labor could create value. Markets for labor and capital were not supposed to exist, and no provision was made for organizing them. As a return to property, interest represented an element foreign to the system and continued to be kept at a negative real level by inflation. Workers were not employees hired at a market wage rate; rather, as members of the OOURs, they shared in the units' net income. Electric power enterprises were, in principle, organized in the same way as other productive activities.

Coincidentally with the disintegration of the business unit, political power was decentralized. Republic consensus on policy under the 1974 constitution translated into the right to veto. Although the Communists maintained their single-party monopoly, decisions were made predominantly on a political basis at a republic, or even local commune, level.

Logically inferior to central planning, because it did not provide for property rights, the new Yugoslav self-management system was nevertheless for a time more successful than its predecessor. For the explanation we have to look to the decentralization of economic decisions and the opportunities for exercising individual initiative. These advantages, however, were not sufficient to allow economic rationality to guide the system. Thanks to its technology and to its inter-republic and international connection, the electric power industry managed to avoid the extreme consequences of enterprise fragmentation and local political autonomy.

Until the onset of an economic crisis in the 1980s, foreign loans financed a relatively high rate of investment and consumption. As a consequence of repayment difficulties, new credits suddenly shrank, leading to a recession. In response, the government in 1982 adopted a stabilization program, which, however, failed to come to grips with the underlying institutional inconsistencies. As the program floundered and the crisis deepened, an awareness finally emerged of the need for radical alterations that would transform Yugoslav institutions into those of a truly market-oriented economy.

Self-management as an official policy was to all intents and purposes abandoned in 1990, but conditions were not favorable for its replacement by a privatized market economy. Four republics took the final step to political independence. Yugoslavia as a state does not now exist, and finds itself in a kind of institutional vacuum in which the process of privatization and organizing a market has been very slow.

Postwar growth of the electric power industry

Following the example of the USSR, in 1946 Yugoslavia nationalized its electric power industry as part of the extended nationalization of business firms and the largest part of private property. Those firms that were partly or completely owned by foreigners were nationalized in 1948; about 42% of power station investment had been held by foreigners in 1938 (Kukoleca, 1941). The economic significance of electric power was recognized in a declaration immediately after nationalization that enterprises in this sector were of national importance.

A basic aim of the First Five-Year Plan (1947–51) was to increase the electric power generating capacity by constructing large hydroelectric units. Thermal power was to be used only to complement hydro production, with thermal plants near mines of low-quality coal. Dependence on hydro required acceptance of a long period for construction so that the full use of the hydro potential was not attained until the 1970s. After that, thermal stations become more important, mainly because of large coal reserves.

At the end of the 1960s new thermal plants were designed to burn liquid fuels. This tendency continued even after the first increase in the price of oil (1974), and especially in those republics where there was insufficient production to satisfy demand for electric energy. By the decade of the 1980s the high cost of liquid fuel consigned these thermal plants to a kind of standby reserve, to be used when there were poor conditions at hydro plants.

Some power plants were built for serving large industrial installations. Industrial electric power plants (self-generators) were important during the period of rapid industrialization. Later on, their output share declined, and they do not usually deliver current to the transmission network, serving mainly the factories where they are installed. In 1990 industrial thermal plants produced 2.7 GWh, or 3.5%, of production. However, these industrial thermal plants frequently provide heat to cities.

Yugoslavia has one nuclear power plant with 632 MW of capacity at the bus bar, which went into service in 1981. The plant was built as a joint project by Slovenia and Croatia at Krsko in Slovenia. It had been intended to construct other nuclear plants, but concerns about safety led to a moratorium on new construction. Proposals for decommissioning the single nuclear plant have not been well received in Croatia, which obtains a sizeable part of its needs from the Krsko station. Plans for building more nuclear plants are uncertain, but Croatia, now an independent state, has located a few sites for eventual future nuclear stations and waste disposal.

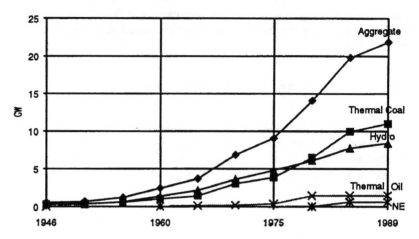

Figure 11-1. Electric power installed capacity (GW), 1946–1989. *Source:* JUGEL (b)

Rated capacity of power stations at the end of 1989 amounted to 21.5 GW, a 40-fold increase since the end of World War II. The maximum rate of growth was registered in 1955–60, when capacity doubled, but expansion slowed to 14% in the years 1985–9. In view of the low stage of exploitation of water power potential from 1945 to 1960, orientation toward hydro plant construction was justified. In comparison with the earlier concentration on building large plants, in the 1970s and 1980s hydro installations were small and the total number of plants built was large. The growth of total capacity and that of each energy source can be seen in Figure 11-1.

A substantial proportion of hydro capacity is run-of-the river, though three pumped storage plants were built in the period after 1980 that now account for about 15% of the hydro capacity. With pumped storage of this magnitude, capacity at peaks has not been a pronounced problem. The storage also made a significant contribution to lowering the cost of thermal plants by using their night capacity for water pumping. At the end of 1989, 132 hydroelectric plants were in operation, of which 63 smaller ones were directly associated with distribution enterprises.

Considerations governing investment in thermal plant construction were the obverse of those determining hydro investment. Initially, in the 1960s, small installations complemented large hydro plants. Later on, larger thermal plants were built, with capacities ranging from 200 to 620 MW, to take advantage of low costs of coal. By 1990, 32 thermal electric plants had been built. For the most part they burned lignite of low caloric value, in which Yugoslavia was rich. The largest reserves of steam coal are in Serbia (12.5 billion tonnes).

Table 11-1. *Size distribution of plants (1989)*

Capacity	To 20 MW	20 to 49 MW	50 to 100 MW	Over 100 MW
Number of hydro plants	71	22	16	20
Capacity	To 100 MW	100 to 199 MW	200 to 500 MW	over 500 MW
Number of thermal plants	5	7	11	9

Source: JUGEL (b)

In the years from 1945 to 1989, production of electricity rose uninterruptedly, although the rate of increase slowed down. The total and the amounts produced by each energy source appear in Figure 11-2. In the years from 1946 to 1960 the yearly growth rate was about 15%, while from 1980 to 1989, it was only 3.7%. As industrialization itself leveled off and rural areas were fully electrified, the decline in the growth rate was inevitable, but the economic stagnation of the 1980s extended also to electric power.

Capacity utilization

The rate of use of maximum installed capacity oscillated between 41 and 50%. Table 11-2 shows a fall in the use of hydro capacity in the period after 1980, and there was a drop in the use of thermal oil-burning capacity immediately after the first oil crisis. Conversely, the use of thermal coal capacity significantly increased. These rates are calculated on the basis of fixed rated capacity. If thermal capacity is adjusted downward to allow for maintenance, capacity use rates would be much higher. Assuming that coal plants' capacity is actually available for only 5,500 hours per year, the capacity use for 1989 would be 78%.

Although generating capacity experienced a dynamic expansion, and the system appeared to have ample reserve margins, it was not always possible to satisfy the rapidly rising demand. Cutbacks in the supply of current were noticeable in the middle of the 1960s, when they amounted to 7.5% of production planned, and at the beginning of the 1980s, when in 1982 they were 5% of planned output. The significance of the shortfalls can be seen in the fact that even aluminum electrolysis suffered cuts. And along with the shortages in the pre-1970s, problems were experienced in the quality of the delivered current.

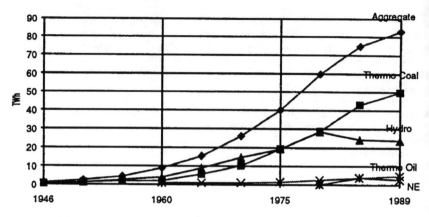

Figure 11-2. Production of electricity (TWh), 1946–1989. *Source:* JUGEL (b)

Large cancellations of deliveries were traceable to delays in construction of power stations and to excessive dependence on hydroelectric power. Those who have examined the question do not blame imperfect forecasting techniques; there was a substantial divergence in growth rates among consumption categories, posing difficulties for forecasting.

Because dependence on hydroelectric plants coincided with poor hydrological conditions, especially in the mid-1960s, large direct customers were the most affected, but the size of the reductions was such that customers served by distribution networks were also seriously impacted. The reductions were carried out simply by cutting off individual areas or direct consumers. Provisions were made for planned cutoffs of individual plants, which received prior notification. Planned reductions had legal authority (Regulation of General Shortages of Electrical Energy) that defined categories of consumers and their hierarchy in reductions. Up to the mid-1970s and economic decentralization, the Federal Executive Council (SIV) had responsibility for carrying out the program of planned cuts; later, administration of load shedding became the responsibility of republic governments (RIVs).

Categories of customers

Data on the structure of consumption that distinguish between direct customers and distribution enterprises are available only from the middle 1960s. In the earlier period, customers were classified as large or small. Large customers benefiting from low prices were denoted as "special customers." When the tariff system was revised in 1965, however, most of the enterprises in the

Table 11-2. *Rate of use of maximum electric power capacity,*
1950–1989 (in percentages)

Year	Hydro	Thermal–coal	Thermal–oil	Nuclear	Total
1950	46	37	—	—	41
1955	47	34	—	—	41
1960	49	30	65	—	41
1965	47	45	70	—	48
1970	46	39	61	—	43
1975	46	47	45	—	50
1980	53	50	20	—	48
1985	36	55	13	69	44
1989	33	57	28	81	46

Source: JUGEL (b)

large customer category were reclassified as direct customers, meaning that they (like distributors) took current directly from high-voltage lines.

The share of direct customers in total consumption in the 1965–89 period ranged between 18 and 28%. Interestingly enough, their number increased from 39 to 53 from 1970 to 1989 (JUGEL b). For each direct customer a special price was established, depending on the volume of consumption and its characteristics. An important decline in the volume of direct consumption took place following 1989, resulting from the sizeable drop in industrial production. Residential consumption in the years 1950–89, as shown in Table 11-3, rose at a 10% annual rate. A relatively rapid growth was registered in transportation as a result of railroad electrification and in electric power consumption by industries connected to the distribution networks.

On account of the continental climate, the highest level of consumption is registered in working days in the winter between 4:00 P.M. and 8:00 P.M. Residential heating by electricity, widespread in Yugoslavia, has significantly contributed to the seasonal peak. Cooking by electricity and working hours from 7:00 A.M. to 3:00 P.M. have also been important factors. Oddly enough, the winter peak was not a problem prior to 1992, because of good relations with neighboring countries in energy exchanges and the availability of pumped storage. On the other hand, there has at times been insufficient capacity for satisfying base-load consumption.

The rapid increase in production capacity was accompanied by an expansion and upgrading of the transmission network. By the end of 1957, through an intensive investment in transmission, the country was completely served with 4,000 kM of 110 KV lines. Shifts to higher voltage levels took place (to 220

Table 11-3. *Electricity consumption by major categories (in GWh)*

Year	In-Plant[a]	Direct customers	Line loss	Distribution Households	Industry	Other	Total
1965	620	4,620	1,676	2,876	5,252	1,678	16,122
1970	1,256	5,513	2,980	6,082	7,442	2,794	26,067
1975	1,897	9,685	4,445	10,351	9,561	3,923	37,972
1980	3,438	11,035	4,858	15,566	18,443	5,299	58,519
1985	4,167	15,540	5,692	17,831	22,760	5,005	70,545
1989	5,372	14,852	7,349	22,190	25,046	6,088	80,997

[a]Includes pumped storage.
Source: JUGEL b

KV in the 1960s and to 380 KV in the 1970s) so that at the end of 1989 there were 3,900 kM in 380 KV transmission lines, plus 5,360 kM of 220 KV lines.

With the construction of these long-distance transmission lines, it was possible to move large amounts of energy from one republic to another. This was especially important where production was far below consumption. Croatia, the most notable deficit republic, had to purchase about 20% of its electricity supply from other republics.

Labor supply

There were few if any examples of limits to growth or current operations of electric power resulting from labor shortages or temporary withdrawal of workers because of disputes over wages or other conditions of employment. Electric power workers' personal incomes ranked among the highest in Yugoslav industries (Dirlam & Plummer, 1973). In the Yugoslav system unions had no bargaining function because, in principle and often in practice, the workers' councils, through their influence on enterprise policy, were in a position to determine incomes and working conditions.

Up to the 1980s strikes against electric utilities were rare. They occurred only in coal mines that were not vertically linked with electric power and where workers were paid personal incomes lower than the average. Local or republic authorities sometimes merged weaker enterprises with stronger ones or with those that enjoyed a monopolistic position, such as electric power. One republic, Slovenia, followed another policy. Mines with losses were simply closed down, and energy requirements were filled with imports or deliveries from other Yugoslav republics. It may be that this policy originated not only because of losses in mines but also in the associated ecological problems.

Vertical integration

Linking coal mining with thermal electric plants is an example of vertical integration. On the other hand, separating electric power distribution from generation and transmission may often appear to be an artificial and indeed uneconomic division. Yet, in Yugoslavia the production and transmission enterprises and their policy-making associations have almost always been organized independently from distribution. The explanation seems to be that distribution was considered to be a municipal service, recognized as legally distinct from the other parts of the electric power industry. Perhaps more important, the fragmented fiscal system stimulated the establishment of independent distribution enterprises. A large number of workers were employed in distribution, taxes on their personal incomes were high, and they were paid partly by the local governments in which the distribution enterprises were organized. Local politicians had a strong incentive to set up independent distribution enterprises as a source of funds.

Economies of scale and domestic technology

Advantages to be realized from economies of scale have influenced decisions about size of units and plants. This is evidenced by the trend toward increasing size of generating units in thermal electric plants and toward higher voltages of transmission lines. From 1970 to 1989, 31 units were installed with more than 200 MW rated capacity, of which three used liquid fuel. Ten were larger than 300 MW, one oil-burning, although only two were larger than 500 MW, both being rated at 620 MW, and installed in the 1980s. It is probable that output would have been concentrated in even fewer and larger units had not political considerations favored keeping investment within republic boundaries.

To determine whether and by how much the electric power industry of Yugoslavia may have been behind that of advanced industrialized countries is not an easy task. Firms specializing in electrical machinery, such as Rade Koncar and Energoinvest, were capable of producing the generating equipment for domestic hydro plants and for transmission and distribution facilities. Their share of deliveries for thermal plant construction and expansion was increasing. Some Yugoslav thermal plants equipped domestically were partly financed by credits from the World Bank following international competition for the installation. The quality of domestically produced equipment mainly was not inferior to foreign. The big electric machinery producers, however, formed a powerful lobby which, together with electric power enterprises, influenced decisions about development and investment options.

Of course, this assessment is valid only for the years when the country was an economic unit. No attempt was made to produce equipment for nuclear stations. Undoubtedly, this was the consequence of the long period in which there was no effective military or economic collaboration with Eastern and Western blocs, and there was continuing isolation from developments in basic research and technology.

Hydroelectric power and average costs

The natural abundance of water flow in Yugoslavia is limited by the extreme climatic variations, which correspondingly affects hydroelectric power potential. There is also a large variation in the flow of water depending on the seasons. Persistent low rainfall was one of the causes of the stagnation of output in the years 1978–89, in spite of additions to capacity. These problems are especially acute when hydro stations in a republic such as Croatia depend on rivers with a large but highly variable flow of water. The flow originates in small watersheds, and the water level is strongly influenced by rainfall that registers great seasonal variations. These factors especially affect not only hydroelectric costs, which are predominantly fixed, but also indirectly have an impact on the costs of thermal plants. In recent years thermal capacity has been sufficient to cover variations in hydro output, which means that at least to this extent new thermal investment was justified. Alterations in the flow of the Danube at the giant Djerdap installation (1.05 GW) have not been significant.

Fuel costs

Trends in fuel consumption in coal-burning plants, as shown in Figure 11-3, have registered continuous improvement. Heat consumption per kWh has dropped for several reasons. In the course of the 1980s, thermal stations using higher-quality coal entered into production, raising boiler efficiency. As an additional factor, the dispatchers took cost parameters into account in choosing the sequence of units to put on line in order to maximize economies of operation. Construction of larger units made economies possible at the plant level, also improving heat consumption. Together these factors brought about a fall in specific heat consumption from 12.5 MJ/kWh in 1970 to about 10.6 MJ/kWh in 1989.

Thermal oil-burning units were in an unfavorable economic position, not because of their heat rate but because oil became relatively expensive. Croatia, the republic where thermal plants were the most dependent upon oil, was at a particular disadvantage. The price of oil was so high in the late 1970s that, even if foreign exchange had been available, it would not have paid to increase the use of capacity and reduce fixed costs per kWh. In later years, coal costs were somewhat below 2 ¢/kWh, while the cost of oil was about 3.9 ¢/kWh (Institute of Social Sciences, 1988).

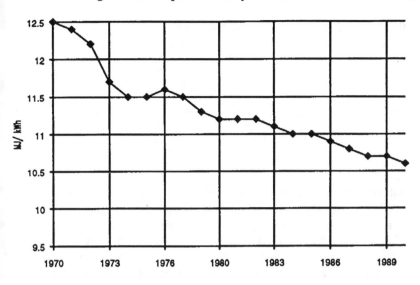

Figure 11-3. Specific heat consumption (MJ/kWh). *Source:* JUGEL (b)

It would be logical to reduce dependence on liquid-fuel thermal plants, first of all those with low-rated capacity. Those that remain should be treated as "cold reserve" capacity but not worth using at peaks. These plants can be of use during major outages, leaving peak consumption to be more economically satisfied from other sources.

Demand management

Apart from rate design, to be discussed later, demand management dates from the 1980s but has been applied only to residential consumption and in only a limited way. Remote control metering made it possible to shift to an optimal daily pattern of consumption of electricity for heat storage, thus reducing demand at the peak, with an increased use of thermal capacity at night, thus helping to reduce unit costs.

Electric power export, import, and exchange

Export, import, and exchange of electric energy became important only during the middle 1970s. Volume and net balance depended on the appearance of surpluses and deficits of electricity in Yugoslavia and in neighboring countries. Hence, no secular trend appears in either net imports or net exports. Nevertheless, the volume of commercial exports (that is, deliveries that were not in

Table 11-4. *Electric power exchanges (in GWh)*

	1960	1965	1970	1975	1980	1985	1989
Export	155	140	152	549	1,710	2,036	2,516
Import	186	407	361	1,642	1,269	2,663	2,188
Total	241	547	513	2,191	2,979	4,699	4,784
Net	69	−267	−209	−1,093	441	−627	328

Source: JUGEL (b)

transit for a fee) grew rapidly. They went to a small number of importing countries, whereas imports tended to be linked to domestic shortages.

In any event, in the past few years the amount of foreign exchanges moved between 5 and 7% of total output. Croatia was the most frequent importer, accounting for 48% of 1990 imports, and Serbia the largest exporter, with 77% of the total. East Europe was the major supplier, and exports flowed to the West, mainly to Italy.

The Yugoslav energy system engaged in permanent parallel synchronized operations in cooperation with UPCTE and temporary "island operations" with electric power systems in East Europe (RWG) (Table 11-4). It should be noted that on account of their geographic position, closer relations with UPCTE and RWG countries led to an increase in transit, or "wheeling," of electric power from foreign countries across Yugoslavia.

Within the boundaries of the federation, there were important exchanges among republics amounting to 20% of total output at the end of the 1980s. As surplus regions, Bosnia–Hercegovina, and particularly Serbia, shipped current to the major deficit republic, Croatia. These relationships began in the mid-1970s and coincided with the construction of large thermal plants in Serbia and Bosnia–Hercegovina, and the hydroelectric installation Djerdap on the Danube in Serbia. Earlier, Serbia had suffered from serious shortages of electric energy.

Interrepublic exchanges for the most part operated on the basis of joint construction of thermal plant capacity, discussed later. These joint ventures accounted for about 75% of the exchanges, the remainder being unplanned, short-term arrangements to cover unexpected outages (Table 11-5).

Research

Throughout the post-1945 years public policy encouraged electric power research. There were ongoing investigations into aspects of estimating and forecasting consumption as well as technical projects. Forecasting consumption

Table 11-5. *Interrepublic exchanges of electricity*

1960	1965	1970	1975	1980	1985	1989
1,990	2,400[a]	4,008	9,551	15,771	16,600	17,930

[a]Estimate.
Source: JUGEL (b)

was assigned initially to an Electric Energy Commission and to research institutes, whose work was coordinated through the Federal Council on Planning (SZP). Together they calculated energy balances at both industry and republic levels of aggregation. Their work was taken over in 1960 by the Federal Planning Council and by the Yugoslav Electric Power Association (JUGEL). The Electric Power Institute (Zagreb) was also wholly occupied with electric power research, both technical and economic.

Major research activities included projects for transmission lines of different voltages, energy transfers over long distances, consumption planning, rationalization of various heating processes, and testing of equipment produced for specific uses. These studies made important contributions to the development of the Yugoslav electric power industry, particularly in connection with the expansion of the 220 and 380 KV transmission networks.

Regulatory institutions and policies

Electric power as an industry had to serve as a basis for the growth of other Yugoslav industries. At the same time, it had to carry out a social function as an integral contributor to rising living standards. This concept of its role dominated almost the entire postwar period. Only in the 1980s did the industry begin to enjoy a limited freedom to make pricing decisions. As a result, electric utilities were required, by furnishing low-priced electricity, to assist in achieving broader goals of economic policy.

At the same time that they almost uninterruptedly maintained downward pressures on electricity prices, governmental regulatory agencies resorted to varying techniques to maintain the industry's financial position within tolerable limits. Only by pervasive subsidies was it possible to hold down price levels over the long run. Although resulting distortions were not always present in every republic, Yugoslav electric prices displayed, over the postwar period, substantial disparities from optimum relationships: (1) with prices of other products; (2) between the cost of electric energy and its selling price; and (3) with internal electric rates in neighboring countries.

Increases in electric energy prices throughout most of the postwar years were held intentionally below the rate of inflation of industrial prices. Prior to the economic reforms of 1965, tariff classes and rate schedules differed depending on the type of activity of the customers. Obviously, this was a technique for stimulating or handicapping certain industrial branches or classes of consumers. From 1958 to 1963, for instance, although the price of electricity consumed by the electrochemical industry increased by 10.5%, the price of electric energy for other uses either stagnated or fell (Gligoric, 1967).

Alterations in basic Yugoslav social and economic structures and ideologies were reflected in shifts in responsibilities of regulatory institutions. Once central planning had been discarded, the electric utility industry was subject to regulation at the federal and republic levels by the executive branch of the government. Controls were exercised also through institutions with differing responsibilities created by statute specifically for electric power, some directly managerial, some nominally advisory. Although the executive branch of the federal government was the ultimate power center, tariff structures and rates were subject to the Federal Price Bureau (SZC). Parallel authorities existed in each of the republics.

To a federal association of electric generating, transmission, and (on a voluntary basis) distribution enterprises (JUGEL) were assigned technical studies, and, with the passage of time, operational responsibilities for assuring growth, economic use of existing capacity, and coordination with international power flows. It was JUGEL that prepared tariff standards and structures for consideration by the government and the SZC. Similar organizations existed in each republic. Their function, like that of JUGEL, was largely that of organizing power pooling. Associations of purchasers of electric current (SIZs in each republic) appeared in the 1970s when centralized controls were unpopular. These associations were officially recognized as participants in rate-making, so that they, too, may be considered as having a semiregulatory status.

In the first regulatory statute to deal specifically with the industry (1958), electric power supply was designated as a public service. In its price and investment behavior the industry was always to take account of its importance in assuring, through its own expansion, the growth of the economy as a whole and an improvement in living standards. Because of its unique role, electric power suffered somewhat less than other sectors from the kaleidoscopic shifts in organization of industry and the vacillations between political centralization and decentralization that kept the economy in constant turmoil. The locus of power and the associated forms of control through the years from 1945 to 1990 are shown in Table 11-6.

Technological considerations and the training and outlook of the engineers in both JUGEL and the republic associations preserved an essential opera-

Table 11-6. *Changes in political policy and regulation, 1946–1990*

Year	Economic organization	Political control	Regulatory institution	Rate structure
1946–52	Central planning, Russian style.	Belgrade	Ministries	Primitive
1952–64	Self-management introduced.	Belgrade	SZC, SZP	Two-part
1965–71	Self-management.	Belgrade	SZC, SZP, SIV, JUGEL	Uniform cost-based
1971–84	Fragmentation. Self-management. Contracting.	Republic	RSIZs, JUGEL	Republic differentiation
1984–9	Abortive introduction of specific ownership.	Tentative decentralization	JUGEL	Partial reimposition of uniform standard
1989–90	Threshold of privatization. OOURs eliminated.	Secession on horizon	JUGEL	Unchanged

SCZ   = Federal Price Bureau
SCP   = Federal Planning Bureau
SIV   = Federal Executive Council
JUGEL = Federal Electric Power Association
RSIZ   = Republic Self-Management Association
OOUR = Basic Organization of Associated Labor

tional coordination during the years when republics were run as almost independent fiefdoms and enterprise cohesion was supposed to be replaced by numerous autonomous decisionmaking units (the OOURs).

Regulation and tariff structure

During the years when a self-management market was being promoted – that is, from the mid-1950s to the early 1970s – the electric utility enterprises had little to say about their pricing practices. The SIV and the Federal Price Bureau proceeded, on the basis of work by JUGEL, to reform the regionally diverse rates structures. At that time, many tariffs still relied on flat rates, did not systematically bill separately for demand, and gave lower rates to favored industries. Tariffs based on energy consumption were the dominant form, with two-part tariffs present to only a limited extent.

Table 11-7. *Average price for delivery from transmission lines, 1970–89 (in ¢/kWh)*

	1970	1975	1980	1985	1989
Direct customers	0.76	1.59	2.44	1.93	2.71
Distributors	1.97	2.07	3.28	3.33	3.53

Source: JUGEL (b)

In 1957, a single nationwide tariff system was imposed, with uniform standards formulated by JUGEL. Two-part tariffs were required, with separate demand and energy charges. Very large customers, however, were not bound by the tariffs. They negotiated special prices, which resulted in serious price discrimination. In 1963, for instance, an aluminum reduction enterprise paid an energy charge of 2.3 dinars/kWh, compared with 25 dinars/kWh by a manufacturer of lighting fixtures (Dirlam & Plummer, 1973). A lower price for energy used at night was introduced in 1963, and specific hours were set for low rates at off-peak periods. With these 1963 tariff innovations, Yugoslavia initiated a wealth of experience with time-of-day tariffs at least a decade before some more highly developed countries.

In a key element of the economic reforms of 1965, the government attempted to reprice all commodities in order to bring them into conformity with world prices – a program that was not wholly successful. Cost-based electric utility tariffs, however, proposed by JUGEL and promulgated under a 1965 amendment to the Electric Power Industry Law, effected a permanent change in tariff structures. Two complementary aims were to assure (1) that all customers would bear the costs they imposed on the system and (2) that they would be stimulated to a more rational use of electric current.

A major reform abolished the practice of establishing customer classes on the basis of use of current, whereby customers in different industries but with identical consumption patterns and amounts could be billed at different rates. Instead, under 1965 schedules, demand and energy tariff rates were differentiated according to delivery voltage, season of the year, time of day, geographic areas, and tariff classes. Seasonal rates applied to all customers. There was a separate rate for reactive energy. Under the cost-based schedules, direct customers should have paid the higher energy prices, but the long-term policy of selective subsidization through low rates was, unfortunately, soon reinstated. As Table 11-7 shows, distributors paid substantially more for current taken directly from transmission lines than the favored direct customers did.

By a 1967 codification of the price control law, wholesale electric rates, like prices of other goods and services of national importance, were to remain under direct government supervision. Direct consumers, however, were subject to levies, described in the section titled "Regulation and investment," to finance electric power investments. Tariffs on sales by distribution enterprises could be set by negotiation between the enterprises and local governments.

As early as 1971, however, the restive republics could no longer be denied a large degree of autonomy, and a constitutional amendment opened the door for redefining the status of the electric power industry. Full regulatory power over wholesale prices was conveyed to the republics in 1973. Four years after the new Constitution of 1974 provided for republic economic autonomy, the regulatory devolution was formalized (1978). Republic institutions – their price bureaus (RZCs) and their customer associations (RSIZs) – promulgated tariff forms and rates. Regulation at the federal level was to be exercised only through JUGEL, which was given additional powers to set standards for reserve capacity, quality, and conditions of interchange. And, hitherto excluded, distribution enterprises could now become JUGEL members.

Under the new dispensation, neither tariff structures nor rates had to be uniform. Cost differences among individual enterprises could be reflected in energy rates and in different limits for the share of demand in the total price for customer categories. These variations were not so pronounced as to lead to significantly different tariff structures. Ceilings on the share of demand in total kWh price constituted a technique for subsidizing customers. Some schedules introduced a third daily period. Although tariff flexibility was unequal, by and large the republics maintained the essential tariff features and principles that had been set earlier by JUGEL. A schematic summary of the institutional changes in the locus of control of electric rates has been shown in Table 11-6.

Even though demand and energy charges were calculated, respectively, by conventional techniques for measuring monthly peak demand and from seasonal and daily variations in the load factor, these procedures could not guarantee that the price of electricity would be equivalent to the real cost of resources used. The price of fuel inputs, the largest single element in thermal plant operating costs, did not include environmental costs. Charges for capacity costs were, at best, determined by fixed costs, which in an inflationary economy were only in the most remote fashion related to actual, or probable future, costs of replacement of plant. And 18 years after the adoption of economic principles of rate making, an inquiry disclosed that average residential rates in Croatia were about 50% less than those in the eight UNIPEDE countries, whereas industrial rates were 35% more, taking into account nontariff obligations and levies.

Regulation and rate levels

Although tariff schedules were being modified to permit increasingly more re-fined assessment of cost among customers, average prices were held at rela-tively low levels. Cost of production was continuously in excess of average selling price in the years from 1958 to 1964 (Gligoric, 1967). There was en-demic inflation, and the authorities feared that higher electric rates would ac-celerate what was regarded as essentially a cost-based phenomenon. Price bu-reaus resisted efforts to bring rates into closer line with industrial prices generally. Representing the industry, JUGEL tried to emphasize the financial and the economic consequences of rates that did not cover cost, thereby creat-ing disparities between electricity prices and other domestic costs, and be-tween Yugoslav rates and those of neighboring countries.

Conflicts between JUGEL and the SIV were especially sharp in the second part of the 1980s when a national energy policy again lodged primary regula-tory authority with the federal government. Efforts were made to reduce dis-crepancies among republic price levels. Rate-making criteria specified in the Social Plan for 1986 provided for weights to be derived from (1) internal and export and import electricity prices in five foreign countries, (2) domestic "standardized" input cots and (3) alternative energy prices. These "combined elements" were supposed to be applied to arrive at an average dinar price in 1987. Over the opposition of JUGEL, and despite proposals for rate increases by republic electric power associations, the SIV drastically cut the weight given to input costs, and by setting maximum prices, prevented rates from ris-ing to economic levels.

Although the device of weighting various factors, each of them a combina-tion of subsidiary prices, seems to have introduced needless complexity into the process of determining an average kWh price, no other procedure was available in the self-management system. Objective external criteria for rate regulation, such as return on investment or cost of capital, could not be used in any economy where there was no capital market, even though enterprises were nominally independent and self-sufficient. Nor was there any incentive or pressure, other than professional pride and the instinct of workmanship (which, of course, should not be underestimated) to insure that the plants would be operated efficiently. On the other hand, there was every inducement to raise prices to increase the personal income residual. Regulators either di-rectly slowed down price increases through rate caps or, as in 1986, put to-gether an average price from several components heavily weighted against input costs.

Only when the 1989 Social Price Control Law freed electric power enter-prises to act independently did their average prices finally rise to economic levels. Controls were not wholly abandoned – the import-export prices in the

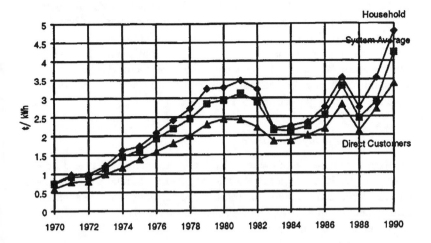

Figure 11-4. Price in ¢/kWh, 1970–1990. *Source:* JUGEL (b)

five index countries combined with their prices to final users still served as a check on monopolistic excesses. In 1989, the new price freedom resulted in an increase of 125%, an average of about 5 ¢/kWh. There were further increases in the real price of electricity in 1990, and 1991 brought it close to world levels, as shown in Figure 11-4.

Both federal and republic rate controls had undesirable effects tending to offset the benefits from introducing rational tariff structures. By imposing price maximals, which during the greater part of the postwar period were usually below average input costs, the SZC and RZCs forced utility enterprises to incur sizeable losses. Sometimes local or republic authorities extracted the necessary funds to maintain incomes and other cash outflows from commercial banks, or even through direct currency emissions from the national bank. On occasion, fiscal and parafiscal relief was provided, such as cutting or eliminating depreciation charges, reducing interest payments, or simply writing off debt.

Engaging in such "financial acrobatics" was not exceptional. Operating losses in the Yugoslav system did not have the connotation, especially for raising funds for expansion or replacement, that they have for western businesses. The casual fashion in which enterprises, including banks, accumulated deficits has remained to plague the economy in the attempted transition to a privatized market-oriented system.

The inescapable conclusion is that, by market economy standards, electricity rates for the whole postwar period were depressed, with little economic justification. Electricity consumption was treated as a unique category of expenditure. Up to the beginning of the 1980s, official parameters for determining price levels either did not exist, or if they did, were not consistently applied. Institutions for price control (federal and republic price bureaus) had discretionary powers with respect to price determination. These powers were exercised alternatively by the federal price bureau and republic price bureaus. Only when it was too late, in 1989, was a reasonable method devised to set a price that would result in more rational consumption and, for the economy as a whole, a lower energy intensity.

Regulation and investment

Somewhat at variance with the introduction of self-management and its supposedly independent enterprises, the federal government retained strict control over selection and financing of investment projects long after the abolition of central planning. Funds from sequestering depreciation accruals and heavy taxes on enterprise and personal incomes were concentrated in federal-level institutions.

These limitations applied *a fortiori* to the electric power industry. In the early postwar years, to 1955, administrative plans determined which individual projects would be built. When indicative, or "global," social plans replaced central planning, the electric power industry, because of its public service character and because of the size of the investments involved, could not select projects and arrange for their financing. It was not until 1966 that the federal government relinquished its preeminent authority over electric utility investments. The enterprises, if not wholly free to make their own investment decisions, could at least secure financing from institutions other than the Federal General Investment Fund.

Expansion and new installations had to be reviewed by federal or republic authorities, depending on the amount of funding and which political level had decisionmaking power at the time. After preparation by JUGEL or the republic buyers' associations (RSIZs), projects went to the Federal Planning Council (SZP) or the republic counterparts for approval. In the analysis of the proposals, JUGEL and the other reviewing bodies applied cost-benefit analysis and conventional discount rates, and calculated an internal rate of return.

In practice, political pressures often overrode conclusions based on economic analysis, so that the most efficient projects, from the standpoint of the whole Yugoslav system, were not necessarily chosen. Almost without exception, target completion dates were not met, with delays often doubling the original estimates of construction time. But the increased financing costs were not accommodated by adjusting prices, because rate levels were controlled and average prices set, as we have seen, with almost complete disregard for the financial condition of the individual utility enterprises. The real cost of the resources invested in electric power installations was, therefore, regarded by the authorities as a charge to be levied on the economy as a whole and as one that did not need to be reflected directly in the price of electricity. Still, through use of excise or similar taxes on electric energy, some of the capital costs were paid by electricity consumers.

Through 1953, investments were financed by nonrepayable grants from federal and republic budgets. From 1954 to 1965, when it was abolished, the Federal General Investment Fund provided low-interest (2%) credits. In subsequent years, utility investments were financed from three major sources, whose relative shares the impenetrability of the published financial statements makes it almost impossible to determine.

What is significant is that though it is a capital-intensive industry, electric power was funded mainly by sources that imposed only nominal capital charges on the industry. Bank loans were paid off in depreciated dinars, although foreign loans were partly repaid by electric energy exports.

Low-voltage customers had to contribute by paying high excise taxes (15 to 20%). These taxes could be regarded as a profit element in price. A special tax was targeted for expanding distribution lines. Large customers – business enterprises – were obliged to contribute supposedly repayable levies related to the volume of their consumption and to their new invested assets (2% in Croatia). These "loans" bore nominal interest rates (0.5%) and were to be repaid only over long periods. In the years of rapid inflation such "loans" were in part gifts to the electric power industry.

Last, funds from noncash charges were the third source for financing investments. They were usually far from sufficient because depreciation accruals were kept low in order to reduce nominal operating costs. Although there were variations from year to year and from republic to republic, it appears that no more than 25% of electric utility investment has been self-financed since 1970.

Outside funding was made available through the RSIZs, which collected the levies and taxes on electric power consumption. The RSIZs tended to funnel money to their respective communal, regional, or republic projects, in order to swell government revenues and create jobs. Nevertheless and in spite of local pressures, there was a remarkable number of interrepublic investments financed by the RSIZs. As a power-deficit republic, and one without local coal reserves, Croatia found that it was economical to contribute to funding large thermal plants in Serbia (Obrenovac) and Bosnia–Hercegovina (Tuzla, Kakanj), and to the nuclear plant in Slovenia (Krsko).

The hodgepodge of regulation failed to provide a normal framework for planning and financing electric power-generating plant construction and equipment. Unnecessarily high outlays were supported by parafiscal mechanisms for channeling funds to the industry. Yet, in spite of the shifts in financing sources and significant changes in the share of electric power in industri-

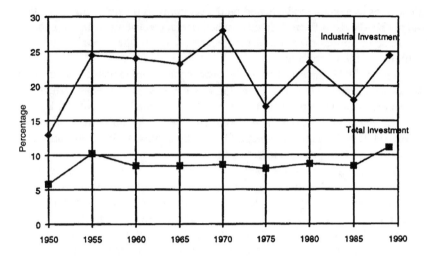

Figure 11-5. Investment in electric power as % of industrial and total investment, 1950–1989. *Source:* Federal Statistical Yearbook

al investment, the industry accounted for a remarkably stable percentage of total investment, as shown by the data displayed in Figure 11-5.

Economic performance

Costs and revenues

In light of the prevalent, and indeed notorious, indifference to profitability in the self-managed economy, an unconcern shared by the principal regulatory institutions, electric enterprise financial losses cannot be traced to poor managerial practices. In their use of resources, the firms may well have been operated as efficiently as they would have been had revenues covered total costs. It is not easy, in any event, to obtain reliable data that put revenue and cost on a kWh basis. Statistical yearbooks and even reports of republic electric power associations do not provide the requisite refinement of financial data to allow a useful breakdown of costs and revenues. Although data on total receipts and on major classes of expenditures are published, they were not usually disclosed in such a way that the information for transmission and for hydro and thermal plant costs can be separated. Besides, distribution enterprises were not always included in the electric power associations, and their financial statements were published separately. In at least one republic, Serbia, revenue appears to have equaled or exceeded reported costs.

Summaries drawn from the financial statements of the electric power associations disclose that for recent years (1985–9), when the enterprises were given a relative amount of autonomy, combined losses for the Yugoslav generating and transmission frequently exceeded "accumulation," a Marxian term that has a distant relationship to profit. This means that for the system as a whole, revenues failed to cover operating costs and reported charges to income. It is interesting that in 1985 the published combined income statement of the Croatian electric power association reported a loss of 14.3 billion dinars on 107.5 billion dinars of revenue. None of the five member generating and transmission enterprises showed a profit (Croatian Electric Power Association, 1985).

Moreover, the compressed financial statements suffer from defects in the underlying data. In order to obtain a useful multiyear comparison of revenues and costs, an inquiry would have to cope with problems arising from combining statements of the working units (the OOURs), each of which enjoyed financial independence. The Zagreb generating enterprise, for instance, was comprised of eight OOURs in 1985. And OOURs might from time to time be reclassified to other industries, such as mining or machinery. Every few years there were revisions of financial accounting to accommodate revisions in the self-management system that altered not only the production units but key accounting and financial terms. The state-imposed system of accounts accordingly redefined items such as enterprise income, the personal income residual (wages), contributions (most of which were actually not discretionary), communal taxes and taxes on income, and accumulation and its opposite, loss.

From a specially commissioned study of Croatian costs and revenues for a 10-year period, using unpublished materials from the constituent OOURs, some conclusions can be drawn with respect to costs and income over the 1979–88 period. It will be seen from Table 11-8 that there were numerous shortfalls, particularly for thermal plants.

In calculating costs in cents, the average yearly exchange rate was applied, using the *Bulletin* of the National Bank of Yugoslavia. During the years in question there was substantial inflation, and a rapid fall in the exchange value of the dinar sometimes exceeded differences in relative prices in the United States and Yugoslavia. Absolute amounts of costs and incomes are therefore probably understated.

The relatively low price paid by direct consumers compared with the wholesale price paid by distributors was shown in Table 11-7. This low price provided a hidden subsidy to the direct consumers that was to some extent offset by taxes and levies. Rates paid by the distributors' customers, however, were high enough to create a surplus cash flow. This was then directed by a variety of fiscal and parafiscal measures to the needs of republics and communes.

Table 11-8. *Electric power costs and income (¢/kWh)*

Year	Hydro Cost	Hydro Income	Thermal Cost	Thermal Income	Transmission Cost	Transmission Income	Distribution Cost[a]	Distribution Income
1979	1.26	1.47	4.14	4.37	0.42	0.46	—	—
1980	1.16	1.54	4.23	4.32	0.37	0.45	—	—
1981	1.12	1.49	4.12	4.21	0.31	0.38	1.62	1.89
1982	1.26	1.68	3.87	3.95	0.32	0.43	1.62	1.46
1983	1.18	1.11	2.67	2.39	0.22	0.23	0.89	0.92
1984	0.95	1.08	2.75	2.67	0.19	0.23	0.73	0.79
1985	0.94	1.02	3.25	3.10	0.19	0.14	0.89	0.93
1986	1.21	1.21	4.26	4.19	0.34	0.25	1.42	1.43
1987	1.47	1.65	4.10	4.14	0.37	0.39	1.11	1.45
1988	1.24	1.28	2.97	2.82	0.29	0.29	0.98	0.99

[a]Distribution costs do not include the purchase cost of electric energy.
Sources: Institute of Social Sciences, 1988. Economic Institute and Electric Power Institute, 1990.

Significant variations in Table 11-8 costs and revenues resulted not only from changes in the dinar exchange rate but from the constant changes in economic policy toward the electric power industry. Although the real price of electric energy was supposed to rise, average revenue per kWh was frequently below the level prevailing at the end of the 1970s.

It is possible that Table 11-8 understates the size of the revenue shortfall. One of the republic enterprises made available, in addition to the requested numbers from its official financial statements, its own estimates of "normal" costs. According to this estimate, "normal" costs were two times larger than the costs derived from income statements prepared according to the official accounting rules.

Operating efficiency

In contrast to government policy that prevented prices from fully reflecting costs, technical regulation by JUGEL in conjunction with the republic electric power associations and their dispatching centers attained a moderate degree of success. By 1971 they were organized as a system through subcenters and generating stations, with the function of maintaining frequency and contractual voltage throughout the country and controlling power exchanges. Dispatching centers (five in all) for their respective power networks existed in every republic except Montenegro, which was controlled from the Serbian center. JUGEL managed the central dispatching center. Continuing parallel activity was employed through 220 kW connections with Italy in 1974, with Austria in 1975, and with Greece in 1979. The republic centers dealt with minor disturbances – accidents or unforeseen equipment problems. Major ones were handled by JUGEL, using hydro stations and foreign interconnections, and arranging for complementary exchanges among the republic networks.

Planning for use of units had two basic elements: forecasting daily needs and distributing load among power stations. Estimates of consumption required analysis of historical statistics and current conditions (temperature, consumption by large customers, atmospheric conditions, and characteristics of needs for specific days). The load for each hour for each unit was obtained. Output of run-of-the-river hydro stations was completely used. Stored power was drawn down during the period when it was most economic to avoid a loss from an overflow of water, or when it was, on balance, cheaper than reliance on higher-cost thermal units. Distribution of load among thermal plants was determined by their specific heat rates.

Additional efficiency was realized by the adoption of the spinning reserves concept in 1981. Enterprises were required to keep in spinning reserves 5% of installed disposable capacity, plus an increase to allow for capacity imported at the time of the peak. In 1988, Austria, Italy, Greece, and Yugoslavia provided for common use of spinning reserves amounting to 300 MW.

Trends in labor productivity

As the electric power industry expanded, larger generating units were installed, and higher voltage transmission lines were built. There was a corresponding rise in output and generating capacity per worker, as shown in Table 11-9. It would be futile, because of the unreliability of reported investment book value and the artificial pricing of sources of primary energy, to try to estimate changes in total factor productivity. Improvement in heat rates has been alluded to earlier. Useful estimates of total factor productivity cannot be made for the industry. For our purposes, the clearly apparent trends are more important than absolute relations between number of workers and the measures of output and capacity. Hiring practices were affected by peculiarities of the self-management system, which led to overmanning. Of greater significance is the sharply rising trend in both series.

The growth in labor productivity as measured by output per worker, 8.5 times for hydro plants, and 20 times for thermal plants, may be considered to be, especially for thermal plants, extremely high. The index reached its maximum at the beginning of the 1980s. Thenceforth, there was a fall in hydro-

Table 11-9. *Labor productivity*

Year	Production (MWh/worker)			Installed capacity (MWh/worker)		
	Hydro	Thermal	Nuclear	Hydro	Thermal	Nuclear
1946	419	128	—	181	60	—
1950	712	170	—	175	53	—
1955	1,400	226	—	342	76	—
1960	1,874	582	—	435	212	—
1965	3,486	1,353	—	844	314	—
1970	3,764	1,743	—	928	501	—
1975	4,570	2,170	—	1,135	444	—
1980	5,137	2,657	—	1,102	676	—
1985	3,780	2,412	6,900	1,206	591	1,134
1989	3,553	2,605	7,116	1,255	594	1,009

Source: JUGEL (b)

electric productivity of about 30%, and thermal productivity stagnated. Changes in the direction of the trend coincided with the onset of stagnation of economic growth generally, which led to a reduction in investments. Coincidentally, pressure was exerted to continue to take on new workers. The drop in the hydroelectric index resulted from a shift in investment to thermal electric plants, and relatively poor weather conditions.

Capital intensity, as measured by kW per worker, reached 1,250 kW in hydroelectric plants and 590 kW in thermal plants. The improvement was more pronounced in thermal plants (10 times by the end of 1989) than in hydro stations (about 7 times).

Social costs of price policy

In estimating social costs of the depressed level of electricity prices, it must be remembered that investment was financed to only a minor degree from electric revenue. Reliance on different mechanisms of financing investment (by the investment funds and from "contributions" levied by the RSIZs) obscure the actual workings of the inflows, although they had some positive effects. It has been estimated that independently of the price of electric energy, significant amounts of assets were drawn into the industry to finance investment. According to one calculation (Institute of Social Sciences, 1988), at the beginning of the 1980s, the money raised by RSIZs amounted to from 32 to 50% of total payments for electricity. Most of these levies were paid by consumers of

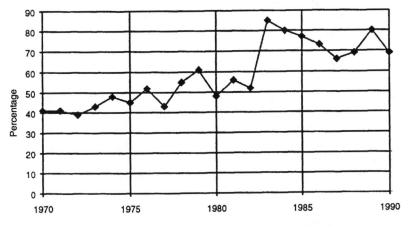

Figure 11-6. Reserve margins (in percentages). *Source:* JUGEL (a)

electric energy, and the same applies to the funds accumulated supposedly for financing all investments. Although the levies may have to some extent compensated for rates that did not fully cover costs, there was a welfare loss stemming from an inadequate distribution of the combined receipts to individual sectors within the electric power industry. And the policy of excessive investment was reflected in reserve margins that reached extremely high levels, as shown in Figure 11-6.

Much larger social costs can be attributed to the influence on industrial structure of the price of energy and the way in which levies (contributions) were calculated for financing investment. The depressed price of electric energy favored energy-intensive technology and neglect of energy-saving procedures, which led to a high rate of consumption of electric energy in relation to the growth of social output. Although Yugoslavia in 1991 had a much lower primary energy intensity than other East European countries (Antic 1994a), consumption of electric energy in 1981 amounted to 1 kWh per $0.95 of GNP, while the index countries' average was 1 kWh per $2.02 of GNP (Institute of Social Sciences, 1988), a relationship that persisted to 1991. The undesirable low price also created large financial losses, which threatened the growth of the industry.

The procedure for assessing the levies for investment also contributed to distorting the structure of industry from the standpoint of energy consumption. The largest share of the "contributions" was based on a percentage of the value of all investment by customers, without regard to their future consumption of energy. As a result, for the same investment value, identical payments were made by the textile industry and the electrometallurgical industry. Because their future consumption of electric energy per unit of investment expenditures would be nowhere similar, additional capacity for future consumers was financed less by those industries that would have a larger share in future consumption. Hence, this source of funds unduly favored energy-intensive branches and technology.

The total damage from the distortions in pricing and investment financing is hard to quantify, but it is certainly far from negligible. Besides other factors, price policy contributed to creating an inefficient economic structure in which – and this is paradoxical – electric power was one of the most progressive of Yugoslav industries. This judgment applies more to its technical level than to economic performance. However, the electric utility industry of at least one republic (Serbia) managed to avoid nominal losses. This suggests that the major adverse consequences of price and investment regulatory policy may well lie in sectors other than the electric power industry.

Appraisal of regulatory policies

Before identifying the shortcomings of electric power regulatory policy, one must keep in mind that two wholly different economic systems prevailed during the postwar years. The first, central planning, but with elements of self-management, lasted from 1945 to 1965. The self-management system evolved into a complete break with centralized planning and established a new form of organization of industry.

In spite of this key difference, the weaknesses in regulatory policy remained largely the same, although in relation to the two systems it changed in importance and role. The leading deficiency of regulatory policy in the centrally planned system was its artificial depression of prices and costs, as well as the vagaries in the organization of the industry. Depressed prices resulted in the electric power industry being treated as a branch that served as a basis for growth of all other industries. The profitability of electric power was not a goal of its activity, and there were frequent changes in organization.

When the legal framework of self-management was altered to weaken the position of management, all enterprises, including those in the electric power industry, were broken up into many smaller parts (OOURs). Republic etatism, made possible by the constitutional amendments of 1971, played a key role in the formation of electric power associations. This policy of excessive decentralization of decisionmaking, however, was less harmful to electric power than to other branches because of its technological links. The relatively good technical understandings and relationships among firms were partially successful in resisting republic and regional fragmentation.

An important policy issue, which did not attract much attention from the regulatory institutions, was that of conservation of energy and the possibilities of reducing energy intensity even though the economy was growing. The electric power system of Yugoslavia did not pass into the phase of energy-saving growth, nor was there a consistent policy of saving electricity. Instead of stimulating saving, price policy led to higher consumption. Saving has not been encouraged by setting appropriate standards for electricity consumption (for example, in kitchen appliances), which sometimes has proved to be an obstacle to export of these items. Reducing consumption has been given priority only when there has been an immediate crisis in supplying electric energy. The problem must be approached in a qualitatively different way, not only by a correction of price levels and relationships, but by a recognition of the experience of countries that have successfully introduced programs for conservation of electric energy. This would contribute to a fall in the rate of growth of consumption of electric energy and to a rise in GNP, and would reverse the unfavorable trend in both variables that has persisted since the beginning of the 1980s.

In the postwar period the electric utility industry benefited from an almost uninterrupted rise in demand. The explanation for its continuous expansion can be found in the unbalanced growth of heavy industry and in demographics. From a backward economy, in which the population was overwhelmingly engaged in agriculture, Yugoslavia has become a country with a largely urban population, a shift that is inevitably reflected in the demand for electricity. Rapid urbanization is also one of the basic causes of the exceptionally rapid growth of household consumption of electricity.

Although the Yugoslavia electric power system, after the shortage crises of the 1960s and early 1980s, accommodated to rising consumption needs, per-capita output ranks substantially below that of western industrially developed economies. The low level of production and consumption of electricity – scarcely a third of that of the United States – reflects the much lower Yugoslav GNP. And despite the countrywide postwar industrialization, three republics (Macedonia, Montenegro, and Bosnia–Hercegovina) remain economically backward. At the bottom is the formerly autonomous Serbian district, Kosovo, where the 1988 GNP was only 27% of the national average.

The basic problems still to be resolved by the industry are those of pricing, internal organization, and financing of investment. Because of its key position in the economy, the industry cannot escape some form of centralized control, if not state ownership. In conditions prevailing in the erstwhile Yugoslavia, privatization and the emergence of management responsibility to investors would surely have a salutary influence on improving business efficiency. Yet, on account of the political and international crises now facing its constituent parts, privatization cannot be anticipated for the near future.

Postscript: The system in transition

The dissolution of Yugoslavia was accompanied by an armed conflict that unfortunately is still continuing at the time of writing. Communications among the former republics are limited. As a consequence, the discussion in this section has perforce to be limited to Serbia during the years 1991–4.

At the end of September 1991, the destruction of the transformers and transmission lines cut the connection between the western and eastern parts of Yugoslavia, so that one part of the UPCTE system, consisting of Serbia, Montenegro, Macedonia, and Greece, became isolated. With the transmission break the long-term growth strategy of the Serbian electric power system suffered an almost mortal blow because the high-capacity transmission links with the former Yugoslav republics and members of UPCTE had assured the delivery of large quantities of energy. The interruption of transmission meant the loss of Serbian export earning of about $100 million yearly. An additional shock came in June 1992 when United Nations sanctions forbade the export and import of goods and services. This left the electric power system of Serbia functioning in parallel only with the tiny Montenegrin system. The sanctions forced the electric power system to supply the predominant share of energy consumption, which had formerly been satisfied by oil and natural gas.

The impossibility of importing these alternative sources of energy has led to a tremendous expansion of consumption of electricity in the winter months. Use of electric heating has been further encouraged by a policy of low prices for current that gives the wrong signals to consumers. Their response, especially in households, has been to buy additional electrical heating appliances, so that consumption at the peak has risen to unprecedented heights. The Serbian electric power system now faces a huge differential of connected demand ranging from a 1.2 GW minimum to a 6.1 GW maximum that threatens the technical and economic existence of the system. In 1990, the ratio of minimum to maximum demand was only about 1:2.

For a good many months, however, surplus capacity was sufficient to satisfy the rise in consumption. The first brownout occurred in February 1993 when there was a breakdown at the most important steam plant and the reserves could not be quickly put on line due to poor maintenance and scarcity of fuel oil. A shortage of repair parts and the continuing rise in consumption resulted in the inability of the system to cope with demand, and current was cut off daily for several hours, beginning in October 1994.

At the beginning of 1992, the Serbian electric power industry was nationalized as a state enterprise under the direction of the Ministry of Energy, moving from social to state ownership. The change in ownership did not involve any transfer of funds, meaning that no compensation was paid. Although the decision can be explained in several ways, it can be justified by the preferability during the initial stage of the transition to a market economy to install a single responsible owner.

As the owner of the system (EPS), the Republic of Serbia controlled assets of about $20 billion with power plants of 8.7 GW, and a yearly output of about 35 TWh. Roughly 60% of the capacity is in coal-fired steam plants, of which some are very large (e.g., Obrenovac with 2.9 GW) that will later prove to be unfavorable, because their capacity cannot be absorbed efficiently in the isolated Serbian system.

Nationalized electric power is completely integrated vertically, from the mining of coal to retail distribution. Outside the system there remain only a small number of industrial power plants with small capacities. Although the Law of Nationalization provides for public (state) enterprises "acting as profit-making businesses, with a majority participation of state capital of 51% and with ownership transfer of the remaining shares," up to now there has been no action taken to transfer the minority share of ownership. The state of Serbia is the sole owner of the EPS, and there has been no move toward issuing stock certificates. To be sure, a proposal has been prepared providing for the sale of part of the enterprise, but the government refuses to act on it. Furthermore, all questions of privatizing part of the EPS and other state enterprises are within the informal authority of the president of the republic. Naturally this leads to questions about the effect of the legislative mandate to privatize.

After nationalization, the EPS was divided into 23 operating units, (four in mining and transport of coal, three hydroelectric plants, four thermal plants, 11 distributors, and one in transmission), but none of them is in any way independent. The EPS is a single enterprise for operating and financial purposes. There is a board of directors appointed on the side of the government, but evidently the key decisions (for example, on pricing) are made informally outside the board through the powerful influence of the political leadership. The choice of managers is completely within the authority of the state, and up to the present not conditioned on the financial results of the EPS.

The price of electric current is strictly controlled. Despite the statutory requirement that the enterprise make a profit, the managerial goal has been to maintain household consumption and to protect living standards by setting low, and sometimes incomprehensible, prices. From a level of only 45% of household rates in Western Europe, the ratio dropped to 8% in December 1992, and still lower in the course of 1993. Destructive hyperinflation quickly rendered valueless the nominal rises in rates, which were put into place in accordance with the rigid control of prices.

In January 1994 the hyperinflation spiral was brought to an end, at least temporarily, but the status of the EPS was not improved. In stressing the social function of electricity prices and in stabilizing the price of current (and other infrastructural services), the authorities established a very low level for revenues. Although the meteoric rise in the general price level has been brought to a halt, the stabilization program has saddled the infrastructural industries, among which is electric power, with a mounting accumulation of uncovered losses. The Serbian stabilization success is therefore linked to discriminatory disparities in prices that can be feasible only in the short run. Although electricity prices have been held for the present at an artificially depressed level, this cannot prevent their ultimate rise with the explanation (or justification) that this must upset the stabilization program. The low average level of electric prices embodied in the tariff system now in force does not reflect relative actual costs. Prices for high-voltage large consumers are now higher than prices to households.

The remaining fields of regulation – investment and ecology – are not for the moment of great interest. It is not clear who will finance investment and from what sources. The results of nationalization have been catastrophic. In the period since 1992 EPS has continuously registered losses. Revenues from operations registered a loss before interest payments and other capital costs that amounted to about $400 million in 1992, $580 million in 1993, and for the first six months of 1994 about $250 million. The total losses, including operations and financial costs, are between two and three times bigger in each of these years. Interestingly enough, none of these losses were included in the republic budget and accordingly have not been covered. The losses reduce *de facto* the assets of EPS.

Although EPS losses have not been made good, subsidies do exist. The EPS is the beneficiary of a subsidy that finances maintenance to enable the enterprise to confront the winter months. These subsidies take different forms. In the hyperinflationary period (1992–3) there were credits that very quickly became valueless. In the period of application of the stabilization program, the EPS issued obligations, and the central bank was the only buyer. It is not clear from which assets the EPS can service the loans or how it can expect that it will be able to pay them off at maturity.

Wartime conditions and UN sanctions resulted in the isolation of the EPS. On account of the lack of imported energy, the electrical power system had to satisfy most of energy needs. To continue from 1991 to 1994 with the policy of relatively low prices adopted in the pre-1990 period was absurd. The absence of any prospective growth, characteristic of a country at war, has led to the gutting of what was once a well-functioning electric power system.

Active participation in gutting the electric utility system has been a key feature of economic policy in the 1990s. Extralegal regulation has in effect created a mechanism for undermining the foundations of the EPS, completely in conflict with the system's economic potential.

REFERENCES

S. Antic (1994a). "Energy: Odyssey 2010." *Southeast Europe Perspectives* No. 6, Ekonomska Politika, Belgrade.

S. Antic (1994b). "An Alternative Approach to Electric Power Regulation." *Ekonomist* 5-6 (available only in Serbo-Croatian).

J. Bendekovic (1975). *"The Basis for Forming Electric Energy Prices,"* Ekonomic Institute, Zagreb, mimeo (available only in Serbo-Croatian).

J. Bendekovic (1971). "Workers and Managerial Decision-making. The Case of the Power Industry in Croatia." Sorento Conference on Labour Productivity, Zagreb.

Croatian Electric Power Association. *Yearbook of Croatian Electric Power Industry.* Selected issues (available only in Serbo-Croatian), Zagreb.

J. Dirlam and J. Plummer (1973). *An Introduction to the Yugoslav Economy,* Merrill.

Ekonomic Institute and Electric Power Institute (1990). "Quantitative and Qualitative Expertise of the Unified Criteria for Determining the Price of Electric Energy and Proposals for Changes and Extension." Mimeo (available only in Serbo-Croatian), Belgrade and Zagreb.

Electric Power Institute (1979). "Study of Unified Methodology for Energy Balances and Optimal Structures I-II." Mimeo (available only in Serbo-Croatian), Zagreb.

Electric Power Institute (1986). "Self-management Organization, Income Linking and Financing of Electric Power Enterprises," mimeo (available only in Serbo-Croation), Zagreb.

Federal Statistical Bureau. *Statistical Yearbook of Yugoslavia.* Selected issues, Belgrade.

R. Gilbert (ed.) (1991). *Regulatory Choices: A Perspective on Developments in Energy Policy.* University of California Press.

P. Gligoric (1967). *Integration in Yugoslav Electric Power Industry,* Savremena administracija, Belgrade (available only in Serbo-Croatian).

Institute of Social Sciences (1988). "Financial and Economic Status of the Croatian Electric Power Industry." Mimeo (available only in Serbo-Croatian), Belgrade.

M. Jamnik (1971.) *The Specificity of System and Policy of Pricing in Electric Power and Traffic.* Institute of Social Sciences (available only in Serbo-Croatian), Belgrade.

JUGEL(a). *Dispatching Report.* Selected issues (available only in Serbo-Croatian).

JUGEL(b). *Yugoslav Electric Power Statistical Yearbook.* Selected issues (available only in Serbo-Croatian).

JUGEL(c). *Yugoslav Thermal Power Stations: Technical and Energy Data,* selected issues (available only in Serbo-Croation).

JUGEL (1990). 380 KV Yugoslav Network (available only in Serbo-Croatian).

S. Kukoleca (1941). *Industry of Yugoslavia 1918-1938* (available only in Serbo-Croatian).

National Bank of Yugoslavia. *Bulletin.* Selected issues.

H. Pozar (1983). *Power and Energy in Electric Energy Systems* (available only in Serbo-Croatian), Zagreb.

Privredni Pregled (1962). *Yugoslav Electric Power Industry* (available only in Serbo-Croatian), Belgrade.

M. Todorovic (1987). "Development and Fixed Assets of Electric Power." JUGEL, mimeo (available only in Serbo-Croatian).

V. Vukotic (1993). *Privatization.* Institute of Social Sciences, Belgrade.

Index